Moyen Orient & Océan Indien
XVIe- XIXe s.

Willem FLOOR

The Persian Textile Industry in Historical Perspective, 1500-1925

11

Société d'Histoire de l'Orient

L'Harmattan
5-7, rue de l'École Polytechnique
75005 Paris - FRANCE

L'Harmattan Inc.
55, rue Saint-Jacques
Montréal (Qc)- CANADA H2Y 1K9

Moyen Orient & Océan Indien
XVIe-XIXe s.
a paru, de 1984 à 1990, comme périodique annuel. La collection est publiée désormais, sous la forme de recueils thématiques ou de monographies sans périodicité fixe, par la Société d'Histoire de l'Orient
aux Editions l'Harmattan
Paris

ISBN : 2-7384-8380-1
ISSN : 0764-5562

Ouvrage publié avec le concours de l'ESA Q8003 du C.N.R.S., Paris
Composition, tableaux, cartographie, mise en page et maquette de couverture :
Jacqueline Calmard

TABLE OF CONTENTS

Illustrations

Tables

AVANT PROPOS

Les tissus persans sont connus et appréciés en Occident chrétien depuis l'Antiquité, notamment par les productions prestigieuses provenant d'ateliers royaux (les fameuses soieries "sassanides"). La Perse islamique continua à être renommée pour ses tissus de qualité et le rafinement des costumes influencés, depuis les invasions mongoles, par des modèles extrême-orientaux. L'établissement de la dynastie safavide (1501-1722) marque un tournant dans la production textile persane, de plus en plus orientée vers l'exportation tant vers l'Inde, l'Asie centrale, la Turquie, la Russie, que vers l'Europe.

Bien qu'un grand nombre d'études aient été consacrées aux tissus et aux vêtements persans, essentiellement par des historiens d'art intéressés surtout par les aspects esthétiques des productions de prestige, dont les tapis, une histoire de l'industrie textile persane depuis le XVIe siècle restait à écrire. Une grande confusion existait dans la terminologie, tant des tissus que des vêtements ou de l'artisanat et des artisans du textile, ainsi que sur les données socio-économiques de la production et de sa commercialisation. Tout en comblant ces lacunes et en relevant de nombreuses erreurs d'interprétation (par exemple en ce qui concerne la commercialisation des tapis), Willem Floor nous fournit ici, dans un exposé clair et concis, l'étude la plus complète à ce jour sur l'histoire socio-économique de l'industrie textile en Perse du XVIe au XIXe siècle. Ce travail est basé sur une profonde connaissance des sources primaires et secondaires persanes et européennes et leur utilisation judicieuse, notamment pour clarifier et ordonner, dans le respect de la chronologie, une terminologie persane d'une grande complexité. Certains chapitres sont nettement novateurs, notamment celui portant sur la production et la commercialisation des châles persans, dont les plus beaux specimens n'avaient rien à envier aux châles de Cachemire; on ne disposait, sur ce sujet, que de données fragmentaires.

Willem Floor a par ailleurs largement prouvé ses compétences par ses nombreuses publications basées sur des recherches approfondies sur l'histoire socio-économique du monde iranien pour lesquelles il utilise abondamment les sources persanes, les archives néerlandaises et d'autres sources et travaux. Sa dernière grande contribution, portant sur la même période que la présente étude, vient d'ailleurs de paraître*, et de nombreuses autres sont sous presse.

Nous tenons tout particulièrement à remercier Willem Floor d'avoir choisi à nouveau notre collection** pour la publication de cette œuvre majeure. Tous nos vœux l'accompagnent pour la poursuite de ses recherches et de ses publications toujours très attendues par la communauté scientifique.

Jean Calmard
Président de la Société d'Histoire de l'Orient

Paris, avril 1999

---

* *A Fiscal History of Iran in the Safavid and Qajar Periods 1500-1925*, dans *Persian Studies Series*, No. 17, Ehsan Yarshater éd., Bibliotheca Persica, New York, 1999.

** Comme il l'a fait pour ses articles parus dans notre publication *Moyen Orient & Océan Indien*, tomes 2/1 (1985), 3(1986), 5(1988), 6(1989), 8(1994).

FOREWORD

My interest in Persian textiles was first awakened by the lack of information about the meaning of the myriad terms by which authors, both local and foreign, referred to all kinds of fabrics. Dictionaries were not very helpful, and this even holds for the huge Dehkhoda dictionary. There are only two specialized Persian textile related dictionaries. The oldest one is that by Maulana Mahmud Nezam Qari Yazdi who wrote the *Divan-e albaseh* towards the end of the 15th century. This dictionary, in verse, which was recently (1980) reprinted, is not very particular about detail, however. Also, its poetic descriptions refer to the situation prior to the Safavid period (1500) which is the starting point of this study. More detail is available in Dozy's *Dictionnaire détaillé des noms des Vêtements chez les Arabes*, which suffers, however, from the fact that it provides only occasional references to the Persia cultural area. It also mainly refers to the situation before 1500. Both are useful, but neither is conclusive enough to enlighten us with regard to many of the textile terms encountered in the Safavid-Qajar period.

I was surprised that my lack of knowledge was shared by those textile specialists whom I bothered with my ignorance. In fact, they urged me to make an effort and try and bring some order and information where only confusion and ignorance exist. A first step in that direction was my contribution to the Washington DC Textile Museum's exhibition of Persian textiles in 1989. Concretely, this meant a chapter in the exhibition's catalogue. However, I was not satisfied with that first step and therefore continued with my research.

The result of this continued endeavor is the present study, which is divided into five parts. In the first part, an analysis is given of the socio-economic dimension of the textile industry. This means that questions are answered such as: where, what was being woven, by whom and what, if any, changes were taking place in the industry over time. Also, the international trade in Persian fabrics is analyzed, and a different view is submitted about the importance of the trade in, for example, Persian carpets than has been the case so far. The same is the case with the analysis of the role of the royal workshops as part of the Persian textile manufacturing complex. In the second part a detailed annotated list of technical terms of fabrics and textile related crafts is offered. The third part provides a detailed overview of male and female clothing terms and offers a head to toe view of the historical development of Persian apparel. The fourth part focuses on one of the most beautiful products of Persian fabrics, the shawl, the best of which rivaled those of Kashmir. A complete overview of production sites, types of shawls, use of shawls, trade in shawls, production of shawls and the ups and final down-turn of the shawl craft is offered. The last and fifth part deals with the production, trade, use and changes therein of kork or Kerman goat down. This product was the most important export commodity, after raw silk, for the Europeans trading in Persia. The study is concluded by an afterword and a bibliography. Because all technical textile and garment terms are alphabetically listed and explained in chapters two and three, and all terms related to shawls are in chapter four, while in chapters 1, 4 and 5 the references to production centers are grouped together for easy reference, it has not been deemed necessary, also for financial reasons, to produce an index.

I do not pretend to have covered all aspects of the Persian textile industry (in fact carpets are only partially dealt with), or even to have been able to answer all my own, let alone the readers', questions on the subject. A major difference with works dealing with the Persian textile industry so far is that this study analyzes this industry, its products and its workers, from a socio-economic historical rather than an artistic point of view. As such it provides the historical background and socio-economic context for art objects, which once, after all, were simply consumer goods. What I have further tried to do is to provide a lexicographic framework, both to help other researchers (especially art historians) in their research as well as to stimulate other researchers to advance our understanding and knowledge on the subject matter even further. I am aware that I may only have been able to show how little I still know about Persian textiles, but there it is. I do not know whether I have succeeded in making Persian textiles more accessible to the textile specialists, the art historians, the Middle Eastern specialist, or just the non-specialist interested readers. Nevertheless, I hope that those who have consulted this publication, in particular its nomenclature part, will be helped in their understanding of the tangled nature of Persian fabric terminology. Furthermore, in having done so, that the study of the art of Persian textiles may be stimulated and deepened as well as that they may be even more appreciated than they already are.

Finally, I would like to thank Mr. Jack Haldane for having read and commented on the manuscript, and Mme Jacqueline Calmard for her commitment and dedication in preparing this text for the printer, which dedication went beyond what one may expect.

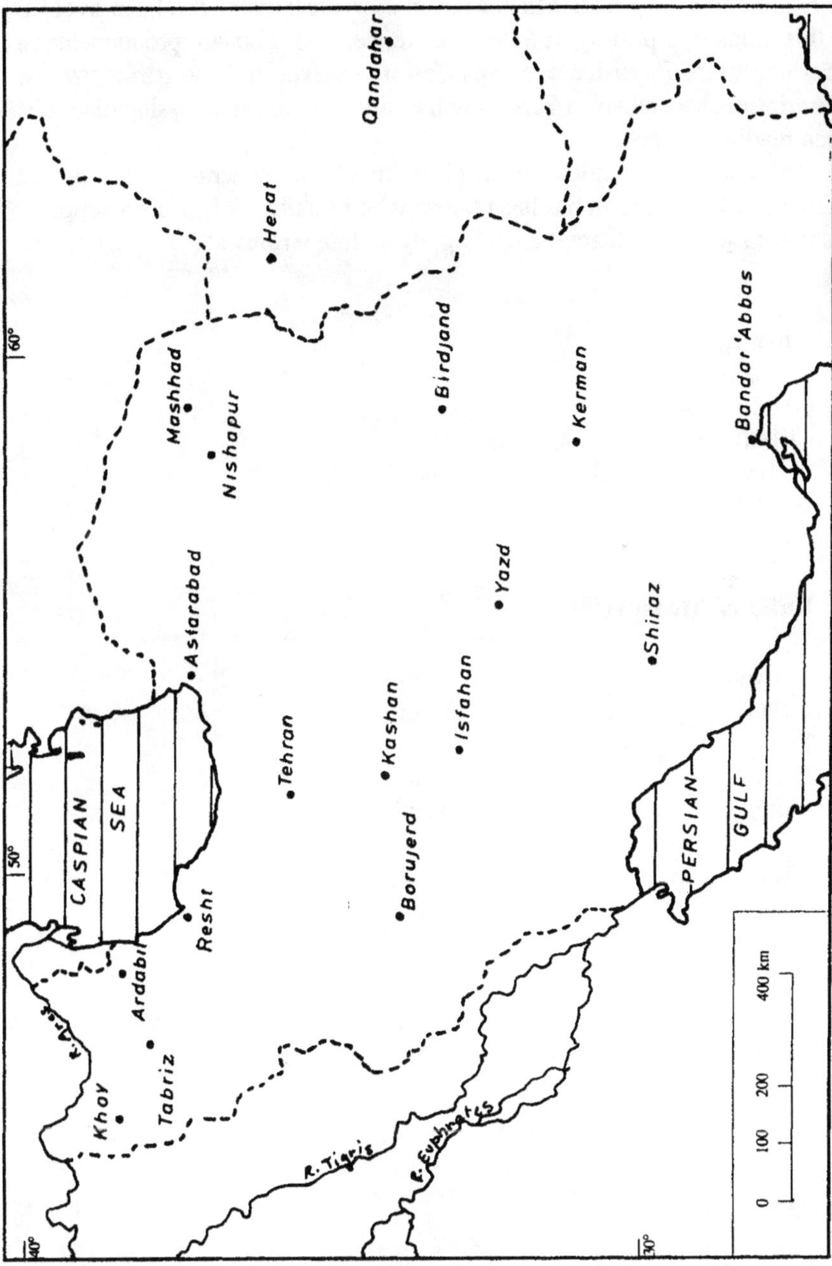

cartographie : Jacqueline Calmard

Main textile production centers in Persia (XVIth-XXth centuries)

Transcription

Studies on the Persian cultural area have been too often burdened by complicated systems of transliteration of the Persian language script (which includes a large number of Arabic and Turkish words). In order to facilitate the reading to a large audience, the use of diacritical marks has been avoided in this book. A priority is given to render the Persian pronounciation according to the English usage. An effort is however made to harmonize the transcription; specialists of Persian will easily visualize the missing diacritics when reading the text.

Although the mention of a plural mark is generally unnecessary whenever a Persian term has been transcribed in italics, it has been supplied in some cases, to facilitate the reading, by adding a roman "s".

Coinage

10.000 dinars	1 toman
1.000 dinars	1 qran
100 dinars	1 mahmudi
50 dinars	1 shahi

Units of Measurement

1 arshin	71 cm
1 dhar'	98 cm
1 gaz	98 cm
1 ell	68 cm
1 cubit	40 cm
1 Tabriz man	2.98 kg
1 methqal	4.6 gram
1 'oqqeh	1.28 kg

I. Introduction

The textile industry was the most important economic activity after agriculture in Safavid, Zand and Qajar Persia. Most rural (sedentary and pastoral) and many peri-urban families were, to a great extent, self-sufficient as far as the satisfaction of their basic needs for textiles were concerned. Polak, for example, writes that *karbas* (coarse cotton cloth) which was used by most people for clothing « is made by craftsmen, but in addition every household weaves enough for its own needs »[1].

International trade in textiles (and to some extent domestic trade as well) served mainly to satisfy the desire for luxury and more comfort rather than to cater for the needs of the common people. A few major textile centers dominated the "export" scene and supplied the domestic market with those cotton, silk and woollen goods that could not be provided by one's own work or the local manufacturing base. Persia itself also exported to the international market, mainly high quality and very expensive silken fabrics. Persian exports were mostly aimed at Russia and Turkey as well as at Central Asian markets. However, contrary to popular belief, Europe was hardly interested in Persian fabrics or its carpets, and in the latter only as of the 1870s. Because nowadays everybody loves Safavid fabrics as well as Persian hand-made carpets, many assume that this same attitude prevailed during the 16th-18th centuries, the golden age of Persian weaving artistry. The more so, because paintings from that era clearly show the use of Middle Eastern carpets as decoration of tables, floors, and walls in the interior of European homes[2]. Also, some of the surviving carpets were made to order for European royalty. Consequently, there is a strong belief, albeit a wrong one, that the trade and export of carpets from Persia to Europe has been an important activity in which Europeans and others were engaged in the 16th-18th century[3]. Imports from India served the luxury market in Persia as to its needs for high quality cottons as well as high quality Kashmir woolen shawls. Europe, first via the Levant, and later also via Russia and the Gulf, supplied the Persian market with woolens such as broad cloth and other kinds of woolen cloths.

---

1. Polak [*Persien*], II, p. 166.
2. See, for example, Ydema.
3. See, for example, in *EIr*, R. Savory, "Carpets, I. Introductory Survey", also D. Walker, *ibid.*, IX, p. 871.

As we will see in what follows the Persian urban textile industry would suffer enormously as a result of both exogenous and endogenous causes. Its importance, especially from a technical and artistic point of view, would grow during the Safavid period, in particular during the 17th century. After the Afghan occupation of Iran (1722-30) the textile industry suffered an enormous blow. Gradually the industry rebuilt itself, but it was never again able to rival the quality of products manufactured during the 17th century. The urban textile industry did recover, but its very existence came under threat in the early 1840s as a consequence of the import of machine-made fabrics from Europe whose low price suited the reduced economic circumstances of the Iranian population. This first wave of European textiles was followed by the silk disease of 1860, high prices of raw silk and cotton on the European market and, finally, a change in fashion in Persia. These factors combined to reduce the urban textile manufacturing base to an estimated 20% of its original strength in cities such as Isfahan. Also by the 1860s, most of the industrial cotton products that were still woven in Iran were made with imported yarns. Other products, such as *qalamkars* or prints, used mostly imported unbleached fabrics. The loss of the fabric industry was partly offset by the unexpected growth of the carpet exports from the 1870s onwards, a role which this commodity had never before played in the Persian economy. The remaining textile industry had to suffer a further onslaught as a result of its use of aniline dyes, which lost Persian textiles their major remaining aesthetic virtue, to wit their lasting colors. This was followed by the Russian tariff Agreement of 1903 which penalized Persian domestic textile products as compared with Russian textile imports. Although a basic weaving *urban* industry was still in place by 1920, the war against imports had been lost. Persia had turned from being an exporter of manufactured fabrics into being an exporter of raw materials (cotton, silk, wool). Even the fabrics that were still woven in Persia mostly used imported yarns and twists rather than the home made product.

The raw materials

In most of Persia's provinces the raw materials needed to produce textiles (cotton, silk and wool) were cultivated. Flax was only cultivated in Gilan and Mazandaran, however, and as far as we know not used outside its production area. Much of these raw materials was processed in the villages for home consumption. In addition, much of the towns' production was meant only for regional consumption. The remainder was left for export outside the region of production, but we have no idea whether the exportable share was large or small relative to total output.

Cotton can be and was grown practically all over Persia. Entire areas were covered with it, and many towns and villages depended for their livelihood on cotton. Much of the cotton production was transformed into fabrics. This was specifically noted by Olearius (in 1637) in Armenia, Erevan, Nakhjevan, all of Qarabagh, Azerbaijan and Khorasan[4] and by Tavernier outside Isfahan. Despite the almost universal production of cotton in Persia the entire harvest was not always turned into fabrics locally. He also mentions that there was a considerable trade in raw cotton[5]. Nasrabadi mentions that in the village of Varnusfa near Isfahan there were 200 cotton ginning shops *(dokkan-e panbeh kani)* which indicates the importance of the local processing of raw materials[6]. The situation remained unchanged under the Qajars (1794-1925), but exports of raw cotton grew to the point where these became dominant after the 1850s[7]. However, in some provinces such as Isfahan the entire crop was still consumed locally, which was not even sufficient to give employment to the existing production capacity of the province[8]. Most of the cotton grown was of the *Gossypium arborescens* variety, especially around Isfahan, Qom and Kashan. Yazd produced a kind of yellowish cotton *(Gossypium religiosum L.)*, which was exclusively used by the Zoroastrian community. This was due to the ban that Zoroastrians wear gaudy clothing. In Sirjan and Sa'idabad, another variety was grown[9]. The cotton was shelled after which the grains were removed. Around 1900 shelling the cotton to remove the grains was still done by hand in Kerman, Shiraz and Yazd, but in Tehran and Isfahan it was undertaken by machine, albeit a very simple, hand-operated, one. This consisted of two cylinders that turned counter-clockwise and was equipped with pins that tore

4. Olearius, p. 566.
5. *Ibid.*
6. Nasrabadi, p. 205.
7. Schneider, p. 166-186.
8. Olmer, p. 32 and DCR 4838 (1911), p. 20-21; DCR 5048 (1912), p. 19-20 for details on cotton growing around 1900.
9. Olmer, p. 32; DCR 1376 (1894), p. 18; Schlimmer, p. 160. « The village Parsis use a natural brown cotton for their garments [which] is partly due to their being debarred from wearing ordinary native garments ». DCR 5048 (1910), p. 50; DCR 5254 (1911), p. 60.

the pod apart and let the grains fall. These grains were either pressed (for their oil, which could be used as a fuel) or mixed in with the fodder given to cattle[10].

Raw silk — although mulberry trees were grown practically all over Persia — was mainly produced in the Northern provinces, bordering the Caspian sea. During the Safavid period the main production areas were Gilan, Mazandaran and the Caucasus. It was also cultivated elsewhere in Persia, in small but inadequate quantities for local industry, such as in Khorasan, Yazd, Kerman-Baluchistan[11], which led to imports from the Caspian provinces to Yazd[12]. Raw silk was even produced in Khuzestan[13]. Herbert (around 1628) describes travelling thirty miles in the forests in Mazandaran in which the principal trees were mulberries[14]. Olearius observed many mulberry trees outside Resht (Gilan) and remarked that the trees were planted together like bushes and not allowed to grow more than 5 1/2 feet high, so that the leaves could be easily reached[15]. The bulk of the production was processed locally, with the remainder being exported to Turkey, Europe, and Russia. Production in the 1650s amounted to some 4,000 bales or 600 tons according to the Dutch, but this declined considerably in late Safavid times to reach a low 200 tons in 1750[16]. The following qualities were distinguished during the Safavid period: *sha'rbafi*; *kadkhoda pesand* or *legi*; *kharvari*; *shirvani*. The *kadkhoda pesand* and *kharvari* varieties were mainly destined for export, the other qualities being used for local manufacturing. Silk from broken cocoons was considered to be the worst kind[17].

During the Qajar period the main production areas were Gilan, Mazandaran, Khorasan and Azerbaijan. In the first half of the 19th century production rose to 1,000 tons, but declined dramatically following the

10. Olmer, p. 32; Schlimmer, p. 162.

11. Floor [Persian Silk], p. 336; Ferrier [An English View], p. 198-199; Vaziri [*Joghrafiya*], p. 176, 105.

12. Bafqi, III, p. 619; *Barbaro and Contarini*, I, p. 73.

13. Stewart, p. 57: « after the hay season came the silk-worm season ».

14. Herbert, p. 171-172.

15. Olearius, p. 702, 579-580.

16. Herzig, p. 61-80; Floor, [Persian Silk], p. 337-343; N. Steensgaard, "Abrisham", in *EIr*, q.v.

17. Chardin, IV, p. 163-165.

incidence of silk worm disease in 1865, with only 99 tons recorded for 1877, increasing very slightly to 104 tons in 1910[18]. Trade during the Qajar period knew the following silk categories: *sha'rbafi* (silk weaver), *a'la* (the best), *tajeri* (trade), *tai* (? unknown meaning), *'alaqehbandi* (used for passementeries); *dovil* (of double cocoons used for coarse silken stuffs); *kej* (waste silk), which term was also used to denote coarse silken fabrics. Silk residues were called *lass*[19]. Silk cocoons were exported in ever increasing quantities from the mid 1860s onwards. By the end of the century very little spun silk was exported and this had a dramatic impact on local employment in the Caspian provinces[20].

Wool has always been found everywhere produced in Persia, most especially with the nomadic tribes and their considerable flocks of sheep, goats and, sometimes, camels. The most sought after wool was that of the Kermani goats. These produced a down (*kork*) which was mainly used for the production of shawls[21]. Next in quality was the wool supplied by the Shirazi and Qomi sheep, while those of Khorasan also were considered to be of good quality. In the South one distinguished the following qualities: *baghdadi*, *shustari*, and Persian. Each of these categories was subdivided according to quality. In Khorasan, the following distinction was made: *julga* for fine wool, *badgashi* for the coarser type of wool. The hair of the goat and wool of the sheep were used separately, never, if possible, were they used together in the making of the same carpet[22]. The clip was once a year at spring time, when the animals are about to start their grazing. One sheep yielded about 750 grams of wool. The custom of *lavage à dos* did not exist. The fleece were collected and washed in a haphazard fashion. Then they were cleaned by hand to remove foreign substances. Thereafter the wool was washed once again in cold water, followed by drying in the open air. Olmer, a French professor who, around 1905, made a study of Persian crafts, comments that he never saw wool being combed as was the practice in Europe. The carding of wool was similar to that of cotton[23].

---

18. Rabino and Lafont, p. 127-128.
19. *Ibid.*, p. 170.
20. Schneider, p. 142-165; Seyf [Technical changes], p. 147.
21. See chapters V and VI; Seyf [Silk Production], p. 66; Rabino and Lafont, p. 166-197.
22. Schneider, p. 187-197.
23. Olmer, p. 34.

The characteristics of the textile industry

The weavers (*nassaj, julah,* or *parchehbaf*) and spinners (*risman-charkh*) were omnipresent in Persia. According to Olearius most artisans in Safavid Persia were weavers and dyers and painters of flowers, who worked with cotton and silk. In Gilan, he also observed that the women spend much of their time spinning and weaving, in addition to their other activities[24]. This is also confirmed by other contemporary travellers in their comments on the economies of other cities, and this situation remained unchanged until well into the 20th century. Wilson, for example, writes in 1895 that « Spinning and weaving dress-goods, carpets, and other fabrics are universal household industries »[25]. This was due to the fact that, driven by poverty and by difficult and irregular access to urban markets, most rural people had to spin their own yarn, weave their own cloth, and make their own clothes. This condition was of course facilitated by the fact that Iran was a predominantly agricultural economy where the raw materials (cotton, wool, and silk) were grown and produced in most parts of the country. Even as late as the early 1900s, a German observer remarks: « However, little the Persian, in general, likes to work in so far as the common people are concerned it is rare to see the women just gossiping without their working at the same time on the spindle or the loom — not unlike our own womenfolk with their knitting. But even the men, if they do not sleep during the day or sit in a tea-house, also start their spinning-wheel during the idle moments, but often more to be occupied rather than out of an urge to be productive »[26].

The weaving technology was also relatively simple. A loom (*kargah* or *dastgah-e nassaji*) required only an investment in wooden beams and ropes. This even held in case of the weaving of costly fabrics such as *zarbaft* or

---

24. Olearius, p. 601, 700.

25. Wilson, p. 129 : « In Gilan and Mazandran nearly every family rears silks worm; and much of the silk thus produced does not come into the markets at all, being manufactured by the women of the family into coarse stuffs used for shirts, trousers, kerchiefs, and the like. In the other districts, where the silk product is less important, every silk-grower also retains a certain quantity of silk for domestic use ». Benjamin, p. 418; see also Bird, II, p. 112, 272; « In one corner two were sitting sewing a garment; others were standing, distaffs in hand, spinning; little girls were drawing out the wool over three or four spikes fastened to a piece of wood. » (Marsh [*The Tennesseean*], p. 68).

26. *Berichte ueber Handel und Industrie*, vol. 14, Heft 7 (June 1910), p. 236.

gold brocade. Nevertheless Shah 'Abbas I, himself an able weaver, marveled at a loom made to weave *sha'rbafi* or expensive silks that could be operated by the weaver while walking. This was demonstrated to the Shah during his visit of Isfahan in 1590, when the weaver walked from the Meidan-e Ilchi Khan to the garden of the Naqsh-e Jahan and wove 2 dhar' or ells of velvet[27]. Du Mans (around the 1680s) marvelled how little hardware was needed to weave these costly and technically complicated fabrics: « Four beams fitting into one another suffice, for here the weavers work at little cost »[28]. Both rural and urban communities knew how to make a loom from materials which were readily available and, even if the result was not always sophisticated, use it with considerable dexterity. Several 19th century observers comment unfavorably on the technical design of looms and spinning-wheels in Persia. The looms are not the best from a technical point of view[29]. Hoeltzer writes about 1875, « For the weaving of *karbas* they use very simple and small looms, which are halfway fixed in the earth. The weaving rooms are generally very dark so that I could not take a picture. Heavy weights and one long weak staff on top of the cloth, big schiffe of age-old construction are the main part of the loom for cotton fabrics. For silk fabrics the looms are better, though old fashioned »[30]. Olmer confirms Hoeltzer's opinion some 30 years later. The silk looms « are less primitive than the cotton and wool looms, and allow the production of a large number of fabrics by hand. The weave mostly used is the taffetas, but always with at least 4 shafts, sometimes as many as 8. This way it is easier to make a fabric, because of the low level of friction of the spool, which is never "à roulettes". Another fabric that the Persians love is the *Casimir* weave with the weft in different colors. The colors are mainly bright aniline ones, and contrasting (rose and green for example), which is hardly to the European's taste. I have seen fabrics with very complicated designs, where the loom had 8, or 10 and even 12 treadles. However, I have never seen the satin weave. The looms that are used are never Jacquard; the comb [beater] is made of wood. The tenter is also of wood

27. Natanzi, p. 373 f.
28. Du Mans, p. 186.
29. Blau, p. 110; Schneider, p. 144; see Wulff, p. 174-177, 205-210 on weaving technology in Persia in general.
30. Hoeltzer, p. 45.

and still exists, although I have never seen it used on wool looms, and where the fabric did not have allover the same size »[31].

Similar observations were made with regard to the technology used for spinning. « All these products are of middling quality, which is mainly due to the silk used and the fact that the weft is badly twisted »[32]. Further, that « The Persian skein of Silk is too long for general use in England, and the thread is usually uneven and knotty ». People were unwilling to alter their machinery[33]. This made Persian silk less valuable than it could have been. « Attempts have been made to persuade the Gheelaunees to use a reel of the proper dimension; the advantages of their so doing have been explained, and measures of the proper size have been given to them, hitherto, however, with little success »[34]. Wilson reports that « wool and silk are sometimes spun by a distaff whirled by hand. More frequently a spinning-wheel is used; the spinner sits on the floor and manages the thread partly with her feet. In many villages there are little shops where the silk is spun on a small machine. The cocoons are thrown into a caldron of boiling water mixed with sour milk. A man turns a wheel, about a yard in diameter, with a foot-treadle, and with one hand stirs the cocoons to loosen the fibers, while with the other hand he draws up the threads to be wound around the wheel »[35]. Silk spinning took place at Yazd, in the same manner as of cotton[36]. We have a description of nomad women weaving from the 1680s which, when compared with a photograph from the 1920s of a similar situation, shows that nothing much had changed[37].

« In Dehgerdu, the women were busy with weaving on their takhta-loom to make their black chaima shelters [*kheimeh* or goat hair tent]. The yarn, of which the fabric is made, is about one straw haulm thick made from black sheep or goat hair, which has been spun by hand. The fabric is 14 paces long and 1 wide, and woven so dense that it is waterproof. One needs 6 pieces of cloth to make an average sized tent. One piece is ready in 12

31. Olmer, p. 39. A tenter is a wooden framework on which cloth is stretched after being milled so that it may dry without shrinking.

32. Blau, p. 75.

33. Schneider, p. 144 quoting FO 60/92. For a picture of silk spinning around 1770, see Gmelin, III, plate XLI.

34. Holmes, p. 100-101, 108-109.

35. Wilson, p. 129-130.

36. Olmer, p. 39.

37. See Norden, p. 84, photo.

days, and is sold for about 60 shahis, more or less depending on the length. Per ell it is sold at 5 shahis. All women make it in the field. They do not have a beam, as do other cotton weavers in Persia, to which they wind the cloth and therefore also no pit, in which they, as other weavers, can sit comfortably. They creep forward as need be, until they have reached the planned woof and the work is ready. The loom is installed on a rough tree branch on the flat earth with wooden poles. Truly, it is a slow and simple operation, the more so with such an inferior material, which serves the poets as proverbial, when they speak about unimportant matters, which however have to provide for hundreds of thousands of families dwelling in Iran and Arabia »[38].

As a result weaving was practiced almost everywhere in Persia and truly can be called its most important industry. Many weavers just started operating in their homes, often apprenticing their own or their neighbor's children, or had a shop in the bazaar, where they worked in rooms that were open to the public view. Generally, these people were in the employ of local investors who owned a small or large number of looms, and who provided them with (colored) yarns, designs and, very important, orders[39]. When such an investor put a number of looms inside a building this was referred to as a manufactory or *kar-khaneh*[40]. The easy entrance level to the industry (low investment and low skill level) resulted in a fluctuating labor force, much of which was in the form of self-employed cottage industry. The weaving craft was a respected one. Many Safavid poets, for example, made their living as weavers or dabbled in this craft[41]. Even royalty such as Shah 'Abbas I could express his pride in his ability at weaving cloth, while Karim Khan Zand could boast of his proficiency in the weaving of stockings, carpets, *gelims* and *jajims*[42]. Especially, in economically troubled times peasants would try to increase their meager income through off-farm employment, including weaving. For example, in 1899, the British political agent in the Gulf reported that « due to poverty of the cultivators, who are the principal customers of cotton goods, caused transactions to be limited. The failure of the crops for three successive years on the Persian coast led

---

38. Kaempfer [*Reisetagebuecher*], p. 90-91, see plate 16.
39. Vaziri [*Joghrafiya*], p. 33-34; Nasrabadi, p. 138; Olearius, p. 495.
40. Shahri, II, p. 1-2.
41. Nasrabadi, p. 49, 71, 144, 258, 299, 356, 360, 369, 371, 380.
42. [*Carmelites*], I, p. 386; Asef, p. 309.

many cultivators to resort more largely to weaving for a livelihood, a demand thereby created for yarn and twist »[43].

However, not the rural areas, but the cities and their immediate surrounding villages were the centers of excellence as far as the textile crafts were concerned. But there was also a difference in quality of output between cities, some of the larger ones dominating the textile industry artistically and qualitatively. Thus there was a kind of hierarchy, with the rural areas at the bottom, smaller cities in an intermediate stage, and some of the major towns leading the industry. For example, it was noted that there was *zelu* production and some *'aba* (in Na'in) as well as block prints, but less artistic than in Isfahan[44]. *Chit* produced in Khonsar was of lesser quality than that of Isfahan and was used for linings (*astar*) of lower quality. On being imported into Isfahan it had to pay a special tax[45]. In the city of Astarabad, *alecheh* was woven which was better than that of the villages[46]. On the other hand fabrics woven outside the cities were cheaper, which may also explain the tax levied on their being imported into the towns. Those able to do so, therefore, got a bargain when they bought fabrics while in the countryside. Near Shiraz, for example, *karbas* was manufactured in the village of Savanat. Ouseley's servants bought the fabric there « at half the price that it would have cost at Shiraz »[47].

Information on the weaving techniques and working conditions of textile weaving is mainly on the textile manufactories, which seems to have been the dominant form of production in urban Safavid and Qajar Persia. In Samarqand, which was part of the Iranian cultural area, we learn of a certain Darya Khan Moltani who operated an extensive textile manufacturing business using skilled Hindu and Moslem artisans from India at the end of the 16th century[48]. In 1663, the Dutch report with regards to carpets that these « are made in a manufactory »[49]. A Persian document from the second half of the 17th century mentions that in Isfahan « the karavansaray-e

43. DCR, 2346 (1899), p. 5.
44. DCR, 5254 (1913), p. 60.
45. Tahvildar, p. 124.
46. [*Astarabadnameh*], p. 27.
47. Ouseley, II, p. 165.
48. Mukminova [*Differentsiatsiia*], p. 53-68.
49. VOC 1243, 28/4/1663, fol. 2035.

'Abbasi is filled with weavers [*julah*] who make karbas and the karavansaray-e Saru Taqi is filled with chitgars »[50].

In Qajar Persia we find the same pattern; textiles were produced both in manufactories and in private dwellings. Consul Abbott reports in 1848 about the situation in Kerman as follows: « The manufacture [of woolen fabrics] is carried on in the private dwellings or premises of the people », while in Kashan « the manufactures are carried on in private houses, and factories »[51]. Since much production was also carried out in the surrounding villages of the main textile towns it seems likely that this was operated as a cottage industry. Sock-making was one such cottage industry, in which, amongst others, Armenian women in Jolfa/Isfahan were engaged. They sat outside their houses on warm evenings in groups knitting. « The knitting is a great industry, and a woman can earn 4 s. a month by it, which is enough to live upon »[52].

In contemporary reports manufactories, because of their easier access, received more attention than the cottage industry. Around 1809, Isfahan had « many silk manufactories. We visited a house where 50 skanes of silk were spun in one day, and were then conducted to seven looms belonging to the same factory, where long black silk handkerchiefs, which the Persian women wear as turbans, were woven »[53]. Silk manufactories (in Yazd in 1876) were « fine, clean, spacious rooms, some containing seventy looms all busily working. The chief patterns were broad striped sheets for the ladies to wear, and black-and-white silk handkerchiefs. Some smaller workshops made a special kind of head-dress for export to Arabia. The silk looked to me poor in quality, and not much better than alpaca; but the weaving was undeniably close, regular, and good, and the colours brillant. The trade is mostly in the hands of the Zoroastrians »[54]. In one such manufactory there were 10 looms, on a level with the floor of the room, the workers sitting in holes conveniently deep to bring them level with the looms[55].

Unfortunately, little information is available on working conditions, wages, output and productivity. Around 1810, Morier writes, « These

50. Gaube and Wirth, p. 272-273, 282; see also Bafqi, III, p. 606.
51. Amanat, p. 83, 75.
52. Bird, I, p. 272.
53. Morier [*A Second Journey*], p. 155.
54. Floyer, p. 353-354.
55. Goldsmid, I, p. 166.

seven looms, employed thirty men. The weavers are paid by the piece; and not by the day. For completing one handkerchief, which is two zers and a quarter square, they receive two piasters (about 3 s.8d.). We were told they could finish one handkerchief in two days »[56]. The British consul observes when reviewing the industries of Yazd, that « weaving is carried on to a very large extent, all kinds of cotton and silk fabrics being manufactured. The hand loom in its most primitive form is the one employed. The warp is set up, and the weft threads are worked through it by shuttles; the treadles, heddles, reeds, and the batten are all of the simplest construction. There are 1,000 looms in the town, the largest proprietors owning from 16 to 20 of them. The operators are boys and men, who receive from 0,5 kran to 2,5 kran a-day; but as the work is paid by the quantity done, the operators are at liberty to work for very long hours. During this time 8 yards of rougher material can be woven daily, and from 4 to 6 yards of the finer class and of silken goods. If we take an average of 6 yards per loom daily, we have 1,878,000 yards of manufactured stuffs turned out of the Yezd looms yearly. This is allowing for no work on Fridays, which is the Persians' weekly holiday. I have visited the various weavers' establishments at different times, and have always found the looms working. It seldom happens, I am told, that a loom lies idle »[57].

In Yazd, one worker made 1.5-2 dhar''(or ells) of fabric per day. In Kashan, 200 looms made 400 pieces of velvet, or 2 pieces per shop, per month. The length of each piece was 13 arshins, and the price was 5-15 qrans per arshin[58]. In Isfahan, the manufactories had usually 30-40 looms each, in all some one thousand[59]. There were 200 looms for making woolen stuffs in Na'in in 1900, with one woman per loom who could produce between a quarter and a half arshin of cloth in 24 hours[60]. In Yazd, the dhar' of 40 inches was used to measure silks, chintzes and other fine goods; the dhar' of 30 inches was only used for coarse articles[61]. However, in Shiraz, silken fabrics were not sold by length but by weight. Curtains, that were sold for a price of 4 tomans to 10 shahis were sold per methqal

56. Morier [*A Second Journey*], p. 155.
57. DCR, 1662 (1894-95), p. 26.
58. Abdullaev, p. 93. See also Curzon, I, p. 369.
59. Abdullaev, p. 100.
60. *Ibid.*, p. 91-92.
61. Amanat, p. 82.

(4.6 g)[62]. Chintzes also were weighed with a view to determine whether it was the real quality product or an adulterated one. « Of course the calico, cotton-cloth, or T-cloth, as it is variously termed, had to be strong and good to stand such a process; and the adulterator had little chance with the wily calico-printer, who had always weighed his cloth prior to purchasing, washed and dried it, and then weighed it again »[63].

The main textile crafts

As stated above, Persia could be described as one big weaving mill, supported by many ancillary crafts. This was particularly the case in the main industrial cities where a major part of the population depended for their livelihood on the weaving industry. Chardin informs us that « all of Kashan's subsistence and wealth depends on the manufacturing of all kinds of silken fabrics, gold and silver brocades [...] One of its villages has one thousand houses of silk weavers »[64]. Yazd also was a town with a large textile industry. In 1757, the Zands recruited an army among its population consisting of *nassaj* and *hallaj* (weavers and wool carders) to fight against the rebel Taqi Khan Dorrani, the self-styled governor of Kerman[65]. In the Qajar period, Tahvildar, when describing the ruin of his town's textile industry, writes in 1294/1877 that « At least 10% of the guilds of this city were weavers, but not one-fifth of them have remained. Almost 5% of the Esfahani unattached widows, mothers or orphans, made ends meet by spinning and were not jobless. But also other big guilds like dyers, cotton dressers and washermen, who were dependent on this guild »[66]. Isfahan was no exception to this rule. A contemporary of Tahvildar, 'Abd ol-Rahman Zarrabi, writing about his town (Kashan) submits: « Silk weaving [*sha'rbafi*] and cotton weaving [*nassaji*] are very important to this town, and many other crafts depend on them. About one-fourth of the population of Kashan belong to this craft »[67]. According to Vaziri, another contemporary author, one-third of the population of Kerman was engaged in weaving.

62. Brugsch, II, p. 104.
63. Wills, p. 194.
64. Chardin III, p. 3-4; confirmed by Tavernier, I, p. 62; see also Afshar [*Yadgarha*], I, p. 132, regarding importance of *sha'rbafi* to Yazd.
65. Vaziri [*Tarikh*], p. 536.
66. Tahvildar, p. 101.
67. Zarrabi, p. 448.

This figure does not include the ancillary crafts[68]. The same holds for Yazd where, in 1865, some 9,000 people were said to be employed in the silk weaving industry alone, or some 25% of the population which was estimated to be about 35,000[69].

How important the ancillary crafts were is clear from another observation from the Kashan area in the 19th century. « Previously, two-third's of the population of Kashan and districts depended for their bread on spinning [*charkh-risi*], now they are all poor. The cotton beater [*hallaj*], starcher [*shudmal*], comber [*dandanehband*], dyer [*sabbagh*] and [other] ancillary crafts were thriving and paying taxes »[70]. A total number of 4,500 people were engaged in dyeing in and around Tabriz[71].

Similar observations also hold for the situation in the nearby villages and small towns, which formed the economic hinterland of important industrial centers. In the 17th century, for example, « the inhabitants of a village near Kashan, Mah-Abad, are all weavers [*julah*] they make *karbas*, their *astara* is also well-known »[72]. In the 19th century, « In the small town of Bidgol, near Kashan, having 40,000 inhabitants, and producing inter alia raw silk, there were around 1280 Q/1860 AD about 1,700 *sha'rbaf* looms which produced fine fabrics such as flowered taffeta [*tafteh-ye goldar*], wavy silk [*harir-e mojdar*], good gold fabric [*zari*], velvet [*makhmal-e porkhvab*], figured satin [*atlas-e moshajjar*], heavy satin [*qotni-ye sangin*], multi-colored cotton-silk fabric [*alecheh-ye rangin*], multi-colored silk-cotton fabric [*qanaviz-e alvan*], soft silk [*qasab-e latif*] and other silken stuffs »[73]. It also had about 300 looms of cotton weavers (*nassaji*) and satin weavers (*qotnibafi*), the others were idle. One quarter was entirely populated with cotton beaters (*hallaj*) and silk drawers (*abrishamkesh*)[74].

The importance of the weaving industry is also indicated by its dominance of parts of the city's landscape. In most cities, certain parts, in particular in the bazaar, were the exclusive domain of textile crafts, despite the fact that much, if not most, work was done in people's homes. For example, in Yazd there was a weaving hall (*khaneh-ye julahan*), a hat-

68. Vaziri [*Joghrafiya*], p. 35.
69. Goldsmid, I, p. 175.
70. Zarrabi, p. 449.
71. Blau, p. 112-113.
72. Gaube and Wirth, p. 270-271.
73. Zarrabi, p. 488.
74. *Ibid.*, p. 493, 495.

makers bazaar (*bazar-e kolahduzan*), a gold-lace makers bazaar (*bazar-e 'alaqehbandan*) a yarn sellers caravanserai (*karavansara-ye risman forushan*) and a starcher's hall (*khaneh-ye shumali*)[75]. In 17th century Isfahan, the karavansara-ye 'Abbasi was filled with weavers (*julah*) who made *karbas*, while the karavansara-ye Saru Taqi was filled with *chitgars* towards the end of the 17th century[76]. In Isfahan there was a linen sellers square (*meidan-e methqal forushi*), while in Kashan, Qom and Isfahan a draper's hall (*bazzaz-khaneh*) is mentioned in the same century[77]. During the 19th century we find in Isfahan the drapers' bazaar (*bazar-e bazzazha*), the dyers' bazaar (the *bazar-e sabbaghan*), the hat makers' bazaar (the *bazar-e kolahduz*), and even two chintz makers' bazaar (*bazar-e chitsazha*)[78]. Especially, the bazaars of the *chit* makers were not only large and extensive, but also were renowned for their architecture[79]. The influx of new products, such as European shirtings or *shelleh*, also left its mark on Isfahan, when a *sara-ye shelleh* was built in the 19th century[80]. In Yazd, we find the drapers bazaar (*bazar-e bazzaz*), *sadri*, gold-lace makers bazar (*bazar-e 'alaqehbandha*), the old hat makers bazaar (*bazar kolahduzan-e qadim*)[81].

The ancillary industries were as important to the local economy as was the weaving industry itself and some of them dominated the urban landscape. « The *chitsaz* occupy two large caravansarais and a number of the best bazaars to do their job, i.e. the karavansaray Qeisarriyeh and Shah are exclusively for their use. 152 *ostads* employ more than 7,000 workers of all kinds, viz. 6452 workers, 195 indigo dyers (*sabbagh-e nil*), 46 dye grinders (*rang-sab*), 95 dye boilers (*rang-paz*), 295 starchers (*aharzan*) and 123 die and wood-block makers (*naqqash-e namuneh-saz va chub-tarash*). In addition, they employ specialized workers such as washermen, porters and muleteers. Annually about 28,000 pieces (*tup*) of cotton are processed. Depending on the nature of their work, the workers [young and old] are distributed over the various cells, closely together. Summer and winter, they

---

75. Bafqi, I, p. 159, 173; III, p. 606, 643-644; Afshar [*Yadgarha*], p. 630.
76. Gaube and Wirth, p. 272-273.
77. Nasrabadi, p. 348, 366, 372; Della Valle [*Voyages*], II, p. 197, 295 ("bazazistan").
78. Esfahani [*Nesf-e jahan*], p. 29, 33, 37, 50-51, 80; Gaube and Wirth, p. 170, 172.
79. Tahvildar, p. 94.
80. Gaube and Wirth, p. 178.
81. Afshar [*Yadgarha*], p. 112, 676, 682, 765-766.

are busy working. It is very dark in these rooms and the simple oil lamps have to help out. They take it all in a stride, for they are well paid, and most of them belong to respectable families »[82].

« The chief industry of Isfahan is calico printing, and it affords a living to a large portion of the population of the town. Except when the Zainderud is in flood, its bed presents a curious sight; for a couple of miles at least is covered with thousands of yards of red coloured cloth, undergoing the various stages of dyeing. To such an extent is this carried out that the waters of the river are discoloured and the stones of its bed at times look as they had been laved in blood. For the most part the work is applied only to the ordinary every day commodities, such as handkerchiefs of various sizes, purdehs (door curtains) coverlets, wrappers, head gear, and suchlike articles »[83].

Spinning, which was also an important ancillary craft for the textile industry, was a cottage industry engaging women and, in winter, men as well[84]. At the other end of the process there was another important industrial activity, viz. the handling and packing of the textiles. Yazd supplied a large portion of Persia with different articles of clothing. About all the women's *chadors* were made in Yazd, both in cotton and silk. « These alone, when finished, afford employment to a large number of hands in packing these in separate paper covers, usually ornamented with gilt pepper. Every piece of this is stuck on with gum, consisting of the gelatine obtained from the sinews of the sheep killed for butcher's meat »[85].

Some ancillary crafts were dominated by marginal groups such as Jews. For example, it was especially Jews who were engaged in silk-spinning in Yazd[86]. In Isfahan, silk assaying (*abrishamkari*) also was an entirely Jewish craft, and it was they who selected silk and distributed it to the *sha'rbaf*, the *meshkibaf*, the *'alaqehband* and other crafts[87]. Mrs. Bishop observes that in Western Persia (Kurdistan), dyeing was often performed by Jews, because it was one of the dirty jobs in which they were

---

82. Hoeltzer, p. 43; see also Gaube and Wirth, p. 170, 172 who mention two *bazar-e chitsaz*.

83. DCR 1376 (1894), p. 48.

84. Kuss, p. 147-148.

85. DCR 1662 (1894-95) p. 7.

86. Olmer, p. 39.

87. Tahvildar, p. 107.

permitted to make a living. She also notes « the solitary Jew dyer, who, with his family is found in all the larger villages on this route »[88].

These observations convey the economic importance of the weaving industry and its ancillary crafts for the urban population. They do not give an idea of the high level of specialization that was peculiar to the weaving industry, however. Although Table 1 reflects the situation in Qajar Persia, most, if not all, of these crafts also existed in Safavid Persia.

In Kerman, for example, the following textile crafts were being carried out in the 17th century: the textile printer (*basmehchigar*), the dyer (*sabbagh*), the *pustinduz*, the carpet weaver (*qalibaf*), the *karbas* seller (*karbas-forush*), the horse blanket maker (*takaltuduz* = *'araq-gir*, *namad-zin*), the sock maker (*jurabduz*), the tailor (*khayyat*), the cotton beater (*hallaj*), the *'alaqehbandi*, the *namad-mal* and the *naqshbandi*[89]. The *'alaqehband* craft was also active in Mazandaran and Resht[90] as well as *sha'rbafi* and *naqshbandi* in Yazd[91].

Other textile or textile related crafts mentioned during the Safavid period include: *namadbaf*, *pustinduz*, *'alaqehband*, *lavvaf*, *bakhyehduz*, *soqralatduz*, *chaqshurduz*, *rangraz*, *tala-kub*, *suzangar*, *basmechi*, *sha'rbaf*, *jurabduz*, *maftul-kesh*, *namad-mal*, *tajduz*, *parchehbaf*, *jula*, *zarbaf*, *golabtunduz*, *naqdehduz*, *chadorshabbaf*, *meshkibaf*, *'ababaf*, *chitsaz*, *darziyan* (tailors), *saqarlatduz*, *londrehduz*, *chaqshurduz*, *jurabduz*, *pustinduz*, *utu-kesh*, *nassaj*, *naddaf*, *longbaf*, *sabbagh* or *gazur*, *shudmal*, *abrishambaf*, *rismanbaf*, *jamehbaf*, *zir-jameh-forush*, *makhmalbaf*[92].

Although the data base is incomplete and sketchy, available statistical data nevertheless provide an idea of the richness and variety of Persian textile crafts. The difference in the lists of enumerated crafts for Isfahan, for example, are only partly due to lack of scientific rigor in collecting these data. More important was the likely change in the nature of the product,

---

88. Bird, II, p. 198, 207.

89. Bastani Parizi [*Ganj*], p. 126, 128, 137, 140, 143, 148, 150, 152-153, 155-158, 160, 162, 171; Bardsiri, p. 236, 473, 520, 531, 680; Nasrabadi, p. 370; Gaube and Wirth, p. 262-282.

90. *Ibid.*, p. 71, 380.

91. Qomi, II, p. 904; Bafqi, III, part 2, p. 697, 703, 709, 719.

92. Golchin Ma'ani, p. 44, 64-65, 113; Kotov, p. 18; Olearius, p. 324; [*'Alamara-ye Shah Tahmasp*], p. 61; Nasrabadi, p. 143-145, 168, 258, 299; Du Mans, p. 180, 205; Richard, II, p. 138, 160; Kaempfer [*Reisetagebuecher*], p. 159; Khaki Khorasani, p. 48; Bafqi, III, part 2, p. 631, 670; Gaube and Wirth, p. 262-284.

which could be woven with the same loom. It also reflects a change in market conditions which engendered the disappearance of certain products and the appearance of others. Finally, the terms employed to denote a certain craft or product are less absolute than it would seem.

Table 1: Textile and ancillary crafts in the major towns of Qajar Persia (Number of master craftsmen engaged in the craft)

Craft	Isfahan 1870	Isfahan 1880	Isfahan 1920	Kashan 1870	Tabriz 1869
ajidehduz			20		
abrisham			-		
abrishambaf				-	
abrishamkar					123
ashrumehduz			64		
'aba or *kishbaf*	20		120		-
'aba-forush			20		
'alaqehband	56		35	-	
'araqchiniduz	-				
baftehbaf	-				
bandzir-jamehbaf	-				
bandabrishamibaf	-				
chadorduz	5				150
chadorshabbaf				-	
charkhtab-abrisham			-		
charkhgari va aqmesheh				-	
charkh-risi	-			-	
charkh-saz				-	
chitsaz			46		
chomushduz				-	
dastar-pich			6		
dukbaf					20
rangraz			100		
gazur		-		-	
golabtunduz		-		-	
golahduz	112				
guniduz					30
haramibaf				-	
jula'i			100		
jurab takht-saz			6		
jurbehbaf	-		-		
kalehbaf			20		
kalehduz			15		
kalijehduz	65				
karbasbaf	-				85
kejbaf	7				

kepehduz			17		
khamakduz				-	
khayyam			20		
khayyat	-				-
kolahduz	40		60	-	
kolahmal			40		
kolijehduz	65				
la'abduz	45				
lavvaf or *labaf*	17		120		
lehafduz			12		
londrehduz	46	-		-	
longbaf			3		
maftulduz				-	
malilehduzi	-				6
malileh-saz					1
mu-tab			6		
naddaf		-			33
namadduz					21
namadmal			20		
naqdehduz	-				
naqshband				-	
nassaj		-		-	
nassaj ba kalimi			40		
pinehduz					200
pulakduz		-		-	
qeitanbaf	-				
qollabduz	-			-	
qollabduz-e charkh			2		
rangraz					100
rishehbaf	-				
rubandehduz	-				
sabbagh-e abrisham			2	-	
sabbagh-e qadak			30		
sekkehduz				-	
shabekehduz				-	
sha'rbaf			100	-	
siyahakduz				-	
taqaltuduz			2		
tarreh	3				
zaribaf			-		
zanjirehbaf			6		
zanjireh-forush			6		

(-) means that only the existence of the craft is mentioned.

Sources: Hoeltzer, p. 21-22; Tahvildar, p. 94-102; Esfahani [*Ketab*], p. 77-79; Zarrabi, p. 226-228, 237-239, 256, 265, 273, 439; Shafi' Javadi, p. 227-229.

Some of these crafts mentioned in Table 1 exclusively employed women such as in the case of: *naqdehduzi* (gold/silver yarn stitcher), *malilehduzi* (silver wrapped yarn stitcher), *qollabduzi* (embroiderer), *'araqchiniduzi* (nightcap stitcher), *rubandehduzi* (veil stitcher), *khayyati* (embroiderer), *qeitanbafi* (makers of strings), *jurabbafi* (sock knitter), *bandzir-jamehbafi* (maker of belts for underwear), *rishehbafi* (cordel maker), *karbasbafi* (weaver of coarse cotton), *bandabrishamibafi* (weaver of silken belts), *charkh-risi* (spinner), *baftehbafi* (weaver of fine cotton). Other crafts also employed men such as *nassaji* (weaver), and *golahduzi* (owning makers), whilst others again only employed men such as *shalbaf* (shawl weaver), *naddaf* (cotton carders), *namad-mal* (felt maker) and *sabbagh* (dyer)[93].

In total, some 90 textile crafts were operative in Persia between 1500 and 1925. Some occured all over Persia, some only in a few places, some were unimportant, others only existed for a brief moment, but together they are proof of the creative powers of Persian artists and weavers who continued to produce beautiful products in a highly competitive market.

The main production centers

Despite the nationwide importance of weaving only a few urban centers dominated the industry. Rural centers of production only acquired some measure of importance either as a supplier to a major urban area, or if it produced a particular product better than anywhere else. For example, « Begistan is famous for the manufacture of a very costly species of cloth made of goat's wool, and called *barak*, and of a cheap silk material, called *chadar-i shahi* »[94]. Kupa is famous for its manufacture of camel's hair-cloth, said to be the best in Persia[95]. The Tunakebun industries consisted of silk manufactories of all sorts, those of Ramak and Kelarabad being celebrated[96].

Because there was no national market until the 1930s, Iran's economy consisted of a number of smaller regional ones, each of which was dominated by its principal urban center. Not all of these centers played an important role on the national scene. In the 19th century, Hamadan, for

---

93. Hoeltzer, p. 21-22.
94. Goldsmid, I, p. 350; see also *Historical Gazetteer*, II, p. 76.
95. Goldsmid, I, p. 166.
96. DCR 4812 (1910-11), p. 12.

example, had manufactories of felts, coarse printed cottons, dyed calicos and canvas[97], while the manufactures of Qazvin were velvets, brocades, *karbas*, and *namads*[98]. Nevertheless neither town was an important textile export center for areas beyond its captive market. The same held for « Sari [which] has no special industry, but almost all the wants of the country are provided for; a rough white cloth, known as kattan and silk stuffs are woven »[99].

Some cities, such as Kerman, only played a role as far as woolen fabrics were concerned. Others, such as Borujerd, temporarily played a role of some importance in the 1840s. But a few major cities (Kashan, Yazd, Isfahan, Tabriz, Mashhad) with their hinterland maintained their importance throughout the entire period between 1500 and 1925. This phenomenon was already observed by Fraser in the 1820s. « It will appear by the foregoing, that there are many articles, as well raw as manufactured, which are common to most provinces; and it is to be understood that there are many fabrics which have no place in it, because they are either entirely consumed at the place of manufacture, or have so little range of export as to be trifling to mention; thus, much silk and cotton is wrought in every village, for the purpose of its own inhabitants »[100].

97. Amanat, p. 94.

98. *Historical Gazetteer*, I, p. 325.

99. Napier, p. 123.

100. Fraser [*Caspian Sea*], p. 357. For a detailed emphasis of Fraser's remark see e.g. Golzari, p. 9, 14, 33, 35, 43, 45, 79, 82, 192, 121, 136, 151, 171, 174-177, 203, 206, 212.

2. 16th century Persian dress

II. Historical Development of the Textile Industry

Safavid-Zand Period

Textile production

The output of Safavid weavers was significant, both in technical variety and high quality artistry. Apart from fabrics with a metal background or mixed with gilt and silver threads (*zarbaft*, *simbaft*) these weavers produced a great variety of silk fabrics such as double cloths, brocaded plain cloths (taffetas), satins, and velvets. Furthermore, they also wove mixed cotton and silk fabrics, as well as woolen stuffs made of fine wool (*taftik*) and down (*kork*), for which Kerman was famous. Only in Gilan and Mazandaran a limited quantity of flax was cultivated and therefore linen fabrics did not constitute a major part of the Safavid weaving technology. In what follows we will discuss: the main production centers and their products; trade in silken, cotton and woolen fabrics; the interest of the Dutch and English East Indies Companies; whether the royal workshop dominated the production of high quality costly fabrics.

• *Sixteenth Century*

The weavers of the 16th century produced a large variety of silken fabrics of high quality. The ones mentioned in various texts bear this out: *alajeh*, *atlas*, *chahar-dhar'i* [*-ye sadeh*], *chahar ghab-e taladuz*, *chit-e qalamkar*, *dara'i*, *dastarha-ye barik*, *diba*, *golabtunduz*, *karbas*, *naqshduzi*, *kamkha*, *khata'i*, *makhmal* [*-e monaqqesh*], *milak*, *qasab*, *qotni* [*-ye sadeh*], *qotni-ye lapehdar va botehdar*, *soqralatha-ye 'amal-e namat*, *tafsileh*, *taladuz*, *suzaniha*, *zarbaf*[*t*], *zarduzi-ye haftrang*[101]. These may not be representative of the textile industry's total composite output. The Persian texts referred to do not focus on textiles which are only mentioned in passing and that rarely, merely to enhance the glory of the shah or magnate who is the subject matter of the text concerned. Thus the fabrics which are

---

101. Afshar, [*'Alamara*], p. 127-128, 137, 249, 250, 394, 400-401, 409, 410, 412, 416; Shirazi, p. 71-72, 120; Monshi, I, p. 260, 431; II, p. 99, 775; Shamlu, I, p. 60, 64, 72, 266.

mentioned were usually only those woven for the rich, for the courtiers, and for court itself.

The costly fabrics produced in Persia were used as part of important public and diplomatic ceremonies. If important magnates or the shah himself came visiting, the bazaars would be festively embellished with costly fabrics[102]. Also a *pay-andazi* (the ceremonial covering of a street or a floor with costly textiles) took place so that the shah would be spared the indignity of walking on dirt[103]. Further, the exchange of costly fabrics during political events, such as embassies and peace negotiations, was a standard procedure. An example of the latter is a tent (*kheimeh*) which had been prepared for Senan Pasha, the Ottoman Soltan's boon companion, with costly carpets, *du-gabbeh* (gold embroidery) and *suzaniha* (embroideries). Also stored in that tent were, inter alia, 300 *tup* (pieces) of *zarbaft*, 1000 *tup* of *makhmal-e frangi*, 1000 *tup* of *motabaq*. Senan Pasha prepared counter gifts consisting of, inter alia, *zarbaft*, *makhmal*, *deq-e Masri*, and *soqralatha-ye 'amal-e nabat.*[104]

The important textile production centers at the end of the 15th century were Kashan, Yazd, Tabriz, Isfahan, Mashhad and Kerman. This does not mean, as I have pointed out in the first section, that in other towns no important weaving activities were taking place, but the latter's activities were mainly of regional importance. The five major towns mentioned, however, produced especially for the national and even international market. The reason their products were in demand beyond their immediate catchment area is partly that their output was far larger but, more important, that their goods were technically and aesthetically superior.

Kashan was the center for silk weaving. It was said that the best trade in all the land was there and its noteworthy fabrics included velvets, satins, damask, girdles and sashes. The velvets were both gold enriched and plain. Kashan « wheare for the more parte they make sylkes and fustians in so great quantitie that he wolde bestowe Xml ducates in a daie may finde enough of that merchandise to bestowe it on »[105]. In 1515, Gomes de Lemos, remarked that Kashan was great in trade and riches, and of great population by reason of the merchandise and foreigners that come to it.

---

102. Khʷondamir, IV, p. 185, 592.

103. *Ibid.*, p. 565; Shamlu, I, p. 65, 333; Bafqi, III, part 1, p. 64; Qomi, II, p. 982, 1012, 1039.

104. [*'Alamara-ye Shah Tahmasp*], p. 127-129.

105. *Barbaro and Contarini*, I, p. 72.

Mestre Afonso, in 1565, observed a large trade in silks, satins, printed cottons, turbans and brocades[106]. Two English merchants in 1569 wrote that they bought a large quantity « of all maner of wrought silk »[107]. However, another English merchant, Edwards, did not have a high opinion of Kashan velvets and other fabrics, for « even though there is some of these wares made in his citie of Cassan, yet nothing like in goodness to those that you may procure for him »[108]. *Zarbaft* from Kashan is mentioned in particular as well as *diba* and *harir*[109].

Yazd was another major center, « a towne of artificers, as makers of sylkes, fustians, chamletts, and other like [...] they all [incl. suburbs] arr wevers and makers of divers kindes of sylkes which came from Straua [Astarabad], from Azzi, and from the cities towardes Zagatai: towards the sea of Bachu [...They] do afterwards furnishe a great art of India, Persia, Zagatai etc. »[110]. In 1457, it was noted that brocade weavers (*sha'rbafan*) were present in Yazd[111], who, in the 16th century, produced inter alia *dibaj*, which was sometimes gold enriched; *khara*, a strong silk stuff of one color; *mushajjar*, a so-called damask, patterned with branches and flowers, and velvet, other plain or gold threaded, the Yazd gold velvet being the most valuable fabric of the period[112]. In addition, Persian chronicles record the use of the following products woven at Yazd, to wit: *jamehha-ye zarbaf*, *zamineh-ye tala va noqreh*, *atlas*, *kamkha*, *makhmal*, *zarbaft*, *alejeh*, and *tafsileh* for the *zir dameni*[113]. Yazd, also « produces cloth made of Cotton »[114].

Tabriz, an important commercial city as well as the initial capital of the Safavid kingdom, was engaged in a « great traffics of divers sorts of merchandises, cloths of gold, of silver, and of silk », and the district was especially famous for its velvets[115].

---

106. Smith, p. 44. Neves Aguas, p. 151-152.

107. Hackluyt, II, p. 123.

108. *Ibid.*, II, p. 51.

109. [*'Alamara-ye Shah Tahmasp*], p. 410; Shamlu, I, p. 72.

110. *Barbaro and Contarini*, I, p. 73.

111. Kateb, p. 109, for the subsequent period see Bafqi, III, p. 697, 709, 711, 719.

112. Pope and Ackerman, III, p. 2174. The velvet and brocade clothes worn by Shah Tahmasp's I courtiers were made of fabrics produced in Yazd. Membré, p. 30.

113. [*'Alamara-ye Shah Tahmasp*], p. 249, 394, 401, 410, 419; Shamlu, I, p. 60, 64, 72.

114. Purchas, VIII, p. 464 (1581).

115. Schefer, p. 85, n.1 citing De Nicolay.

At Isfahan a variety of silks including cloth of gold was produced. It was also the center of a silk-producing district. In Isfahan « the people are industrious and curious in all Sciences, but especially in weaving Girdles and Sashes, in making velvets, Sattens, Dammasks, very good Ormuzines, and Persian Carpets of a wonderfull fineness »[116]. Persian sources mention the production of *chahar dhar'i* and *methqali* in Isfahan[117].

Although Mashhad is not singled out as a major center, the silken fabrics and especially the velvets of Khorasan were famous, for they « are equal in excellence to the Genoese; in other parts they work on smoothen stuffs and damask, but not with the finish they have in Italy »[118]. The *A'in-e Akbari* mentions that both Mashhad and Herat continued to produce silk without gold (plain silk?), satin and velvet both with and without gold, while Mashhad also exported a silken fabric without gold (plain silk?)[119]. *Dara'i* made in Mashhad and Khavaf was used in making royal robes of honor; further *makhmal* is mentioned as well as *karbas* made in Tabas[120].

Secondary centers mentioned were Shiraz, « wheare they make sylkes and other like workes »[121], and nearby Hormuz whose inhabitants allegedly « arr great makers of sylkes [as were those of] Tessu and Zerister that generally make fustians, lynen clothes, fryses, many rugges, and a litell sylke »[122]. It is more likely that the inhabitants of Hormuz sold silken textiles rather than making these themselves. In fact, it may well be that the reference to Shiraz and/or Hormuz may refer to Lar (and other smaller rural towns), which was an important secondary textile production center in the 17th and 18th century. Tenreiro for example, in 1523, observes that north of Lar groups of Torkoman nomads lived, who « weave very fine carpets of silk »[123]. However, he neither other Portuguese travelers who passed through Lar mention textile production in Lar itself. In Shamakhi silk called « Talamana and other of a light texture are made, as well as satins »[124],

---

116. Purchas, III, p. 86 (1609).

117. [*'Alamara-ye Shah Tahmasp*], p. 410, 420; Shamlu, I, p. 61; Nava'i [*Shah Tahmasp*], p. 55.

118. *Barbaro and Contarini*, II, p. 225, 218.

119. 'Allami, I, p. 92-93.

120. [*'Alamara-ye Shah Tahmasp*], p. 419-420; Shamlu, I, p. 60.

121. *Barbaro and Contarini*, I, p. 74.

122. *Ibid.*, p. 79, 86.

123. Smith, p. 66.

124. *Ibid.*, p. 144.

while in Russian sources taffetas from Shamakhi are mentioned[125]. Other production centers mentioned were Kesar, which produced *alejeh-ye kesari*, and Qazvin, whose *qasab* was well-known[126]. The mentioning of *diba-ye shustari* and *atlas-e shushtari* suggests that Shushtar also produced good quality textile products[127]. Finally, Resht also produced silken fabrics, although there is no textual evidence so far. However, a silken fabric dated 952/1545 mentions that it was made in Resht thus making a tangible case for Resht's role as a silken producing center[128].

How many silken fabrics were made is not known, but of Yazd it was said that « They saie that towne requireth every daie twoo sompters of sylkes: which, aftre or. maner, amounteth to Xml. weight. s for chamletts, fustians, and such other, I saie nothing; for, by the sylke they make, it may easelie be gessed how much more they make of those »[129]. Kashan was in the same league. There « The people are very industrious and curious in all sciences, but especially in weaving Girdles and Shashes, in making Velvets, Sattins, Damaskes, very good Ormuzenes, and Persian Carpets of wonderfull finenesse; in a word, it is the very Magazeen and Ware-house of all the Persian Cities for these stuffs [you may buy] also all sorts of Silkes, as well wrought as raw. I am perswaded, that ine one yeare there is more Silke brought into Cassan, then is of Broad-cloath brought into the Citie of London »[130].

• *Seventeenth Century*

The situation in the 17th century was not basically different from that of the 16th century neither in the geographical distribution of the most important textile production centers nor in the rich and varied output by Persian weavers. The wardrobe of Soltan Hosein (1696-1722) provides us with a short list of the kind of important fabrics produced during that period. It was stocked with *dara'i*, *atlas*, *diba*, *kamkha*, *parniyan*, *qasab*, *alicheh*, *zarbaft*, *qalamkar*, *awrangshahi*, *bekras*, *mahut*, *soqralat*, *kattan*, *harir*, and *qotni*, thus containing both domestically produced as well as imported

125. Chenciner and Mogomdkhanov, p. 125.
126. [*'Alamara-ye Shah Tahmasp*], p. 410.
127. Kh^{w}ondamir, IV, p. 565; Bafqi, III, p. 125; Qomi, II, p. 628.
128. Pope and Ackerman, III, p. 2076.
129. *Barbaro and Contarini*, I, p. 74.
130. Purchas, VIII, p. 510 (1603).

fabrics. Other sources mention the production of *atlas-e botehdar-e zartari, atlas-e Tabriz, zarbaft-e talabaft, zarbaft-e noqrehbaft, zarbaft-e dasti, makhmal, motabeq-e qotni, tuni-ye qotni, dara'i-ye Kashan, tafsileh-ye sabzevari* and *yazdi*[131].

It was alleged that the royal wardrobe was so well-stocked that it could clothe an army of 100,000. The used clothes of the shah, princes and his harem were allegedly burned every seven years and their gold and silver collected[132]. It would seem that the situation had changed with regard to the 16th century when Shah Tahmasp I, for example, sold his old clothes to his courtiers, which seemed to have been a more profitable undertaking[133]. This custom of burning the royal wardrobe is not mentioned nor even referred to by contemporary observers, who certainly would have commented upon such a wasteful activity. In fact, as is clear from several reports, 'Abbas I, Soleiman and Soltan Hosein were in the habit of rewarding deserving courtiers with a gifts of their used clothes[134].

According to Tavernier there were more people engaged in silk weaving than any other trade. Many artisans were capable of making silk fabrics, brocades, carpets which did not lose their lustre. They made many qualities depending on their final use. There were those who only worked in applying gold and silver flowers with gumwater on the taffetas with which the women made chemises and trousers[135]. The superior qualities of silken stuffs were mainly produced in Kashan and Yazd and, perhaps as a result of the presence of the *karkhanajat-e boyutat* or royal workshops, increasingly also in Isfahan[136]. Kerman and Yazd were also noted for their woolen products[137].

John Cartwright in 1603 observes that the craftsmen of Kashan are very good « in weaving Girdles and Shashes, in making Velvets, Sattins, Damaskes, very good Ormuzenes, and Persian Carpets of wonderfull

131. [*Asnad-e Siyasi*], p. 5, 87.

132. Asef, p. 89.

133. *Barbaro and Contarini*, II, p. 218. Kakasch, p. 117f.

134. Riazul Islam, [*Calender*], I, p. 399, 443; Du Mans, p. 55; Richard, II, p. 41 reports that Shah Soleiman gave the clothes that he wore during the ten days of 'Ashura to his barber, the *khass sar-tarash*; Mirza Rafi'a, for similar gifts to the *beglerbegi* of Bakhtiyari, the *qurchi-bashi*, and the *monajjem-bashi*, p. 18, 24, 56.

135. Tavernier, I, p. 606.

136. Chardin, III, p. 3-4; IV, 152-154; Tavernier, I, p. 62, 135; *Don Juan*, p. 40, Olearius, p. 601.

137. Tavernier, II, p. 95, 105; Du Mans, p. 12.

finenesse »[138]. The Carmelites noted in 1607 that in Kashan they make very fine carpets of silk and gold, brocades, velvets and other stuffs as well as tissues of the Arras kind [*gelims*?] and so does Della Valle, who singles out *zarbaft* and *milek* and adds that also cotton and cotton-silk fabrics are woven there, in particular *qotni*[139]. Ferrier mentions the production of velvets, figured velvets, *milek*, satins, damasks, taffetas and gold and silver cloth[140]. *Chit* was also manufactured in Kashan[141]. Herbert remarked that in Kashan there « are full manufactures of silks, satins, and cloth of gold curiously wrought and coloured, no better in the world and in such plenty »[142]. Kotov reports that in Kashan striped and checkered silken fabrics were made as well as *makhmal* and *zarbaft*[143]. Tavernier writes that there are many silk weavers in Kashan who produce a great variety of the best and most beautiful gold and silver in Persia[144]. In 1683, Kaempfer observes the sale of silk and silver brocade fabrics in the bazaar of Kashan, which was made not only in Kashan itself, but also in a village three miles outside the city, which is corroborated by Chardin[145]. The inhabitants of a village near Kashan, Mah-Abad, are all weavers (*julah*), they make *karbas*, their *astara* is also well-known, while *zarbaft*, *qotni*, *alecheh*, *tafsileh* and *chaharkari* (or rather *chahar-zari*) from Kashan were sold in the Isfahan bazaar[146]. Du Mans submits that the largest group of artisans were constituted by the silk weavers of *sha'rbaf*[147].

Yazd likewise remained an important silk weaving center. In Yazd silk « is made into Taffetas, Sattens and Damaskes »[148] and *sha'rbafi* is specifically mentioned a few times in the *Jame'-ye Mofidi*, which adds velvets and gold and silver cloth[149]. Von Poser observes in the 1620s that

138. "Observations of Master John Cartwright", Purchas, VIII, p. 509-510.
139. [*Carmelites*], I, p. 120; Della Valle [*Voyages*], II, p. 197, 199, 201.
140. Ferrier [An English View], p. 200-201.
141. Nasrabadi, p. 369.
142. Herbert, p. 218.
143. Kotov, p. 61; also Gopal, p. 17 (in 1638).
144. Tavernier, I, p. 62.
145. Kaempfer [*Reisetagebuecher*], p. 79; Chardin, III, p. 3-4.
146. Gaube and Wirth, p. 270-271, 282-283.
147. Du Mans, p. 195; Richard, II, p. 152.
148. Purchas, IV, p. 275-276 [1615].
149. Bafqi, p. 697, 709, 711, 719; see also Ferrier [An English View], p. 200-201; Afshar, p. 635 (*makhmalbaf*).

large quantites of silk [fabrics] were being manufactured in Yazd[150]. According to Tavernier, in Yazd silken fabrics, interwoven with gold and silver, were made which were called *zarbaft*; further Yazd produced fabrics of pure silk called *dara'i*, which were like the French single- or multi-colored taffetas. « They also make them of mixed silk and cotton as well as of pure cotton, which resembles our futains as well as a very fine woolen serge »[151]. Du Mans remarks that in Yazd the brass wire is drawn so delicately that when it is interwoven with the fabric, during six months, one has the greatest difficulty to distinguish it from real gold wire[152]. *Alecheh, tafsileh, zarbaft*, and *mandilha-ye zartar* from Yazd are also mentioned around 1680, as well as *qotni* some decades later[153].

Some art historians have submitted that Isfahan's role was strengthened through the establishment of the royal workshops (*karkhanajat-e boyutat*), although there is no evidence for that. Whatever the truth of the matter, the new capital remained a strong and important textile producing center. Kotov observed the dyeing of patterned fabrics, and also the sale of *methqal* from India and Arabia in Isfahan in the 1620s. Also, the manufacturing of cotton fabrics. People wore clothes such as *azyami* (male overcoat with wide sleeves), *kindachi* (flower patterned garment), *dargili* (striped checkered fabric), *kumachi* (red, leaning towards blue, cotton fabric), *kutiniya* (probably *qotni*), and *kaftans*. Also shawls around their waist and around their heads[154]. Don Juan writes that « in the district round Isfahan silk-worms are reared, and many silk stuffs are very skillfully woven here »[155]. *Zarbaft* and *simbaft* were also made in Isfahan[156]. Du Mans also mentions the production of figured silks, in particular *zarbaft* in Isfahan. In fact, he states that the main artisans are *sha'rbaf* or brocade weavers. Its product surpass those in the West, he opines, although he admits that *zarbaft* from Venice are more expensive and more wanted in Isfahan than in its own domestic product, which is lighter for it has less gold and silver[157]. Isfahan

150. Kochwasser, p. 87.

151. Tavernier, I, p. 105; see also Nasrabadi, p. 49. Yazd also exported cotton fabrics and raw cotton to Kashan, "The Voyage of Master John Newbery", Purchas, VIII, p. 464.

152. Du Mans, p. 195; Richard, II, p. 152. Afshar [*Yadgarha*], p. 131-132.

153. Zarinehbaf-Shahr, p. 190; Gaube and Wirth, p. 282-283.

154. Kotov, p. 65-66, 83-84.

155. *Don Juan*, p. 40.

156. Ferrier [An English View], p. 201.

157. Du Mans, p. 186; Richard, II, p. 145; see also Nasrabadi, p. 336.

also produced *chits* with all kinds of flowers and in all kinds of colors. Du Mans worried about those people living next to the *chit* makers' establishments, because of the bad smells[158].

Tabriz also remained an important economic center, second only to Isfahan in importance and population, where, Chardin was told, 6,000 bales of silk were processed annually (which seems unlikely), and the best turbans in Persia were reputedly made there. The town was further full with weavers of cotton and silken fabrics[159]. This is also confirmed by Schillinger around 1702, who remarks that both in the city and its hinterland costly silken fabrics and all kinds of figured cottons (*chits*?) were being woven[160]. Other sources mention the production of *dara'i* and the export of Tabrizi dresses to Russia[161], while in 1721, *atlas-e Tabriz* formed part of the presents made the Ottoman grand vizier[162].

Mashhad is not mentioned very much, although the production of *namads* in Jam and Mashhad has been recorded[163], while the English mention the production of *zarbaft*, *simbaft* and "sylke Stuffes" in Khorasan[164].

In Shamakhi people dyed silk, which was mostly exported, while it « is mostly sold to the natives, and consumed in stuffs for their own use » in 1716[165]. Kaempfer observes that in Baku in 1684, the weaving of wool and cotton was done rather poorly[166]. In Nakhjevan *qalamkar* was made[167], while Schillinger, in 1702, reports that Nakhjevan was mostly inhabited by Armenians who made a living in trading raw silk and silken fabrics. The silken stuffs woven at Nakhjevan he adds were sold all over the world[168]. In Ardabil, *jajim*, *gelim*[169] and *chit* were produced in the 1630s,

---

158. Du Mans, p. 203; Richard, II, p. 158. Nasrabadi, p. 360 also mentions *chit* production in Isfahan.
159. Chardin, II, p. 327-328; see also Tavernier, II, p. 51-52.
160. Schillinger, p. 149.
161. Gaube and Wirth, p. 262; Gopal, p. 17.
162. [*Asnad-e Siyasi*], p. 87.
163. Gaube and Wirth, p. 278-279.
164. Ferrier [An English View], p. 199, 201.
165. Bell, VII, p. 291.
166. Kaempfer [*Reisetagebuecher*], p. 50; Kotov, p. 46.
167. Pope and Ackerman, III, p. 2167.
168. Schillinger, p. 140.
169. Gaube and Wirth, p. 262-263.

while silk fabrics were also woven in Gilan[170]. In Tabriz there was a lively trade in raw silk in 1716, as well as of « manufactories of silk and cotton stuffs »[171].

Della Valle, writing in 1617-8, reports that deported Georgians cultivated and manufactured silk in Mazandaran. Also, that Gilan produced silken fabrics, while *tafsileh*, made in Gilan, was sold in Isfahan around the 1680s[172]. Olearius mentions that women in Gilan spent much of their time spinning and weaving. He also mentions that the bazaar of Resht housed many crafts, which he unfortunately does not list[173]. In 1638, the Dutch report that Gilan consumed 150 bales of silk, and Resht and Kashan 600 bales of silk for the production of fabrics[174].

In Isfahan, *qasab* and *zir-damani-ye nawshi* from Qazvin which women used as garments; from Ardistan *methqal* and *karbas* and *astar* and *chador* for women; *karbas* from Qom; *karbas* and *methqal* from Natanz; and *khan va khancheh* from Mahallat (a village near Kashan) which is used as a table cloth (*sofreh*), were for sale in the bazaar[175]. Schillinger also notes that there were silk and cotton spinners in Qom[176]. Shushtar continued to produce *diba* and *atlas* as in previous centuries[177]. Lar also was a center of some importance. Dutch sources refer to it as a town where many people were engaged in weaving around 1625[178], while in 1638 they report that Isfahan and Lar consume 200 bales of silk for the production of silk fabrics[179]. Tavernier reports that the town of Lar owes its repute to the silk products, in particular their beautiful girdles, woven by its mainly Jewish inhabitants. He also notes that there was no silk manufacturing at Shiraz at all[180]. Struys, in 1672, observes that the town of Scharim (Jahrom) was « full of weevers »[181]. In 1702, and two decades later (although the

---

170. Gopal, p. 17.
171. Bell, p. 295.
172. Della Valle [Extract], VII, p. 51, 311; Gaube and Wirth, p. 266.
173. Olearius, p. 700-701.
174. Dunlop, p. 612.
175. Gaube and Wirth, p. 266-269, 270-271, 276-277.
176. Schillinger, p. 175.
177. Shushtari, p. 491; Qomi, II, p. 628; Bafqi, III, part 1, p. 125.
178. ARA, Collectie Geleynsen de Jonge, Anonymous, "Description of Persia", unfoliated; Dunlop, p. 612.
179. *Ibid.*
180. Tavernier, I, p. 675.
181. Stranszens, p. 193.

information may have referred to an earlier period), Lar was still described as a town with a large Jewish population, who made their living by making many fine silken fabrics[182].

Attention has long been focussed on the major textile production centers, who depended for much of their imputed output on the production of the villages in their hinterland, and whose importance as secondary centers has been seriously under-estimated. Steele and Crowther, in 1603, for example, report that the main occupation of villages along the Mashhad-Birjand-Yazd road was the making of carpets and the production of silk, as much as 3,000 mans of silk per year to be delivered to Yazd silk weavers[183]. Around the same time, Don Juan mentions that « in the district round Isfahan silk-worms are reared, and many silk-stuffs are very skillfully woven here, as likewise elsewhere in the outlying districts of the towns of Ardistan, Kashan, and Yezd, Qum and Savah »[184]. Olearius, referring to the situation in 1637, mentions 1460 villages in the vicinity of Isfahan which housed many weavers[185]. In 1680, the Dutch report that « in the surrounding villages [of Isfahan] a great quantity of cotton cloth is being woven which is more profitable for the common man than the coarse Salampouries. Much effort is put into the cultivation of cotton and the establishment of weaving looms takes place with incredible energy. They have made so much progress with this that they now are able to manufacture silk stuffs such as allegeas, handkerchiefs, etc. which exceed the Bengal assortment not just in quality but also in color and fineness, for which reason the secklassies and roumaels, except for the extraordinary ones of lemon or gold-yellow color, with neat red or ash-gray stripes and little white stripes running in between [...] find a slack market and have significantly dropped in price »[186]. In 1683, Kaempfer observes the sale of silk and silver brocade fabrics in the bazaar of Kashan, which were made not only in Kashan itself, but also in a village three miles outside the city, which is

182. Schillinger, p. 266 Valentyn, V, p. 226.

183. Purchas, IV, p. 274-275; this also confirmed by Bafqi, III, p. 697, 709, 711, 719.

184. *Don Juan*, p. 40.

185. Olearius, p. 563.

186. VOC 1343, 27/2/80, fol. 602r; also VOC 1360, fol. 1933r.

corroborated by Chardin[187]. Schillinger specifically mentions the Tabriz hinterland as the producer of silken stuffs and carpets in 1702[188].

These remarks by independent observers indicate that textile related activities were strongly represented in the rural economy, as one would expect. Ackerman thus is wrong to ascribe these activities to the various cities rather than to their rural districts[189].

Likewise, the secondary textile centers often also played a role beyond their captive market. In a document, probably dating from about 1680, describing the caravansarais in Isfahan, much useful information is found about what textiles were traded locally, whence they came, and for what purpose they were used. *Qasab* from Qazvin, *dara'i* from Tabriz, *jajim* and *gelim* from Ardabil; in the days of 'Abbas I they sold Indian fabrics for *mandils*, further *kattan* from Baghdad, *'abas*; *ja-namaz, tafsileh* from Gilan out of which male *qabas* are made; *qasab* and *zir-damani-ye nawshi* from Qazvin which women use as garments, from Ardistan *methqal, karbas, astar* and *chador* for women; *karbas* from Qom, *karbas* and *astar* from Mahabad; *karbas* and *methqal* from Natanz; *khan va khancheh* from Mahallat which is used as *sofreh,* some Moslems and Armenians are active in *londreh-forush* and *londrehduz, mammal-e mandil, alecheh* and *chit-e qalamkar* from India; *namad* from Jam and Mashhad; *alecheh, tafsileh* and *zarbaft, mandilha-ye zartar* from Yazd; *zarbaft, qotni, alecheh, tafsileh,* and *chaharkari* (or rather *chahar-zari*) from Kashan[190].

By the end of the Safavid period, the earlier situation seems not to have undergone much change. Schillinger, in 1702, notes the importance of the textile industry in Tabriz. This is also clear from the fact that taxes were paid on textile production such as *sha'rbaf-khaneh* and *tamgha-ye aqmesheh*[191]. Bell, in 1716, also notes that a lot of the silk produced in Resht was used for local consumption[192]. In 1704, de Bruijn mentions that in Kashan « where they make most of the silk and gold and silver stuffs in such quantity that they every day use seven bales of silk, which weigh one

187. Kaempfer [*Reisetagebuecher*], p. 79. Chardin, IV, p. 154. Gaube and Wirth, p. 270-271.

188. Schillinger, p. 149.

189. Pope and Ackerman, III, p. 2174.

190. Gaube and Wirth, p. 262-283.

191. Zarinebaf-Shahr, p. 123-126.

192. Bell, p. 311.

thousand five hundred and twelve pounds »[193]. As to the Armenian suburb of Isfahan, Jolfa, he writes, that one of its quarters is « full of weavers and artificers in stuffs, among whom there are some Frenchmen »[194]. Bell observes that « the common manufactures of Persia are found here [Kashan], viz. silk and cotton stuffs, carpets, besides some other articles which makes this place of considerable trade »[195]. Also, that « at Isfahan there are many manufactories of silk and cotton, and a great many silk-worms in the neighbourhood. As the consumption of silk is considerable at this place, little of it is exported »[196].

• *Post-Safavid period - Eighteenth century*

In the eighteenth century we note a continuation of textile production in the same centers as in the earlier centuries.

The industry did not undergo a structural change, although in quantitative and qualitative terms the textile industry suffered enormously due to the destruction of Persia by the Afghan invasion (1720-1730). In terms of types of fabrics produced there was no change either and the typical Safavid textile of silk, of silk and cotton mixed, and of wool was still being produced.

Fabrics mentioned during this period by Persian sources include *atlas-e frangi*, *badeleh*, which was also made at Isfahan, *begras*, *parcheh-ye frangi*, *dara'i*, *zarbaft-e khata'i*, *soqralat*, *qadak-e abi*, *kamkha*, *golabtun*, *makhmal-e irani* and *khata'i*, and *namad-e kermani*[197].

The fall of the Safavid dynasty in 1722 and the subsequent Afghan rape and occupation of Iran, followed by the incessant years of warfare under Nader Shah and the power struggle for absolute dominance between various parties between 1750-1790 dealt the textile industry a terrible blow. In 1723, the Dutch Agent in Isfahan reports that « the few remaining merchants and textile shopkeepers have been charged to supply [Mahmud Khan Afghan] with 4.000 tomans worth in gold and silver cloth. Those

193. Le Bruyn, I, p. 179. Bell, VII, p. 298, writes that « the common manufactures of Persia are found here, viz. silk and cotton stuff, carpets, beside other articles ».

194. Le Bruyn, I, p. 225 (should be p. 229).

195. Bell, p. 298.

196. *Ibid.*, p. 307.

197. Mervi, p. 90, 119, 268, 370, 377, 448, 477, 480, 544, 624, 740, 743, 761, 771, 785, 795, 799, 918, 1140, 1148, 1164.

merchants who had fled, but had left their wife and children behind, were also made responsible for this impost. It is impossible, however, to find these fabrics now. There are no workers [=weavers], so that this city will be smothered by its own ruin »[198]. The Dutch implied that the weavers and other silk weaving industry workers fled or died during the siege. According to Krusinksi the Afghan invasion had an even more devastating and structural impact on the art of silk weaving. He reports that « experts in weaving, endowed with land, transmit the secret of their art as an inheritance to their sons, and if they have none of their own, they adopt them. [...] During the siege of Isfahan, when the weavers were stricken with famine, the special technique of interweaving silk tissues with a silver thread [...] was completely lost. It was certain that if any of the experts of the weaver's art had been left alive or had managed to escape this art would have revived under the reign of the Afghans »[199]. Reports from the post-Afghan period as well as surviving fabrics from this later period fortunately prove Krusinski to be wrong. Silver and gold wrought fabrics and carpets were still being made in Persia after 1730 in, for example, Isfahan, Yazd and Kashan. Among presents sent by Nader Shah to Soltan Mahmud we note: *zarbaft-e talabaft*, *zarbaft-e noqrehbaft*, *zarbaft-e mahamarat-e talabaft*, *zarbaft-e mahamarat-e noqrehbaft*, *atlas-e zarbaft-e noqrehbaft*, *dara'i-ye zarbaft-e yazdi-ye talabaft* and *noqrehbaft*, *atlas-e alwanan-e sadeh*. Also, a coverlet for the imperial throne made from *zarbaft-e badeleh* in Turkish design, with a lining of azure *atlas* with false hems of silver fir-cone (*boteh*) patterned *atlas* and golden *golabtuns* fringes. Further, one large (*rashidi*) *zarbaft* tent, on the inside *zarbaft* with a lining of red broad cloth consisting of 24 khaneh or section; each khaneh was 2 dhar' and the entire circumference measures 48 dhar'. Finally, a tent carpet of *zarbaft*, and an under-carpet of *londreh* lining, *qotni* and *qadak* were also mentioned[200].

After the expulsion of the Afghans at the end of 1729 the economic situation improved slightly, but not significantly. The Dutch report in 1737 about the situation in Isfahan as follows: « there are over 200 sjarbaff conas [*sha'rbaf-khanehs*] or silk weaving manufacturies, but only about 20 have remained in this famous city, in which light fabrics are woven for every body's needs [*gerief*], with the exception of the Shah. There are also few

198. KA 1908, 17/8/1723, fol. 151.
199. Mankowski, p. 2431-2432.
200. Nasiri, p. 100, 164.

weavers to be found in these [troubled] times, who are willing to work for a reasonable price »[201].

This statement stands in contrast with that made by Mohammad Kazem, who writes that Nader Shah gave orders to make 100,000 *khel'ats* or robes of honor for his coronation in 1736, « and in the course of one whole month, they brought so much *badeleh, diba, kamkha, atlas, chahar-dhar'i, begras* and colored silk material, and so many accoutrements from the provinces that one could not imagine »[202]. It is indeed difficult to imagine that this actually happened in view of the reduced output of the textile industry since 1722 as well as the reduced level of foreign trade. In 1740, for example, Nader Shah ordered broad cloth and shawls from Kerman which were not available there[203]. A Jesuit priest reported in 1744 that « the manufacturing of golden and silver [wrought] fabrics has almost totally ceased, and the number of workers who are engaged [in making] those luxurious carpets which we, in Europe, so much admire, has diminished considerably »[204]. However, Otter mentions that in the 1740s, in the bazaar of Isfahan, « everything necessary for living was sold, even the superfluous such as beautiful silk carpets, fabrics, gold and silver cloth » and in the Mint « one still makes gold [wire] for fabrics for which Gilan provides the silk »[205].

In the 1740s, woolen stuffs were difficult to obtain. Moreover, Nader Shah seemed to have prohibited the use of good quality woolens by his troops. According to Hanway, not one-third of his army wore European cloth[206]. After his death, therefore, there was sudden surge in demand for woolen broadcloth which the EIC and VOC were only too willing to satisfy. After a few years, demand dropped off again due to the economic recession in Persia as a result of the internecine warfare[207].

Abu'l Fath Khan, beglerbegi of Isfahan in 1750, allegedly gave orders to burn the wardrobe of old clothes [*zobl-khaneh*] of the Safavid shahs and to gather up the remaining gold and silver to be converted into gold (dinars)

201. VOC 2448, 14/4/37, fol. 1309.
202. Mervi, II, p. 448.
203. VOC 2511, 28/1/1740, fol. 134.
204. "Lettre écrite de Julfa par le Père Desvignes [26/5/1744]" in *Nouveaux Mémoires*, p. 134.
205. Otter, I, p. 208, 210.
206. Hanway, II, p. 27.
207. *Ibid*., p. 88; Floor [The Decline], p. 54.

and silver (derhams) coins. Therewith a force of 25,000 men was gathered to oppose 'Ali Mardan Khan. When the latter took Isfahan a *pay-andazi* or spreading of textiles in his path was part of his triumphal entry ceremonies. Amongst the textiles used were mentioned: gold brocades, satin silks, silk brocade, muslin and damask[208]. This story does not seem to be based in fact. The costly fabrics were more valuable than the little gold and silver they contained. Sale of the fabrics themselves would have raised more money than that of the gilt and silver thread they contained. The author also does not report where the fabrics for the *pay-andazi* came from after the bon-fire of the royal wardrobe. That such a line of action is more likely is for example borne out by Mahmud Khan's (the conqueror of Isfahan in 1722) behavior, who when in desperate need for cash after the fall of Isfahan offered costly Persian and Gujarati textiles for sale[209].

A Russian document detailing imports from Persia via Astrakhan around the 1750s provides an overview of what type of products were produced by which cities. Unfortunately, I have been unable to trace the published Russian text, which was used by Ackerman through an unpublished English translation. The main production centers were Kashan, Yazd, Isfahan, and Tabriz. Secondary production centers were Gilan (Resht), Ardabil, Shamakhi, Hamadan, Kessar, Kerman, Tehran, Shiraz, Qom and Shustar. Gmelin remarks that especially the products from Kashan were excellent. However, those produced in Gilan were of inferior quality, and products from other Persian towns also were better[210]. Hanway mentions the production of silken fabrics in Resht and Kashan. He adds that the weavers of those towns preferred first quality or *sha'rbafi* silk. However, « what generally goes for the Persian fabrics at Cashan is the finest sort, the threads of which are more split; this is usually all white, whereas the other is white and yellow; nor is it wound so short, so that though finer we do not esteem it as much as Sherbaff »[211]. Du Cerceau reports that « the best Manufactures of Silken-stuffs in all Persia are carried on in » Kashan. He also states that « Tauris is famous in Persia for the beautiful Turbans »[212]. Cook mentions that « formerly the greatest part of the inhabitants [of Kaskar in Gilan] were silk-weavers. They still continue

208. Asef, p. 247-248, 441.
209. KA 1891, fol. 486 (18/11/1722).
210. Gmelin, III, p. 419.
211. Hanway, II, p. 16.
212. Cerceau, I, p. 12, 22.

to cultivate silk, but the bulk of the weavers are fled or killed »[213]. Yazd also was a town with a large textile industry. In 1757, the Zands recruited an army among its population of *nassaj* and *hallaj* (weavers and wool carders) to fight against the rebel Taqi Khan Dorrani, the self-styled governor of Kerman[214].

« Kashan made veils of thin, close textured *doroi*, and also Alexandrian red half-silk veils with white hems. An equivalent quality was made in Gilan. Kashan also made silk and half-silk belts, sold resp. at 2,4 and 1,25 rubles, and full silk *doroi* kerchiefs dyed cherry color. Silk kerchiefs were also made in Temizhan and both silk and half-silk ones were made in Gilan, Ardabil, Qazvin and Tehran, the quality of the last two being poor. *Movni* kerchiefs were made in Shamakhi; and a silk called *bogadtz*, dyed black and sized, was also used for kerchiefs. Taffeta kerchiefs, very thin and loosely woven and sized, came in two qualities, while Tabriz, Shamakhi and Ardabil made an even thinner and flimsier quality called *gundelbev*. In the Gilani dialect *gundelbev* means "rough weave". Isfahan made silk and gold belts and Gilan red silk striped belts. Chequered silk kerchiefs were made in Gilan, Rasht, Lahijan, and Kashan. Probably like the kerchiefs made now at Yazd, they were made with small checks defined by a warp twill and a weft twill alternating. *Konovat* was used for kerchief and was made into blanket covers in Isfahan and Mazandaran »[215].

The Russian data is confirmed by other European sources dating from the 1770-90 period. In Kashan many silken fabrics were produced, for which it was famous, as well as cotton ones[216]. Persian craftsmen still produced « fabrics of pure silk, of mixed silk and cotton, of silk and silver or gold, of cotton and of cotton and wool. In Yazd, Kashan and Isfahan they produce brocades, velvets, taffetas, satins and almost all silken fabrics that we know. Although the royal manufactories do not make gold or silver-threaded carpets any more the art has not been lost »[217]. Isfahan produced all kinds of fabrics, especially gold and silver brocades, while Kashan is

213. Cook, II, p. 414.
214. Vaziri [*Tarikh*], p. 536.
215. Pope and Ackerman, III, p. 2169-2170.
216. Olivier, V, p. 169.
217. *Ibid.*, p. 305; De la Harpe, VI, p. 22.

famous for its silken stuffs[218]. Abiana, Tabriz and Ardabil also produced silken fabrics, but the quality of the latter two centers left to be desired[219].

Table 2: Prices of textiles in Isfahan around 1770

Product	Type	Price (dinars)
qadak	18 chelleh of Isfahani *abreh** 1st quality	1,500
qadak	16 " of Isfahani *abreh*	500
qadak	14 " "	700
karbas	12 " "	500
tafti	top quality *abreh* 1st quality	1,000
alicheh yazdi	1st quality *abreh*	1,500
qasab-e yazdi	1st quality per dhar'	600
begras	1st quality "	500
mahut	top quality "	2,000
khazz	good, one *jamehvar*	1,500

**Abreh* is the opposite of *astar* or lining, thus the outside of a fabric.
Source: Asef, p. 315-316.

The manufacturing of silken fabrics was also undertaken in places outside the traditional centers, mainly for local use. Olivier, for example, notes about Hamadan production « also, some kind of nankeen with cotton on the contrée. The production of these fabrics are in a slump now »[220]. Lar, too, was famous for a time for its velvets and taffetas[221] as was Shamakhi whose silk fabrics were well-known. This town had been destroyed in the 1720s, but was revived by Nader Shah. Mohammad Sa'id Khan had taken 100 Tabrizi master weavers, who were known to be the best at that time, to Shamakhi. However, after that town was taken by Fath 'Ali Khan these master weavers returned to Tabriz which led to the decline of Shamakhi which thereafter turned out a lower quality product. This was partly due to the fact that the weavers lacked good lasting dyes[222]. In N.E. Persia « coarse woollens of a strong texture are manufactured in the adjacent districts, a great part of which, made into garments, are exported into various parts of Northern Persia »[223].

218. Ferrières-Sauvebœuf, II, p. 37, 41.
219. De la Harpe, VI, p. 22.
220. Olivier, V, p. 52.
221. Ferrières-Sauveboeuf, II, p. 28.
222. Gmelin, III, p. 68.
223. "Extract from Forster's Travels in N. Persia (1784)", in Pinkerton, VII, p. 286.

Although 18th century European travellers record the presence of textile production in the various Persian cities they were not as enthusiastic about its quality as their 17th century forerunners. Hanway reports that van Mierop, a merchant of the Russian Company, received Persian manufactures in partial payment of his own goods, « which no reason but the absolute impossibility of obtaining money induced him to accept »[224]. Gmelin, writing about Gilani textiles, opines that « Persian fabrics are not attractive; the silk ones are so stiff and strong that it is hard to believe that one holds silk. The reason for this is that the manufacturers are too wasteful with this material and use 1.5 instead of 1 ell, more than is needed. However, it is undeniable that these fabrics become so strong that one can hardly tear them. But there is another defect. The yarns are uneven and knotted due to negligence during spinning and weaving. Also, the fabrics lack exterior beauty and flashiness. The dyers acknowledge that they do not excell in their craft. These fabrics are therefore more interesting rather than made for the European market. A French *gros de Tours* is to a *mokhoyar* like the day to the night. The mixed fabrics fray badly and the cotton ones do not last long. Other Persian fabrics are better than the Gilani ones, and especially the ones from Kashan excel »[225].

Olivier, although less detailed, shares Gmelin's opinion. « Persia does not make muslins, perses, or the very fines cottons which we have imported from Isfahan for so long. The Persian cotton is not fine enough and does not have sufficient consistence to give it, while spinning, that tenacity that the fabrics which we mentioned require. All cotton fabrics in Persia are rather coarse or ordinary to be used by everybody. They are very cheap. The same holds for the Indian cottons used by the rich »[226].

Carpets and felts

• *Manufacturing of carpets*

Safavid carpet (*qali*[*cheh*], *farsh*) production was a continuation of Timurid practice and was no creation *ex nihilo* as Spuhler has rightly argued[227]. Nor were Safavid carpets a borrowing of Anatolian

224. Hanway, I, p. 25.
225. Gmelin, III, p. 419.
226. Olivier, V, p. 306.
227. *Cambridge History of Iran*, VI, p. 697.

craftsmanship as some art historians have suggested[228]. The Italian traveller Barbaro, for example, observed in the 1470s that the floor of the large tents pitched for Uzun Hasan and his court was covered with the « most beautiful carpetts, betwene which carpetts and those of Cairo and Borsa (in my iudgement), there is as much difference as betweene the clothes made of Englishe woolles and those of Saint Mathewes »[229]. This clearly marks Persian carpets off from those of the Levant and Anatolia. These beautiful carpets, mentioned by Barbaro, probably were silk carpets which Uzun Hasan had shown Barbaro on an earlier occasion, « which were mervailouse faire »[230]. Khʷondamir also mentions the use of silken carpets around the same time in Eastern Persia, while the use of multi-colored and silken carpets is also attested around 1500 in Mazandaran[231]. Barbaro not only had an eye for the beauty, but also for the cost of these carpets. He noted that « they haue carpetts lyed vnder their feete better worthe than a hundreth ducates a peece »[232]. Carpets covered floors and were used for sitting, but none were used to cover walls[233].

Although pile carpets, flat weaves (*gelims*, *jejims*), and felt carpets (*namads*) were made everywhere in Persia as a significant part of the country's cottage industry in textiles, mostly it was for the workers' own needs or for local use. High quality goods seem to have been woven in a few specific areas of which the most often mentioned are Kerman, Khorasan and Yazd. This does not mean that good carpets were not woven elsewhere, of course, since other provinces are sometimes mentioned as well. However, Safavid chronicles single out these three areas as a recurrent theme and in a consistent manner. Also, 17th century European sources confirm these areas as the centers of excellence.

According to Persian sources carpets were woven in Kerman, Qa'en and Jaushaqan [between Kashan and Isfahan] in the 16th century[234]. These Kermani carpets were also very much appreciated abroad, for Abu'l-Fazl mentions that carpets were still being imported from Kerman, Jaushaqan,

228. Helfgott, p.110.
229. *Barbaro and Contarini*, I, p. 60.
230. *Ibid.*, p. 59.
231. Khʷondamir, IV, p. 190; Mar'ashi, p. 55.
232. *Barbaro and Contarini*, I, p. 48.
233. *Ibid.*, p. 52, 57, 130; Du Mans, p. 97.
234. Monshi, I, p. 102, 578; Shamlu, I, p. 72.

Khuzestan, and Sabzavar into India in Akbar's time[235]. Carpets from Khorasan were clearly also very much appreciated, because Shah Tahmasp gave instructions that « *qaliha-ye kar-e Khorasan-e abrishami* [silken khorasani carpets] gold embroidered cloth [*du-gabeh*] and felt carpets from Jam » be made available for the Great Moghul Homayun's quarters in 1540[236]. Carpets from Hamadan and Dargazin (in Khorasan) were considered to be good enough to be given as presents to the Ottoman Soltan[237]. Van Linschoten also mentions that carpets from Khorasan were an important trading commodity[238]. Pedro Texeira reports that the richest and most refined carpets were from Yazd, followed by those from Kerman and, finally, those from Khorasan[239].

In the 17th century, the earliest English reports submit that carpets « are made in divers partes of this kingdome, but the best and greatest quantety is made [in Khorasan] where they make them eyther of wooll or sylke, or both »[240] although « sondry places nerer » Isfahan and Kashan are also mentioned as production centers[241]. Joseph Salbancke, an English merchant, reports in 1609, that a large village called Vea (between Qandahar and Yazd) was « a store of Felts and Carpets ». Further a town called Gora, near Isfahan, was a store « of raw Silkes, Quilts, Silke-Carpets, and Turkeshes »[242]. Steele and Crowther, a few years later, report that the main occupation of villages along the Mashhad-Birjand-Tabas-Yazd road was, inter alia, the making of carpets and felts. They also report that « Carpets of all sorts, Silke and Gold, Silke and Silver, halfe Silke halfe Cotton, &c. » were a chief commodity of Persia[243].

Olearius mentions that Herat (which was then part of the province of Khorasan) was the best carpet producing center[244]. Khorasani carpets indeed continued to be sold in the market and were available in the Isfahan bazaar around 1680[245]. The Dutch understood that carpets were made in

235. Blochman, p. 55.
236. ['*Alamara-ye Shah Tahmasp*], p. 409.
237. Von Hammer, III, p. 520.
238. Van Linschoten, I, p. 47, 166.
239. Texeira, p. 243.
240. Ferrier [*British-Persian Relations*], p. 354; Ferrier [An English View], p. 200.
241. Purchas, III, p. 86 and VIII, p. 510.
242. Purchas, III, "The Voyage of M. Joseph Salbancke", p. 85.
243. Purchas, IV, p. 274-275, 277.
244. Olearius, p. 199.
245. Gaube and Wirth, p. 278.

Isfahan and Yazd, which were said to be better than those of Isfahan. They also reported that carpets were made in Isfahan, Kashan and in the villages between these two cities[246]. The Carmelites also report the production of silk and gold (wire) carpets at Kashan in 1607[247]. Figueroa observes in 1618 that the carpets made in Kashan were the most beautiful in Persia and equal to those in Isfahan[248]. English reports also mention the existence of Kerman carpets, as do some Safavid sources[249]. According to Chardin, Kerman was the town that produced the best carpets and even better were the carpets from Seistan[250], while Kaempfer also states that woolen carpets from Kerman were the best[251].

The Seistan carpets mentioned by Chardin probably were from Birjand where the Silesian traveller von Poser noted in the early 1620s the manufacturing of « artful carpets and the [floor] coverings made from goat's hair that are so common in Persia and Turkey »[252]. In Turkey, Persian woolen carpets seem to have been equated with Kerman carpets. When the Hungarian prince, George Rakoczi, wanted to have woolen carpets in 1646, he was informed that the Turkish merchant « has to send his own men to Karamania to have them made. Here [Istanbul] the Turks do not buy that type of rugs »[253]. There is a carpet, dated 1066-67/1665-6, produced by *ostad* Mo'min son of Qotb al-Din Mahani, Mahan being a town close to Kerman[254]. Carpet weavers from Jaushaqan worked in a caravansaray in Isfahan during Shah Soleiman's reign. In the same building carpets made in Mahallat (near Kashan) were also sold[255]. Schillinger reports that carpets with vivid colors [starck gedruckte Teppiche] were also produced in Tabriz and its immediate surroundings in 1702[256]. Krusinski mentions the role of Kashan as a production center of carpets in the early

246. Dunlop, p. 629.

247. [*Carmelites*], I, p. 120.

248. Figueroa, p. 210; see also Della Valle [Extract], VII, p. 298.

249. Ferrier [An English View], p. 200, n. 81; Bardsiri, p. 520, 531; Bastani Parizi [*Ganj*], p. 128, 137, 140, 148.

250. Chardin, IV, p. 154. This confirms earlier Persian and English observations of carpets production in Birjand, Qa'en and Tabas and surrounding villages, see *supra*.

251. Kaempfer [*Am Hofe*], p. 202; see also Fryer, III, p. 8.

252. Kochwasser, p. 88.

253. Gervers, p. 31.

254. Ferrier [*The Arts*], p. 128.

255. Gaube and Wirth, p. 274.

256. Schillinger, p. 149.

18th century and so does John Bell[257]. The latter also mentions that in Isfahan, « the making of carpets, however, employs the greatest number of hands, for which the demand is great; as they are preferable in quality, design, and colour to any made elsewhere »[258].

Helfgott maintains that no carpets were produced in the Kerman area during the 18th century, but his assertion is not borne out by the facts[259]. Several sources mention Kerman carpets. For example, Lockyer mentions that carpets were among the chief commodities of Bandar 'Abbas in the early 18th century and adds « these are in great measure the product of Carmenia [Kerman] »[260]. Mohammad Kazem Mervi also mentions the production of carpets in Kerman during the Nader Shah period[261]. Francklin mentions that Yazd and Kerman were exporting carpets in the 1780s[262]. There is even a carpet dated 1172/1758 which was woven by *ostad* Mohammad Sharif Kermani, although this by itself does not constitute convincing evidence. Housego even goes so far as to dub the 1750s as « the decade of the Kirmani carpet » for which, however, there is no evidence at all[263]. Niebuhr reports the production of small carpets by a Torkman tribe in the Shiraz area, « of which so many are exported from Persia each year »[264]. Ferrières de Sauveboeuf reports that gold threaded carpets were woven in Khorasan[265]. This type of costly carpets was amongst other things given as a gift to the Karbala-Najaf shrine by 'Ali Morad Khan Zand[266]. British East Indies Company reports also mention the manufacturing of carpets in various Persian towns[267]. One report suggests that the Khorasani carpets were the best Persia had to offer, « for the brightness of their colours and the elegance of their workmanship are deservedly in high estimation all over the world »[268].

---

257. Mankowski, p. 2432-2433; Bell, p. 298.
258. *Ibid.*, p. 315.
259. Helfgott, p. 115.
260. Lockyer, p. 219.
261. Mervi, p. 410, 454, 892.
262. Francklin, p. 148.
263. Housego, p. 44, 46.
264. Niebuhr, part 2, p. 130.
265. Ferrières de Sauvebœuf, II, p. 8.
266. [*Ruznameh*], p. 82; Fasa'i, I, p. 224.
267. Issawi, p. 88, 262-263.
268. Housego, p. 48 quoting a Report on British Trade with Persia and Arabia, 1790, EIC Factory records, G/29/21, 1987.

• *Size, Price and Use of Carpets*

As far as prices of carpets are concerned the Dutch observe that those bought in the market were cheaper than those made to order[269]. Also, those bought by local people were cheaper than those bought by Europeans. Further, that carpets bought outside of Isfahan were also cheaper[270]. According to Russian sources the price of a so-called Polonaise carpet was 30 rubles for a gold-silver threaded carpet of 5 x 3 arshins, and 10 rubles for a rug with a white ground of the same size towards the end of the 16th century[271]. Prices, of course, differed per size, quality of work, and the type of carpet (wool, silk, gold and silver wrought). Although we do not know any particulars of the carpets listed in Table 4 we may conclude that the difference in price of these carpets resulted from their size and quality. Also, that for some destinations cheaper carpets were bought than for others. The same holds for some carpets sold by the English in London, viz. seven carpets in 1685 at £15 each. In 1687, 14 carpets were sold at the same price, while in 1688, 17 carpets were sold for £7 each[272].

Carpets came in all sizes: big, middle, and small[273]. In the first part of the 16th century mention is made of silken carpets with gold-wrapped threaded fringes (*risheh-ye golabtun*)[274], as well as of carpets with standard sizes of 12, 10, 7 and 5 dhar' or ells. Some of these were further specified as being *davazdeh dhar'i-ye jushkani* [from Jaushaqan]. The production of very expensive small silken gold-wrought velvet embroidered carpets (*qalicheh-ye makhmal-e du-khabeh-ye talabaf*) are also mentioned. Furthermore, that carpets were counted, and probably sold, per *zouj* or pair[275]. Carpets were also sold by the square ell or gaz, at a price which normally amounted to 5-8 gold ducats per ell, depending how much

269. VOC 1243, 28/8/1663, fol. 2035.

270. VOC 1239, 31/12/1662, fol. 1210v.

271. Chenciner and Mogomdkhanov, p. 125.

272. Ferrier [*British-Persian Relations*], p. 395, quoting B/38, p. 38, 3/8/1685; B/39, p. 75, 2/11/1687; B/39, p. 152, 11/9/1688.

273. Shamlu, I, p. 72, 194.

274. [*'Alamara-ye Shah Esma'il*], p. 168.

275. [*'Alamara-ye Shah Tahmasp*], p. 294: *davazdeh zouj qali-ye davazdeh dhar'i va deh dhar'i va haft dhar'i* and *haft zouj qali-ye panj dhar'i* (*ibid.*, p. 403); 12 *zouj-e qali-ye davazdeh dhar'i va deh dhar'i* and 5 *zouj-e qali-ye panj dhar'i* (*ibid.*, p. 423). « The one idea that is distinctive with these people [carpet weavers of Birjand] is that of symmetry. The larger rugs are woven in pairs exactly alike, and a pair of these always lies symmetrically at the far end of a reception room » (Hale p. 84).

goldwire had been used, the Dutch write in 1636[276]. The English report that, in January 1620 a pair of carpets, of 11,5 x 4,5 covids, were transported by the EIC which cost 4,000 shahis, i.e. £100 the pair, or about £1 per sq. covid or gaz[277]. A « one payre verrie fine and lardge carpets of Kirman » were bought in Isfahan for 40 tomans in 1624; its expected sales price in India was 60 tomans[278]. Two pair of gold-enriched silk carpets were valued at 1500 reals of eight in 1631[279].

In 1663, the Dutch report that the price of silver and gold wrought silk carpets in Isfahan was 150 mahmudis per square gaz. This price only held for those carpets with the following sizes:

length in ells	width in ells
4.5	2 9/16
5	3 1/8
6	3 7/8
6.5	3 3/4
7	4
8	4 3/4

However, one carpet, that was ordered at the same time, but which had a size of 8 x 4,75 ell cost 20 mahmudis more per square gaz[280]. Persian silk carpets, bought for prince Rakoczi in Istanbul in 1639, which measured 5 cubits long and 3 cubits wide, cost between 50 and 70 thalers each. A gold and silver threaded silken Persian carpet, 3 cubits and one "fertaly" long and two cubits and one "fertaly" wide, cost 125 thalers. « It depicts two pairs of peacocks, or I should say pelikans, there is a nice large flower, and their faces are worked in gold and silver thread. Above their heads, there is a nice large flower, and even the fringes contain some silver thread »[281]. Around

276. Dunlop, p. 452.
277. Ferrier [*British-Persian Relations*], p. 354, quoting B.M. Egerton Mss. 2123, fol. 14.
278. Ferrier [An English View], p. 200, n. 81.
279. Dunlop, p. 26.
280. VOC 1239, 31/12/1663, fol. 1210v.
281. Gervers, p. 30.

1780, a good carpet cost 1300 dinars per dhar' and a good *gelim* 700 dinars per dhar' in the bazaar of Isfahan[282].

The carpets bought by the Dutch were either for use in the Netherlands as table cloth and interior decoration, or to be used as presents to Asian princes such as the emperor of Japan, the kings of Siam and Tonkin, and various Indian and Indonesian princes. Persian silk carpets and fabrics were held in particular esteem at the Japanese, Siamese and Tonkinese courts, which is why the VOC included them in the annual presents to the rulers and important courtiers[283]. If carpets had not been included in the annual present, or because the court wanted to make sure that it received a particular type of carpet, it was made known to the Dutch that these had to be included next year[284]. In Iran itself carpets played a prominent role. Apart from floor covering[285] or decoration of the interior, carpets were considered to be of sufficient status to be brought as presents to the Shah and foreign princes[286]. Musa Beg, the first Persian ambassador to the Netherlands, for example, brought amongst other things 6 carpets as a present with him[287], and so did Sir Anthony Sherley when he returned to England with a mission from Shah 'Abbas I. Carpets were also used as a form of payment, *beh rasm-e qalein* or a pair, to provide funds to dignitaries and/or their families, which was also referred to as *zar-e qalein*[288]. Moreover, carpets were of sufficient value to be used as security for debts, as an instance reported in 1629 shows, or to be singled out as booty[289].

• *Felts*

Felt carpets or *namads* also were produced in Iran. Shah Esma'il I used *takiyeh-namadha-ye divani* in addition to silken carpets for his court

282. Asef, p. 317.

283. Hotz, p. 68; Coolhaas, I, p. 483; II, p. 293, 421, 650, 700, 756, 788; III, p. 177, 306; IV, p. 158; V, p. 222.

284. *Ibid.*, II, p. 650, 700; V, p. 222. The Japanese court liked large carpets and the silver-gold wrought ones.

285. Hotz, p. 23 (tent floor covered with carpets), p. 149 (during an audience Shah 'Abbas II was seated on two finely woven woollen carpets), p. 188 (carpets used as floor covering during picnic); Le Bruyn, I, p. 149, 167 (mosque covered with carpets), p. 231 (house covered with carpets). Also [*'Alamara-ye Shah Esma'il*], p. 86, 168.

286. Qomi, I, p. 390.

287. Dunlop, p. 142, 144, 691.

288. Qomi, I, p. 415; II, p. 1088.

289. Dunlop, p. 296; Fumeni, p. 110; Shamlu, I, p. 175.

councils[290]. In 1540 Shah Tahmasp I (1524-1576) ordered that the household goods for Homayun, the refugee Great-Moghul, should include felt carpets or *namad-e takiyeh-ye korki-ye astar-e atlas* (felts for reclining purposes made of Kerman down and lined with *atlas*, a silken fabric) had to be included[291]. In the same decade, Membré mentions that Shah Tahmasp I was seated on a "techioneme", or a « very expensive felt [carpet] from Khorasan »[292]. Bayazid, the Turkish prince seeking refuge at the Safavid court also sat down on a *namad-e takiyeh*[293]. These probably are also referred to in a description by Paul Simon, a Carmelite friar, in 1607, « The house was furnished with rich carpets; around the room on the ground over the carpets were certain pieces of very fine cloth, folded in four, which in their tongue they call "Tishenamak" (and would cost 150 to 200 sequins for a good one) on which they sit »[294].

Membré further mentions the trade in « zambelotti e mocajari » or woolen fabrics made of camel wool and fine sheep wool (mohair), in Mingrelia in Georgia in the 1540s[295]. In addition to Khorasan (Mashhad and Jam) Kerman and Yazd also were known for their *namads* in the 17th century[296]. Du Mans also mentions the production of *namads*, without telling us where. These *namads* had a length of 4-5 ells and a width of 1-1,5 ells. They were so well made and so uniform allover that one thought it was English cloth. This impression was even reinforced when one felt the *namads*, for it was as soft as *londreh*. Felt was also finished with cotton on one side. These were used to make chamber robes, which would not dishonor an honest man[297].

290. [*'Alamara-ye Shah Esma'il*], p. 168.

291. [*'Alamara-ye Shah Tahmasp*], p. 294, see also p. 409, which specifies that the felts were from Jam; these type of felts are also mentioned by Membré, p. 56, 72. The editor of the *Divan-e albeseh*, Mirza Habib Esfahani, specifically states that he cannot explain the word *takiyeh*. See Qari. For a possible explanation of the origin of the use of the word *takiyeh* in connection with a floor covering, see Kashefi p. 196-197.

292. Membré, p. 23.

293. Qomi, I, p. 406.

294. [*Carmelites*], I, p. 117.

295. Membré, p. 12, 14.

296. Bardsiri, p. 236; Afshar [*Yadgar*], p. 633; Shamlu, I, p. 72; Purchas, III, p. 85; IV, p. 275.

297. Du Mans, p. 248; Richard, II, p. 192.

Chardin mentions the production of, inter alia, felt capes for the common people[298], known as *yapanchis*, which indeed were sold in the Isfahan bazaars during Shah Soleiman's reign[299]. According to Tavernier large felt rain coats in various colours were made in Kerman and, in a coarser quality, in Lar[300]. This highly serviceable item of clothing also was exported, even by Europeans as, for example, the Dutch who shipped 100 *yapanchis* to Ceylon and 1200 to Cochin in 1666[301]. It is also reported that 100 *corges* (one corge = a pack of 20 fabrics) of *yapanchis* were exported to Konkan (W. India) in the 1670s[302]. *Namads* were also produced in the 18th century, in particular the Kerman and Yazd ones are mentioned[303]. A good felt horse coverlet (*namad-e sarkesh-e khub-e asb*) cost 750 dinars in the bazaar of Isfahan around 1780[304]. Felt caps were the common head gear for villagers and servants in the towns[305].

The trade

• *The international textile trade with Persia*

Both prior to the Safavid dynasty as well as during its reign over Persia foreign textiles were imported for use by the wealthy. Persian texts mention the use of Chinese, Japanese, Levantine (Turkish, Syrian and Egyptian), Indian and European fabrics. Shops were dressed up with *dibaha-ye chin* (Chinese brocades), *makhmal-e frang* (European velvet), *atlas-e khata'i* (Chinese satin), *parniyan* (Chinese silk) and *taqcheh-ye haftrang*. For *pay-andazi, atlas-e mesri* and *khata'i* (Egyptian and Chinese satin), *diba-ye shushtari* (brocades from Shustar), and *dara'i* was used[306]. In addition, foreign fabrics are mentioned such as *makhmal-e frangi, makhmal va deq-e*

---

298. Chardin, IV, p. 155.

299. Gaube and Wirth, p. 278 who misread "papunchi". They are also mentioned by Du Mans, p. 248; Richard, II, p. 192, and Fryer, II, p. 184, 316.

300. Tavernier, I, p. 676.

301. VOC 1264, fol. 647v.

302. Floor [A Description], p. 44, n. 205, where "japancies" were wrongly identified.

303. Mervi, p. 410, 454, 892; Francklin, p. 148.

304. Asef, p. 317.

305. Du Mans, p. 248; Richard, II, p. 192. *Kolah-e namad*, or felt caps, were also made, Nasrabadi, p. 350.

306. Khʷondamir, IV, p. 83, 178, 185, 219, 473, 565, 592 (*diba-ye rum* and *zarbaft-e chin, diba-ye rum* and *frang, zarduzi-ye haftrang*).

mesri, atlas-e frangi, atlas-e khata'i, kamkha-ye rangin-e frangi, tafteh-ye shami, mandilha-ye zartar-e kar-e foton, alajeh-ye mov-e kar-e Hend[307].

The frequent occurrence of foreign textiles in Persian chronicles suggests that there was a ready market for high quality and costly fabrics in Persia. Foreign merchants availed themselves of course of this demand. English merchants, for example, looking for the possibility to export raw silk from Persia did not overlook the opportunity to sell European textiles to the Persian market either. For example, in 1609, the English merchant Shalbanck reports that the following goods could be imported from England: « broadcloth for the merchants and the better sort of people, also carsies for the Common people; blacke clothes for womens garments, good Chamlets and Velvets died in graine, with purple colours, and fine reds: cloth of Gold and Tissue, Velvets embroydered with Gold, fine Holland cloth for the King and Sultans. The colours of Cloth must be Scarlets Violets in graine, fie Reds, Blacks, brown Blues, London Russets, Tawnies, Lyon colours, faire lively Greenes »[308].

The import of foreign fabrics did not mean that there was no export market for Persian fabrics, but this market was limited to high quality products and to neighboring countries only. Persian textiles (gold brocades, and worked cotton and silk fabrics) were mainly exported to Ottoman Turkey, Central Asia, Trans-Caucasia, Russia and India[309].

Exports to India were mainly of costly silken fabrics such as *zarbaft* and rich carpets. The English mention that « Damasks, Carpetts, Velvetts, Taffeties, Sattins, Cloth of gould and sondrye other sylke stuffs carryed in great quantetyes for Indya »[310]. The situation that Tavernier referred to, viz. that in the past Persian textiles were in demand in Europe, is reflected in the prices that European velvets obtained as compared to Persian ones in the 16th century as reported by the *A'in-e Akbari.* Persian velvets obtained

307. [*'Alamara-ye Shah Tahmasp*], p. 127, 394, 401, 408, 410; Shamlu, I, p. 64, 72; Monshi, p. 783.

308. Purchas, III, p. 86 (1609); Purchas, VIII, p. 510 (1603). For similar remarks on market prospects for English textiles 15 years later see Ferrier [An English View], p. 210-211.

309. Chardin, IV, p. 166; *Barbaro and Contarini*, I, p. 151; Schillinger, p. 277.

310. Ferrier [An English View], p. 203. See also Purchas, III, p. 88, « Here [Hormuz] is a very great trade of all sorts of [...] Silkes, cloth of Silke, fines Tapistries of Persia [...] which serve for all India ».

better prices than European ones, a situation that apparently was reversed several decades later when Tavernier made his comments[311].

Origin	Brocaded velvet per piece/*mohur*	Plain silk velvet per yard/*mohur*
Yazd	15 - 150	2 - 5
Europe	10 - 70	1 - 4
Gujarat	10 - 50	-.-
Kashan	10 - 40	2 - 7
Mashhad	-.-	2 - 4
Herat	10 - 40	1.5 - 3
Lahore	10 - 40	-.-

Such was the appreciation in India for Persian velvets that when Sir Thomas Roe presented Shah Jahangir with a coach upholstered with Chinese velvet the Shah had this replaced by « gould Persian veluett »[312]. However, the English considered Persian velvets "trash" when compared with European velvets[313]. A French proposal to promote trade between Persia and the East Indies indicated exports would include inter alia carpets, satins, *zarbafts* and brocades which they expected to sell in India[314].

Trade with Turkey was dominated by the silk trade. However, Ottoman Turkey also imported various kinds of Persian silken fabrics, mainly *qotni* and *zarbaft*.. Also, but also in diminishing quantities in the 18th century Persian *karbas* and *alecheh* [315].

Russia was a major trading partner taking both raw materials (silk and cotton) and finished products (silk and cotton fabrics and manufactured goods such as belts, sashes, kaftans, wearing apparel and, of course, carpets). In particular *zarbaft* is mentioned in Russian sources as a main export article in addition to *kamkha* (brocade), "dorogo", "mov", velvets, *qotni*, taffetas and figured cottons (*kiseya*, *methqal*, *kindyak*) as well as Indian textiles[316]. Russian, Indian and Persian nationals were all involved in this export trade. Indeed, a treaty of 1667 even « gave the Armenian

311. Tavernier, I, p. 609; 'Allami, I, p. 98.

312. Roe, p. 118, 322-323.

313. Ferrier [An English View], p. 200.

314. Du Mans, p. 358, also p. 366.

315. Zarinehbaf-Shahr, p. 172-179.

316. Chenchiner and Mogomdkhanov, p. 124-125; Bushev [Besposhlinnaya torgovliya], p. 78-90; Bushev [Iranskii kuptsina], p. 166-180; Kukanova, p. 72-83; Gopal, p. 17, 19, 72; Mueller, III, p. 489.

traders a concession to transport goods, mainly cloth, hides and silk, from Asia to Europe via Astrakhan and Archangel for a duty of 5 per cent »[317]. Cook describing Astrakhan, observes that, « the produce of Persia, Armenia, Georgia, India, Buchar, and Chiva, are imported by the Caspian sea from all these countries; such as silks, sattins, velvets, brocades, cotton cloaths of all denominations »[318]. As of 1729 Persian traders enjoyed free trade in Russia as did Russian traders in Persia. In Astrakhan, Persian traders even enjoyed extra-territorial privileges and were allowed to be judged by their own judges[319]. The situation continued largely unchanged until the very beginning of the 19th century. « The important goods coming from Persia, are silk from Shemakha and Gilan and woven cotton fabric from Mazanderan and Isfahan and Derbent. Among other goods received [here] are: various silken and half-silken goods, drugs, also sometime wine from Shiraz, Isfahan, Shemakha and Derbent »[320]. However, it would seem that trade in silken belts, which had been an important luxury export to Poland, came to a halt. Either because of the Afghan occupation, which reduced trade and textile production and/or internal Polish conditions, these silken belts were henceforth manufactured in Poland and were as rich and beautiful as the original Persian models[321].

The export of Persian high quality textiles suffered a substantial set-back in the 1670s. Formerly, Du Mans notes, *zarbaft* was a popular export article to India. But now, he writes, « this trade has been reduced considerably due to the fact that it has been forbidden to adorn normal palanquins with that fabric in India. A master silk weaver or charbafe, who had 20 or 30 looms working, could not keep more than two or three, and even those did not enable them to make a living. The majority of these weavers, therefore, have begun to weave cloth or joula and taffetas »[322]. The same employment crisis is mentioned by Jan Struys who passed through Kashan in January 1672 and who observed how many of the

317. Chenchiner and Mogomdkhanov, p. 124-125; Gopal, p. 70, 99, 101, 104, 112, 118-119, 124, 158, 206.

318. Cook, I, p. 348.

319. Gopal, p. 170, 206.

320. Gopal, p. 244.

321. *Ceintures et Costumes Polonais*, Exhibition Catalogue, Mulhouse, 1972.

322. Du Mans, p. 186-187; Richard, II, p. 145; Sanson, p. 116.

numerous gold cloth and carpet looms were standing idle[323]. The reduced circumstances of the Persian weavers, the most important part of the urban labor class, also had consequences for the larger population's purchasing power, and thus for imports. The Dutch, for example, observed that in the 1670s, a linen cloth was woven in Yazd, which constituted a cheaper alternative to imported Indian (Coromandel) textiles such as Guinea cloth and Salempouries, which were used for the making of *qaba*s or garments for the poor[324].

The Yazd example was not an exceptional occurrence, for the same happened around Shiraz and Isfahan. Tavernier reported, for example, that there was no manufactories to be found in Shiraz and its surroundings districts. Meanwhile local weaving of coarse *chit*s to supply the needs of the poor had only recently begun[325]. This caused serious inroads into the exports of similar cloth from Bengal and Coromandel, both of which suffered in consequence. Though Lockyer noted that, in 1700, the « chief commodities of Gamron are [...] Rich silks and Carpets »[326], it may have been but a temporary respite since in 1115/1703 the silk weavers (*sha'rbafan*) of Yazd were driven by their distressed condition to petition Shah Soltan Hosein[327].

The set-back also had consequences for the import of Indian textiles which continued to be imported as in the previous century. The Indian textiles were both for local consumption as well as for transit trade to Russia, the Khanates and Ottoman Turkey.

Persia mainly produced a coarse cotton fabric, *karbas*, although other kinds (some of which were partly silken) such as *chit*s were also manufactured. However, due to its cheapness and quality large quantities of cotton textiles were imported from India. « They make also Calico Cloth very reasonable; but they make none fine, because they have it cheaper out of the Indies than they can make it [...] They understand also the painting of Linnen, but not so well as the Indians, because they buy in the Indies the finest painted Linnen so cheap, that they would get nothing by improving

323. Stranszens, p. 176.
324. VOC 1315, 12/11/76, fol. 75-76; Tavernier, I, p. 116-117.
325. *Ibid.*, I, p. 660.
326. Lockyer, p. 218; Gopal, p. 77.
327. Afshar [*Yadgarha*], I, p. 132.

themselves in that Manufacture »[328]. Consequently, local production of cottons seems to have been mainly for the poor, which, moreover, were of a coarse type and badly made[329]. These local cottons were often *chits*, which were made in Isfahan and Kashan[330] and, probably, in Tabriz[331]. Tavernier comments that the production of *chits* in Shiraz was a recent development and he also noted that fustian-like cottons were being produced in Yazd[332].

Nevertheless, Safavid weavers also produced a better-type of cotton cloth. The best cottons were mixed with silk with which Persian weavers produced a good quality fabric ("tela"), which in Europe was referred to as linens ("menu linge", "biancheria"). This term referred to many coloured fabrics, which were as good as Dutch cloth, according to Della Valle. Consequently this type of cloth was often exported[333]. Shah 'Abbas I (1590-1629) had tried to stimulate the production of high quality fabrics to reduce the import of Indian textiles, but apparently no measures were taken by successive governments to imitate this obviously failed policy. Failed policy or not textile production in Persia continued to be an important economic activity. Olearius also confirms this, when he observes that « in Yazd and Kashan they have good weavers, using artful figures even by writing it. If not used for making clothes it is sold at great profit abroad »[334].

Unfortunately we do not know how many Indian textiles were imported from India. Although quantified data from the European companies are available we do not know how big, or small, their market share was. According to a Dutch report from 1634 some 375,000 pieces of cotton stuffs from Gujarat and Coromandel were exported to Persia by sea and some 217,000 cotton pieces from the Punjab, Awadh and Bihar. Thus altogether some 590,000 pieces of cotton stuffs were imported into Persia, which is an enormous number given the estimated size of its population[335]. Data from a later date indicate that considerable quantities of cotton stuffs continued to be imported, although its volume fluctuated of course with the

328. Chardin, VI, p. 155-6.
329. Du Mans, p. 14; Richard, II, p. 9.
330. Nasrabadi, p. 360, 369.
331. Schillinger, p. 149.
332. Tavernier, I, p. 105, 660.
333. Della Valle [*Voyages*], II, p. 201.
334. Olearius, p. 601.
335. Dunlop, p. 494, 484-485.

ups and downs in the economies of the two countries. In January 1641, for example, the Dutch report that a caravan of about 800 camels coming from Lahore arrived here, bringing mostly coarse fabrics such as « jalaelsey, sephtanga, s'joutaers, ketsiaes, duppetas »[336]. In 1644, a number of caravans with 6,000 camels in all arrived in Isfahan resulting in a fall in demand for VOC cotton fabrics[337]. In 1645, a caravan of 400 camels arrived in Isfahan in December with cloth from Agra and indigo[338].

The European Companies only held part of the textile market, and their market share was under constant downward pressure due to heavy competition by Persian and Indian merchants. The VOC, for example, had the following standard order for fabrics from Coromandel and Bengal in the 1650-60s, in all some 90,000 cotton stuffs. If the 1637 estimate is correct also for this period it means that the VOC only held some 15% share of the textile market. The English probably held a similar market share.

Import : From Coromandel	From Surat
10,000 p. bleached allegias bethilles	16,000 p. sioutsaer deryabaddi
6,000 p. painted chits	12,000 p. sephtanga de calpy
6,000 p. bleached dongris	12,000 p. Jalaelsy
10,000 p. bleached salempourys	16,000 p. duppetas de Jalaelpoer[339].
3,000 p. bleached Chavonys	

Source : ARA, *Hooge Regering Batavia* no. 896, Instructie Sarcerius, 1/5/49, fol. 593. Allegias=*Alecheh* (q.v.); Bethilles=kind of muslin; Dongris=inferior cotton cloth; Sioutsaer deryabadi=cheap fabrics from Gujarat, in this case from Daryabadi in India; Sephtanga de Calpy=cotton fabrics from Agra and Surat; Jalaelsy=simple fabrics from Jalalpore in Gujarat; Salempoeries=a kind of multi-colored chintz; Chavonys=white cotton light fabrics with silken buttons if various colors; Duppetas=do-pattah, a fabric of two "breadths", a cotton sheet.

Although ships and caravans continued to arrive for Indian, Persian and European merchants we have no idea about the total volume of imports as the information that we have is impressionistic and irregular. For example, in 1666, there was an unusually large import of goods from India: « by way of Qandahar is arrived lately at Spahaun neare 1000 camells load of

336. KA 1044, van Oostende to Geleynssen de Jonge, Isfahan 12/2/41.
337. Van Santen, p. 65; Coolhaas, II, p. 247.
338. VOC 1183, Dagreghister Bastijncq, 13/12/1645, fol. 249.
339. ARA, *Hooge Regering Batavia* no. 896, Instructie Sarcerius, 1/5/49, fol. 593.

cloth and indigo which hath caused said commodities to fall in price 15 p. cent »[340]. This interesting piece of information is qualitative in nature and we learn nothing about how many textiles it brought and whether this was the only caravan to arrive. Chardin mentions that the Qandahar caravan trade represented a multi-million toman affair[341], although Tavernier observes that the Qandahar trade had fallen off by the 1650s compared with previous times[342].

We know that there was a continuous traffic by sea as well as overland where hundreds of camels bore fabrics from India to Persia. But even if we would know how many pieces of textiles were imported into Persia we still would not know how many were consumed locally. Available evidence suggests that a large quantity of the Indian textiles was only in transit in Persia and were in fact destined for the Ottoman Turkish markets[343]. One Dutch report strongly suggests that the textile trade was essentially a transit trade, with the Persian market being a side-effect only. « For the last two years we have seen a large quantity of textiles in Isfahan, but little or no trade in them, because during that time few merchants from Turkey had arrived. The Jolphalines [Armenian merchants] occasionally buy a substantial quantity of textiles, but for the most part they bring these for their own account from Lahore to Isfahan, whence they transport them to Turkey »[344].

The export of Indian textiles to Persia was so important that Fryer notes in 1673 that « the Persians have planted themselves here through the intercourse of traffick »[345]. Not only *chitgars* emigrated to Coromandel, but also carpet weavers, who arrived there around the 1560s and continued to make good carpets in the Persian fashion. In Elloor, « where are made the best Carpets after manner of those in Persia, by a race of Persians,

340. Matthee [*Politics*], p. 392, quoting EIC, G/36/104, letter 24/2/1666, fol. 348; see also VOC 1251, 30/1/66, fol. 212-213; for an earlier instance VOC 1224, 3/9/57, fol. 315.

341. Chardin, II, p. 347-349.

342. Tavernier, 1711 ed., I, p. 771.

343. Du Mans, p. 180; Richard, II, p. 138.

344. Dunlop, p. 670 (report by merchant Nicolaes Jacobsz. Overschie with regards to the trade in Persia 15/12/1638); see also *ibid.*, p. 566; see also KA 1071 bis, Sarcerius to GG 29/3/1650, fol.

345. Fryer, I , p. 86.

which they told us came over above 100 years ago » wrote Master Streynsham, chief of the EIC on the Coromandel coast in 1680[346].

Many of the imported textiles were specially made for the Persian market, down to patterns and colors. Also, coarse cloth imported from Surat was dyed and made into surcoats (*qabas*) in Persia itself[347]. Consequently, many of the fabrics imported from India, which included both coarse and high quality pieces, were unbleached.

Over the bed-covers Persians use a « Cloath painted with flowers and other Trifles; these they call Indian Cloath, because most of them are made in the Indies, nevertheless, a great many are also made in Persia, and the Flowers and other paints are stamped upon them with a mould besmeared with Colours »[348]. In fact according to Tavernier « They make so many of those taffetas that they do not care anymore for the fabrics imported from India, though these are superior », which probably referred to the situation of the 1670s when local production surged due to adverse economic conditions. Labrosse mentions that one reason why the *chits* were so popular is that the colors did not run and remained clear when washed or bleached[349].

• *The trade with Dutch and English East Indies companies*

- Woolens

Woolen goods were much admired and in demand in Persia. Shawls made of *kork* or goat hair were made in Kerman and Yazd, while elsewhere, such as in Hamadan, shawls were made of sheep wool. High quality shawls were also imported from Kashmir in India[350]. Other woolen products such as coats, hats and socks also were woven in Persia of goat wool (*taftik*), sheep and camel wool (*pashm*) as well as made from imported European cloth. There was a lively trade in raw goat wool and goat hair from Kurdistan, Yazd and especially Kerman, for the hatting and fulling industry

346. Records of Fort St. George: Diary and Consultation Book 1679-80, Madras, 1912, p. 100.

347. VOC 1349, 25/11/1679, fol. 1713v.

348. Thévenot, II, p. 94.

349. Bastiaensen, p. 96. The same justification (colors and good designs) is given by Schillinger, p. 277 some 30 years later.

350. See chapters V and VI.

in Europe[351]. According to a French report from the 1680s, the first quality of [goat] wool originated from Kerman, the second quality from Mashhad, and the third from Tabriz[352].

Because Persian weavers were not able to produce good broad-cloth, quality woolen goods were imported from Europe. « Persians are not good at working with wool and cloth, though they love broadcloth for which they pay 8-12 Reichsthaler per ell in Isfahan »[353]. Chardin confirms Olearius' evaluation and adds that the *taftik* and *kork* products made by Yazd and Kerman were soft, were not firm and lacked body. Good goat hair fabrics were made in Hyrcania, but the best were produced along the Persian Gulf littoral, especially in Douraq, which produced excellent *'abas*. Coarse serges and épaisses (probably felt coats or *yapanchi*) were made in the Moghan area (Northern Azerbaijan) which were used by the common people[354]. This is confirmed by the report on the Isfahan bazaars which notes that *gelims* and *jajims* from Ardabil as well as *jajims* and *yapanchis* from Khorasan were sold in the days of Shah Soleiman[355]. Tavernier disagreed with this view, for he claimed that the fine woolen products of Kerman and Yazd (by which he meant their shawls) were so well made and soft that they were better than silk fabrics and more expensive[356]. Kaempfer mentions that in the royal sock making workshop (*jurabbafi*) socks were woven with European woolens, because these could not be made in Asia, to serve the needs in socks of the royal court[357].

Prior to the arrival of the EIC and VOC Armenians were the main importers of (broad) cloth. This term referred to several types of cloth[358]. The best quality was known as *begras*; broad cloth was known as *mahut*, while *londreh* was a dyed, lower quality, cloth. The Armenians bought or bartered these various cloths in Aleppo and other Levantine towns for cash or silk. Europeans (especially the English) did their utmost to bypass the Armenian merchants, but these managed to survive successfully albeit with

351. Du Mans, p. 187; Richard, II, p. 145.
352. Du Mans, p. 367. In general on the *kork* trade see chapter VI.
353. Olearius, p. 601.
354. Chardin, IV, p. 155.
355. Gaube and Wirth, p. 262, 278.
356. Tavernier, I, p. 95, 105; see also chapter V.
357. Kaempfer [*Am Hofe*], p. 121.
358. See e.g. Ferrier [An English View], p. 210-211; Hackluyt, II, p. 44-45, 111.

a diminished share of the market. The importation of European cloth across Russia to Astrakhan by Russian traders had, at the time, only a marginal impact on the market[359]. Despite the long and severe Persian winters demand for woolens was low compared with cotton goods, because only a minority could afford these expensive fabrics. Consequently, trade patterns in this commodity was cyclical or rather erratic, where one season demand and thus prices were high and the next one demand would be low.

The VOC director in 1636 commented that « Cloth does not sell well here. It is only useful to hurt the [market] position of English cloth. We barter it for silk. The Armenians bring a lot of it from Aleppo too, which they take in barter for silk. Therefore we do not need more than 400 p.[ieces] per year, mostly red and green, also brown, but no orange, yellow or other light colors »[360]. Although English cloth compared unfavorably with Dutch cloth, the English had more of it and were more or less stuck with the Persian market, one of the few Asian market outlets for their product. For the EIC the cloth trade was a necessity, while for the VOC it was and remained a marginal activity[361].

The English sold cloth at very low prices in Gamron, because there was a lot of cloth from Aleppo in the market in 1642. The Dutch, therefore, decided that their broad cloth would be stored till winter time, unless it could be bartered with Shah for silk[362]. The English likewise blamed slow and disappointing sales on the Armenians, who had glutted the market in 1651[363]. Thus, the cloth trade carried on by the Europeans fluctuated and imports were intermittent[364]. Chardin when discussing the *londreh-forush* bazaar states unequivocally that Armenians dominate the cloth trade and that until the reign of Shah Soleiman they had been exclusively engaged in it, which as we have already seen is not entirely true[365]. The English made a last major effort after 1689 to increase their sales of cloth in Persia. The EIC even went so far as to conclude an agreement with Armenian merchants to

359. Gopal, p. 108-109, 128.

360. Dunlop, p. 584 (15/5/1636).

361. Ferrier [*English-Persian Relations*], p. 336.

362. KA 1044, Geleynsen to Governor-General, 25/10/1641, fol. 699; KA 1046, Geleynsen to LXVII, 20/2/1642, fol. 565; KA 1077, Sarcerius to Governor-General, 25/4/1651, fol. 584.

363. Ferrier [*British-Persian Relations*], p. 339-340.

364. *Ibid.*, p. 376-380.

365. Chardin, VII, p. 367; see also Gaube and Wirth.

boost its sales. However, the competition from Aleppo remained too strong and by the end of the Safavid period the EIC practically ended its attempts to gain control of the cloth trade in Persia[366].

Broad cloth and other woolens also were imported during the 18th century. Armenian, Greek and Russian merchants played an important role in this and other types of trade[367]. The EIC was compelled to play a role in this trade as well, because Persia remained one of the few Asian markets for this commodity[368]. In fact, one third of all the EIC's export of woolens was absorbed by the Persian Gulf between 1750-1770. Both broad cloths and long ells also called perpets (long lasting) in various designs and colors were marketed[369].

The Dutch occasionally dabbled in this trade, but found its profits too low, partly due to the higher price for their high quality product. The acting VOC director, Carel Clement, writes in 1742 that: « Cloth can be sold as soon as winter begins and the merchants come down from the uplands. The Persians prefer Dutch cloth to the English product, which can only be used to make cabaayen [*qaba* or overcoat], but from the heavy Dutch cloth, which they call begras, they can make hats, socks, rain coats, cattebies [*qatebi* or fur lined coat] and cordies [*kordi*, a small fur lined sleeveless coat]. This would be a good line of trade, but cloth is brought directly by private merchants from Amsterdam via Russia and the Volga [to Persia]. In Isfahan it is sold cheaper than the merchants can buy it here. That is the reason why the cloth that is bought here is mostly destined for Kerman, Herat and Khorasan »[370].

Hanway confirms Persian preference for Dutch cloth, although his discussion of the import of European goods suggests that English cloth, which was bought in larger quantities because it was cheaper, also was referred to as *begras*. In addition, Persians also imported white Gloucester cloth, which the Persians called « maghoot and ordinary Yorkshire dyed cloth, which was known as "londora". Furthermore, in good times, shalloon was imported as well as some rich silks, gold and silver lace, velvets and other rich manufactures »[371].

366. Ferrier [*British-Persian Relations*], p. 405-412.
367. Hanway, I, p. 374; II, p. 18, 24, 30.
368. *Ibid.*, II, p. 55, 60.
369. Amin, p. 120.
370. VOC 2593, Clement to Governor-General, 31/10/1742, fol. 1674-v.
371. Hanway, II, p. 19-20.

- Silken fabrics

West Europeans did not invest much in Persian silken goods and practically nothing in Persian woolen and cotton goods. Della Valle remarks that although weavers in Kashan produced all kinds of fabrics, none were as good as those produced in Europe. In particular, he notes, that the colours were richer and the dyes more beautiful. Della Valle singles out velvets and silken satins in general, which were not well made in Persia, because they had not invented how to properly weave it. He makes the point that good Christian weavers could make a lot of money in Persia by teaching their Persian counterparts how to make top quality products. Della Valle notes that Shah 'Abbas I had sent as far as Venice for European craftsmen to come to Persia and weave satins, but so far only one, a Greek weaver, had the courage to come. Della Valle had seen his work, but it was not good enough compared with the work of Naples in his opinion[372]. The English in 1618 state that velvets and satins were trash compared to the European product, while damask was not comparable to its European counterparts. Figured velvets would not be marketable in England, not being fashionable, so only taffetas were considered to be as good as the European fabric[373]. According to Tavernier, in the past there had been some export of taffetas, brocades and velvets from Persia to Europe. Most of the velvets went to Russia and Poland. Now these fabrics were made cheaper and were more beautiful in Europe[374]. Tavernier adds that the French used to admire Persian carpets, brocades and silken fabrics, but now the roles had been reversed and it was the Persians who were admiring the new rich fabrics made in France[375]. Tavernier's claims, though confirmed by reality, are contested by an anonymous French author who claims that Persian brocades, silk and cotton fabrics were better made than French ones and that they were brighter. They did not lose their color, and if these started to fade one only had to wash them. « Wait till the rain has stopped and the water is still not clear, and then immediately wash your fabric. Let it dry and then wash it three or four times. But the last time wash it in a vessel and out one-eighth part of a lemon in your water. When it is dry smooth it with some pieces of marble.

372. Della Valle [*Voyages*], II, p. 193-194.

373. Ferrier [An English View], p. 200-201.

374. Tavernier, I, p. 609.

375. Tavernier, I, p. 698; the same situation also held for Turkey that imported French silken fabrics, see Evans, p. 28-31.

[The result is that] the fabric is more beautiful and brighter than it was ever before »[376]. Another anonymous French author supports this view indirectly fot he argued that Persian carpets and fabrics should not be imported because these would compete with French manufactured goods[377].

It is unfortunate that most of the quantified data comes from the records of the European East Indies companies whose share of the trade in Persian textiles was relatively insignificant. In 1648, the EIC gave orders to contract, on the basis of a pattern sent to Persia, for 14 pieces of 70 covids, 60 ells each long, which were to cost 4 'abbasis a covid, or equivalent to about 6s.3/4d. per half ell. Twenty-eight half pieces were sent, one green, the other blue, in 1648. The order had been difficult to execute, because « lengths more than 30 or 34 covetts will be to these people somewhat troublesom [...] if no more then 20 in each would please you doubtless their goodness would be needed »[378]. The factors claimed that Persian taffetas were better than Florentine ones which could be purchased for 11 shahis per covid and sarcenet such as imported into Great Britain from France for 7 shahis per covid. They also were thought to be better made than the Indian ones, though the colors faded[379]. In 1687, the EIC again tried its hand with taffetas and ordered « a sort of plain white glossy Persian Sarcenet or Taffety [...] the buying of 1,000 pieces for an experiment »[380].

In 1681, the EIC bought some velvet cushions embroidered with gold and silver[381]. The EIC wanted to barter English manufactures for wrought silks. The EIC ordered over 2,000 pieces costing under £3 a piece, 1,000 pieces costing £3-5, and 500 costing £5-6 a piece and a few costing £6-8. Orders were given that the colours should not be « uncouth or tadry, as the Ladies call them, such as redd and yellow mixt or striped »[382]. « The most hopefull Silke Commodity was Millicks [*milek*] Single and double, being a kind of Lutestring, some with Silver, but most with Gold flowers [...] sold

376. Du Mans, p. 343.

377. Du Mans, p. 355; see also p. 367, which lists profitable goods for export by the French EIC which only includes raw materials.

378. Ferrier [*British-Persian Relations*], p. 355, quoting E/3/21/2082 and 2086.

379. *Ibid.*, p. 356, quoting E/3/21/2131 and E/3/22/ 2147.

380. *Ibid.*, p. 394 quoting B/38, p. 203.

381. *Ibid.*, p. 393 quoting E/3/89.

382. *Ibid.*, p. 393 quoting E/3/90.

from 25-100 Abassees the piece » the EIC opined in 1682[383]. However, the batch sent was not appreciated[384].

In 1695, the EIC ordered the purchase of 10,000 pounds of Isfahan chintzes, 15 yards in length and nearly 3/4 yard broad and « the more variety of Work, and Colours of all sorts, stripes, flowers or otherwise the better, provided there be not less twenty pieces of one Sort » in case they should be wanted for furnishing a bedroom[385]. In all the order came down to 8,240 pieces which were shipped on 23/7/1697[386]. In 1699, the EIC shipped another 5,000 chintzes, which were well liked in London[387]. However, the Surat factory opined that the Persian chintzes « come out much dearer and worse than many we provide in these parts » and suggested to end these purchases. The last chintzes sent by the EIC was a lot of 6,000 in 1699 « to be sold for Exportation [...] in Lieu [...] of getting Returns in Raw Silk »[388].

Thus, of the fabrics the EIC only considered taffetas to be of interest. Other fabrics also were exported, but the Persians did not want to upset their traditional markets and alter designs for the uncertainty of new markets. Moreover, the qualities, the fashion, and the prices were not to the liking of the EIC or the European market, which could always get a better buy with the purchase of Indian textiles. Finally, the Act of 1701, prohibiting the import of wrought silks from India and Persia into Great-Britain, prevented any further EIC experimentation with or interest in silken Persian fabrics[389].

The Dutch likewise showed no interest in Persian textiles. The small quantities that they exported were used as presents for Asian princes. After a first purchase of Persian textiles in 1623 the VOC only showed marginal interest in these fabrics[390]. Table 3 gives an indication of the marginal importance of this trade during the hey-day of Dutch trade with Iran as well as the destination of the fabrics. As far as I have been able to ascertain none

383. Ferrier [*British-Persian Relations*], p. 394 quoting E/3/90.

384. *Ibid.*, p. 394 quoting E/3/91.

385. Ferrier [*British-Persian Relations*], p. 418 quoting E/3/92.

386. *Ibid.*, p. 419 quoting E/3//92.

387. *Ibid.*, p. 419 quoting E/3/92 and E/3/93.

388. *Ibid.*, p. 419 quoting E/3/99.

389. *Ibid.*, p. 354.

390. « I also bought some Persian fabrics: 69 silk taficielen [*tafsileh*] at 11 'abbasis per piece; 3 p.[ieces] of flowered meleck [*milek*] at 30 'abbasis per piece; 1 p.[iece] of blue-white striped at 20 'abbasis, and 2 cottony [*qotni*], printed with flowers at 2 r[eals] per piece or 13 'abbasis for two » (Dunlop, p. 78).

Table 3: Dutch export of Persian fabrics to Asian destinations

Destination	Fabrics	Cost in Dfl*
Export 1658		
Japan	3 gold cloth	656
Coromandel	14 velvets	436
	2 gold, silver cloth	269
Bengal	6 velvets	n.a.
	12 silk darayen	n.a.
Export 1659		
Ceylon	10 velvets	n.a.
Coromandel	some velvets and silk fabrics	n.a.
Paliacatta	10 velvets	299
	2 gold cloth	276
Bengal	12 silk darayen	109
Export 1660		
Ceylon	26 velvets+some silk fabrics	n.a.
Export 1662		
Ceylon	12 velvets	367
	2 small silver cloth	205
Bengal	20 velvets	595
Ceylon	18 velvets	527
Bengal	12 darayen	133
Batavia	4 gold + silver cloth	n.a.
Ceylon	8 velvets	n.a.
Export 1663		
Batavia	6 gold+silver cloth	607
Ceylon	25 darayen	227
	80 taffetas	819
Export 1664		
Coromandel	2 gold+silver cloth	343
	20 velvets	535
	12 darayen	104
	6 brocades	210
	8 heavy taffetas	109
Bengal	18 velvets	490
	12 col. darayen	121
	10 gold+silver cloth	1389
Export 1665		
Malabar	4 velvets	111
	4 darayen	53
	16 taffetas	56
	2 gold cloth bad quality	82
Batavia	12 velvets	357
Export 1666		
Ceylon	20 velvets	667
Coromandel	30 velvets	1598
	11 brocades	941
	6 gold silver cloth	787
	40 various satins	2324
Batavia	12 colored velvets	384
	6 gold and silver cloth	728

[* Dutch guilders; darayen = *dara'i*; n.a. = not available]

Sources: VOC 1226, fol. 805v; VOC 1226, fol. 816 (for 1658) - VOC 1229, fol. 870v; VOC 1224, fol. 296v-297 (for 1659) - VOC 1235, fol. 16 (for 1660) - VOC 1240, fol. 420, 1420v, 1422 (for 1662) - VOC 1243, fol. 2034 (for 1663) - VOC 1242, fol. 1087 (for 1664) - VOC 1252, fol. 700, 709 (for 1665) - VOC 1259, fol. 3363-64; VOC 1264, fol. 647v (for 1666).

were exported to the Netherlands, for those listed as destination "Batavia" either were sent on to Japan or were used as presents for Indonesian princes.

From Table 3 it is clear that gold cloth was the most expensive fabric, from Dfl. 138 per piece to Dfl. 218 for the cheapest. The next most expensive were the gold-silver cloths (average price of Dfl. 135), while silver cloth was priced at Dfl. 103 per piece. Brocades came into several varieties, the most expensive cost Dfl. 86 per piece. A less costly variety cost only Dfl. 35. Satins were not cheap either and obtained a price of Dfl. 58 per piece. Velvets show a very stable price level of on average Dfl. 29 per piece, although one variety was priced at Dfl. 53. *Dara'is* and taffetas were both Dfl. 10, although the *dara'is* tended to be cheaper. A heavy taffeta obtained Dfl. 14 per piece. Lacking information on size, pattern and weight much more cannot be said about these data.

Small quantities of Persian textiles continued to be exported by the Dutch throughout the Safavid period. The last time probably was in November 1721 when 32 phelpen or velvets (blue, green and red colored) were sent to Batavia[391]. This practice was continued in the post-Safavid era, but on an even smaller and more irregular scale. In 1740, for example, 19 gold and silver fabrics were bought to be used as a present for the king of Siam, also some velvets for Coromandel were bought[392]. In 1748, three velvets for Ceylon and 5 red velvets for Coromandel were exported[393], after which date no other textile exports are recorded.

- Carpets

Of the two major European East Indies companies only the VOC showed some, if marginal, interest in the purchase of Persian carpets. However, even during the years that the VOC bought a large number of carpets their value never exceeded 0.1% of its total annual turnover in Persia. Nevertheless, the companies were quite aware of the value of Persian carpets.

The EIC preferred not to trade in carpets, because Persian carpets were considered to be expensive and of small esteem in England. Most English purchases, therefore, were private deals made by EIC staff on their own

391. KA 1785, 9/11/1721, fol. 241.
392. VOC 2511, 11/8/1740, fol. 201.
393. VOC 2705, 21/3/1746, fol. 140.

account[394]. In 1624, for example, 12 carpets were bought by the EIC at 30 shahis per covid. Another carpet bought by one of the EIC staff in 1625, in Isfahan, was « one payre verrie fine and lardge carpets of Kirman » for which he paid 40 tomans. He was expecting to sell it for 60 tomans in India[395]. It would seem that the EIC carried on trade in carpets elsewhere in Asia, viz. in India. The Dutch report, for example, that the EIC bought large quantities of carpets in Coromandel such as a lot of 1500 carpets in 1683[396].

The VOC became a regular buyer of Persian carpets, although of a limited number only. The Company ordered some 800 Persian carpets early during its presence in Persia. Their dimensions had to be 4 by 5 ell. The VOC also wanted 40 carpets of 7 x 2,5 and of 8 x 3,5 ell. The carpets had to be of a good quality. The Company instructed its staff that if Indian carpets were cheaper and better than the Persian ones then they had better buy the former. In that case, they should acquire 100 Indian carpets to enable them to test the market. Thus altogether 900 carpets[397]. This bulk order seems to have been an exception, for no other such large demand for Persian carpets is mentioned in the VOC archives. Henceforth, the VOC concentrated on a small number of mainly woolen carpets, i.e. between 25 and 100 carpets per year, as well as a few silk carpets, sometimes wrought with gold and silver wire. Like the English Company's staff their Dutch counterparts sometimes also traded for their own private account in carpets. For example, Huybert Visnich, the first VOC director in Persia (1623-30), sent 2 bales of carpets to Aleppo for private gain[398]. The appearance of Persian carpets in Dutch paintings coincides with the beginning of VOC trade relations with Persia[399]. However, their appearance in these pictures did not necessarily mean that in each self-respecting bourgeois home there was a carpet. For, in some cases, a carpet was rented as a prop to complete the proper interior background of the patron's house, as is clear from the text of a 1645 bill. « Paid to Abraham Pietersen Dfl. 6.3.- rent for a carpet for a period of five

394. Ferrier [*British-Persian Relations*], p. 354, quoting G/29/1, p. 210, Surat to Gombroon, 7/12/1626 and E/3/10/1165, Isfahan to EIC, 28/8/1624.

395. *Ibid.*, p. 354, quoting E/3/10/1178, Barker, Gombroon to John Bangham, Agra, 12/2/1625.

396. Coolhaas, IV, p. 630.

397. Dunlop, p. 130.

398. *Ibid.*, p. 297.

399. Ydema, p. 60.

weeks and 3 days [used] for brother Nicolaes' [Spiller, an Amsterdam merchant] painting »[400].

The Dutch sometimes tried to buy Indian carpets from Ahmadabad if Persia could not supply them with the required number of carpets within a certain timeframe. However, they recognized that the Persian carpets were "curieuzer" or more interesting[401]. The English were also regular buyers of small quantities of Indian carpets during the first half of the 17th century, after which their interest faded away[402].

In Table 4, a list is given of the number and type of carpets, and, where available, their cost and destination, and where to exported by the VOC between 1651 and 1666[403]. As the VOC's records for this period are not complete, there are inevitably gaps in the table. It is therefore possible that more carpets were exported, although their number cannot have been much higher than indicated here. In 1651, for example, the company's order (or "eis") for carpets from Persia was 75 carpets. Except in the case of Batavia the final destination has been given for all carpets. When Batavia is referred to as final destination this does not necessarily mean that the carpets remained there. A number of carpets were shipped to the Netherlands as well as to Japan, Malacca, Siam and Tonkin. The remainder was destined to be used in the Indonesian archipelago.

Table 4: Carpets exported by the VOC between 1651-1666

Year	No. and type of carpet	Price in Dfl.	Destination
1651	111 woolen carpets	2891	Batavia
	2 silk carpets	1255	Netherlands
1652	49 woolen carpets	830	Netherlands
	37 woolen carpets	818	Batavia
	47 woolen carpets	801	Batavia

400. Ydema, p. 124.

401. VOC 1239, 31/12/1662, fol. 1210v; the VOC indeed seems to have bought Indian carpets, made in Ahmadabad, regularly. In 1651, a carpet for the emperor of Japan, had rotted away on its voyage from Surat to Nagasaki. A new carpet was ordered from Ahmadabad (Coolhaas, II, p. 549).

402. MacAllan, p. 105-115; see Ydema for Indian carpets in Dutch and Flemish paintings.

403. These include 49 carpets exported by Joan Cunaeus, the Dutch ambassador to Shah 'Abbas II in 1651. Of these 49 carpets 25 were square carpets, the remainder of different sizes (Hotz, p. 340, 346).

1653	67 woolen carpets	n.a.	Batavia
	6 silk carpets	n.a.	Batavia
1657	12 woolen carpets	428	Batavia
1658	12 woolen carpets	428	Batavia
1659	20 woolen carpets	n.a.	Batavia
	6 woolen carpets	n.a.	Ceylon
	some woolen carpets	n.a.	Coromandel
	2 silk carpets	n.a.	Batavia
	8 woolen carpets	564	Paliacatta
1660	20 woolen carpets	739	Batavia
	10 woolen carpets	n.a.	Ceylon
	3 silk carpets	265	Batavia
1662	4 wool carpets	214	Masulipatnam
	10 woolen carpets	328	Ceylon
	16 wool carpets	n.a.	Batavia
1663	21 wool carpets	747	Batavia
	6 wool carpets	840	Ceylon
	7 silk carpets	939	Batavia
	4 silk carpets wrought with gold	2731	Netherlands
1664	2 woolen carpets	362	Coromandel
	10 woolen carpets	674	Bengal
	7 woolen carpets	236	Malacca
	1 woolen carpet	74	Ceylon
	8 silk carpets wrought with gold	1493	Netherlands
1665	6 wool carpets	158	Malacca
1666	12 wool carpets	429	Ceylon
	28 woolen carpets	1826	Batavia
	16 of which		for Mallaca

Source: ARA, KA 1077, 3/9/1651, fol. 531-539; KA 1086, 20/8/1652, fol. 830; KA 1086, 22/5/1652, fol. 818; KA 1086, 30/3/1652, fol. 801; KA 1092, 16/8/1653, fol. 821-38; KA 1092, 30/9/1653, fol. 839f.; VOC 1124, 14/5/1657, fol. 305v; VOC 1224, 21/4/1659, fol. 296v-297; VOC 1233, 13/3/1660, fol. 84v; VOC 1235, 2/9/1660, fol. 16; VOC 1240, 12/4/1662, fol. 420; VOC 1240, 13/5/1662, fol. 701-702; VOC 1240, 30/8/1662, fol. 1420v, 1422; VOC 1243, 28/6/1663, fol. 2034; VOC 1242, 20/6/1674, fol. 1087v-89; VOC 1253, 8/9/1665, fol. 1702; VOC 1259, 14/6/1666, fol. 3363-3364.

We cannot draw any conclusions from this table other than that the Dutch exported carpets regularly, albeit in insignificant quantities. Because the records fail to show any information as to quality or sizes, the apparent unit cost is a figure of little significance.

Carpets are mentioned as export commodities to Russia, India and Ottoman Turkey[404]. In fact, many of the Turkish carpets sold in Europe were manufactured in Persia. « Many of the Istanbul dealers were probably no more knowledgeable about centres of rug-making than their modern counterparts who describe everything as being "Anadolu" »[405]. Around the 1670s, Du Mans mentions that although this trade of "Turkish carpets" persisted it did not really turn a profit[406]. The EIC had totally lost interest in Persian carpets by that time. Its agent in Persia was instructed « You must never send us anymore Persian Carpets, for those we had last by way of Surat will not yield us here above a third of what they cost in Persia, which gives us just that cause to fear that we were abused in the price of these, the greater cause of our loss being that such carpets are now grown much out of use in Europe »[407]. This lack of interest in Persian carpets around the 1680s is also clear from the fact that Persian carpets disappear from Dutch paintings, where they had been prominent for decades[408]. This lack of interest probably was also due to the development of a European carpet industry that produced tailored designs in harmony with the interior (in terms of color, pattern, and size of the rooms) of the homes in which the carpets had to be used[409]. Although not a major trading item, carpets were found in Bandar 'Abbas in 1700 as one of its main goods for sale[410].

Thus, contrary to popular and widespread belief, even among students of Safavid history and art historians, there was neither a great European interest nor trade in either Persian fabrics or carpets during the 16th-18th and most of the 19th century period. In both cases Persian textiles were considered to be too expensive compared with those produced for example in India. Also, despite their artistry, Persian textiles were sometimes considered too gaudy. Europeans bought Persian textiles, but in small quantities and more often than not, certainly in the case of the Dutch, to be used as presents for Asian princes rather than for the European market.

---

404. Chenciner and Mogomdkhanov, p. 125; Ferrier [An English View], p. 203; Gervers, p. 30-31.

405. Gervers, p. 30; Ydema, p. 51.

406. Du Mans, p. 187.

407. Irwin [Indian Textile], p. 18 f.

408. Ydema, p. 60.

409. Housego, p. 40.

410. Lockyer, p. 218.

Towards the end of the 17th century English interest in Persian carpets was even further reduced for « such rich Carpets, are now grown much out of use in Europe »[411]. The English bought even less carpets than before, and finally none at all. Although the Dutch still bought carpets their number was very insignificant, and finally no purchases were reported anymore. For example, in 1715 only two woolen carpets were shipped to Batavia, in 1717 eleven, in 1718 only four (destined for Banda and Ternate) and in 1719 ten woolen carpets for Ceylon[412]. After that date carpets are not mentioned in the correspondence with an occasional exception such as in 1746 when 13 carpets were bought for use in Ceylon[413].

Market demand for Persian carpets cannot have been increased significantly due to incremental demand from Europe. The derisory volume of carpets purchased by the Dutch and the English East Indies companies evidently did not affect Persia's carpet market in any significant manner, since during their century long period of activity there nothing changed: the range of merchandise on offer was as restricted as ever, nor was there any development in the market's structure or method of working. In case of unusual demands the master weavers still required longer time spans to produce carpets that were specially ordered. In 1713, for example, the Dutch report that « the woolen carpets, i.e. in the desired size and pattern, destined for the emperor of Japan are not available in the market. The golden and silver fabrics for the king of Siam, of the required length and width, will demand about one year [to produce] according to the weavers. For each sample they will have to mount a separate weaving loom, so that these fabrics will become very expensive »[414].

One, therefore, cannot but conclude that Europeans recognized the special artistic merits of Persian carpets. However, European taste and interest seems to have been tempered by the price of Persian carpets as well as by that of its competitors, viz. Indian and Turkish carpets. Trade in Persian carpets, therefore, was an insignificant and marginal activity for the European Companies. Most of the Persian carpets bought by the VOC, the

411. Ferrier [*British-Persian Relations*], p. 395, quoting E/3/91, Company to Persia, 3/9/1686.

412. KA 1735, 13.5.1715, fol. 3280; KA 1805, 13.12.1717, fol. 59; KA 1796, 7.11.1718, fol. 2357; KA 1796, 20.3.1719, fol. 2440.

413. VOC 2705, van der Welle to Governor-General, 20/7/1746, fol. 149.

414. KA 1710, 27/4/1713, fol. 243.

more important company of the two, did not find their way to Europe, but rather to other Asian countries such as Japan, Siam, and Indonesia.

• *Production for the state or for the market?*

Since the silken fabrics, gold and silver brocades and carpets were very expensive, and therefore their cost could only be borne by the rich and well-to-do, it has been suggested that the production capacity to cater for these needs could only exist under state patronage. The existence of the royal workshops producing these textiles gives credence to the validity of such a conviction. The truth of this matter is the subject of this section.

Following age-old tradition, Shah Esma'il I (1500-1530), the founder of the Safavid state, established 33 royal workshops or *karkhanajat* and appointed heads to each one of them in 915/1509-10[415]. Among these royal workshops were a number of silk and cotton fabric manufacturies[416], as well a tailoring department. The attendance at court of *ostad* Allahverdi Khayyat with a staff of 14 of the tailoring workshop or *khayyat-khaneh* with four packages of colored *londreh* and five *pustinduz* (pelisse makers) and one *kharvar* of Bokharan lamb skins is mentioned[417]. But it was not only the royal court that kept special workshops to satisfy its needs, but so did important governors to satisfy the needs of their own provincial establishments. A rebellious upstart, who gave himself royal airs, kept workshops « just like kings and magnates »[418]. That this instance was not an exceptional situation induced by *hubris* is not only clear from the statement quoted, but also by other reports that mention the existence of workshops operated by provincial governors. For example, a governor of Seistan had several workshops, amongst which the *qeichaji-khaneh* or tailoring department[419]. Nasrabadi mentions that an exceptionally skillful weaver, Na'ima, worked in the tailoring department of Emam Qoli Khan,

415. Astarabadi, p. 44, which is confirmed by [*'Alamara-ye Shah Tahmasp*], p. 82. See also Shamlu, I, p. 57, 72, 287, 300, 414. The number 33 or 32 most likely is a symbolic one which recurs in connection with Persian crafts, see e.g. Khᵂondamir, IV, p. 84 and Floor [Guilds and futuvvat], p. 106-114.

416. Safavi, p. 64.

417. [*'Alamara-ye Shah Tahmasp*], p. 410.

418. *Ibid.*, p. 82, 118.

419. Sistani, p. 434.

governor of Fars from 1022-1042/1613-1633[420]. Gurgin Khan, governor of Qandahar around 1700, also had several workshops[421].

Art historians have maintained and repeated that royal manufacturies existed in Isfahan, Kashan, Kerman and maybe elsewhere, such as in Tabriz. However, most of the sources they adduce to prove their point of view actually do not say anything about royal workshops[422].

There are only two European travellers to wit, Della Valle and Krusinksi, who report that royal workshops existed in many towns, of which Krusinski is the only source who lists specific geographical locations of royal workshops other than those at Isfahan. A *kar-khaneh*, according to Della Valle, referred to two different types of things. First, it meant a workshop in which certain craft type activities, such as the weaving of silk fabrics, were undertaken. Second, it referred to the baggage that was taken along by the shah or members of the elite when they went on a journey[423]. In Persian texts the word is used in both meanings[424]. Della Valle reports that « the king has these car-chane in all of his important cities »[425]. Krusinski states that « Shah 'Abbas the Great caused numerous and manifold factories to be established in the provinces of Shirvan, Qara-bagh, Gilan, Kashan, Mashhad and Astarabad »[426]. However, if true, it is not clear whether all these factories were still financed by the royal court after the death of Shah 'Abbas I in 1629. For his successors, who did not have the same interest in trade and commerce, abolished the silk export monopoly, and pursued a policy that left in effect the operation of the economy to the private sector. All subsequent shahs followed the same line of policy as well. So, the establishment of these factories seems to be at odds with the policy pursued by Shah 'Abbas I to rely for the production of high quality silk fabrics on the private sector. Della Valle explicitly states

420. Nasrabadi, p. 294.

421. Mar'ashi Safavi, p. 7.

422. Beattie, p. 9; Erdmann, p. 37, 41-2; R. Savory, "Carpet. I", *EIr*, IV, p. 836; Niño Jesus, p. 102; Tavernier, I, p. 397, 589; Mankowski, p. 2431-2433.

423. Della Valle [*Voyages*], II, p. 223, 395.

424. See for example Qomi, I, p. 121, 140.

425. *Ibid.*, II, p. 223.

426. Mankowski, p. 2431. Sanson's statement (p. 116) that « Manufactures are establish'd at Ispahan, Cachan, Tauris, and Masched; but these Manufactures, where they work very fine and rich Silks, are made only for the use of the Kingdom; for the Great Mogul, to hinder the utterance of 'em in his Empire, has forbid his Subjects to wear 'em » does not necessarily refer to royal workshops, as many have assumed.

that « only persons of consequence can legitimately own them; thus, a number of people own various car chane [workshops] in different places, from which they draw substantial revenues; and consequently, they maintain various looms to produce these silken fabrics and all kinds of outstanding craftsmen, but above all [to work] that silk »[427]. Della Valle's statement means that most of the royal workshops were in fact privately owned workshops, but had a royal patent permitting them to be engaged in the business of producing costly silken and other fabrics for the court.

Whatever the case may have been Shah 'Abbas I was not the initiator of the royal workshops as Krusinski states, because as we have seen these were created by Shah Esma'il I at the very beginning of the Safavid dynasty. Management of the royal workshops had been delegated to trusted individuals whose overseers exercised a strict supervision according to Krusinski[428]. This observation seems to be borne out by what we know about the function of head of the tailoring department. This workshop was headed by a *qeichachi-bashi*, who was assisted by *qeichachis*. It would seem that this was not a humble function, as is usually submitted, but a normal court function granted to members of the elite such as the son of the governor of Shiraz[429]. In addition to craftsmen, the tailoring department also employed clerical staff. For example, the chief clerk or *'azab bashi-ye qeichachi-khaneh-ye khasseh* is mentioned during Shah Safi's I reign[430]. In the case of the workshops that were attached to the Mashhad and Qom shrines these managers were the custodians of the shrines, but what these workshops produced is not known. It is more than likely that these workshops only served to assist the operation and maintenance of the shrines and their activities, and that no textile production took place there[431]. Kaempfer states that the *malek al-tojjar*, or chief of the merchants, was charged with the supervision of the royal weaving, tailoring, dyeing, and silk embroidering workshops as agent for the steward of the royal

427. Della Valle [*Voyages*], II, p. 223.

428. Mankowski, p. 2431.

429. Qomi, I, p. 397, and II, p. 623, 1034 for other examples. We even have a *qeichachi* serve as ambassador for Shah 'Abbas I to the Great Moghul, see Riazul Islam, II, p. 138. For the view that the *qeichachi* was a humble function see e.g. Matthee [The Career], p. 20.

430. Esfahani [*Kholasat*], p. 39, see also p. 73 for the mentioning of the weaving department.

431. Mirza Rafi'a, p. 35-37.

palace or *nazer-e boyutat*[432]. Tavernier mentions that the *malek al-tojjar* was responsible to supply the royal court with its needs in fabrics to which end he gave the necessary materials to the weavers[433]. He further mentions the existence of a royal workshop in Isfahan, where « one side of a large court yard is reserved for the manufacturing of gold and silk carpets and of gold brocades, which the Shah maintains for his own needs »[434].

There were seven textile-related royal workshops, i.e.: *sha'rbaf-khaneh* (silk weaving workshop), *khayyat-khaneh* (tailors workshop), *jurabbaf-khaneh* (sock knitting workshop), *pustinduz-khaneh* (sheepskin coat making workshop), *taladuz-khaneh* (goldbrocading workshop), *kafshduz-khaneh* (shoemaking workshop) and *hallaj-khaneh* (carding workshop)[435]. Kuznetsova mentions that the workers in the royal workshops were formerly called *darbasteh*, probably referring to bonded labor or slaves bought for specific functions[436]. For example, Shah Tahmasp I employed, amongst others, slaves whom he had specially bought to make gold embroideries or *zarduz* and had them placed among the *zarduzan* of Tabriz, who were free and independent artisans[437]. Della Valle when describing the *kar-khaneh* in Qazvin mentions that the looms were operated by slaves[438]. Chardin mentions that an artisan once he had been engaged to work for the royal workshops was employed for life. They received a very good treatment and their work load was not very heavy. Their only obligation in addition to produce those products that the shah desired was to follow the shah whenever he went on a trip[439]. There was even a Greek weaver working in the royal workshop[440]. This was not exceptional for foreign artisans were also hired for other royal workshops, while in Jolfa some

---

432. Kaempfer [*Am Hofe*], p. 86.

433. Tavernier, I, p. 588.

434. *Ibid.*, I, p. 397; see also p. 589 where he mentions that in the royal workshop manufactures « beautiful gold and silver carpets, silk and cotton fabrics, brocades of gold and silver, velvets and taffetas of various kinds ».

435. [*Tadhkirat al-Muluk*], p. 30, 95.

436. Kuznetsova [Urban Industry], p. 313 which is an abridged version of Kuznetsova [*O genezise*].

437. Shirazi, p. 71; [*Tadhkereh*], p. 19; Qomi, I, p. 215.

438. Della Valle [*Voyages*], II, p. 394-395.

439. Chardin, VII, p. 332-333.

440. See *supra* n. 372; Sanson (p. 52) notes even Chinese craftsmen among the foreigners employed by the Shah.

French textile workers were active in 1704[441]. In the 1530s the staff of royal workshops (*'amaleh-ye boyutat*) numbered 3,800 persons[442]. According to Chardin, each of the *kar-khanehs* employed an average of about 150 men, thus a total of 5,000 people in the 32 royal workshops. The tailors workshop, however, employed only 80 people around 1670[443]. In Isfahan the royal carpet workshop was situated between the Chehel Sotun and the Meidan-e Shah[444]. Krusinski reports that carpets were made here for the royal court[445], which Tavernier confirms for an earlier period[446].

Kaempfer describes the royal workshops in Isfahan as follows: « The court weaving workshop consists of several looms on which silken fabrics as well as gold and silver brocades are woven. The supervision over the royal weaving workshop is exercised by the malek al-tojjar. He also selects the designs, the preparation of the raw materials as well as the storage and guarding of the finished products. In addition he is in charge of all those workshops that supply the court's needs for clothes »[447]. Kaempfer further supplies short notes of the fulling workshop, the tailoring workshop, the sock making workshop, and the embroidery workshop[448].

Although they played a much diminished role there were still some royal workshops (*karkhanajat-ye saltanat* [or *ye-shahi* or *-ye sarkar*] during Nader Shah's days[449]. These accompanied the Shah on his military campaigns[450], just as the *ordu-ye bazar*, or the army's supply center, which was an entirely private sector undertaking, however[451]. One of Nader Shah's royal workshops is even mentioned by name, viz. the *qeichachi-khaneh* or tailoring department[452].

The royal workshops produced not only for the court, but also to sell their surplus output in the market. Della Valle writes that the royal workshops (*kar-khaneh*) signify « certain locations, in which silken fabrics

---

441. Le Bruyn, I, p. 225 (should be p. 229).
442. Qomi, I, p. 203.
443. Chardin, VII, p. 329.
444. Tavernier, I, p. 444.
445. Mankowski, p. 2431 and n. 5.
446. Tavernier I, p. 397, 589.
447. Kaempfer [*Am Hofe*], p. 121.
448. *Ibid.*
449. Mervi, p. 100, 295, 456, 554, 1053, 1198.
450. *Ibid.*, p. 294.
451. *Ibid.*, p. 385, 468, 481.
452. *Ibid.*, p. 118, 336, 866, 1089.

are made, as well as certain products which they use in particular, also to make money with them; in fact, they display these for sale to whomever wants to buy them »[453].

Krusinksi notes that « these factories not only produce what is necessary for the court and the courtiers with small expense to the Treasury, beyond the cost of the silver thread, but they also enrich not a little the royal Treasury, for the more precious silk weavings and the textiles that are enriched with gold and silver threads are sent with government salesmen for sale to Europe and even more to India by whole shiploads »[454]. However, the reality may have been different. In fact, the artisans of the royal workshops often had little or nothing to do, so that they could produce four times as much than they were asked to by the royal court. They therefore worked, for their own account, for anyone who wanted to make use of and pay for their services, according to Chardin[455]. Krusinski, however, maintains that the royal weavers were constantly making rugs and fabrics for the royal court[456]. However, Chardin reports that the royal silk-weaving workshops had finally been discontinued (this is corroborated by the *Tadhkirat al-Muluk*) so his description of what was happening is more likely to reflect the truth of the situation than Krusinski's.

However, despite their important and privileged role (viz. producing for the royal court and thus having a major market for luxury products) this did not mean that the royal workshops monopolized the textile crafts. Around 1473, silken fabrics were being sold in the market just as other consumer goods. « An howre aftre the sonne ryseng certain go about wth sylkes and other wares on their armes, passeng rounde abouth without speaking. And the merchaunts, if they see ought that pleaseth them, call the seller, and looke on his wares; the price whereof is written on a paper sowed unto it »[457]. John Cartwright, in 1603, reports about Qazvin that in some of its bazaars « you may buy Shasses and Tulipnats, and Indian cloath, of wonderfull finenesse: in others Silkes of all sorts, as Velvets, Damaskes, Cloath of Gold and Silver »[458]. The Carmelite Paul Simon, four years

453. Della Valle [*Voyages*], II, p. 223.
454. Mankowski, p. 2431-2432.
455. Chardin, VII, p. 333.
456. Mankowski, p. 2431.
457. *Barbaro and Contarini*, I, p. 73.
458. Purchas, VIII, p. 507. For a similar situation in Isfahan in 1609 see *Ibid.*, III, p. 86.

later, notes that Qazvin « is much frequented for trade, as there is an abundance of silk, carpets, brocades »[459], which is confirmed by Della Valle, who in addition notes that silken fabrics woven in Kashan were sold in the Bazazistan, an enclosed room in the bazaar[460]. Herbert, some 20 years later, observed that « the bazar [of Kashan] is spacious and uniform, furnished with silks, damasks, and carpets of silk, silk and gold, and of coarse thrummed [i.e. fringed] wool; no part of the world having better or better-coloured »[461]. Fryer reports that « besides these common Buzzars, there are others set apart for choice Commodities, as Silks and Velvets, Sarbaff [*sha'rbaf*], that is, Gold and Silver Cloth, Embroidery, Persian carpets, both Woolen and Silk, intermixed with Gold and Silver very costly, which are the peculiar Manufacture of the Country »[462]. Tavernier makes similar remarks: « from the end of the Porticos that touch the North-side of the Mosque, live the shop-keepers that sell Sowing-silk, and small manufactures of Silk, as Ribands, Laces, Garters, and other things of the same nature »[463]. The textile bazaars made quite an impression on contemporary visitors. Fryer writes: « the Commodities of all the Earth are seen in distinct Buzzars in this one City [Isfahan], as Cheap as in their separate Homes. For beholding the Sack-cloth Buzzar, for so they call English Cloth, I thought it exceeded Blackwell-Hall, or any Cloth-Fair in England, being piled in huge Quantities both in their Shops around the Buzzar, and Heaps amidst thereof, of all Sorts, Colours, and Conditions; where I bought a Coat of Broad-Cloth to line with Furrs against the Winter, for Fourteen Shillings the Cobit, almost equal with our Yard, for what I am sure I have paid Twenty Shillings the Yard at home »[464]. Tavernier remarks that the bazaar of Tabriz was filled with rich merchandise, while Olearius reports that in the Qeisarriyeh of the Ardabil bazaar costly products such as gold and silver fabrics were for sale[465].

One, therefore, may assume that only some of the most costly fabrics were made in the royal workshops. However, in general, the production of

---

459. [*Carmelites*], I, p. 119.

460. Della Valle [*Voyages*], II, p. 197, 295; see *Ibid*, II, p. 394 for the situation in the Qazvin bazaar.

461. Herbert, p. 218; see also Kaempfer [*Reisetagebuecher*], p. 79.

462. Fryer, II, p. 248.

463. Tavernier, I, p. 403.

464. Fryer, II, p. 249-50.

465. Tavernier, II, p. 51; Olearius, p. 463.

costly fabrics and carpets was for the market by privately owned workshops. This is borne out by Dutch sources, who report in 1663 that the asymmetrical headings of some silk carpets bought by the VOC could « not be corrected, for this type [of pattern] is seldom produced for the market. If we had ordered them, instead of bought them ready made, they would have been more expensive »[466]. In Isfahan, for example, carpets were made in a manufactory. Here one could order carpets to be made of a specific pattern and size. In ordering carpets one had to be very specific. In one case the « borders ["hooftwerk"] of some silk carpets do not correspond with one another. This cannot be helped, because they seldom do. If one wants it that way one has to order that specifically, because the Moors do not pay much attention to this »[467]. The same situation also existed in late Safavid times when the Dutch report in 1713 that « the woolen carpets for the emperor of Japan, i.e. with that particular design and size, is not available in the bazaar »[468]. In 1738, the French reported that beautiful carpets of silk and wool could be bought in Bandar 'Abbas[469].

Already in the beginning of the 17th century the royal dye-works had been abolished. All necessary work was contracted out by the state, against fixed tariffs, to the existing private sector crafts. This held whether it was for dyeing of cloth, the production of silk, gold and silver fabrics, or the manufacture of brocades, velvets, carpets and the like. This system was technically referred to as *tahvil-e asnaf* or « payment by the guilds »[470]. Several workshops such as the dyeing workshop and silk weaving workshop had been closed under Soleiman or earlier, and their products were bought in the market[471]. Chardin, writing about 1672, states that « formerly there were more workshops » when he refers to the abolition of the dyeing and silk weaving workshop[472]. Bardsiri mentions that Kerman was visited by a certain Hatem Beg, *sha'rbaf-e khasseh* (royal silk-weaver), bearer of the letter of Shah Safi's II (= Soleiman) accession to the throne in 1076/1666[473]. This may imply that the *sha'rbaf-khaneh* still existed, or that

466. VOC 1243, 28/4/1663, fol. 2035.
467. *Ibid.*, 28/8/1663, fol. 2035.
468. VOC 1818, 27/4/1713, fol. 243.
469. Housego, p. 40.
470. [*Tadhkirat al-Muluk*], p. 30, 95.
471. Kaempfer [*Am Hofe*], p. 125; [*Tadhkirat al-Muluk*], p. 48a.
472. Chardin, IV, p. 330 f.
473. Bardsiri, p. 319.

the official referred to had a supervisory role with regards the *sha'rbaf* products received by the royal court and produced for its account in Kerman. The latter seems likely in view of a plea addressed to Shah Soltan Hosein by the vizier of Yazd, Mirza Mohammad Hasan, in 1113/1703, to show compassion to the silk weavers (*sha'rbaf*). For the formulation of the request implies that the Yazd silk weavers probably were suppliers of the royal workshops, or worked under contract for them. It was a request for exemption of payment of fees or *rosum* to the military garrison, which was granted[474]. Also, selected rural villagers worked under contract for the royal court to produce carpets and received in lieu of wages tenure of crown lands, for which the rent had to be paid in carpets[475]. The *Dastur al-Muluk*, a state manual written in 1725, leaves no doubt about the fact that the royal court obtained its textile requirements in the open market. When discussing the role of the *nazer-e boyutat* or Overseer of the Workshops the *Dastur al-Muluk* states that one of his tasks was « the purchase of fabrics at the recommendation of the *malek al-tojjar* and other merchants as well as [other] experts »[476].

As is clear from Nader Shah's regular orders with the Kerman weavers for the production of woolen products for his army most products were obtained in the market. The textile products ordered by Nader Shah included items such as shawls, caps, *qabas*, stockings, trousers, carpets, shirts, and waist bands in the 1730s[477].

However, there is no doubt either that the weavers themselves were, in most, if not all, cases, incapable of pre-financing the production of luxury objects. If the shah or some other rich client did not supply them with the raw materials and payment of regular wages during the production of the fabrics or carpets this role was taken over by one or more leading merchants. One such merchant was the *malek al-tojjar*, or chief merchant, who formally was the state's supervisor of the textile guilds and royal workshops. But there were also other merchants. For example, a group of merchants specialized in the production and sale of embroidered garments, who were known as *naqshineh-forush* in the 19th century[478]. But there were also individuals who invested in one or more looms to cash in on the

474. Afshar [*Yadgarha*], I, p. 132-133.
475. Chardin, VII, p. 330-333.
476. Mirza Rafi'a, p. 54.
477. Floor [*Hokumat*], p. 106, 110, 116-117.
478. Tahvildar, p. 99.

weaving boom[479]. Tavernier also notes in the bazaar of Isfahan that the cloth merchants and the merchants who sell silver and gold brocades and other rich fabrics share the same location, which he identifies[480]. In fact it could be anyone, for Chardin states that « they also work for anyone who employs them »[481]. Undoubtedly, a similar situation existed for the production and sale of other costly garments and fabrics.

Nevertheless, production for the market was limited. This was due to both the long production times and the high costs of the final products (fabrics, carpets), and consequently to the small size of the market as well as the relatively small number of master weavers engaged in the luxury textile crafts. The Dutch remarked that the number of master weavers was limited and therefore it was difficult to order out-of-the ordinary products.

The Dutch found that, for example, good carpets were difficult to obtain[482]. They were either available in the market or had to be specially made[483]. Also, if Europeans bought them they paid more than if a local representative bought it for them. Often the order of carpets could not be satisfied, because there were not enough masters ("werkbazen") in Isfahan[484]. It was therefore recommended to buy carpets in Kashan or in the villages between Kashan and Isfahan[485], which contradicts statements by many art historians that the carpet industry was an urban one.

In one particular case the Dutch ordered specifically square carpets of 4 x 4 ells. These could not be bought in the market, but had to be specially ordered. Therefore, their price was higher than normal. It also took longer to obtain them[486]. Carel Constant, VOC director in Persia (1642-45), reports that if one had to order a carpet the price was 25% more expensive than when one bought a similar carpet in the market. The English had the same problem. The EIC factory in Surat had ordered a carpet « lively and fresh colours of Carmane to be 7,5 yards long and 3,5 broad [which

479. Nasrabadi, p. 138
480. Tavernier, II, p. 403.
481. Chardin VII, p. 332-333.
482. KA 1077, 3/9/1651, fol. 535.
483. This is also reported by the English, Ferrier [*British-Persian Relations*], p. 394.
484. KA 1092, 30/9/1653, fol. 839f.
485. KA 1079 A, Instructie to Willemsen, 14/6/1652.
486. KA 1077, 29/8/1650, fol. 619.

however was not] procurable ready made [...] a pair of that size would cost £100 and likewise a long time before they would be finished »[487].

3. Qajar head dress (around 1840)

487. Ferrier [*British-Persian Relations*], p. 395, quoting E/3/34/3947, Surat to Persia, March 1673/4 and E/3/37/4136, Isfahan to Surat, 22/11/1675.

Qajar Period

During the Qajar period the main textile production centers were the same as in previous centuries, i.e. Yazd, Kashan, Isfahan, Tabriz, Kerman and a relative newcomer Resht, which only drew the attention of Gmelin around 1770 as an important production center of silken fabrics. Kerman, of course, continued to play its role as the center par excellence for woolens, due to a great extent to its superior *kork* or goat hair. As such it was famous for its shawls, felts, and carpets. The manufacturing base in other towns was broader and this enabled them to offer a wider selection of products, to wit: silken, cotton, cotton-silk and woolen fabrics. However, neither technically nor artistically were Persian weavers able to rival their Safavid predecessors. In what follows we will discuss: the main production centers and their products; the decline of the Persian textile industry. Carpet weaving will only be referred to tangentially.

The revival of the textile industry

With the establishment of the Qajar dynasty in 1794, which brought internal security in its train, manufacturing industry and trade started to increase again. After his mission to Persia in 1801, Sir John Malcolm reported, inter alia, on the Persian textile industry as follows: « Isfahan, is still the first city in Persia. Its manufactures are gold brocades, which are lately brought to great perfection, coarse cotton cloths, plain and coloured [...] Yazd produces silk, carpets, nummuds, shawls made of Karmania wool, and coarse cotton cloth. Shiraz only coarse cloth [...] Kashan is famous for its silk and carpet manufactures. Imitations of velvet and some other manufactures of Europe are made with tolerable success in this city [...] Hamadan, coarse cloth and nummuds [...] The silks manufactured at Resht, are more esteemed than any other in Persia. They bear a higher price than those of Cashaun and Yezd, and their consumption is therefore not so great »[488].

This EIC and subsequent reports by other observers demonstrate that a great variety of textiles, including the more costly ones, were still produced all over Persia. According to Fraser the main silken goods around 1825 were « allejahs, dereis, cussabs, peerahuns, tafetas, handkerchiefs »[489]. The main cotton good manufactured were « chintzes or printed cottons, and

488. Issawi, p. 262-263.

489. Fraser [*Caspian Sea*], p. 360.

culumcars, perahuns shahees, kudduks, kherboz, Isfahan stripes, with a few intermediate varieties »[490]. Bélanger mentions the costly fabrics of *zarbaf, zarbaft-e doru'i* and *makhmal-e zarbaft* that were for sale in the Tabriz bazaar[491].

Thus, textile production increased, but initially it seems to have been mainly for local and regional consumption. Trade in textiles was moreover mainly restricted to domestic markets. Only a few articles such as *chits*, *qadaks*, *karbas*, Kerman shawls and some silken fabrics were exported, mainly to Russia and the Central Asia Khanates. In 1802, according to Waring, « there are manufactories of silk at Kashan and Yezd; but they do not fabricate more than supplies the consumption of the country. The cloths, however, of Isfahan, Kashan and Yezd, are exported from Persia into Russia, whence they bring in return broad cloths, velvets, satins, and cutlery.... There are many cities in Persia which supply the adjacent towns with the produce of their manufactories. [...] But speaking generally, they rely almost entirely on foreigners for furnishing them with articles of dress and luxury »[492].

Waring's statement is borne out by other contemporary observers such as Morier and Fraser. « Nine-tenth's of Isfahan cotton is consumed on the spot, the rest in exported. Their principal cotton manufacture is the kadek, a strong and excellent cloth, which resembles nankeen, and which is worn by all ranks of people, from the King to the peasant. Also exported to Russia, for use as the undress of the Russian soldiers. Kerbas of which shirts and drawers of the lower orders are generally made. Stronger qualities are used to make tent coverings etc. They paint cotton stuffs with a hand stamp, then called chit, and washed etc. in the river »[493]. But elsewhere the situation was not much different. « Mashed, its velvets are esteemed as the best of Persia. [...] Silk and cotton cloths are fabricated and dyed here, as in all other Persian towns, but of these there is no export »[494].

Russian customs records corroborate the above observations, for these list "sukno" (broadcloth in yellow, red and blue), "beyaz" (white cloth for underwear), carpets, *zarbaft*, *karbas*, silk cloth, silk headscarves, "vyboika" (printed cloth), "koshma" (felt mats), socks, "sitets" (*chit*? cottons), quilted

490. Fraser [*Caspian Sea*], p. 362. See also Bélanger, II, p. 321.
491. *Ibid.*, II, p. 334.
492. Waring, p. 76.
493. Morier [*A Second Journey*], p. 156.
494. Fraser [*Narrative*], p. 468.

woolen and cotton burmets, *termali* (saddle cloth or figured silk), *burmet* (cotton), *badamu* (cloth), and *alajeh* as Persian imports in 1812[495].

Textile production surged not only due to greater security and thus greater possibilities for trade, but also due to court patronage. Fath 'Ali Shah (1797-1834) promoted the production of *sha'rbafi*. He spent large sums of money on the purchase of silken fabrics. This is a clear indication that the royal court did not maintain court manufactories for the weaving of fabrics. The *khel'ats*, or robes of honor, that the Shah bestowed upon deserving officials were all made by the private sector. The production of *khel'ats* was part of the tax burden of particular cities and thus formed a continuation of the *tahvil-e asnaf* practice initiated by the Safavids. Morier states that the *khel'ats* « are furnished in specified contribution, by particular cities, (Yezd, Shiraz, and Ispahan), and by the ameen-ad-doulah. [...] The number of kalaats is reckoned at nine hundred »[496]. Fraser, some twenty years later, estimates that the number of robes of honor ran in the thousands[497].

This did not mean that the royal court no longer had any textile-related workshops: the shah's wardrobe and tailoring department was as essential to the proper functioning of the court as was the kitchen. However, there was no silk weaving manufactory (*sha'rbaf-khaneh*) or any other weaving workshop attached to the court. Mostaufi describes the *sanduq-khaneh* and *rakhtdar-khaneh* in which fabrics (*shal, barak, khaz, sanjab, zari, qalamkar, qadak*) and clothes (especially robes of honor or *khel'ats*), were kept for shah's personal use and to give away[498].

Fath 'Ali Shah nevertheless kept a direct interest in the welfare of the weaving industry. Molla 'Ali, Lesan al-Molk Sepehr's father, was appointed to supervise the weaving industry and to collect such goods as were destined for the royal wardrobe. The craft of *sha'rbafi* and its ancillary crafts were exempted from paying taxes. As a result several thousand *sha'rbafi* looms were operating in Kashan, including some 1,500

495. Chenciner and Mogomedkhanov, p. 128; Gopal, p. 244.
496. Morier [*A Journey*], p. 206.
497. Fraser [*Winter's Journey*]; Tahvildar (p. 97) claims Isfahan was main producer of *khel'ats*.
498. Mostaufi, I, p. 408-9; see also Fraser [*Winter's Journey*], II, p. 51-52.

manufactories (*kar-khaneh*) which had been idle and inoperative and which started working again[499].

The major production centers

As a result of this development various sources mention the positive developments in Kashan. « Cashan is remarkable for the excellence of its weavers; for its various manufactures of silk and cotton stuffs, and velvets »[500]. The author of the *Zeinat al-Majales* wrote « the craft of *sha'rbafi* is very widespread in Kashan. Both the elite and the commoners were engaged in it. None of the old crafts did have looms numerous as this craft or had so many varied ancillary crafts related to *sha'rbafi* »[501].

However, it was neither Kashan nor Isfahan that was the main industrial textile center of Qajar Persia. This position was claimed by Yazd which held it till the beginning of the 20th century. In the beginning of the 19th century according to Morier « the manufacturing towns are Yezd, silken stuffs, stuffs of silk and cotton; Kashan, silks; Resht, silks, coarse woolen-cloths of which the *tekmis* are made; Isfahan, brocades, cotton-cloths, Kerman shawls »[502]. Fifteen years later Fraser confirms Morier's assessment. « The best manufacturing centers were Yazd and those at Isfahan, Kashan and Tabriz ».

Yazd mainly manufactured silk stuffs (which were famous) such as: « aleedjahs, cassubs, dereis, taftehs, mookhyyehs, handkerchiefs, and other articles of women's attire ». Some silk was produced locally in the Yazd area, but most was imported from Gilan. There was also manufacturing of cotton stuffs. *Namads* were made in the vicinity, those of Taft, were reputed to be equal to those of Birjand, Qa'en and Kerman[503].

The fabrics originating from the traditional weaving centers were not all made in those cities, however. Many of these cities were the hub of a network of surrounding villages which made the same product as the famous urban regional center, or supplied it with inputs such as (dyed) yarns and *karbas*. Colored cottons made at Dihergan and Oulgurd in

499. Naraqi, p. 244.

500. Ouseley, III, p. 92; Kashan famous for its silks; Morier [*Second Journey*], p. 162.

501. Naraqi, p. 216.

502. Morier [*A Journey*], p. 231; on *tekmis* (*tekmen*) see *ibid.*, p. 243; also Tancoigne, p. 203; see also chapter IV.

503. Fraser [*Caspian Sea*], p. 360.

Azerbaijan and in Kerman and Isfahan were mainly sent to Russia[504]. The production of Kashan silks was relatively speaking even more important in Bidgol than it was in Kashan[505]. In the 1850s, according to Blau, the center of cotton manufacturing was Tabriz and its districts (such as Gunish, Salmas, Kaldiran, and the villages Dilman, Disa-Halil, Khosroushah, Tesuj and Dehikurgan) as well as Yazd and its surroundings[506]. In Isfahan also the manufacture of cotton goods was carried on to greater extent. « Many people in and outside Spahan earn their living with it »[507].

In addition to the major industrial centers there were some smaller centers which carved out a niche for themselves with a particular product. The latter's popularity ensured the continued place in the market for these secondary production centers. « Begistan is famous for the manufacture of a cheap silk material, called *chadar-i shahi* »[508]. Woven woolen socks, esp. the Kashmir type, was supplied by Mashhad and partly made with Indian wool. Ordinary stuff was also made in Tabriz, Khoy and other towns. These also produced braids, tassles, fringes, etc.[509]. Although producing an ordinary product, Khoy was nevertheless celebrated for its worsted socks which were striped and variegated with many colors; they occupied many extensive quarters[510].

The textile trade also reflected this large and geographically widespread variety of production centers. For example, printed cottons used in Caspian provinces were imported from Borujerd, Khonsar, Yazd etc. Also coarse calico from Astarabad, Yazd and Semnan[511]. Silk scarfs from Yazd and Kashan; plain silks from Mashhad and Yazd also were imported by the Caspian provinces. *Qadak* used in the Caspian provinces, for example, was imported from Kashan and Natanz[512].

The principal products of the province of Qa'en were « a cloth called barak, kirbas, unmanufactured silk. These are exported to Karman, Yazd,

504. DCR 241, 1887, p. 5.
505. Naraqi, p. 276.
506. Blau, p. 110.
507. Amanat, p. 76.
508. Goldsmid, I, p. 350.
509. Blau, p. 109.
510. Stuart, p. 130-131. Silk sock making is an industry peculiar to Bujnurd, Kuchan and Sabzevar (Polak [*Persien*], I, p. 171); Socks, principally knitted at Isfahan (Wills, p. 320).
511. Amanat, p. 40.
512. *Ibid.*

Mashhad, Tehran, Herat, Bandar Abbas etc. and the province receives in exchange from Karman the coarser species of shawl manufactures, abas or cloaks, and kurk, from Yazd manufactured silk, turbans called Imamas, a substance known as kadak »[513]. Thus, each major province had an output that was varied and mostly for domestic consumption. The situation of Khorasan is, in this respect, representative. In 1828, Stirling records that « the artificial products [of Khorasan] may be stated to be: woollen of various descriptions, numdahs [*namad*], carpets, stuffs for habits [and] clothes which bear some resemblance to those of Cashmere, [...] and species of serges, stockings, the fine woolen cloths of Birun [Berjand] and remarkable for their doftness. Silk cloths of various descriptions, among which may be reckoned plain silk and coloured piece silk chadars [head coverings], eating cloths, napkins, handkerchiefs of various colours of which black is very common I believe. Mixed silk and woolen stuffs, velvets, silk worked on cotton clothes, silk piece destined for Bokhara and home consumption, which are employed in making the large habits worn in general but more particularly by the Toorkomans ». Coarse cottons also were made in Khorasan which served for the dresses of the lower classes and the peasants[514].

The impact of European imports

• *The beginning*

Although the majority of the Persian population still consumed mainly Indian and Persian products « a taste for European goods is but arising » Fraser observed in the mid-1820s[515]. This not only held for woolen goods, which traditionally had been imported from Europe, but also for printed cotton goods, of which the superior qualities had been imported from India, and even European printed goods made inroads on the market. Persian printed goods were gradually being superseded by Indian and European ones, and manufacturers were reported to have petitioned Fath 'Ali Shah to prohibit further importation[516]. « Chintzes and Prints are manufactured in many places, but they are coarse, both in texture and pattern, and are only used for inferior purposes. The printed cottons of India and Europe,

513. Goldsmid, I, p. 337.
514. Stirling, p. 173-174.
515. Fraser [*Caspian Sea*], p. 378.
516. *Ibid.*, p. 368.

particular the latter, had superseded them so much, that the manufacturers were said to have petitioned the king to prohibit further importations. A protecting duty was talked of. They are largely exported to Russia »[517].

The result of this request is not known, but around 1809 Fath 'Ali Shah had restricted the import of Kashmir shawls into Persia to encourage the domestic shawl weaving industry, showing that the central government took an interest in such matters[518]. What happened in Azerbaijan, where the majority of the urban population was reported as wearing clothes made of European fabrics, confirms this new policy. For, as part of his modernization drive, the heir-apparent, 'Abbas Mirza, stimulated the production of broad cloth (*mahut*) in Khoy. His object was to substitute the Persian product for the European cloth that was used for the uniforms of his army at that time. Because the artisans had difficulty in producing a comparable quality of cloth, 'Abbas Mirza had the necessary know-how and machinery imported from Russia. He also ordered the Persian ambassador in London to engage a cloth manufacturer. Though this effort was restricted to a small group and a narrow range of products, the *mahut* factory proved a failure[519].

Despite this set-back, another Qajar prince, Malek Qasem Mirza, set up improved European looms some ten years later in Shishevan. These were « for weaving a variety of cotton, silk, and worsted goods. However, his object is amusement, rather than profit, one can hardly expect the merchant of Gilan to adopt his improvements »[520]. Although Rawlinson was right that no merchant adopted his improvements, Malek Qasem Mirza apparently did a thriving business. Blau reports in 1856 that the prince's dye-works at Urmiyeh, for which he paid 200 tomans in rent, enabled him to make a good profit[521].

Europeans realized that to be able to sell textiles in Persia these had to cater to the taste of the market. Fraser had already drawn attention to the need for careful planning of both design and colors in the 1820s. « The colours preferred in Persia were fawn, brown, green, yellow, purple, scarlet, and light colors in general. The Persians preferred the flashy, good-looking types of woolens to really good quality broad-cloth. The cheaper

517. Fraser [*Caspian Sea*], p. 361-362.
518. See chapter V.
519. Donboli, p. 143; Issawi, p. 290, 296.
520. Rawlinson, p. 6.
521. Blau, p. 113.

varieties therefore dominated, while the better qualities were only found in the women's quarters and among the rich. In the early 19th century woolens were especially used as birunis and ummahs. [He also pointed out that] The inhabitants will reject an excellent article merely because the pattern does not please them, while they give an extravagant price for goods of a very inferior description, merely because their gay colors happen to suit their fancy. For some time before I was in Persia, the long rich, running patterns, resembling striped shawls, were most approved of, and such chintzes, of moderate quality, would fetch from 5 to 8 reals (6s. 8d. to 10s. 8d.) per yard of 39 inches. At the time I was there, these had begun to lose ground, and those patterns which resembled spotted shawls, with larger or smaller pines, upon a black, blue, green, or yellow ground, had the preference »[522].

Burgess, in 1833, had to learn this lesson the painful way. He writes « Chintzes are good if properly chosen (ours were none of them suited to the Persian taste and consequently did not sell well) the only way to do well in Chintz and Cotton prints is to go about the caravansaraies (Public warehouses where the merchants resort) and learn, from observation, what goods are most in demand, obtain patterns, and send them off to England along with money to purchase »[523].

Although relatively unimportant, imports of European fabrics increased and became a real avalanche by the 1840s. Persia had no means to create trade barriers, however, due to the Treaty of Torkmanchai, which determined a fixed ad valorem rate of 5% on Russian imports and *pari passu* on imports from European countries enjoying the "most-favored-nation" status. Nevertheless, Mohammad Shah (1834-1848) tried to check the consumption of European goods and to promote the use of Persian ones. In fact, when he acceded to the throne, Mohammad Shah allegedly stated that he would not allow the population to import what they needed from abroad, but would teach them how to produce it themselves[524]. « To effect the latter purpose he has recently advanced money, and offered rewards to the makers of chintz, and he has insisted that the courtiers shall gradually substitute Persian woollens and Kerman shawls for the broadcloth now used in their

522. Fraser [*Caspian Sea*], p. 367.
523. [*Burgess*], p. 34, 84.
524. E'tezad al-Saltaneh, p. 209.

dress »[525]. In 1836, Mohammad Shah commanded his subjects to have their clothes made only of Persian manufactured cloth. To implement this royal order, he instructed that all his courtiers adopt a new style of dress, viz. European trousers and redingote. Those refusing to do so would loose their government salary. Once this change had taken place the shah intended to bring about the same change in dress for the rest of the population[526]. However, apart from the unfavorable legal and economic context in which the Persian domestic industry had to operate, Persian consumers also had to pay more for the Persian goods and this resulted in the failure of the shah's efforts despite some success to produce some new good quality products such as *khara* and *manganeh*.[527]. Moreover, the shah himself did not set a good example, for he sent some of his own people to buy goods « of which he had himself so lately forbidden the purchase »[528].

When merchants, in 1837, protested against the establishment of European trading houses in Persia because these could hurt their business, Mohammad Shah remarked « that people were told not to purchase European goods, but that they did so secretly notwithstanding »[529]. He therefore had given up the unequal battle and was content to reap the benefits of the higher customs revenues due to increased European imports. Nevertheless, in 1844, Persian merchants asked the Government to ban their importation « on the ground principally of the ruin Persian manufacturers are reduced to by the constant and immense importation of foreign goods »[530]. The merchants were, however, unable to achieve their objective as were traders and manufacturers of Kashan in 1845[531]. It therefore comes as no surprise that Consul Abbott reports ten years later that « hitherto, no encouragement has been shewn to native industry in Persia »[532].

As a result of cheap European imports and the reduced economic circumstances of the population, the silk manufacturing industry suffered a

525. Issawi, p. 78-79, see also Sepehr, II, p. 90.
526. Boré, II, p. 127, 129-30; for a translation of the royal command see *ibid.*, p. 134-138; see also chapter four, the *nezami* dress.
527. E'tezad al-Saltaneh, p. 209.
528. Stuart, p. 226.
529. Issawi, p. 212.
530. *Ibid.*, p. 76 quoting FO/107, letters 28/8/1844 and 29/7/1844.
531. *Ibid.*, p. 76 quoting FO 60/117, letter 31/3/1845.
532. Amanat, p. 85.

substantial decline. It started already in the 1830s, for when Flandin and Coste passed through Kashan and observed in 1841 they remarked: « If a few industries have still survived, the majority of them are unfortunately inactive only waiting to vanish altogether » [533]. Abbott reports that in 1848, Kashan which formerly boasted of 8,000 silk looms now only had 800 silk looms. Of these « 100 are for plain, figured and gold-tissued velvets, the remainder for brocades and plain and figured silks of various denominations »[534]. Isfahan did not escape the decline either, for « manufactures have also undergone great decline [in producing cotton twist] and its silk manufactures appear to employ now only about 200 looms. The manufacture of cotton goods is carried on to greater extent »[535]. Of Yazd he writes: « Yazd is seat of various silk, cotton manufactures. Its manufacture has also undergone decline, but they still retain the reputation of excellence of their designs and patterns. For silk, mixed silks and cotton fabrics about 300-350 looms and for cottons of various kinds 1300 looms »[536]. As to Kerman he submits that it « derives its little importance from shawl and other woolen fabrics. Though limited, its woolens seem to thrive, since increased attention has been given to the production of the finer kinds of shawls »[537].

He further stated that « the manufactures of England have in a great measure superseded the use of the Cotton and Silk fabrics of this country, owing to their cheapness, the superiority of style and execution of the designs, and the greater variety of patterns, which enabled people to make a more frequent change of dress » and, elsewhere, that this led to the « detriment and ruin of many branches of native industry »[538]. This judgement is also confirmed by Holmes, who, in 1844, observed that, « Formerly a large quantity of prints were manufactured in the vicinity of Tabreez and other parts of Persia, the designs being executed both on cloth of the country and English calicoes brought for the purpose; but, nearly all these designs having been imitated in England, the Persians can now get a cheaper article than they can make themselves. The native prints and dyed calicoes, however, continue to be manufactured, in a more limited quantity,

533. Flandin and Coste, I, p. 267-268.
534. *Ibid.*, p. 75, mainly used in Persia and Caucasia.
535. *Ibid.*, p. 76.
536. *Ibid.*, I, p. 79.
537. *Ibid.*, p. 84.
538. Issawi, p. 258-259.

for the supply of the Georgian market, where the importation of British goods is strictly prohibited by the Russian Government. The dyed native calicoe from Ispahaun and Yezd is more durable, though dearer, than the English manufacture »[539].

• *The efforts to reduce European imports*

Under the dynamic prime minister, Mirza Taqi Khan (1848-1851), the Persian government tried to assist its domestic industry. Its stated purpose was to counter the penetration of European goods. In Tehran, a calico and broadcloth factory were built as well as a spinning factory, while in Kashan and Milan a silk weaving factory were erected around 1852[540]. These policies were continued by Naser al-Din Shah despite Mirza Taqi Khan's ouster from office (November 1851) and sudden execution (January 1852). According to his official chronicler, Mirza Mohammad Hasan E'temad al-Saltaneh, Naser al-Din Shah took a number of measures to boost the ailing national textile industry. The Shah was reputed to have ordered the army to wear uniforms made of locally produced materials, and to have ordered cloth from both Kerman and Kashan for this purpose which, indirectly, helped to revive the ailing textile industry in Yazd, Mashhad and Shiraz. He also promoted *malilehduzi*, *maftulduzi* and *sormehduzi* for official dress[541], the making of the *kolah-e mahut-e meshki* (blue cloth cap), which because it was cheap, became accepted by everybody; silken *'abas* based on the Najaf and Kerbela models in Kashan; and weaving in general in Isfahan[542].

Others followed the shah's lead but did so in a limited and half-hearted manner. Hajji Mohammad Hosein Kashani, for example, developed a fabric made of cotton and refuse silk (*kej*) which was almost as thick as broadcloth (*mahut*), but much suppler and more durable. The government took an interest in this fabric and ordered 2,000 coats of the material for the military. The price per hat was 4.5 qrans, thus the government only spent 850 tomans. There is no report for additional orders of these hats[543]. However, after the initial interest in the product the Government lost it, despite local opinion that such Government orders would have saved part of their textile

539. Holmes, p. 390.

540. Floor [Traditional], p. 334, table 2; see also Issawi, p. 292-295 and chapter V.

541. E'temad al-Saltaneh [*Ma'ather*], p. 106.

542. *Ibid.*

543. Naraqi, p. 259-260; E'temad al-Saltaneh [*Ma'ather*], p. 63, 103; E'temad al-Saltaneh [*Montazam*], III, p. 232, 280, 380.

industry[544]. These may have been the same fabrics that Lady Sheil referred to, viz. mixed silk-cotton *qadak* and *qotni*[545].

Individual governors also tried to stimulate the industry in their province. For example, « in the time of the former governor, Muhammad Khan [1865], who greatly encouraged the silk trade, there were 1,800 silk manufactories in Yazd, employing probably 9,000 hands. Since his removal, only 300 were in work. The silk so extensively manufactured in these parts is considered by some persons to be the best in all Persia »[546].

The Government acquired the services of some Russian experts to build and equip a cotton spinning factory some 3,5 miles outside Tehran which opened in May 1859. It was a large, three-story building (68 m long, 24 m wide and 6 m high) and it was reputedly equipped with 30,000 spools. Payments both to the 150 strong labor force, and the Russian manager, were frequently in arrears which probably explains why, between 1863 and 1866, the plant was often completely idle. Even when it was working, this was never more than two days a week and, in any case, a mere 1,600 spools were ever used. Energy cost (and other overheads) were high and combined with an input of inferior raw materials meant that the principal customer (the Isfahan weaving industry) was supplied with inferior yarns. Failure here was inevitable and there was also failure in the other projects mentioned above by the late 1860s. All this unfortunately implicit by the silence of the records in these matters after 1868[547].

The Persian craftsmen did not give in easily either and tried to compete with the European products by imitating them and by developing new products. This was no easy task, because Persian weavers started with a handicap of quality of raw materials. « In general, silk fabrics are lasting and of lively colors. Through binding of the yarns during dyeing the Persians know how to get nuanced designs. Their brightness and evenness of color is not equal to the European yarns, however »[548]. Kashani weavers also developed a new variety of *dara'i*, which was very attractive from the point of view of pattern and colors[549].

---

544. Naraqi, p. 260; Bastani Parizi [*Farmanfarma*], p. 251.
545. Sheil, p. 378.
546. Goldsmid, I, p. 175 (Mohammad Khan Vali was governor in 1282/1865-6).
547. Schneider, p. 138-139; see Floor [Traditional], on the industrialization policy in general.
548. Polak [*Persien*], II, p. 171-172.
549. Naraqi, p. 260.

Not only Kashan was active, but so was Yazd. It was here that Persia's most beautiful silken shawl, the Hosein Qoli Khan shawl, was developed by a native of Kerman. Kashani weavers also developed new silk-cotton fabrics of the *qadak* and *qotni* variety. Especially well-known became a fabric known as *'aba-ye posht-e mashhadi*, which was used to make winter clothes and was reputedly almost as fine as *kork* shawls[550]. In Isfahan, the chintz makers (*chitsaz*) made « from *qalamkar* (calico) *qalamzar*, a superior and more expensive form of Sadras calico »[551]. In 1882, the author of the *Esfahan Nesf-e Jahan* writes: « Thriving is the *qalamkar* craft where good quality has regained it such popularity that our *qalamkar-e sadras* has broken the market of the *Machli* (Madras imports) and the handicrafts of Isfahan, *chit*, *zari*, *qalamkar* are carried to most of the cities of Iran and are very well received ». He blames the later decline on the cheating of many of the makers which gave a foothold to foreign imports[552].

However, despite these creative efforts, artistically the weavers failed to turn the tide or to emulate the superior qualities of their Safavid forbears. Tahvildar reports that « the gold brocade [*zari*] which since the time of Shah 'Abbas Safavi till now has been losing its gold, still retains its design. Master painters admit their inability to imitate this design and method, and say that nowadays master painters are not able to imitate this style, let alone the weavers [*zaribaf*] »[553]. In the case of another marketable product, embroideries, the craftswomen « imitate the old patterns, but none are as good as the old ones. The old fabrics are all color fast, lasting and well done »[554].

Production in many cities and towns of a wide variety of textiles diminished through the 1850s and 1860s. *Karbas* was manufactured at Qom, Semnan and Abadeh, while *qadak* was made in Isfahan, Kashan and Yazd. *Barak* was made in Kerman and Isfahan, while silks were made in particular at Kashan and Yazd, but also in Isfahan, Tabriz and Mashhad. « The best plain taffetas are made in Mashhad and Kashan; colorful, checkered-design bed covers in Yezd and Isfahan; and door-curtain in

550. Naraqi, p. 259-260; Posht-e Mashhadi was an urban quarter in Kashan; see also chapter V.

551. Tahvildar, p. 94.

552. Esfahani [*Nesf-e jahan*], p. 124. The term *Machli* refers to the town of Machhilipatan, or fish-town, which is better known as Masulipatam, a town near Madras.

553. Tahvildar, p. 97. Other examples, Issawi, p. 295.

554. Greenfield, p. 312.

Gilan. Atlas is produced only in Kashan, where also gold brocades are made. In Yazd silken stuffs were made, above all its chadors were well-known »[555]. There was also production of silken stuffs in Kashan and Kerman, and some in Isfahan and Shiraz (where only recently silk culture had begun). « The perdehs, invariably sold with the unavoidable cypress tree pattern, and the termeh-nama, or the hardly lasting silk fabric with shawl-like patterns and figured weave, and some brocades are the best liked products. Embroideries are still widespread, above all the Resht work is good. The embroideries on horse blankets, table and chair covers, cushions, hats, and others on woolen fabrics are beautiful »[556].

Blau reports in 1858, that « the prints are made on both local and imported fabrics. The art of printing is inferior to that practiced elsewhere. In Persia cylinder print is unknown, they only use block print. This has consequences for the weft as to the regularity of pattern and the production of multi-color prints. Indian qalamkars had already been ably imitated by the Persians. But now the British are producing imitation chintz in Manchester and are pushing both the Indian and Persian qalamkars from the market since two years. Unless Persia decides to import European machines and technology this branch of industry will disappear »[557]. As a result, most of the cottons (*chits*) used in Persia were mainly imported from Great Britain in the 1860s, while people preferred *qadak* woven from British yarns[558]. « Since it is no longer in demand, it is no longer made. [...] Their products are still used allover Persia, but the European textiles have ruined their market and not even half of the original number remain »[559].

Despite these efforts there was a considerable downturn in the importance of the textile industry. « The Persian silk industry is not as flourishing as before and cannot keep up with its European counterpart. Therefore it served the domestic market as well Turkey, Russia and the Khanates. There is hardly any export to Europe, only as a kind of curiosity »[560]. This was also due to the fact that Persian textiles were not considered to be as good as European ones. There continued to be a considerable export of silken textiles to Russia, however. In 1855,

555. Polak [*Persien*], II, p. 172.
556. Brugsch, II, p. 90.
557. Blau, p. 113.
558. Polak [*Persien*], II, p. 167. They use imported cloth to print; Greenfield, p. 311.
559. Tahvildar, p. 94.
560. Blau, p. 109.

according to Russian trade statistics, some 486,570 rubles were imported by Transcaucasia. This was partly due to the force of tradition, partly to their low price. Especially, the embroideries or *golduzi* played an important role in these exports to Russia. These embroideries came originally from Isfahan, but as of the 1850s in particular from Resht, while inferior qualities from Tabriz also were exported[561].

According to de Gobineau, « today, all this is far from having survived, but a little remains of everything »[562]. Indeed, silk fabrics were still produced in Yazd, Kashan, Isfahan and Resht and were exported to neighboring countries, in particular to Russia. The silk embroideries were most beautiful in Resht, less so in Isfahan[563]. Although in absolute terms the production of silken fabrics had been reduced considerably, in relative terms it still remained an important local industry. In fact silk weaving was still very important for cities such as Kashan, where, with copper it was the chief produce. Its annual silk output was about 1,400 mans, which was sent in manufactured state to Russia around 1870[564].

According to de Rochechouart, in 1862, Yazd was the most industrial town of Persia where, in addition to the cotton, sugar and opium industries, the manufacturing of silken fabrics was of especial importance. In the Yazd area some 24,000 kg of silk was produced; a further 6,000 kg was imported from Khorasan and 1,900 kg from Kashan. This silk was woven into silken fabrics such as *tafteh*, *qasab*, *alejeh al-katon*; *alejeh-ye dal*; *alejeh-ye atlas*; *ormek*; "moiré"; "glacé" (= shot); *dara'i*; and satin, and exported allover Persia. A total of about 60 manufactories ("fabriques") were operating in Yazd, most of which were owned by Zoroastrians[565]. Silk manufacturing remained the chief industry in Yazd, which continued to get much of its silk raw material from its surrounding villages, but large quantities were also brought from Mashhad and Herat to be woven[566]. Houtum-Schindler states « in Yazd, the main manufactories are namad production, silk, and a kind of nankin look-alike, which is an important product, and made from the

561. Blau, p. 110.
562. Issawi, p. 38 quoting Gobineau.
563. Stolze and Andreas, p. 25-26.
564. Goldsmid, I, p. 154.
565. MAE, Rochechouart to Gobineau, Yezd, 26/10/1862 (unfoliated).
566. Floyer, p. 353-354 [1876].

native yellow cotton [kind of *Gossypium herbaceum*], which is only used by the Parsis »[567].

In Kerman, apart from shawls, large quantities of other woolens such as *barak* and *patu* were produced. There were 180 looms which produced only *patu* and *barak*, each loom produced two pieces per day and was never idle. According to de Rochechouart, Kerman exported some 2,5 million francs worth of these woolens, which represented about 50% of total exports from that city[568]. However, 10 years later the number of looms had been halved. For according to Houtum-Schindler there were 90 looms for *barak*, 6 *namad* manufactories and 18 dye manufactories in Kerman[569].

For Resht, the center of Persian sericulture, silk weaving also remained an important part of its economic lifeblood. Embroidery played an especially important role amounting to about 10% of Gilan's exports in the 1870s. « One of the few articles of Resht industry exported from this place, as well as to the interior of Persia and to the Caucasus and other parts of Russia, is the silk embroidery on cloth, for which Resht has acquired a certain reputation »[570].

Furthermore, the textile fabrics produced in Persia continued to find a ready sale in Turkey, Georgia and the south of Russia, generally. « Last year £280,000 sold at the fair of Nizni-Novgorod. The thick blue cotton cloths called "charchsvs" [*charqad*] worn as wrappers by the Persian women are woven in Yezd, and fetch a high price, from 35 s. to 80 s. each. In Azerbaijan there are no manufactures of cloth, but a large trade is carried on with Georgia in printed cottons, which are imported plain from Manchester, and receive coloured patterns in Tabreez »[571].

The decline of the Persian textile industry

• *The reasons why*

- Cheap European imports

Despite efforts both by government and industry the weavers were not successful in slowing down the disappearance of their craft. This failure was due to a number of interdependent and self-reinforcing factors. The

567. Houtum-Schindler [*Reisen*], p. 321.

568. MAE, Rochechouart to Gobineau, Kerman 5/11/1862.

569. Houtum-Schindler [*Reisen*], p. 331.

570. AP 1876, "Report by Consul Churchill on the Trade and Commerce of the Provinces of Ghilan and Astarabad for the years 1874 and 1875", p. 1498.

571. AP 29, LXV (1873), p. 240.

most important factor was an economic one; people were poor and had to chose between a cheap and more attractive European fabric, or a more expensive inferior quality Persian product. Economics won out, even when the nationalist Moslem drum was beaten to buy Persian products only. Consul-General Jones (Tabriz) observed in 1873 in this regard, « cheapness is above all the characteristic which finds favour with Persian customers, and to this they are prepared to sacrifice every other consideration »[572]. But not only the poor changed their minds. « Qanavuz, khara, atlas etc. » that formerly were used by the rich for their clothing have been displaced by European imports, Greenfield reports[573].

In addition to European imports, there was also a small, but thriving, trade in the very much appreciated Indian cottons. « Persian craftsmen were settled [in Masulipatam] in order to insure production of the type of fabrics needed for the Persian market, and this explains why many of the nineteenth century Masulipatam fabrics bear Persian inscriptions »[574]. In 1886 an eyewitness states « elsewhere in India, printed cloths are produced which rival Persian work in delicacy and minuteness of pattern, while in remote Madras, the descendants of Persian immigrants are still making chintzes exactly similar in texture, finish and pattern, to those of Tehran »[575]. Linings for clothes, with tiny botehs, were made in India and, later, by the cheaper Russian printing machines.

- Use of aniline dyes

Apart from cheap European imports there was the increased use of European aniline dyes by Persian artisans. Initially, despite all its setbacks, the Isfahan *chit* industry had been able to build up a small export trade of *qalamkars* to Europe. « These qalamkars were mainly used for decorative purposes and were especially appreciated in France. However, due to the deterioration of the use of dyes such as Prussian blue (*nil-e sanduqi*) and bad and unsound reds which all wash out and run together, the *qalamkars* were no longer in demand »[576].

Persian natural dyes were famous for their quality and durability. However, their preparation was labor intensive and not cheap and therefore

572. Issawi, p. 114 quoting AP 1873, 67, p. 366.
573. Greenfield, p. 309.
574. Irwin and Hall, I, p. 43.
575. *Ibid.*, p. 45.
576. DCR 1593 (1895-96), p. 7. Greenfield, p. 309.

increasingly felt the competition from chemical anilines. Although the import of aniline dyes had been forbidden, they were offered for sale in the bazaar without any problem. « If the user had an idea how to properly use the anilines the damage would not be so bad. But this is not the case, especially the nomads do not know how use them, and therefore Persian fabrics are inferior and not durable. Colors are running through. Real indigo is still used at large scale. For red, madder is used, for yellow, berries, and also vine leaves »[577].

- Manufacturing of inferior products

The lack of Persian competition was reinforced by the fact that, instead of building on their strengths (good dyes, durability) Persian weavers sacrificed these on the altar of cheapness. Sacrificing quality for cheapness may be was the intelligent thing to do to compete with low-cost European textiles, but it was at the cost of giving up the one thing that distinguished their product competitively from the imported article. « These [Persian] stuffs are of cotton, of silk, and of wool; they all possess one quality in common, which cannot be said of all European manufactures, - durability » states Benjamin[578]. But the Persian public, forced by economic conditions, chose cheap articles rather than quality products. « The Persian wants something cheap, which presents a good appearance to the eye at the first sent off. The better class of goods, really good broadcloths, are only to be found in the women's quarters of the well-to-do people »[579].

The result was that Persian textile products became even less attractive, not only at home, but also abroad. Mrs. Bishop, for example, observed that Kashan was noted for its silks and velvets, « but the modern productions are regarded by judges as degenerate »[580]. The fact that these often shoddy products could still be sold in Russia and the Khanates had to do with the fact that cheap products catered for a segment of the market that looked for such products. However, it was a dwindling market for, due to Russian protectionist economic policy and its fast growing textile industry, Persian textiles were increasingly being displaced by Russian ones. « Exports of Iranian textiles to Russia, which had averaged 649,000 rubles in 1875-78,

577. Kuss, p. 149-150.
578. Benjamin, p. 427.
579. DCR 1662 (1895-6), p. 9.
580. Bird, I, p. 230.

fell to 197,000 in 1885-87, and declined further during the 1890s, at a time when total Iranian exports to Russia were advancing very rapidly »[581].

- Reduced availability of raw materials

Another economic factor that in a major way contributed to the ruin of the Persian textile industry was the reduction in the availability of raw materials, especially the export of raw silk to Europe, whose own silk disease had led to high prices there. Persia's silk weaving industry suffered a further set-back when the silk-disease started so to affect local sericulture that many farmers abandoned silk in favor of opium and other crops[582]. Silk production in Persia fell from 1,000 tons to about 100 tons due to the silk disease of 1864[583]. This greatly reduced the capacity to produce silken fabrics, which, on top of this constraint, also had to face growing competition from silken fabrics from abroad.

A similar development took place with regard to cotton where people found it more profitable to sell the raw material rather than manufacture fabrics[584]. The same problem faced the weavers of cottons. The fact that Russian agents organized an effective credit-purchasing system in the rural areas also assisted this development[585]. In addition, of course, there was the competition of foreign fabrics, as a result of which cotton fabrics were imported on a large scale.

- Change in fashion

Finally, there was the change in fashion. Several products that had been a standard component of Persian dress went out of fashion, and almost disappeared altogether. European producers were also much more alert to react to fashion changes and the need for to market new or adapted products, colors and designs. The tradition-ridden textile industry could not keep up with the new developments, and lost much business as a consequence.

Change in fashion too had its impact on the reduction in or disappearance of the production of certain fabrics and/or products. For example, Tahvildar lists a great number of these products for which there

581. Issawi, p. 300-301 quoting Glukhohed, p. 23.
582. Jamalzadeh, p. 79; Polak [*Persien*], II, p. 171-172.
583. Issawi, p. 231-232; Seyf [Silk Production], p. 51-72.
584. Issawi, p. 245; Tahvildar, p. 101.
585. Issawi, p. 246.

was little or no demand. « Formerly, besides those in Persia, the *sha'rbaf* or silk weavers had customers in Turkey and Russia, but now their product is very little in demand [...] Formerly, there was not a woman in Persia who did not wear a *meshki* piece of fabric on her head [...] Now it has fallen into disuse [...] The *jahkbaf* weave women's lace out of material such as *jahk, muzhegan, muj*, and *purchuk* [...] Some of their products for the town ladies have fallen into disuse now and have become old fashioned »[586]. « Formerly, gold brocade weaving (*zaribaf*) was very widespread and gold brocade was one of the high quality cloths in Persia [...] Now this guild and its craft have been ruined and fallen into disuse and its craftsmen are insignificant and its production is small. What buyers there are come from foreign countries. In Persia it is very little used indeed »[587]. « The trade of *naqdehduz* has gradually declined and most of the remaining artisans have gone to Tehran and Tabriz [...] The same description holds for the group of *qollabduz* or crocheters [...] The group of sewers of *londreh* cloth [*londrehduz*] are now few in Persia [...] The work of the *kolahduz* is not much in demand and their guild is ruined [...] Formerly, *kolechehduzi* was much in demand »[588]. « Most *naqshduzi* was sold to customers in Turkey, Egypt, India, Turkistan, and Afghanistan; some was also sold to Europe. From the time of the late Shah [Mohammad Shah 1834-1848] to the present day the trade had gradually declined and fallen into disuse »[589].

« Formerly, goldlace was much in demand and the number of goldlace spinners great; now they only number only a few and their products are not much in demand »[590]. As a consequence, imports of gold and silver thread and lace, from Bavaria, were reduced significantly at the end of the 19th century, because the fashion of embroidering coats and mantles (*'abas*) with these materials had almost disappeared in North and Central Iran. In 1903, only inferior grades (down to half fine) of gold and silver thread were in demand (mainly for the Arab population of the Gulf), where formerly high grades of thread (up to 900 fine) were wanted[591]. In 1904, a British commercial commission concluded that « the extremely gaudy native socks

586. Tahvildar, p. 102.
587. *Ibid.*, p. 97.
588. Tahvildar, p. 98.
589. *Ibid.*, p. 99.
590. *Ibid.*, p. 94.
591. DCR 1662 (1894-95), p. 7-10, 18; MacLean, p. 36, 39, 42; Gleadow-Newcomen, p. 71; Greenfield, p. 309.

or jurrab is, however, going out of fashion, natives preferring European-made socks of grey or black »[592].

As a result of the growing imports of cheap and attractive European fabrics and the failure of the Persian industry to meet the challenge by producing inferior and unattractive products, and using aniline dyes, as well as a change in fashion, the Persian textile industry received a major set-back in the 1870s when most of its remaining capacity was forced out of business. Tahvildar, a contemporary observer, ascribes this defeat, inter alia, as follows:

« Formerly when European textiles were not common, everyone from high to low, even high government officials and some princes, wore clothes made of *qadak*. Therefore, *qadak* of superior quality of 8 till even 30 chelleh (warp) was woven in Isfahan. The yarn for both warp and woof was spun in Isfahan too. When the colors, made by Isfahani dyers, were added to this it produced a softness like *dara'i*, in all its beauty. The more it was used, it would become so stiff that it dissolved like dried whey [*kashak*] and it would become downy like *mahut* [broad cloth]. The more it would be twisted, the woollier and brighter its color would get. The poor could use one *qaba* for two to three years. Which European cloth does not loose its stiffness and color after one time of washing [*tashviyeh*]. For the past few years yellow and red european cloth, which is soft on the inside [*baten-e sost*] has become popular. Every time these [European] textiles had a new pattern and each of them had the look of novelty about it. The Persian people lost their senses and only had eyes for the outward appearance. In fact, this path led to ruin, but they did not realize it. Especially now when cheap clothes are not sufficiently economical and lasting.

This is the reason why the products of the weavers' guild are hardly sold. Therefore, they imitated the European style but neglected durability [of their product] and turned to superficial prettiness. Because of its nice appearance and the convenience [*sohulat-e amr*] European yarn was used for the weft of the *qadak*, but these fabrics turned out badly. Composed [*morakkaban*] as it was of a mixture of Persian and European style their weaving became faulty all at once. When it was worn it became ragged. It also lost its stiffness, woolliness and durability. The yarn spinners [*risandehha-ye rismanha*] became jobless and found themselves in difficult

592. Gleadowe-Newcomen, p. 94.

straits and misery. Russian did not buy textiles anymore, and the Persians lost interest in their own product. The weavers' guild was completely ruined. As a consequence everyone has suffered damage, according to his share.

At least 10% of the guilds of this city were weavers, but not 1/5th of them have remained. Almost 5% of the Isfahani unattached widows, mothers or orphans, made ends meet by spinning and were not jobless. But also other big guilds like dyers, cotton dressers and washermen, who were dependent on this guild, were almost completely ruined. The other classes of people also suffered from this ruin, especially the farmers, who, because there was no price fixing for cotton, lost on all their produce. Just like a few years ago, when this situation also occurred, when [cotton] prices rose and foreigners bought it all. This caused a rise in prices of other goods and everyone profited therefrom. But what is the use, « it shone brightly but it was soon over ». The relation between loss and profit concern all products and individuals. Their influence is to be noticed in all things and persons to the extent of their involvement. All parts of the world are like the members of one body, having but one soul. 'When misfortune has befallen one member [of the body], the other members will not go unscathed'. When it prospered many will share in the profit and will it be the cause of the preservation of the species »[593].

Tahvildar was not alone in this opinion which was shared by Mohammad Mehdi, a contemporary and fellow-Isfahani: « Some other products of Isfahan such as *qalamkar*, *chit*, *zari* and some other woven stuffs are exported to most [other parts] of Iran where they are traded. Because of cheating some of the products, both where their manufacturing and trading is concerned, have suffered a decline and become unimportant [*ruy be kami avardand*]. European products have taken their place, and this situation still persists »[594].

The impact of the ruin of the Persian textile industry has been most graphically described for Isfahan, where there was hardly a craft which had not suffered ruin or a much reduced state due to cheaper European imports and inferior product. As we have seen of the total weaving population only some 20% was able to hold on to their jobs, while the impact was most severe in crafts that were sensitive to changes in fashion as well as those that

593. Tahvildar, p. 101.
594. Esfahani [*Nesf-e jahan*], p. 125-126.

produced costly fabrics. Hoeltzer, a long-time resident of Isfahan, confirms Tahvildar's somber picture when he informs us that « formerly weaving was the main occupation of the Isfahan populace. They made *karbas*, *qamis*, *nashur*, *shal*, *piremshahi*, *malmal* and silk and other fine or coarse fabrics. But due to European imports the number of looms has been reduced. Now one finds only a few in Isfahan and the surrounding villages. Mostly some old women still weave as well as the rural population during winter time »[595].

Nor was Isfahan the only textile producing center to lose a major share of its market: in the 1840s Borujerd had been renowned for the excellence of its printed cotton goods, yet, barely four decades later, was reduced to import these from Isfahan[596].

Silk fabrics continued to be manufactured all over the country, but on a reduced scale. The principal centers were Yazd (which produced the best fabrics) and Kashan, followed by Isfahan, Tabriz and Mashhad whose pre-1865 capacity had been 1,200 looms, now reduced to 150-200 looms. Even Yazd, whose 1,800 looms had employed 9,000 workers, had suffered in a similar manner (see Table 5).

Silk weaving was reduced significantly in most non-silk producing areas. In Isfahan, for example, « little of it is left. Most of the [silk weavers] weave shawls and abas, a small group the richer garments for the wealthy, but only on orders. Silk comes mostly from Rasht, Yazd and Kashan. In Isfahan only some landlords still are engaged in sericulture as a hobby »[597].

Table 5: Decline of the number of silk looms in major cities

City / Year	1830	1848	1860	1870	1890	1900	1915
Kashan	8000	800	400	-	-	200	262
Bidgol (Kashan)	-	-	1700	-	-	-	50
Isfahan	1250	460	249	-	12	-	-
Yazd	-	350	1800	300	100	700	
Mashhad	-	-	1200	-	700	200	-

595. Hoeltzer, p. 45.

596. *Historical Gazetteer*, I, p. 112; see also, for other examples, Qazvini, p. 44, 50-51, 82.

597. Hoeltzer, p. 45.

Sources: Amanat, p. 76, 79, 93; Polak [*Persiens*], II, p. 171; Naraqi, p. 275, 488, 495; Abdullaev, p. 93, 95; Sykes [*Ten Thousand*], p. 423; Curzon, I, p. 167; *Historical Gazetteer*, I, p. 694, II, p. 489; Tahvildar, p. 102; Jamalzadeh, p. 79.

« Some ten years ago », an Armenian commentator wrote in 1881, « the gain from the weaving industry was plentiful, to the extent that weavers not only supported their families moderately, but also amassed riches in addition to necessities, now earning only 10 shahis a day. Annually 140,00 sheets of linen and 25,000 pairs of socks per year were produced in Jolfa »[598].

Not only cotton prints and silken stuffs, but also another successful export product, *rashtduzi* or embroideries, suffered an important set-back, due to a deterioration in the quality of its output. « The beautiful Persian embroideries which in times past stocked the bazaars of Stamboul have now almost disappeared, and it is difficult for any but a resident in the country, employing dellals to ransack the native houses, to procure good specimens. At Resht is manufactured a showy but somewhat vulgar embroidery, consisting of a species of coloured cloth patchwork, richly covered with broidered designs; and glittering arabesques of gold and silver, on backgrounds of black, green, and crimson velvet, are worked elsewhere. Nevertheless, to the traveller who has made an inspection of the excellent and representative collection purchased for the South Kensington Museum by Sir R. Murdoch Smith, a visit to modern Persia will probably prove a great disappointment »[599]. This beautiful silk embroidery was done by men and used for table and chair covers, cushions, stools, carpets etc. in all varieties and colors[600].

The disappearance of quality textile products was also brought home to those travellers who had come to Persia to look for these products. One such traveller mentions that, when in Kashan, he looked in vain for its costly silken stuffs in the bazaar[601]. Mrs. Bishop found a similar situation in Kermanshah in 1891, when she reports that « no rich carpets or other goods are exposed to view for fear of exactions. A buyer wanting such things must send word privately, and have them brought to his house »[602].

---

598. Issawi, p. 60.
599. Curzon, II, p. 525-526.
600. Marsh [*A Ride*], p. 61.
601. de Windt, p. 122.
602. Bird, I, p. 103; see also p. 185 with regards to the situation in Tehran.

• *Some textile products do well*

Despite the decline and ruin of many Persian crafts some textile crafts prospered. One example is that of the weavers of *'abas* (*'ababafs*), who prior to 1870 had been a small group. By the end of the 19th century, 30,000 looms were in production and gave employment to the women of the villages around Isfahan. « Local cotton crop is nearly all used in Isfahan. It is used locally in weaving of karbas, the rest is used in making ropes, yarn, bags, 'abas, and uniforms for the troops. It gives employment to the women of the districts, some 30,000 looms it is said in the villages, in the town itself there are none. They are underutilized and could use more cotton »[603].

Another example is that some crafts and/or textile centers were still able to export. In Azerbaijan, due to the inability to export its inferior quality cotton, people in Salmas, Urmiyeh and Tabriz provinces started turning it into a cheap cotton coarse cloth, which because of its cheapness was very much appreciated in the Caucasus[604].

The situation in Yazd, the major silk weaving center was not different. « The silk stuffs of Yazd are very good and are much thought of by Persians, they are very widely in demand all over Persia and even into Russia. They are made up into curtains, handkerchiefs and dress pieces. Weavers imitate successfully European products. They turn out these goods as occasion demands. Some 75,000 lb of silk is imported from Resht »[605].

However, a total outsider, carpet weaving, was to become the most important and a very successful textile craft in Persia. Carpets had never played a role in Persian exports before, but the position changed radically in the 1870s partly because European merchants were looking for a suitable commodity to export from Iran, but mainly because of the growing interest for old and antique carpets in Europe. Demand for carpets increased dramatically after the World Trade Fair of 1873. Demand between 1872 and 1874 increased by 100%. Carpet production was still carried out in weavers' homes so, to be able to satisfy this new and rapidly growing demand, it became essential to re-organize manufacturing methods and European firms alone had the know-how and the capital to do so. Their

603. DCR 1662 (1894-95), p. 9-10; Tahvildar, p. 102.
604. Issawi, p. 301.
605. DCR 1376 (1893-94), p. 20-21.

influence was mostly exercised in the Soltanabad (Arak) area, and led to far stricter control of materials, qualities, designs and sizes than had ever been experienced in Persian industry. Their paramount situations in the towns was soon emulated and threatened by largely similar factories set up in surrounding villages by enterprising merchants from Tabriz. Both where output and employment were concerned carpet weaving was a success-story for by 1910 at least 65,000 persons were directly employed in this craft, as compared with only 1,000 around 1860. Carpets were also important for the economy as a whole; in 1850 they did not figure among exports, however, by 1912 they accounted for no less than 12% of total Persian exports[606].

Table 6: Main textile exports of Iran (in %)

Product	1850	1880s	1911-13
silk and products	38	18	5
cotton and woolen cloth	23	1	1
raw cotton	1	7	19
carpets	-	4	12

Source: Issawi, p. 136.

Despite the general failure of European type factories to prosper in Persia some investors were able to hold their own. « There is a steam spinning establishment at Resht owned by Haji Mohamed Hassan, the late mint-master at Tehran. His looms produce a very fair quality of silk, which is consumed in the country itself and also exported to Marseilles and Moscow »[607].

However, for textiles in general, the situation deteriorated (see Table 6). Even once popular fabrics, such as ubiquitous *karbas*, were woven in far smaller quantities to the point where they had been completely replaced by European fabrics (the so-called "Mexican" cotton goods) in Kurdestan, Borujerd and Sauj Bolagh. A British print known as Seyd Abdul Khassemi, a six-coloured print, was doing well in Khorasan, as a heavy-striped print (*tampush*) in Kermanshah[608].

606. See Floor [Traditional]; Wirth; Issawi, p. 301-05; "Carpets", in *EIr*, q.v.

607. DCR 1189, "Persia - Resht Report on the Trade and Commerce of the Province of Ghilan for the Year 1891", p. 3. See also Ashraf, p. 82-86.

608. MacLean, p. 40.

• *Popular reaction*

Such was the impact of the ruin of the weaving industry on the laboring population that street urchins sang the following lines:

harkehra karash bud bafandegi
mordanesh behtar bud az zendegani[609].
[Everyone who earned his bread with weaving
Would be better off dead than living].

The failure of the government to stop the European onslaught fuelled nationalism and resentment. The nationalist reform movement gained importance and agitated against the growing dependence on imports of basic goods. In the satire *Ketab-e Ahmad* the writer asserts « if we wore cotton cloth [*qadak*] of Isfahan and made clothes from the woolen cloth [*shal*] of Yazd and Isfahan; if instead of the felt of the foreigner, we made hats out of the skins (*pust*) of Shirazi, Iran might make progress »[610].

As a result of the structural changes in the Persian economy the call for action and change increased. Naser al-Din Shah was not interested any more in fighting what he considered to be a lost battle. The initiative taken by Persian investors in the establishment of a silk reeling factories (Resht) in the 1880s and of a spinning mill in Tehran in 1895, however much appreciated, clearly did not satisfy the reformists. A group among them founded in 1897 the Oriental Society (*anjoman-e sharqi*) in Isfahan, whose aim was to promote the consumption of Persian goods. Around the same time (*Dhu'l-Qa'deh* 1316 / March 1899) a similar organization was founded known as the Islamic Society (*anjoman-e eslami*). As part of this movement many other trading companies were founded, but only one of which explicitly aimed at the production, trade and sale of Persian goods, and in fact this company was forbidden to trade in foreign goods.

The Islamic Company (*sherkat-e eslami*) as this new company was called, was founded by the backers of the two previously mentioned societies. The company constructed weaving facilities in Ardestan and produced cloth which was known as Islamic cloth (*parcheh-ye eslami*). The weaving was done on handlooms and the workmanship was generally considered to be poor, according to the British consul. According to Majd al-Eslam Kermani many of the leading olama used only Islamic cloth for

609. Malekzadeh, I, p. 174.
610. Talibof, quoted by Bakhash, p. 351.

their clothes and even for their turban. Although the company was financed by the leading olama, who « use every available opportunity to compel the Persians to purchase their goods rather than go to Europeans, whose goods they declare to be unclean », it went bankrupt. Apart from embezzlement of funds the main reason seems to have been that the consumers preferred the cheaper and better foreign textiles[611].

Despite this failure, the reformists continued to have an interest in the "buy Iranian goods only" movement. In 1900 a book appeared, *Lebas al-taqva* (Dress of the Devout), written by one of the leading constitutionalists of the 1906 revolution, which exhorted people to use Persian goods only[612]. This and similar activities seem to have caused an increased interest in local textiles, for as the British consul in Yazd reports « here seems to be an increasing demand for cotton and silk stuffs of local manufacture, due it is said, to efforts by the majles to induce natives to encourage home industries by wearing garments the materials of which are of local manufacture »[613]. Because economic reality rather than ideology was the guiding principle for the poor in Persia such efforts only had a passing effect and the "buy Persian goods" movement failed to make any permanent impact on the domestic market.

• *The end of the Persian textile industry*

The textile industry was the hardest hit of Persia's traditional industries, due to a combination of factors[614]. These were cheap European imports of machine-made fabrics with changing designs and colors. To compete the Persian industry only had been able to put up a weak defense by giving up quality through the use of inferior materials and the use of aniline dyes. Finally, a change in fashion reduced and wiped out markets for certain specialized products. Government support was weak and ineffectual, and appeals to buy Persian goods only fell on deaf ears.

By 1900, Persia's most important textile producing centers had by no means lost their manufacturing industry. All kinds of woven fabrics, from the most expensive velvet and satin to the coarsest nankin and calico were,

611. Floor [The merchants], p. 128; Ashraf, p. 100; DCR 3923, Isfahan (1906), p. 7; Kermani [*Tarikh*], II, p. 311-315.

612. Floor [The Merchants], p. 128; for a short discussion of the contents of this book see Saba, p. 103 ff.

613. DCR 3923, Yazd (1906), p. 13.

614. See Floor [Traditional], in general.

and/or could, still be manufactured. Of Yazd, the most important center of the textile industry[615] it is reported that « the most important industry of Yazd still remained weaving. There are fully 1,000 looms, the most important articles were chadars for women and all sorts of cotton, cotton and silk, and silk materials. Cloth printing and dyeing were carried on to a considerable extent. Shoe making and felt making are also done. The Yazd felt carpets are very good and substantial, but they are only made to order »[616].

Other towns also still had a textile industrial base, albeit with a large underutilized capacity. Cotton prints were not only made in Yazd, but also in Isfahan. In Yazd, for example, there were 800 cotton manufactories with 2,000 looms, although Sykes states there were only 700. They produced 100,000 tomans of value around the turn of the century. In Isfahan, at the beginning of the 20th century, there were still some 2,000 cotton looms, or 3-4 looms per shop, thus, in all, 500-600 manufactories. In Kashan, there were about 100 cotton manufactories[617]. According to Rittikh there was export of woolens from Yazd to other cities in Persia, but also to Turkey[618]. In 1900, were exported from Isfahan some 2,000 *'aba*s at a value of 6,000 tomans[619].

However, all these *chit* producing activities could not hide the fact that « the shirting on which the pattern is stamped is now for the most part imported into the country, while an imitation article is turned out by machinery in Manchester »[620].

There was also still some considerable production in the hinterland of the main textile producing centers. McLean reports that « Yazd still produces large quantities of cotton tissues, also Khorasan, although the latter is losing ground as cotton or mixed suitings and trouserings are taking the place of the plain home-made cotton tissues (karbaz). In the Yazd and Isfahan districts the weaving industry in cotton tissues is very extensive, though it is all house work, on cottage looms, and in articles of certain

---

615. Greenfield, p. 239.

616. *Historical Gazetteer*, I, p. 694.

617. Abdullaev , p. 93, 97-98; Sykes [*Ten Thousand*], p. 423; See also Curzon, II, p. 42, 245, MacLean, p. 47.

618. Rittikh, I, p. 181.

619. Abdullaev, p. 92.

620. Curzon, II, p. 525. There was also some velvet production in Shiraz (Forsat, p. 500.

dimensions, such as kerchiefs, napkins, shawls, scarfs, braids, tapes, cords, etc. Cotton longcloth, or karbaz, has already been noted. Yazd also produces a thick cotton drugget "zeloo" »[621].

Part of the output of the remaining active textile industry was still being exported, although in diminishing quantities. « Persian cloaks (abas), socks, cotton shoes (givehs), gloves, handkerchiefs, etc, are exported from Azerbaijan to Caucasia and Turkey, and find a market amongst the Muhammadan population in those regions »[622].

The situation with regards to the production of silk fabrics was not much different from that of cotton fabrics. The main difference was that whereas cotton yarns and fabrics were imported, silk yarns were still being made locally in Persia. « There is a large consumption of reeled and waste silk in Persia; perhaps one-half of the production in ordinary years is forwarded to Tabriz, Kashan, Isfahan, Yazd, Kerman, Mashed and via Kermanshah to Baghdad. There is also a considerable manufacture of coarse silk tissues in Gilan. Imports to Kerman are amongst other things for silk tissues of many sorts, kerchiefs, sashes, cloaks (abas) and brocades. Kashan has long been famous for its varied silk tissues, from handkerchiefs to velvets, brocades and carpets. In the Yazd, Kashan and Urmiya districts silk is cultivated but in much smaller quantities than required for local consumption. Khorasan grows silk, particularly near Turbat, but not sufficient for the weaving industries, much is imported from Resht »[623]. « In Kashan the silk yarn comes from Resht or Europe, and the same holds for Yazd. However, one also uses much filoselle, i.e. waste silk »[624].

Kashan, Isfahan, Tabriz and Resht were the centers of the silk-weaving industry. In Resht, *dara'i* was made, a very compact/close fabric with patterns (figures), red or yellow zigzag, not unlike a Bokhara robe. In Tabriz they made *dara'i futa*. Yazd also produced *termeh-nama*, a not so very durable fabric[625]. Particoloured velvets were manufactured at

621. MacLean, p. 42. A drugget is a common cloth, usually tabby, with a wool weft on a linen or cotton warp. Also, simple floor covering, often made of a mixture of wool and cotton.

622. *Ibid.*, p. 18.

623. *Ibid.*, p. 43. There are, perhaps, 500 hands employed in spinning [silk] in Mashhad. *Ibid.*, p. 44.

624. Olmer, p. 39.

625. Abdullaev, p. 94.

Mashhad, Kashan and Isfahan, gold and silver brocades at Kashan and Yazd. *Namads* were principally made at Yazd, Kerman and Isfahan[626]. The main producers of *tafteh* were Tabriz, Yazd, Mashhad, Astarabad and Sabzavar, and for velvet, mainly Kashan, Resht and Isfahan[627]. « The silk tissues manufactured in Yazd and Khorasan are exported from the latter to Transcaspia, Afghanistan and India. A larger trade in similar articles, handkerchiefs, shawls for turbans, and girdles, striped and coloured tissues, etc. exists from Tabriz to Caucasia »[628].

But all these activities, the seemingly large number of available looms, and the ongoing exports could not hide the fact that the curtain had fallen for the Persian textile industry. « The once flourishing printing and dyeing industry of Isfahan still exists, but is no longer flourishing [...] The local prints were more costly than foreign machine-made prints, and are consumed by the middle and upper classes »[629]. The imports of foreign Russian cottons, especially a printed variety, became very popular among the well-to-do, who used them as carpet covers (*rufarsh*). Jobs were also lost due to change in fashion.

The heavier duty on white and grey goods (compared with printed goods) as a result of the new disadvantageous Russian 1903 tariff, as well as on dyes, dealt a heavy blow to the already depressed printing and dyeing industries of Persia. « The chitsaz, or native printer, and the dyer had been badly hit by the increased 1903 tariff. White goods were mainly imported for re-dying, but since the tariff is on weight and not ad valorem the expensive goods are less taxed than the cheap white ones. Consequently there was a decrease in demand for these goods, that came mainly from Great-Britain. Thus native dying is being killed. Demand for shirtings is roughly half that for printed and dyed tissues, and mostly supplied by Great-Britain »[630].

In Isfahan, where despite heavy competition the *qalamkar* industry had been still thriving, although at a much reduced level, finally was hit once more. The market for *qalamkars* was the rural and nomad population, who used these products for shirts and trousers. These also used the undyed product as underclothing. The middle class was still using it, but only

626. Curzon, II, p. 525.
627. Abdullaev, p. 93; Curzon, II, p. 13, 525.
628. MacLean, p. 44.
629. *Ibid.*, p. 37.
630. Gleadowe-Newcomen, p. 70; see also Jamalzadeh, p. 79.

imported products. This especially held for the more expensive Indian hand printed cottons (twice to four times the price of the local product), which were especially appreciated by the mollahs, and other well-to-do people, who used them for lining their clothes. Indian printed cottons remained a small market also in the 20th century as it was too expensive[631].

To improve their market share, *chit* makers in Isfahan tried to make prints that were more suited for the European market. In 1910 « experiments made on local [Kashani] silk tissues have been attended with a certain measure of success. Better results have been obtained from Chinese silk or European twills, the colours being found not to run on these as they are apt to do on native silk tissues. A French firm exports these to France »[632].

Encouraged by the early experiments the *chit* makers also attempted « to reproduce (on cotton tissues) some old Genoese designs with a certain measure of success ». However, the final result was that the prints were more of interest from artistic point than of commercial point of view[633].

Efforts to boost output also continued in Yazd. For example, around 1905, workers from Resht came to Yazd to establish manufactories and its adjacent villages, mainly at Mohammadabad[634]. But this and other efforts were to no avail. « Most local industries in Yazd are gradually declining, as imported articles can be retailed cheaper than articles of local manufacture. Foreign manufacturers therefore imitate the silk tissues of Yazd exactly. An important factor to cause this decline is the excessive taxation levied by the local authorities on the industries, most of which did not reach the national treasury, but was pocketed by the tax collectors »[635]. In 1906, excessive taxation also led to the closure of the indigo plant in Dizful, where, around 1900, « some of the inhabitants are occupied in the stamping of designs on cloth with wooden blocks, in dyeing. Dizful indigo, though inferior to imported Indian, enjoys local favor »[636].

The situation in Yazd deteriorated in such a manner that by 1908 only a few weavers were able to continue thanks to imported cotton yarn and some

631. DCR 3923 (1906), p. 4.
632. DCR 5048 (1912), p. 23.
633. DCR 5254 (1913), p. 32. See also DCR 5521 (1914), p. 28.
634. Olmer, p. 38.
635. DCR 3748 (1905-06), p. 9.
636. Lorimer, p. 485.

to work in silk with imports from Gilan. But the quality of what they produced continued downwards because of market pressure on prices[637]. However, increased European imports combined with closure of the trade routes due to their insecurity had such an effect on the textile industry of Yazd « that many weavers can barely earn enough to support themselves and their families. Coarse kinds of canvas of closer or finer texture are manufactured in the villages and used for villagers' clothing, the yarn being spun on an ancient spinning wheel »[638]. For want of a change for the better either in the general economic and political situation internally or, in particular, in the security of the roads and communications, Yazd's textile industry continued to have to pay high prices for its imports, suffered from contracting markets, was forced to reduce production (with inevitable reductions in employment) and thus found itself in a desperate situation.

Kashan also provided a picture of a dying textile industry. Until the end of the 19th century the production of velvet and silks was very widespread and successful in Kashan, as was the weaving of expensive fabrics. Thereafter they turned to weave middle and inferior grade dark blue silken stuffs, that were cheap, known as *meshkibafi*, which were sold to the tribes and neighboring countries. But as of 1900 due to insecurity on the roads and political instability *sha'rbafi* was stopped, and only a few looms producing cotton fabrics continued. Just after the fall of Na'eb Hosein in 1919, of the 7,000 *sha'rbaf* looms only 750 silk looms (*vatanibaf*) and 262 *abrishambaf* were still operational, while the annual consumption of silk was only 11,174 Tabriz mans[639].

Bidgol, a large village supplying Kashan, also suffered, because there was neither support nor demand for its products. Only 50 of the previous 1,700 looms were still working around 1930 making beautiful *alejeh-ye meshki, mahramat-e moharami-ye kabriti-ye alvan-e thabet rang*, the type of *kebrit*, ideal for soldiers trousers, and also *qotni-ye sangin, shalha-ye kamar kenareh-ye abrisham, khaqani-ye khosh-rang, mahramat-e sefid va meshki*[640].

By 1910, « the weaving center is Yazd, followed by Kerman, and Mashhad, while Kashan is important for the finer fabrics. The brocade industry that was important in the past, is all but disappeared, though here

637. DCR 4838, p. 32.
638. DCR 5048, p. 50; DCR 5254, p. 60.
639. Naraqi, p. 275-276; see also *ibid.*, p. 448.
640. Zarrabi, p. 495.

and there still to be found in Kashan. Half silk stuffs are produced in great quantities by Yazd and Mashhad. Woolen fabrics are made in Yazd, but also in Mashhad and Berjand, and mostly in very good quality. The latter are mostly for Persian cloaks »[641]. The cotton weaving industry had almost totally disappeared, since cheap Manchester stuffs flooded the market[642].

The reduction in output and in diversity had a knock-on effect on intermediate products such as yarns which had, in the past, mainly originated in Persia. Now — especially for fine fabrics — these came increasingly from abroad: India, which had replaced England and Europe for cotton. For weaving woolen cloth and carpets, British yarns were paramount. Only in silk fabrics were local materials still used, occasionally ignored in favor of Chinese silk[643].

The unsettled and insecure period that followed the Persian Revolution of 1906 was not conducive to the development, let alone the thriving, of the textile industry. As we have seen insecurity on the roads negatively affected the textile industry in both Kashan and Yazd. The advent of the first World War and the military activities that were its consequence brought a halt even to the carpet industry in, for example, Birjand and Kerman. The 1917 famine and the aftermath of the World War I also had a negative impact on textile production[644].

Towards the end of the Qajar period there was still some weaving of silk and cotton fabrics, but the Persian market relied on imports for most of its needs. In 1921-22, the imports of cotton tissues of all kinds represented 25% of total imports[645]. During that same period, there was still some export of both cotton (0.9%) and silk fabrics (0.5%), but carpets with 14% of total exports were a much more important textile product[646]. This situation did not change, despite the fact that in 1922 the Majles tried to stimulate the national spinning and weaving industry, « by passing a law making it compulsory for all employees of the Government and for such Government departments as the army, to wear only cloth made in Persia. As a result a considerable fillip has been given to weaving, though at present

641. Kuss, p. 147.
642. *Ibid.*, p. 147-148.
643. *Ibid.*
644. Hale, p. 58, 136, 217-218; Dillon, p. 293, quoting FO 416/61 No. 172.
645. Temple, p. 4.
646. Temple, p. 9.

the majority of the yarn is of foreign make since it cannot be spun in Persia and it is uncertain whether Persia can produce enough cloth to supply her needs »[647]. According to Millspaugh, the law really had the intended effect, for a number of spinning and weaving machinery was imported[648]. However, neither the diligent implementation of the law (*Qanun-e este'mal-e albeseh-ye vatani* of 29 *Dalv* 1301 / 7 February 1922), nor the subsequent industrialization and import-substitution program of the Reza Shah government could structurally change the dependence on foreign textile imports. In fact, cotton imports were, relatively speaking, even higher than before, representing 30% of total imports in the period of 1923-27. The law making it compulsory for Government employees to wear Persian-made cloth during office hours or when in uniform (i.e. in the army, police and gendarmerie) had a negative effect for « the expense and poor wearing qualities of the local material has militated against any but a patriotic acceptance of the extra burden involved by a large class of very lowly paid minor employees »[649]. Not only the shoddy work and use of inferior materials, but also the continued use of aniline dyes harmed the reputation of the Persian fabrics. The import of aniline dyes had been forbidden in 1909, but it was freely and everywhere available in Persia[650]. The problem was not so much the use of aniline dyes, for « Other countries also make use of aniline dyes for cheap qualities, but there the yarn is dyed properly and the dyes themselves are superior in quality to the Congo red and fuchsine which the Persian weaver is apt to use in such abundance »[651].

---

647. Hadow [1923], p. 9.
648. Millspaugh, p. 264.
649. Hadow [1925], p. 17, 20, 34-35.
650. Kuss, p. 149-150.
651. Lingeman, p. 15. For an analysis of the subsequent industrialization policy under Reza Shah see Floor [*Industrialization*].

4. 17th century Persian dress

III. Nomenclature of Persian Textile Products and Crafts

In what follows an attempt has been made to give as detailed a description as possible of many of the terms referring to mainly Persian fabrics and the crafts[men] making them. Thus far, the most detailed source of information on textiles was Pope and Ackerman's *Survey of Persian Art*, in particular the various notes made on the basis of a Russian customs document[652]. Although containing much useful information Ackerman did neither supply the reference to the original Russian source nor reproduce Klein's translation of this document. Not having access to either document (although I tried, in vain, to trace the Russian source) makes it impossible to determine what the document states and where Ackerman's (sometimes questionable) interpretation begins. For that reason, I have only reproduced elements of the Klein and Ackerman document where there was other independent information available. Where Ackerman's interpretation seemed guess work I have not used her material, and the reader therefore should consult that material him/herself.

• ***'Ababaf*** or weaver of a sleeveless male overcoat made of camel hair. The group of *'ababaf* constituted a guild in Isfahan in the 1870s, which, formerly, was small and of no account, Tahvildar wrote « nowadays it is large and successful. Their products are sold all over Persia »[653]. In 1870, there were about 20 of them in Isfahan, and 50 in Tabriz[654]. In 1920, the group of the *'ababaf,* which included a group of so-called *kishbaf* or cotton cloth weavers, was 120 men large in Isfahan, while there were 20 *'aba* sellers in Isfahan[655]. *'Ababaf* were also to be found elsewhere in Persia such as in Kashan and Sari, while in Shiraz there were *'aba-duz*[656].

However, other towns were even more well-known for their *'aba*s. « Kupa is famous for its manufacture of camel's hair-cloth, said to be the best in Persia. The cloth is made of cotton and camel's hair, the warp being

---

652. Klein and Ackerman, p. 2163-2174.
653. Tahvildar, p. 102.
654. Hoeltzer, p. 21; Shafi' Javadi, p. 226, 228.
655. Janab, p. 79. *Kisehduz* were also found (Afshar [*Yadgarha*], p. 134).
656. Zarrabi, p. 248; Golzari, p. 102; Forsat, p. 502.

cotton, the woof camel's hair, and it is woven very close together, so as, in fact, to be quite impervious to rain. The camel hair, we were informed, is chiefly brought from Shiraz, where the camels are shorn twice a year. The hair is carded in the same way as cotton, and spun into thread with the fingers. An ordinary coat made of this material costs about three and half tumans, but some better descriptions of cloth are made which are very much dearer »[657]. In fact, Majd al-Islam had bought a top quality Kerman *'aba* for 12 tomans in 1904[658]. The cost-price of camel cloth, from Herat, 2 meters wide, was 2 qrans per arshin, in the Tabriz bazaar in 1857[659].

Olmer, in 1908, reports that in Yazd, Kerman, and Na'in « I have seen the weaving of *'aba*s. The fabric is very tight, very warm and waterproof. The warp is of sheep's wool, and the yarns are very tight. There are only two heddles moved by two threadles. The woof is from camel's wool, but the pick (of the weft) is not perpendicular to the warp's yarn. The course of the spool is a very regular half-circle. After each shoot (of the weft), the weaver beats it several times with the beater which is very heavy. The fabric, therefore, is much thicker and acquires a bit the semblance of a fabric that has been exposed to carding. I have never seen this done in Europe »[660].

• ***Abrishamduzi***, see *golduzi*.

• ***Abrishamkar*** are the silk assayers, who formed a guild in Isfahan, and probably also in Kashan, Tabriz (where they were also called *ipekchi*) and elsewhere, in Qajar Persia. In Isfahan, they were « a group of Jews who select pure silk and distribute it to the guilds of the *sha'rbaf*, the *meshkibaf*, the *'alaqehband* [lace makers] and others »[661]. *Abrishamkar* is also a term used to refer to a broad range of various embroidery techniques such as *'alaqehband* and *yaraqbafi*[662].

• ***Abrishambaf*** or silk fabric weavers, who belonged to the group of the silk weavers (*sha'rbaf*), of which there were some 80 looms in Tabriz in

657. Goldsmid, I, p. 166.
658. Kermani [*Tarikh*], I, p. 34.
659. Blau, p. 121-122.
660. Olmer, p. 34.
661. Tahvildar, p. 107; see also Shafi' Javadi, p. 228; Naraqi, p. 238.
662. Golriz, p. 734.

1869[663]. Around 1918, there were 262 *abrishambaf* operational in Kashan with an annual consumption of 11,174 Tabriz mans[664].

• ***Aharzan***, clothes starcher, see *shu[d]mal.*

• ***Ajidehduzi***, a special kind of embroidery, where the crasftsmen or women stitched the fabric with fine parallel lines creating raised or *barjasteh* patterns. It seems to have been a very fashionable type of embroidery in the 19th century. For *lutis* or sharpers were proud to be known that their shirts had *ajideh* embroidery better than anybody else, even going so far as to be able to name the embroideress[665]. In Isfahan, 20 masters of this craft were left in 1920[666]. Gluck mentions that this type of work was still being practised in Mahan on dervish caps in the 1960s[667].

• ***'Alaqehband*** is someone who twists braids (*qeitan*), using silk and cotton yarn. They also used lesser quality material (e.g. waste silk), passing it off as real silk, to make more money[668]. The craft was found in Gilan and Mazandaran in the 17th century[669], as well as in Kerman[670]. Asef mentions the existence of an *'alaqehband-bashi*, who was in charge of the royal workshop making *'alaqehband* under Shah Soltan Hosein[671]. There were 5 *'alaqehband* in 1870 in Isfahan and 35 in 1920[672].

• ***Alecheh*** or ***Alejeh*** was a very popular striped, silk or silk-cotton, fabric, probably *ikat*, i.e. the warp and/or wefts were resist-dyed prior to weaving. *Ala* (Turkish) means motley, variegated, parti-colored. This type of silk, silk-cotton or cotton fabric was an important and major product of the Persian textile industry down to modern times. According to the *A'in-e*

---

663. Tahvildar, p. 102; Shafi' Javadi, p. 227; Zarrabi, p. 273.
664. Naraqi, p. 276.
665. Shafi' Javadi, p. 175.
666. Janab, p. 77.
667. Gluck and Gluck, p. 222. For a picture see Bier, p. 285.
668. Shahri, II, p. 26.
669. Nasrabadi, p. 71, 380.
670. Bastani Parizi [*Ganj*], p. 156; see also Golchin Ma'ani, p. 64.
671. Asef, p. 101.
672. Hoeltzer, p. 21; Janab, p. 79. For a detailed discussion of the *'alaqehbandi* craft and its implements 'Ala'i, p. 51-62.

Akbari it was a warp-striped fabric, i.e. *tahrdar* or corded, and therefore probably repp woven[673].

In early Safavid times mention is made of *alecheh-ye kesari* and *alecheh-ye yazdi*, referring to two well-known textile producing towns[674]. *Alecheh* was also produced in Central Asia, especially in Samarqand, where there was even an *alecheh* bazaar. Here weavers produced a so-called *alecheh-ye kattan-e mesri*, made from Alexandrian [= red] colored cotton mixed with silk[675]. Early in the 16th century, Persian products also experienced competition from Indian products. Around 1540 mention is made of an *alecheh-ye mov kar-e Hend* or an *alecheh* made in India[676]. *Alecheh* was also found in the royal wardrobe such as that of Shah Soltan Hosein[677].

Alecheh is mentioned as a product of Kashan around 1680[678], but throughout the Safavid period native woven *alecheh* had to compete with "allegias" imported from Coromandel.

Alecheh was produced at Khiva, Bokhara, Tabriz (in particular, the Alexandrian type), Qazvin, Ardabil, Resht, Kesmin and Yazd around 1750. Khiva also made a chequered version, and likewise variegated belts of thick cotton of very poor quality. Isfahan allegedly did not produce any *alecheh*[679]. However, in late Safavid and early Qajar times, *alecheh* or stripes were produced in Isfahan. *Alecheh* made in Yazd cost 1,500 dinars in case of first quality *abreh* in Isfahan towards the end of the 18th century[680].

Alecheh, around 1770, is described as a striped fabric, that was either made entirely of cotton or of silk with a cotton cross weave. Its length was 5 arshins and its width 0.75 arshin[681].

---

673. 'Allami, p. 97, 100 n. 1.

674. ['*Alamara-ye Shah Tahmasp*], p. 410.

675. Mukminova [*Ocherki*], p. 51; see also Kh^{w}ondamir, IV, p. 566. « Alexandrian, which ranges closest to violets than the true reds. It was developped from various species of lichens, the so-called Orchilla red (*Rocella tinctoria*), which also yields litmus » (Pope and Ackerman, III, p. 2166).

676. ['*Alamara-ye Shah Tahmasp*], p. 410; for the term *mov* see *infra*.

677. Asef, p. 89.

678. Gaube and Wirth, p. 283.

679. Pope and Ackerman, III, p. 2167.

680. Asef, p. 315-316.

681. Gmelin, III, p. 415. Also mentioned by Asef, p. 89, 359, 382.

Around 1820, Fraser provides the following descriptions : « *Allejahs* are made in pieces of 2 yards 25 inches long, by 25 inches wide, and resemble stout lutestrings, but are fully closer in their texture. The wholesale price of those from Yezd was 7 reals (9s.4d.); those from other quarters about 4.5 reals (6s.) per piece. They were dyed either blue or red. They are used for men and women's shirts, one piece making a shirt »[682]. « Mingled with a little silk, and more elaborately wrought, it [kharboz = *karbas*] forms a stuff called aleejah, of a striped pattern, of which they make long-skirted vests (called *ulquluchs*) »[683]. « The aleedjahs are used for shirts and trowsers[684]. Stripes of Isfahan, another coarse cloth, striped blue, purple or grey, which costs about 2.5 reals (3s.4d.) a piece, and are taken in great quantities by the Russians »[685].

In the 1840-50s, *alecheh* was produced in Mazandaran and Astarabad. It was a striped manufacture of mixed silk and cotton of 9.5 yards by 14-15 inches. it was also made with waste silk or *kej*. The price was respectively 10-20 sahebqerans and 5 sahebqerans per piece. In Astarabad it was of the refuse silk variety, and used by Torkoman women for shirts. Its length was 8 yards by 14 inches. It was sold for 4 sahebqrans per piece[686].

According to Blau, in 1858, *alecheh* was all produced with half silk, mixed with cotton. He further remarked that *alecheh* was like canevas (q.v. *qanavat*), but smoother, striped and chequered. It was 45 inches, but mostly 66 inches wide, and was produced in Yazd and Tabriz. It was woven in various colours such as red, green, yellow, brown, lilac, and blue[687]. The 45 inches variety (Tabriz) was sold at 2 qrans per arshin in 1857, and the 60-66 inches Tabriz variety for 2 qrans and 12 shahis and the Yazd 66 inches variety for 2 qrans and 5 shahis per arshin in that same year[688].

682. Fraser [*Caspian Sea*], p. 361.

683. Fraser [*Winter's Journey*], II, p. 152. *Ulquluch* is a bastardization of the word *arkhaliq* or a tight vest, see *infra*.

684. Fraser [*Narrative*], App. B., p. 22.

685. Fraser [*Caspian Sea*], p. 362. *Alejeh* in Syrian style also was produced during Mohammad Shah's reign (E'tezad al-Saltaneh, p. 209).

686. Amanat, p. 23, 25; see also McKenzie, p. 214.

687. Blau, p. 109.

688. *Ibid.*, p. 121.

In 1862, in Yazd three types of *alecheh* were made, to wit: *alecheh al-katon* 0.75 m width, 2 tomans 90 per meter; *alecheh-ye dal* 0.60 m width, 2 tomans; *alecheh-ye atlas* 0.60 m width, 2 tomans 90[689].

Zarrabi reports around 1870 that *alecheh* was made of silk or cotton (*alecheh-ye abrishami, alecheh-ye rismani*), while he further implies that the main production centers were Kashan, Yazd and Mazandaran (*alecheh-ye kashi, alecheh-ye mazandarani, alecheh-ye yazdi*)[690]. *Alecheh*, when imported was referred to as « fancy stripes »[691]. It was still woven at Sari around 1910[692].

• ***Aqabanu*** is a floral patterned cambric, a pseudo-muslin, which came in three varieties, according to Gmelin around 1770. The first one was embroidered. The second had a floral pattern, which usually was yellow of color. The flowers were dyed with the Indian herb *mungi*. The third one had white flowers, made of cotton. The sizes were not fixed[693]. This fabric also occurs in the official correspondance between the Safavids and Moghuls[694]. *Aqabanu* was still being used around 1870[695].

• ***Atlas*** or ***qotni*** (also referred to in European language texts as *kutna, kutniya, gutna* and *gatni*) is a mixed silken-cotton fabric, often also referred to as satin. According to Gmelin, around 1770, « atlas, is woven in the same manner as gutna. The difference, however, is that atlas is unstriped. Its length is 5 arshins and its width 0.75 arshin »[696]. Ackerman also suggests that *qotni* was a satin striped, variegated, reversible cloth[697]. True muslin was not made in Persia or Transoxiania, however, according to the Russians around 1750. A flismy quality of *karbas* served as such. Another pseudo-muslin was *aqabanu*[698].

---

689. MAE, Rochechouart to Gobineau, Yazd, 26/10/1862; see figures 3, 4, 5 in that letter.

690. Zarrabi, p. 248-250.

691. Rabino [Kermanshah],p. 67.

692. DCR 4812, p. 19.

693. Gmelin, III, p. 423; Pope and Ackerman, III, p. 2165. *Mungi*, properly *manjith*, or so-called Bengal madder.

694. Riazul Islam, [*Calender*], II, p. 364.

695. Zarrabi, p. 249.

696. Gmelin, III, p. 415.

697. Pope and Ackerman, III, p. 1070.

698. *Ibid.*, p. 2165.

Early Safavid texts suggest that *atlas* indeed was a single color fabric (red), which also was found in brocaded (*atlas-e zarbaft*) varieties[699]. It also was manufactured patterned with gold and silver flowers[700]. Yazd is mentioned as a city making high quality *atlas* in the 16th century[701], but so is Tabriz, where there « is a kind of silke Sattin, called Atlas, of nine or ten Gasse long every piece, and it is sold for three merchel and a halfe the piece, and the best for foure Croysh »[702].

Safavid 16th century sources also mention *qotni*, *qotni-ye botehdar* (with *boteh* design), *qotni-ye sadeh* (unfigured), and *qotni-ye lappehdar* (wavy, may be shot?)[703].

Atlas was also imported, for fabrics such as *atlas-e khata'i* and *atlas-e frangi* are mentioned[704]. These and other high quality *atlas* and *qotni* were used by royalty and their courtiers. Both *atlas* and *qotni* were fabrics that were included in Shah Soltan Hosein's wardrobe, for example[705]. Satins were made in large quantities in Yazd and Kashan around 1618, and priced according to quality. « The ordinary kind 40-70 shahis per piece. Some of them are almost as good as Lucca satins, but trash compared with Florence or Genoese satin. Its width is 5,5-6 covids »[706]. In the late 17th century, Kashan is also mentioned as producing *qotni*[707].

In addition to simple satins, Persian weavers also made very expensive gold and silver brocaded ones. This is clear from a list of presents offered to the Ottoman grand vazir in 1721, which included « *atlas-e zarbaft-e noqrehbaft* [silver and gold brocaded atlas] and *atlas-e alwanan-e sadeh* [single-colored]. Also, a coverlet for the imperial throne made from *zarbaft-e badeleh* in the Turkish design, with a lining of azure *atlas* with false hems of silver *boteh* [fir-cones] patterned *atlas* and golden *golabtun* fringes »[708].

Qotni, around 1750, was made especially in Kashan, Tabriz and Resht. An inferior quality made at Hamadan, flimsy, and of thick thread, was

699. [*'Alamara-ye Shah Tahmasp*], p. 410, 398; Riazul Islam, [*Calender*], I, p. 75.

700. VOC 2254, fol. 874.

701. [*'Alamara-ye Shah Tahmasp*], p. 394, 416.

702. Purchas, VIII, p. 468 (1581).

703. [*'Alamara-ye Shah Tahmasp*], p. 410; for *qotni* see also Monshi, p. 775. *Atlas-e mesri* and *khata'i* (Khʷondamir, IV, p. 565-566).

704. *Ibid.*, IV, p. 408; [*'Alamara-ye Shah Tahmasp*], p. 394, 416.

705. Asef, p. 89.

706. Ferrier [An English View], p. 201.

707. Gaube and Wirth, p. 282.

708. Nasiri, p. 100, 164.

known as Turkish satin. That imported from India was superior in quality to that made in Tabriz, but it had cotton intermixed. Plain *qotni* came in various colours and there was likewise a multicolor unfigured "shot" satin, evidently an all-over *ikat* type. This was made in Kashan (Persians traditionally attributed all the fine *ikat* to Kashan). A poor quality was made in Gilan, a poorer one in Shamakhi, and the poorest in Ardabil. These *ikat* satins were made of silk and cotton mixed so that the surface was silken. *Qotni* shawls of a very poor quality were exported from Kashan, and of an even poorer quality from Tabriz. No *qotni* was made in Qazvin, Tehran or Kasmin, and no export of the satin made at Avan (maybe Abiana)[709].

« *Kutna*, is a silken fabric with a cotton cross weave. Its length is 5 arshins and its width 0.5 arshin. *Kutna* from Tabriz is prefered to the Gilan variety. It is made with more silk and less cotton. Its length and width vary »[710].

« *Atlas* is a satin, very firm stuff, used for making their outward coat, the caba. It is produced in Isfahan »[711]. « Satin is also made, but not I think, of so fine a quality; that from China is much preferred », states Fraser in 1826[712]. Around 1850, Blau referred to *atlas* as a silken fabric, although he added that « nowadays all atlas is produced with half silk, mixed with cotton »[713]. *Atlas* was 50 inches wide and manufactured at Kashan and Kerman. Its price was 2 qrans, 10 shahis per arshin in the Tabriz bazaar in July 1857[714].

According to Polak, by the 1860s, the production of *atlas* or "gatni" was limited to Kashan only, it was never made of pure silk, but always mixed with some cotton[715]. This, however, is not true, for de Rochechouart mentions the production of satin in Yazd in 1862, woven in pieces of 0,60 m wide, and sold at 4 tomans per meter as well as a fabric, referred to as "glacé" or shot, sold in pieces of 1 m width at 9 tomans per meter[716].

---

709. Pope and Ackerman, III, p. 2170-2171.
710. Gmelin, III, p. 415.
711. Morier [*A Second Journey*], p. 155.
712. Fraser [*Caspian Sea*], p. 362.
713. Blau, p. 109.
714. *Ibid.*, p. 121.
715. Polak [*Persien*], II, p. 172.
716. MAE, Rochechouart to Gobineau, Yezd, 26/10/1862; see figures 8 and 10 in this letter.

Zarrabi refers to two kinds of *atlas*, i.e. simple *atlas* and *nazem al-molki atlas* which were used for making clothes[717].

• ***Aurangshahi***, a silk or half-silk scrape[718]. This fabric is also mentioned in Persian texts as *avrangshahi*, inter alia, as part of Shah Soltan Hosein's wardrobe[719]. It is also mentioned as one of the presents offered to the Ottoman Soltan Mahmud Khan I by the Moghul emperor Mohammad Shah and thus, probably, it is not of Persian, but of Indian origin[720]. However, according to Russian records, the crapy fabric called "avranschaj" also came brocaded. This was made in Gilan, Khiva, Bokhara and India. The Indian type, which was striped, was also called "aurangschtschagi" and "abrashaj", the latter suggesting *ikat*. It was made of either silk or silk mixed with cotton and glass fibre[721].

• ***Baba Ahmad***, was a white cotton cloth made in two qualities with even yarn in Tabriz and Tehran around 1750. The better quality was 35 inches (88.8 cm) wide and 31 yards 4 inches (28.44 m) long. The inferior kind only 28 inches (71.1 cm) wide and 18 2/3 to 20 yards 5 inches (17-18.4 m) long. Because of its unusual length Ackerman has suggested that it may have been the Persian equivalent of the Indian longcloth[722].

• ***Badileh*** was a gold-wire enriched fabric, but less rich than *diba* (q.v.). Its measurements were not fixed. It was made in Kashan, around 1770[723]. It was also manufactured in Isfahan[724] and in other places.

• ***Baftehbaf***, weaver of better quality cotton fabric or of ribbons. Blau reports that *bafteh*, as sold in the bazaar of Tabriz in 1857, had a width varying from 0.25, 0.5 to 1 inch wide. It was sold, per arshin, at 6-10 shahis[725].

---

717. Zarrabi, p. 227-228, 249, 381; *atlas-e nezam al-molki*, (Zarrabi, p. 250) as well as to *qotni*, (*ibid.*, p. 227-8, 249, 381).
718. Pope and Ackerman, III, p. 2170.
719. Asef, p. 89.
720. Riazul Islam [*Calender*], I, p. 75.
721. Pope and Ackerman, III, p. 2172.
722. *Ibid.*, p. 1263.
723. Gmelin, III, p. 420.
724. Mervi, p. 1148 and p. 90, 119, 370, 448, 624, 799.
725. Blau, p. 122, July 1857, Tabriz; see also Hoeltzer, p. 21-22.

• ***Bakhyehduz***, stitchers, see under *golchehduz*.

• ***Barak*** is a soft flanel-like fabric woven from fine camel hair. Supple, warm and lasting it took the place of broad cloth for the Persian. « The best kind comes from Afghanistan, from the Hazara tribe, but in Khorasan they also manufacture a good quality »[726].

Only one decade later, Stolze and Andreas, however, maintain that « The fabrics woven from camel hair or barak are mostly woven in Khorasan (Bojnurd, Bijistan, Tun) and are also used as broadcloth »[727]. This seems to be borne out by other observations. Bojnurd produced amongst other things « striped silks as are made elsewhere in northern Khorasan, also woolen and silk socks, gloves and purses »[728]. « Bushruyeh produced barak, a soft warm material made from the hair of goats »[729].

Barak had the same advantages as *patu* (q.v.), but it was lighter and its colors were more varied, according to de Rochechouart. « Its width is 40 cm and its length 9 meters, which piece sold for 6-36 francs or 5 qrans-3 tomans in 1862. *Barak* is also used for making winter clothing and used by all Persians »[730]. In 1900, it was described as a woolen fabric of 6 dhar‘ [9 arshins] length and 3/4 dhar‘ [1 arshin] width, costing 1-2 tomans[731].

By the beginning of the 20th century *barak* was the main fabric made with wool in Persia, according Olmer. He judged the looms on which *barak* was woven to be primitive and the fabric to be similar to the merino type woven with a cross weave ("armuré croisé") or a Batavia weave[732].

• ***Bas*** or *baz*, a coarse cotton fabric. See under *karbas* and *kaskarnas*.

• ***Basmehchigar*** or block-printer[733], see *chit*.

726. Polak [*Persien*], II, p. 171.
727. Stolze and Andreas, p. 25.
728. *Historical Gazetteer*, II, p. 95.
729. *Ibid.*, p. 98.
730. MAE, Rochechourt to Gobineau, 5/11/1862; see figures 12-15 in this letter.
731. Rittikh, I, p. 157.
732. Olmer, p. 34.
733. Bastani Parizi [*Ganj*], p. 148; Golchin Ma'ani, p. 64.

• ***Begras*** or high quality, especially Dutch, broadcloth[734].

• ***Burmet*** is a glazed red cotton, which in Turkish means corded, suggesting that the dye had first become familiar in a repp. *Burmet* was exported from Darband, Baku, Tiflis, Karagan, Ardabil, Tabriz, Mazandaran, Gilan, Qom, Qazvin, Tehran, Isfahan, Kashan, Shushtar, Kerman and Khiva around 1750[735]. Around 1770, the best *burmet*, *kurschaki* and *kottun* were made in Isfahan, according to Gmelin[736].

Quilted woolen and cotton *burmet*, and normal cotton *burmet* are mentioned as Persian imports into Russia in 1812[737]. *Burmet* was still produced in Talesh and Gilan around 1860 together with *shalvar*, *sardari* and *chukheh*[738], where the fabric was described as « a dyed karbas. Its dimensions were those of karbas, viz. 7 yards by 30 inches »[739].

• ***Chador*** **(1)** or *Kheimeh* a tent or pavillion. Despite the splendor of their palaces, even the most settled of Persian kings was constantly on the move, and so never lost touch with the tent life of his ancestors. Over the centuries royal tents were developed in size and artistic merit to the point where some were truely outstanding. Great skill went into the making of these canvass houses, some of which were so large as to include several distinct apartments. When travelling, or on an outing for pleasure or hunting, the Shahs were wont to have tents for themselves and their court[740]. These royal tents were often of one particular color such as green, white or red[741], while its material could be variously *atlas*, *makhmal* or some other fabric[742].

---

734. VOC 2477 (1739) fol. 692; Asef, p. 89, 356; Mervi, p. 377, 448, 469, 522, 785.

735. Pope and Ackerman, III, p. 2166.

736. Gmelin, III, p. 420.

737. Chenciner and Mogomedkhanov, p. 128.

738. Bastani Parizi [*Farmanfarma*], p. 214.

739. McKenzie, p. 215.

740. [*'Alamara-ye Shah Tahmasp*], p. 397, 399, 403, 417, 419, 420, 423; see also Qomi (II, p. 630), who mentions *kheimehha* and *khargahha*. Kh^{w}ondamir (IV, p. 219) makes mention of « *kheimeh, khargah, sarapardeh* [screens] and *bargah* ».

741. [*'Alamara-ye Shah Tahmasp*], p. 394, 417, a *chador-e sabz*; on p. 394 and 416 a *chador-e sefid*, and on p. 394 and 416, a *chador-e qermezi*.

742. *Ibid.*, p. 398, 420.

Mention is made of a tent of red *atlas* (*chador-e atlas-e qermez*) of which the middle was made of *karbas-e tabasi* and the top of *methqali-ye esfahani*[743].

For Homayun's party Shah Tahmasp ordered the preparation of 50 *chadors*, 20 *sabiyans* (shades) and a *chador-e bozorg-e alaboteh* (flowered of *nimrang-e sorkh*)[744]. Hakim 'Ali Kashani, known as Hakim-e Kuchek, ordered the making of a tent made of felt under which a bathtub had to be erected so as to give a steam bath in which the shah could recuperate[745].

Also mentioned are a *kheimeh-e lashkari* (soldier's tent) and a *gol chadori*, which refers to a bell-shaped form of tent, usually also a soldier's tent[746]. Sometimes, the city's guilds were ordered to pitch tents (*kheimeh, sayeban* and *khargah*) as part of a *pay-andazi*[747].

Royal tents could be very costly. In the *Takmelat al-akhbar* it is mentioned that an embroidered royal tent (*kheimeh-ye naqshduzi-ye khasseh-ye sharifeh*) was kept in the servants department (*farrashkhaneh*) in Tabriz[748]. Mention is also made of a beautiful tent, made in Turkey, embellished with trees, beautiful faces, and birds done in *maftulbafi*, that allegedly had cost 140,000 tomans to make, which is hard to believe[749]. A tent and screens made of gold brocade and costly silks (*kheimeh va sarpardeh az zarbaft, khata'i* and *deq*) are also mentioned as part of the royal train[750]. A tent made for Shah 'Abbas I, and consequently still known during his successor's reign was known as *chador-e 'Abbasi*. It was made of brocaded velvet and had cost 4,000 tomans to make[751]. Among presents sent by Nader Shah to Soltan Mahmud we note one large (*rashidi*) *zarbaft* tent, on the inside *zarbaft* with a lining of red broad cloth consisting of 24 *khaneh* or sections; each *khaneh* was 2 dhar' and the entire circumference measured 48 dhar'. Finally, a tent carpet of *zarbaft*, and an under-carpet of *londreh* lining, while *qotni* and *qadak* are also mentioned[752].

---

743. Shamlu, I, p. 61. *Kheimeh, sayeban* and *khargah* made of *soqrelat, makhmal* and *atlas* (Qomi, II, p. 1039). For a picture of a circular rich velvet fragment from the ceiling of such a tent, see Bier, p. 195, 198.

744. Shamlu, I, p. 66.

745. *Ibid.*, p. 168.

746. *Ibid.*, p. 218.

747. Qomi, II, p. 982.

748. Shirazi, p. 72.

749. [*'Alamara-ye Shah Esma'il*], p. 297-298; see also *ibid.*, p. 145.

750. [*'Alamara-ye Safavi*], p. 119. *Kheimeh-ye zarkesh* (Qomi, I, p. 268).

751. Esfahani [*Kholasat*], p. 309.

752. Nasiri, p. 100, 164.

Golestaneh speaks about tents made in Isfahan of *dara'i*, *zarnegari* and *atlas*[753]. Francklin says that the tent of Ja'far Khan Zand's minister was lined on the inside with a fine chintz, and walls had a curious open work; his own tent was lined on the inside throughout with a beautiful clouded silk, and had open work much the same as the minister's[754]. The same situation existed under the Qajars. « Those of the Shah and his courtiers are lined with embroidered cashmere. It is common to use for linings a cloth stamped with picturesque designs representing hunting-scenes decoratively treated. Such tents are called "kalemkar". The external colour is generally dark blue, crimson reserved for the Shah alone »[755].

Isfahan was the most important production center for tents in Persia. The shah, the governors and tribal leaders all bought them there. Here they were made in various degrees of luxury, type, and size. The fabric and cords were of cotton, the pegs of wood, often from cast iron. The simple tent for soldiers was bell shaped, the better varieties were square; while the best ones were octagonal in shape, with double walls and top, and with nice and easy add-on compartments with separate entrances[756]. There were, however, only five *chadorduz* in Isfahan, while there were 150 of them in Tabriz[757]. In Isfahan, the group of *chadorduz* (makers of tents) formed a guild. « They make sash window curtains for Isfahan buildings, coverings for passion play theatres, tents for soldiers, screens for the royal court, and the like. This group has not been reduced in number compared with before and their number is of average proportion »[758]. In 1920, there were still 20 *khayyam* or tent makers in Isfahan[759].

---

753. Golestaneh, p. 196.

754. Francklin, p. 193, 196.

755. Benjamin, p. 195, see also p. 269. For a detailed description see Dhabiyan, p. 180. « Chador, a tent surrounded with red ser perdehs, or screens, as is the custom with all of the royal family » (Fraser [*Winter's Journey*], II, p. 181). On the comfort of a tent, see Morier [*A Journey*], p. 106. Freygang, p. 282, 284. For a photograph, see Anet, p. 108. The production of *chador-parcheh* and *parcheh-ye sarbazi* under Mohammad Shah was claimed to be of better quality than the European products (E'tezad al-Saltaneh, p. 209).

756. Hoeltzer, p. 60.

757. *Ibid.*, p. 22; Shafi' Javadi, p. 279.

758. Tahvildar, p. 100. For a discussion and pictures of royal tents and separate embroidered interior panels, see Toby Falk, "The Shah's Tents", in *Hali*, 59 (1991), p. 118-123.

759. Janab, p. 78.

• ***Chador*** (2) the outdoor apparel for women which covers the entire body. These, in general, were « thick white cotton chuddars [*chador*] 32-45 inches wide [0.81-1.14 m] and 3 yards 33 inches long (3.55 m) » were exported from Tehran, while Isfahan and Kashan made a thinner grade around 1750. White cotton *kadifeh* (*qatifeh*) 45 inches wide (1.14 m) and 2 1/3 yards long (2.13 m), some plain, some lace-edged, were imported into Russia from India, Kashan, Shushtar and Bandar Abbas, the Indian fabric obtaining twice as much as the Persian one. A *kadifeh* is described as a « bath-house curtain », for which purpose it is used indeed. A *qatifeh*, in that case, could be made from brocade to cotton, and was used as a kind of large bath mat[760].

• ***Chadorshab*** is a « plaid of cotton woven in Mazandaran, 2,5 yards square, which sells at 2 to 3 sahebqrans per piece. If woven of silk it sells at 25 to 30 sahebqrans per piece »[761]. *Chadorshab* was exported in great quantities to Russia[762]. It was a square shaped cotton fabric, according to McKenzie[763]. In Isfahan, the *chadorshabbaf* « wove silk head veils and the like for women. They are a type of *sha'rbaf* »[764].

• ***Chahar-gaz*** also *chahar-dhar'i* was a sash of four ells long as the term indicates. These were often made of very rich fabrics, but *chahar-dhar'i-ye sadeh* or a single-colored variety was also found[765]. The term "tsjaargessier" (*chahar-gaz*) is used by the Dutch, who translated it as meaning "middelbanden" or waist bands[766].

• ***Chalvar*** was a tightly woven cotton fabric, of a quality that was superior to *karbas* (q.v.). *Chalvar-e mina'i* or dark-blue dyed cotton, was used by those of the religious class who were a seyyed as material for their turban[767].

---

760. Pope and Ackerman, III, p. 2165.
761. Amanat, p. 24.
762. Stolze and Andreas, p. 25.
763. McKenzie, p. 215.
764. Tahvildar, p. 102. See also Zarrabi, p. 239.
765. [*'Alamara-ye Shah Tahmasp*], p. 410; Monshi, I, p. 260 and II, p. 775, 783.
766. VOC 2448, fol. 1343.
767. Zarrabi, p. 248.

• ***Charkhtab*** or twiners, who constituted a guild in Isfahan, « transfer untwisted silks from the skein [*guridag*] and wind them on the twining-wheel »[768]. In Kashan, there was a special group known as *charkhtab-e abrisham*[769].

Cotton yarn was supplied, amongst others, by Tabriz and its surrounding areas, mostly undyed. According to Blau, spools were completely deficient. « This deficiency, of course, has its impact on the local final product. In Tabriz, and elsewhere, they also make cotton ribbons, trimmings, and braids, as well as sock fabrics from Isfahan, Kashan and Tabriz »[770]. A great deal of cotton twist was spun, resulting in exports of 1500 mule loads to Astrakhan alone in 1848[771]. Cotton yarn from Kashan was used in the Caspian provinces[772]. Cotton twist were also made in Borujerd[773].

Other silken products were *khayyateh* or embroidery, and sewing silk yarn, produced in Resht and Tabriz. Braids (*qeitan*), ribbons (*bafteh*), fringes (*risheh*), made in Tabriz and Yazd, all of which were of inferior quality[774]. Sewing silk cost 25 qrans; cotton yarn made in Tabriz, 7 qrans per 640 methqals or 8 qrans if these had been indigo or madder (red) dyed; cords and braids of one inch width, cost 2 shahis per arshin, while those that were one-quarter of an inch width cost 1 shahi, in July 1857 in the Tabriz bazaar[775].

"Alangbandee" silk is Gilan silk manufactured into sewing-silk, which is used for trimmings, laces, fringes, cords and similar stuffs. When ready for use and dyed of different colors it costs at Resht 16-18 qrans per pound[776].

• ***Chit*** is a cotton fabric on which designs have been printed through the use of a wooden stamp. It would seem that Persians did not make a distinction between *chit* and *qalamkar* although, both linguistically and

768. Tahvildar, p. 121.
769. Zarrabi, p. 239.
770. Blau, p. 110-111.
771. Amanat, p. 75.
772. *Ibid.*, p. 40.
773. *Historical Gazetteer*, I, p. 112.
774. Blau, p. 110.
775. *Ibid.*, p. 121. A *kelaf* or skein of twist (yarn) was sold per load (DCR, Misc. Series, n° 590, p. 67).
776. Benjamin, p. 420.

practically, the two imply two different processes. *Chit* refers to the block-printing of a piece of cloth, while *qalamkar* (pen-drawing) implies the use of a different technique, in particular that of *batik*. However in early Safavid times we find already references to the term *chit-e qalamkar*[777]. *Qalamkar*, therefore, is a cotton fabric on which designs were either painted, or block-printed. Textual evidence, indicates that there was nevertheless a difference between *chits* and *qalamkars*, the one a block-print, the other a painted print. In fact, the *chitgar* was also referred to in early Safavid times as *basmehchi* or *bashmehgar* or literally block-printer.

Chit and *qalamkar* manufacturing was the heir of pre-Safavid technology, which is the reason why we find these products also being made in former Timurid areas such as in Bokhara and Samarqand. Craftsmen in these cities produced, for example, a *parcheh-ye chit-e porband-e haft rang*, which was 12 gaz long and one gaz wide. A *chit* of a similar size had a *parcheh-ye malun-e porband*, although its width was 6.5 cm shorter. Other types of *chits* mentioned were *chit-e bikchi* (1 gaz by 14 gaz) and *chit-e shahri* (3 x 15 gaz). They were sold per *'adad* or piece, though the term *tup* is also found. *Chits* were printed on *karbas* (q.v.) and produced by *chitgars* in a *chitgar-khaneh*. Indian *chits* were called *chit-e hendi*[778].

Mukminova's remark on *chit-e hendi* shows that there was a serious and long-established trade between India and Persia, in amongst other things, *chits*. Thévenot, for example, observes that Persians use bed-covers decorated with flowers and other paints stamped upon them with a mould[779], clearly refering here to blockprints. But an observation by Chardin makes it clear that both block-printing and painting of fabrics was practised.

Chardin states « they make also Calico Cloth very reasonable; but they make none fine, because they have it cheaper out of the Indies than they can make it [...] They understand also the painting of Linnen, but not so well as the Indians, because they buy in the Indies finest painted Linnen so cheap, that they would get nothing by improving themselves in that Manufacture »[780].

---

777. [*'Alamara-ye Shah Tahmasp*], p. 410, 412. On *chit* and *qalamkar* see Irwin and Brett.

778. Mukminova [*Ocherki*], p. 62-67.

779. Thévenot, II, p. 94.

780. Chardin, IV, p. 156.

But Persians did not simply import Indian *chits*, they also directed and managed both their production and sale. In 1673, Fryer reports that in Masulipatam « the Persians have planted themselves here through the intercourse of traffick [...] As for their dealings in the world, they are well skill'd [...] having accomplishment in the Art of Staining Calicuts here beyond any other place in the East Indies (for that they are upon washing rather clearer and livelier at first, and this is it that makes this port so frequented) »[781].

From a Russian document, reflecting the situation around 1750, it is clear that *chit* and *qalamkar* manufacturing was almost universal in Persia. « Printed cottons made of thick thread were exported from Tehran around 1750. These were 14 inches (35.4 cm) wide and about 5.5 yards (c. 5 m) to a piece, while a second quality, of inferior yarn, was narrower but twice as long. Similar qualities, varying in width came from Qom, Kashan, Hamadan, Ardabil, Qazvin, Tabriz, Shushtar, Mazandaran, Samiran, Khiva and Bokhara. None were produced at Shiraz, Masjad, Gilan, Lahejan, Shamakhi or Baku. Printed *baft* was exported from Kashan, Isfahan and Tehran. Printed cotton handkerchiefs, 4 to a *batcha*, came from Isfahan, Kashan, Gilan and Khiva »[782].

Printed calico curtains were made in Isfahan, Kashan, Tabriz, Tehran and Shushtar. Those from Isfahan were from 5 feet 10 inches to 7 feet (1.78-2.13 m) wide, made of three widths of cotton sewed together, and from 7 to 8 feet 2 inches (2.13-2.49 m) long. Mazandaran produced a poor quality of cotton print, thick and flimsily woven. Samiran made thin, very large table cloths from 3 yards 4 inches to 3 yards 32 inches (2.84-3.55 m) wide and from 3 yards 32 inches to 7 yards 28 inches (3.55-7.11 m) long. Bokhara and Khiva made the poorest quality. None were made in Yazd, Qazvin or Gilan. Bandar 'Abbas cotton *kadifeh* sometimes had flowered hems[783].

Gmelin confirms the production of *chit* in the 1770s. « Schitt (*chit*) or Kattun is made from *karbas*. Its quality determines the length and width of a piece »[784]. He also observes that many Indian *qalamkars* were sold in Persia and beyond.

781. Fryer, I, p. 86.
782. Pope and Ackerman, III, p. 2167.
783. Pope and Ackerman, III, p. 2167-2168.
784. Gmelin, III, p. 418.

Sadras qalamkar is a « *ziz* [*chit*] in which the flowers have been painted ». Its length was 5.5-6 arshins, while its width varied. *Sadrasnama qalamkar* was a printed *chit.* Its length is 5.5 arshins, its width varies. *Jenischla Kandar qalamkar* was a printed *chit*, but coarser than the previous one. Its length was 5.5 arshins. *Wetendis* (probably *walandis*) *qalamkar* was an even coarser printed textile. Its length was 5.5 arshins. Bedspreads made of all these *chits* were exported to Russia[785].

Sadras does not mean, as Gluck[786] has it, 100 colors, but the term is derived from the name of the town of Sadras (Tamil: Shathurangappatanam or City of the four arms) 40 miles south of Madras, a major textile production center.

Early in the 19th century, Fraser also makes a distinction between *chit* and *qalamkar*, although he does not report anything about their production process. « Culumcars are that sort of print, the pattern of which consists of wreathed and consecutive flowers in gay colours, sparsely thrown upon a ground, white, blue, red, fawn colour; they are used for particular purposes, as inner vests, lining of robes, etc. and are often of high price, according to the beauty of the pattern »[787].

Chits or « Chintzes with a pattern of light and gaily-coloured flowers, wandering over a red, fawn, or light blue ground, and of no great finess, were sold, according to the beauty of the pattern from 4 to 6 reals (5s.4d. to 8s.) a yard of 39 inches »[788]. It is claimed that *qalamkar-e sadras* was made better in Iran than in India during Mohammad Shah's reign in Isfahan, but especially in Borujerd. In this town a master weaver, Ostad Naqd 'Ali al-Haqq, excelled in producing this fabric[789].

Indian cotton fabrics were sought out, and were much loved, especially in the eastern provinces, which is why many of their designs were copied on *qalamkar*. Isfahan carved a niche for itself by producing a good fabric, a little bit narrower than the Indian product (18 inches against 19 inches), and

785. Gmelin, III, p. 423-424.
786. Gluck and Gluck, p. 190.
787. Fraser [*Caspian Sea*], p. 362.
788. *Ibid.*, p. 367.
789. E'tezad al-Saltaneh, p. 209.

12.5% lower in price. India was also the source of European red-dyed yarns[790].

« These are the so-called *Indiennes* or *Pars*, which is a fine fabric with patterns of small arabesques embellished with flowers. Also, the many-colored flowery striped *Ahram* cottons. Their production is difficult and time-consuming, because the colours are each separately applied by hand blocks »[791].

Although *chits* and *qalamkars* were produced in a different manner they were nevertheless manufactured by the same craftsmen, to wit: « The group of *chitsaz* (textile printers). This is a very important craft; formerly its members formed a big group and their product was in great demand. Compared to former times it has now considerably declined. From *qalamkar* (calico) they made *qalamzar*, a superior and more expensive form of Sadras calico. Since it is no longer in demand, it is no longer made. This guild has four connecting bazaars. One of its gates is situated at the Qeisariyyeh [market-hall] on the Meidan-e Shah, between the bazaars, five karavansarays and *timcheh* are situated one of which is the Sara-ye Shah. All of them are workshops of the *chitsaz* and they comprise 284 shops, *hojreh* [stores] and *kar-khaneh* [manufacturies]. Their products are still used allover Persia, but the European textiles have ruined their market and not even half of the original number remain »[792].

Qalamkar was used for door and window curtains, table cloths, bed covers, curtains, hangings (with which to cover the house on the occasion of a marriage) and as bier-coverings. « The blocks measure 15 x 20 cm. The main production centers are Isfahan, Yazd and Hamadan, but Isfahan is the most important. Isfahan qalamkars measure 4 m long x 1.20 m wide. The Yazd ones, also called kerbaz, are coarse and were only 0.70 m wide. To compete with Isfahan the two are darned together. Old products are easy to spot, because of their coarse weave. Now only machine-made manchester shirting are used ». Older pieces had their appearance rejuvenated by a process involving gum, so as to improve their saleability. This treatment was especially useful on pieces destined to adorn houses. In the 18th

790. Blau, p. 111. The real *qalamkars*, which were one yard and seven inches wide, cost 2 qrans, 10 shahis per arshin or 10 shahis more than the Esfahani imitations (Blau, p. 121, Tabriz, July 1857).

791. Polak [*Persien*], II, p. 167.

792. Tahvildar, p. 94; see also Wulff, p. 224-227.

century, silk fabrics also got handblocked. Samples, as such, are very rare[793].

Both the Moslem population and the minorities used *qalamkar* to decorate their homes on festive occasions. For example, « The walls [of the Nestorian church] were tapestried from top to bottom with hangings of calico and coarse silk, and scores of old lamps and bells were strung upon cords from one side to the other »[794].

A special kind of *chit* was the *chit-e dola'i-ye fatileh kesh*[795]. A very common *chit* was the *chit-e frangi* or the European *chit*[796]. Of the latter type there were many varieties. *Chit-e astari* or print lining was sold in lengths of 12 yards. Further, there was *chit-e meshki* or black lining; and *chit-e atlas a'la* or glazed prints (first quality), *alvan* (mixed) and *vasat* (inferior quality). Finally, the *zomorrudi* (emerald); *kamruti*; and *muskofi* (Moscow) type were found[797].

« The once flourishing printing and dyeing industry of Isfahan still exists, but is no longer flourishing. Grey goods are indigo dyed, black or blue, or printed with blue and red ground, as blouses, trouserings, etc. for the rural and nomad population, who also use the same material, undyed, as undershirts, drawers, etc. doubtless part of their purchases being dyed in the villagers. The nomads buy mostly in the spring and autumn, the seasons for changing camp. Prints are by handblock. These prints are seldom prepared in the piece for retail by the yard, but are printed as articles such as handkerchiefs, napkins, table cloths, curtains, etc. (the cloth being previously seamed to the desired width), or as material for undercoats, vests and linings. etc, in lengths for one garment. They are more costly than foreign machine-made prints, and are consumed by the middle and upper classes. [...] Indigo dyeing is a special branch of the trade usually carried on apart; the other colours are hand-blocked by the printer »[798].

---

793. D'Allemagne, II, p. 153; see also DCR 1376 (1894), p. 48. For a comprehensive technical, artistic and historical pictorial overview of Persian *qalamkars*, see Ehsani.

794. Marsh [*The Tennesseean*], p. 69.

795. Zarrabi, p. 249.

796. *Ibid.*, p. 248, 250.

797. Rabino [Kermanshah], p. 67.

798. McLean, p. 37; see also Gleadow-Newcomen, p. 77; Kuss, p. 150.

• ***Chukheh*** or *chokeh* or *Hazar Jarib* (see also under *burmet* and chapter V), is a coarse woollen fabric or felt cloak made for and by the peasantry. It was made all over Persia, but under this term, in particular, in the Caspian provinces[799]. « It was much in demand by the people of Mazanderan and Astarabad, who make of it their winter clothing. There are three qualities of this chukha: made of silk refuse and wool, and known as abai; made of wool and European cotton thread; thick coarse, made of wool and native cotton thread »[800].

• ***Dah-yekduzi*** is primarily a filling consisting of one or more gold threads, metal strip silver gilt, gilded, wound around a core of cotton or silk, which are laid and couched with small couching stitches regularly placed to make a pattern. Also made in Qazvin, but the metal thread was not as fine, being made of half copper, half silver, called *balandizi*[801].

The *dah-yekduz* formed a guild in Isfahan. « They, like the *naqdehduzis* [q.v.], sew with silver and gold threads, which contain one-tenth [*dah-yek*] of *golabtun* [goldlace], on silk cloth and the like »[802].

• ***Dandani*** or *gol-e khord* is tie-and-dye technique traditionally associated with the Zoroastrian community in Yazd. It is a simple, if laborious, technique of resist dyeing. The resist is provided by tightly tying up the cloth in little knots. Thus the basic design element resembles a simple flower or sunburst and may range from pinheads to gigantic medallions. Strips of tie-and-dye are traditionally used as inserts for shirts or trousering alternating with bands of embroidery or silk brocades[803].

• ***Dara'i*** is an unfigured or figured fabric woven from simple silk. To make the stripes clear in both the unfigured as well as the striped variety one mixes some brightly colored stripes with the ground yarn. The latter then form the stripes. It measured 5 by 0.75 arshin. "Muchojar" [*mokhayyar*] is the same as *dara'i* with the difference that a double ground yarn is used. If

799. Amanat, p. 40; DCR, 4812, p. 12. It was also made in Sari, Savad Kuh and Yakhkesh. *Ibid.*, p. 16, 19. For further details see chapter V.

800. DCR 4812, p. 17. At Sari, *chukeh* was produced, a woollen tissue, head coverings or *bashluk* (*ibid.*, p. 19).

801. Gluck and Gluck, p. 234.

802. Tahvildar, p. 99.

803. Gluck and Gluck, p. 196; see also Wulff, p. 219.

one uses silk of various colors, as is usually the case, the fabric then becomes shot. It is made in the size that one wants[804].

Dara'i is mentioned from the beginning of the Safavid period as an important and costly fabric. Centers of *dara'i* production that are mentioned include Mashhad, Khavaf and Yazd[805].

According to Ackerman, *mokhayyar* was a kind of brocade. « This was either silk or half silk and half cotton, and was used for garments. It was 35 inches (89 cm) wide and the piece varied in length from 2 yards 16 inches to 27 yards 16 inches (2.23-25.1 m) »[806].

According to Fraser « Dereis are 3 yards 29 inches long, by 29 inches wide, of similar manufacture to alejas, and of different fineness; those of Yazd sell at 10 reals (13s.4d.) others for 8 reals (10s. 8d.). They are used for abas, the Persian outer vest »[807].« The dereis for the kabbas or gowns worn by men »[808].

In 1862, *dara'i* was sold at Yazd for 4 tomans per meter and was woven in pieces of 0.75 m wide[809]. « At the beginning of this century, a silken fabric much of which is made at Yazd, but less so now, and still made at Kashan, is called dara'i or portières [door curtain]. The weave is serge [worsted?], while dropping a yarn at each shoot [of the weft]. This way one has an inside and an outside with two different effects. The originality is in the manner in which the warp's yarn is dyed. Once the yarns are arranged, part of them are soaked in the dye vats, so that prior to weaving the taut warp has spots of different colors. The contours of these spots are totally haphazard. This way, after the weaving of the design, one gets a flame effect, with vague and nuanced contours, which gives a pleasant effect »[810].

- ***Dastar*** is very loosely woven fabric, like ordinary calico, of a thick yarn and highly glazed. It was called "tastar" or "tager", in a Russian document

804. Gmelin, III, p. 417.
805. [*'Alamara-ye Shah Tahmasp*], p. 397, 419 mentions *dara'i-ye khavafi* and *dara'i-ye mashhadi*; Monshi, p. 99, 775; Khʷondamir, IV, p. 474, 565; Asef, p. 89, 382; *dara'i-ye zarbaft-e yazdi-ye talabaft* and *noqrehbaft* (Nasiri, p. 100, 164).
806. Pope and Ackerman, III, p. 2073.
807. Fraser [*Caspian Sea*], p. 362.
808. Fraser [*Narrative*], Appendix B, p. 22.
809. MAE, Rochechouart to Gobineau, Yezd, 26/10/1862; see figure 9 in this letter.
810. Olmer, p. 40; Rabino and Lafont, p. 171. See also Gluck and Gluck, p. 202.

of around 1750. According to Ackerman it was used for canopies, not for turbans as *dastar* seems to imply[811]. However, the mention of a *dastar-e barik*[812], and of *dastar-e sar zard*, both show that the term and fabric was used as a turban[813].

• ***Dastkesh*** or gloves are a recent introduction, probably dating from the early Qajar period. In July 1857, gloves made in Isfahan cost 10 shahis in the Tabriz bazaar[814]. Rice reports that women in the early 20th century wore white cotton gloves, sometimes embroidered, often with rings on the outside[815].

• ***Dastmal*** refers to Persian simple silken handkerchiefs that were woven either unfigured or striped. They measured 1 by 1 arshin[816]. Cotton handkerchiefs of a poor quality were exported from Tehran and Qazvin around 1750. These were sold uncut in a unit of varying size, ranging from 4 to 15 handkerchiefs. Sometimes this was refered to as *topa* (*tup*) or as *batsha* (or *buqcha*), meaning a good-sized square of any kind of cloth used to carry things, the four corners being gathered up to make an informal bag[817].

Handkerchiefs, black, rather less than 1.5 yard square, coarse, and twilled like Barcelone handkerchiefs, were manufactured everywhere, and served for women's head-dresses; sold at 3,5 reals (4s.8d.); if dyed in crimson, at 4.5 reals (6s.) each[818]. Handkerchiefs of very flimsy texture, about yard square, spotted yellow, red, brown, blue, or green, upon grounds of the same colours to match, sold from 1 to 1.5 real (1s.4d. to 2s.) each. Others of a better texture, spotted or flowered on a black, red, blue, green or brown ground, with borders to match, 1.75 yards square, sold for 4.5 to 5 reals (6s to 6s.8d.). A small sort, very coarse and flimsy,

811. Pope and Ackerman, III, p. 2164.
812. [*'Alamara-ye Shah Tahmasp*], p. 410.
813. Monshi, II, p. 775.
814. Blau, p. 121.
815. Rice, p. 164-165.
816. Gmelin, III, p. 417 (dassmal).
817. Pope and Ackerman, III, p. 2165.
818. Fraser [*Caspian Sea*], p. 362.

checked, red, grey, yellow, green, blue, or white, 0.5 to 0.75 of a yard square, sold as low as half a real[819].

In 1857, silk handkerchiefs cost 24 shahis per piece in Tabriz[820]. By the turn of the century, red (*dastmal-e goli*) and black (*meshki*) handkerchief were imported[821]. In 1913, handkerchiefs are described as having fringed hems, being often unbleached, with a blue streak, or chequered pattern in two colors[822].

Handkerchiefs were not used for the same purpose in Persia as they did in Europe. According to Della Valle in 1617, « to wash one's hands, as sometimes one needs to [while eating], use is made of the handkerchief everyone always carries in his belt, which is either of very fine multi-coloured Indian linen or worked in silk and gold »[823]. Polack, around 1860, comments that « Men also use a dastmal or handkerchief not so much for cleaning their nose, but to hold all kinds of objects handed to them [letter, document, meat, vegetables etc]. Pocket-handkerchiefs are never used, save by the rich or the Teheranis »[824].

• ***Deq*** was a costly fabric, of which the Egyptian and Turkish varieties were most well-known[825].

• ***Diba[j]*** is the richest grade of *sha'rbaf* (q.v) and originally meant a moiré silk, but the term was also used to denote any very rich fabric[826]. Khʷondamir mentions *diba-ye Rum* (made in Turkey), *diba-ye haftrang* (multi-colored) as well as *diba-ye shushtari* (made in Shustar)[827]. Around 1750, *diba* was made in Kashan[828]. Gmelin, around 1770, identifies

819. Fraser [*Caspian Sea*], p. 362.
820. Blau, p. 121.
821. Rabino [Kermanshah],p. 67.
822. Rabino and Lafont, p. 171.
823. Della Valle [Extract], p. 155.
824. Polak, I, p. 144; Wills, p. 322.
825. [*'Alamara-ye Safavi*], p. 119; [*'Alamara-ye Shah Tahmasp*], p. 127 (*deq-e mesri*).
826. Pope and Ackerman, III, p. 2172.
827. Khʷondamir, IV, p. 63, 473, 565; see also [*'Alamara-ye Shah Tahmasp*], p. 250; Esfahani [*Kholasat*], p. 187, 232, 246, 294.
828. Pope and Ackerman, III, p. 2172.

"dirba" as a very rich golden fabric. Its measures were not fixed and it was made in Kashan[829].

• ***Dubahr*** was a term used for white mulls, a kind of Indian chintz which was 20-22 yards in length[830].

• ***Ehramibaf*** were a special group of weavers who formed a guild in Isfahan. « Formerly they wove very fine and long lasting ehrami carpet covers. They had several looms in town. The appearance of European carpet covers made of linen, ruined their market reducing them to two looms, which are continually inactive and idle »[831]. In Kashan, there were also *haramibaf*, who probably were the same as the *ehramibaf*[832].

• ***Embroidery***, see *naqshduz*, *golabtunduz*, *qollabduz*, etc.

• ***Estifa-ye zari*** is gold brocade, while *estifa-ye frangi* is gold brocade of European origin. It is not known in which way *estifa* differed from *zari* (q.v.)[833].

• ***Fastuni*** or light cotton and wool trousering and suitings[834].

• ***Gazur***, washermen or rinsers, formed a guild in Isfahan. « The workers of the washer manufactury have in Isfahan itself one manufactury. With many operators they wash *qadak*. There is another group which are the workers of the *chit* or textile printers manufactory. They bring the calicoed cloth to the river for bleaching it [there] »[835]. « During the summer the large gravel banks were covered with long strips of printed calico placed closely together; at dawn the rinsers came down the bazaars with many donkey-loads of dyed cotton cloths; the beasts used for the carriage were the lame, the halt, and the blind of the asses and mules of Isfahan. Along the

829. Gmelin, III, p. 420. *Diba* is mentioned by Asef, p. 89, 441, 407.
830. DCR 3951 (1906-07), Bushire, p. 12.
831. Tahvildar, p. 102-103; see also Zarrabi, p. 251, *patu* made of *kork* was also used as carpet cover.
832. *Ibid.*, p. 239.
833. *Ibid.*, p. 250.
834. DCR 4179 (1907-08), Bushire, p. 11.
835. Tahvildar, p. 117; see also Zarrabi, p. 238.

edges of the channels between the gravel banks stood rows of old millstones; im front of each stone was a rinser up to his knees in the river. Taking a piece of dyed cloth half wrung out, which had been thoroughly soaked in water, in his hands — and the pieces were at times twenty yards long he proceeded to thwack the rol of cloth against the stone with his whole strength, keeping time to a loud song until he was out of breath. As these men worked in rows, and the coths were full of water, the noise and splashing were something tremendous. The work was heavy in the extreme, and as they can only get to the river when low, some seven months in the year, the pay is good. [...] As each piece had the water thus throroughly beaten out of it, a boy on the bank seized it and proceeded to spread it on the gravel, fixing the edges and corners with a stone; his duty was never to let the wrung cloth get dry, which he managed to do by constantly dashing water over the outspread rows of dyed cloths with a pan. Often the process had to be repeated several times, as the cloths are sent down from the printers at various stages »[836].

« Each rinser has his watchdog to guards the cottons on the bank, and between the banging, splashing, and singing, the barking of the dogs and the shouts of the boys, it is a noisy and cheery scene »[837].

« Of course the calico, cotton-cloth, or T-cloth, as it is variously termed, had to be strong and good to stand such a process; and the adulterator had little chance with the wily calico-printer, who had always weighed his cloth prior to purchasing, washed and dried it, and then weighed it again; the consequence is that, save of the best quality, little cotton-cloth is sold at Isfahan. certain brands known for their genuineness command a high figure, such as that of the Ace of Spades, though they are soon closely imitated by ubscrupulous makers. However, the calico-printer is generally quite a match for the adulterator [...] Many of the rinsers make litle hovels of brushwood and earth, and live altogether on the banks of gravel, and in February, when the waters suddenly rise, the scene is exciting as they collect their traps at the last moment, and a few seconds after, their huts are swept away »[838].

« During the day there is a constant traffic of pack animals with fabrics coming and going to the river. During the summer, standing on the Chaharbagh bridge, one sees an endless field of fabrics and people washing

836. Wills, p. 193-194.
837. Bird, I, p. 259.
838. Wills, p. 194; see also Bird, I, p. 258-259.

and wringing and bleaching. The washermen have a flat stone, often an old mills stone with a hole in the middle, with which they strike the fabrics hard until they are dry. The noise is audible throughout the day, winter and summer. Only in spring when the river floods have the workers to flee. During the night guards with dogs patrol the area, for whom mud huts have been built. The washermen are standing with uncovered feet till their hips in the ice cold water »[839].

• ***Golabtun*** was a gold-silver wrapped thread used for a special kind of costly embroidery and *zaribafi*[840]. First a certain quantity of silver would be heated, then poured into a crucible and made into ingots of 20 sq. cm. These ingots were given to an *ahangar* or blacksmith who would turn them into round wire of 35 cm. These would then be filed (*souhan*) and thus made thinner. A thin sheet of gold (*varaqeh*) then would be twisted around the silver wire and secured with a cotton thread. The silver wire would be rolled on a flat surface and thus be burnished (*mohreh-keshi*). The gold and silver would be merged through another phase of filing. Then the wire would be held in fire to burn off the cotton thread, after which it would be burnished using an agate stone. If the gold would not stick to the silver wire the latter would be heated and once again be burnished. After this phase the gold-silver wire was given to the blacksmith to make it into a wire of 2 to 2.5 m long with a diameter of about 11 mm. This wire would then acquire a 1 mm diameter through the use of a *charkh-e jabr-al thaqir* or a wire-drawing wheel and a *hadideh* or a wire die, which is a metal sheet with small holes through which the wire is drawn. After this the wire was twisted through a *tuqeh* or a copper mould, which is a band around a pinion wheel. This process, which is called *hadideh-keshi* or wire-drawing, required that the wire be heated again to allow the thread to pass through the small holes. When properly heated the wire was drawn through a *chahar-pa* or a wire drawing device, so that it would become 8 mm wide. This is the last time the wire is drawn and it was then twisted around a copper mould and heated again to become malleable. The wire was then spun, using the *charkhnakh koni* or the wire spinning bench, and acquired a diameter of 2 mm. Now the thread was ready to be twined with silk thread to which end the *charkhnakh*

839. Hoeltzer, p. 43-44; see also various pictures.

840. Zarrabi, p. 239, 250; also [*'Alamara-ye Shah Tahmasp*], p. 409, 411, 421.

tabi or the twinning wheel was used. The result of this was the golabtun thread which could be used for *zaribafi* and *golabtunduzi*[841].

• ***Golabtunduzi*** was practised by the upper and middle class, and even by the lower class, in the past. They made various products such as *taqpardeh* and *taqpush* for their trousseau. The *taqpardeh* was made of *turi* [lace, tulle] and was hung above the recesses in the groom's room so that these half covered them and one could still see what was in them. There were two kinds of *taqcheh-push*. One that covered the floor of the recess which was made of *shelleh* (q.v.; a red, cheap and simple fabric). The outside of the recess was covered with *golbatunduzi* for 10 cm wide and its entire length was made from red or blue embroidered velvet. It was stitched to the *shelleh* floor piece of the recess. Painters drew on special paper three cm thick figures such as flowers, *boteh*, sparrow, or some other bird which was glued on the velvet. It was on this paper that the *golabtunduzi* was applied. Apart from *taqcheh-push* they also embroidered small boxes on three sides. They also did it on shoes, on cases for prayer stones, on boxes, on small and large table covers, as well as on the Ashureh banners[842].

The group of the *golabtunduz* (goldlace stitchers) formed a guild in Isfahan. « Formerly, goldlace was much in demand and the number of goldlace makers great; now they only number only a few and their products are not much in demand »[843]. The custom of embroidering coats and mantles (*'abas*) had almost disappeared in Northern and Central Persia, for which gold and silver thread and lace was imported from Bavaria. By 1900, it was used by the mostly Arab population in the littoral[844]. By 1913, *golabtunduzi*, or embroidery with gilt or gold-silver thread, had become obsolete[845].

• ***Gol[cheh]duzi*** was a kind of embroidery of which there were various types in Persia such as « the group of *golchehduz* (flower sewers). They were and [still] are a group of men and women, who sewed silk flowers onto small caps and *termeh* night caps »[846]. In Resht, *golduzi* was done on

841. Sharifzadeh [Golabtun], p. 34-35.
842. Golriz, p. 733-734.
843. Tahvildar, p. 97.
844. McLean, p. 42.
845. Rabino and Lafont, p. 172.
846. *Ibid.*

black or colored cloth (*mahut*). Its flowers (*gols*) were mostly multicolored or of one color or gold. The fabrics, in particular quilted carpets, which have been subjected to *golduzi* are called *suzani*[847]. This was an old technique already known in the 16th and 17th century. In early Safavid times mention is made of *namad-e suzani*[848]. In the 1670s, Fryer reports that « they takes their Seats on Susanees, a rich Tapestry of Needle-Work that borders the carpets, behind which are placed huge Velvet Bolsters »[849]. The mats of cotton cloth (*karbas* or muslin) embroidered with flowers and circles and quilted were called *suzani* and came from Kashan. Inferior qualities came from Qazvin and Ardabil. They were not made in Tabriz or Gilan. Isfahan was not mentioned. The only other embroideries mentioned were the embroidered bed-covers from Khiva[850]. In Isfahan, in 1870, there were 112 so-called *suzanduzi*, to wit: 12 men and 100 women[851].

Silk embroideries or *abrishamduzi*, brocades (*zarbafi*, *maftulduzi*, *golabtunduzi* etc.), openworked embroidery on white cotton (*qermeh*), passements, etc., were well made in Persia. Especially good were the embroideries from Resht (table cloths, door curtains, cushion covers)[852]. The silk embroideries, for which Kerman also was famous, and which were already noted by Marco Polo, also used *kork* or goat hair. In fact, Kermani darners (*rafugars*) were induced to emigrate to Kashmir to bolster the quality of its needlework[853]. Abbott states that in the 1840s this art was « performed with great skill and beauty in Kirman, but to a limited extent »[854].The *naqshduz*, or the embroiderers, in Esfahan used silk and *kork* to make their beautiful needlework[855].

There was another kind of *golduzi* known as *khatemi*, which formerly was very widespread, but slowly disappearing. This craft used small pieces of fabric that were of different color and of many forms, and its art consisted in darning these pieces together in such a way that they seemed to

847. Jamalzadeh, p. 79.
848. [*'Alamara-ye Shah Tahmasp*], p. 409.
849. Fryer, III, p. 136.
850. Pope and Ackerman, III, p. 2175.
851. Hoeltzer, p. 21.
852. Greenfield, p. 312.
853. See chapter V.
854. Amanat, p. 83.
855. Tahvildar, p. 99.

be like Kashmir shawls. D'Allemagne mentions the production of *khatemi* without using this term. He further mentions the use of embroideries on silk, or shawl, while the poorest artisans use cotton cloth. He also states that it was used inside the house to adorn the walls during festive days such as marriage. Especially Resht produced good work[856]. The embroidery was varied and original according to contemporary observers. In 1913, it is reported that « the "mosaique" design has become obsolete. It consists of putting small pieces of fabric together to imitate Kashmir shawls. The darnings are covered with artistic embroideries »[857].

Stitchers or *bakhyehduzis* also made use of the colored silken *golduzi* products. One piece of such a fabric measuring 5-6 dhar' would cost 50-60 tomans, and some curtains [*pardeh*] would cost 100-250 tomans, and a saddle cover from 25-125 tomans. In Isfahan there were many types *golduzi* practiced such as *turiduzi* (lace, veil making), *naqdehduzi* and *golabtunduzi*, while there was also silken *golduzi* in Kashan[858].

« Richly embroidered covers with gold and silver are used by high dignitaries as back pillows. Smaller and narrow strips are used as wall hangings for recesses. Others are used to cover fine garments and underwear. Persian ladies showed them off in the baths and when sending presents. Very remarkable were the women's trousers that were worn in the past. They were made of one piece of cloth, which has been embroidered very closely with fine silk in a small diagonal stripe. It required a lot of patience that is not available anymore nowadays. Of the same type are the small Yazdi covers embroidered with red, blue and yellow silk in bigger and broken patterns. One still find old samples, but they are not made anymore »[859].

Some of the prices quoted for embroideries in 1857 were the following. For brocade (*tafruk-sary*) from Kashan, for a piece of 47 inches, per arshin, 6 qrans. For silk embroidery from Resht, per 100 methqals, 20 qrans; while for the same product and quantity, but made in Ordubad, 12 qrans was paid[860].

---

856. D'Allemagne II, p. 155-156, 158-160.
857. Rabino and Lafont, p. 172; see also Brugsch, II, p. 89.
858. Jamalzadeh, p. 80; see also Golchin Ma'ani, p. 64.
859. Hoeltzer, p. 59.
860. Blau, p. 122.

• ***Guniduzi*** where those who stitched canvass bags. There were 30 masters in Tabriz in 1869[861].

• ***Hakisteri*** was a black or white ground print, which in the rural areas and by tribesmen were used for clothing, displacing *dubahr* prints. It also replaced *lamsa* prints for the inner coats of the upper-class Persians[862].

• ***Halab***, a silken fabric manufactured by silk weavers (*sha'rbaf*)[863].

• ***Hascha*** (probably *hashiyeh* or hem) is an entirely silken, striped fabric. It was made in Kashan in 1770[864].

• ***Jahkbaf*** or ribbon weavers formed a guild in Isfahan. « They weave women's lace out of material such as *jahk*, *muzhegan*, *muj*, and *purchuk*. The weaving of *astarabadi* and ribbons is the work of the same people who make bedsheet bands. Some of their products for the town ladies have fallen into disuse now and have become old fashioned. These are now bought by the village women »[865].

• ***Jimbaf*** were a kind of *sha'rbaf* who wove plain and dark silken fabrics[866].

• ***Jorab*** or socks were woven from wool. In Safavid times, people usually wore puttees. Socks were a recent introduction according to Chardin. However, even in a remote town such as Kerman there was a *jurabduz* in the beginning of the 17th century[867]. In liveliness of color and beauty of pattern, Persian socks rivalled the aesthetics of Kashmir shawls. The best were produced in Shiraz and Khoy[868]. The price for Kashmir like woolen socks knitted in Mashhad amounted to 18 qrans per pair. Khoy socks cost 2 qrans per pair, while a similar pair knitted in Tabriz cost only 10 shahis.

---

861. Shafi' Javadi, p. 228; they were also in Kashan, Zarrabi, p. 229.
862. Report on the trade of the consular district of Bushire (1910-11), p. 10.
863. Tahvildar, p. 102.
864. Gmelin, III, p. 421.
865. Tahvildar, p. 102.
866. Sharifzadeh [Sha'rbafi], p. 57-58.
867. Bastani Parizi [*Ganj*], p. 150.
868. Polak [*Persien*], II, p. 171; see also chapters II and V.

Isfahan socks cost 18 shahis per pair, while a similar pair made in Tabriz cost only 10 shahis[869].

• ***Kalehbaf*** were those who wove a fabric from which, amongst other things, tents were made. There were 20 of them in Isfahan in 1920, and 15 of *kalehduz*, i.e. those who turned *kaleh* into consumer goods[870].

• ***Kamkha*** or *kamkhab* is a costly gold brocade. The term has been borrowed from the Chinese (*kin-hwa*)[871]. Although it is regularly mentioned till the end of the Zand period, the term seems to have become obsolete during the Qajar period[872].

• ***Karbas*** (from Sanskrit *karpassi*: cotton) was the Persian word for the most common cotton fabric woven in the Iranian culture area. In Uzbek it was called *baz* or *buz*. A probably better quality of *karbas* was referred to as *karbas-e do-nimbandi*. It was usually sold per *jameh*, i.e. the size of one normal garment, although its size is unknown. It was also sold per dhar', e.g. 4.5 gaz of *karbas* measured as the Samarqand gaz. Central Asian *karbas* was exported to Russia[873]. There were also *karbas-forush* (*karbas* sellers) in Safavid Persia[874].

Karbas (also referred to as *bias*, and *baz*) could be either white or grey (doubtless unbleached) and it varied in quality of yarn, in width and in length of the piece. The bolt ranging from 4 2/3 yards to 15 yards 20 inches (4.26-14.22 m). *Karbas* was made all over the country, but Isfahan made the best quality, for it was sold for 5 rubles per 100 arshins (71.11 m) while the other *bias* was sold only for three. In Russia *karbas* was used by the Moslem population for shirts and linings. It was also referred to as *baft*, the Persian word for "woven". "Baft", "bafteh", "bofta" or "boffeta" was used in the 17th-18th India trade to refer to fine cottons[875].

869. Blau, p. 121. All the prices refer to July 1857.

870. Janab, p. 79; *galehduz*, there were 122 of them in 1870 (Hoeltzer, p. 21).

871. Laufer, p. 539.

872. [*'Alamara-ye Shah Tahmasp*], p. 250, 401, 421 (*frangi*); 397, 401, 419, 421 (*yazdi*); Riazul Islam [*Calender*], I, p. 75; Mervi, p. 377, 448, 544, 477, 480, 761, 771, 785, 918, 1164; Asef, p. 89, 441.

873. Mukminova [*Ocherki*], p. 46-50. Monshi, I, p. 383, 504; [*'Alamara-ye Safavi*], p. 308, 454. *Karbas* made in Tabas (Shamlu, I, p. 61).

874. Bastani Parizi [*Ganj*], p. 150, 160; Bardsiri, p. 389.

875. Pope and Ackerman, III, p. 2163-2164. See also *Hobson-Jobson*, q.v. *bafta*.

According to Gmelin, "baessen" (*baz*, *karbas*) is a cotton fabric. Depending on the quality, the size of *karbas* differed. The best quality measured 10 by 1 arshin, while an inferior piece measured 5 by 0.5 arshin[876]. « Kherboz, a coarse white cloth of a loose fabric, varying in quality. It is used by the poorer classes in many articles of clothing, and as lining for the garments of the better sirts. It is made for home-use in every village, and an immense quantity is taken off by the Russians »[877]. « Karbas, a coarse cotton cloth or calico made in Mazandaran and Astarabad. It is 30 inches wide, and the price is 5 shahis per Persian yard of 41 inches. If 9 inches wide and length 8 yards it sells at 15 shahis to 1 sahibqran per piece »[878]. According to McKenzie, *karbas* made in Mazandaran measured 7 yards by 30 inches[879].

Most of the cotton (*panbeh*) produced in Persia, until recently, according to Polak, was used to make *karbas*, which served as the main fabric for making the clothing of the middle class, but mostly to be used as tent material. Production was mostly concentrated in Qom, Semnan, Abadeh as a manufacturing craft, but households wove as much as they need for their own use. *Karbas* was sold per *tup* of 6-8 meters[880]. Mrs. Bishop observed that the women, when making clothes « sew backwards, i.e. from left to right, and seem to use none but a running stitch. Everywhere they have been delighted with gifts of English needles and thread, steel thimbles, and scissors »[881]. « The group of *karbas-forush* (*karbas* sellers). Compared with old times there is not much difference [in size]. In Isfahan and some other provinces *karbas* is generally used for tents, pavillions (*khargah*), shelters (*chador*), covering (*push*), etc. »[882]. There were 120 *karbasbafs* in Isfahan, and 8 *ostads* with 16 workers in Jolfa[883], and 85 *karbasis* in Tabriz, around 1870, who also were called *qadakchis* implying that they also made *qadak* (q.v.)[884].

876. Gmelin, III, p. 417.
877. Fraser [*Caspian Sea*], p. 362.
878. Amanat, p. 24-25.
879. McKenzie, p. 215.
880. Polak [*Persien*], II, p. 166.
881. Bird, I, p. 112.
882. Tahvildar, p. 115.
883. Hoeltzer, p. 22, 81.
884. Shafi' Javadi, p. 228.

Karbas « is 23 yards long and 18 inches wide and is sold at 8 qrans per piece. The inferior qualities of *qalamkar* are done on it »[885]. « Plain and rough tissues, called Karbaz, are woven in Persia, but in decreasing quantities, from home-made and imported twist »[886]. *Karbas*, from home and imported cotton twist, but the extensive markets formerly found for those fabrics in such disticts such as Burujird, Kurdistan, and Soujbulak have been largely captured by imported Mexicans, and this formerly large trade is now of little account[887]. « The weave is always taffetas, i.e. the loom has but two pedals. The looming is always continuous looming ("remettage suivi"). If the weave is square and the fabric not tightly woven then it is called *karbas*. These fabrics are used as tent material, and in Yazd, as coarse curtains which are called *qalamkars*. In Yazd I have seen them weave a nankin fabric, and at Tehran they used a serge weave. But in the latter case the looms are European imports »[888].

• ***Kasavari*** was a term used to refer to Indian so-called "Mexicans" when these were dyed with indigo. Most of these were mull. This fabric was used mostly by the poorer classes for both winter and summer clothing, especially for shirts. However, dyed shirting was only used in the cold season and during the months of mourning, Moharram and Safar. These fabrics went up country in their white state, where they were too thin for much wear, reason why nainsooks were preferred there. The tribesmen in the South used the *kasavaris* for trousering, but by 1910 it was substituted by dyed nainsooks of 22 yards, known as *pirahanshahi-ye siyah*[889].

• ***Kaskarmas*** was a fabric woven from boiled and twined simple silk. It was entirely unfigured, and it was made in all kinds of colors. It was only used for *karbas*. Its measurements differed, for they were made to order in any size[890].

885. McKenzie, p. 215; Amanat, p. 24.
886. Gleadowe-Newcomen, p. 70.
887. McLean, p. 36.
888. Olmer, p. 33.
889. DCR 3941 (1906-07), Bushire, p. 12; DCR 4179 (1907-08), Bushire, p. 12. Report on the trade of the consular district of Bushire (1910-11), p. 10.
890. Gmelin, III, p. 417.

• ***Kattan*** was a linen fabric used for making garments and matresses. It was used by the aristocracy, and Soltan Hosein Baiqara wore a *jameh-e kattan*. Also, it was used to make *bastar-e kattan*. Egyptian and Turkish *kattan* are mentioned in particular[891].

Kattan or linen was only grown and woven in Mazandaran. It was used for scarfs, shawls, handkerchiefs, shirting, waist bands, and shammed (for pulling over people in warm weather during sleep), made chiefly in Barforush[892]. There were 15 *kattanbafis* in Tabriz in 1869[893].

The term *kattan* also refers to cotton fabrics, may be under the influence of European terminology. For example, the best "kottun" was made in Isfahan, according to Gmelin[894]. Also, "katan roofarshi" or cotton chintz prints are mentioned in a British consular report[895].

• ***Kejin*** was « a common fabric woven in Mazandaran of waste silk (*kej*) alone. It is 5 yards and 25 inches by 10 to 15 inches, and is used for women's shirts, underwear, and handkerchiefs. It was sold at 2 to 3,5 sahibqrans per piece »[896]. From *kej* another fabric was made referred to as "tool". It was seen by Abbott at Mohammarah, but is was unclear where it had been manufactured[897]. According to Rabino, the best *kejin* fabrics were made in the South and Central Persia[898]. *Kejbaf* or waste silk weavers, of which there were seven in Isfahan around 1870, manufactured this fabric[899].

Kejin was probably the same as "ketschbaff" (mentioned in a Russian document), which term probably referred to more than one fabric according to Ackerman. *Kejbaf* or diagonal weave, obviously twill, was close in texture; there were two grades. In general it ranged from 14 to 28 inches (35.5-71.1 cm) in width and there were 3 yards 4 inches to 5 yards 16

---

891. Mukminova [*Ocherki*], p. 57; Khʷondamir, IV, p. 555, mentions *kattan-e Rum*.

892. Amanat, p. 24; McKenzie, p. 215; *Kattan-e mazandarani*, Zarrabi, p. 248-249. DCR 4812 (1911), p. 10; *ibid.*, p. 12, coarse linen or *katan*, and p. 16, in Savad Kuh.

893. Shafi' Javadi, p. 227.

894. Gmelin, III, p. 421.

895. DCR, Misc. Series, n° 590, p. 67.

896. Amanat, p. 24; Rabino and Lafont, p. 172.

897. Amanat, p. 92.

898. Rabino and Lafont, p. 172.

899. Hoeltzer, p. 21.

inches (2.84-4.97) in a piece. It was made in Gilan, Kashan and Shamakhi in the 1750s[900].

• ***Kepehduz***, of which there were 17 in Isfahan in 1920, were those who made the modern hats or "kepis"[901].

• ***Kepenek***, see chapter V.

• ***Kham-khalat*** was a woolen or cotton fabric, exported in great quantities to Russia[902]. However, according to Abbott, *kham-kalat* consisted part of English calicoes dyed in Persia, of dyed Persian calico called *qadak*, and a great variety of printed and dyed cottons of native manufacture[903].

A 1903 customs list mentions a number of related imported fabrics, mostly referred to as Mexicans which were all 48 yards long, and only differed in width. *Kham-sefid-e 'ariz* (wide); *kham-sefid-e kam 'arz* (narrow); *kham-mahuti-ye 'ariz* (wide); *kham-mahuti-ye kam 'arz* (narrow). Further there was *kham-kerbassi*, or so-called shirtings, grey, and *kham-sormei* or dyed mexicans[904].

• ***Khamakduz*** is mentioned as a craft in Kashan around 1870[905]. This craft may be the same as *khamehduzi*, or embroidery with silk or cotton thread on cotton fabrics. « The background is filled with many patterns. These patterns are done either in a flat satin stitch tightly pulled with the "basket weave" or in a braided stitch with a ridge on one side. Small spaces of material are left free in between these different patterns creating an effect of low relief. It is used on articles of clothing, prayer mats, cases for prayer stones, male skull caps. Many of these *khamehduz* pieces are finished of with *siyahduzi*, a black button hole-stitch edging forming spaced triangles, which is a speciality of Zabul »[906].

---

900. Pope and Ackerman, III, p. 2168.
901. Janab, p. 79.
902. Stolze and Andreas, p. 25.
903. AP 29, LXVIII (1867-68), p. 502.
904. Rabino [Kermanshah], p. 67.
905. Zarrabi, p. 273.
906. Gluck and Gluck, p. 260.

• ***Khan*** and *khʷancheh-ye naqqashi*, or floor coverings, were produced in the village of Mahallat (near Kashan) in the 17th century[907].

• ***Khaqan*** (or *chakan*) is described as a close textured silk with flowers. This was made in Kashan around 1750. It was 28 inches (71.1 cm) wide and there were 3 yards 4 inches to 5 yards 16 inches (2.84-4.98 m) in a piece[908]. *Khaghani* is also mentioned in a customs list of 1903[909]. It was still produced in Bidgol (near Kashan) at the turn of this century[910].

• ***Khara*** was a silken fabric which formed part of the fabrics worn by Safavid and Zand courtiers[911]. *Khara* was made in Tabriz, Khorasan, Kashan and Yazd in the 19th century, and woven from silk and cotton, often in equal proportions[912]. It was woven in moiré and façonné form, in which case it was 54-62 inches wide. It was sold for 2-3 qrans per arshin. Red or flowered (*goli*) *khara* was 56 inches wide and sold for 5 qrans per arshin. A better quality *khara*, probably ponceau colored, was 67 inches wide and also sold for 5 qrans per arshin[913]. Moirés (*khara* and *darah*) were quite equal to the European product in every respect, according to Polak in 1865. *Khara* was used for making trousers (*zir-jameh*)[914].

• ***Khata'i*** was made in two varieties. One had a silken ground and was covered with golden flowers. The other was also flowered, but was entirely woven from silk. Its length was 7 to 8 arshins, its width was not fixed. It was made in Kashan in 1770[915]. It was also used (and produced?) in Safavid Persia[916], as well as in Qajar Persia[917].

• ***Khatemi***, see *golduzi*.

---

907. Gaube and Wirth, p. 274-275.
908. Pope and Ackerman, III, p. 2172.
909. Rabino [Kermanshah], p. 67.
910. Naraqi, p. 495.
911. [*'Alamara-ye Shah Tahmasp*], p. 421; Nami, p. 47.
912. Blau, p. 109.
913. *Ibid.*, p. 109, 120-121 (Tabriz, July 1857).
914. Polak [*Persien*], II, p. 172.
915. Gmelin, III, p. 420.
916. Monshi, I, p. 99; [*'Alamara-ye Safavi*], p. 119.
917. Zarrabi, p. 228, 249-250.

• ***Khaz*** was a silken fabric that is recorded being in use during Shah Tahmasp I regime[918]. In Isfahan, in the Qajar period, the *khazduz* formed a guild. « In this city there are no more than two men, formerly there were more »[919].

• ***Kheimeh***, see *chador*.

• ***Kolahduz*** or hat makers formed a guild in Isfahan. « They have a special bazaar next to the Meidan-e Shah-e Naqsh-Jahan. Their work is not much in demand and their guild is ruined »[920]. There were 40 of them in 1870[921], and 60 in 1920. The *kolah-mal*, of which there were 40 in Isfahan in 1920, prepared the fabric out of which the hats were made[922].

• ***Kolechehduz*** or overcoat makers (see chapter V) formed a guild in Isfahan. « They make fur coats. Formerly, their product was much in demand and they were numerous, but now the *kolechehduz* have become few [in number] »[923]. There were 65 of them in 1870[924].

• ***Komash*** (also *qomash*) was an unglazed red cotton, dyed *bias* or *karbas*. Isfahan and Kashan produced three grades, the best of which was thick. Shamakhi and Tehran made inferior grades. It was also produced in Gilan, Qazvin and Hamadan, the latter being thin[925]. According to Gmelin, Tabriz also produced *komash*, which he defined as an "ungekletterter" (unglazed?) *burmet*[926].

• ***Kord***, a silken fabric, and a product of the *sha'rbaf*[927].

• ***Kork*** « (or mohair) is hand spun from the underhair of the goat in natural animal colors. It is spun in bolts of 20 to 30 cm wide and 15 m long.

918. [*'Alamara-ye Shah Tahmasp*], p. 410.
919. Tahvildar, p. 102.
920. *Ibid.*, p. 98.
921. Hoeltzer, p. 21.
922. Janab, p. 79.
923. Tahvildar, p. 98.
924. Hoeltzer, p. 21.
925. Pope and Ackerman, III, p. 2166.
926. Gmelin, III, p. 420.
927. Tahvildar, p. 102.

In Kurdistan it is called *buzu*, In Azerbaijan *shol*, *ariz* in Hutak and *barak* in most other places. Wool is used for the unseen warp, the mohair only in the surface weft »[928].

• ***Kurshaki*** is silk or half silk *karbas*. The best *kurshaki* was made in Isfahan, according to Gmelin[929]. These were silken belts of one color only. In 1913, this was a speciality of Lashteneshah in Gilan. The entire production was exported, because these belts formed an essential part of the Georgian costume[930].

• ***Koshmah*** is a woolen cloth, which represented the major industrial activity of Nishapur around 1910[931].

• ***La'abduz*** were makers of quilted bed covers. There were 45 masters in Isfahan in 1870[932]. They may be the same as the *lehafduz*, of whom there were 12 in the 1920s[933].

• ***Labaf*** or *lavvaf* or is a rope maker or tent material maker. They formed a guild in Isfahan. « They twist sack-makers' thread [*qatimeh*], rope [*tanab*], and weave tent materials [*galeh*], nets [*tur*], bags [*khur*], large sacks [*juval*], saddle bags [*khurjin*] and the like. This group has not declined »[934]. There were 17 of them in 1870[935], and 120 in 1920[936].

• ***Londreh*** was London cloth, which was introduced into Persia in the 1560s. Prior to that date mostly Venetian cloth was used[937]. *Londrehduzi* and *londreh-forushi* (*londreh* sellers) were, for example, to be found in Isfahan karavansarais around the 1680s[938]. English cloth was used for

928. Gluck and Gluck, p. 184; for more details see chapter five.
929. Gmelin, III, p. 420-1; see also *sarbaw*.
930. Rabino and Lafont, p. 172.
931. D'Allemagne, III, p. 122-123 (with pictures).
932. Hoeltzer, p. 21.
933. Janab, p. 79.
934. Tahvildar, p. 104; see also *galehduz*.
935. Hoeltzer, p. 21.
936. Janab, p. 79.
937. Hackluyt, II, p. 42; [*'Alamara-ye Shah Tahmasp*], p. 410.
938. Gaube and Wirth, p. 276.

making trousers, *kurdi* and *chaqshur*[939]. Persians called ordinary Yorkshire dyed cloth "londora" in the 1740s[940]. *Londrehduzi* and *saqerlatduzi* was still an active craft in the second half of the 18th century[941]. In Isfahan, around 1870, there was a guild of « sewers of *londreh* cloth [*londrehduz*]. They sew broadcloth [*mahut*], *barak* and the like. They are few now in Persia »[942]. According to Gluck, *londrehduzi* signified patch work needle work, i.e. « pieces of cloth of various shapes and colors are joined together in a patchwork mosaic, not appliqué like Rashti duzi »[943], for which there is no textual evidence. Gluck may have confused this with *khatemi* (q.v.).

• ***Longbaf*** or the loincloth weavers formed a guild in Isfahan. « They weave the silk clothes used in bathhouses »[944]. There were still three of them in 1920[945]. The *long* was a rectangular chequered cotton cloth (usually red with dark blue) worn as a loin cloth in the *hammam*.

• ***Maftulduzi***, also *maftulbafi*, seems to have been a craft that made fabrics with highly decorative and figurative designs[946].

• ***Mahmudi*** was a silken fabric. From the Shamakhi area came not only raw silk, but also some *mamodee* (*mahmudi*), which is a kind of silken fabric[947]. In the *A'in-e Akbari* it is mentioned as a low priced cotton fabric. Steingass states that it is a kind of muslin[948]. However, another contemporary source leaves no doubt of the silken character of this fabric. Eres, near Shamakhi, « hath yeelded in times past great store of those fine white Silkes, commonly termed by the Merchants Mamodean Silkes,

---

939. Du Mans, p. 187; Richard, II, p. 146.
940. Hanway, II, p. 19-20.
941. Asef, p. 159, 409.
942. Tahvildar, p. 98. There were 46 of them around 1870 (Hoeltzer, p. 21); see also Zarrabi, p. 238.
943. Gluck and Gluck, p. 226.
944. Tahvildar, p. 102.
945. Janab, p. 79.
946. [*'Alamara-ye Shah Esma'il*], p. 297; Asef, p. 159; Zarrabi, p. 256.
947. Membré, p. 151.
948. *Hobson-Jobson*, p. 707; 'Allami, I, p. 100.

whereof at this day, there is not to be found, no, not a very small quantitie, by reason of the monstrous ruines and overthrowes »[949].

• ***Mahramat*** is a multi-colored, striped cotton fabric. There were several varieties such as *mahramat-e soltani*, white and black (*meshki*) fabrics. One type is especially mentioned, because it was touted as being ideal for military trousers. It was a sulphur colored, color-fast *mahramat* fabric (*mahramat-e moharami-ye kabriti-ye alvan-e thabet rang*), produced in Bidgol (near Kashan) at the beginning of the 20th century[950].

• ***Mahut*** or broadcloth. As the Persians did not know how to make this cloth, which was in considerable demand, they always had to import it. Around 1750, white Gloucester cloth, was called "maghoot" (*mahut*)[951]. « A factory established in Azerbaijan 30 years ago (1830 or thereabouts) soon went out of business. All *mahut* is imported, mostly from Austria, though it is sold as *mahut-e valandi*s or Dutch broad cloth. The Persian is more interested in quality than price, because he is accustomed to a lifetime of 6-10 years of his woolens. There are a lot of complaints about its lasting quality. For a cloak 3,25 meters are used. *Mahut* is appreciated as a present, especially blue, chamois and olive-green colored cloth »[952].

Because good cloth was imported Mrs. Bishop « saw scarcely any rough woolen goods or shoddy. The Persian wears superfine, smooth, costly cloth, chiefly black and fawn, stiff in texture, and with a dull shine upon it. The best comes exclusively from Austria, a slightly inferior quality from Germany »[953].

After the 1830's failure Persian investors tried again to make broad cloth at the beginning of this century. « The Persians do not make cloth, except for Tehran where they are trying to do so at present. But they use looms imported from Russia, with Russian weavers. The result is very much a fabric that is called camelot in France »[954].

---

949. Minadoi, p. 64, which was copied by Purchas, "Observations of Master John Cartwright", VIII, p. 500-501.

950. Zarrabi, p. 228, 249, 250, 495.

951. Hanway, II, p. 19-20.

952. Polak [*Persien*], II, p. 171. Gluck and Gluck, p. 218, prefer to identify *mahut* as wool flanel. Zarrabi, p. 248-249, 448.

953. Bird, I, p. 186.

954. Olmer, p. 34.

• ***Makhmal*** or velvets are known to have been produced in Persia since the 14th century, being invented simultaneously in China, Italy and Persia[955]. This tradition was continued and improved upon by weavers during the Safavid period. The most important centers of velvet production were Yazd, Kashan, Isfahan, Khorasan (Mashhad, Herat) and Tabriz. Yazd was famed for its gold velvets or *makhmal-e yazdi*[956], but so were the velvets of Khorasan, for they « are equal in excellence to the Genoese »[957]. The *A'in-e Akbari* mentions that both Herat and Mashhad produced velvets, both with and without golden grounds[958]. Good velvet was also produced in Kashan, both gold enriched and plain velvets[959], while Isfahan is also mentioned[960]. In 1618, the English report that velvets were made in Yazd and Kashan in all prices and colors and sold at prices from 120 to 160 shahis per piece of 6,75 yards long. The ordinary kinds of velvet sold for 8-10 pieces of gold or 160 to 200 shahis. « All silk stuffs are made between 5,6 and 6,5 covids, just the right size for an upper betles. However, they can make them any size we want. Figured velvets with gold and maleeks [*milek*, see *zari* q.v.] of silk and gold is also to be had there, same length and width, same price and quality, but I suppose not vendible in England »[961].

The Tabriz area was also known for its excellent velvets[962]. According to Chardin the most important velvet production centers were Yazd, Kashan and Isfahan[963]. The production of figured velvet or *makhmal-e monaqqesh* is especially mentioned, which means that figurative velvets probably were already woven before 1500[964].

Velvets, which came in various colors, although mostly green, red, and blue[965], formed an integral part of court life[966], and was used to make

955. Gluck and Gluck, p. 206; Pope and Ackerman, III, p. 2061.
956. [*'Alamara-ye Shah Tahmasp*], p. 401.
957. *Barbaro and Contarini*, part 2, p. 225.
958. 'Allami, I, p. 92-93.
959. *Barbaro and Contarini*, part 1, p. 72; Purchas, VIII, p. 510.
960. *Ibid.*, III, p. 86.
961. Ferrier [An English View], p. 200 (betles appear to be some kind of hangings).
962. Schefer, p. 85, n. 1.
963. Chardin, IV, p. 154.
964. [*'Alamara-ye Shah Tahmasp*], p. 400.
965. *Ibid.*, *makhmal-e sabz*, *makhmal-e sorkh*, p. 400; Qomi, II, p. 1042, 1050.
966. [*'Alamara-ye Shah Tahmasp*] mentions *makhmal*, p. 394, 397, 400, 401, 408, 416, 421. Monshi, I, p. 99; II, p. 775.

clothes such as a *balapush* (upper coat) of a robe of honor[967], as well as for normal silken clothes[968]. Velvets were still being used as material for garments such as the the robe of honor in the 1650s. The Dutch ambassador Joan Cuneaus, for example, received in 1653 a *balapush* made of gold-wrought velvet, while the VOC director, Sarcerius, received a golden velvet *balapush*[969]. Velvets were also used to decorate the shops in the bazaar on the occasion of a visit of the king or a governor[970]. Velvets were included among presents given to and by the king. For example, Senan Pasha's gifts to Shah Tahmasp I included velvets, and the shah reprocicated with, amongst other things, 1000 *tup-e makhmal-e frangi*[971].

However, despite the high quality of Persian velvets many were also imported from abroad. The presence at court or the use of foreign velvets by elite members is mentioned in Persian texts. Not only *makhmal-e frangi*, but also *makhmal va deq-e mesri* and *mahkmal-e khata'i* are mentioned[972]. The English merchant Shalbank, therefore, recommended in 1609, for example, the export to Persia of « Velvets died in graine, with purple colours, and fine reds [...] Velvets embroydered with Gold »[973].

Tavernier submits that in the past Europeans admired Persian silken fabrics but that, in his time, the roles were reversed and it was the Persians who were admiring the then new French products[974]. The earlier period is corroborated by prices recorded in the *A'in-e Akbari*. Persian velvets obtained better prices than European ones, a situation that apparently was reversed several decades later when Tavernier made his comments[975].

---

967. [*'Alamara-ye Shah Tahmasp*], p. 419.

968. *Ibid.*, p. 401.

969. Hotz, p. 257-258.

970. Khʷondamir, IV, p. 185.

971. [*'Alamara-ye Shah Tahmasp*], p. 127-128; Monshi, II, p. 783. *Makhmal* as a present to Ottoman grand vizier in 1721 (Nava'i, p. 87).

972. [*'Alamara-ye Shah Tahmasp*], p. 127; Monshi, II, p. 783; Khʷondamir, IV, p. 185, 219.

973. Purchas, III, p. 86.

974. Tavernier I, p. 698.

975. 'Allami, p. 98; Tavernier, I, p. 609.

origin	brocaded velvet per piece/mohur	plain silk velvet per yard/mohur
Yazd	15-150	2 - 5
Europe	10- 70	1 - 4
Gujarat	10- 50	-.-
Kashan	10- 40	2 - 7
Mashhad	-.-	2 - 4
Herat	10- 40	1,5 - 3
Lahore	10- 40	-.-

Such was the appreciation in India for Persian velvets that when Sir Thomas Roe presented Shah Jahangir with an upholstered coach, the Shah replaced the original Chinese velvet with « gould Persian veluett »[976]. Appreciation in Europe was, however, marginal. Chardin is the only one who writes admiringly about the *makhmal-e zarbaft* or golden brocaded velvet, especially the frisé or curled variety, which was one of the most expensive fabrics in the world costing up to 50 tomans per gaz or ell. Not surprising when, to produce it, 30 different shuttles were needed (instead of the usual two) and this required six weavers to operate the loom. The finished article was in universal use made up as curtains and portières. These fabrics, moreover, Chardin comments, last forever as it were, and its gold or silver work lasts as long as the fabric itself does, always keeping its shine and color. The silver tarnishes at length, after some 20-30 years, but it keeps and does not fall off, which Chardin ascribed to the climate in Persia as well as the quality of work[977].

Della Valle, however, observes that generally velvets and silken satins were not well made in Persia; none were as good as those made in Europe, because Persian weavers do not know how to make them properly, he explains. He adds that European weavers could make money in Persia by teaching their Persian counterparts how to make top quality products[978]. This opinion was shared by English merchants who report in 1618 that the quality of Persian velvets was considered to be bad compared to that of European velvets, « trash to it in goodnesse »[979]. Tavernier notes that velvets were made better and more beautiful in Europe and that Persian

976. Roe, p. 118, 322-323.
977. Chardin, IV, p. 152-154. See picture in Bier, p. 166.
978. Della Valle [*Voyages*], II, p. 193.
979. Ferrier [An English View], p. 200.

velvets were mainly exported to Russia and Poland[980]. European velvets were also appreciated by the Persian king and the elite. Shah Safi I, e.g. asked the Dutch in 1636 to send him ten pieces of good Dutch velvets of the following colors: crimson, purple and black[981]. The EIC bought some velvet cushions embroidered with gold and silver in 1681[982], while the VOC regularly exported some velvets (but never more than 20 per year) to be used as presents for Asian princes. These came in various colours such as green and red[983]. This lack of European interest in Persian fabrics in general and velvets in particular explains why our knowledge about them is so insignificant.

Although gold velvets were costly fabrics, normal velvets were relatively cheap as compared with gold and silver fabrics and brocades. The average price of velvets exported by the VOC, for example, was Dfl. 29 per piece, although some could cost as much as Dfl. 53 per piece. The cheapest gold cloth cost exported by the Dutch cost Dfl. 138 per piece[984].

Around 1750, velvet was of two kinds: shaggy, made in Kashan, and smooth but thick, made in Kashan, Isfahan, Pir-e Bakran, Tabriz and Gilan. It was only 21 inches (53.3 cm) wide, might be entirely of silk or of half silk, and was considered inferior in quality to the European mockado[985].

Velvets of very great beauty were made at Mashhad, and in various other places such as Isfahan, Kashan and Tabriz in the early 19th century[986]. By the 1850s, according to Blau, velvet was produced with half silk, mixed with cotton[987]. Polak mentions that velvets were woven in Kashan in the 1860s. They were inferior to French ones in terms of solidity, but as good in softness and colors. Some color nuances such as blue-black the Persians could not make. The best kind that they produced were orange

980. Tavernier, I, p. 609.
981. Dunlop, p. 528, 554.
982. Ferrier [*British-Persian Relations*], p. 393.
983. Dunlop, p. 572, 629; see also chapter II.
984. *Ibid.*
985. Pope and Ackerman, III, p. 2173.
986. Fraser [*Caspian Sea*], p. 362.
987. Blau, p. 109.

and ponceau colored[988]. In 1857, Kashan silk velvet cost 10 qrans per piece (47 inches wide)[989].

At the beginning of the 20th century only single-colored velvets were still made in Yazd and Kashan, of which the latter were better known. Usually they were made of silk, although often the warp was of cotton. In Yazd, so-called peluches were made[990]. « These velvets are so-called velvets "de chaîne" [warp velvets]. I.e. there are two warps, one ground (de fond) and the other "de poils". There are also two "trames" [wefts], i.e. two spools. Sometimes the trame is of cotton or "en fil". The two warps are always of silk. The armure has 4 "lisses" [warps] and "remettage à suivi". It is the most simple system and the velvet is always single-colored. One uses two copper rings, but instead of a knife, guided by a watch, the weaver cuts the warp's yarn directly with a normal knife. This type of work is demanding and a waste of time »[991].

• ***Malileh*** or *sermeh* is a thin metal strip silver gilt, wound around a core of cotton or silk thread. The *malileh*, or silver gilt strip, was made by the *malileh-saz*. The designs, made by the *malilehduz*, are often raised by inserting cotton stuffing into such parts of the design as the petals of flowers. Usually done on black velvet backed with coarse cloth, or waxed for hangings, belts, collars and pockets. Pieces of *termeh* are also ornamented with this in combination with seed pearls or *marvaridduzi*[992].

• ***Mandil*** was a term that referred to a striped cotton, according to Ackerman. However, by the mid-17th century it was referred to as a fabric. A French inventory mentions « a petticoat of black mandil ». However, a Safavid document does not speak of *mandil* as a fabric, but rather implies that it is a fabric for turbans, that was imported from India. Also, the usual meaning of the term *mandil*, when used in contemporary texts, is turban[993].

---

988. Polak [*Persien*], II, p. 172; Zarrabi, p. 227-228, 250, 381 mentions that both Kashan and European velvets were used to make clothes; see also Mrs. Bishop who mentions that Kashan velvet was of inferior quality (Bird, I, p. 230).

989. Blau, p. 121-122 (Tabriz, July 1857).

990. Rabino and Lafont, p. 171.

991. Olmer, p. 40.

992. Gluck and Gluck, p. 233; Shafi' Javadi, p. 228; Sani' al-Douleh, p. 105.

993. [*'Alamara-ye Shah Tahmasp*], p. 410 mentions a *mandil-e zartar*. Monshi, I, p. 329, 388; see also *chahar-dhar'i*, which was sometimes added to the *mandil* (*ibid*, II, p. 775). Ibn Batutta states that a *mandil* was a sash or turban. Dozy q.v. *mandil*.

• ***Managaneh-ye moshajjar*** was a kind of new fabric that was allegedly invented during Mohammad Shah's reign (1834-48) about which no further particulars are known[994].

• ***Marmar*** is described by Gmelin in 1773 as a piece of cambric « a coarser variety of Dschunay » and of the same size. He describes « Dschunay as a very fine white, cotton fabric, what we may call an Indian cambric [kammertuch] ». Its length was 18 arshins, while its width varied. Other fabrics, of the same quality as cambric, although coarser, were: "Tscherbate", "Bisson", "Chassa" (which was even coarser), "Maderpork", with a length of 13 arshins and a varying width; "Humay" (length 12 arshins, width varies); and "Sahan" (length 12 arshins, width varies)[995]. The term "maderpork", mentioned by Gmelin, may be the same as *maderbaf*, which was a thin cotton made of poor yarn and flimsily woven. The term probably means "Madras woven". The Russian document, used by Ackerman, also lists it as *materpak*[996]. Zarrabi, about 100 year later, mentions *marmar* as a fabric used to make a turban for the olama[997].

• ***Meshkibaf*** was an average or inferior type of black silk fabric that was made in Kashan and Isfahan, and sold to tribal people and abroad[998]. These weavers formed a guild in Isfahan. « They wove the dark-bay silk cloth [*meshki*] used by women to cover their head [*charqad*]. Many of their products were sold abroad. Formerly, there was not a women in Persia who did not wear a *meshki* piece of fabric on her head. It lasted 40 to 50 years and was not without beauty and charm. Now it has fallen into disuse. This guild is also a type of *sha'rbaf*. They were very numerous, but now there are only a few and their trade is ruined »[999].

• ***Meshmesh***, was the name given by the drapers [*bazzaz*] to a very thin, starched piece of cloth. It was many-colored and was for several years very popular during the summer, to such an extent that the women even used this

994. E'tezad al-Saltaneh, p. 209.
995. Gmelin, III, p. 422-424.
996. Pope and Ackerman, III, p. 2165.
997. Zarrabi, p. 248.
998. Naraqi, p. 275-276.
999. Tahvildar, p. 102.

fabric to make their *charqad* in winter[1000]. In a customs list of of 1903 the term is translated as muslin, while the term *meshmesh*, or large size handkerchief, also occurs in the same list[1001].

• ***Methqal***, also *metqal*, or a kind of muslin. The *Divan-e albaseh*[1002] describes *methqali* as a thin, fine and very delicate fabric at the end of the 15th century. Around 1540, mention is made of a « *bala-ye methqali-ye Isfahani* » or a top of a tent made of *methqal* from Isfahan. Apparently *methqal* had become a sturdier fabric[1003]. Also found as *metqal*, it was white and used to make a purse or *kiseh*[1004]. There was a *bazar-e methqal-forushha* or *methqal* sellers bazaar in Isfahan, which sold the fabric, which was used to make surcoats or *qaba*[1005]. *Methqal* was also made in Natanz in the 1680s[1006].

Methqal is referred to around 1750 as a calico, a kind of *baba ahmad*. It was heavy, being woven of a thick yarn. Isfahan made the best quality, despite the use of poor yarn. Tehran, Yazd and Qazvin also made a good quality; the former's produce described as being "thick and glossy". Kashan, Mazandaran, Qazvin, Bokhara and Khiva also produced an inferior quality. The Gujerat *mishkal* was considered to be superior to the Persian variety. *Mishkal* measured 14-21 inches (35.5-53.3 cm) wide and there were from 7 yards 14 inches to 7 yards 28 inches (4.97-7.11 m) to the piece. Different measures are also given, viz. 25 inches (88.8 cm) wide and 9 1/3 to 12 yards 16 inches (8.5-11.37 m) in a piece. The Russians used *mishkal* for shirts and veils, while the Moslem population used it for smocks (*beschmet*). Another quality was blockprinted and made into bedcovers and thus exported. This quality was also called *saygan* or *sagan*, which was also used to refer to a thin flimsy calico from India, made of poor yarn. The latter was also refered to as *umay*, *umaya* or *umaj*[1007].

1000. Mostaufi, I, p. 472, n. 1.
1001. Rabino [Kermanshah], p. 67.
1002. Qari, p. 203.
1003. [*'Alamara-ye Shah Tahmasp*], p. 398, 420; see also Shamlu, I, p. 61.
1004. Qomi, II, p. 1055; see also Shamlu, I, p. 61.
1005. Esfahani [*Nesf-e jahan*], p. 53.
1006. Gaube and Wirth, p. 272-273.
1007. Pope and Ackerman, III, p. 2164; see also *marmar* [q.v.] for the term *sahan*.

Methqal still existed in the Qajar period and was used for trousers (*zir-jameh*)[1008].

• ***Milek***, see *zarbaft*.

• ***Mokhayyar***, see *dara'i*.

• ***Mov*** is a fabric usually woven from pure silk, but sometimes found in a silk and cotton mix. It is referred to in early Safavid times, when mention is made of an *alecheh-ye mov kar-e Hend*, or a *mov-alecheh* made in India[1009]. It is probably the same as "movny", 35 inches (88 cm) wide, which was woven in Ardabil, Qazvin, Kashan, Tabriz, Kessar, Gilan and Shamakhi, who also produced the best quality. It was dyed in various colours, the most expensive was dipped in saffron. This was 2.5 rubles a piece, while the ordinary yellow and the red were 1.5 and all other qualities 1/5th[1010]. Gmelin mentions that its length was 3 to 3.5 arshins, while its width was not fixed. Tabriz also produced both silk and half silken *mov*[1011].

Pirahan-e karmar or *mov* was woven with red simple silk, it was entirely unfigured. It measured 3 by 0.75 arshin. A *pirahan-e karish* was a silken *mov* with a silken cross weave. It measured 3 by 0.75 arshin. *Pirahani* was a striped, entirely cotton fabric. All three fabrics were used, as indicated by their trade name, for the making of shirts[1012].

• ***Motabeq***, also *motabeq-e qotni*, an expensive silken fabric[1013].

• ***Namad*** is felt of which various products were made, notably carpets, but also tents, *kavajeh-push*, clothes[1014] and horse blankets[1015]. This was the work of the *namadduz* or *namadbaf*[1016]. *Namad* was not ironed, but

1008. Zarrabi, p. 249; Janab, p. 79.
1009. ['*Alamara-ye Shah Tahmasp*], p. 410.
1010. Pope and Ackerman, III, p. 2168.
1011. Gmelin, III, p. 420.
1012. *Ibid.*, p. 416-417.
1013. Monshi, II, p. 775; Nava'i, p. 87.
1014. Qomi, II, p. 955, 1002.
1015. Bird, I, p. 185.
1016. There were 21 of them in Tabriz in 1869; also called *kechehchi* in Azeri. Shafi' Javadi, p. 228.

beaten with a stone to make it ready for sale in the bazaar. The quality of a *namad* depended on the quality of wool used. The best *namad* were made of *kork* or down, the worst, of wool of old animals. Inferior qualities were not only rolled, but also beaten. The *namadmal* cheated sometimes by using good wool on the upper side of the *namad,* whilst using bad wool, cotton and other stuff on the inside, or by making the borders firm and thick, while the middle was made thin or, again instead of rolling it was pounded[1017]. Du Mans said that the *namads* were so well made that one mistook them for cloth or *londreh*[1018].

Namads or fine felt carpets, were sometimes of great beauty, but they were dear, and apt to get moth eaten[1019]. *Namads* kept their natural color, and came with or without gaudy embellishment. They were often 4 cm thick, but nevertheless of incredible softness. There was no export of *namad* to Europe. « The felts are self-colored, with a small amount of stamped pattern. They have not got cut edges, but are made in one piece, consequently the shape is very inaccurate. They cost nearly as much as good carpets, and are protected with druggets in the same way »[1020].

Namads were already made prior to the Safavid era, so it does not come as a surprise to find mention of this product throughout that period[1021]. The same holds true of course for the Qajar period.

The best felt carpets were made in and about Kerman[1022]. Hamadan was famous for its *namads* or felts, which were used as carpets and horse-coverings and as great-coats by the peasants, as well as by the Lurs. A good carpet of Hamadan manufacture was an inch thick, but some made at Yazd reached two inches. For rich men's houses they were made to order to fit rooms. The largest Mrs. Bishop saw in Tehran was 120 x 80 feet and formed 14 mule loads; 60 x 40 feet is not an uncommon size and makes 8 mule loads. Due to their bulk and weight *namads* were not exported. The best made at Hamadan cost about 20 s. per sq. yard. Chairs spoil them and

---

1017. Shahri, II, p. 24; Janab, p. 79.

1018. Du Mans, p. 248; Richard, II, p. 192.

1019. Fraser [*Caspian Sea*], p. 362.

1020. Malcolm [*Five Years*], p. 22.

1021. *Namadmal, namadzin* and *namadbaf* (Bastani Parizi [*Ganj*], p. 152, 157); Bardsiri, p. 236; Golchin-Ma'ani, p. 44. *Namadzin* (['*Alamara-ye Safavi*], p. 530); *kolah-e namadi* and *namad-push* (Monshi, p. 201).

1022. Goldsmid, I, p. 101; see also DCR 1376, (1893-4), p. 20-21; p. 32, *namads* and felts in Kerman, which were considered the best.

therefore the manufacture of these magnificent floor-covering will probably die[1023].

« I have seen a *namad*, or felt carpet, eighty feet long and fifty feet wide, without a seam. The name of the maker is woven in it — as the painter puts his name on the painting. The great weight of these felt carpets forbid their exportation. Indeed, the chief item of expense connected with them is the cost of transportation from Yezd and Ispahan, where they are made, to the residence of the purchaser. But nothing in the way of a carpet can be so luxurious and suggestive of comfort as a Persian *namad* an inch thick »[1024].

« A very beautiful one, covered with an intricate geometrical pattern in blue, red, and green worsted. [...] In an inner room, carefully protected from the wind, is a polished plaster form. On this pieces of coloured worsted are arranged in the desired pattern, with some sort of size. A very thin felt is then carefully pressed over them, and at once removed, carrying on its face the pieces of worsted in their proper place. This thin felt is laid on the thicker felt of the carpet, and the two incorporated with blows of the mallet »[1025].

Namads were made in a great many towns in Persia. In addition to Kerman, Yazd and Hamadan there was also a considerable production in Astarabad[1026] and Isfahan[1027].

• ***Namnamduzi*** (also *monjuqduzi*) refers to the sewing of imported beads of various colors[1028] onto prayer cloths, prayer stone cases, men's comb cases, toothbrush holders, scissors cases, holders for *sormeh*, purses, etc. This craft fell into disuse around the turn of the century[1029].

1023. Bird, II, p. 151-152; *ibid.*, I, p. 207, and Benjamin, p. 277.

1024. *Ibid.*, p. 277; « The banquetting hall is of immense size, and the floor is covered with a darn fawn named three-quarters of an inch thick, made, I understood, in one piece eighty feet long by fifty broad » (Bird, I, p. 207).

1025. Goldsmid, I, p. 101-102.

1026. Astarabad exports felts, *namad*, and horse coverings (*jhul*) manufactured by the Torkomans (*Historical Gazetteer*, I, p. 92). They make good *namads* at Astarabad in 1903 (Dhabihi, p. 27).

1027. There were 30 *namad-mal* in Isfahan (Hoeltzer, p. 22).

1028. Already in use since Sassanian times, see also Gluck and Gluck, p. 236.

1029. Golriz, p. 734.

• ***Naqdehduzi*** is embroidery with silver or gilt-wired thread. It is mainly used for clothing, as for a taffeta skirt (*shaliteh*). The thread is a flat strip gilt silver. The embroidery is the same front and back, in a double-sided satin stitch[1030].

In Isfahan there was a *naqdehduz* (silver brocade makers) guild. « Formerly, *naqdehduzi* was highly esteemed and noteworthy and many men and women were engaged in making silver brocade. First, the painters would make excellent intricate designs on cloth and then the *naqdehduz* would sew on the designs. The old products, which have lasted till our days, are spoken off very highly. Now this trade has gradually declined and most of the remaining artisans have gone to Tehran and Tabriz »[1031].

• ***Naqshduzi*** or embroideries were, according to Blau, usually done on unpatterned native woolen fabrics, often on shawls, but in Rasht mostly on Russian colored fabrics. The most common patterns were brightly colored arabesques, flowers, and animals. The embroideries were turned into table cloths, saddle cloths, chair covers, shoes, slippers, *kolah-e shab* etc. and were exported to Turkey and Russia[1032]. The embroideries served also as marriage presents and were always well cared for. These were often made by the women of the family themselves, when time and money played no role. The best silk embroideries hailed from Mazandaran and Gilan, the second best from Kashan.

The *naqsh* or *zileh* used for women trousering throughout the 19th century, were embroidered in diagonal parallel bands, using tent stitch, a short slanting stitch with each stitch crossing diagonally an intersection of the foundation. Fine work used silk threads on a cotton foundation[1033].

They differed from Indian embroideries in two respects, one being their richer range of colors, and the other their weaving technique. Due to the close integration of the appliqué work to the base material, the mosaic-like result appears virtually seamless. The price of Rashti embroidery was 20-40 German marks per square meter in the early 1880s[1034].

The British consul Churchill agreed with Stolze-Andreas' assessment of the artistic value of Rasht embroideries. « Horse-cloths, table-covers, and

1030. Gluck and Gluck, p. 232.
1031. Tahvildar, p. 97-98; Hoeltzer, p. 59.
1032. Blau, p. 110.
1033. Gluck and Gluck, p. 226.
1034. Stolze and Andreas, p. 25-26.

carpets are made of this really most beautiful embroidery, in which great taste is displayed both in the design and in the disposition of colours. It surpasses by a good way, in fineness, embroidery of the same kind produced in the Bombay presidency, and its price is from 2,5 to 5 tomans the square dhar', which is a trifle larger than the square meter »[1035].

According to Benjamin there were distinct elaborate schools of embroidery, to wit: those of Shiraz, Resht, and Qaradagh. « The main features are massive and intricate designs wrought with silk in chain-stitch, with a wonderful massing of brilliant colors on broadcloth, which is generally scarlet or gray, though sometimes black. The richer specimens are distinguished by having the design partly made of small bits of cloth of other colors, sewed into apertures cut into the groundwork. In the Shiraz embroideries, the inserted pieces are generally of velvet ». Sometimes entire carpets are made on this elaborate scale, which are very expensive. Old designs were more artistic, and no artificial colors used. Also, the old gold and silver embroideries of the past[1036]. Wills noticed that « the needlework of the Persians is very beautiful, silk being used for sewing to the total exclusion of cotton »[1037].

Like so many other crafts, that of embroidery fell into disuse around 1870. What happened in Isfahan is typical of what was happening all over Iran. « The group of the *naqshduz*. Formerly, this guild had many members and both men and women were engaged in making embroideries. This article sold well. Everything the painters designed was drawn on *qadak*, *chalvari*, etc. and these designs were embroidered completely with a needle, in either pure silk, in *kork*, or in cotton yarns of different colors. The price of these embroideries varied in accordance with the material used. One piece of Kashmir of the size of a man's *nezami* [European] trousers or equal to a women's *zir-jameh* [tight trousers], which was in common use in those times, cost from six to eight *riyals* up to forty tomans. Their product lasts sixty to seventy years and pieces which were not much used, have lasted for 200 years or longer and remained beautiful. The best were worn by the nobles, the average quality by middle class women. This cloth had

1035. "Report Churchill on the Trade and Commerce of the Provinces of Ghilan and Astarabad for the years 1874 and 1875", p. 1498. The price per square yard of Gilan embroidery was 1 pound 10 shillings in 1876 and 1 pound 8 shillings in 1877 (AP 29, (1876), p. 696). These silk embroideries were done by men (Marsh [*A Ride*], p. 61).

1036. Benjamin, p. 335.

1037. Wills, p. 333-334.

other uses too, such as mantel shelve coverings [*taqcheh-push*], cradles [*na'ini*], swadling clothes [*qandaqeh*], portofolios [*mahfazeh*] cushions for the room's place of honor [*pushtiha-ye bala-ye otaq*], pack saddles [*palan*] and the like. Most of it was sold to customers in Turkey, Egypt, India, Turkistan, and Afghanistan; some was also sold to Europe. From the time of the late Shah [Mohammad Shah 1834-1848] to the present day the trade had gradually declined and fallen into disuse. There were merchants known as *naqshineh-forush,* who specially engaged in the selling and buying of this article. They were wealthy and formed a large group and were all esteemed. Of their line hardly any is left, except for Hajji Hosein, son of the late well-known Hajji Mohammad Ebrahim and some others who are engaged in trading other merchandise »[1038].

The demise of the crafts is also recorded by Western contemporaries such as Benjamin. *Naqsh*, or embroidery, is no longer practised. The female house custom has undergone changes and the embroidered pantaletes, or "nacsh", has been discarded. « These nacsh are about two feet long and sixteen inches wide, more or less. They consist of some superb pattern embroidered entirely in silk, so formly and solidly that they are like carpets in miniature. Their durability is phenomenal. Some old preserved pattern have acquired a soft, gray tone. These nacsh are becoming rare. The more recent embroideries are coarser in texture and less delicious in tone, and wrought especially to meet the foreign demand for Persian goods. Old pieces are retouched with new colors, which come off when moistened. Another form of embroidery, that on linen of prayer carpets and of veils for streetwear is nearly extinct. The design is produced by working a pattern with white silk and drawing the threads, the result being a raised pattern in silk lighted by open-lattice-like spaces »[1039].

• ***Nashur*** was a white cotton fabric, which was finer than *karbas* and more like *methqal* (q.v.), but coarser than *chalvar*. It was woven in towns such as Isfahan, but after 1870 it was replaced by imported, mainly grey, shirtings[1040].

1038. Tahvildar, p. 99.
1039. Benjamin, p. 333-334; see also Gluck and Gluck, p. 226.
1040. Rabino [Kermanshah], p. 67.

• ***Nimtan*** is a term used to denote a kind of flowered silk, though *nimtaneh* actually is a short jacket[1041]. This silk (probably a brocaded taffeta) was made in Kashan and Isfahan, but not in Yazd. It could have either large or small flowers, and was sometimes striped. One kind of *nimtan* was called "anbarbu" and another with large flowers "sranturovy"[1042].

Nimtan is also described as a kind of or *sha'rbaf*. This type of flowered silk was used for belts, hence it was either a compound cloth or compound twill. A *nimtan* was a kind of *rasuli*, it must have been compound cloth. It was produced in Kashan. The flowers were either large or small and it was sometimes striped. It was 28 inches (71.1 cm) wide, with 5 yards 16 inches (4.97 m) to the piece. It was also made in Shiraz and Shushtar, and *sha'rbaf* belts of various qualities were made in Gilan and Isfahan, but it was not made in Tehran. *Sha'rbaf* was used in Russia for clothes and church vestments[1043].

• ***Noqrehbaft***, see *zarbaft*.

• ***Ormek***, is a silk-cotton fabric, woven in Yazd. It was 50-56 inches wide, and sold in July 1857 for 1 qran per arshin in the Tabriz bazaar[1044]. In 1862, its length was 0.90 m and sold at 1 toman per meter in Yazd[1045]. Although it is not mentioned prior to the 1850s we know that the craft of *ormekbaf* existed just prior to the Safavid period, and that *ormekbafi* was an important craft because various draft letters, of the *ensha* variety, exist addressed to various master *ormek* weavers. Ostad Jalal al-Din Mohammad is mentioned as having produced 24 dhar' or ells (16.8 m) of *ormek* from 44 methqals (202 gr) of raw material[1046].

• ***Palas*** was a coarse woolen cloth, which was still being woven by groups of herders, mainly in the Qazvin area in the 1870s[1047].

• ***Pardeh***, originally a silken fabric, but by the 1850s was made of half silk mixed with cotton, was produced in Rasht in pieces, that were mostly

1041. See e.g. [*'Alamara-ye Safavi*], p. 161.
1042. Pope and Ackerman, III, p. 2171.
1043. *Ibid.*, III, p. 2171.
1044. Blau, p. 109, 121.
1045. MAE, Rochechouart to Gobineau, Yezd, 26/10/1862; see figure 6 in this letter.
1046. Khavafi, I, p. 255-263.
1047. Golzari, p. 33, 175-177.

used as door coverings, etc. and therefore made in the appropriate sizes of 8/4 and 9/4 wide, and 2.5 arshins long. They were woven in pairs. In July 1857, a pair of *pardeh* made in Rasht cost 30 qrans in the Tabriz bazaar[1048].

• ***Pargaleh***, (variously rendered as "parkallen", "percalls", "pargula") was a cambric, similar to *methqal* (q.v.), with a length of 9 arshins long, and *bafteh* (12 arshins long), which were two varieties of cambric[1049]. The term "parkalla" already occurs in Middle-Dutch, which implies that this fabric was known in Europe during the high Middle-Ages.

• ***Patehduzi*** or *selselehduzi* is a kind of fine silk embroidery. The thread is usually of fine wool, with which silk is sometimes combined. The finer embroideries were used for *kursi* covers, coverlets, women's veils, borders on men's robes (*'aba*), small table covers, etc. The stitches used are mainly stem stitch, darning stitch and the running stitch which forms the trade mark of this embroidery — a row of small squares or boxes outlining the motifs. The patterns consist usually of a central medallion and a special design such as the *boteh* in each of the four corners. Sometimes the smaller covers are quilted (*pambehduzi*) in a simple running stitch in spaced rows[1050]. This fine embroidery was still practised in Kerman in the 1970s « (although this is rarer among contemporary women) on finely woven *kurk* or other cloth. These are known in Kirman as *pateh* »[1051].

• ***Patu*** is a beautiful, natural colored and motley, waterproof, extremely light and soft felt flannel-like fabric, that was woven from goat hair (*patu*), in particular in Kerman[1052]. Blau contests that *patu* is like flannel. He states that « As far as I know one does not know combing wool and combing yarn in Persia. Therefore there is no cloth, Casimir, flanel or other similar stuffs in Persia. The only cloth like fabric is the camel-cloth known as *patu*. This comes from Herat to Mashhad. With a width of 80 cm it is used for covers, cloaks and packing material. It is soft, elastic, and lasting, but is not

1048. Blau, p. 109, 121.
1049. Gmelin, III, p. 423; Borhan-e Qate', q.v. *pargaleh*.
1050. Gluck and Gluck, p. 222.
1051. Dillon, p. 267, n. 4.
1052. Stolze and Andreas, p. 25.

exported but for the Khanates. From camel and goat hair in all provinces they make for domestic consumption drellstofe, sacks, etc. »[1053].

Patu, according to de Rochechouart, was a kind of coarse woolen cloth, which was very supple and used to make winter garments. Its width was 1.50 m and its length 3.50 m. Each piece was sold at 1 to 10 tomans. Those pieces of fabrics that were too thick to make into garments, or of which the color was too bright, were made into carpets. It was a very good cloth, very warm; it kept its color, and was pleasant to wear. He thought it would sell well in Europe, and he estimated that Kerman could produce as much as one wanted. The wool for the *patu* was supplied by the herds from Seistan and Baluchistan[1054].

• ***Pirahani*** (see also *mov*) is a striped, entirely cotton fabric. It was used for the making of shirts[1055]. « Peerahun shaees (or king's shirts) resemble English long-cloth, which has entirely superseded them »[1056]. « Peerahuns are made in pieces of 2 yards 25 inches long, by 25 inches wide, and resemble stout lutestrings, but are fully closer in their texture. The wholesale price of those from Yezd was 7 reals (9s. 4d.); those from other quarters about 4,5 reals (6s.) per piece. They were dyed either blue or red. They were nearly 30% dearer than alejehs, because cochineal was used in dyeing them. They are both used for men and women's shirts, one piece making a shirt »[1057].

• ***Pulakduzi*** refers to sewing golden, silver or gilt sequins or *pulak*, which were round with a hole in the middle, on silk or cotton, but mainly on *qanaviz* fabrics, with all kinds of patterns, sometimes brocaded. Additional motifs were worked in chain stitch. It was used for *taq-pardehs*, plate covers, boxes, cases for prayer stones, etc.[1058]. In Isfahan there was a sequin sewers guild (*pulakduz*), « They sewed gold or gilt sequins onto cloth. Formerly the clothes of Their Royals Highnesses the Princes and special royal robes of honor for the governors and others were sewn with

1053. Blau, p. 109.

1054. MAE, Rochechouart to Gobineau, 5/11/1862, see figures 8-11 in this letter. See also Zarrabi, p. 251.

1055. Gmelin, III, p. 416.

1056. Fraser [*Caspian Sea*], p. 362.

1057. *Ibid.*, p. 361.

1058. Golriz, p. 734; Gluck and Gluck, p. 234.

sequins. It was also often used for women's clothes. In one way it was beneficial that its manufacture was discontinued, for in spite of its splendor, it was not economical and did not last long. Some of the original group of the *pulak-forush* [sequin sellers] have left, and are now engaged in other work »[1059].

• ***Qadak***, meaning "of a person's size" (*be andazeh-ye qad*), was a tightly woven Persian cotton fabric which is also referred to as nankin. It is mentioned in the 18th century for the first time. It came in various qualities and width ranging from 14 to 18 chelleh[1060]. A Russian report documents that « imitations, dyed buff with a weak solution of iron salts, usurped the name of nankin. It is described as not being silk. It had undulating stripes and flowers. It was made in Kashan, but not in Isfahan, Tabriz or Rasht »[1061].

« ["Kudduks"] are narrow cloths, of a fabric resembling nankeen, of all colours, and of a size suited to make a single kabba (the Persian upper vest, which sits close to the body, as far down as the waist and has long skirts) for which they are entirely used. They cost from 3 to 6 reals (4s. to 8s.) according to fineness. Those of Isfahan are most esteemed, and are largely exported to Russia »[1062]. « In Qomisha caduck is made, a better sort of that coarse linen called kerbas, which is made in every village »[1063]. « The best manufacture is caduck; of this there is an exportation to Turkey. The finest is manufactured in Isfahan »[1064]. At the end of the 1840s, consul Abbott mentions the production of *qadak*, which he refers to as colored calico, in Isfahan, Yazd and Natanz[1065].

« The only tightly woven Persian cotton fabric, in its best quality is a nanking type of fabric, which is made in Yazd; a more ordinary quality (Tabriz, Gunish) is more like a common cotton fabric. During the weaving each weft yarn alternatively takes a warp yarn over it and then under it. This fabric is called qadak and is woven in width between 40 inches-52 inches, at a price varying between 3.5-6 shahis per arshin. This fabric is used for male

---

1059. Tahvildar, p. 99-100; Zarrabi, p. 256.
1060. Asef, p. 316, 380-381.
1061. Pope and Ackerman, III, p. 2172.
1062. Fraser [*Caspian Sea*], p. 362.
1063. Morier [*A Journey*], p. 161.
1064. *Ibid.*, p. 231.
1065. Amanat, p. 20, 40.

and female clothes allover Persia and the neighbouring Russian provinces. Prior to the onslaught of European textiles qadak was exported in large quantities there and found a willing market. Its manufacturing, however, falls year by year, because of European competition »[1066].

Qadak from Yazd was the most appreciated in the 1850s. Prices naturally varied per quality. For example, in July 1857, prices in the Tabriz bazaar were as follows[1067] :

1st quality,	45-48 inches wide	7 qrans 10 shahis per arshin
2nd quality	50 inches wide	- 6 qrans per arshin
3rd quality	52 inches wide	- 4 qrans per arshin

Qadak was still produced in Isfahan, Yazd, Kashan and, in small quantities, in Bushire, in the 1860s. It was described as a tightly and evenly woven fabric of which the colors were quite fast. *Qadak*, therefore, was much appreciated in Persia and the Caucasus for making summer clothing. « Formerly, the naturally yellow cotton, also was used to make qadak, the so-called qadak-e khodrang [of natural color]. However, because this type of cotton is very brittle it is difficult to spin a smooth yarn from it. Therefore, nowadays British yarn is preferred to make qadak. Because of this the price as well as the quality has gone down »[1068]. *Qadak* was exported in great quantities to Russia[1069]. *Qadak* is « a sort of nankeen, much used in dress »[1070]. There were 25 *qadakbaf* in Isfahan[1071].

• ***Qalamkar***, see *chit*.

• ***Qalamzar***, see *qalamkar*.

• ***Qamis*** or cotton shirt or shift and the material it was made of. It was still made in Isfahan and Kashan until the 1870s[1072].

1066. Blau, p. 111.
1067. *Ibid.*, p. 122.
1068. Polak [*Persien*], II, p. 166-167.
1069. Stolze and Andreas, p. 25.
1070. Curzon, I, p. 42; Zarrabi, p. 227-228, 248-249, 448.
1071. Hoeltzer, p. 21; see also *sabbagh* and *karbas*.
1072. Hoeltzer, p. 45; Zarrabi, p. 250-251, 259.

• ***Qanavat*** or *qanaviz* was a silk cloth of close texture. The word is a fistored form of canvas. In the 1750s, it came in three qualities and was unusually wide: 56 or even 84 inches (1.42 to 2.13 m), though that from Gilan was only 35 inches (89 cm) wide. A half silk quality, known as *palu-qanavat,* was made in Lahijan, and the poorest quality was made at Shamakhi, and was refered to as "donluk", which in Turkish means a women's gown. It is also referred to as "parcheh", Russian for brocade, and is sometimes qualified as nankin[1073]. Gilan *qanavat* also came with either broad or narrow stripes, and one type that was "shot" had likewise wide plain stripes[1074].

Qanavat is a fabric, which is made from simple silk. The best quality pieces measure from 5 arshins by 0.75 arshin. Lesser qualities are 4.5 x 0.75 arshin. This fabric comes in diamond and striped pattern as well as with a cross weave with a golden yarn. There are also unfigured and figured varieties, of which Gmelin list the following:

- *Foti,* a diamond patterned and embroidered *qanavat* with an additional warp of gold thread. Russian women use this fabric as a head covering. Its length is 2 arshins by 1.25 arshin.

- *Boqcha* is a diamond patterned, brocaded/ embroidered *qanavat* without a golden yarn. The Persians use these as kerchiefs. The fabric measures 1.5 by 1.5 arshin.

- *Darpardeh qanavat,* is a diamond patterned *qanavat* that is used as a cover for doors and the like. It is made to order.

- *Makhmal-e qanavat* is a striped *qanavat.* Its measurements are 3.5 by 0.75 arshin[1075].

Qanavat, « a striped silk and cotton manufacture, 9 yards in length and various qualities produced in Astarabad. It sells per 8 to 10 sahebqrans per piece »[1076]. Cannevas is a plain, single-colored piece of silk-cotton fabric for making garments, it was 50-53-56 inches wide and was produced in Yazd and Tabriz. Its price was 2 qrans, 10 shahis per arshin. There was also a broader version, 66-68 inches wide, which was produced in Yazd, Kashan and Khorasan. Its price was 3 qrans for the Yazd, and 2 qrans per

1073. Pope and Ackerman, III, p. 2169.
1074. *Ibid.*, III, p. 1070.
1075. Gmelin, III, p. 415-416.
1076. Amanat, p. 25.

arshin for the Kashan product[1077]. Qanaviz, both in striped and single-colored form, were still produced in Khorasan around 1910[1078].

• ***Qasab*** is a silken and a silk-cotton fabric. The term existed prior to the Safavid era, when it meant a fine linen. Qazvin is one of the towns mentioned as producing *qasab* in early Safavid times. Also, the existence of the *qasabbaf* or weaver is mentioned[1079]. According to Ackerman, *qasab* is the same as "doroi". It was made in Isfahan, Kashan, Qazvin, Kassarlam, Kasmin, and Shamakhi in 1750. When made of half silk and cotton, it was called half, *palu-qasab*. Whatever the grade, it was always 35 inches (89 cm) wide[1080]. Gmelin described *qasab* as an unfigured fabric that is woven from double (twisted?) silk yarn. There were two varieties. One was entirely silken, while the other had a cotton crossweave. The Persians used this fabric to make trousers. It measured 3 by 0.75 arshin[1081].

« Cussabs, 7 yards 2 inches long, by 29 inches wide, somewhat stouter than aleejahs and dereis, but similar in fabric, sell at about 22 reals (29s.4d.) a piece. They are used for men and women's trowsers »[1082]. *Qasab* was woven in Yazd, 1.30 m long, and sold at a price of 9 tomans per meter in 1862[1083]. « The cassubs are used for shirts and trowsers »[1084]. Zarrabi mentions in particular red (*qermez*) colored *qasab*[1085]. *Qasab*, described as a very strong blue or ponceau colored fabric, of which high quality trousers were made, were still manufactured in Persia around 1910[1086].

• ***Qeitanbafi*** was the making of *qeitan* (braid, cord) that was embroidered around the hems of male and female clothing to make it beautiful and solid. Another was the making of the *zonar* (girdle that distinguished Jews and

1077. Blau, p. 109, 121; see also Zarrabi, p. 250 for the same production centers.
1078. Rabino and Lafont, p. 171.
1079. [*'Alamara-ye Shah Tahmasp*], p. 400, 410.
1080. Pope and Ackerman, III, p. 2169.
1081. Gmelin, III, p. 416; *Qasab* is also mentioned by Asef, p. 89, 316, 367, 382, 441.
1082. Fraser [*Caspian Sea*], p. 362.
1083. MAE, Rochechouart to Gobineau, Yezd, 26/10/1862, see figure 2 in the same letter.
1084. Fraser [*Narrative*], App. B, p. 22.
1085. Zarrabi, p. 248.
1086. Rabino and Lafont, p. 171.

Christians from Moslems) which were sewed on the hem and collar of the *sardari* (over coat), or *qaba* or *labadeh* (long male outer garment) and also for the girdle of the young. The young *lutis* in particular made much of their *zonarduzi*, i.e. on the back and front of their *sardari* from top to middle there were beautiful flowers, and on their breast hung two silken tassels. But it was also applied on *taq-pardeh, boghcheh, sar-e hammam*, as well as female trousers. It was also used for the case for the prayer stone, purse, *band-e kaghaz* (the paper tube that *mostaufi*s carried with them) and the *shamsheh* for the rosary, as well as silken buttons. Many men and women made a living with this in the past[1087]. Braids, ribbons, fringes (*risheh*s) and cordels cost 6 shahis in July 1857, in Tabriz[1088].

• ***Qollabduzi*** or embroidery using the chain stitch only, was employed in overall embroidery; it was also known as *Rashtduzi*. Hoeltzer implies that is was a kind of patch-work embroidery, because several fabrics were joined. It is characterized by its use of the foundation materials (*mahut*), flannel wool, felted to appear like a fine grade of felt, embroidered in firmly twisted silk thread. It was the work of women, working at home and using the *mil-e qollab*. With the introduction of the sewing machine (*chark golduzi* and *qollabduzi*) it gradually became a man's job, while it changed from a cottage industry into one performed in shops. It was especially in use during the months of mourning (Moharram and Safar) and throughout the year in pilgrimage towns such as Mashhad and Qom. It was used for banners, boxes, holders, place mats, and to adorn clothing. The *qollabduzi* was sewed on velvet, fine cotton (*chalvar*), and mostly on *makhmal-e meshki* and *albalu'i* and other dark colors. Usually fine silken thread was used, though thick artificial silken yarns were also used. Hoeltzer observed that in the 1870s, the traditional natural dyes were not used anymore, while also European rather than traditional Persian designs were used, which he regretted[1089]. It was also woven, in the red variety, in the Caspian provinces[1090].

1087. Golriz, p. 436-437; see also Hoeltzer, p. 21.

1088. Blau, p. 121.

1089. Shahri, II, p. 28; Gluck and Gluck, p. 218; Wulff, p. 219; Hoeltzer, p. 59-60; Ness, p. 263; Golzari, p. 171.

1090. Golzari, p. 33.

The same description (as for the *naqdehduz*) holds for the group of *qollabduz* or crocheters in Isfahan[1091].

• ***Qotni***, see *atlas*.

• ***Reshteh*** is a fabric used already during early Safavid times. *Reshteh-ye khata'i* is mentioned as being used for garments. The qualifier *khata'i* probably meant that it had a Chinese pattern[1092]. The fabric was still produced at Kashan, Tabriz, Qazvin, Ardabil, Hamadan and Shamakhi around 1750. The Kashan variety was the superior quality[1093].

• ***Rubandi***, « white silk handkerchiefs are cheap and fairly good, and the finest embroidery in silk can be purchased at almost nominal prices; it is known as Rubandi and is most effective »[1094]. It was most suitable for use as a face veil, since one could see through its lattice work[1095]. Wills marvelled at « The networks on white silk, done with the needle on the "rubanda", or veils, at the part covering the eyes, being done wholly with the needle, are almost monuments of art work »[1096]. Finally, the fine white embroidery for the female veil used simple arabesques, for the rest simply flat. The bed covers are all made of cotton, covered with printed cotton or silks and nicely done in various patterns. It is of course all hand work[1097].

• ***Sabbagh*** or dyer, who dyed the yarns and fabrics. The various natural dyes were first ground by the *rang-sab*, and then prepared through boiling by the *rang-paz*[1098]. Once the dye was ready the *rang-raz* or *sabbagh* would use them to dye the various yarns and fabrics. Of the *sabbagh* there were several specialities. For example, there was « the group of *sabbagh-e risman* [cotton yarn dyers] [in Isfahan]. They are a group other than the dyers of *qadak*, who dye cotton for the weavers and tailors »[1099].

1091. Tahvildar, p. 98.
1092. [*'Alamara-ye Shah Tahmasp*], p. 397, 418.
1093. Pope and Ackerman, III, p. 2166-2167
1094. Sykes [*Ten Thousand*], p. 423. See also *sokmehduzi*.
1095. See Chardin, IV, p. 11; Mostaufi, I, p. 510; Rice, p. 163-164; also *rubandeh-duz*, see Hoeltzer, p. 22.
1096. Wills, p. 333-334.
1097. Hoeltzer, p. 59-60.
1098. *Ibid.*, p. 43.
1099. Tahvildar, p. 117.

According to Hoeltzer there were 1456 *rangraz* in Isfahan in 1870[1100]. In the same town there was also « the group of *sabbagh-e abrisham* [silk dyers]. They form a separate group who dye silk. Anybody wanting the finest quality of *qadak*, which has the best color, gives it to the silk dyers »[1101]. There were only two of them left in 1920[1102]. Further, there existed « the group of the *sabbagh-e qadak* [which was] a big guild. Formerly it had many members, but now its has been halved. The members of this guild occupy very long connecting bazaars with high arched vaults which contain 136 shops. Every shop has a site and buildings [*a'yani*] similar to a big house. The buildings are clean and pleasant. There are benches, winter and summer sleeping places, ponds, waterpools, wells, cisterns and apparatus for dyeing and fulling. More than 1500 tomans have been spent for the construction of some shops belonging to the head of the guild. For similar buildings in other provinces one would have to spend more than 3,000 tomans. Formerly most of the merchants and officials of the *divan*, who had dealings or were acquainted with the dignitaries of the guild, came to these shops for their daily repose. Apart from these two bazaars which are next to the Meidan-e Naqsh-e Jahan, there are a lot of dyeing shops spread out over the bazaars and the meidans »[1103]. There were still 30 of them in 1920[1104].

Persia's favorable conditions for dyeing textiles (a dry climate, clean water and good natural dyes) was recognized as far away as Europe. Indeed the English even tried to obtain the trade secrets of the Persian dyers. Richard Hakluyt gave instructions to Morgan Hubblethorne, Dyer, when he was sent to Persia in 1579 to learn everything about the Persian art of dyeing to improve the market for British cloth. « In Persia you shall finde carpets of course thrummed wooll, the best of the world, and excellent coloured: those cities & townes you must repaire to, and you must use meanes to learne all the order of the dying of those thrummes, which are so died as neither raine, wine, nor yet vinegar can staine: and if you may attaine to that cunning, you shall not need to feare dying of cloth: For if the colour holde in yarne and thrumme, it will holde much better in cloth.

1100. Hoeltzer, p. 21; 100 *rangraz* in Tabriz in 1869 (Shafi' Javadi, p. 228).

1101. Tahvildar, p. 117-118.

1102. Janab, p. 78.

1103. Tahvildar, p. 93. The rolling shafts (*chubeh*) used by the dyers in Isfahan were imported from Azerbaijan, on which local taxes had to be paid (*ibid.*, p. 124).

1104. Esfahani [*Ketab*], p. 79.

4. For that in Persia they have great colouring of silks, it behooves you to learne that also, for that cloth dying & silke dying have certaine affinity, and your merchants mind to bring much raw silke into the Realme, and therefore it is more requisit you learne the same.

5. In Persia there are that staine linnen cloth: it is not amisse you learne it if you can: it hath bene an olde trade in England, whereof some excellent clothes yet remaine: but the arte is now lost, and not to be found in the Realme »[1105].

He was further instructed to learn the same in Russia or from Chinese dyers present in Persia. Also to procure the herb for aniline, « either by seed or by plant » to take it the England to learn how to make it. Also, « make daily trials in your arte, as you shall from time to time learne ought among them ». He had to write down in detail what he would learn so that he would not forget, for if he would die, the information would be lost.

The same favorable situation still existed in the 19th century. However, by 1860, natural dyes were being substituted by chemical dyes by more than 50%. According to Blau, « All fabrics [silk, cotton, wool] were either dyed as a piece, or its yarns were dyed. The dye industry for silk and wool was concentrated where the weaving industries were. In Azerbeijan, cotton dyeing was mostly done on the banks of the Adschi Tschai, which runs through Tabriz; or in Disa Halil and Dehikurgan as well as Nasly Chay and Shahir Su in the Urmiya area. Also in Tesuj and Dilman. Their main occupation is the dyeing of imported British and Swiss long shirts, white and grey shirtings, which are known as tela americana, though local cottons are also dyed. These are imported undyed and are only dyed in Persia. Persians prefer fabrics dyed in Persia, efforts to import dyed cottons have failed. Also, because dyeing in and around Tabriz is cheaper than in Europe. The most universal color, in Persia, the Russian provinces and Bokhara, is hell blue, which is made with indigo ».

Cost of dyeing in Tabriz in the summer of 1857

	width (inches)	length (yards)	price (per piece)
long cloths	39-39	36	5
shirtings *chalvar*	36-38	40	4
shirtings	18	40	4
T shirtings	32-40	24	2

Source: Blau, p. 112.

1105. Hakluyt, II, p. 202-203.

The prices were lower if large quantities were involved. Even at these prices the dyers made a considerable profit. For example, Malek Qasem Mirza, founder and owner of a dyeing factory in Urmiya, employing 18 people, paid 200 tomans per year in rent[1106].

The cost of dyeing had increased considerably 40 years later (or it reflects another location's condition) for the cost were 10 shahis per yard in 1894 in Yazd[1107].

According to Hoeltzer the process of textile printing, as observed in Isfahan in the 1870s, was as follows:

- The undyed fabric is soaked for three days in a warm liquid of sheep stomachs, after which it is well washed.

- Then the fabrics are dipped in a watery liquid of *hellilah siyah* (*Myrobalanum nigrae*) and then dried.

- Now the various colors can be applied to the fabric, which are colorfast. First the black print made of ferrous sulfate, mixed with iron and gum resin.

- Then red dye made of red earth from a nearby village, mixed with *Myrobalanum*, hot oil and alum.

- Then the fabrics are well washed in the river, and boiled twice in a big copper vessel with *runusa* (*Rubia tinctoria*). Then washed again in a liquid made of cowdung and then bleached for as long as it takes the red dye to look white again.

- The fabrics go to the indigo dyer (*nilkesh*) who makes blue, mixed with *nil* and yellow and *Myrobalanum*. Then the fabric is dipped into tanning water (*ab-e kahleh*) and then quickly and thorougly washed in ordinary water. If it remains too long then the indigo and the other dyes run through one another. Per *tup* one needs 15 methqals of *nil* or indigo[1108].

All dyes were printed one after another on the areas that had been drawn onto the fabric beforehand. The block patterns were made out of pear tree wood and walnut tree wood and were used with a leather band attached to the hand for short runs, and attached to the lower arm for long runs. The entire process lasted from one to three months, according to the weather.

1106. Blau, p. 112-113.

1107. DCR 1662 (1894-5), p. 29.

1108. Hoeltzer, p. 43-44; see Gluck and Gluck p. 192 for a description of the dyeing process. « The runah tree of Yazd supplies the red color, the green color is realized by using the skins of grenades or *pusht-e anar*, also black, both made with water in which *sang-e ahan* or iron has been laying for one month » (Brugsch, II, p. 46).

« The dyer in Persia drives a roaring trade, as the cotton cloth, shirting, or long cloth, as the case may be, is often bought and afterwards dyed. The dyer, or rangraz, may always be known by his arms, which are stained a deep blue, or other colour, generally blue, as indigo is most used; all the shulwar [trousers] of the men and veils of the women, and most of the shirts of the lower orders, being dyed fast by indigo. The Persians dislike dyes that are not fast, as the analine, and prefer the old ones such as madder and indigo »[1109]. In Western Iran (Kurdistan), dyeing was often performed by Jews, because it was one of the dirty jobs in which they were permit to make a living. Mrs. Bishop remarks « the solitary Jew dyer, who, with his family, is found in all the larger villages on this route »[1110].

« There is a very large dyeing trade carried on [in Isfahan]. Two bazaars alone are occupied by the Guild of Dyers. They are chiefly employed in converting white shirtings, etc. into those sombre cloths which are so affected by the Persian ladies in their outdoor costumes. They also dye muslins to various tints of blue or light green, for the use of the descendants of the Prophet, who use them either as a turban or Kamar band [belt] »[1111]. « The nil dyers get as black as crows, because when stirring the large copper vat with long sticks and hop around it while squatting and at the least breeze they are covered by the smoke that leaves the small chimney of the hut that they working in. One needs good lungs to work there for a long time »[1112].

The printed pieces are practically never prepared for retail in the piece or for sale by the yard, but only in single articles, such as handkerchiefs, curtains, etc. or in made-up lengths suitable for various garments[1113].

• ***Sandalbaf*** was a thin cotton with narrow strips, maybe with the warps and wefts equally exposed. *Sandalbaf* was 21-28 inches (53.3-71.1 cm) wide and there as only 55-86 inches (1.42-2.13 m) to the piece. One kind of

1109. Wills, p. 190-191; see also Wulff, p. 193-194.

1110. Bird, II, p. 198, also p. 207.

1111. DCR 1376, p. 49; see also Gaube and Wirth who mention a *bazar-e sabbaghan* (p. 178) and two *bazar-e rangraz* (p. 179-180); also a *saraye-nilchi* (p. 180). « Heavy cottons of village make and unbleached cottons of Manchester make being brought here to be dyed and printed » (Bird, II, p. 258).

1112. Hoeltzer, p. 43.

1113. Gleadowe-Newcomen, p. 71.

burmet was evidently similar in weave for it was called *sendal*, probably a variant of the same term[1114].

• ***Saqerlat*** (also *sakkalat*, *soqralat*) was a sackcloth or an English broadcloth[1115]. Usually red in color, though blue is also recorded[1116]. It was used for making trousers, *taj* and boots during the Safavid period[1117].

• ***Sarbaw*** is a fabric with either golden stripes or flowers. Its length was 5.5 to 7.5 arshins, while its width was not fixed[1118]. *Sarbaw kurschaki* were gold lace braid and trimmings. Its length and width were all different. It was made in Kashan[1119].

• ***Sekkehduz*** or sewing different fabrics together and decorating this with mirror work, shells, and coins, and probably lining it with felt[1120].

• ***Selselehduzi***, see *patehduzi*.

• ***Sha'rbaf***, with many variant forms in European languages, was a term widely used for various kinds of Persian silk[1121]. Damask or *sha'rbaf* was made in large quantities in Yazd and Kashan, in lengths of 5,75-6 covids, in 0.75 covid wide and in all colors and prices. But it was not as good as European products[1122]. This variety of fabrics indicates that *sha'rbafi* was a generic term to refer to the weaving of expensive silken fabrics[1123].

According to Ackerman « The poorest quality of "isorbaff" is designated as "tschergat" [...] which is simply the same word as *sherbaff* with an Indian suffix substituted for the Persian », which is wrong.

1114. Pope and Ackerman, vol. 3, p. 2167.
1115. *Hobson-Jobson*, p. 861.
1116. [*'Alamara-ye Safavi*], p. 30 : *saqerlat-e sorkh*; Qomi, I, p. 442 : *saqerlat-e kabud.*
1117. *Chekmehha-ye saqerlat-e qermez* (Khʷondamir, IV, p. 474). It was the stuff the *taj-e heidari* was made of (*ibid.*, p. 426-427); see also chapter IV. Astarabadi, p. 26; Asef, p. 89, 159, 369, 382; Monshi, I, p. 19.
1118. Gmelin, III, p. 415-420.
1119. *Ibid.*, p. 420.
1120. Gluck and Gluck, p. 258 (and p. 254-255 for examples); Zarrabi, p. 273.
1121. Tahvildar, p. 102.
1122. Ferrier [An English View], p. 199.
1123. Sharifzadeh [Sha'rbafi], p. 55.

Undoubtedly, "tschergat" refers to the Persian word *charqad*. « The richest grade of *isorbaff* [*shar'baf*] is called *dyby*, and this was made also in Kashan. *Dyby* [*diba*] or *dibaj* orginally meant a moiré silk, but the term was also used to denote any very rich fabric »[1124]. *Diba* is mentioned as a Persian textile product from the early Safavid period onwards[1125].

Silken fabrics were woven, seldom single-colored, but mostly striped or flamed around 1900[1126]. « That known as Husein Kuli Khan, after its originator, who was a native of Kerman, consists of a fir-cone pattern on a plum-coloured ground, and is far from cheap, costing about 7s.6d. per yard. The other silks are not particularly pleasing, and are mainly used for linings »[1127].

In Isfahan the group of *sha'rbaf* or silk weavers constituted a guild. « This guild uses silk as their raw material and their work is approximately the same as that of the weavers who use cotton. They were a large group whose number and looms as well as their profits were not less than those of the weavers. What has been said about the weavers is completely applicable to them. Their products were used both in the country and abroad. The decline of this guild is worse than that of other guilds, nay it has even completely gone to pieces, and there are now only a few of them left. It is said that they were very numerous in the times of the Safavid kings, and that during the reign of the late *khaqan* [Fath 'Ali Shah, 1799-1834] there were 1250 looms. During the reign of the late Shahinshah [Mohammad Shah, 1834-1848] there were 460 manufacturies [*kar-khaneh*], in the beginning of this eternal empire 249, which now have been reduced to 12. The products of the abovementioned guild are: damask of several colors, *dara'i* of all qualities, [silk] cloth such as *halab*, *kord*, *qasab*, *alicheh*, *shal*, *abrishami* and the like. Formerly, besides those in Persia, they had customers in Turkey and Russia, but now their product is very little in demand »[1128]. There were still 100 of them in 1920[1129].

1124. Pope and Ackerman, III, p. 2172.

1125. See sections on 16th, 17th, and 18th century in chapter II; see also Asef, p. 89, 407, 441.

1126. Kuss, p. 147.

1127. Sykes [*Ten Thousand*], p. 423.

1128. Tahvildar, p. 102; Zarrabi, p. 227, 239.

1129. Janab, p. 78.

• ***Shelleh*** was twilled English cotton cloth, which came in various colors (red or *goli* and black or *meshki*) as well as multi-colored (*alvan*). Usually it was imported in wide bolts of 50 yards[1130].

• ***Shir-panir*** was woven in the Caspian provinces using cotton and waste silk. According to Abbott it was a narrow cloth (13 to 15 inches), always 17 feet long and used for shirts. Its price was 2.5 sahebqrans per piece[1131]. McKenzie agrees on the width (he mentions 13 inches) but differs on the length quite dramaticallly: just over 50 yards if unmixed with silk, but only 7 foot long when silk is incorporated[1132].

• ***Siyahakduzi*** probably is the same as *siyahduzi,* a black button hole-stitch edging forming spaced triangles[1133].

• ***Suf*** a woolen cloth used to make garments[1134].

• ***Sokmehduzi,*** or drawn work « is patiently worked in fine linen table cloths, napkins, lamp shades and doyleys. It involves drawing out certain weft and/or warp threads in a given area. After drawing the required number of threads, embroidery stitches are taken to fill the open spaces thus created with lacy looking embroidery which at the same time binds the loosened warps and wefts into a definite pattern. The junction where the threads are cut is carefully "held" by various stitches »[1135].

In Isfahan the group of the *sokmehduz* formed a guild. « They are those men and women, who make the open-worked part of women's face veils [*shabikeh-ye ruband*]. Their number has remained the same as before », i.e. they did not suffer too much from the foreign imports[1136].

• ***Shudmali*** is the synonym of the *aharzan*, i.e. the starcher, he who made the size (*ahar*) and prepared and applied the starch which was made from a

1130. Amanat, p. 108; Rabino [Kermanshah], p. 67.
1131. Amanat, p. 24.
1132. McKenzie, p. 215.
1133. Zarrabi, p. 273; see also *khamakduzi* (q.v.)
1134. Zarrabi, p. 227-228, 249.
1135. Gluck and Gluck, p. 22.
1136. Tahvildar, p. 100. This craft was referred to as *shabekeh duz* in Kashan (Zarrabi, p. 273).

boiled mixture of wheatmeal and bran[1137]. In Yazd, this craft was carried out in a *shumal-khaneh* or starcher's hall in the 17th century[1138].

• ***Suzani***, see *golduzi*.

• ***Tafsileh*** was a fabric used to make surcoats or *qabas*. In the 16th century, Yazd is named as a production center[1139], while in the 17th century it was produced in Yazd, Kashan and Gilan[1140].

• ***Tafteh*** or taffeta, was a silken fabric. We hardly have any data on *tafteh* production in the early Safavid period. In fact, only an imported product *tafteh-ye shami* is mentioned[1141]. This may have been caused by the fact that « Cloth painted with flowers and other taftehs, those they call Indian cloaths, because most of them are made in the Indies, nevertheless, a great many are also made in Persia and other paints are stamped upon them with a mould besmeared with colours »[1142]. In 1618, the English report that « Tafetas are made in great quantities, long 6.75 yards per piece, wide 0.75 yard less 2 inches. Those of Yazd are worth 48 shahis. In addition, other kinds of silken stuffs were made, which were as good as any European lustred taffeta, although they are more watered, i.e. moiré. They are of light and pleasing colors, long 5.5-6 covids and wide 26 inches. They cannot make them changeable, i.e. shot silks. Their value is 40-48 shahis per piece, none are in "grayne" [a fast scarlet dye in the wool before making up into cloth], crimson and carnation »[1143].

The EIC staff reported that taffetas were mostly made in Yazd and Kashan and only this fabric was of interest and comparable to European standards, « beinge as good in my oppinion as any lustre taffeties of Christendome onely they are sumwhat more watered, of light and pleasing Colors, leangth about 5,5 and 6 Coveds, bredth 126 inches of a yard, they

---

1137. Wulff, p. 196; Afshar [*Yadgarha*], p. 143, 346, and *shumal-khaneh*, p. 630. see also Ja'fari, p. 118 and 'Ali-ye Kateb, p. 192.

1138. Afshar [*Yadgarha*], p. 630.

1139. [*'Alamara-ye Shah Tahmasp*], p. 410.

1140. Gaube and Wirth, p. 266-267; p. 282-283; p. 282-283. Dunlop, p. 78.

1141. [*'Alamara-ye Shah Tahmasp*], p. 401, 421.

1142. Thévenot, II, p. 94.

1143. Ferrier [An English View], p. 201. For a picture see Bier, p. 160.

have not the arte to make changeable, worth 40:44:46 Shahees a peece, none in grayne, Crimsone and Carnatione excelent good colors »[1144].

Another kind of floral brocade is referred to as "Rassuly" (*rasuli*). A typical Shah 'Abbas taffeta brocaded with large rose trees which passed through the Isfahan market carried the weaver's signature "Raisul", and this name became associated with the whole type[1145].

In the early Qajar period, Fraser observes that « tafetas, a fabric similar to, but stouter than the same stuff with us, in size and price is the same as the aleejahs »[1146]. Consul Abbott, some 20 years later, made rather detailed remarks on this fabric. « Tafteh is a manufacture of pure silk, of various shapes and measures. It is used for women's scarfs and shirts. Those of Barforush measuring 3 yards 15 inches by 31 inches when divided into two pieces and sown together for women's scarfs sell for 10 to 15 sahibqran per scarf. Other plain silks mixed with cotton used for riding dresses, etc. measuring 5 yards and 25 inches by 18 inches 5 to 7 sahibqrans per piece. Ditto, 6 yards and 30 inches by 18 inches sell at 6-8 sahibqrans per piece »[1147]. In Astarabad it was of plain silk, 18 inches wide and white of color. Per Persian yard of 42 inches it sold at 1 sahibqran per piece. If colored, at 1.25 to 1.5 sahibqran per piece[1148]. According to McKenzie, taffeta was silken fabric, of various sizes, used by women for head dress and shirt[1149].

According to Polak, around 1860, « tafta or kaenavis are best produced smooth in Mashhad and Kashan and in motley squares in Yazd and Isfahan to serve a bed covers, and in Gilan as door curtain [*pardeh*] »[1150]. In Yazd, *tafteh* of 109 cm wide was sold at 4 tomans per meter. Also, moiré, 0,75 m wide, and sold at 2-9 tomans per meter.[1151].

They were still produced at the beginning of this century. Although durable, their quality was not very high and the fabrics were very coarse, so

1144. Ferrier [*British-Persian Relations*], p. 354-5 quoting E/3/6/699. For a picture see Bier, p. 241.

1145. Pope and Ackerman, III, p. 2131 and plate 1046, and p. 2171.

1146. Fraser [*Caspian Sea*], p. 361.

1147. Amanat, p. 24.

1148. *Ibid.*, p. 25.

1149. McKenzie, p. 215.

1150. Polak [*Persien*], II, p. 172; also produced in Kashan, Zarrabi, p. 381.

1151. MAE, Rochechouart to Gobineau, Yezd, 26/10/1862, see figures 1 and 7 in the same letter.

that one would not say they had been woven with silk. Many varieties were made, of which the moiré and the colored moirés were used to make door covers or so-called *pardeh-ye dara'i*, very much appreciated. Moiré and popeline varieties, mixing silk and wool, were also manufactured[1152].

• ***Taftik*** is the Turkish name for the fine goat hair and the cloth woven from it. It came mainly from Khorasan and Kerman[1153].

• ***Termeh-nama*** was a kind of look-alike silken shawl, or imitation *termeh*. In 1858, Blau reports that « nowadays [*termeh-nama* is] all produced with half silk, mixed with cotton »[1154]. It was exported to India and Turkey around 1850. According to Brugsch *termeh-nama* was a silken fabric with a figured weave of shawl-like patterns which was not durable, although it was well liked by the public[1155]. First quality *termeh-nama*, made in Isfahan, was sold at 6 qrans per arshin in July 1857 in Tabriz. A lower quality sold at 4 qrans[1156].

• ***Tikehduzi*** or appliqué work constituted various elements of the designs, i.e. different colors for petals of flowers, feathers of birds. This chain stitch is on velvet or leather saddle cloths, cushion covers, table covers, wall hangings, bed covers and garments. This has traditionally been men's work and still is[1157].

• ***Utu-kesh*** or « ironer, is employed to ornamentally iron the dresses of the lower orders that are made of coloured calico or longcloth. This he does by ironing a pattern upon them with the edges of his iron, generally a box-iron filled with charcoal; often, however, merely a heated rod. He irons

---

1152. Rabino and Lafont, p. 171-172.

1153. See chapter VI.

1154. Blau, p. 109.

1155. Amanat, p. 109, 114; Blau, p. 109. Brugsch, II, p. 90 says about the *termeh-nama* that it was a silken fabric with a figured weave of shawl-like patterns which was not durable, although it was well liked by the public. It may already have been manufactured in the 1830s, Stuart (p. 226) mentions that Kerman shawls and "Tirmalaman" (error for *termeh-nama* or simply for *termeh*?) are really to be admired.

1156. Blau, p. 121 (July 1857, Tabriz).

1157. Gluck and Gluck, p. 218.

upon a large jar, which he holds between his knees. He also marks the stuffs that are to be quilted for under-garments »[1158].

• ***Vatanibaf*** was silk weaver. In 1298/1919, in Kashan, only 750 *vatanibafs* were left. They were part of the *sha'rbaf* group[1159].

• ***Zanjirehbaf*** or string weavers constituted a guild in Isfahan. « They weave *zanjir* [strings] of goldlace for women's clothes »[1160]. There were only 6 of them left in 1920. There were also 6 string sellers[1161].

• ***Zarbaft*** or gold brocaded fabrics were already made prior to the Safavid dynasty. The same holds for *noqrehbaft* or silver brocade. This explains why its use is already mentioned during the early years of Safavid rule[1162].

The metal yarns used in these fabrics are mainly of silver, or silver with a thin layer of gold (see *zarkesh*). *Zari*, or metal-thread enriched silks, occur throughout the Safavid - Qajar period. Sometimes the term refers to the fact that fabrics were enriched with gold, silver, tinsel or all of them. Sometimes it referred to the fact that a costly fabric such as *diba* had either a silver or a gold ground and the flowers were in silk or silk together with the other metal not used in the ground[1163].

In 1618, the English report that « Cloth of gold and silver was made in Isfahan, Kashan, Khorasan and other parts. Its price was 200 shahis to 2000 shahis depending on its quality per piece of 7 yards. Plain was not to be had, but wrought in silk variety »[1164]. According to Chardin gold brocade (*zarbaft*) was the most expensive fabric in the world, costing up to 50 tomans per gez (70 cm). Ordinary *zarbaft* came in about 100 varieties, but the real luxury items were *zarbaft-e do ruy*, or two-faced gold brocade, so called because it had no reverse side, as well as (*zarbaft-e*) *makhmal* or gold velvet[1165]. In Persian texts the following varieties of *zarbaft* are

---

1158. Wills, p. 191.
1159. Naraqi, p. 276.
1160. Tahvildar, p. 102.
1161. Janab, p. 78.
1162. [*'Alamara-ye Shah Tahmasp*], p. 408, 410. Also, *zarbaft-e chin* (Khwondamir, IV, p. 83). In addition to *zarbaft* there was also *zartar* (Sepehr, III, p. 164).
1163. Pope and Ackerman, III, p. 2173.
1164. Ferrier [An English View], p. 202.
1165. Chardin, IV, p. 152-156.

mentioned. Although their number is far short of the 100 varieties mentioned by Chardin these few items show the great sophistication and variety of the *zarbaft* weavers' output. We find, for example, *zarbaft-e dasti*, *zarbaft-e talabaft* (gold embroidery on a golden fond), *zarbaft-e noqrehbaft* (gold embroidery on a silver fond), *zarbaft-e mahamarat-e talabaft* (gold embroidery on striped golden fond), *zarbaft-e mahamarat-e noqrehbaft* (striped silver fond), *atlas-e zarbaft-e noqrehbaft* (mixed silver or gold-silver brocade on *atlas*), *dara'i-ye zarbaft-e yazdi-ye talabaft va noqrehbaft*. These costly textiles were mentioned within the context of a list of presents given to Ottoman prime-ministers[1166].To produce these costly fabrics six weavers worked at the same time at the loom, using as many as 24 to 30 shuttles instead of the usual two to make the intricate patterns. Persian weavers also had developed a technique to press gold and silver on cloth, taffetas and satins to which end they used moulds. The results were such that the final product looked as if it were gold brocade[1167]. Olearius notes that most artisans are weavers and dyers or flower painters on cotton and silk as well as producers of gold cloth of a maximum length of 10-12 ells which is the right size for making a Persian coat[1168].

Della Valle observes that in Kashan the silk weavers produced three types of silk fabrics. The first kind were long wide sashes for men which were wound four times around the body and into which sometimes gold, stripes and delicate leaf and flower patterns were woven. The second type, called *milek*, resembled the first type, and was called in Naples « toiles Indiennes à deux envers » or reversible materials, but it was much more beautiful. The *milek* fabric was embellished with all kinds of intricate designs, and even entire Persian verses and inscriptions and figures such as men and women and animals. The third type of fabric, called *zarbaft* or *milek-e zarbaf*, only differed from the two other types of fabrics in that it was made with silk interwoven with gold and silver wire. The latter was used for women's garments, cushions, bed curtains and similar domestic uses[1169]. « The richest manufacture of Isfahan is the *zari* or brocade. They do not equal the *kincobs* of India or the goldstuffs of France. They are used for making *khel'ats*. A piece of 0.75 dhar' wide and 5 dhar' long costs 5-10

1166. Nasiri, p. 100; Nava'i, p. 87.

1167. Chardin, IV, p. 152-156.

1168. Olearius, p. 601.

1169. Della Valle [*Voyages*], II, p. 199-200. Floral *milek* is also mentioned by Visnich in 1623 (Dunlop, p. 78); see also Monshi, II, p. 775 (see *khel'at*, q.v.).

tomans »[1170]. By 1858, brocades were all produced with half silk, mixed with cotton[1171]. Around 1860, brocades were only woven in Kashan, the so-called *zarbaft*, with woven golden flowers but, according to Polak, nowhere the near the once so famous brocades[1172].

However, Isfahan continued to be a center of *zarbaft* production as well. In fact, in Isfahan, the brocade weavers (*zaribaf*) formed a guild. « Formerly, gold brocade weaving was very widespread and gold brocade was one of the high quality cloths in Persia. The elegant golden clothes of the nobles and princes and the precious royal robes of honour came especially from Isfahan. It is an art in which the Europeans have not been able till now to achieve the perfection of the Isfahan [work]. The gold brocade which since the time of Shah 'Abbas [I] Safavi till now has been loosing its gold, still retains its design. master painters admit their inability to imitate this design and method, and say that nowadays master painters are not able to imitate this style, let alone the weavers. Now this guild and its craft have been ruined and fallen into disuse and its craftmen are insignificant and its production is small. What buyers there are come from foreign countries. In Persia it is very little used indeed »[1173].

Mostaufi recounts that so-called *zari-ye naseri-ye goli* was woven in Isfahan. Mirza Fath Ali Khan Sahebqeran, when he was governor of Isfahan, favored this fabric, and as part of the New Year's gift to the shah he sent some of this *zari*. To distinguish it from *zari-ye gujarati* it was called *zari-ye naseri*. Its silken ground was neutral and somewhat thinner or thicker, but not inferior to the Gujarat variety. « The *zari* bought for my *qaba* had golden flowers in between *khaneh-ye masdas*. The color of the flowers and their ground was *barq* [flashy], very beautiful, and the choicest fabric of its day »[1174]. However, according E'temad al-Saltaneh, this fabric was promoted by Naser al-Din Shah and his son Zell al-Soltan, governor of Isfahan. The Shah is reputed also to have promoted the weaving of velvet (*makhmalbafi*) and of silk (*harirbafi*) in Kashan and Tabriz, as well as the weaving of Kashmir-type shawls in Mashhad[1175].

1170. Morier [*Second Journey*], p. 155.
1171. Blau, p. 109.
1172. Polak [*Persien*], II, p. 17.
1173. Tahvildar, p. 97.
1174. Mostaufi, I, p. 510.
1175. E'temad al-Saltaneh, p. 101.

The so-called *zari-ye qalebi*, or gold brocade made to the buyers's form and shape, also found a ready market where *zari* was still used for the official dress as well as other outdoor garments[1176].

• ***Zarkesh*** or « the Gold Wire-Drawers and Thread-Twisters, are very dextrous Workmen. They draw an Ingot, weighing a Mescal, or Drachm, nine hundred Guezes, or Persian Ells long, each Guez being five and thirty Inches long. Their Tools of several sizes, are like our Wire-drawing Irons: They wind on Bobins and Drums, and buy at the Mint, the small Wire of the bigness of a Pin: Their Thread is the best and the smoothest that can be imagined. All the Art they use to give it that lively and lasting Colour, is to guild the Wire very fine and very thick »[1177]. This description by Chardin is borne out by what modern technical studies have revealed about the use of metal yarns in Safavid textiles. « Based on microscopic analysis, the strips seem to have been made in one of two ways: by hammering two layers of foil together and then cutting the result into strip, or by drawing metal wire into fine diameters and then flattening them by rollers »[1178].

In Isfahan, where the *zarkesh* formed a guild in the 19th century, « formerly, when the weaving of gold brocade [*zari*] was important, gold wire drawing was also esteemed. The gold wire drawing craft is one of the better professions Isfahan has produced. They have sophisticated equipment and very precise instruments. The precision which they had attained in former times was such that they made 1200 dhar‘ [1200 meters] gold lace [*golabtun*] out of one methqal [4.6 gram] of gold. Now the same would be possible if only there would be customers »[1179]. The same situation held for the *simkesh* or silver wire drawers. There had been many of them when demand for *naqdehduzi*, *golabtun* and *dah-yek* cloth had been high, and silver and gold wire had been woven together. By 1870, only a few of these craftsmen were left[1180].

• ***Zilu*** was a flat-weave floor covering (similar to *gelim* or *jajim*) which was made of cotton or silk, or a combination of both. It was produced especially in the Yazd area, although it was used beyond its location of

1176. Zarrabi, p. 227-228, 250, 381.
1177. Chardin, IV, p. 131.
1178. Hardin and Duffied, quoted in Bier, p. 171.
1179. Tahvildar, p. 97.
1180. *Ibid.*

manufacture[1181]. In 1893, it is reported that « A good quantity of twist was locally produced and mixed with that imported from India in the making of *zilu*, a carpet made solely in Yazd and its districts »[1182]. Nowadays, the *zilu* is described as a flat-stitch carpet, made principally for mosques[1183].

1181. Khʷondamir, IV, p. 219, mentions *zilucheha-ye abrishamin*; Bafqi, III, part 1, p. 171, in Yazd. For a discussion and much detail on the occurrence of the *zilu* prior to the Safavid era see Afshar [Zilu], p. 31-36.

1182. DCR 1376 (1894), p. 20.

1183. Gluck and Gluck, p. 276.

IV. The Persian Dress, 16th-19th Centuries

So far attempts to describe Persian dress during the Safavid and Qajar periods have been very incomplete. Few contemporary Persian sources have been consulted and even where European ones are concerned attention has been focussed on but a limited number[1184]. As for miniatures, their study to date has been haphazard and, so far, without systemic analysis. The result, therefore, is that the picture of the variety and development of Persian dress is still in its early stages. This point is also being made, *ex silencio*, by the paucity, and the sometimes erroneous nature of, information offered in the articles "*Libas* - Iran" in the *Encyclopedia of Islam* and "Clothes - Safavid, Qajar period" in the *Encyclopaedia Iranica.* Here an attempt will be made to bring our knowledge a step further. The information offered here is based solely on the study of Persian texts and European travelogues. Unfortunately, I was unable to make a study of contemporary miniatures and surviving artifacts, or to interest an art historian to participate in this multi-disciplinary endeavor, which, undoubtedly, would have yielded additional information on details and trends in fashion. This is for example clear from a recent study on Iranian headdesses, which however is not detailed and elaborate enough in its use of miniatures and very liited in its use of written source material. Nevertheless, the study has the merit that it shows that there xas a great variety in headdress, or the manner in which a turban was folded[1185]

For convenience the material is presented in five sections: 1. the 16th century; 2. the 17th-18th century; 3. the Afsharid period; 4. the Zand period and 5. the Qajar period. Each section is further divided into seven sub-sections (headwear; shirts; outer garments; trousers; socks; shoes and other items), and the whole is followed by a section on the "*taj*" and another on the "*khel'at*". Within each sub-section priority is given to mens wear, since most material refers to this, followed by comments where applicable on women's clothing and the clothing of the poor. With a few exceptions, mainly in respect of the rural poor, the material relates to prosperous Moslem urban dwellers. Although the texts used include some information

1184. A recent example is given by Shari'at-Niya [*Orupa'iha*].
1185. Shahanshahi [*Tarikhcheh*].

of minorities (Armenians, Zoroastrians) I have decided not to include that due to the incomplete nature of the available material.

Although Persian dress was relatively simple and Chardin remarked that since Timur's time early Safavid dress had not changed we will see that there was some change nevertheless[1186]. There was also clearly identifiable social stratification in dress. This was not only evident from the costliness of materials used, but also from choice in cut and type of garments chosen. « The dress of the men of the sword is quite different from what is worn by the men of the robe »[1187]. There was, for example, also something like merchants dress or *lebas-e tajer*[1188]. There also existed distinct regional dress that even foreign observers were able to distinguish from the "normal" Persian dress. Della Valle reports that Shah 'Abbas' I pages were all dressed « in the garb of Mazandaran, namely long, stretched stockings, like those of Pantaloon in the comedies, and a gown (or whatever we would call it) half-way down the thighs, tight-fitted to the chest, with a large flap hanging down from the waist down over the stockings, serving simultaneously as a great coat and a cassock »[1189]. Further mention is made of Armenian, Georgian, Zoroastrian and Kurdish dress or pieces thereof, while we will see that dress in the Persian Gulf area differed from the rest of the country. Mention is also made of darvish clothes, *lebas-e darvishi*[1190], of beggars clothes or *lebas-e geda'i*[1191], and of praying clothes or *lebas-e namazi*[1192].

Historical evolution

Safavid period

• *16th century*

Because we have very few contemporary sources that describe Safavid dress during the 16th century, and because Persian texts, as usual, are

---

1186. See for similar remarks, Bier, p. 215-216.

1187. Le Bruyn, I, p. 212. The habit of the most considerable of the men of the robe is in plate 86.

1188. [*'Alamara-ye Shah Esma'il*], p. 87.

1189. Della Valle [*Voyages*], II, p. 202.

1190. Qomi, I, p. 273. *pashmineh-push* or *sufi* (Bafqi, III, part 1, p. 87).

1191. *Ibid.*, I, p. 173.

1192. *Ibid.*, p. 306. The Chagatay cavalry was referred to as *abchin-push* or dressed in towels of the washers of the dead (*ibid.*, p. 169).

mostly silent on thc subject, miniatures provide most of the information to fill our knowledge gap for that period.

The most striking and beautiful part of Safavid male garments was the head dress. This was due to its gaudiness and not to the fact that one could recognize people's "ethnicity" as in Turkey, according to Chardin. However, there are indications (which seem to be borne out by what we know about later periods) that some groups or areas in Persia were characterized by a headdress peculiar to them.

Safavid dress was loose fitting. Membré comments: « Their clothes are not tight like those of the Ottomans, but wide, as if they are wearing paigiami [pyjamas] »[1193]. Early Safavid dress was also rich in its use of colors and costliness of fabrics. This was enhanced by the use of silver and gold metal enriched fabrics as well as by their elaborate designs and patterns. They also wore layers of garments in striking variations of colors and patterns[1194]. Contemporary Italian visitors commented on the richness of early Safavid dress[1195]. Finally, Persian texts state that the emirs were all dressed in gold brocade (*zarbaft-push*) or in velvet and silk (*makhmal-push*, *diba-push*) garments, with gem-studded swords, daggers and belts[1196].

Scarce suggests that in early Safavid dress « jewelry, apart from the clasps and mounts of belts and weapons, was relatively discreet, usually little more than a pair of gold hoop pierced earrings and an occasional gold ring on thumb or fourth finger »[1197]. If we leave aside the *khel'at*, which was a very costly garment, we notice that Persian sources maintain that the dress of Safavid dignitaries was a veritable display of wealth and not discreet at all. Shah Esma'il I, for example, put the *taj-e Joneid* on Soltan Morad's head and gave him proper *Qezelbash* clothing (*lebas-e khub-e qezelbash*), which meant *morassa'-push* or gem-studded[1198]. Also very costly *bazubands* or arm clasps of great value were worn[1199]. Another text states that « everybody, Turk, Persian, or Georgian, was dressed in golden

1193. Membré, p. 30-31. English translation, see Morton, p. 27.

1194. Scarce [Vesture], p. 35.

1195. *Barbaro and Contarini*, II, p. 172, « There are robes of silk; some of crimson cloth, velvet, and cloth of gold, according to the condition of the wearer ».

1196. [*'Alamara-ye Shah Esma'il*], p. 146; Afshar [*'Alamara*] p. 249-50.

1197. Scarce [Vesture], p. 38.

1198. [*'Alamara-ye Shah Esma'il*], p. 510.

1199. *Ibid.*, p. 382; [*'Alamara-ye Safavi*], p. 197, 199.

garments or *taskpush* »[1200]. Tenreiro noted that « the men wore their best garments that they have, to wit: cabayas of silk, robes of velvet, and scarlet, and violet cloths; and those that who lack silk, [dress] with very fine quilted white and blue linen, and lined blue cloaks of [or from] London, leggings upon draws of cloth, likewise blue ». He further remarked that « They make a good impression and dress in satins, from which they make their quilted garments, and [with] cloth of scarlet-in-grain in their cloaks, with many and rich frogs of gold, and with silk, and with very noble linings, which are worth much in this land » [1201]. Membré writes that the courtiers were dressed in velvet and brocade, wore swords with golden handles and sheaths while their garments, and above all their head gear, were dressed up with turquoises and rubies[1202].

Those not belonging to the leading class of Safavid society were dressed more soberly, but not necessarily cheaply. The English merchant Edwards reports in 1566, that « the people are given much to weare cloth: the common people specially weare karseis, and the merchants of more wealth weare broad cloth ». « He also wished for good velvets and chamlets [...] because these are most worne»[1203]. As to the kind of cloth worn by Persians, Edwards comments that « here is much Venice cloth worne, being cromplisted [*sic*] a yard and a halfe broad, and sold here from 24. to 30. shaughes their arshine, being longer by two inches then the Russian arshine is »[1204].

Despite the preponderance of Venetian cloth, there was much « interest in London clothes [*londreh*], being well shorne and drest. [...] They talk much of London clothes and they know the wearing, are desirous of them before the cloth of the womens making, for they find it nothing durable. For when it commeth to weare on the threed, it renteth like paper »[1205]. As to the colors that Persians liked, Edwards recommended that his principals send some « Violets in graine and fine reds must be worne [...] blacks for womens garments, with some Orenge colours and tawnies »[1206]. Upper class women also had their clothes made of *aksun*, an expensive satin, that

1200. Qomi, I, p. 255.
1201. Smith, p. 75, 85; Neves Aguas, p. 169-170.
1202. Membré, p. 31.
1203. Hackluyt, II, p. 42, 40.
1204. *Ibid.*, p. 42.
1205. *Ibid.*
1206. *Ibid.*

was often black and was made in Egypt[1207]. Apart from the fact that women had to wear black when they menstruated, it was also the color of mourning[1208].

The poor wore simply *karbas*, or coarse cottons. In wintertime people wore quilted garments (*jamehha-ye panbehdar*) and cheap dressed skins (*pustin-e arzani*)[1209]. Those who wanted to appear humble, or did not want to attract attention also wore *karbas*[1210]. From an annual gift by an amir to the needy and the poor we get a good idea in what elements basic Safavid dress consisted of. He gave: 500 pieces of surcoats (*qaba*), 500 shirts (*pirahan*), 500 trousers (*zir-jameh*), 500 dressed skin coats (*pustin*), 500 slippers (*'arabi papush*), 500 felt overcoats (*kepenek*), 500 head cloths (*futeh-ye sar tartib*)[1211]. That these garments were typical for the poor is clear from the fact that Mirza Soltan Abu Sa'id, for example, said that « I took this *velayat* as a *kepenek-push* », showing how low in status he had been and how high he had risen[1212]. A coat similar to the *kepenek* was the *yapanchi*, which also was a felt cloak or great coat used to protect the wearer against the cold and rain[1213]. Tenreiro described the dress worn by Torkoman nomads in the vicinity of Lar in 1523. « They wear linen of quilted cotton and much cotton and some fitted garments reaching to the ankles. In winter they wear linings of lamb and rabbit skin » which refers to the *pustin*. Of the urban lower class in Lar he recorded that « They wear cloths of linen, with quilted cotton in winter, and in the summer they gird it about themselves, and draws, [and] shoes with points turned upwards. They are made of strips of cotton cloth, thus the pieces, as the soles, and they wear for a long time ». This description also holds for the urban population of Shiraz and Tabriz, although here the shoes were shod with many pieces of metal[1214].

1207. [*'Alamara-ye Safavi*], p. 119.

1208. Tavernier, p. 271; Qomi, I, p. 285.

1209. Astarabadi, p. 216; Qomi, I, p. 168. These skins usually were those of lambs, foxes, sheep and rabbits (Smith, p. 66, 83).

1210. [*'Alamara-ye Shah Tahmasp*], p. 124, 351.

1211. Qomi, II, p. 1051.

1212. Khʷondamir, p. 52; *kepenk* is a garment made of out felt, which the poor wore during winter (Rumlu, p. 473); A young man, *kepenk-push* (Astarabadi, p. 37). Guards dressed in felts or *namad* against the rain (Qomi, I, p. 398).

1213. Asef, p. 359; Du Mans, p. 248; Richard, II, p. 192; [*'Alamara-ye Safavi*], p. 374, 505.

1214. Smith, p. 66, 79, 81.

Male dress

Headgear

In addition to the *taj* or "crown" (about which later), Safavid males wore turbans, mostly referred to as *mandil*, and sometimes as *dastar* in Persian texts. Membré also mentions the turban, which was adorned with precious stones in the case of royal courtiers[1215]. In the case of the well-to-do, these, of course, were multi-colored and gold and/or silver brocaded[1216]. Another form of head dress referred to is the *qalansuh*, which probably was a cap with a high cone though it could also be a small cap with a slightly turned rim, notched in front. A wrap around sash was optional[1217]. During the early Safavid period the turban was first rather round; about 1530 it became narrower and higher, while finally « the length of the scarf increased rapidly, so that it became broader and broader, and at the same time very low »[1218]. It is the difference in the shape and size of the turban that is the principal difference between the early items and those of the following century about which there appear to be far more detailed records. It would therefore appear (admittedly without any hard evidence) that most of what is written in the section on the 17th century will be equally applicable to the headdress of the 16th century.

Shirt or pirahan

Safavid males wore a shirt (*pirahan*) which was worn belted over, or tucked in, a pair of long trousers (*zir-jameh*), tapered towards the ankles. It was also used as an undershirt. The under garments usually also served as bed clothes. Only the very rich seem to have worn separate night clothes such as Esma'il I who wore white garments or *lebas-e sefid* in his bed[1219]. Also, bed clothes or *lebas-e khʷabi* are mentioned during the early reign of Tahmasp I[1220].

Jacket or arkhaliq

Based on a study of a selection of 16th century miniatures, Scarce suggested that the jacket that was worn by males was close fitting and reached till just above the knees. Its sleeves tapered to the wrist and an

1215. Membré, p. 30.
1216. [*'Alamara-ye Shah Tahmasp*], p. 410, 421.
1217. Shirazi, p. 126.
1218. Goetz p. 2247.
1219. [*'Alamara-ye Shah Esma'il*], p. 621.
1220. Qomi, I, p. 177.

oblique wrapover front fastened under the right arm. « Sleeves are cut separately and joined at right angles to the center piece, from shoulder to the underarm. The wrapover front is achieved by seaming a separate piece, with obliquely cut neck, to the left front, leaving a vent from waist to hem. Underarm, sleeve, and side seams are then sewn together, leaving a short slit from mid-thigh to hem. All raw edges are faced with strips of bias-cut trim binding »[1221]. Membré mentions that Shah Tahmasp, in the morning, wore a short scarlet vest[1222]. It should be noted that the Persian vest is a piece of clothing worn between the shirt and the jacket.

Scarce's description is in agreement with descriptions of 17th century Safavid dress, but not necessarily of 16th century dress. Goetz stresses the loose and untight nature of early Safavid dress, continuing Timurid fashion. This also is borne out by Italian visitors. I have not studied the miniatures, but I would recommend that, at long last, art historians start a real systematic and all-encompassing study of these pictures rather than just haphazardly selecting a few. I understand it will be a tedious job, but somebody has to do it. Art historians cannot afford to continue to write about the subject of Persian dress without finally really tackling this and other similar issues.

Overcoat or qaba

Various overcoats were worn over this shirt and trouser ensemble. Most frequently seen was an ankle-length belted robe, with long sleeves and wrapover front. It was slit at the front from the waist to ankle and on the sides, beginning at mid-calf. « Their dress is the same as always has been - the Persian costume — wearing it open at the breast, showing their bosoms and even their bodies »[1223]. According to Goetz, however, the outercoat was shorter than the *arkhaliq*, and « was often worn open, and in many cases the sleeves were short, but when long, they were frequently allowed to hang down empty, the arm coming out through a slit in front »[1224]. This overcoat undoubtedly was the *qaba* which was worn universally[1225]. For the rich the *qaba* was, of course, made of gold brocade[1226]. The *qaba*, was wider from the waist downwards for it had both an undergarment and a

1221. Scarce [Vesture], p. 36.
1222. Membré, p. 31.
1223. *Barbaro and Contarini*, II, p. 172.
1224. Goetz, p. 2246.
1225. Qomi, I, p. 175.
1226. *Ibid.*, p. 216, *qaba-ye zarduzi* and a *mojavvazeh-ye taladuzi.*

corresponding part of the dress that fell wide from the waist, for mention is made of the use of a *zir-daman*, which was made of *tafsileh-ye Yazd*[1227], although it is believed that this type of dress was only introduced in the 17th century (see below).

Long overcoat, tekmeh and balapush

A long coat, which was optional, completed the costume. According to Scarce there were two types, all with simple front openings without wrapovers. The first type falls in a straight, unshaped line from the shoulder, interrupted only by side slits from knee to ankle. Wide, elbow length sleeves are attached separately, with the neckline either emerging smoothly into the front border or finishing with a short upstanding collar. It is usually worn belted[1228]. This may have been the *tekmeh* (see below), which in case of high ranking persons was made of *golabtun* (gold-threaded fringes) and *talabaft* (gold brocade)[1229].

The second type of coat, « worn unbelted [...] in cut and construction was similar to the first type of coat, but its exaggerated sleeve extensions are slit horizontally at mid-upper-arm level. The wearer could either insert his arms into the sleeves so as to conceal his hands, or he could simply hang the coat over his shoulders like a cloak »[1230]. This may have been a *balapush*, which often was made of velvet (*makhmal*)[1231]. In addition, there was a large overcoat with long sleeves that was probably worn in case of inclement weather[1232]

Waistband

« The girdle was at first a leather scrap with large, richly engraved metal plaques and knobs, but this was supplanted more and more by a smartly draped scarf »[1233]. This scarf or *kamarband*, of which the *chahar-dhar'i* (see below) was a particularly expensive variety, became gradually the universal method to gird the loins[1234].

1227. ['*Alamara-ye Shah Tahmasp*], p. 410.
1228. Scarce [Vesture], p. 36.
1229. ['*Alamara-ye Shah Tahmasp*], p. 421.
1230. Scarce [Vesture], p. 36-37.
1231. ['*Alamara-ye Shah Tahmasp*], p. 137, 419.
1232. Dickinson and Welch, I, p. 91, fig. 129.
1233. Goetz, p. 2247.
1234. ['*Alamara-ye Shah Tahmasp*], p. 410.

Shoes and boots

The dress was completed with simple footwear; flat-soled shoes of black, white, or red leather, often over long red and orange cloth stockings secured at the knees with string garters. Cuban-heeled clogs were worn out-of-doors[1235]. This is borne out by a contemporary account. « [Quelli che sono apresso del Re portano scarpuzzo de veludo negro e de rosso e de verde, quali sono li piu amici del Re, che quelli molte volte razona e piglia piacer] Those who are close to the king, those most loved by him, with whom he often talks and takes his pleasure, wear caps of black, red or green velvet »[1236]. According to Tenreiro the men wore « very sturdy shoes of leather, and the soles fastened with numerous small iron nails, and at the heels an attached plate of iron, with a point of one inch, which serves as [a] spur »[1237]. Military officers also wore *chekmeh* boots[1238]. For foot wear in general see below on the situation in the 17th century, which, probably also reflected 16th century reality.

Female dress

Women's clothes were similar to male garments in cut and decoration, although their construction was simpler with no full-length center front opening and therefore no need for a wrapover extension, according to Scarce. Tenreiro wrote that « in their attire they do not dress differently than the men, save they wear some head-dresses on their head with braids in back, and the face veiled »[1239]. According to Contarini, a contemporary observer, « All the Persian women wear men's robes, and put them over their heads, covering them altogether »[1240].

Head dress

Indoors women wore a *lachak*[1241], a neat white triangular scarf as a head covering. A second headscarf, of a light patterned fabric, was often pinned over the white scarf and worn with pointed ends framing the face

1235. Scarce [Vesture], p. 37.
1236. Membré, p. 30.
1237. Smith, p. 75.
1238. Khʷondamir, IV, p. 518.
1239. Smith, p. 75.
1240. *Barbaro and Contarini*, II, p. 172.
1241. [*'Alamara-ye Safavi*], p. 161.

and falling to the shoulders. This scarf was probably known as *rupak*[1242]. Often, women wore a small cap under it. Some jewellery including an aigrette was worn[1243]. When outside, women covered themselves from head to toe in an all-embracing *chador*. « I saw [one of the Shahs wives] her face covered with a black veil, riding like a man »[1244]. However, some of the royal women only covered their hair, but not their face. « The women wear robes of silk, veils on their head, and show their face openly »[1245]. Women wore head-pieces of *framegas* according to Simoes and Tenreiro states that they wear on their head some braids with covering[1246].

Shirt or pirahan

The basic item was a white undershirt, which with rare exceptions is visible at the neck only. It has a simple round neck fastened with a single clasp and a deep, center front opening. It is also seen ankle-length, with full long sleeves. Although, it looked very much like a male shirt the use of the term *pirahan-e zananeh* indicates that the female shirt was clearly distinct from its male counterpart[1247]. It may have been made of *khalkhal*, a fine thin cloth[1248]. Tenreiro observed that female garments were « very tight through the sleeves, and embroidered on the arms, fitted to the body, and they reach to the foot, [and] open in front from the breasts to the waist, and thus even the blouses; and underneath draws of silk worked in gold and seed-pearls on the front side »[1249].

Vest

Women also wore a short vest over their shirt, which probably did not reach as far as their calves. It was referred to as *nim-taneh*[1250]. Simoes referred to « quilted shirts of silk upon shirts of taffeta »[1251].

1242. [*'Alamara-ye Safavi*], p. 161.
1243. Vecellio, p. 451-453 (with pictures); Goetz, p. 2248.
1244. *Barbaro and Contarini*, II, p. 217.
1245. *Barbaro and Contarini*, II, p. 223.
1246. Smith, p. 49, 86.
1247. [*'Alamara-ye Safavi*], p. 161.
1248. *Ibid.*
1249. Smith, p. 86.
1250. *Ibid.*
1251. *Ibid.*, p. 49.

Overcoat

Invariably, a robe was worn over the shirt, falling in loose, straight lines to an ankle-length hem. One style had a high, round neck from which fell a deep front opening fastened by two or three gold clasps. Long, tight sleeves were gathered in folds and creases at the wrist. The second type was identical to the first but cut with a deep V-shaped neckline extending to the waist and revealing the undergarment. A variation of this robe has wide, elbow-length sleeves and embroidered scroll designs around the neck and shoulders. « All these were worn loose and unbelted. A third type of coat, with wrist-length sleeves and plain colors, was worn with a contrasting scarf knotted around the hips. Flat-soled shoes in black or yellow are seen beneath the trailing hems of the layers of garments »[1252]. Simoes mentioned « French cloaks of brocade, velvets, satins, damask, cloth of scarlet-in-grain » while Tenreiro observed that « over these garments they wear some upper garment fitted with tight and long sleeves, which hang free. They are lined with ermine and marten and with other linings »[1253].

We have no contemporary description of female clothes, but a superficial general assessment of the costliness of their garments. « These are robes of silk, some of crimson cloth, woolen cloth, velvet, and gold cloth, according to the condition of the wearer »[1254]. Contarini's opinion is borne out by contemporary Persian sources who state that the women of Shah Esma'il I all were *zarbaftpush* or dressed in gold brocade[1255].

• *18th century*

The luxuriousness of Safavid dress continued in the 17th and 18th century. « In Persia the clothes of all folk, to speak generally, are made of coloured stuffs, and there are a few who do not wear silk, for this is quite cheap. Thus velvet of double and a half pile will hardly cost ten reals the yard, and eight yards of coloured taffetas, which may of pearl colour, can be had for five reals. The price of muslin and linen goods which same are imported in great abundance from India, is so moderate that 20 yards of

1252. Scarce [Vesture], p. 39.
1253. Smith, p. 47, 86.
1254. *Barbaro and Contarini*, II, p. 172.
1255. [*'Alamara-ye Shah Esma'il*], p. 83.

either may be bought for a sum not exceeding four reals, and this material be as fine as our holland of cambray »[1256].

Speelman, the secretary of the Dutch embassy of 1651-52, reports for example, that the governor of Lar was dressed in a "Cabay" of striped Surat *atlas*, a black satin, embroidered with gold and with costly sable fur lined coat, and a gold-striped turban. The governor of Isfahan was dressed in a golden *balapush* or long cloak[1257]. Sanson submits that « Their under Vests glitter extreamly; for they, as well as their Sashes, are of Brocard, with Gold or Silver Ground. Their Upper Coats are of Scarlet Cloth, lac'd all over with Gold, and lined with the richest Sables »[1258]. In Shamakhi, for example, Kaempfer noticed that the courtiers were dressed in gold and silver fabrics. The guards of the governor, during the audience, wore clothes made of *atlas* with a gold flower design[1259].

Fryer observed that rich dress was mainly worn during official occasions, and that otherwise the « nobles, being of the same make with the meaner Multitude, only their everyday Cloaths surpass in Richness, being Surbaffs, or Cloaths of Silver or Gold, and the middle Sort only appear so on great days, otherwise they are Habited alike, unless Business, or Necessity of the Weather create a difference [...] within doors they are clad more carelessly, as also when they are on Foot near their own Homes [...] In the Winter, they wrap themselves in Furs, and in Summertime go in looser as well as lighter Garments »[1260].

Persians of all ages dressed in any color they liked (except for black), presenting a colorful, if sometimes flashy, picture to the European contemporary observer. « They take especial care that every part of their dress shall be of a different colour, in this varying from our practice; nor do they choose common colours, such as blue, green and the like, but compound and whimsical tints, such as bronze colour, that of the camel, of wine leaves, olive and similar; but of all, that which in my esteem is the most brilliant is a flame colour, by the side of which our liveliest scarlet or carnation appears as nothing, and among their darker colours, a certain deep green pleased me more highly than the most fashionable of any in the East.

1256. *Don Juan*, p. 49.
1257. Hotz, p. 45-46, 86.
1258. Sanson, p. 47; see also Fryer, III, p. 120.
1259. Kaempfer [*Die Reisetagebuecher*], p. 44.
1260. Fryer, III, p. 120-121.

It is called Negti or Neft, from its similitude of tint to that of a certain oil exuded from the earth in the neighbourhood of Backu »[1261].

Persians not only wore colorful clothes but, unlike contemporary Europeans, sported a wide and varying combination of colors at the same time. Each individual piece therefore had a different color. « Persians like to have different part of the clothes all of a different color, esp. the women. The sash and turban always need to be of striped fabric. Only the mollahs have clothes of one colour. They use black taffetas when women have their monthly courses, then they put on a black shirt of taffeta. Dancers at a party wearing a black shirt are allowed to dance but nobody approaches them and they eat apart »[1262].

Clothes played an important part in the life of the Safavid elite. A courtier with an income of 7-8 tomans per year spent 4-5 tomans on clothes; this luxury also increasingly touched the common people, comments Chardin, so that it was often difficult to distinguish between master and servant. Feathers made the man also in Persia. While 'Abbas I only allowed people to dress in accordance with their station, 'Abbas II allowed disorder[1263]. « One of the Kzel-Baches shall content himself with a piece of Bread, and a little sowre Milk, so that he can but accoutre himself and his Horse better than ordinary »[1264].

Not only had dignitaries to keep up appearances at all cost, but they were also very particular about the cleanliness of their garments. « Dress is less confortable, but gaier than Turk. In Iran one needs a servant to tie the strings of the qaba, therefore most tie but one of them and leave the rest hanging. Is also more expensive. Turks wear it several years, Persians no longer than they find a spot on them. Therefore they are neat, take off the qaba when at home, and change qaba everyday. At 6 months they take one those qabas they have worn already, which is thought to be new, because nobody remembers having seen it before. They value a man for his neatness and good clothes »[1265]. The rich change every day their robe, because these are dyed and do not keep their colour. If water drop falls on it

1261. Della Valle [Extract], IX, p. 42.

1262. Tavernier, p. 269; On black color see also Kashefi, p. 193. Black is not worn, which is color of mourning. They don all colours at all ages (Chardin, IV, p. 9).

1263. Chardin, IV, p. 18.

1264. Sanson, p. 47.

1265. Thévenot, II, p. 93

becomes a spot[1266]. Persians are very clean and keep their clothes proper. The rich do take off their clothes when dirtied. The poor have them weekly washed[1267].

The middle class, instead of brocade, wore Dutch and British broadcloth, while the lower class wore cotton and other coarse fabrics of various colours, normally violet, blue, green, etc. with the exception of black. The lower classes only wore these clothes, because spots did not show easily on them. In winter, furs were worn, the poor used sheep and fox skins; the middle class Yazd and Kirman lambskins, or cat skins. Rich men used marten furs from Russia, costing up to 500 écus[1268].

Men's robes, according to Diba, became much shorter during the 17th century. But more striking was the change in the cut of the robe, which was worn close-fitted around the torso, stiffended at the hips and cuffs with quilting, with a flaring, bell-shaped skirt[1269]. She is supported in her conclusion by a statement in a Persian text that Shah 'Abbas I was the inventor of, inter alia, the *qaba-ye damandar* (robe with bell-shaped skirts)[1270]. However, there is a miniature of Shah Mohammad Khodabandeh, Shah 'Abbas' father, which shows him wearing a *qaba-ye damandar*[1271].

Other fashion changes were the adoption of Georgian style robes, opening front with buttons and loops. There was also some experimentation with the wearing of European clothes, but this had more the nature of a charade than anything else[1272]. The Europeans, on various occasions supplied the shahs with European clothes, most likely for his harem women to have some fun[1273].

1266. Tavernier, p. 631.

1267. Olearius, p. 589.

1268. Tavernier, I, p. 632. Most an end their Stockins and upper Jerkins are made of English Broad Cloth (Fryer, III, p. 121).

1269. Diba, p. 791.

1270. Astarabadi, p. 134.

1271. Falsafi, I, p. 56.

1272. « Young men wearing full trousers, either billowing to the ankle or are tucked into shaped, knee-length stockings, worn with snug, hip-length belted jackets that resemble contemporary European doublets. A feathered hat with tall crown and wide brim is worn instead of the turban or cap » (Scarce [Vesture], p. 44); for pictures, see Falsafi, II, p. 88, 104.

1273. Pacifique de Provins, p. 261.

Male dress

Head dress

The normal or more universal head dress that was invariably observed by Europeans was the turban (Turkish: *dulvent* or *tulbent*, Persian *dulband*, or rope), which was a most distinctive form of head gear. « Their Head-Attire gives 'em so noble an Air, that the Ottoman Turbans appear ridiculous to 'em »[1274]. The turban was also referred to by the terms *mandil* and *dastar*[1275]. A *mandil* and lamb skin hat were worn summer and winter by everybody, Olearius remarks[1276]. Around 1670, Fryer, described normal Safavid headgear as follows: « A large Turban is placed upon his crown, of divers Colours, either Silk or Cotton, in the Figure of an overgrown-Cabage, with a great broad Leaf a top, which is wrought of Gold and Silver, and spread to make a shew »[1277]. Despite its distinctiveness the turban did not mark any distinction of rank[1278].

The head was covered with a skull-cap stuffed or stitched with cotton, which was sometimes made of broad-cloth or leather, over which they wrapped a coarse white cloth. It was always so large as to conceal the little cap in the middle. Sometimes, the turban was just wrapped around the naked head, even by persons appearing before the shah[1279]. The skull-cap cum wrapper served as the basic form on which the remainder of the work of art, which consisted of silk or cotton fabrics, was "built". The fabrics used to wrap around the "base" were multi-colored, often wrought with silver and gold-thread, of an average length of 16 to 18 ells. Only mollahs and *hajji*s wore high quality white muslin turbans. The cheapest cost 20 écus, but those of the shah and the magnates would cost 400-500 écus. Upper class men often embellished their turban by wearing precious stones on them, while less fortunate persons made the same with less costly fabrics[1280].

Because of the length of the fabric the turbans appeared to be very big, and, moreover, they were very heavy. According to Chardin, who in the

1274. Sanson, p. 46.

1275. Monshi, I, p. 329, 775: *mandil-e zartari*.

1276. Olearius, p. 586.

1277. Frye, III, p. 120. Tavernier also says it looks like a fruit.

1278. Della Valle [Extract], IX, p. 42.

1279. *Ibid.*, p. 42; Falsafi, I, p. 212.

1280. Tavernier, p. 268; see also Herbert, p. 232-233; According to Du Mans (p. 101) the length of the turban sash was 2 to 3 gaz.

beginning had difficulties wearing one, some turbans weighed 12 to 15 pounds, the lightest weighing as much as 6 pounds[1281]. The size of the turban was really meant to be impressive. According to a contemporary Persian cleric: « One day I was in the mosque, and a man entered, dressed in white and wearing a turban so large that it looked like a small dome. He meant to give everyone the impression that he was a great scholar »[1282]. Darvishes made fun of the large turbans worn by many members of the olama, saying: « the larger the turban, the less brains under it »[1283]. In this respect the famous poem by Sa'eb is also instructive:

« If hugeness of the turban is an indication of learning
The dome of the Shah Mosque would be the greatest of scholars
Let not, Oh Sa'eb, the ascetic's turban pass with you for learning
For, as in a dome, hollowness of the head creates much echo. »

The end of the sash, a strip varying in length of 20 to 30 cm, was either worn in the form of a plume of feathers on top of the turban (15-20 cm) or was hanging down the back of the bearer (40-50 cm). In the latter case this strip would be green of color in the case of a seyyed[1284]. According to Du Mans, those who wrapped their turban in such a way that it was crowned by a cockscomb, wanted to show that they were men of some importance[1285].

Both Moslems and non-Moslems wore the turban[1286], but not always in the same manner. Shah 'Abbas I, for example, wore his turban « fancifully in reverse way from the others: that is to say, it is worn back to front, and in Persia, apart from him, no one can wear it in this fashion »[1287]. « The dress of the men of the sword is quite different from what is worn by the men of the robe [...] The Mandiel or turbant they wear upon the head varies also; they are of all sorts of colours, some striped, some wrought with gold and silver, and some white. The churchmen wear them much larger than any others, but extremely neat, and very nicely folded up; in a word their dress is very magnificant, and their garments

1281. Chardin, IV, p. 7-8; Thévenot, II, p. 92.
1282. Stewart, p. 57.
1283. Gramlich, III, p. 6, n. 17.
1284. Chardin (aigrette); Tavernier (bouquet); Olearius, p. 586.
1285. Du Mans, p. 247; Richard, p. 191.
1286. Della valle [Extract], IX, p. 42; Thévenot, II, p. 92; [*Carmelites*], I, p. 462; Olearius, p. 586.
1287. Della Valle [Extract], IX, p. 62; see also [*Carmelites*], I, p. 287.

mostly flowered »[1288]. Asef mentions that court officials of Shah Soltan Hosein's royal workshops wore intricately patterned so-called *khalil-khani* silk turbans, fine leather shoes, Kurdish trousers, and gold brocade waist sashes[1289].

Apart from the skull-cap, Persian males also wore another cap under their turban. « Many in the winter time, when very cold, wear a large pointed bonnet under the turban, the extremity of which appears above, and the lower parts serves to keep the head and ears warm. It is of the same description as Xenephon describes the Thracians to have worn in his time. Some wear this cap alone, but these are only the common people; except, indeed, the Georgians, who, having the turban in abhorrence, wear it indiscriminately, both high and low »[1290]. Della Valle probably referred to the *qalansuh*, which indeed was a normal headgear under Shah 'Abbas I and his successors[1291].

The *taj* and the turban were not the only type of head wear worn in Safavid Persia. Della Valle reports, for example, « On their head [the king's pages] wear, not a turban, but a small cap of silk and fur, rising to a point from a wide rim; and for fancy's sake, in the modern way invented by the king, they wear them inside out, namely with the fur on the outside, and the rim turned back to show the face of the cloth, instead of fur. These small caps, called *bork* in Persia, are very common here, and are the same as those I said before are worn at home instead of a turban, for greater convenience. And although they may not be worn out of doors by mature men, nonetheless for servants and for pages they are often used and most acceptable »[1292]. These *bork* caps probably referred to the caps made of Bokharan or some other kind of lamb skin. Eskander Beg Monshi mentions the use of the *kolah-e sammuri* or a hat made of sable skin[1293].

Della Valle's observation is borne out by other contemporary observers later in the century, who note that « lower class people wore long and sharp pointed caps of white felt, with a little slit before and behind just like

1288. Le Bruyn, I, p. 212.

1289. Asef, p. 100-101.

1290. Della Valle [Extract], IX, p. 42.

1291. Shirazi, p. 126; Monajjem, p. 436, 445; see also Sanson, engraving frontispiece, with a picture of this cap.

1292. Della Valle [Extract], IX, p. 62. However, the Torkman hat or *qalpaq*, which was made of felt, also was trimmed with fur, Goetz, p. 2242.

1293. Monshi, I, p. 13.

English caps. They also turn them inside out in the same manner. They often put a sorry turban around this cap. Indoors they do not wear turbans, but only long pointed caps, lined with lambskin. Apart from the turban, members of the upper class also wore hats made of Bokhara lamb skin, both inside and outside the house, which were very popular »[1294]. The felt caps mentioned by Thévenot undoubtedly were the *kolah-e namadi* mentioned by Persian and other European sources[1295]. The use of the so-called *kolah-e khʷari* is also mentioned[1296], but nothing is further known about this head gear.

Shirt or pirahan

« Next to their skin they wear smocks, or demi-shirts, of cotton, in colour resembling Scotch plaid »[1297]. Other travellers confirm this and report that the shirts were made of calico, or a colored cotton, because there was no linen in Persia. The shirts were seldom pure white, and commonly of divers colours. Their shirts had no collar, but only a hem[1298]. The shirt was normally not seen when covered by the vest[1299]. Neither men nor women wore silk around the neck[1300].

According to Tavernier people wore a cotton shirt with quilted flowers, while the shirt was also made of silk, in various colors, because linen is worn as little as possible « because soap is so scarce in Persia; moreover they are not very good at bleaching. When we come from India to Persia we take for 6 months needs of underwear ["linge blanc"] and take it back to India where they are better at bleaching »[1301]. According to Du Mans the reason why the shirts were sometimes of colored silk was because dirt does not show that soon and it lasts longer[1302].

The shirt had a slit above, not in front, but on the right side; it was tied upon the right shoulder with a string on each side; it had a slit on the sides

1294. Thévenot, II, p. 92; see also Olearius, p. 586 who states that the lamb skin hats were very popular and that their price was 16 Reichsthaler.

1295. Monshi, I, p. 201; Nasrabadi, p. 350, *kolah-e namadi*.

1296. Bafqi, III, part 1, p. 191.

1297. Herbert, p. 232.

1298. Thévenot, II, p. 191; Herbert, p. 174. Over this hung a shirt, mostly red colored (Olearius, p. 587).

1299. Della Valle [Extract], IX, p. 41.

1300. Chardin, IV, p. 2.

1301. Tavernier, I, p. 630.

1302. Du Mans, p. 101; Richard, II, p. 77.

below just like French shirts[1303]. The shirt was long, went down to the knees, and was worn over the trousers. Rich women, and sometimes men, bordered the collar with large pearls[1304] or *yaqeh-ye pirahan-e duri*, of which Shah 'Abbas I reputedly was the inventor as he was of the *yaqeh-ye qalami*[1305].

Although the majority of the people did not have sleeping garments, « the night-dress customarily worn [by the rich], is a shirt and drawers, or rather trousers reaching to the feet »[1306].

Outer garments

Over the shirt an outervest was worn, which was called *jobbeh* or *arkhaliq*. Over this vest the Safavid male wore a *qaba*, a long coat. Over the *qaba* he wore in summer a *kurdi* (a sleeveless short cape), and in winter a *qatebi* (a similar coat but long, furred or quilted). When going out another garment or surcoat was worn over the *qaba* called Ya'qub Khani.

Jubbeh, arkhaliq

« Next, upon his Body is a Shirt, which he covers with a Vest, tied double on his Breast, and strait to his Body as far as the Waste, from whence it hangs in Pleats to his Ancles, sometimes Quilted, sometimes not »[1307]. « Their *jobbeh* or outervest is usually of calico stitched with silk or quilted with cotton. The better sort have vestes polymitae, garments of party-coloured silks; some being satin, some gold and silver chamlets, and some of bodkin and rich cloth of gold figured, for variety best pleases them. No colour displeases, but black, which is not worn, because they hold it dismal and unlucky. The sleeves are straight and long; their close coat usually reaches to their calves, and bears round »[1308]. « They wear a waist-coat quilted with cotton and set thick with Oilet-holes that comes down to the middle of their thigh; that waiste coat is of white cotton-cloth or of cloth painted with flowers and birds, and they call it arcalick »[1309].

1303. Thévenot, II, p. 91-92.

1304. Chardin, IV, p. 2; see e.g. the pictures showing embroidered hem-collars in Falsafi, I, p. 166, 174.

1305. Astarabadi, p. 134, and not, as Diba (p. 791) mistakenly has it, 'Abbas II.

1306. Della Valle [Extract], IX, p. 61.

1307. Fryer, III, p. 121.

1308. Herbert, p. 174-175.

1309. Thévenot, II, p. 90; see also Olearius, p. 587-588 (also pictures) who gives a similar description and adds that « in front it is closed one over the other and closed under the left arm » [this seems to be the first time that this term is used; see Diba, p. 857;

Qaba

Over the *arkhaliq* « they have a vest which they call caba, made commonly of very fine cotton, dyed red, yellow, green, or any other color according to their fancy, and so slacked that it seems satin. This vest is quilted and set thick with oilet-holes, and reaches down to the calf of the leg. It is cut very round before, so that the right side of it reaches over the stomack, and is tied with strings under the left arm, the left side slapping over it and fastened with four strings on the right side, with one hanging loose over the rest. So the stomack is well covered and close girt, for it fits very well and is straight to the girdle from the girdle downward it grows wider and wider, so that it looks like a bell, below, standing routed as if it had a ring of iron in it, and that is because of the cotton it is stuffed with. The sleeves fit close to the arm, but are much longer; therefore they pleat them that they may not hang over the wrist. Many have them close at the wrist and without the button. Those who wish more comfort use a button, many do so now, learnt from Europeans. The cabas commonly are of one colour type, of cloth only. Persians of quality wear them also many time of satin or Zerbaft (brocade of Persia) and in summer many have of Aldgia and not quilted »[1310].

Cavaliers also wore the Georgian *qaba*, the only difference with the normal *qaba* was that the former was open at the stomach, with buttons and loops. Though this vest was lightly closed, one secured it with 2-3 sashes which were used as pockets[1311].

In general, « these vests or coats are made of Indian cloth stained of a single colour, but the figures are whimsical, and are therefore so much the more prized. When these cloths are new, they are as glossy and lustrous as satin »[1312].

« Le dessus est l'arkalou comme chemisole et ce de toile fine à pointe double et entre deux du coton picqué. La doublure, aster, est d'ordinaire de grosse toile a treillis » (Du Mans, p. 101; Richard, II, p. 76). For pictures see Bier, p. 214-219.

1310. Thévenot, II, p. 90-91; see also Tavernier and Della Valle [Extract], IX, p. 41-42, who, however, states that it is laced on the right side, for a similar description. He also adds (p. 63) that Shah 'Abbas I and his entourage sometimes laced the *kurdi* in front with laces. See also Chardin, IV, p. 3-4 and his plate XXXII.

1311. *Ibid.*, p. 3; « La cabaye qui, comme une hongreline, doibt passer de demi pied les genoux » (Du Mans, p. 101; Richard, II, p. 76).

1312. Della Valle [Extract], IX, p. 42.

'Aba

The *'aba* is a sleeveless male overcoat, that is open in the front and has large armholes. In the 17th century *'aba*s were imported from Baghdad[1313]. It probably was only worn by members of the religious class.

Kurdi, Ya'qub Khani

« Over the *qaba* they put a Just a Cor [juste-au-corps or tight fitting jacket] or cloath which in summer has no sleeves or fur, and reaches down to the middle of the thigh; they call that garment Courdy. In spring and autumn it is furred; but in winter they make it with close sleeves and so long as it reaches down to the calf of the leg and they call it Cabebis [*qatebi*]. It is not buttoned before, though it has commonly 6 long buttons on the one side, and as many loops of the same fashion on the other, but that is only for ornament, and the Coordies have none. This Just a Cor is commonly lined with fur in winter; the rich use sable, the meaner content themselves with lambskin, the wool of it is long, finer than the shortest hair, and full of rings and curls. They line their coordies with another sort that has short wool, but rings in the same manner. Round the neck on the outside they put upon the stuff an ornament 6 fingers broad, that comes down a foot length on each side. These lambs skins come from Yezd and Kirman, the second sort comes from Shiraz »[1314].

The *Kurdi* was a short jacket without sleeves, while the *qatebi* was a long jacket with sleeves. The choice of wearing one of them depended on the season. They were both made of broad cloth, gold brocade or satin, and were embellished with lace, gold or either marten or Khorasan sheep skins with fine hair. Either jacket was seldom buttoned[1315]. Della Valle offers a similar detailed description and adds that the *kurdi* is very short, « so much so, that it scarcely flaps the haunches of the horse when they ride; the common people wear it somewhat longer, but never to reach lower than the bend of the knee. It is principally of cloth, but of a curious colour, different from that of the vest, and trimmed with cords and silk frogs »[1316]. The *kurdi* and *qatebi* were made of various fabrics. The outside either of

1313. Gaube and Wirth, p. 265-266.

1314. Thévenot, II, p. 91-92; see also Olearius, p. 587-588. Tavernier mentions that sheepskin from Khorasan was used in particular; also Della Valle [Extract], IX, p. 42; Chardin, IV, p. 3-5; Fryer, III, p. 121.

1315. Chardin, IV, p. 3-5; also Du Mans, p. 102; Richard, II, p. 76-77.

1316. Della Valle [Extract], IX, p. 42.

« Scarlet, or the finest Wool of Europe, or Cloath of Silver or Gold of their own Manufactory »[1317].

« When they go out walking or riding they wear over this outfit another cloack, mostly of silk, worked with golden flowers, which is called Jakub Cahni, called in remembrance of a king who first wore it »[1318].

Waistband or kamarband

« Their waists are girt with fine towels of silk and gold about 8 yards long; those and the sashes distinguish the quality of those that wear them; dukes and others of the nobles sort have them woven with gold, merchants and qezelbash with silver; of silk and wool those of inferior rank »[1319]. According to Olearius the waist sash was called « Tzarkesi, because it is 4 ell long. When they are well-to-do they in addition carry another sash of silk, called shal. This one like the mandil are bought from the Indians, because their colours are more lasting. A molla, when he wore such a silk sash, had to take it off when he wanted to pray »[1320]. Important people wore a *chahar-dhar'i* or *chahar-gaz*, which is a strip of 4 ells (dhar' or gaz) long and not a robe of 4 ells long as Diba wrongly has it[1321].

The waistband arrangement was important. Not only did it give an indication of the social position of the wearer, but it also served a functional purpose, i.e. as pockets. « In the sashes they often keep a dagger, *dastmal* or money; in the case of a secretary, his writing implements and letters »[1322]. Important people wore special sashes, and more often than the common people. Putting on a waist band was not a simple matter either, for the uninitiated. « This vest is girt with 2 girdles of which the first, which is the broadest and the longest, is a kind of stuff purposely of brocade, some of silk with gold, and others of silk. But persons of quality have them always with gold. They double its many plies till it be but 4-5 fingers broad, and they bring it 3 x 4 times about their body. The other is shorter and narrower and is commonly of goats or camel hair, and only of one colour. They fold it till it be no more but 3 fingers broad at most, and it is put over

1317. Fryer, III, p. 122; for a detailed discussion of a *qatebi* see Dal Farra, p. 81-90.

1318. Olearius, p. 587-588.

1319. Herbert, p. 175.

1320. Olearius, p. 587-588.

1321. *EIr*, p. 787. See also Monshi, II, p. 775; Du Mans, p. 102.

1322. Olearius, p. 587-588; see also Fryer, III, p. 121: « his Loins are Girt with Phrigian Girdles, or rich Sashes, above which his Belt carried a Falched Sword or Scimitar »; Chardin also mentioned the use of the sash as "pocket".

the other, so that it covers but part of the breadth, and therefore it goes but twice round the body, so that both are seen »[1323]. Other observers also note that two to three sashes, amongst which one of woolen shawl, were worn, of which the silk one often was embellished with gold and/or silver flowers. Also, that the sash made of wool, « is not in less esteem, being often times of greater value than those made of silk ». Further, the use of a sash of only one color served to better show the beauty of the other[1324].

Trousers, zir-jameh or tomban

Persians wore loose cotton or London sackcloth trousers, of any color, which were narrow below the knees and went down till the ankles and did not respect the shape of the leg. They were worn on the naked skin, and were held together by a rope[1325]. Their trousers, referred to as *tomban* were also of silk, often with small squares, but were not open like the European ones.« It has no opening in front and has to be unknotted and down to relieve oneself »[1326].

Only after the Dutch and the English started trading in Persia were cloth or woolen stockings worn. Before that time, everybody, even the Shah, did like the soldiers, servants, carriers, villagers, and most of the common people still did: they swaddled their legs with linen cloth 6 fingers wide and 3-4 ells long. It was easy and comfortable, light and heavy depending on the season. In winter, the feet were wrapped like the leg. In summer, the feet went naked into shoes[1327].

Socks or jurab

Socks or *jurab* were only used by the well-to-do, but during winter time by most people. « The stockings falls not always into their shoes, but from the ankle down gives to the eye two inches of the leg naked »[1328]. Their stockings were of cloth, very wide and big, i.e. they do not tightly fit the form of the leg, and therefore appear shoddy. They reach up to the knees,

---

1323. Thévenot, II, p. 91-92.

1324. Della Valle [Extract], IX, p. 42; Chardin, IV, p. 7; Tavernier, I, p. 633; Du Mans, p. 102; Richard, II, p. 77. For pictures of the rich silk brocaded and figured sashes see Pope and Ackerman, III, *passim*.

1325. Olearius, p. 587; Fryer, III, p. 121.

1326. Chardin, IV, p. 5; for a similar description see Thévenot, II, p. 91-92; Du Mans, p. 102; Richard, II, p. 77.

1327. Chardin, IV, p. 2; for a similar account, see Tavernier, I, p. 633. For a picture showing a soldiers' dress with leggings see Falsafi, I, p. 120.

1328. Herbert, p. 232.

and are tied under it. They sew a piece of red leather to the heel of the stocking to prevent wearing out[1329]. Often stockings were green of colour, which the Turks found horrible[1330].

Chaqshur

Only Herbert mentions that Persian wore breeches or *chaqshur*. « Their breeches have hose and stockings, sewed together »[1331]. Other authors are explicit about the fact that Persians did not have or use breeches, even in winter time[1332]. However, Herbert is right, for Persians did have breeches, as is for example clear from Eskander Beg[1333]. Shah 'Abbas I is reputedly the inventor of the *chaqshur-e londreh* (London cloth stockings)[1334], although the reference in Eskander Beg would make that unlikely.

Even Du Mans, who also stated that Persians did not have breeches, mentions their existence, this implies a later development. « Their long trousers, which ended in stockings, or chackhour [*chaqshur*] are made of English cloth, are of the same length »[1335].

Shoes or kafsh

« Their shoes are of leather well sewed, but without latchets, and of what colour you can fancy, sharp at the toe and turning upwards, the heels high and small, shod with iron spikes or nails ingraited »[1336]. Shah 'Abbas I reputedly was the inventor of the *kafsh-e pashnehdar* or the high-heeled shoe[1337]. Their shoes or *kafsh* are « of the best Shagreen Leather, mostly Green, with narrow Toes, high narrow Heels, shod with neat Iron Half-moons, without Shoe-ties or Quarters to pull up about their Heels, being the readier to slipp off and on as occasion requires »[1338]. According to Du Mans, green was the normal color of shoes, and blue and white was for the

1329. Thévenot, II, p. 91-92; Chardin, IV, p. 5-6; Du Mans, p. 102 (Richard, II, p. 77), states that they were knitted woollen socks.

1330. Olearius, p. 587-588.

1331. Herbert, p. 231-232.

1332. Du Mans, p. 102; Richard, II, p. 77; Chardin, IV, p. 6.

1333. Monshi, I, p. 184.

1334. Astarabadi, p. 134.

1335. Du Mans, p. 102; Richard, II, p. 77. There were also *chaqshurduzan* (Keyvani, p. 50).

1336. Herbert, p. 233; Della Valle [Extract], IX, p. 43 and p. 63, Shah 'Abbas I wearing orange colored shagreen shoes.

1337. Astarabadi, p. 134.

1338. Fryer, III, p. 122; very much like slippers with low heels (Olearius, p. 587-588).

general public, whose shoes had no heels[1339]. They were all with *nal* (*na'l*) [nails], but only on the narrow high heels[1340]. Also, European and Georgian style shoes were introduced[1341]. Costly Russian shoes were peculiar enough to be included in a present for Shah 'Abbas I[1342].

The military or « the [nobles] Ride shorter, and are booted over their Stockins, with a kind of Buskin with flat heels, only shod with an Iron Horse-shoe »[1343].

Gloves are of no esteem to them[1344], instead of gloves they tincture not only their hands, but feet, with *henna.* They only use gloves when they carry their hawks on their fists[1345]. Neither men nor women wear gloves[1346]. « They use no napkins, but in lieu wipe their hands on large handkerchiefs of painted linen, embroidered with silk or gold, suspended from the waist »[1347].

Female dress

Women's costume from 17th century onwards develops a more curved and voluptuous line accentuated by carefully chosen accessories. In miniatures flimsy white shirts with loose sleeves and center front openings, slit to the navel are seen[1348]. The dress was « very simple, and without ornament, although the rich are not sparing in having a variety of cloth, silk, and gold, with handsome tissue of various kinds. Their dress is much less loose than that of Turkish ladies, and in my esteem is not so becoming »[1349].

1339. Du Mans, p. 102; Richard, II p. 77.

1340. *Ibid.*, p. 103. For picture of high narrow heels on shoes see Falsafi, II, p. 174; for slippers see Falsafi, p. 70, picture of Aqa Reza Mossavar Kashi in undress; also p. 88. There were *pashneh-sazan* or shoe-heel makers.

1341. Keyvani, p. 51, 267.

1342. Monshi, II, p. 989.

1343. Fryer, III, p. 121, which refers to the use of the *chekmeh*, or the knee-high riding boots, which were in use at least since early Safavid times. *Chekmeh* were high leather boots worn since the beginning of Safavid period (Monshi, I, p. 382); Mervi, II, p. 568, 772. Qomi, I, p. 586 mentions a *chekmehduz*.

1344. Herbert, p. 233.

1345. Fryer, III, p. 120.

1346. Chardin, IV, p. 12-13.

1347. Della Valle [Extract], IX, p. 20.

1348. Scarce [Vesture], p. 4.

1349. Della Valle [Extract], IX, p. 43.

Head dress

« Their Garments differ no farther from the Mens than Convenience requires »[1350], although female clothing was thinner than men's[1351]. « On their head they have small bonnets, sticking out like a small turret, embellished with stones in accordance with their means. From this bonnet hangs down [with some] a silk veil, while their hair in tresses till their shoulders »[1352]. The head is well covered, over which they carry a veil which falls down on their shoulders and covers their neck and bosom[1353]. It resembles « that of the women of Bagdad, and is tied in the same manner in front, but trains to the ground on each side: it is of various colours, extremely fanciful and extraordinary »[1354]. On their heads the women wore no particular jewelry, according to Olearius[1355].

Shirt

The shirt called "camiss" (*qamis*), was open in front up to the navel. Their vests were longer and hang almost to the ankles[1356], open in front and it did not pass their calfs. Their sleeves were just up to the wrists[1357]. These shirts could be very expensive. The secretary of the Dutch ambassador in 1691 saw one for which 4 tomans had been paid. He was told that there were women who wore shirts that cost even more[1358].

Vest, qaba and qatebi

The women, like the men, also wore a *qaba* and a *qatebi*, which were heavily gold brocaded and lined with sable fur[1359].

Belt

« Their sash is tied very low, almost below the haunches, [and] is not so becoming »[1360]. The belt was narrow about one inch[1361], and not belted fast, but dropping casually[1362].

1350. Fryer, III, p. 127; also Chardin, IV, p. 10.
1351. Olearius, p. 588-589.
1352. Tavernier, p. 272-273; della Valle [Extract], IX, p. 43.
1353. Chardin, IV, p. 10.
1354. Della Valle [Extract], IX, p. 43.
1355. Olearius, p. 588-589, which contradicts other travellers (see picture p. 585).
1356. Chardin, IV, p. 10.
1357. Tavernier, I, p. 635.
1358. Valentyn, V, p. 257.
1359. *Ibid.*
1360. Della Valle [Extract], IX, p. 43.
1361. Chardin, IV, p. 10.

Trousers

Women wore drawers and shoes like the men. Their socks were in general red or green velvet[1363]. They wore their trousers down to the ankles, but the leg part was longer, straighter and thicker, because the women did not wear stockings. They covered their feet with a buskin which went four fingers above the ankle, and made of embroidery or the richest fabric[1364].

Veils

Women going out in street were covered from head to foot in white textile. At face level they held a split open through which they looked. « When outside women are covered with White Sheets, with Holes for their Eyes and Nose. Those that desire to be reputed Whores have large Borders [to their *chador*], and wear them as a Sign of their Trade »[1365].

Women wore 4 veils, 2 at home and 2 when outside. The first one was a head dress, which fell at the back as ornament; the second passed around the chin and covered the bosom; the third was the white veil which covered them from head to foot; the fourth was a kind of kerchief which they held in front of their face and was fastened at the temples[1366].

The dress of the men of the sword is quite different from what is worn by the men of the robe, and the same it is with regard to their wives. There is also a wide difference between the dress of the married and the unmarried women; of women advanced in years and young women[1367].

« The wives of the men of the robe wear a forehead-band adorned allover with pearls and precious stones; it is four finger broad, and goes but half way round the head; but the wives of the councillor of state, wear it all round the head, in the nature of a crown, and call it borshiboroe; and upon it they have several plumes of black heron feathers, aigrettes, and bunches of flowers with golden leaves. To this band or diadem they have a jewel which falls upon the forehead, and they fasten it on with a rope of pearl which comes under the chin, and their hair falls down in several tresses. They

1362. Tavernier, I, p. I, p. 635.

1363. Olearius, p. 588-589.

1364. Chardin, IV, p. 10-11; see also Tavernier, I, p. 635.

1365. Fryer, III, p. 128; della Valle [Extract], IX, p. 43. Chardin, IV, p. 10-11; Valentyn, V, p. 257. Herbert, p. 237 for a description of a prostitute's clothes.

1366. Chardin, IV, p. 12-13; two types of veils, one tied at the top like a sack (Herbert, p. 48) the other included a face-veil.

1367. Le Bruyn, I, p. 212.

wear also a white veil, embroidered with gold which falls over her shoulders, necklaces of precious stones and pearls, and golden chains which fall down to their girdle with a box of perfume. Their upper garment is of brocade of gold or silver, it is also sometimes quite plain, and under it they wear a vest which falls down beneath the girdle; their shifts are of taffaty, or some other fine silk embroidered with gold. They wear also drawers and under petticoats made in the loom; buskins which come up four fingers above the ankle, which are of embroidery, velvet or some richer stuff. Their slippers of green or red shagreen, pointed, and with a heel raised of the same colour, lined, and adorned with little flowers. Their girdle which is two or three inches broad, is adorned with pearls and precious stones, and upon the breast they wear certain ribbons which fall down to the girdle. Over all this, in winter, they wear a gown lined with a cotton-cloth, which falls down a foot below the girdle, and when it is very cold indeed, they wear a gown of gold or silver brocade, lined with sables or some other fur. When they go abroad they are from head to foot covered with a white veil, which shows nothing but their eyes. This veil is commonly all of one piece; they wear also bracelets of precious stones, and have their fingers loaded with rings. The women of a middling rank, dress themselves in proportion to their means, and the wives of the nobility and the men of the sword wear over their clothes a silk net, or something of the kind, which has a very pretty effect »[1368].

The Poor

« The villagers go clad in course Cloths underneath, above with Felts, kneaded into the form of a Coat, and are covered with Hats of the same, but their Hats are grey, bound up with Linnen Cloth either of White, Green or Blew; their Coats are of what Colour they please, but mostly Blew; their Hats are high-crowned, and the brim slit before and behind, which if it be cold, they pull down and bind with their Cloth; if the Sun offend their Eyes, they draw it over their Faces, or cock up when it is shady: When they rest, the upper Garment is put on with Sleeves, armed with an undressed Sheep's-skin against the injury of the Weather; their Shirt next to their Skin is rugged enough; over it a plain Jirkin is tied with a hard Linnen Girdle of the same wooft with their Shirt: About the Calves of their Legs they bind

1368. Le Bruyn, I, p. 214; see one of these ladies, going abroad, on plate 87. Bier, p. 239, with a picture of woman with pearl-jewel hairnet.

Rowlers for want of Stockins [something like the modern puttee] and their Shoes are soled with Wood, and the upper part wrought with Packthread »[1369].

« Racte [*rakht*] or *lebas* of peasants are made of coarse cloth, karbas, normally of blue color. The clothes are coarse, but nevertheless, they are just like those in town as per their size and pattern. Some of them use a sash on their head just like in town, but they do not wear a tepeh (that which cover the top of the head), which is at the extreme end of the cloth, which is made in silk or silk or a fringe of the same stuff. When wrapping the turban a plume sticks out on top like a bunch or roses. However, the villager and the artisan, esnaf, hide this end of the turban »[1370]. Because people were poor they often had only one shirt, which was seldom washed and vermin infested[1371].

Ordinarily, the villagers went barefoot; they did not even have wooden clogs. They used so-called *charuq*; these were pieces of green leather, which with cords, were bound around the leg, and which fitted the form of the leg. For breeches they used *pataveh*, which were bands of cloth, in which they swaddled their legs. They also had coats made of felt or *namad*, of which material servants, peasants and boys also wore caps. « Felt is very well made here and you find little difference with londere »[1372].

The clothes of the people in the Persian Gulf coastal area was, of course, different from elsewhere in Persia, because of different climatic conditions. The children of the poor only wore a loin cloth, while those in better circumstances nevertheless wore the lightest dress imaginable. The women, « in general, only wear a simple shift, which covers half the arms and the body to the waist, and from the waist downwards wrap themselves round with a large piece of silk or cotton of different colours, which breadthwise reaches to the feet, and is long enough to wrap round the body twice. [...] Their headdress is a piece of silk or cloth, similar to that worn round the lower part of their body but smaller, which, thrown over head, hangs down in part on the shoulders behind, and fall over the face after the

1369. Fryer, III, p. 124.

1370. Du Mans, p. 247; Richard, II, p. 191; see further Mokamalli. For a picture of peasant dress see Falsafi, I, p, 152, 360, portrait of a *chupan* or herder.

1371. "Mémoire de la Province du Sirvan" in *Nouveaux Mémoires*, IV, p. 358.

1372. Du Mans, p. 248; Richard, II, p. 192.

manner of the Persians »[1373]. They also wore on their feet no stockings, but very peculiar sandals.

At Tarom, in the Persian Gulf littoral, Della Valle observed that « the sandals worn by the people being made of woven palm leaves, of which the sole is made tolerably thick, the upper part consisting only of two strings interwoven with similar leaves, which clasp the foot pretty tight, and join in the middle towards the point, which they pass between the great toe, and thus keep the sandal firm on the foot. Among the villagers on the sea side this sort of sandal is in general use »[1374].

Afsharid period

The 18th century, in the post-Safavid period, saw no major changes in fashion. Although surviving garments are rare, they do not show major differences with the preceding period. Clothes were generally less sumptuous and rich, but still considered to be elegant though simple[1375]. What did not change either was the fact that « even the meanest sort are usually very clean in their cloaths, which have seldom any rent, but if it was not for their repeated bathings, the want of changing their shirts would render their persons indelicate »[1376].

The major change in fashion was the use of the *kolah-e naderi*, a four-pointed cap. According to Otter, Nader Shah invented this new *kolah*[1377] probably to mark the end of the Safavid dynasty. Du Cerceau, confirms Otter's statement, when he writes that Nader Shah « also made some Alterations in the Dress of the Persians, and, instead of Mundels, gave them Caps of Drab-cloth resembling those of our Grenadiers »[1378]. Often, like in the case of the *taj*, a sash or shawl was wrapped around it. Whether this hat was really a new type of head gear is questionable. If, for example, the frontispiece picture in Father Sanson's book, representing a number of Persians, is a reliable rendering of Persian fashion, it would seem that the four-pointed hat was already worn under Shah Soleiman. However,

1373. Della Valle [Extract], IX, p. 117. Women of Ormuz due to the heat, only wore trousers with a shirt (Tavernier, I, p. 690); See Kaempfer, p. 160, all dresses pictures.

1374. Della Valle [Extract], IX, p. 114, see also p. 117.

1375. Hanway, I, p. 228-229; Otter, I, p. 39.

1376. *Ibid.*, p. 335.

1377. Otter, I, p. 39-40. Otter does not state that Nader Shah forced the Persians to wear this new *kolah* as Lockhart has submitted.

1378. De Cerceau, II, p. 128-129.

whether this is true or not (more research is required) a fact is that Nader Shah made the four-pointed cap the new head attire during his reign. In this connection it is of interest that the Dutch report in October 1736 that Nader Shah put « his Afshar hat aside and now wears a mandil (which he continues to wear) after his coronation [*jahantazi*] more in the Arab than in the Lor fashion. He wears the aigrette in the middle and not on the right side as was done formerly by the Safavids »[1379].

Male dress

Head dress

« Most of them have caps of cloth, which rise ten to twelve inches, and terminate on the top in four corners. They have a shorter cap for summer, faced with gray Bokharian lambskins. Crimson is a colour they much affect in their caps, as well in their outer garments; and it makes a grand appearance: deep blue, which is seldom seen worn, except in coarse cloths, is their mourning colour. The better sort of people wear a sash of Khermania wool, wrapped around their heads as turbands; some of these are so exceeding fine as to cost 100 crowns [25£] »[1380].

Shirt

« Their shirts for the most part, are made of checkered silk and cotton; these have neither wrist bands nor collars, for they always go bare-necked »[1381].

Outer clothes

« In general they wear two or three light vestments, which reach only to their knees; so that their dress gives them a great advantage over the Turks, who wear long effiminate robes. Besides their cloth garments of the ordinary sort, which are much esteemed, some have them lined with furs, as ermins, squirrels or sables, which are worn for warmth, and very often for state also; for it is common to see a great man sit in his sable coat in the height of summer; but it must be observed that these coats reach no farther than the waist, thus demonstrating the judicious distinction not to load themselves with a superfluous weight of cloaths »[1382]. Cook adds that the

---

1379. VOC 2416, 26/10/1736, fol. 2543.
1380. Hanway, I, p. 331; for a similar description see Cook, II, p. 439, 331.
1381. Hanway, I, p. 332.
1382. *Ibid.*, p. 331-332.

Persian chiefs were dressed in brocades, silks and cloths of gold[1383]. Hanway also submits that « silk is worn in summer by man of fashion, esp. for under garments; but these as well as their cotton and woollen undergarments are quilted, which renders them very warm without being heavy »[1384]. The sleeves of their upper-garments reached down to their fingers. The outward garment of the common sort of people, is a slight cotton[1385]. *Qabas* made of *qadak* were worn by the common people of Merv[1386].

Belt

« Under the rich shashes round the waist they carry a pointed knife in a case of wood or leather which is mounted with gold, silver and gems, as is the handle. [...] Their writers carry their ink and pens about them in a case which they put under their sash, or in their pocket under their arm »[1387].

Trousers

« Their drawers, or rather trowsers are more convenient than breeches in a hot country, being without any tight ligaments »[1388]. Cook submits that they wear « long drawers and hose made of cloath »[1389].

Socks

« They sometimes wear cloth-stockings, which set loose like boots; but for the most part they only use socks of wool, which reach over the ankles »[1390].

Shoes

« They wear slippers like women's shoes without quarters; these are of shagreen made with the skin of horse rumps, which are prepared hard and rough like a seal's skin. The heels being high, they are calculated to carry one out of the dirt, but they are extremely uneasy to those who are not accustomed to them »[1391].

1383. Cook, II, p. 331.
1384. Hanway, I, p. 332.
1385. *Ibid.*
1386. Mervi, II, p. 743.
1387. *Ibid.*, I, p. 332; Cook, II, p. 439.
1388. Hanway, I, p. 332.
1389. Cook, II, p. 439.
1390. Hanway, I, p. 332.
1391. *Ibid.*; see also Cook, II, p. 439.

Female dress

« The dress of women is simple, differing from the men rather for the distinction of sexes, than by affecting any form shocking to nature [ornaments, hair]. [...] Their shirts, as well as the men's, are of a thin manufacture of silk and cotton, but they are open at the breast in the manner of men's shirts in Europe, whilst the men's are supported on the left shoulder by a small button; the women also wear drawers and slippers as the men »[1392]. « They are all dressed in long gowns of silk or cotton: They all wear silk and cotton drawers, which reach down to their ancles; they wear bracelets of gold about their ancles and wrists; and the foremost part of their shifts; which are commonly of silk, from a point immediately below the navel, are embroidered down to the bottom with gold or silver figures forming a large triangle whose upper angle is acute »[1393]. When going outside the house « they are vailed with white linen, but have a piece of net-work before their eyes »[1394].

Zand period

Clothes in the Zand period did not change that much as compared with the previous period. Persians continued to wear three to four tight garments over one another which reached a little below the knee[1395]. The most important change being that the *kolah-e naderi* went out of fashion and was replaced by a tall conical hat or the Bokharan lamb skin hat, wrapped with a shawl sash.

Moreover the downward trend in the luxuriousness of garments, begun under the Afsharids, continued during the second half of the 18th century. For clothes worn by people during the Zand period were generally of lower quality and less costly than during the Safavid and Afsharid period. The dominant material was cotton fabric. Ferrières-Sauvebœuf states that « the entire nation seems to have sworn off luxury; both masters and servants dress in simple cotton fabrics »[1396]. Contemporaries remark at the simplicity, even poor manner of Karim Khan's dress; his sleeves were even often darned, while his summer dress was made of *chit*, and his lining of

1392. Hanway, I, p. 334.
1393. Cook, II, p. 444.
1394. *Ibid.*, p. 445.
1395. Gmelin, III, p. 157.
1396. Ferrières-Sauveboeuf, II, p. 58; see also Morier [*A Second Journey*], II, p. 156 and Dhoka', p. 9 f.

karbas[1397]. Poor men were dressed in cheap *karbas* and *pashmineh* clothes, and the very poor in just a thin *'aba*[1398].

However, this alleged simplicity of dress of Karim Khan Zand was not representative for his court and the elite in general. The Safavid shahs, generally, also dressed less sumptuously than their courtiers. Successful people during the Zand period, such as the main officers of Mir Mohanna, wore *zarbaft*, *atlas*, *dara'i*, *alicheh*, *qasab* and *londreh*, though the chieftain himself, to mark off his distinctiveness, wore only blue *qadak* and used a cotton cloth (*futeh-ye rismani*) on his head and as a girdle[1399]. The same held true for Karim Khan's successors who dressed up as well. For example, Ja'far Khan Zand wore « an orange-coloured cuba [*qaba*] or coat, made of silk, and quilted, and had his scimitar on »[1400]. « In Persia, the general and favourite colour is green, even to their shoes; and people of all persuasions and denominations wear it as they please »[1401].

Male dress

Head dress

Men wore a hat, mostly of red broad-cloth, which was covered on the outside with black lambskin. They also wore skull-caps of white or blue embellished with silk embroidery; others wore a leathern cap. Wealthy men wrapped a Kashmir or Kerman shawl around it. The latter cost from 30 rubles, for an inferior quality, to up to 200 rubles[1402]. Karim Khan's head dress was a tall hat bound with a Kashmir shawl, which tall cylindrical cap replaced the *kolah-e naderi*[1403]. High officials wore a similar head dress. However, a hat made of lambskin, bound with a shawl was more frequent[1404]. The common Persian wore a hat which was very wide at the bottom, had two edges on each side, and was probably a *kolah-e namadi*[1405]. Merchants generally wore a coarse cap without a sash; leading

1397. Qajar, p. 136; Fasa'i, p. 219.
1398. Asef, p. 407-408.
1399. *Ibid.*, p. 382.
1400. Francklin, p. 197.
1401. *Ibid.*, p. 184.
1402. Gmelin, III, p. 156; Olivier, III, p. 2, 280; Niebuhr, p. 108.
1403. Fasa'i, I, p. 219.
1404. Niebuhr, II, p. 175; Ferrières-Sauvebœuf, II, p. 47; some courtiers wore striped shawls (Asef, p. 387).
1405. Niebuhr, II, p. 176.

merchants, however, wound a shawl around their hat[1406]. Princes and magnates wore their hat tilted, while the common people wore it straight on their head[1407].

Shirt

The shirt was of both silk and cotton and had wide sleeves, with the slit at the shoulders, which was fastened either on the left or the right. The neck was left entirely bare[1408]. « They therefore also wear generally shirts of striped cottons »[1409].

Vest

The vest was made of silk, in case of important people, and was quilted with cotton[1410].

Outercoat or qaba

The overcoat was made of gold brocade, often lined with sable furs. Those worn by middle class and lower people were made either of cotton or silk, depending on the person's means. It reached down and was fastened by a hook to the hips. The sleeves reached down to the fingers, and were adorned with numerous small buttons. On the underside both the sleeves were open[1411]. Niebuhr reports that « the Persian manner of clothing is totally different from that of the Arabs and Turks. [...] All wear a jacket, which reaches down till the calves [...] The sleeves are long, and generally closed over the hands. Around the waist they wear a sash as all Orientals do. [...] The clothes of a leading citizen only differs from the above in that he wears an over coat, which in winter time generally is lined with furs »[1412]. In winter time, Karim Khan, for example, wore garments made of *qadak* and *atlas*, lined with furs[1413]. Merchants generally wore a coarse cap without a sash, and a short fur jacket (probably a *pustin*) without sleeves[1414].

1406. Niebuhr, II, p. 176.
1407. Asef, p. 365; Waring, p. 58.
1408. Gmelin, III, p. 156.
1409. Niebuhr, II, p. 175 ff.
1410. Gmelin, III, p. 157.
1411. *Ibid.*, p. 157-158.
1412. Niebuhr, II, p. 175 f.
1413. Fasa'i, I, p. 219; furs were popular with the rich for collars and sleeves, especially sable (Gulestaneh, p. 341); Hedayat [*Rouzat*], IX, p. 206.
1414. Niebuhr, II, p. 176.

In addition to the *qaba*, large coats were worn, especially red of color, which were greatly loved. These were worn on solemn occasions and against the rain[1415]. These great coats probably were the *tekmeh* (see below). In addition, an *'aba* was worn. According to Olivier *'aba*s were « goat fleece fabrics that more than other stuffs resists the rain. They are sometimes as fine as our best camelottes, though they are close to our *bouracans* due to their coarseness. They are called habba »[1416].

Belt

People wore a silk sash over which they wore either a silk or a cotton sash or, if they could afford it, a Kerman shawl[1417]. Karim Khan girded his garments with a *termeh* sash[1418].

Trousers

Trousers were wide, like that of a Dutch sailor[1419]. Karim Khan wore red trousers, which was a very popular piece of dress among the well-to-do[1420].

Stockings

Important people wore crimson red stockings, whilst others only used floral woolen socks which reached as far as the ankles[1421].

Shoes

Generally slippers were worn with high heels[1422].

Boots or chakmeh

In the 18th century *chakmeh*, leathern, knee-high riding boots with tapering heels were worn. Especially cavalry officers used them, but would take them off as soon as they dismounted because it was very difficult to walk in them. Courtiers wore black calf *chakmeh*s which were comfortable to wear as well as durable. Often letters and handkerchiefs were carried in these boots[1423].

1415. Gmelin, III, p. 158.
1416. Olivier, V, p. 305.
1417. Gmelin, III, p. 158.
1418. Fasa'i, I, p. 219.
1419. Gmelin, III, p. 158.
1420. Morier [*Journey*], I, p. 244, 247.
1421. Gmelin, III, p. 158.
1422. *Ibid.*
1423. Niebuhr, II, p. 176; Olivier, III, p. 222.

Female dress

Women's style also reflected the Safavid style. Women wore hip-length, long-sleeved jackets over long robes. « Hip-length undershirts are worn over wide, straight trousers embroidered and woven with oblique stripes of floral motives. Long robes are replaced by tight, short jackets that flare over the hips »[1424]. Male and female dress also was in many respects similar during the Zand period. When going outside their house women were, of course, entirely covered by a veil with a *ruband* to allow them to see where they went[1425].

Head dress

Women wore a small skull-cap, sometimes decorated with pearls or coins[1426]. This was covered with a large silken kerchief of two square royal arshins of various colors. This kerchief was first folded in the form of a double triangle, the center of which was put on the head, so that one part was hanging down at the back, while the two other ends were tied up at the nape of the neck[1427].

Shirt

Women wore narrow shirts, varying in length, made of cotton or silk (crimson taffetas), which were open in front. Some wore see-through shirts[1428]. In front there was a slit, which was closed at the neck with a button or ribbon. The female shirt differed from that of the men in that it was fastened under the neck and not on the shoulder like that of the men. Further, the female shirt reached down to the navel. The female shirt was also adorned with a silken black hem and a silken cord, which were intertwined, and covered with thin round or square pieces of silver or bronze[1429].

Vest or arkhaliq

Like the men the women protected themselves against the cold with quilted jackets or *arkhaliq*, with puffed-up sleeves, or short sleeved lambskin vests which were closed in front by a clasp and by a wrap-around

1424. Scarce [Vesture], p. 46.
1425. Ferrières-Sauvebœuf, II, p. 57; Gmelin, III, p. 159.
1426. Ferrières-Sauvebœuf, II, p. 58.
1427. Gmelin, III, p. 158.
1428. See contemporary drawing in Waring, p. 61.
1429. Gmelin, III, p. 158; Ferrières-Sauvebœuf, II, p. 58.

sash[1430]. The vest was shorter than that of the men and, in the case of ladies of quality, it was made of expensive materials such as broad-cloth and *burmet* or silk. If in addition they were rich they had them covered with golden and silver loops and large buttons on both sides all the way from the neck to the navel, just like the men. Poor women wore even shorter vests, which were very tight (like that of their husbands) and open under the armpits[1431]. A long coat was worn over this vest which, if its owner was a woman of quality, would be made of gold brocade[1432].

Trousers

Under the shirt they wore trousers. These were often designed with diagonal parallel bands and lined with another fabric[1433]. According to Ferrières-Sauvebœuf, this trouser fashion hailed from Shiraz. These trousers were filled with so much cotton and layers that they looked like two monstrous pillars. Ladies of quality had them made of gold brocade and/or embroidered[1434]. This fashion did not seem to have yet reached the Qajar north by 1770, because Gmelin only mentions that the trousers tapered towards the feet[1435].

Stockings

No stockings were worn, for women wore leggings (*puttaveh*) up to their knees. These were made of white cotton bands, which were stuffed with cotton, which made them very thick[1436].

Shoes

Rich women wore slippers, just like the men, with high heels (without quarter) as well as boots made of saffran colored leather[1437].

Qajar Period

The dress of the men has changed very materially within the last century, Malcolm concluded around 1810[1438]. That the Qajar period had

1430. Dhoka', p. 13; Ferrières-Sauvebœuf, II, p. 58-59; Waring, p. 57.

1431. Gmelin, III, p. 158-159.

1432. Dhoka', p. 13; Ferrières-Sauvebœuf, II, p. 58-59; Waring. p. 57.

1433. Dhoka', p. 12 f; Olivier, p. 155; Ferrières-Sauvebœuf, II, p. 57; also quilted with wool (Niebuhr, II, p. 177).

1434. Ferrières-Sauvebœuf, II, p. 57-58.

1435. Gmelin, III, p. 159.

1436. *Ibid.*

1437. Ferrières-Sauvebœuf, II, p. 59; Gmelin, III, p. 159.

started was clear where people's dress was concerned. « The Qajars preside over fashion, and everything which is supposed to be near or elegant, is called *Qujjuree* or à la Qajar »[1439]. « The dress of the Persian is very expensive, frequently amounting to sixty or one hundred guineas, in proportion to their capacity to bear this expence »[1440].

« The inhabitants of the principal towns are fond of dressing richly. Their upper garments are either made of chintz, silk, or cloth, and are often trimmed with gold or silver lace: they also wear brocade: and in winter their clothes are lined with furs, of which they import a great variety. It is not customary for any person, except the king, to wear jewels »[1441].

« The Persians reserve their luxury and magnificence entirely for those parts of the dress which are exposed, for they attach no importance to such as are not visible. Thus it is that their clothes of gold cloth, or silk, are lined with the coarsest linen; in fact, they place no value on the fineness of that article »[1442].

Morier remarks on the great difference in dress compared with Safavids. The Persians had adopted for their apparel the dark and somber colours, which were universal among all ranks, while under the Zands light colours were much in vogue. Browns, dark olives, bottle greens, and dark blues, were the colours most worn. Red they allegedly disliked[1443]. « The Persian costume is not the liveliest; the colours used in dress are for the greater part sober blues, browns, greens, greys, chiefly of neem-rungs, or middle tints, as they are called »[1444]. « The colours preferred in Persia are fawns, browns, greens, yellows, purples, scarlets, and light colors in general. Blues and black are little used, and the lighter qualities of cloth, as ladies' cloth, are I think most in request »[1445].

By now, red was not in general use by the public. This was not because they disliked the color — after all, it had been very popular in the 18th century — but because it was now reserved for royalty. « The merchants

1438. Malcolm [*History*], II, p. 594.
1439. Waring, p. 57.
1440. *Ibid.*, p. 60.
1441. Malcolm [*History*], II, p. 594; Porter, I, pictures of women (p. 454) and *khan* (p. 448).
1442. Tancoigne p. 203-206.
1443. Morier [*Journey*], p. 242.
1444. Fraser [*Winter's Journey*], II, p. 87.
1445. Fraser [*Caspian Sea*], p. 366.

are prohibited wearing either scarlet or crimson cloths, and also using silver or golden buttons to their robes. Anyway it is never done »[1446]. The *sardar* of Erivan's « wives travel clothed in scarlet; a superb sort of raiment, not permitted in Persia to any women but those of the family of the King, or of his sons. He has, also, the privilege of covering the baggage carried by his mules, with highly ornamented cloths of blue or red, which are badges of royal equipage »[1447].

« Woolen fabrics are less in demand in Southern Persia than seems natural in a country where the winters are long and severe. Only a very small percentage of the population can, however, afford any other than cotton clothing, and in the winter, instead of wearing warm woollen clothes, the people put on many layers of cotton garments. Demand is growing, but most the cheapest and most shoddy description due to poverty of the people. Most in demand is broadcloth, recently fancy suiting and trouserings have become popular »[1448].

In the previous period, Europeans had been very positive about the cleanliness of the Persians and their clothes. However, in the Qajar period the opposite sentiment prevailed, which may have been caused by the fact that Europeans themselves were cleaner and more hygienic than they had been in the previous period. « Great filthiness is the inevitable result of this negligence. The rich as well as the poor are devoured with vermin; they wear the same shirt day and night during whole months, putting it on again when coming out of the bath, and never changing it until it quits them by falling into rags »[1449]. They very seldom changed their garments according to Waring[1450]. Lady Sheil is only somewhat more positive, writing that « the only time Persians change their clothes is when they go to the bath. They take their clothes off at night; but generally they lie down just as they are, and even in cold weather they wear their chaddor, at night »[1451]. This opinion persisted throughout the century. « The people [...] have a total disregard of cleanliness of person, clothing, and dwellings. Whether they are actually too poor to have anything warmer than cotton clothing, or whether they have buried hoards I do not know; but even in this severe

1446. Waring, p. 60.
1447. Porter, I, p. 202.
1448. Gleadow-Newcomen, p. 81. People in the north were richer (*ibid*, p. 82).
1449. Tancoigne, p. 205-206.
1450. Waring, p. 58.
1451. Sheil, p. 204-205.

weather the women of this region have nothing on their feet, and their short blue cotton trousers, short, loose, open jackets, short open chemises, and the thin blue sheet or chadar over their heads, are a mere apology for clothing »[1452].

By the end of the 19th century, fashion began to change. « The ordinary costume of the well-to-do men at Bushehr now consists of a long coat, waistcoat, pantaloons, woollen socks and imported shoes; but elderly and religious persons still affect the robe confined at the waist by a Kashmir or Calcutta shawl, the loose drawers, the white Shiraz socks, and the broad-cloth cloak which were universal 20 years ago »[1453]. In 1922, according to a census carried out in Tehran, men wore the following clothes :

Type of clothes	No. of males in %% or '000
Fekli [tie and spats]	3,000
Vest and trousers	2,000
'Abba qaba'i [overcoat]	35%
Sardari and *Moradbegi* [knee-length overcoat]	14%
Zhendeh push [clad in rags]	38%
'Ur bedun-e tan push [without proper clothes]	8%

Source : Shahri, I, p. 88.

Male dress

Head dress or kolah

The most characteristic article of Persian garb was the head dress, which identified the wearer's "ethnicity". According to Polak in 1865, each tribe and many cities and provinces had different head gear[1454]. However, most other European observers noticed little variation in head dress. The most common types of head gear were the following: « one is the familiar felt hat or *kulah-i namadi*, which may be black, grey or white, another is the *kolah-i mahuti* or black broad-cloth mounted on cardboard; a third is the light cloth cap or *araqchin*, or perspiration catcher, and worn with a coloured Masqat turban. There are also a *kulah-i tierma* or soft hat, which goes with a white turban styled *'amamah* or *shal*, and a *kulah-e sefid* made

---

1452. Bird, I, p. 136.
1453. Lorimer, p. 344-345.
1454. Polak [*Persien*], I, p. 140; Lorimer, p. 344; note the contrast with Chardin's statement for the 17th century.

of white shirting; the latter is used by mullahs and merchants and is covered by a white turban of local pattern »[1455].

Continuing the change of fashion started in the 18th century, the head-dress of every Persian was composed of one substance, a cap of jet black lambskin, from Bokhara or Astrakhan, about one foot and a half high. « The Persians give this [lambskin cap] an almost conical form by flattening the upper part, generally terminated by a point of red cloth or velvet, or simply a white skin. This dress is called Burk or Koulah, and is common to all classes, from the king to the peasant »[1456]. The only distinction in the head-dress of Persia is that of a shawl wrapped round the cap, which custom was very general according to Malcolm[1457], although Waring limits its use to the more educated class. « It is the custom for the military men to press their caps down on one side; the Mirza twist a shawl about them, and the artificers, tradesmen etc. wear their cap upright »[1458]. However, shortly, after Waring's visit this distinction was confined to the king, to the princes his sons, and to some of the nobility and great officers of state. « Cashmere shawls have been discouraged of late, in order to promote the domestic manufacture of brocade shawls »[1459]. « The nobility and officers of state wear, on occasions of ceremony only, a cap of the same skin, the wool of which is shorter, round this is bound a cachemire shawl of a palm pattern »[1460].

Not only the choice of material or the sash used, but also the way in which the *kolah* was worn, reflected a person's attunement to fashion. The 23 year old prince Hosein ʻAli Mirza, governor of Shiraz, had his cap sideways, according to a fashion among the younger Persians[1461]. One of his courtiers was a « perfect model of fashion [...] his cap was never seen in a perpendicular situation on his head; it inclined either to the left or the right, or was pushed backwards with a careless air »[1462].

1455. Lorimer, p. 344-345.

1456. Tancoigne, p. 206; see also Waring, p. 57.

1457. Malcolm [*History*], II, p. 594.

1458. Waring, p. 58.

1459. Morier [*Journey*], p. 244-245; see also Malcolm [*History*], II, p. 594.

1460. Tancoigne, p. 203-206; Viziers of Fath ʻAli Shah wore the full-dress turbans, of fine Indian shawls (Ouseley, III, p. 134).

1461. Ouseley, II, p. 13.

1462. *Ibid.*, II, p. 56; see also p. 13.

By 1820, the use of caps of lambskin was almost universal among the Persians, following the Qajar fashion[1463]. However, Mollahs « wrap their heads in a shawl, or long piece of white linen. The descendants of the Prophet use green »[1464].

According to Malcolm, « The turban, as a headdress, is now worn by none but the Arabian inhabitants of that country »[1465], in which he is wrong. Polak confirms that the turban (*'amameh, delband*) was not universally worn anymore. However, its prevalence was wider than Malcolm would have us believe. For the turban was still worn by some tribes (Kurds, Afghans, Baluch) and some classes of people. In particular, the merchant, tradesmen, mollah, *seyyed, tollab*, physician, and chemist (*'attar*) class wore turbans. The olama used generally a white one, consisting of many yards of muslin or *marmar*. Grass-green or indigo-blue, nearly black, dyed cotton (*chalvar-e sabz-e mina'i*) turbans were only worn by *seyyeds*. Merchants also affected the turban, usually of muslin, embroidered in colors, or of a yellow patterned or straw-coloured muslin, or of calico, or at times of Yazd shawl[1466]. Members of the religious class (olama, *tollab, va'ezin*), like their Safavid predecessors, also wanted to create the impression that a big turban hid big brains and much intelligence. The more important an *'alem* was the bigger his turban, so much so that the heavy turban would slide from left to right when the wearer was walking[1467]. Under Mohammad Shah the military were ordered to wear a shorter hat, much like the double-faced Khorasani hat, with a height of two *charak*[1468].

Polak confirms the universal popularity of the familiar lambskin hat or *kolah* in the 1850-60s. « It was about 15 inches high, in the form of a cone, slightly suppressed on the top. That part was worn slightly sideways or forward. The entire hat was mounted on card-board and covered with red cotton. The *kolah* of the rich was made out of the finest Bokhara lambskin, especially from the best part on the back. Less rich people had it made out of domestic sheepskin, mainly from Shiraz or Qom »[1469]. « The most

1463. Ouseley, I, p. 301.
1464. Porter, I, p. 466.
1465. Malcolm [*History*], II, p. 594.
1466. Wills, p. 320; Zarrabi, p. 248.
1467. Kermani [*Tarikh*], I, p. 34-35.
1468. Mustaufi, I, p. 87, 99 (also for more details on military dress).
1469. Polak [*Persien*], I, p. 140; Zarrabi, p. 250.

expensive are those made of foetal lamb. These skins usually go to Europe — Leipzig to be dyed. The commoner wears colored lambskin hats, or even sheep skin with the wool long. The fashions in hats change yearly; they are generally affected by the military and servant class, by courtiers and beaux, and are usually worn with a knowing cock. The Isfahani merchants, and the Armenians, at times wear very tall ones »[1470].

The *kolah* was, although fashionable, very inappropriate for riding, it fell off and, if worn in the rain, it folded. It had to be renewed 3-4 times a year, which was a costly affair. Skins from Bokhara were used to make the best quality *kolah*, which then cost from 10-14 ducats, but when local skins were used the price dropped to between 2-5 ducats. The high cost of these better *kolahs* so concerned Naser al-Din Shah that he encouraged the use of local lambskins, and had articles printed in the newspapers to exhort people to change their head dressing habits. The police checked in the street whether people stuck to the prescribed length of *kolah*. However, fashion was stronger than the shah. Only in the military around 1850, a new short, so-called *kolah-e nezami* (European type hat) was prescribed. The *kolah* had to be worn in- and outdoors and had to cover the greater part of the ears. When travelling a leather *aftab-gardan* was worn to serve as protection against the sun. In general the neck was not covered[1471].

The middle class wore a *kolah-e mahut*, or a hat made of broad-cloth, in which group government officials were included, as well as some of the lower class[1472]. The laboring class wore the familiar felt hat or *kolah-e namadi* [black, grey, or white of color] which was also the name by which this class of people were known (cup-shaped caps of felt). They also wore cheap animal skin hats (*astar-e pust*)[1473]. The peasant might or might not wear it with a turban. In the south colored Masqat turbans were worn. There was also a *kolah-e termeh* or soft hat which was combined with a white turban style *'amameh* or *shal*, and a *kolah-e sefid* made of white shirting. The latter was used by mollahs and merchants and was covered by a white turban of local pattern (white or blue muslin). Richer ones had shawl, especially a *termeh-e selseleh*, in the same color, or of *aqabanu* (a silk fabric), wrapped around it[1474]. Under this head cover a light cotton or cloth

1470. Wills, p. 320-321.
1471. Polak [*Persien*], I, p. 143.
1472. Zarrabi, p. 248, 250.
1473. *Ibid.*, p. 250.
1474. *Ibid.* p. 143, 249.

embroidered skull-cap or *araqchin* was worn, which was especially made in Isfahan by women[1475].

« Inside their homes, most Persians affect a *shab-e kolah*, or night hat. This is a loose, baggy cap, of shawl or quilted material; it is often embroidered by the ladies and presents of night hats are as frequent with them as our ones of embroidered slippers »[1476].

In 1922, according to a census carried out in Tehran, the following headwear was in use by the male population:

Name of headwear	no. of persons wearing it %%
'Amameh (turban)	20
Finah (fez)	3
Kolah-e namadi (felt hat)	25
Kolah-e meqva'i (cardboard hat)	2
Shir shekari (silken hat)	1
'Araqchin (skull-cap)	4
Sabz o siyah ("green and black ")	18
Kepi	1
Various (kerchief [*dastmal*], shawl, fur hat, patched fabric (*parcheh-ye pareh*), etc.)	15

Four per cent of the male population went bare headed[1477].

Shirt or pirahan

The shirt, or *pirahan*, was of unstarched linen, cotton (*chalvari*, *karbas*), red or blue silk; being open on the right breast, it was fastened at the same side, on the shoulder, with two or three small buttons, and descended only to the waist, and was worn by all classes[1478]. The shirt reached a few inches below the hips, and « goes close round the lower part of the neck, where it is sometimes ornamented by a ribband or thin cord of silk. The opening of the shirt extends to the bottom of the ribs »[1479]. « The shirt was sewn with white silk, cotton as a sewing material being unknown; it is often, particularly in the south of Persia, elaborately embroidered

1475. Polak [*Persien*], I, p. 40.
1476. Wills, p. 322.
1477. Shahri, I, p. 88.
1478. Tancoigne, p. 203; also Waring, p. 57; Drouville, I, p. 26; Zarrabi, p. 248.
1479. Morier [*Journey*], p. 269-270.

around the neck. There is no collar, and the sleeves are quite loose, and are not confined at the wrist »[1480].

The poor had only one shirt, while the well-to-do had two. The rich did not wash them, but gave them to their servants and just bought a new one. The lower orders, particularly the villagers, often had them dyed blue, whereas the upper classes — and their servants — invariably wore white shirts. In the Caspian sea area a silk shirt was worn, while at court a so-called European shirt, or *pirahan-e nezami*, was worn[1481]. « Silk shirts used to be worn, but are now seldom seen on men. Among the very religious during Moharram the shirt is at times dyed black »[1482]. In the south, Persian tribesmen wore a long undershirt (*jameh-juma* or *pirahan*) made of nainsooks (white or dyed black), or white mulls or *kasavari*. In winter time white shirtings were used[1483].

Outer garments

Persians did not wear loose fitting clothes, but rather those that accentuated the form of the body and arms. Men wore a quilted vest which was closed only around the hips, leaving the chest open to be covered by their coats. These fitted snugly down to the waist and were then flared down to the ankles[1484]. « The Shah wore an open shawl surcoat, lined with fur, reaches about half way down the thigh, the sleeves are cut off a little below the elbow. These surcoats cost less than 25£ often much more. Under this a light gown is worn, reaching nearly to the ancle, and open on the sides for about a foot from the bottom. These gowns, likewise an universal dress, have slits left open under the arms and inside the elbows. A shawl is tied round the waist. In cities, the surcoat is usually laid aside, and in winter a cloak of cloth is substituted »[1485].

Vest or arkhaliq

Over the shirt (*pirahan*) and the trousers (*zir-jameh*), a tight vest or skirted coat called *arkhaliq* was worn. It was buttoned in front, generally made of quilted *chit* or cotton cloth, velvet, satin, and silk, sometimes of fine shawl, open at the breast, which tied at the side, and reached normally

1480. Wills, p. 317 f.
1481. Polak [*Persien*], I, p. 144.
1482. Wills, p. 317 f.
1483. Report on the trade of the consular district of Bushire, (1911-12), p. 11.
1484. Drouville, I, p. 26.
1485. Stuart, p. 185.

to the knee, but could go as low as the thin part of the calf of the leg. It had sleeves extending to the wrist, but open from the elbow[1486]. This closely fitting garment was collarless, with tight sleeves to the elbow. The lower arm was open but could be closed in winter with a number of metal buttons[1487]. When the vest was made of *qalamkar* the most appreciated material was produced in Benares. Inferior qualities came from Isfahan, Shiraz and Borujerd, and fabrics from Britain were also used. Rich people had their *arkhaliq* made of woolen cloth made in Europe, or of *kork* or *barak*[1488].

The olama wore an *arkhaliq* made of *qalamkar* or European *chit*, as well as of *alecheh*. Government officials wore a so-called *arkhaliq-e hasani*, made of cotton (*qalamkar*) or of various silk fabrics such as *atlas-e mahramat*, *atlas-e khata'i* and *alecheh*. The difference between the summer and winter *arkhaliq* is that in winter it was quilted (*panbeh-dar*), while in summer it was doubled (*dula'i*). Middle class males wore an *arkhaliq* made of European *chit* or *alejeh* from Kashan and Yazd[1489]. Tribesmen in the south had their *arkhaliq* commonly made of *astari*, *lamseh*, and Russian (*orusi*) prints, or of black and white discharge, purple and chocolate *dubahrs* and crimps[1490].

Qaba

Over the *arkhaliq*, especially in cold weather, a second jacket or *qaba* was worn, made of cloth or *barak*. The *qaba* always had one color (green, yellow, blue, violet, red, etc.) and was made of *qadak* (domestic nankin) or of Yazd and Kashan silk (taffeta) of which the moiré variety (*khara* and *dara'i*) in particular were very much liked. However, the rich had their *qaba* made of brocade (*zarbaft*). The two jackets reached halfway between knee and ankle. They were wide and had to cover the private parts, otherwise one's dress was considered to be improper[1491].

1486. Morier [*Journey*], p. 269-270; Waring, p. 57; Tancoigne, p. 203-206; Polak [*Persien*].

1487. Wills, p. 318.

1488. Polak [*Persien*], I, p. 145. Other European renderings of this term include alcalock, alkaluk; « alcaloks : vestes de dessous en indiennes matelassées » (Bélanger, I, p. 333).

1489. Zarrabi, p. 248-250.

1490. Report on the trade of the consular district of Bushire, (1911-12), p. 11.

1491. Polak [*Persien*], I, p. 145.

« The caba: which is a long vest descending to the ancle, but fitting tight to the body as far only as the hips: it then buttons at the side. The sleeves go over those of the alcalock, and from the elbow are closed by buttons only, that they may be opened thus far for the purpose of ablution, when the namaz or prayer is said »[1492]. « The qaba, is likewise open on the breast, and ornamented before with two pieces of gold or silver lace, and buttons of the same metal: this falls as low as the ancle »[1493]. The olama wore a *qaba* made of cloth (*mahut*) or dyed nankin (*qadak*). In summer, the *qadak* would be of better quality such as from Kashan and Yazd. Government officials and leading merchants wore a so-called *qaba-ye band-e hoseini*, usually made of broadcloth (*mahut*) or *barak*. During the winter, they wore a *qaba-ye 'aqeri* or one made of *kashmir shekan*, while during the summer, the *qaba* was made of silk fabrics such as *dara'i*, *qotni*, *suf* or *qadak*. Middle class males wore a *qaba* made of *barak* or *qadak-e hoseini*, while in summer it was made of *qadak*[1494]. The quality of the fabric used depended, of course, on the wealth of the wearer. The lowest class wore *abreh*, i.e. pieces of five yards of Liepmann's shirting, which was dyed in various colors by local dyers. The better-off class had it made of white shirting in summer, and in winter of black and colored Italian prints (*dabit*). Nomads used a variety of fabrics such as *fastuni*, suitings, sateens, and also plushes, velvets and silk[1495].

There was another kind of *qaba*, « called the bagalee, which crosses over the breast, and fastens all down the side by a range of buttons to the hip. This is generally made of cloth, or of shawl or cotton quilted, and as the warmer, is most used in winter »[1496]. Less important merchants were in the habit of wearing a *qaba-ye baghali* and *bargeh-dar*[1497].

« The outside robe, or Quba, is made of various kind of cloths, some of which are magnificent and expensive »[1498]. The Shah's « robe was of fine gold brocade. His undergarments were composed of red Kashmere shawl of the richest work. Another shawl, of deeper hues, but of greater

1492. Morier [*Journey*], p. 242.
1493. Tancoigne, p. 203-206.
1494. Zarrabi, p. 248-250.
1495. Report on the trade of the consular district of Bushire, (1911-12), p. 11.
1496. Morier [*Journey*], p. 242. Kabas and bagalis are practically the same (Bélanger, I, p. 333).
1497. Zarrabi, p. 250.
1498. Waring, p. 57; see also Tancoigne, p. 203-206.

value, bound his waist »[1499]. 'Abbas Mirza wore a *qaba* made of *qadak* with a Kashmir shawl[1500].

« Above this is the coat, or "kemmercheen", a tunic of coloured calico, silk, satin, moiré, cloth, cashmere, or Kerman shawl, gold embroidered silk, satin, or velvet, according to the time of the year and the purse or position of the wearer. This, like the "alkaluk", is open in front and shows the shirt. It has a small standing collar at times, and is double-breasted. It has a pocket hole on either side, giving access to the pockets, which are always in the "alkaluk", in which garment is the breast-pocket, where watch, money, jewels, and seals are kept. The length of the "kemmercheen" denotes the class of the wearer. The military and official classes and the various "noker" or servants, from the king's valet, who also may be prime minister, wear them short; that is to say, to the knee, while fops and "lutis" (sharpers) wear them shorter even than this. The priest, and merchants, and the villagers, esp. around Shiraz, and the townsmen and shopkeepers, with doctors and lawyers, wear them very long, often to their heels »[1501].

Long over coat, tekmeh, uymeh and baruni

The outer coat is always made of cloth, and is worn or thrown off according to the heat of the weather. Of this dress there are many sorts - the *tekmeh, uymeh* and *baruni*. The *tekmeh* which has sleeves open from the elbow, but which are yet so fashionable as to admit occasionally the lower part also of the arm. These sleeves are generally permitted to hang behind. The coat itself is quite round, buttons before, and drops like a petticoat over the shawl that goes round the waist[1502]. « On a journey or with the army, they replace the bala pouch by the tikme, a tartar coat of green cloth, fitted close to the shape, with sleeves open to above the wrist, at which part they become narrower. The tikme is also worn by the common people »[1503].

1499. Porter, I, p. 355.
1500. Bélanger, I, p. 357.
1501. Wills, p. 318.
1502. Morier [*Journey*], p. 242.
1503. Tancoigne, p. 204-205. The tekmis is made of silk or coarse woollen-cloths, Morier [*Journey*], p. 231. His *qaba* was held by a shawl-girdle, and covered by a « tekmeh, robe de drap de couleur claire. Cette robe, boutonnée sur la poitrine, tombait comme un jupon par dessus le chale, qui, augmentant au niveau des reins l'ampleur de la tekmeh » (Bélanger, I, p. 212). « tekmeh, oymeh: redingotes à peu près semblables » (*ibid.*, p. 333).

The *uymeh*, which was like the *tekmeh*, except that from the hip downwards, it is open at the sides[1504]. The *uymeh* was more used, and was more exclusively calculated for riding. It somewhat resembled a lady's riding habit, fitting tight to the shape, from the neck to the waist; where it was gathered into plaits, and swells out above the girdle, falling in ample folds to the feet. It is generally made of broad-cloth, varying in quality, as well as richness of the embroidery with which it is ornamented, according to the ability of the owner[1505].

The *baruni*, which was a loose and ample robe, with proportionally ample arms, generally made of cloth, and faced with velvet, and thrown negligently over the shoulders[1506]. The *baruni*, according to Fraser, was confined to men of some rank, « is an ample cloak, with large sleeves, that shrouds the whole person. It is made, according to the fancy and means of the wearer, of coarse or fine broad-cloth, of shawl, or even of velvet, it is lined with every kind of material, from the richest furs down to the coarsest chintz, and embroidered (often very richly) with gold, silver, or silk »[1507]. Persians to warm themselves, fold themselves in a fur pelisse, or a barounee, which is a handsome robe of crimson cloth, lined with shawls or velvets[1508]. The so-called *chukeh-barani* was part of the official court dress[1509].

Kolejeh, kurdi

The *kolejeh* was a knee-length coat, somewhat shorter than the similar *sardari*. It was fitted at the waist and open under the armpits to facilitate movements, or with empty sleeves dangling[1510]. « They also have a short jacket, called the koordee, which fits close to the body, but with loose flaps

1504. Morier [*Journey*], p. 242-243.

1505. Fraser [*Narrative*], p. 69-70.

1506. Morier [*Journey*], p. 242-243.

1507. Fraser [*Narrative*], p. 69-70.

1508. Kinneir, p. 24. « The governor of Fasa dressed in his barani or immense cloak of scarlet cloth » (Ouseley, II, p. 94). « Fath Ali Shah wore an orange coloured barouni or cloak, while the princes were in sky-blue velvet riding dress » (Fraser [*Winter's Journey*], II, p. 77). « Nasakchi and Yasavuls in their scarlet barounies » (*ibid.*, p. 80); « the yasawuls have a brass ornament in their caps to distinguish them from the nasaqachis » (*ibid.*, p. 88). « Beroune = manteau en drap, ample et à large manches » (Bélanger, I, p. 333).

1509. Soltan-Ahmad Mirza, p. 62.

1510. Mostaufi, I, p. 510.

as low as the commencement of the swell of the thigh »[1511]. It was mainly worn during cold weather[1512]. In winter many wore a cloak or jacket (*kolejeh*) of cloth, Kashmir or Kerman shawl or *barak* (camel hair flanel) with short sleeves till elbows. These are often lined with otter or squirrel fur (*pustin*) which is imported from Russia[1513]. But during summer-time, it was also used, if only for a short while. « Over the kemercheen is worn the kolajah, or coat. This is as a rule cast off in summer, save on official occasions, as when the wearer is performing his functions or making a call, and is often borne by a servant or carried over the shoulders by the owner himself. They are of cloth, shawl, or camel hair cloth, and are invariably lined throughout with either silk or cloth, flannel or even fur. They are like the Turkish frock-coat, made with a very loose sleeve, and with many plaits behind. They have lappels, as with us, and are trimmed with gold lace (derbeeri), shawl, or fur, or at times quite plain; they have a roll collar and false pockets »[1514]. The olama wore a *kolejeh* made of *mahut* or of *barak-e dula'i* with a Bokharan lambskin lining. Government officials and merchants, wore a *kolejeh* and *sardari* made of *mahut* or *termeh-ye dula'i*, with a lining of *pust-e khaz* or beaver fur[1515], similar to the *kolejeh*, reaching to the knees. Those of magnates were made of silk brocade with ornamental froggings rather than buttons. The *sardari* was a frock cloak, double-breasted, with a high collar (also referred to as greatcoat or waistcoat), similar to the *kolejeh*, reaching to the knees. Those of magnates were made of silk brocade with ornamental froggings rather than buttons. It was worn by the middle and upper classes and was made of quite plain or dark materials either suitings or black Italians (*dabit*). Chiefs and wealthy people wore sardaris made of broadcloth. The *sardari-ye nezami* was a garment corresponding with the European frock-coat, but with pleats below the waist at the back[1516]. The *sardari* was made of various materials such as *shamsehdar* (flowery) *'aqeri-ye shekari* (?) *termeh-ye laki*, *-sefid*, *-lajevardi*, and *-goli* (red, white, blue and flowered shawl)[1517].

1511. Morier [*Journey*], p. 243.

1512. Mostaufi, I, p. 510.

1513. Polak [*Persien*], I, p. 147.

1514. Wills, p. 318.

1515. Zarrabi, p. 248-250. The *sardari* was a frock cloak.

1516. Golzari, p. 203; Marsh, p. 101; Report on the trade of the consular district of Bushire, (1911-12), p. 11.

1517. Amin-Lashkar, p. 24, 40, 44, 48, 56, 61, 86, 165.

« Zill ol-Soltan deep yellow satin or velvet kabba, over which a scarlet kulaejeh, or vest, of a peculiar form, worn only by the royal family, and called koordee, the back, shoulders, and breast of which are splendidly mailed with pearls and precious stones »[1518].

By the 1870s the *kolejeh* went out of fashion. Tahvildar writes « formerly their product was much in demand and they were numerous, but now the kolichehduz have become few »[1519].

Qatebi, jobbeh, balapush

Besides the outer coats mentioned they have also coats trimmed with fur. « Such is the catabee, which is an uncommonly rich dress, covering the whole of the body, with fur over the back and shoulders, fur at the cuffs, and fur inside. It is made of cloth of gold and brocades, with large ornaments of gold lace in front, and forms altogether the most dignified among the habits that I remarked in Persia »[1520].

A special cloak, when on official occasions, is the *jabbeh* made of shawl, *mahut* or *aghri*, which covers the wearer from top to toe and has long sleeves. When out walking or visiting the loose *aba* or cloak of cloth or *barak*, or Kashmir is thrown over the shoulder[1521].

« The khans and mirzas are dressed. on occasions of ceremony, each in a long pelisse of gold cloth, with lace and large buttons of the same metal. At all other times they wear a wide capote of red cloth, which is called bala pouch, the cape of it being quilted and embroidered with silk of the same colour, garnished with large silk covered buttons, and falling as low as the waist »[1522].

Pustin

Those who could not afford these more suitable and expensive garments, protected themselves from the cold by cloaks of felt, or coarse woolen fabrics, or sheepskin pelisses, which reached down to the thighs; and, occasionally, by ample wrappers made of the same materials having the leathery side worn outwards (called *pustins*)[1523]. « The skins are used in making pelisses, though I am not certain, as the Persians are very

---

1518. Fraser [*Winter's Journey*], II, p. 91.
1519. Tahvildar, p. 98.
1520. Morier [*Journey*], p. 243.
1521. Polak [*Persien*], I, p. 149; Amir-Lashkar, p. 156, 238.
1522. Tancoigne, p. 203-206; Amir-Lashkar, p. 59, 71, 93.
1523. Fraser [*Narrative*], p. 69-70.

scrupulous in the use of furs, some of which they will not wear; of these they say, "Namaz ne darad", literally "It has not prayer", meaning that it is not lawful to pray in that kind of a skin. If, on the contrary, it is not forbidden, they say "Namaz derad", "It has prayer". The fur of the polecat is their most usual and favourite wear »[1524].

« The warmest of their dresses is a sheep-skin with the fur inside, and the leather part outside. It is called, from its sudoforic qualities, the *hummum* or bath, but it is more generally named the pooshtee. The better sheep skins come from Bokhara and are covered with the finest wool certainly that I ever saw »[1525].

« The undress consists of a little pelisse (furlined coat) covered with cloth or silk stuff, embroidered with gold or silver, and which has the same form as the *tikme*. It is not uncommon to see the greatest noblemen, especially in winter, dressed in a simple pelisse of sheepskin, similar to that of the shepherds »[1526]. Lastly, a small pelisse or *poustin* which did not go below the waist[1527]. A *nim-taneh*, made of a heavy, warm fabric such as *barak*, was worn in combination with a *pustin* during winter time[1528].

« The Afghan pustin, full-length, are only worn by travellers and the sick and aged. The neemtan or the common sheepskin jacket, with short sleeves, used by shopkeepers and the lower class of servants, grooms etc., in winter. They are mostly seen in Isfahan. The Afghan pustin is warm and used both as bed and as bedding. Its skin is dyed yellow; the fur is a naturally brown. An ample cloak is made with very long sleeves, which act as gloves, the hands not being protruded. They are often elaborately embroidered with yellow silk, and are worth in Tehran, where they are very common, from four pounds [ten tomans] to sixteen pounds [forty tomans] »[1529].

By the 1870s the *pustinduz*, which had been a numerous craft in Isfahan, were reduced to a only a few. They used local sheep skins and also lined cloth like *kharqeh* (quilted cloth) when it was of good quality[1530].

1524. Holmes, p. 278.
1525. Morier [*Journey*], p. 244.
1526. Tancoigne, p. 205.
1527. *Ibid.*
1528. Mostaufi, I, p. 238.
1529. Wills, p. 319.
1530. Tahvildar, p. 98.

« In winter they have large cloaks, which are called kork. They also have a morning coat; when not dressed to receive people. Superior ones are made of scarlet broad-cloth, but these were only for princes, nobles and high officials. Other classes wore blue, green or brown. Both male and female members of rich class had fur coats for winter. The poorer class only had a sheepskin, which was open at the front, with sleeves till the elbow »[1531].

Yapanchi

Besides the *balapush* or overcoats there was « the yapunjah, the woolen Kurdish cloak. This is a kind of felt, having a shaggy side, of immense thickness. It looks like a bearskin and is of great weight. It is a half-circle in shape; a strap at the neck holds it on. The wearer, generally a shepherd, uses it as a great-coat, bed and bedding »[1532]. « There is also the felt coat of the villager, a very warm and inexpensive garment. It is from half an inch to one inch thick and enables the villager to defy the severest weather. It costs from 5 to 15 krans »[1533].

The cossacks « wearing their yaponchas, a short cloack of goat-skin, with long hair, movable round the neck to face the wind and rain from any quarter »[1534]. « The felt coats, which protect equally from the rain and old, are dark and seamless, and cost from 10 s to 20s. They have sleeves closed at the end to form a glove, and with a slit below the elbow through which the hand can be protruded and used. The coats are cloak like, the sleeve is as long as the coat, and they are often worn merely suspended from the neck »[1535]. «The *yapuncha* was known among the Torkomans as *kusgun*. As many as four sheepskins were used to make a *kusgun*. A good coat cost from 15 to 20 shillings in 1880. When the hide was of lamb, or the wool was of fines quality, the price rose in proportion, especially when the front was stamped or embroidered, in which case five to eight pounds were paid.»[1536].

1531. Drouville, I, p. 26.
1532. Wills, p. 320.
1533. *Ibid.*
1534. Sheil, p. 43.
1535. Bird, II, p. 151-152.
1536. O'Donovan, I, p. 246-248.

Paltu

As a result of European fashion the traditional overcoats gradually disappeared and were displaced towards the end of the Qajar period by the *paltu*, which in the second half of the 19th century gradually was adopted by a growing number of courtiers. These overcoats were either made of dark cloth or of *termeh* in various colors[1537].

'Aba

The *'aba* is a sleeveless male overcoat, that is open in the front and has large armholes. Although some state that the *'aba* was made of goat wool, others state simply that it was made of camel and even sheep wool. Rabino even states that it was made of refuse silk, sometimes mixed with cotton[1538]. Fraser reports that it was made « of camel's hair, white, or black, or striped, white, brown, and black, clasped on the breast »[1539]. Abbott submits that they were of black wool, made in Hazar Jarib, and were 3 yards 15 inches wide by 30 inches[1540]. According to Polak, *abas* were made from camel hair in Kerman and Isfahan. « They are adorned by gold lace. They are very light, water proof and indestructible. They cost from 3 to 8 ducats. They can be used both in winter and summer, and are very practical when travelling, better than a rubber overcoat, because they protect against rain and sun, heat and cold »[1541].

« The abba, or camel-hair cloak of the Arab, is often worn by travellers, priests or horsemen. The priests particularly affect it; it is warm, and waterproof, also very light. Some of these abbas are very expensive, though plain; while the others, much embroidered in gold, are given as dresses of honor to the middle classes and priests, and are used at weddings, etc. »[1542]. In winter the olama wore an *'aba-ye mahut* or an *'aba-ye bushehri* or from some other place of origin such as Najaf. In summer, they wore an *'aba-ye kashmir shekan*. Government officials also wore an *'aba*, which in winter was likewise made of cloth or *mahut*, or the Bushehri or the Kermani type[1543].

1537. Amin-Lashkar, p. 40, 44, 48.
1538. Rabino and Lafont, p. 172.
1539. Fraser [*Travels*], I, p. 86.
1540. Amanat, p. 24; also McKenzie, p. 215.
1541. Polak [*Persien*], II, p. 171.
1542. Wills, p. 319.
1543. Zarrabi, p. 248. « Their ['olama] aba is made in Kurdestan, near Kermanshah » (Porter, I, p. 467).

In Kurdistan the *'aba* was a recent introduction in the 1830s. Fraser reports that a Kurdish chief commented that « the abba is not our regular dress, it is an adoption of recent days. We get them from Baghdad, or make them here now. They are cheap, and we are poor. Formerly no one ever dared to appear in the presence of a great man without a handsome cloak of broad cloth; but now, go to the Khan's dewan-khaneh, and nothing but abbas will you see »[1544].

Other woolen articles were also produced in small quantities. In particular « a butter-nut coloured, narrow-width fabric resembling Kashmiri *pashmina*, and a somewhat coarser and thinner variety with a crepe surface, which is used to making of *Abas*, the cloak in universal request among the Persians as a wrap »[1545].

Belt or kamarband

« Over the caba comes the shal kemer, which is the bandage around the waist. This is made either of cashmer shawl, or the common shawl of Kerman, or of English chintz, or of lowered muslin. The proper size is about eight yards long and one broad »[1546]. « The king and the chahzedehs alone enjoy the privilege of wearing shawl, those of the nobility are of gold cloth »[1547]. « Round their hips they wear a girdle; that for the lower class of cotton or linen and, for the rich, of kashmir shawl »[1548].

« To this is fastened (by a string neatly tied around it) a *kunjur*, or dagger, ornamented according to the wealth of its possessor, from an enamelled pummel set in precious stones, to a common handle of bone or wood »[1549]. Next comes the shawl or girdle, which is worn over the *qaba*. Military men always have a dagger in their girdles; the literati have a simple roll of paper instead of arms[1550]. It consists of a long robe, reaching nearly to the feet, and a high cap, which when covered with a shawl, has some resemblance to the ancient tiara. A sash is bound round the waist: in this a

1544. Fraser [*Travels*], I, p. 112.
1545. Gleadowe-Newcomen, p. 94.
1546. Morier [*Journey*], p. 244.
1547. Tancoigne, p. 203-206.
1548. Drouville, I, p. 26. The Shah and princes with their shawl-girdles and brocaded vests (Porter, I, p. 324).
1549. Morier [*Journey*], p. 244.
1550. Tancoigne, p. 203-206.

small dagger is stuck; and no person ever conceives himself dressed without his sword[1551].

The waist belt was not just functional, but was also an object of fashion. Prince Hosein 'Ali Mirza, governor of Shiraz, was observed with his « girdle being worn very low, according to a fashion among the younger Persians » he also had his cap sideways[1552]. One of the courtiers was a « perfect model of fashion; his sash was low and rather loosely tied, yet his waist was contracted to a narrow compass »[1553].

During the 1870s a change of fashion was slowly, but certainly asserting itself, although the *kamarband* was still almost universally worn. « The kemmerbund, or belt, is also characteristic of the class. It is made of muslin, shawl, cotton cloth among the priests, merchants and traders, and bazaar people; shawls and muslins are also affected by the secretary class and the more aged or old-fashioned among the great Government employees. In it is carried by the literati and merchants the penance and a role of paper, and its voluminous folds are used as pockets, by the bazaar people, villagers, porters and merchants's servants a small sheath knife is stuck in it, while by the farrashes a khanjar or dagger, less for use than a badge of office »[1554]. The *seyyed* usually also wore a *kamarband* of green muslin shawl, or cotton cloth[1555]. In summer, government officials and merchants wore a *shal-e kamar* made of Mazandaran cotton (or *kattan*?), and during winter one made of *termeh-ye selseleh* or of *mahramat*[1556]. Tribesmen universally, and the majority of townspeople wore a *shal-e kamar* or a heavy thick roll, usually consisting of an entire piece of mulls (22 yards long) or of colored drill, or of purple twill when in mourning. It was wound over the *pirahan*, *zir-jameh* and the *arkhaliq*[1557].

However, the distinctive mark of the courtier, military and upper servant class is the belt, generally of varnished leather, black in colour, with a brass clasp, usually of Russian manufacture. The princes and courtiers often replace the brass clasp by a huge round ornament of cut stones[1558].

1551. Kinneir, p. 23-24.
1552. Ouseley, II, p. 13.
1553. *Ibid.*, p. 56.
1554. Wills, p. 320.
1555. *Ibid.*
1556. Zarrabi, p. 248-249.
1557. Report on the trade of the consular district of Bushire, (1911-12), p. 11.
1558. Wills, p. 320.

Naser al-Din Shah gave close officials and military men leather belts with a clasp which was embossed with diamonds or precious stones. These could cost up to 2,000 ducats[1559].

Trousers or zir-jameh

« The zeer jumah: a pair of very wide, long and light trowsers, either of red silk or blue cotton or taffetas [rose or crimson], according to the quality of the person. They reaching below the ancle, where they are wider then on the thigh. They do not have trousers. They are fastened by a string which passes through the top, and is tied before on the hips under the shirt »[1560]. Those trousers worn in the hot weather were sometimes of flax[1561].

By mid century some minor changes had taken place. The trousers were still very loose, and were worn to accommodate kneeling according to Polak, and were still mostly made of cotton, dyed purple black, blue (*shalvar*), but they now had a slit in front[1562].

« The zerejumah or trousers, are of cloth among the higher classes, particularly those of the military order, who affect a garment of a tightness approaching that worn by Europeans »[1563]. « But the ordinary zerejumah is of cotton, white or dyed blue, or at times red, cut very loose, and exactly similar to the pyjamas worn by Europeans in India. They are held up by a thin cord of red or green silk or cotton round the waist, and the labouring classes, when engaged in heavy or dirty work, or when running, generally tuck up the end of these garments in under the cord, which leaves their legs bare and free to the middle of the thigh »[1564]. The olama and the majority of merchants wore trousers made of indigo dyed cotton (*chalvar-e nili*), while government officials and leading merchants wore one of red silk (*qasab-e qermez*). Middle class males wore trousers made of *qadak* or of indigo dyed cotton (*methqali-e nili*)[1565].

« For riding a pair of very wide trowsers, of any colour, but frequently of red color, which envelope in their folds a large proportion of his under garments, and which, tied around the ancles by a band for the purpose,

1559. Polak [*Persien*], I, p. 146.
1560. Morier [*Journey*], p. 243; Tancoigne, p. 203-206; Drouville, I, p. 26.
1561. Waring, p. 57; Bélanger: Ja'far Khan wore a *zir-jameh* or silk trousers.
1562. Polak [*Persien*], I, p. 147.
1563. Wills, p. 317.
1564. *Ibid.*, p. 318.
1565. Zarrabi, p. 248-250.

becomes capable of being thrust into a very wide and clumsy pair of boots, made of reddish leather, or, if the owner can afford it, of bhulkhal or Russian leather [corruption of *bulghar*]. It gives a peculiar bunch-like appearance. He also crams everything into it »[1566]. « With boots are worn *shulwar*, or baggy riding breeches. These are very loose, and tied at the ankle by a string; a sort of kilt is worn by the courtiers »[1567].

Socks or jurab

Socks and shoes complete the attire. Thick cotton or woollen socks, *jurab*, or stockings of red cloth are also worn in winter. The first are of various colours, and an attempt is made to imitate, in their patterns, those of the striped Cachemire shawls; to these are added slippers of green Morocco leather, with high heels, for wearing in town; and on journey, they bind their feet and legs with a long bandage of cloth, which they increase with the advance of the cold[1568], but also for both journeys, or for military expeditions, they wear long boots of brown leather, which rise above the knee[1569]. According to Polak, socks were very short and only reach till the ankles, they were also made of silk[1570]. Wills writes that the socks are about two inches long in the leg. The rich, however, affect a longer sock: white cotton ones are worn in summer, and coloured worsted in winter. The patterns of these worsted socks are often very pretty and effective. The villagers wear only socks on state occasions, as at a wedding, *Nawruz* etc.[1571]. Government officials and merchants wore black or green socks matching the color of their shoes. During summer their socks were of white Shiraz yarns, and during winter, they were of Khoy or Fazeki wool. Middle class males wore black socks[1572]. By the turn of the century « the extremely gaudy socks or jurrab are going out of fashion. The natives preferring European made socks of grey or black »[1573].

Shoes, kafsh

People wore three different kinds of shoes: A green slipper, with a heel about an inch and a half high, with a painted piece of bone at the top. These

1566. Fraser [*Narrative*], p. 69; see also Morier [*Journey*], p. 245.
1567. Wills, p. 321; Polack, I, p. 148.
1568. Morier [*Journey*], p. 245.
1569. Tancoigne, p. 203-206.
1570. Polak [*Persien*], I, p. 148.
1571. Wills, p. 320.
1572. Zarrabi, p. 248-250.
1573. Gleadowe-Newcomen, p. 94.

are worn by the higher classes, and by all before the king; A flat slipper, either of red or yellow leather, with a little iron shoe under the heel, and with a piece of bone over that shoe, on which, as in the first instance the heel rests; A stout shoe (with a flat sole, turning up at the toe) which cover the whole foot, and is made either of leather, or of thick-quilted cotton. It is worn by the peasants, and by the chatters or walking footmen[1574].

The olama always wore clogs of Arab yellow colored donkey skin, while government officials and merchants wore black or green shagreen shoes[1575]. The priests affect a peculiar heavy shoe, with an ivory or wooden lining at the heel. Green shagreen shoes are very common at Isfahan. Blacking is unknown to Persians generally, but a European's servant may always be recognized by his polished shoes[1576].

Middle class males wore Russian type (*orusi*) black shoes[1577]. The *orusi* or Russian shoe, similar to our children's shoe, but without the strap, is the most common[1578]. Poor people wore leather shoes and those made of black dyed goat skin (*timaj*) during winter time, while in summer they wore *giveh* or *ajideh* slippers[1579]. « Next, the *kafsh*, or slippers of various kinds. The heel is folded down, and remains so »[1580]. Shoes are made of native leather (*kafsh*) and are like slippers, with elastic sides so as to allow easy taking off when entering a house or mosque. Peasants and the laboring class wear the *giveh* or cotton shoes, made of rag soles with uppers of corded cotton kept clean by pipe clay[1581].

The guild of the *pashneh-saz* cut leather shoe heels out of black cow horn, white ivory bones and fish teeth, but by 1870 its number had decreased considerably indicating a change in fashion[1582]. Likewise the number of *na'lband* or shoe smiths[1583]. But these were not the only shoes that went out of fashion. The *gorjiduz* guild, who made Georgian women's shoes, and of which the men's version had been in common use, had fallen

1574. Morier [*Journey*], p. 245.
1575. Zarrabi, p. 248.
1576. Wills, p. 321.
1577. Zarrabi, p. 248-250.
1578. Wills, p. 321.
1579. Zarrabi, p. 248-250.
1580. Wills, p. 321.
1581. Polak [*Persien*], I, p. 148.
1582. Tahvildar, p. 110.
1583. *Ibid.*, p. 104.

in total disuse[1584]. The same held true for the *charmiduz* who made leather shoes that used to be in great demand. Most of the olama and all the merchants and artisans wore them. « Now they are only worn by some mollahs and most merchants »[1585]. The same fate hit the *sagheriduz*, who made shoes that in the past were worn by the ranking people and women, « but had now gone entirely out of fashion »[1586]. This guild was also referred to as *kafshduz*. These *sagheri* shoes or slippers, « only barely reached the commencement of the heel, and when new are very elegant. They are shod with iron heels, which are a separate trade of themselves »[1587]. *Sagheri* was commonly dyed green[1588].

This was due to the use of the *orusi* shoe, which by the 1870s was in common use in Isfahan, and probably elsewhere as well. Tahvildar writes that in Isfahan the guild of *orusiduz*, around 1870, was a new guild, which did not exist before, and « forms now a large group »[1589]. Wills calls the « orosi duz a riding-boot maker; these boots are always made loose enough to kick off, and are practically better for long journeys on horseback than European boots »[1590].

« Then there were a lot of *giveh-chin* (*giveh* makers) and *giveh* sellers. Most nobles also wore supply *giveh*, mainly when amusing and diverting themselves. A pair made on order did cost 3 tomans or more. It is said that the well-known Hajji Ebrahim, the former *kadkhoda* of Karladan-Lenjan, made of pair of *givehs* for the late Shah, which weighed 12 methqals (55,7 grams) and cost 24 tomans. Formerly, the Isfahan *givehs* were used allover Iran, now not even one-tenth is used in this town [Isfahan] and the other cities. Only a few people are in this guild », which was also referred to as *rassaf*[1591]. In addition to the *giveh* there was also the « malakee [which] is rounded off at the toes »[1592].

1584. Tahvildar, p. 98.
1585. *Ibid.*, p. 98.
1586. *Ibid.*, p. 99.
1587. Wills, p. 190.
1588. Binning, I, p. 250.
1589. Tahvildar, p. 98.
1590. Wills, p. 190.
1591. Tahvildar, p. 104.
1592. Binning, II, p. 71. For further information on *giveh* see Wills, p. 190, « cost: two kerans to five kerans for an ordinary pair; it is possible to give a pound for an elaborate or embroidered pair ». See for a technical discussion Wulff, p. 228-230.

Charuk, is « a sort of raw leather sandal much like the Highland brogue »[1593]. *Zangal*, « or leggings made of leather, and cover the space between the knee and ankle; they are affected by tribesmen, grooms, and muleteers as being cheaper than boots and as useful. They are often elaborately ornamented with embroidered leather. They are worn with ghevas, sandals, or coarse shoes »[1594].

Boots or chekmeh

The different kinds of boots were: A very large pair with high heels turned up at the toe, made generally of Russian leather, and covering the leg; A smaller and tighter kind, buttoning at the side, and reaching only to the calf of the leg.

« When the Persian ride, they put on a loose trowsers of cloth, called *shalwar*, into which they insert the skirts of the *alcalock*, as well as silken trowsers; so that the whole looks like an inflated bladder. The *shalwar* is very useful in carrying light baggage, as handkerchiefs, small books etc. not infrequently a light meal »[1595]. Boots are only used by horsemen, and are then worn much too large, for ease. Those worn by courtiers often come up the thigh, and are similar to those used by our sewer-men[1596]. The guild of the *chekmehduz* « was very large, when, as in the past, soldiers wore boots and the provincial government employed many servants and the province was well populated, but now the guild has been reduced to almost nothing »[1597].

Formerly, gloves or *dastkesh* were only worn when travelling, but never of leather, always of cotton or silk[1598]. Some woolen articles were also produced in small quantities. « Woollen socks, comforters, and gloves are produced from home-grown and home-dyed wool »[1599]. Pocket-handkerchiefs are never used, save by the rich or the Tehranis[1600].

1593. Fraser [*Travels*], II, p. 157.
1594. Wills, p. 321; See Wulff, p. 234.
1595. Morier [*Journey*], p. 245.
1596. Wills, p. 321.
1597. Tahvildar, p. 98-99.
1598. Polak [*Persien*], I, p. 148.
1599. Gleadowe-Newcomen, p. 94.
1600. Wills, p. 322.

The poor

The poor people wear no cap and had very little clothes; when the cold weather comes on, they make dresses out of sheep skin, etc.[1601]. In general the poor are miserably clad; the children have scarcely anything to cover them but a shirt of coarse linen, which hardly reaches their middle; and the women wear nothing but a shirt, a pair of drawers, a jacket, and a veil, which covers their head, and serves them on all occasions[1602]. The poor wore cotton clothes (*bafteh-ye rismani*), and when they married wore from head to foot European *chit*[1603].

Peasants wore a cotton short jacket of quilted cotton (*qaba*) or of simple cotton, a *kamarband* and *giveh* without socks. During winter they often wore a *pustin*[1604]. « The peasantry in this part of the province [near Mashhadisar] generally wear a sort of jerkin of a dark brown colour, instead of the "Kabba", the women wrap their cloaks round their faces instead of concealing then by the "chedar" »[1605].

« The clothing of men and women is a common blue cotton, made up with little difference in style, except that the women's costume reaches only to the knees, leaving limbs and feet bare. But the head-dress is distinctive: only men wear hats, while women have handkerchiefs of red — the favorite color — and in the street are enveloped in the chudder of checked white and blue cotton [farmers dress] »[1606].

Female dress

« The dress of the women is extremely simple. It is composed, in the summer season, of a silk or muslin shift, a loose pair of velvet trowsers, and an ulkhaliq, or vest. The head is covered with a large black turban, over which a Cashmerian shawl is gracefully thrown, to answer the purpose of a veil. In the cold weather, a close-bodied robe, hanging to the knees, and fastened in front by large gold buttons, is worn over the vest. This is made of velvet or kimcob, and sometimes ornamented with jewels »[1607].

1601. Waring, p. 60.
1602. Morier [*Journey*], p. 269-270.
1603. Zarrabi, p. 250.
1604. Polak [*Persien*], I, p. 152.
1605. Stuart, p. 278.
1606. Wilson, p. 269.
1607. Kinneir, p. 24; see also Mostaufi, I, p. 510 for a similar description.

Head dress

Women wore, like in the 18th century, a small cap, that went out of fashion at the Qajar court after Naser al-Din Shah travelled to Europe. It was replaced by the *charqad* or *lachak*, which had been derived from European fashion. On the head, women wore a small shawl, pinned under the chin. On the shawl were fastened strings of pearls and diamond sprigs[1608].

« The head is usually covered with a chargat, or large square of silk or cotton, embroidered. These chargat are folded, as were shawls amongst us a few years ago, thus displaying the corners, two in front and two behind. It is fastened under the chin by a brooch. It is often of considerable value, being of cashmere shawl, embroidered gauze, etc. A jika, or jewelled feather-like ornament, is often worn at the side of the head, etc. »[1609].

As to the women of olama, officials and merchants, they wore a *charqad* inside during wintertime[1610]. « Had she been in another house she would have worn a large square of gold-embroidered silk, with the points in front and behind, and fastened under the chin. Under the crêpe square there was a small skull-cap of gold-embroidered velvet, matching her little zouave jacket, with an aigrette of gems at the side. Her arms were covered with bracelets, and a number of valuable necklaces set off the beauty of her dazzlingly white neck »[1611].

« Beneath the chargat is generally a small kerchief of dark material, worn to offset the complexion, and preserve the chargat; only the edge is visible. The ends of the chargat cover the shoulders, but the gauze *perhan*, quite transparent, leaves nothing to the imagination. The breasts and chest are very visible, and the abdomen is quite bare »[1612].

Shirt or pirahan

« During summer, the Persian ladies, in the interior of their houses, wear no more clothes than a light shift of linen or silk, the Peerahun is but concealment visible to the rest of their persons »[1613]. Women like men wore very short shirts, without collar, closed in the middle with on top a golden button or pearl. Usually, they were made of brocaded muslin, with 2 or 3 rows of pearls on the collar. They let it fall, like the men, on the

1608. Sheil, p. 132-134.
1609. Wills, p. 323.
1610. Zarrabi, p. 250.
1611. Bird, I, p. 217.
1612. Wills, p. 324.
1613. Waring, p. 61; Tancoigne, p. 203-206.

trousers. « The chemise or perhan; it is, with the lower orders, of calico, white or blue, and comes down to the middle of the thigh, leaving the leg nude. Among the upper classes it is frequently of silk. At Shiraz it is often of fine cotton, and elaborately ornamented with black embroidery; among the rich it is frequently of gauze, and much embroidered with the gold thread, pearls, etc. With them it often only reaches to the navel »[1614].

This type of shirt was worn by everybody. For example, the women of olama, officials and merchants, wore a shirt of white *qamis* inside during wintertime. Middle-class women wore a shirt of white *qamis* or *chitha-ye rizah-ye naqsh-e parcheh-ye sefid* (of white figured chintz)[1615]. Upper-class women, of course, wore a shirt that reflected the wealth of their family. The shah's mother, for example, « had a thin blue crepe chemisette, also trimmed with pearls; this chemisette hang down a little below the waist, nearly meeting the top of the trousers, which are fastened by a running string. As there was nothing under the thin gauze, the result of course was more display than is usual in Europe »[1616].

Vest or arkhaliq, kolejeh, nim-taneh

Women wore large vests usually made of quilted satin, tunics without colar, open in the front, showing the breasts, and closed by 3 buttons only. Long armpits make them look larger than they are. Under the buttons the chapkin closes from left to right with large wrapovers[1617]. A small jacket of velvet was worn over the shirt, reaching to the waist, but not made to close in front[1618]. « A very short jacket of gay colour, quite open in the front, and not covering the bosom, with tight sleeves with many metal buttons, is usually worn in summer: a lined outer coat in cold winter. In winter a pair of very short white cotton socks are used, and tiny slippers with a high heel; in summer in the house ladies go often barefoot »[1619]. The *arkhaliq*, usually was worn during the summer, while in wintertime women wore a *kolejeh* to keep warm[1620].

During the winter the women of olama, government officials and merchants wore indoors an *arkhaliq*, or vest of Kerman shawl (*termeh-ye*

1614. Drouville, I, p. 26.
1615. Zarrabi, p. 251.
1616. Sheil, p. 132-134.
1617. Drouville, I, p. 26 and plate 8 (*arkhaliq*).
1618. Sheil, p. 132-134.
1619. Wills, p. 324.
1620. Mostaufi, I, p. 510.

kermani), of Kashani velvet, or a *sardari* made of Kerman shawl, broad cloth or flanel. Middle-class women wear a *kolejeh-e kamarchin*, or juste-au-corps, of the same description. They also wore an *arkhaliq* made of silk (*qanavat*) or a silk-cotton fabric in particular the Yazd variety[1621].

The *arkhaliq* and *kolejeh* went out of fashion after about 1880. Naser al-Din Shah, who had introduced other changes in fashion among his harem women, also insisted that they wear henceforth a *nim-taneh*, of gold brocade, velvet, cashmere or European worsted[1622].

The neat zouave jacket, with sleeves, breast and back profusely embroidered in gold, or with pearls is called the *yel* (*yal*). When lady friends come visiting, a long veil is fastened to the belt and, supported on the projecting skirt hangs down to the feet. Sometimes it is left to drag. It is quite transparent[1623], and partly closed on the breast by frogs and loops, hardly reaching the waist[1624].

The trousers

They also wore « large pantaloons of gold cloth or Cachemire stuff, wadded with cotton » or silk work with gold or silver and often pearls[1625]. Their legs and parts of their bodies, imprisoned in those two heavy columns, contrived so as to embarrass all their movements, must necessarily be unfit for long walks. This is their summer apparel; in the winter they wear garments made of shawls, silks stuffed with cotton, and if they can afford it, cloaks made of sable[1626].

« The queen's dress was rendered cumbersome by the quantity of jewels embroidered upon it, that she could scarcely move under its weight. Her trowsers in particular, were so engrafted with pearls, that they looked more like a piece of mosaic than a wearing apparel. Padded with cotton inside, stiffened by cloth of gold on the out, they were so fashioned as to exclude the possibility of discovering the shape of the leg. The brocade trowsers were so stiff they could stand up right in the middle of the room »[1627].

1621. Zarrabi, p. 251.
1622. Mostaufi, I, p. 511.
1623. Savage-Landor, I, p. 212.
1624. Feuvrier, p. 158.
1625. Drouville, I, p. 26, (also plates 1-12).
1626. Waring, p. 61; Tancoigne, p. 203-206.
1627. Morier [*Second Journey*], p. 61-62.

« I do not admire Persian female dress. The shah's mother wore a pair of trousers made of gold brocade. They are very wide, each leg being, when the means of the bearer allows it, wider than the skirt of the gown, so that they have the effect of an exceedingly simple petticoat; and as crinoline are unknown, the elegant wear ten and eleven pairs of trousers, one over the other in order to make up for the want of the above important invention. The trousers were edged with a border of pearls embroidered on braid »[1628].

These trousers went out of fashion in the 1870s, after Naser al-Din Shah had seen the ballerina dress during his first tour of Europe. On his return he insisted that his harem women wear similar dress. Because fashion was determined by the royal court, women in the harems of other members of the elite soon followed suit. The *zir-jameh* became so short, that even Naser al-Din Shah was upset. He forbade the wearing of the short *zir-jameh* and decreed the wearing of the *nim-taneh* and the *chador-e namaz*. The old *zir-jamehs* were cut up and used to make the new style garments, or were sold to collectors[1629].

« The rest of the costume is composed of the *tumbun* or *shulwar*; these are simple short skirts of great width, held by a running string; the outer one usually of silk, velvet, or Cahsmere shawl, often trimmed with gold lace, according to the purse of the wearer; or among the poor, of loud-patterned chintz. Beneath these are innumerable other garments of the same shape, and varying in texture from silk and satin to print. The whole is very short indeed; among the women of fashion merely extending to the thigh, and as the number of these garments is amazing, and they are much bouffe, the effect of a lady sitting down astonishes the beholder [...] The indoor dress is very much like a corps de ballet, but shorter; while in winter a garment like the kolajah of the man, with short sleeves, and trimmed with fur is worn, which gives it a graceful appearance »[1630].

The *shalita* is a short, loose skirt with many pleats, worn by women over the trousers, and derived from European tutus. « The undergarment very much in evidence, is a short chemise of tinselled silk gauze, or gold-embroidered muslin so transparent as to leave nothing to the imagination. This lady wore a skirt of flowered silver brocade, enormously full, ten or twelve yards wide, made to stand nearly straight out by some frills or skirts of vary stiff starched cotton underneath, the whole, not even on a waist

1628. Sheil, p. 132-134, 204.

1629. Mostaufi, I, p. 511; Benjamin, p. 332.

1630. Wills, p. 324-325.

band around the waist, but drawn by strings, and suspended over the hips, the skirts coming down to within a few inches of the knee, leaving the white rounded limbs uncovered. [...] White socks are worn. Over the transparent pirahan, or chemise, she wore a velvet jacket beautifully embroidered in gold, with its fronts about ten inches apart, so as to show the flowered chemise. [... her hair] was all but concealed by a small white square of silk crepe on the head and brow and fastened under the chin by a brooch »[1631].

Naser al-Din Shah, when the new short skirt became too short, insisted on his women wearing a *nim-taneh* (see above) with a *chador-e namaz*. This veil was made of the same material as the *nim-taneh*. It was often wrapped around the waist, while part of the veil trailed at the back. Because the *chador-e namaz* was fastened with buttons or clasp to the waist it was worn like to-day's skirts. Thus, the *chador-e namaz* gradually took over the role of the long traditional trousers (*zir-jameh*) and the short drawers (*tomban*). The old heavily brocaded and embroidered *arkhaliqs* and *zir-jamehs* were cut up and tailors and stitchers made *nim-tanehs* and *chador-e namaz* out of them[1632]. Another kind of *chador-e namaz* is the veil which was kept especially for prayer at home. The quality of the veil (cotton or silk) depended on the family's wealth. Rice reports that a bead, a small button, or a knot or thread was sometimes sewn on the selvage to mark the section held over the nose[1633].

« First of all one's eye is caught by a 'bundle' of short skirts - usually of very bright colours- a tricking out at the hips, not unlike the familiar attire of our ballet girls, only shorter. These skirts are made of cotton, silk or cotton, according to the lady's wealth or position. These skirts are occasionally very elaborate, with heavy gold braiding all over them with small pearls. Under the skirt appear two heavy, shapeless legs, in long foreign stockings with garters, or in tight trousers of cotton or other light material - most unseemly sight »[1634].

As to the women of olama, officials and merchants, they wore various trousers of european *chit*, or from *khara*, *qanaviz-e kashi* or *yazdi* or *khorasani* inside during wintertime. Middle-class women wore trousers that were made of European *chit*[1635].

1631. Bird, I, p. 216-217.
1632. Mostaufi, I, p. 511.
1633. *Ibid.*, p. 511; Rice, p. 162.
1634. Savage-Landor, I, p. 211-212.
1635. Zarrabi, p. 251.

Shoes

Leg coverings are now being introduced, which Persian women in the past also wore[1636]. As to the women of olama, officials and merchants they wore shoes of red, green or blue Hamadan dyed goat-skin (*timaj*) and/or black leather *orusi* shoes during winter time indoors. Middle-class women wore shoes of colored Hamadan dyed goat-skin[1637]. The Shah's mother « wore no shoes, her feet being covered with fine Cashmere stockings »[1638]. In winter a pair of very short white cotton socks are used, and tiny slippers with a high heel; in summer in the house ladies go often barefoot. Women's feet were « socked in white or blue, and she toddles on dainty slippers with no back to the heel »[1639]. Those of the lower classes had stockings of yellow leather called *chakmeh*[1640].

When visiting

« Before going out a huge pair of loose trousers or bloomers - the *chakchur* - fastened at the waist and pulled in at the ankle, are assumed, and a *ruhband* -- a thick calico or cotton piece of cloth about a yard wide, hangs in front of the face, a small slit some three to four inches long and one and a half wide, very daintily netted with heavy embroidery, being left for ventilation's sake and as a lookout window. This is fastened by means of a hook behind the head to prevents its falling and is held down with one hand at the lower part. Over all this the *chudder* - a black or blue piece of silk or cotton about two yards square and matching the colour of the trousers - covers the whole from head to foot, and just leaves enough room in front for the ventilating parallelogram »[1641].

Chaqshur are long, often black trousers of thin fabric, worn by women. One type consisted of loose trousers ending in stockings, which covered the body from waist to toes. it was held up by a waist band and strap. The other type resembled a pair of leggings tied with tapes under the insteps. This second type required less cloth and was lighter and more confortable. In the 2nd half of the 19th century it was considered old-fashioned, and was seldom worn by upper-class women. It was also part of the official Qajar

1636. Wills, p. 325.

1637. Zarrabi, p. 251. When walking in the streets women wore iron-shod heels, which slapped up and down at each step. James, p. 14; O'Donovan, I, p. 170.

1638. Sheil, p. 132.

1639. Savage-Landor, I, p. 214.

1640. Lorimer, p. 344-345.

1641. Savage-Landor, I, p. 215.

dress in bright red broad cloth[1642]. Those of the upper classes used, outside their houses, a kind of silken trouser which fitted like a stocking over the foot and lower leg and was baggy over the knee[1643].

When going outside they wear four thick veils, and are covered from head to foot with a long piece of white linen, having some small openings opposite the eyes; their faces and hands are invisible. The latter is sometimes worked like a net, or else two holes are made in the cloak for their eyes[1644].

The outdoor dress is a large blue sheet, with a yard of linen as a veil, perforated for two inches square with minute holes, the feet thrust into two huge bags of coloured stuff. The dress is all the same; save in quality or costliness[1645]. The all-enveloping mantle of calico which shrouded a women from head to heel, was called *feridgi* in Astarabad[1646].

If they go out to visit, they, of course, put on their best garments[1647]. When a princess, for example, came visiting she « came in the black silk sheet with a suggestion of gold about its border which is the street disguise of women of the richer classes, and she wore huge bag-like violet trousers, into which her voluminous skirts were tucked. [....she wore] rose and silver brocade skirts, a rose velvet jacket embroidered in silver, a transparent white muslin pirahan with silver stars on it, and a chargat of white muslin embroidered in rose silk »[1648].

When the women of olama, government officials and merchants visited each other they wore « a *charqad*, a shirt of *qamis-e dur dukhteh* with *golabtun* or *abrisham-e meshki*, or coloured, or silken *golabtun*. Their *arkhaliq* of kashmir *termeh* or of *mahkmal* and *estifa-ye frangi* or of *selseleh* or *zari-e mahramat-e soltani*; the *kolejeh* and *sardari* of *termeh-ye kashmir* or of european velvet or european gold brocade [*estifa*] or various stuffs [*yaraqha*] of *golabtun* or *shenel-e mahut* or *mahkmal* or *termeh*. Their trousers of coloured european *qanaviz* or of *atlas-e nezam al-molki* or of velvet or *zarri-ye qalebi* etc. with various accoutrements of *golabtun* and

1642. Rice, p. 162; Mostaufi, I, p. 98; Soltan-Ahmad, p. 62.

1643. Lorimer, p. 344-345.

1644. Waring, p. 62; outside the chador and the veil or *ruband* is worn (see plates 1-12, Drouville, I, p. 26). The chador or wrapper of white, or chequered blue-and-white cotton. (Porter, I, p. 208, with a drawing of a Persian lady).

1645. Wills, p. 418-425.

1646. O'Donovan, I, p. 170.

1647. Sheil, p. 204-205.

1648. Bird, I, p. 218.

various golden trinklets and jewellery on ears, head, neck, hands and feet »[1649].

Middle-class women, when visiting, wore a *qamis* shirt knitted (*dur dukhteh*) with *abrisham-e meshki* and an *arkhaliq* of *khata'i* or *atlas-e mahramat* or *termeh-e kermani* or *makhmal-e kashi*. The *kolejeh-e kamarchin* was made of the same fabrics; their trousers were of european *chit* and *qanaviz* and *khari-ye kashi* or *yazdi* or *khorasani*[1650].

The Taj

In addition to "normal" head dress, there were several kinds of *taj* (or crown), whose origin pre-date the Safavid era[1651]. As part of the *khel'at* or robe of honor [see below] rulers bestowed a *taj-e zarduzi* or gold embroidered head dress to deserving courtiers and important visitors. These head dresses are referred to as *taj-e zarnegar* or as *taj-e zarduzi-ye doulat athar*[1652].

A special kind of head dress was the so-called *taj-e nawruzi*, which we may assume was given during the New Year period of the year. We do not know, in what way, this *taj* differed from the other ones. There was also a *taj-e saruq*[1653], and the *taj-e morassa'* or the *taj* studded with precious stones, which formed part of the *khel'at* where all the other accoutrements of the gift also were often gem-studded[1654].

However, the most well-known *taj* was that worn by members of the Safavid sufi order. According to Safavid tradition a *taj* or crown with 12 *tark* or gores, commemorating the twelve Shi'i Emams, was devised by either sheikh Safi or sheikh Heidar, who were instructed in a dream by the first Emam 'Ali to do so[1655]. According to Safavid tradition Sheikh Heidar received an instruction from the Emam 'Ali to make a 12 gored *taj* and give this to his followers to wear, and for this reason the *taj* became known as the *taj-e heidari* or the *taj-e davazdeh tark-e heidari*[1656]. In one single

1649. Zarrabi, p. 250.
1650. *Ibid.*, p. 251.
1651. For a discussion of the Timurid *taj*, see Goetz, p. 2243-2244.
1652. Khʷondamir, IV, p. 388, 454, 480, 496, 505.
1653. Qomi, II, p. 623, 749; also found as *taj va saruq*, (['*Alamara-ye Safavi*], p. 356).
1654. See e.g. Qomi, II, p. 676, 690, 857, 887, 1002, 1018, 1078.
1655. Falsafi, I, p. 159-160.
1656. ['*Alamara-ye Shah Esma'il*], p. 26; Shamlu, p. 33; Qomi, I, p. 44-45.

instance it was also referred to as *taj-e Joneid*[1657]. Because of its red or crimson color it was also called *taj-e sorkhi* and the wearer as *qezelbash* or red head[1658]. Shah Esma'il I sometimes also wore a red kerchief (*dastmal-e sorkh*) on his head[1659].

According to Membré, who visited Shah Tahmasp's court in 1539-40, « all the Sophians, that is men of the Sophy, wear the red cap, with twelve sections, by day, and by night the Sultan-Haidari, which Sultan-Haidari was worn by his grandfather. The Shah Isma'il altered the fashion and made another form of cap, that is of the form which appears below: the *taj* is a roll of scarlet, more than half an ell long, with twelve sections. Sultan-Haidari with twelve sections of cloth. This is worn in diverse colours but the *taj* can only be worn in red »[1660]. When Shah Tahmasp went fishing, for

5. *Taj* (16th c.)

1657. ['*Alamara-ye Shah Esma'il*], p. 510.
1658. *Ibid.*, p. 42; ['*Alamara-ye Safavi*], p. 46.
1659. Qomi, I, p. 75.
1660. Membré, p. 26; Morton, p. 26.

example, he wore a Sultan-Haidari on his head. « The Shah wears his cap [*taj*] with the turban-cloth, that is, the cap is covered to its top by the cloth, which is twisted round it from the bottom and ties up the whole of it. So, all those who receive a cloth as a favour wear it so for three or four days and then tie it another way. They call this manner of tying it *Shah-desturi*; the Sayyids of Usku wear the *taj* as the Shah does, also Qadi-yi Jahan, the Shah's brothers and the *qurchis* [royal guards] but not the others. And none can wear a velvet *taj* unless the Shah gives it »[1661].

Scarce and Falsafi[1662] have suggested that the Safavid *taj* was made of felt, however, there is no literary evidence for that in Persian texts. Kashefi mentions that the dervish *taj* was normally made of felt, but other materials were also used[1663]. Only two European authors mention that the *taj-e heidari* was made of felt[1664]. What Persian textual evidence there is suggests that the Safavid *taj* was made of *saqarlat* in a crimson or red color (*taji az saqarlat-e qermezi-ye davazdeh tark*) the wearer therefore was known as *qezelbash* or red-head[1665]. It is not true as Diba has it that « the cap was most often red, but other colors were sometimes worn to coordinate with the costume as a whole »[1666].

Neither the idea of the *taj* nor that of the *taj* with 12 gores was new. Members of dervish and *fottovat* orders were in the habit of wearing a *taj* prior to Sheikh Heidar's divine inspiration. In fact, there was quite a variety of the sufi *taj*. According to Kashefi, the normal sufi *taj* was called *taj-e maulavi*, referring to the first person who wore the *taj*, the prophet Moses. This *taj* was made of felt. But there were also other varieties such as the *taj-e pust* or the *taj* made of skin as well as the *taj-e hazar bakhiyeh*, *taj-e qoreish*, *taj-e maftul*, *taj-e pashmineh*, *taj-e kalleh-push*, and *taj-e muzavvajah*. Each type of *taj* had an esoteric significance. Although Kashefi mentions the 12 gored *taj* and says he will discuss it he does not do so[1667]. The

1661. Membré, p. 27, 41.

1662. Scarce [Vesture], p. 37; Falsafi, I, p. 160.

1663. Kashefi, p. 184.

1664. Figueroa, p. 87; Kaempfer [*Am Hofe*], p. 47.

1665. Khʷondamir, IV, p. 426-427; [*'Alamara-ye Safavi*], p. 30; see also Falsafi, I, p. 159, n. 2, who refers to *saqarlat-e sorkh*.

1666. Diba, p. 788. See e.g. Membré, p. 26; Morton, p. 27.

1667. Kashefi, p. 184-189. See also, for more details, Gramlich, III, p. 5-6, 29, who also mentions that a *taj-e heidariyeh* existed prior to Sheikh Heidar's creation.

Ne'matollahi dervishes also wore a *taj* that was embroidered, a practice probably initiated by Sheikh Qotb al-Din Ebrahim[1668].

Nor was the 12-gored *taj* an innovation since the Bektashi dervishes had worn a so-called *Hoseini taj* with 12 gores (symbolizing the 12 Emams) since the 13th century. Ironically, the Turkish janissaries, the main adversaries of the *Qezelbash*, also wore a hat with 12 gores[1669]. The color red also had a long usage in Persian sectarian history, not only among early Shi'ite *ghulat* or sectarian groups (e.g. the *Khorrami* or *Mohammirah*), but even going back as far as Mazdak[1670]. The color of the *taj* worn by members of the "regular" sufi orders were white, green, blue, or of natural color[1671].

As to the form of the *taj*, Contarini mentions that the *qizilbash* wore a « red caftan, coming half a cubit over the head, which widens at the part which covers the head; it gets narrower towards the top, and it is made of twelve fringes, a finger in thickness, symbolizing the twelve Sacraments of their religion »[1672]. According to a Carmelite report, around the year 1553, « the red cap [...] which they wear on their heads, and which stand out half an arm's length beyond the head and is of red cloth quilted in rolls lengthwise, and of a thickness that it can be grasped with one hand »[1673]. A sash or *dastar* of white silk (green silk for a seyyed) was wrapped round the felt or *saqarlat* hat in such a way as to make a bulge at the front[1674].

Diba submits that the Safavid followers had to wear the red *taj* at all times « except in battle, when a helmet was worn », which is wrong. The

---

1668. It is also possible that the *taj* referred to here is in fact a piece of fabric, that presumably could be put on one's head as a *vasleh* around a cap (Bafqi, III, part 2, p. 605, n. 2), reading *tach* in stead of *taj*, which in Yazdi dialect means a piece of fabric. See also Khʷondamir, IV, p. 185, who mentions *tacheh-ye haftrang* that was used to embellish the bazaar, which clearly shows that it was used in the sense of "fabric" which seems also be the case when Khʷondamir (IV, p. 566) mentions the use *tajha-ye haftrang* for a similar purpose.

1669. Birge, p. 37, 46, 50-51, 232-233 and illustrations. on p. 26, 236.

1670. Abdulbaki Golpinari, "Kızıl-baş", in *Islâm Ansiklopedisi*. Browne [*History*], I, p. 310-313.

1671. Kashefi, p. 193-195.

1672. *Barbaro and Contarini*, II, p. 115.

1673. [*Carmelites*], I, p. 36.

1674. See Falsafi, I, p. 160, n. 1, 209. The *taj* had a frontward bulge comparable with a tongue as is clear from a 17th century poem which hails the virtues of the *taj* maker (*tajduz*) (Keyvani, p. 292-293), or had colored brocades rolled in a thick tube and coiled.

Spanish ambassador Figueroa states that the *Qezelbash* had quilted their felt hat to make a sword cut slide off their head[1675]. To protect themselves better when they went into battle, the sufis used to put an iron cap under their tightly wrapped *kolah* cum-turban[1676]. Such was their devotion to the *taj* that according to Shah Esma'il I if their head was cut in battle the *taj* would not be separated from it[1677]. The same point, in reverse, was made in case of wrong doers. In 1590, Eskander Beg Monshi mentions that in case of two executions the executors first removed their victims' *qezelbash* hat and only then slew them[1678].

This was done, because the *taj* was held in great veneration, a point that the Ottoman Turks, for example, used to embarrass their enemies. « To show his contempt for them [two Persian spies] the Pasha had removed the red caps, which they wear on their heads »[1679]. But prudence often overcame religious zeal, and many of the Safavid adherents would hide their red hat when their area had been overrun by enemy forces. For example, when the Ottomans had extended their sway over northern Azerbaijan during Mohammad Khodabandeh's reign people hid their red hat. But when 'Abbas I retook the area in 1012/1603, the population of Tabriz as soon as they saw the *qezelbash* troops, rushed to demonstrate their « love of the shah » by donning their *taj-e heidari*, which for fear of the Ottomans they had kept hidden in the basements and other places during the occupation[1680]. Also, when Shah 'Abbas I prostrated himself on arrival at Tabriz, his troops threw their caps in the air and cheered lustily[1681].

The wearing of the red hat was a symbol of the political and religious authority of the Safavids, and their leaders tried to impose its wear on secular rulers. The first one that allegedly was targeted was Uzun Hasan, the Aq Qoyunlu ruler of Persia. He is said to have kissed the red *taj* when it was first shown to him by Sheikh Heidar, which according to Safavid tradition occurred in 893/1487 when Uzun Hasan had been dead for 11 years. However, true or not, after his death his son and successor Ya'qub

1675. Diba, p. 794. Figueroa, p. 87; also see picture in Falsafi, I, p. 208.
1676. Falsafi, I, p. 210.
1677. [*Tadhkereh*], p. 45.
1678. Monshi, I, p. 384. Ya'qub Khan bound Mehdiqoli Khan's hands and removed his qezelbash hat, dragged him out, and slew him on the spot.
1679. [*Carmelites*], I, p. 36.
1680. Monshi, II, p. 639.
1681. *Ibid.*, p. 752.

allegedly forbade the wearing of the Heidari *taj* by the Safavid sufis and by his subjects in general[1682]. Shah Esma'il I tried to have Babur, then not yet Moghul emperor, to put on the *taj*[1683]. Tahmasp I, who himself wore the *taj*[1684], also tried to have Babur's son, the exile seeking Moghul emperor Homayun, and his entourage accept the *taj*. Homayun when pressed to don the *taj* by Tahmasp finally gave in « saying that it was a *taj* of honour for him », thus making it clear that he did not want to make the politico-religious statement that Tahmasp wanted him to[1685]. For this reason all regional chiefs and rulers, such as the ruler of Lar, Khʷarezm, and Kurdish chiefs, who subjected themselves to Safavid rule accepted the *taj* as a sign of their fealty[1686]. Not wearing the hat or refusing to do so was an act of defiance and opposition. When Alqas Mirza fled to the arch-enemy, the Ottoman Soltan, this event was therefore referred to as « throwing down his *taj* »[1687]. It could also be a sign of grief such as when Hamzeh Mirza died the emirs removed their *taj* and hurled them on the ground[1688].

The Safavid *taj* as shown in manuscript miniatures is a turban with a thick red baton some 25 cm high. The batons have faceted sections, likely 12 in number. According to Barbara Schmitz, who studied manuscript miniatures of the *taj*, under Tahmasp I the *taj* became more graceful. The red baton, became longer and more slender, and appears round rather than faceted. By the end of his reign pictures show a very large baton and enveloping scarf which, she surmises, must have been very difficult to wear. Under his immediate successors, Esma'il II and Khodabandeh, a new *taj* with a low gored hat or *kolah* was worn, and this smaller turban permanently replaced the larger one with the tall red *kolah*[1689].

Schmitz submits that the Safavid supporters stopped wearing the symbolic tall hats with their slim batons soon after Shah Tahmasp's

---

1682. Savory, "Kizilbash", *EI*, q.v.; Savory, p. 19-20; [*'Alamara-ye Safavi*], p. 30.

1683. [*'Alamara-ye Safavi*], p. 238-239.

1684. Membré, p. 31.

1685. Riazul Islam [*Relations*], p. 31, see also p. 29-30.

1686. Membré, p. 36-37, 44, 48; some other tribal groups renewed their allegiance to the shah and donned the twelve-gored hats of the twelver shi'ahs, Monshi, II, p. 648.

1687. Qomi, I, p. 321; see also [*Tadhkereh*], p. 45; Monshi, I, p. 320.

1688. [*'Alamara-ye 'Abbasi*], I, p. 484. For a picture of such an occurrence see the "Lamentation on the event of Eskander's death", in Dickson and Welch, I, p. 174, fig. 232.

1689. Schmitz, p. 104.

death[1690]. However, this is not borne out by the facts which show that the *taj* was worn during 'Abbas I reign, for example. She therefore assumes that Shah 'Abbas I « after a lapse of several decades, reinstated the custom of wearing » a special Safavid *taj*. She argues that the 'Abbasi *taj* was based on the wide Khorasan turban with a thick baton. This *taj* appeared in miniatures for the first time around 1600. Other later miniatures show high officials of Shah 'Abbas I wearing a similar *taj*, though it is less frequently found depicted after 1600 than in miniatures from the period prior to 1590[1691].

Pictorial evidence implies that the *taj* changed its appearance look, according to Schmitz. « Not only the red baton of the *kulah* is visible, but the top of the cap to which it is affixed can also be seen. The *kulah* itself no longer fits the hat snugly, as it apparently had fitted earlier, but it is noticeably wider at the crown than at the brim. The turban wrappings have been substantially reduced, and the narrow fabric is no longer needed and has been discarded. All of the turban cloths are now made of plaid fabric. The black brushes, as found on the earlier models, are still present, but there is a new ornament of strings of pearls and jewel-studded gold pins on the side of the *taj* »[1692]. Falsafi also mentions that under Shah Tahmasp the *taj* became more and more embellished with gems and feathers[1693].

One may question whether Schmitz is right, however. In the first place, the early Safavid *taj* was as richly studded as were the later ones. The normal reference in Safavid texts is to the *taj-e morassa'* or jewel-studded crown[1694]. For example, Shah Esma'il I gave his own *taj va tumar* to Akhi Soltan, which had a value of 5,000 tomans, which was an enormous amount[1695]. Also, the jewel-studded gold pin Schmitz refers to may be nothing else than the *jiqeh* or aigrette, which was a standard part of the *khel'at* or robe of honour, about which later[1696].

So, the *taj* continued to be worn by the *qezelbash* or Safavid followers in continuation of tradition without any rupture between the reign of

1690. Schmitz, p. 105.
1691. *Ibid.*, p. 106-107.
1692. *Ibid.*, p. 107.
1693. Falsafi, I, p. 120.
1694. Qomi, II, p. 623, 676, 690, 857, 887; [*'Alamara-ye Esma'il*], p. 72, 196, 231, 238. See also Membré, p. 27.
1695. *Ibid.*, p. 355; [*'Alamara-ye Safavi*], p. 298.
1696. See picture of a *qurchi* with a *taj*, in Falsafi, I, p. 208.

Tahmasp I and 'Abbas I. Roemer is wrong when he writes that under Tahmasp I the wearing of the *taj* dwindled and became rare[1697]. Both Balbi's (the Venetian consul in Syria) report of 1582 and an anonymous Venetian report of 1587 mention that part of the Persian army personnel wore the *taj*[1698]. Don Juan, the shi'ite courtier turned roman catholic, writes: « The difference in dress which distinguishes the nobles from the common folk, is that the nobles alone are allowed to wear as their headgear the Turban ornamented with Twelve Points, known in Persian as the Taj or crown »[1699]. Throughout the 17th century till the end of the dynasty the granting of the *taj* to deserving courtiers is mentioned in Persian chronicles. European pictorial evidence also shows that Persian ambassadors wore the *taj* when abroad. The feathers in the *taj* may have had, at first, a functional purpose. Della Valle reports that « the Jasachi [*yasaqchi*], or the King's guards, wearing the tag and an arrow, the point fixed in the turban, and the feather pointing upward »[1700]. Initially, the plumes on the head could only be worn when the Shah had given them[1701].

Schmitz is right, however, where the changing form of the *taj* is concerned. The early *taj* was conical with a wide base which narrowed upwards, the 17th century *taj* « was shaped like a kettle narrowing downwards; its sides formed twelve scallops in memory of the Twelve Imams; in the centre of its top there was a point somewhat similar to a chess pawn »[1702].

According to Falsafi until the reign of 'Abbas I only followers of the Safavid sufi order were allowed to wear the *taj-e Heidari*. 'Abbas I gave the non-Turk *gholam* officers of Caucasian extraction the right to wear the *taj-e Heidari*. However, this innovation may have already been introduced under Shah Mohammad Khodabandeh, Shah 'Abbas' I father or even earlier, for it is reported that the Georgian king Simon when he was thrown off his horse in battle in 1583 wore a « guilt Torbant with his Golden Horne »[1703]. The golden horn most likely refers to the red (*qezel* = red or gold) *taj*. Whether

1697. Roemer, p. 250.

1698. Berchet, p. 288, 290.

1699. *Don Juan*, p. 49; see also Della Valle [Extract], IX, p. 28, 42.

1700. *Ibid.*, p. 71. However, Membré, p. 19 reports that Bahram Mirza's *yasaqchi*, around 1540, also wore an arrow upon his turban-cloth.

1701. Membré, p. 41.

1702. [*Tadhkirat al-Muluk*], p. 32, n.3; Houtum-Schindler [Shah Isma'il], p. 114-117.

1703. Minadoi, p. 247.

true or not, a Persian source also reports that the Christian *vali* of Georgia was given the *taj va tumar*[1704]. Della Valle mentions that « The King's slaves are allowed on certain occasions to wear the tag »[1705]. The right to wear the *taj*, therefore, became a royal discretionary rather than an inherited right. It would seem that even foreigners sometimes received the *taj*, as was claimed by Robert Sherley, although this seems highly unlikely. However, Pietro della Valle reports: « Sometimes, His Majesty, as a token of esteem for a foreigner, makes him a Kizilbashi, by bestowing on him the tag, this, however, is rarely the case ». In fact the only person, he learnt, to whom had befallen this honor was Robert Sherley[1706]. Nevertheless, Father Sanson around 1680, submits that only members of the Safavid order were allowed to wear the *taj*[1707].

The *taj* continued to be worn by those Safavid followers, who were the members of the *Qezelbash* tribes, until the end of the dynasty. However, the *taj* gradually went out of fashion, though whether this was because of its uncomfortable weight, as Schmitz has it, is questionable since normal turbans were also very heavy (see section "head dress"). A more likely reason may be "secularization" (if one may use that term) arising from the reduced role of the Safavid order and credo in state policy. It was eventually only worn on official occasions such as royal councils. At all other times the normal turban was worn, even during routine appearances at court. Della Valle reports that « on some solemn occasions, I understand it is usual for the King himself to wear this red cap, called tag, or crown, which is the mark of the wearer belonging to the army, and of nobility »[1708]. Most royal officials, however, continued to wear the *taj ex-officio* when present at court. The *qurchis*, were seldom without the *taj*[1709].

The *taj* remained in use under Shahs Safi I, 'Abbas II and Soleiman. For example, the formal initiation rite of entry into the Safavid sufi order which, as we will see later, included the granting of the *taj*, was being

---

1704. [*'Alamara-ye Safavi*], p. 584. See also picture of Emamqoli Khan and a *gholam* with a *taj*, in Falsafi, I, p. 394; Alexander Khan was granted a robe of honor, a *taj*, etc. (Monshi, II, p. 670); King Kustandil of Kartli (Georgia) and his emirs also received jeweled *qezelbash* hats (*ibid.*, p. 681).

1705. Della Valle [Extract], IX, p. 79.

1706. *Ibid.*, p. 28.

1707. Sanson, p. 27-28.

1708. Della Valle [Extract], IX, p. 28.

1709. *Ibid.*, p. 80.

practised at Shah Safi's I court[1710]. The *qurchis* under 'Abbas II continued to wear the *taj*[1711]. During the audience granted to the Dutch ambassador, Joan Cuneaus, in 1651, « 'Abbas II was dressed in a apple blossom colored armosine cabay, which was embellished with ribbons studded with diamonds and precious stones in front, on his head a cap with a protruding cone, which also was studded with various precious stones as well as dressed up with black bird feathers. The E'temad al-Douleh sat next to the Shah with a beautiful turban (for a cap such as the king wears, he is not allowed to wear, because he is not of noble but of scribe's descent, for only nobles, royal guards and the sufis [are allowed to wear it]) »[1712].

It is not true as Schmitz has it that by 1666 the « origin of this peculiar crown had apparently been generally forgotten », nor is true when she surmises that only royal guards and the Shah during his coronation still wore the *taj*[1713]. She based this supposition on the fact that pictures in Kaempfer's travelogue show that the guards during Soleiman's enthronement wore the *taj* as they do in pictures by de Bruyn.

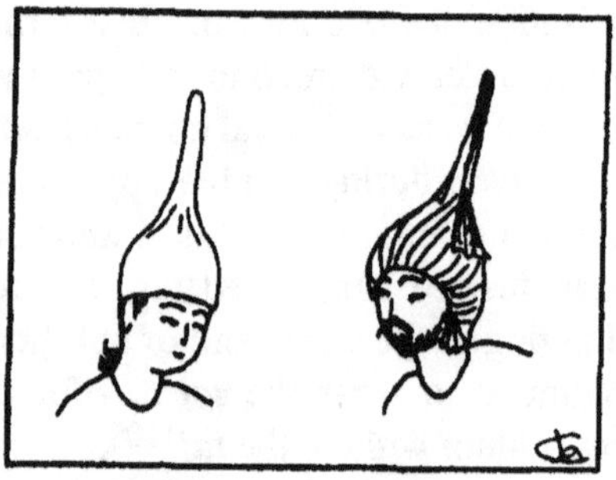

6. Red *taj* without and with turban

A particular and unique kind of *taj* was the royal head dress or *taj-e shahi*[1714]. In this context the term *taj* had a totally secular meaning. For when Heidar Mirza wanted to take the throne after Tahmasp's I death this

1710. Esfahani [*Kholasat*], p. 96, 251.
1711. Falsafi, I, p. 208.
1712. Hotz, p. 149.
1713. Schmitz, p. 107-108.
1714. Shamlu, I, p. 129 Mohammad Khodabandeh put it on his son's head, or *taj-e padeshahi* (*ibid.*, I, p. 414 ('Abbas II)).

was referred to as his desire for crown and throne (*taj va takht*)[1715]. According to Minadoi, writing in 1587, « the chiefe of these Califes [*khalifat al-kholafa*] is he that putteth the Horne [= *taj*] upon the kinges head, when he is first inthronized »[1716]. The royal *taj* used at Soleiman's coronation was covered with pearls and jewels and, according to Kaempfer, was valued by expert jewelers at more than 100,000 tomans[1717].

Chardin reports that, during festive and solemn days, the magnates would wear the 12-gored *taj*, embellished with aigrettes and heron's feathers and covered allover with gems. Some of these he valued at 3,000 francs[1718]. This is also confirmed by Kaempfer who states that the peculiarly formed felt cap or *taj* is worn on solemn occasions by the courtiers, who have it made of gold brocade and covered with jewels. Kaempfer makes a distinction between this *taj*, which is a wrap-around turban, and worn by the guards and sufis. These wore only a simple red *taj*, which fits tightly on the head, then becomes wider and is flat on top. The 12 gores were clearly visible, and out of the midst of this *taj* rose the cone-like staff[1719].

The royal guards, composed of *Qezelbash* troops, wore the *taj* as a standard part of their costume. Around the red hat they wrapped a white sash[1720]. In addition to the guards, the royal runners (*yasavol*) also wore the red *taj*, with a white light wrap-around, and three closely packed feathers, as a regular item[1721]. The sufis of the Safavid order formed part of the cavalcade that accompanied the Shah on his arrival in, and departure from a city[1722]. These wore a red *taj*, sometimes embellished, sometimes plain. Kaempfer also provides us with a description of the adoption of some officials into the Safavid sufi sect, which, amongst other things, involved receiving the *taj* at the end of the ceremony. The chief royal master of ceremonies, who wore a normal turban until the start of the initiation ceremony, would leave the hall and return decked out in sufi dress and *taj*,

1715. Qomi, I, p. 601. For earlier instances see [*'Alamara-ye Safavi*], p. 52, 149, (*taj o takht-e othmani*) p. 180, (*taj o takht-e moruthi*) p. 264.

1716. Minadoi, p. 67; John Cartwright, an English merchant visiting Persia in 1609, copies this statement in his own report (Purchas, VIII, p. 513).

1717. Kaempfer [*Am Hofe*], p. 41.

1718. Chardin, V, p. 473, 300; for a picture see plates 22 and 29.

1719. Kaempfer [*Am Hofe*], p. 47-48.

1720. *Ibid.*, p. 71.

1721. *Ibid.*, p. 85, 201.

1722. *Ibid.*, p. 187.

changing back into his normal dress after the completion of the ceremony[1723].

Du Mans' statement, that only the poor sufis, remnants of the Safavid order, who were employed to sweep the area around the royal palace, still wore the ancient *taj* around 1680, is not true either[1724]. Although these sufis may have been the only ones who wore the *taj* on a regular and daily basis, others also still wore the *taj* when occasion demanded it as is clear from a report by a contemporary of Du Mans. Father Sanson writes, for example, the *mehmendar-bashi*, « wears the Tadge upon his Head, which is a great green Cap brocarded over, and with a long Steeple-crown: It has a great many little white Feathers about the sides of it, whose lower parts are all over enrich'd with Gold and precious Stones, as likewise the Torse of the Cap, and the Steeple-part is all beset with Heron and Crane's Feathers. This sort of Head-attire is in great Veneration; for, they say, it is consecrated to the Twelve Imans, or Saints of Persia. All Kans and Kzel-Bachi's wear this Cap on Days of Ceremony: But the Tats being of the Long-Robe, cannot, nay, even the Etmadaulet himself, because he is no soldier »[1725]. In 1691, the secretary of the Dutch ambassador noted that « nobody presents himself at court, or he wears the hat with the heron and crane feathers, which is heavily studded with gold, pearls and gems »[1726]. Nasiri, an important court official also mentions the wearing by and granting of the *taj-e vahhaj* (resplendent hat) to courtiers in the 1690s[1727].

In 1702, according to Cornelis de Bruyn: « Most of the Lords, invited upon this occasion [*Nawruz*], wear a sort of turban adorned with pearls and precious stones; they call it Tha-eits-timear [*taj va tumar*], and they are sometimes adorned with herons feathers of great beauty. They take them off when the are out of the hall where the feast is, and put on those they commonly have upon their heads: a servant carries it before them »[1728]. Since the *taj* is part of the *khel'at*, de Bruyn's description of such an event is also of interest. He submits that « the Khan before he assumed the robe,

---

1723. Kaempfer [*Am Hofe*], p. 216.

1724. Du Mans, p. 16, 86-87; Richard, II, p. 11, 65.

1725. Sanson (p. 27) adds « The Tats are natives, while the Kzel-Bachi's are Soldiers that always come Slaves or Refugees into the Country: There is an abundance of them from Damascus and Hungary ».

1726. Valentyn, V, p. 257, see also p. 254.

1727. Nasiri, p. 56, 106, 110, 153, 305, 321.

1728. Le Bruyn, I, p. 186.

covered himself with the gold cap, which was adorned with precious stones, closed at the top, and carried at a small distance before him on horseback. They pretend that this cap presents the arms of the prophet Ali, who was wont to wear such an one. The Khan took it off when he put on his robe, and it was carried before him in going back, as it had been in coming »[1729].

In the *Tadhkirat al-Muluk*, mention is made of a special head dress, that was presented to the emirs, viz. of gold brocade on a gold base (*taj-e wahhaj az zarbaft-e bum-ezar*), which is the same as the 12 gored *taj*[1730]. Mirza Rafi'a mentions that all the members of the royal council wore the *taj va tumar* when they sat in council[1731].

There is no mention of the *taj* in the post-Afghan period and the *taj-e Heidari* disappeared with the fall of the Safavid dynasty.

A final word about the term *tumar*. The term usually occurs in combination with the word *taj*. According to the dictionaries that I have consulted the only meaning of this term is "scroll", in fact a meaning of the term that is peculiar for Persian only. However, I find this explanation unsatisfactory. The more so, because one text even refers to the *tumar-e morassa'* or a gem-studded scroll, which does not make sense[1732]. The same dictionaries also make the point that the *tumar* or scroll had the form of a *luleh* or tube. Therefore, I submit, that *tumar* may have referred to the red baton (which has the form of a tube) that sticks out of the turban as shown in miniatures. This wooden baton was four fingers long and one finger wide, it was also red, and flat on the top[1733]. This is also clear from a story that Nasrabadi tells about a *shahnameh-khʷan* (reciter of the *Shahnameh*), who came into a coffee-house with a *tumar* firmly pressed on his head[1734]. A similar description is also offered by Brosset in his translation of contemporary Georgian texts[1735].

1729. Le Bruyn, I, p. 148.
1730. [*Tadhkirat al-Muluk*], p. 66, 136.
1731. Mirza Rafi'a, p. 102 f.
1732. [*'Alamara-ye Safavi*], p. 197.
1733. Figueroa, p. 268.
1734. Nasrabadi, p. 145.
1735. Brosset, vol. II/1, p. 530, n. 1; vol. II/2, p. 33, n. 3.

The Khel'at

The granting of a *khel'at* or robe of honor was part of the political process. Deserving followers were rewarded, while erring magnates were received back into the fold and received a *khel'at* to clinch the deal. Visiting royalty, ambassadors, and other dignitaries, including Europeans, also received robes of honor[1736]. The royal favor could take the form of a dress, but also a jewel, or an amount of money. The custom persisted till the very end of the Qajar dynasty, although after the 1890s, the custom seems to have been a less regular affair. Throughout the Safavid and the Qajar period we have descriptions of the *khel'at* receiving ceremony by provincial governors. For « it is the custom in Persia to send all governors, royal personages, and ministers, a yearly present from the king, to show the royal satisfaction. These presents are all termed kalaats (or dresses of honour), even though the gift may be in jewellery, or even specie; a dress or robe of greater value, or a jewelled weapon, being the general kalaat. The withholding of the yearly robe of honour to a provincial governor is generally the sign of the royal disfavour, and the dispatching of it often the

7. 18th century Persian dress

1736. [*Carmelites*], I, p. 480, 559; Hotz, p. 257-258.

token of the recipient's confirmation in office, though at times it is what gilds the bitter pill of his recall. The kalaat is usually sent from the capital by the hands of some person of consequence, generally some favoured servant of the Shah, and this man is sent down that he may receive a present, generally large in amount, from the recipient, and may bring back the usual bribe to the Prime Minister for retention of power, or even the same thing to the king himself. The New Year's festival is generally the time of the despatch of the official dresses of honour from the capital »[1737].

Although the above description has succinctly described the several different sorts of *khel'at*, we will delve a little bit deeper into this subject. The short description of Shah Esma'il's I grant of a *khel'at* to his son tells it in a nut-shell where a high ranking person was concerned. The Shah gave his son a full complement of *khel'at*, to wit: a *taj*, an aigrette (*jiqeh*), a mace (*gorz*), a dagger (*khanjar*), a gem-studded sword, and a pure bred Arab horse with golden reins[1738]. Therefore, let's have a closer look at the *khel'at* accoutrements.

Members of the Safavid sufi order were given the *taj* and *tumar* which, as we have seen in the case of important persons, were usually gold brocaded and studded with gems. This could be further embellished by a gem-studded *jiqeh* or aigrette. What the texts usually refer to as the *khel'at* proper (also *khela'-ye molamma'* or gilt robes of honor) could take various forms. Those especially honored would receive a *khel'at-e khass*, which was a robe worn by the Shah himself, or from his wardrobe[1739]. On the occasion of *Nawruz*, the Shah handed out so-called *khel'at-e nawruzi*[1740]. Sometimes, in case of a special official, the Shah bestowed a *khel'at-e sardari*, as in the case of the Gilan ruler[1741]. The garment that constituted the robe of honour was usually referred to as a *balapush*, surtout or long overcoat. It also took various other forms such as *dagal-ha-ye makhmal-e frang* (Europan imtation velvets) or a multicolored *qaba-ye diba*[1742].

1737. Wills, p. 255-256; p. 256-258 contain a detailed description of the festivities accompanying the receipt of the robe of honor and of the entire ceremony.

1738. [*'Alamara-ye Shah Esma'il*], p. 30, see also p. 62.

1739. Kh^{w}ondamir, IV, p. 388, 454, 480, 496; Esma'il I gave the new *vali* of Howeizeh a *khel'at-e khass* ([*'Alamara-ye Shah Esma'il*], p. 188).

1740. Qomi, II, p. 1021.

1741. [*'Alamara-ye Shah Esma'il*], p. 157.

1742. Kh^{w}ondamir, IV, p. 505; upper coats or surtouts (*jabbeh*) made of muslin (*kish*), ermine (*sinjab*) and *alta'i*, and *qabas* of *diba*, *qotni* and *dara'i* (*ibid.*, p. 518); *taj-e zarduzi*, *qaba-ye molamma'* (Qomi, I, p. 57); a *chaharqab* and *qaba-ye zarbaft* (Qomi, II, p. 623).

Sometimes, boots or *chekmeh* made of red *saqarlat* were added[1743]. It was not the custom to give a *chahar-qab* to a Tajik or Persian at that time[1744].

The *khel'at* itself was further adorned by a *kamar-e morassa'* or a gem-studded belt, which was completed by the grant of a gem-studded dagger (*khanjar*). Sometimes a studded sword, in particular an Egyptian one, was granted as well, while in some cases a mace (or *gorz*) was added for special high-ranking persons. In the 16th century the *khel'at* was not complete if the grant did not include one or more Arab horses (*asb-e tazi*) with gold and gem-studded reins[1745]. The Turkish ambassador in 970/1562-63 brought horses covered with blankets (*jol*) made of *zarbaft* and velvet[1746].

The accoutrements received by the Georgian *vali*, which consisted of a belt (*kamar*), a dagger (*khanjar*), a gold and studded sword (*shamshir-e zarrin morassa'*), an aigrette (*jiqeh*), a horse (*asb*), and a gold brocaded overcoat adorned with beaver pelt (*balapush-e taladuz-e samsur*) corroborate this[1747]. It seems that robes of honor ceremonies became less elaborate with the passage of time in that only the robe of honor, without the belts, daggers and horses, was given, or it may be that these later records only referred to grants to lower ranking officials. The *khel'at* given to Bardsiri (around 1670), for example, consisted of a surcoat or *qaba*, a turban or *mandil* and a sash or *chahar-dhar'i*[1748]. Molla Jalal, in the early 17th century, says of the *khel'at* that it consisted of a *qaba*, a *balapush* and a *mandil*[1749]. However, in the 16th century, grants that were restricted to only the *taj* and *khel'at* also were given[1750]. In 971/1563-64 some Mashhadi seyyeds were given a present (*be rasm khel'at*) of *saqarlat-e kabud*[1751]. However, the trend was towards simplification and lower cost. Kaempfer reports that « The robe of honor consisted of a double surcoat, both parts of which reach till the calfs,

---

1743. Khʷondamir, p. 518. Also, *astar, taj, saruq, qaba va balapush* and *pustin* were given (Qomi, II, p.1002); royal *khel'ats* consisting of *taj, saruq*, and *chaharqab* were given (*ibid.*, p. 1018); *taj, saruq, lebas-e noqrehbaft* such as *qaba* and *balapush* (*ibid.*, p. 1078).

1744. Rumlu, p. 56.

1745. Khʷondamir, IV, p. 505, 516, 518, 556, 566; [*'Alamara-ye Shah Esma'il*], p. 72, 196, 231, 238; Qomi, II, p. 623, 676, 690, 749, 857, 887, 1078.

1746. Shirazi, p. 120.

1747. Qomi, II, p. 716.

1748. Bardsiri, p. 467.

1749. Monajjem, p. 389.

1750. Khʷondamir, IV, p. 598, 602; Bafqi, III, part 1, p. 222 *khel'at az mandil, kamarband, qaba va balapush.*

1751. Qomi, I, p. 442.

and is made of gold or silver brocade, or of a costly fabric embellished with flowers. Sometimes also a turban and a sash are given, however, very seldom a golden sword ». He adds that often, « these robes of honor were passed on to other people by the recipients, to reward a service rendered to them »[1752].

It is clear from these descriptions that *khel'at* grants were an expensive custom. Mansur Beg Qepchaq, for example, received a *khel'at,* together with a studded *taj va tumar*, a studded *jiqeh*, an Arab horse with studded reins, all of which amounted in value to around 12,000 tomans[1753]. But even if not everybody received such an expensive robe of honor sometimes the sheer number of the grants also added up to substantial sums. For example, Shah Esma'il I gave 4,000 *Qezelbash* a *khel'at* each, at a total cost of 30,000 tomans, or 7.5 tomans per person, which for many was more than an annual salary[1754]. All emirs were given a *jiqeh*, a *kamar*, a *khanjar*, and a *shamshir-e morassa'* and a *khel'at*[1755], while the entire Talesh army received a *khel'at*[1756]. Shah 'Abbas II gave almost 8,000 *khel'at*s each consisting of: gold brocaded velvet coats lined with sable fur; gold brocaded overcoats (*balapush*) made of gold and silver cloth and *dara'i*; turbans entirely made of gold and [...] cloth; gold brocaded and single-colored *chahar-dhar'i*; and costly fabrics of many colors in 1038/1638-39[1757].

In the highly stratified Safavid society great attention was given to have the presents reflect the status of the recipient. What might look like a number of gaudy dresses to an uninformed observer were signs of different social status to a Safavid courtier. This is clear from a description provided to us by Eskander Beg Monshi. Shah 'Abbas I on the occasion of « the defection of the Jalali tribe from Diyar Bekr, bestowed 2,000 *khel'at*s! The leading magnates received a gold brocaded and gilt surcoat [*qaba-ye zarbaft talabaf*], a gold brocaded velvet long overcoat [*balapush-e makhmal zarbaft*], a gold

1752. Kaempfer [*Am Hofe*], p. 66; [*Carmelites*], I, p. 480 « a girdle, and surcoat, and a head dress, all of silk fringed with gold and silver » (Hotz, p.).

1753. [*'Alamara-ye Shah Esma'il*], p. 148; in addition to the *khel'at* etc. he also received an *'alam* and some dresses with *mandil*s entirely of gold and a *qaba-ye zarbaft* (*ibid.*, p. 239).

1754. *Ibid.*, p. 544.

1755. Qomi, II, p. 804.

1756. [*'Alamara-ye Shah Esma'il*], p. 359; on that day some 50-60 jewel studded belts and daggers were given away (Qomi, II, p. 627).

1757. Esfahani [*Kholasat*], p. 47.

brocaded sash of 4 ell long [*mandil-e sarasar-e chahar-dhar'i-ye talabaf*], and a gem-studded aigrette [*jiqeh-ye morassa'*]. Other high ranking persons, though lower in rank, received a gold brocaded *dara'i* surcoat [*qaba-ye zarbaft-e dara'ibaf*] and a long overcoat made of figured and unfigured velvet [*balapush-e makhmal-e monaqqesh-e makhmal-e sadeh*] and a many-colored turban sash [*mandil-e alvan*], and some received an additional *chahar-dhar'i* or waist sash. The middle ranks received a surcoat made of *milek* and other middle quality silken fabrics [*qaba-ye milek, motabeq, na'lband, khoftan-e makhmal*], and head sashes [*dastarha-ye sarzard*]; while the lower ranks received a silken surcoat made of *qotni* and *dara'i* [*qaba-ye qotni* and *dara'i*], and a single-colored head sash [*dastar-e sadeh*] »[1758]. This stratification continued to exist under Nader Shah, where the cost of a robe of honor for the highest category (*a'la*) was 100 tomans, for the medium (*vasat*) category 50 tomans, and for the lowest category (*forutar*) was 10-20 tomans[1759].

The ceremonial procedure as well as the nature of the *khel'at* present did not change during the 18th century. *Khel'ats* were handed out with *balapush-e zarbaf-e sangin va tazayyon*[1760]. Nami also mentions that *sanadeq-atlas, khara, zarbaf* and *diba* were stored by the Zand court for the making of *khel'ats*[1761]. They were made by the private sector, mainly in Yazd, Kashan, Shiraz and Isfahan, as part of the city's tax burden. In the Qajar period the number of robes of honor handed out each year numbered in the thousands[1762].

The robe of honour (*jobbeh*) is a wide cloak with long sleeves in which one can hide the hands, only donned when visiting high dignitaries, when it is worn over the *qaba*. It is made of shawl, in many cases adorned with pearl tresses and gold galons, which raised its value substantially[1763]. « This ample and majestic garment is affected by mirzas (secretaries), Government employees of high rank, as ministers, farmers of taxes, courtiers, physicians, priests. The wearers carry a staff as a rule. The jubas are made of the finest cloth, very amply cut. They have a standing collar and

---

1758. Monshi, II, p. 775. See also Chardin, V, p. 272.

1759. Mervi, III, p. 1088.

1760. Gulestaneh, p. 266; Nami, (p. 120) mentions *khel'at-e noqrehbaft, taladuz va thiyab-e guharnegar zar-anduz*.

1761. *Ibid.*, p. 47.

1762. Morier [*Journey*], p. 206; Fraser [*Travels*].

1763. Hotz, p. 19, note.

long sleeves. These sleeves are from one to two feet longer than the arm, and are often allowed to hang down empty when the garment is worn out of doors; but when in actual presence of guests or a grandee, they are used to keep the hands hidden (as a token of respect to those present), and the many wrinkles formed by the excessive length of these sleeves are supposed to be their beauty »[1764]. « It is customary for the person to whom the dress is sent to meet the bearer of it a short distance from the town. In some places there is a house built for the purpose, called a khallat-pooshaun, as at Tabreez; but, where there is none such, the nearest village on the road by which the messenger arrives is generally the appointed place »[1765].

However, the ceremony of the grant of the *khel'at* became less important after the 1870s also, due to the influence of the European fashion, the *jobbeh* went out of fashion[1766]. The inevitable consequence was that most of those craftsmen whose livelihood depended on the *khel'at* —namely the *zaribaf*, or gold brocade weavers, of Isfahan and others like them — went out of business. The same held for the shawl weavers in Kerman, since most of their production had been on orders from Tehran to be used at the New Year *khel'at* presentation ceremonies[1767]. A timid effort to bolster the *khel'at* custom, in particular the use of shawl, provided some temporary relief to remaining craftsmen, but could not hide the fact that the custom had lost its social and political function. In 1928, the *khel'at* ceremony was formally abolished by the Government[1768].

1764. Wills, p. 319.
1765. Holmes, p. 177, with description of accompanying festivities.
1766. Mostaufi, I, p. 98.
1767. Tahvildar, p. 97.
1768. See chapter V.

V. The Persian Shawl

Shawls made in Persia and India have attracted, and continue to attract, the admiration and appreciation of the public as well as textile experts. The 19th century witnessed a large-scale adoption by Europeans and Americans of the Kashmir shawl, imported as an item of fashionable apparel; later, with the introduction of the Jacquard loom, the European products ended up beating out their original models. Shawls were appreciated mainly for their beauty as female adornments in the West, and in Persia (as in India), where their use was not restricted to women, the appreciation was not any less. Besides, the sale of shawls was the mainstay of a large segment of the population in production centers. But despite their economic importance, the artistic appreciation they enjoy, and the influence they have exercised on Western fashion, relatively little is known about Persian shawls. They have received cursory mention in general surveys of Persian art[1769]. One study says about Persian shawls: « Up to the present time only nineteenth-century examples have been known, and these are difficult to distinguish with any confidence from the Kashmiri productions »[1770]. Other works offer hardly anything more substantial. Aside from redressing such scholarly neglect, this study aims to delve into the following relevant questions: what constitutes a shawl; what kinds of shawls are there; what purposes shawls have served; when and where shawls were made and who made them; how did the Persian shawl industry fared in the 19th and 20th centuries and what were the differences between Kerman and Kashmir shawls are.

The Shawl characteristics

• *Semantic Background*

The etymology of the word *shal* is unknown. It may be a bastardization of the word *sa'r*, which in Syriac denotes fine hair, silk, or of *sha'r* (hair) in

1769. There are several studies on Kashmir shawls and their contribution to European art and culture. See, among others, Ames [Fashion]; Ames [*Kashmir*]; Cassin; Irwin [*Kashmir*]; Levi-Strauss; Mikosch; Mossman; Nicolas; Rennicke; Rowe; [*The Indian Heritage*]; [*The Kashmir Shawl*]. Literature on Persian shawls is scantier and offers little detail. For representative samples see [*Ketabshenasi*]; Anavian and Anavian; Qandahari and Lotfi; Scarce [Persian Shawl].

1770. Pope and Ackerman, III, p. 2153-2154.

Arabic. The Syriac *sha'raa* (soft hair, down, wool) complicates the issue, because normally the Arabic 'sh' become 's' in Syriac and vice versa. The use of the term *shal* to denote a woolen fabric is attested as early as the 10th century by Ibn Hawqal, and in the 11th century in poems by Sana'i and 'Onsori[1771]. A *shal* was originally a coarse woolen fabric used by men for clothing; it was also used to cover animals, tents and floors. *Loghat al-Fors* (completed 1332) defines *shal* as a small woolen *gelim*[1772]. It is also reported that the poet Sa'di was a *shal-pushi,* one dressed in coarse woolen cloth[1773]. The wearing of woolen garments was a trademark of those in Persian society who had adopted the life-style of a dervish, a life-style that might entail working with textiles, as was the case with Shaykh Qotb al-Din Ebrahim who took pleasure in embroidering woolens from Rasht[1774]. A *shal* garment was also known as *chukheh* (woolen surplice) or *pashmineh,* which, in medieval texts, denoted a coat made of rough woolen cloth or raincoat. Muslim dervishes were not the only ones who wore the *chukheh;* Christian monks did, too[1775]. It would seem, therefore, that the *shal* was principally a homespun fabric that had not yet reached the level of artistic excellence it would attain from the 16th century onwards.

In addition to the Kashmir shawl, there continues to exist a completely different variety, also made of wool. This type of *shal* is a rough, thick fabric, rather felt- and cloth-like. It is the major textile product of mountainous regions such as Khalkhal, Talesh, Gilan, Eastern Azerbaijan, and the Caucasus (Daghestan). It is used primarily to make winter clothing for men, such as coats, trousers, and hats (in which case only sheep wool is used); or wrappers, horse blankets, and other animal coverings (in which case wool is mixed with goat hair). When used as a roof covering or awning (*chador*), the material consists only of goat hair. Because of its functional

---

1771. Ibn Hawqal referred to shawl production in Bam (Barthold, p. 139); Dehkhoda, q.v. *shal.*

1772. See Tusi. This definition is supported by other early literary sources (see Dehkhoda, who cites, among others, Sana'i, 'Onsori, the *Sehah al-Fors*, the *Sharafnameh-ye Maniri, Bahar-e 'ajam* and *Anandraj*).

1773. [*'Alamara-ye Safavi*], p. 10. According to Dehkhoda, the term *shal-pushi* could refer to someone who donned a shawl, to an article of dress of the poor, or to a horse blanket.

1774. Bafqi, III, p. 605. On the obligatory use of woollen or cotton clothes by dervishes see, for example, Kashefi, p. 170-171.

1775. Kermani [*Manaqeb*], p. 38; *Borhan-e qate'*, II, p. 669; Doerfer, III, p. 110-111; Dozy p. 122-125; [*Maqalat*], p. 150, 1003.

nature and rough exterior, this type of fabric is seldom dyed and therefore retains its natural colors of black and brown. Its use is typical among some herders in the northern mountains[1776].

As a fabric, *chukheh* evolved over the course of years, and so did the uses to which it was put. It is reported that Shah Soltan Hosein Safavi included an overcoat (*qaba*) made of *chukheh* from Astarabad or Khafi in his design for his soldiers' uniforms[1777]. Around the 1770s, *chukheh* and *pashmineh* are referred to as fabrics for the upper classes by Asef Hosein, who writes that Hosein Qoli Khan made a comparison between his wardrobe and that of his vassal Mehdi Khan, and scornfully pointed out to his audience that his *qaba* was made solely of *chukheh* and *pashmineh* and his *shal-e kamarband* was of linen, while those of Mehdi Khan were made entirely of shawl (*termeh*)[1778]. We learn from another source that *'abas* made of Mazandaran goat hair were sold in the bazaar of Tabriz around 1826[1779]. Shawls blended with waste silk and known as *chukheh, hazar jarib,* or simply *shal,* were made at Hazar Jarib, Savadkuh and Nur in Mazandaran in the 1840s. These were 10 yards 9 inches by 18 inches, and sold for 4 to 10 sahebqrans per piece, according to quality[1780]. Around 1860, a Persian traveler reported amongst other things that Talesh, Asalam, and Gorgan-Rud produced *shal-e chukheh*[1781]. The so-called *chukheh-ye barani* was also part of the required dress for royal audiences in the early Qajar period, according to Soltan Ahmad Mirza[1782]. A peculiar variety of textile was the *shal-e khar*, a horse-cloth or pack-saddle made of cotton and gunny or sack-cloth. It has been suggested that the choice of wording in this case has a political connotation: it is intended to ridicule the elite's receiving of robes of honor[1783]. While this may have been the case in certain poems, such was certainly not the term's generic use. Naser al-Din Shah (r. 1848-

1776. Bazin *et al*; Bazin, II, p. 51; Dehkhoda, *shal*, q.v. Abdullaev, p. 88; Agashirunova, p. 64-67.

1777. Nava'i, p. 5.

1778. Asef, p. 359.

1779. Bélanger, II, p. 336.

1780. Amanat, p. 24; McKenzie, p. 215. McKenzie states that this type of woollen-silk shawl was woven in Hazar Jarib, Savadkuh and Nur and measured 3 yards 15 inches in length and 3 inches in width.

1781. Bastani Parizi [*Farmanfarma*], p. 214, quoting [*Safarnameh*].

1782. Soltan-Ahmad Mirza, p. 62.

1783. Bastani Parizi [*Farmanfarma*], p. 300, and the amusing and well-known story on p. 303 n. 1, of which other variants exist.

96), or rather his first prime minister, Mirza Taqi Khan Amir Kabir, realized the importance of the coarse shawl and made efforts to promote the Mazandaran variety for the making of army uniforms in 1266/1850[1784]. In 1911 Rabino described this type of coarse shawl as « Chukha, a woolen stuff manufactured at Yakhkesh [Savadkuh] [which] is much in demand by the people of Mazanderan and Astarabad, who make of it their winter clothing. There are three qualities of this chukha: made of silk refuse and wool, and known as abai; made of wool and European cotton thread; thick coarse, made of wool and native cotton thread »[1785]. Also produced in Tonekabon and Sari, this fabric was referred to as a felt cloak. In Tonekabon, too, a fabric known as *shal* was manufactured; as is clear from Abbott's report, this was probably a different name for *chukheh*. *Chukheh* (also *chuqeh*), made from goat hair or sheep wool, is still woven in Mazandaran, although, like other traditional fabrics and forms of dress, it is gradually disappearing[1786].

The same kind of coarse *shal* was produced by the Kurds and used by herders to make great-coats and bedding. « Most of their [the Kurds of Baneh] clothes are made of stuffs woven locally of wool of sheep and goats and called "shal", and some of these are of very fine texture », reports a late-19th century traveler[1787]. When made of goat hair, such shawls are known as *maras* and are still produced in Kermanshah. The material of the *maras* was also used to make shirts, known as *chukhehs*, worn by women of the Jaf tribe[1788]. The shawl as a girdle is still a standard part of the male dress of the Jaf Kurds[1789]. In northern Khorasan (Shirvan district) both *chukheh* and *shal-e gardan* are still woven[1790]. In the southwestern Bakhtiyari area, the term *shal* refers both to a covering for animals used during cold weather and to a cotton sash used to gird men's trousers[1791].

1784. E'temad al-Saltaneh, p. 103; Adamiyat, p. 220.

1785. Rabino [Barfrush], p. 12, 16, 17, 19.

1786. Barsavush, p. 130.

1787. Wills, p. 319. See also *Historical Gazetteer*, I p. 87; Tavakkol (p. 22) states that weaving shawls for making clothes is a craft still pursued by the Baneh Kurds.

1788. Soltani, p. 180, 262.

1789. *Ibid.*, p. 253, 254, 261.

1790. Moqimi, p. 220. Shalchi, p. 206, states that a *shal* is understood to be a *patu* (felt-like material) made by the Hazaras of Afghanistan, while a *shal va shalmeh* is a gift and robe of honor.

1791. Digard, p. 53, 212-214. The use of the cotton shawl to gird the trousers occurred among the Papi Lors; see Feilberg, p. 115.

By the 1970s, in Gilan, this variety of coarse *shal* was woven either on a simple horizontal loom or on a loom with two pedals. It is partly a cottage industry (using the simple loom), partly an aesthetic one — such a division of labor being determined by geography. The production of this coarse type of *shal* has never become an organized industry as was the case with the more costly Kerman shawls. Even the artisans who make this type of *shal* work only on demand from their clients, who bring them the raw materials. The warp and woof are of wool, and the fabric is usually washed in soapy or warm water with a view to making the material more felt-like. After soaking, the fabric shrinks to one-fifth its size. As a result, it becomes thick, strong, and water resistant, and closely resembles the material referred to in Europe as "loden". It is from this material that the various types of winter clothing, sacks, blankets, and coverings are made[1792]. Although related to — if not indeed the forerunner of — the high quality Kerman and Kashmir shawl, this type of coarse *shal* will not be discussed here further. Our attention will turn instead to the fine and superb twilled tapestries produced in Persia. Henceforth the term shawl is used to refer to these and not to the coarse varieties, unless otherwise indicated.

Although shawls were woven during the 16th and 17th centuries in Persia, we do not have many particulars about them. Around 1540, an edict (*farman*) by Shah Tahmasp I (1528-1574) gave detailed instructions for the reception of the Moghul emperor Homayun, then in exile in Persia, as well as for the supplies to be provided to him. Among the fabrics made available to Homayun's entourage were mentioned *shal-e termeh* and *shal-e Kashmir*[1793]. Unfortunately we do not know whether the *termeh* had been woven in Persia or in India. Of the man who ousted Homayun, Shir Khan, it is said that Shah Ibrahim Lodi found him in front of his palace with an old shawl wrapped around his head[1794]. Shir Khan's captor, Shahverdi Khan, put on garments of black *shal* to mourn the death of Soltan Morad Mirza[1795]. It is also reported that around the 1560s Shah Tahmasp I demanded « twenty-five loads of cloth and shawls » as tribute from the population of Zutta, chiefly Armenians[1796]. In a poem written for Begtash Khan, governor of Kerman (996-98/1587-89), in which he satirizes the

1792. Bazin *et al*, p. 69-72. See also Bazin, II, p. 50.
1793. [*'Alamara-ye Shah Tahmasp*], p. 410.
1794. *Ibid.*, p. 228.
1795. *Ibid.*
1796. *Barbaro and Contarini*, part 2, p. 219.

inhabitants of Yazd, the Safavid poet Vahshi Bafqi refers to various fabrics including the shawl[1797]. We learn further that in India people had richly-colored clothes « as in Persia they call Scial, and use for girdles, but the Indians wear them cross the shoulders »[1798]. The Russian merchant Kotov, visiting Persia in 1623, mentions that Persians wore shawls around the head and waist[1799]. Another source tells us about « a beautiful silk sash, which they call Schal. This, like the sash used for the turban, is brought by the Indians into Persia, because [their products] are better and more durable than the Persian ones »[1800]. Meanwhile, production of coarse shawl or *chukheh* continued. Various poets lived as dervishes and opted for a *shal-pushi* life-style in the 16th and 17th century[1801].

The word "shawl" is presumably of Persian origin[1802], but the 17th-century authors quoted here indicate that shawls were mostly imported from India, particularly Kashmir, and that a similar fabric produced in Persia was of inferior quality. Shah 'Abbas I reportedly ordered a courtier to don only a *balapush* (overcoat) made of Kashmir shawl[1803]. Although never using the word shawl, another European traveler confirms that such fabrics were manufactured in Kerman and Yazd. The Zoroastrians of Kerman, he writes, « have the trade of wool which they also process. They make girdles which are used [all over] Persia as well as some small pieces of serge, which are almost as soft and as bright as if they were made of silk »[1804]. As for Yazd, he remarks: « They also make serge of a particular type of wool, which is so fine and so delicate that the fabric is more beautiful and more expensive than if it were made of silk »[1805]. From yet another source we learn that Kerman goat hair was used « to weave both Cloth and Carpets very fine, which they sell at dear Rates »[1806]. Persians, we are told, wore two girdles, of which « the other is shorter and narrower and is commonly

1797. Bastani Parizi [*Farmanfarm*], p. 290.

1798. Della Valle [Extract], p. 123; Parodi, p. 325.

1799. Kotov, p. 54, 90.

1800. Olearius, p. 587, implies here that shawls were made in Persia.

1801. Nasrabadi, p. 33, 52, 395-396, 419, 432.

1802. The etymology of the word shawl is unknown. Bastani Parizi (*Farmanfarma*], p. 194-201, 293-296, has suggested that it may be a bastardization of *shar*, which in Syriac denotes silk (*Makhzan al-adwiyah*, index).

1803. Monajjem, p. 427.

1804. Tavernier, I, p. 95-96.

1805. *Ibid.*, p. 105.

1806. Fryer, III, p. 8.

of goat or camel hair, and only of one colour »[1807]. Du Mans, translates the word chal as "ceinture", i.e. girdle or sash[1808].

That shawls were indeed produced in Persia is made clear from a report by the British East India Company that mentions that, in March 1685, « 15 shawls from Kirman, 20 of various coloured ones sold for 24/- each, 8 striped for 8/6, 23 camel coloured for 9/- and 28 white ones for 20/- »[1809]. Apparently, there existed a shawl weavers' quarter (*mahalleh-ye shalbafan*) in Hamadan in 1017/1608-09[1810]. We also learn that in the last quarter of the 17th century the population of the village of Saghand was making its living by weaving shawls[1811]. The trade had become important enough for individuals to be identified with it, as in the case of one 'Abd al-Ghani, son of Kh^{w}ajeh Gheyath Shalbaf[1812], and in the early decades of the 18th century, the return of the shawl merchants to Isfahan after the departure of the Afghans was significant enough to merit mention[1813]. Shah Soltan Hosein included the shawl (undoubtedly the coarse variety, to be used as a waist band) as part of the uniform that he had designed for his soldiers, and among presents to the Ottoman grand vizier in 1721 we find 9 pieces of *shal-e termeh*[1814]. Because shawls were expensive fabrics, they were offered for sale by specialized shawl sellers in the Qeisariyeh, the most exclusive section of the Isfahan bazaar[1815].

European Company agents mention the existence of shawl weavers for the first time in 1677, and observe a growing competition from their side for goat wool[1816]. This is not surprising because shawls were woven from silk or from goat hair (*kork*)[1817]. In 1684, *kork* had become scarce, a scarcity « occasioned by the yearly encrease of weavers, who gett their liveing by

1807. Thévenot, II, p. 92.

1808. Du Mans, p. 190; Richard, II, p. 148.

1809. Ferrier [*British-Persian Relations*], p. 394, quoting B/38, p. 203, 17 March 1685/6.

1810. Monajjem, p. 346.

1811. Bafqi, III, p. 662.

1812. Bardsiri, p. 589. Although the son is referred to in 1691, it means that his shawl-weaving father must have exercised his craft some 40 years prior to that date, around 1650.

1813. ARA, KA 1856, fol. 299 (18/7/1720).

1814. Nava'i, p. 87.

1815. Nasrabadi, p. 426.

1816. VOC 1328, fol. 674v (12/8/1677).

1817. Du Mans, p. 366.

weaving that comodity »[1818]. Some ten years later, a conflict about the sale of *kork* broke out between the European companies and the weavers of Kerman, because the latter « must all starve, there being not enough left for them to work upon, in makeing namatts [felt carpets], shauls, capps, etc. »[1819]. This problem remained unsolved and was a recurring irritant in the local politics of Kerman. We learn, for instance, of the resentment the shawl weavers of Kerman felt towards the wool-gathering privileges that the European companies enjoyed[1820]. Although the Dutch East Indies Company did not trade in Persian shawls, the company's Persian correspondence contains references to them. On 13 February 1728 it is reported that « 12 pieces of very beautiful shawls or turbans [hoofdwindsels] » were presented to Zabardast Khan, the Afghan general, in Bandar 'Abbas[1821]. In 1732, a VOC document refers to « halssluiers or sjala doesandaz [*shal-e duz andaz*], also called sjaals tirma and camerband »[1822].

In 1153/1741, among the presents that he sent to the Ottoman Sultan Mahmud, Nader Shah included a number of beautiful Kashmir shawls; on an earlier occasion he had sent 27 pieces of *shal-e termeh-ye kamarband* and *shal-e reza'i*[1823]. In a Russian report about the import of Persian textiles in the 1740s, no mention is made about woolen shawls, though there is a reference to *taftik* (Turkish for fine goat wool, or the cloth woven from it)[1824]. A European traveler observed that « the better sort of people wear a sash of Khermania wool, wrapped about their heads as turbands; some of these are so exceeding fine as to cost 100 crowns [£25], and the common price for such as are good is 8 to 10 crowns »[1825]. In the early 1770s, the chiefs of Darband exported « a thin type of cloth, called Ruberschi Schal »,

1818. Matthee [East India], p. 358, citing India Office G/36/109, fol. 90 (14/1/1684).

1819. *Ibid.*, citing India Office E/3/5/6066, fol. 18 (9/8/1695). For a similar complaint see E/3/50/5920 (8/8/1694).

1820. VOC 2042, Resolutie Gamron, fol. 3960 (13/4/1726).

1821. VOC 2080, fol. 3522 r and v.

1822. VOC 2254, fol. 825 (29/5/1732). See also KA 1926, fol. 198 (9/3/1725) informing Zabardast Khan, Afghan governor of Shiraz, that the VOC cannot supply him with *shal-e termeh*, because it does not trade in that commodity; also KA 1891, fol. 593 (30/3/1723) reporting the theft of a shawl from the VOC agent in Kerman, and VOC 2322, fol. 313 (28/10/32) which mentions that « chits, shawls, and Yazdi fabrics were prepared as presents » for Nader Shah.

1823. Nasiri, I, p. 100, 110.

1824. Pope and Ackerman, III, p. 2171, 2172, 2174.

1825. Hanway, I, p. 330.

to pay for the import of silken and cotton fabrics[1826]. This may have been the type of shawl referred to in a Persian document dating from the second half of the 17th century, namely, *shal-e kar-e Ardabil,* or a shawl made in Ardabil. Both may have been shawls of the coarse variety[1827]. Under the Afshar and Zand rulers the so-called *shal-e termeh-ye patehduzi-ye hashiyehdar* (a *termeh* shawl with embroidered borders) was wrapped around the hat[1828]. During Karim Khan Zand's reign *shal-e gush pich* and *shal-e reza'i,* both high-quality fabrics, were sold at Isfahan for 25,000 dinars and 15,000 dinars a piece, respectively. Both kinds were wrapped around the head. There was also trade in a very expensive *shal-e ebra* (?), (six tomans per piece)[1829]. By the last decades of the 18th century, all woolen manufactures came from Kerman and Yazd, and these undoubtedly included shawls[1830]. This seems the more likely, because around that time mention is made of Jamal Shalbaf in Kerman, as well as of Ostad Taqi Shalbaf, who probably worked in Isfahan[1831]. Around the same time, Kashmir woolens were used as turbans and girdles as well as female garments. In Kerman « they imitate Kashmir shawls, although these are not so soft as the former »[1832]. In the 1770s the girdle of the Persian dress was still made of Kerman goat wool[1833]. Shawls were also made in Yazd, and though inferior to the Kashmir shawls, they were good enough to be sought by the rich[1834]. The British make mention of shawls again in 1790, reporting that Ja'far Khan Zand prohibited the export of *kork* and that increasingly the wool was being used for shawl making[1835].

• *What is a Shawl?*

The product that stands out among the woolen textiles made in Persia is the shawl. A twill woven tapestry, it is finely made from spun wool. As

1826. Gmelin, III, p. 15. Perhaps Gmelin means *rufarshi* (carpet covering).
1827. Gaube and Wirth, p. 262-263.
1828. Mostaufi, I, p. 98. *Shal-e fatehduzi* was still made in Kerman at the end of the 19th century (Vaziri, p. 37). On the craft of *patehduzi*, see Gluck and Gluck, p. 222.
1829. Asef, p. 316.
1830. Francklin, p. 148.
1831. Nami Esfahani, p. 140.
1832. Ferrières-Sauvebœuf, II, p. 11, 13.
1833. Gmelin, III, p. 158.
1834. Olivier, V, p. 305.
1835. Lorimer, p. 167.

Irwin describes it: « The technique of Kashmir shawl-brocading is known to historians as the twill-tapestry weave, because of its basic similarity with the technique traditionally employed in western Europe for tapestry weaving. According to this, the wefts of the patterned part of the fabric were inserted by means of wooden spools, without the use of a shuttle. Weft threads alone form the pattern; these do not run the full width of the cloth, being woven back and forth round the warp threads only where each particular colour is needed. The only significant difference between the technique as employed in Europe and India is that in the former case the ground is a plain weave, whereas in Kashmir it is a twill »[1836].

In Europe a shawl is understood to be a square, oblong, or triangular protective or ornamental article of dress, worn generally by women over the shoulders, neck, or head. This meaning of shawl stands in contrast to its Persian denotation — *shal* meaning the material rather than a particular article of dress[1837]. In the latter part of the 19th century, a European observer was able to distinguish three types of shawls:

- « The "Shal" is a woolen cloth which is made up into lengths of from 3 to 5 yards, with a width of about 42 inches, of various tints and thickness. It is used for coats and cloaks, and costs about from 20 krans to 50 krans apiece.

- Better qualities are embroidered in various designs and colours and form lovely articles, being used for curtains, coverlets, table cloths, and wrappers. This is known as Tirmah.

- A further development comes out in the shape of the shawl, which is so widely renowned, and is only surpassed by the celebrated ones from Cashmere »[1838].

Shawls were used as garments (cloaks, hats, caps, turbans, waist bands), bed coverings, pillow cases and other household items[1839]. It has

1836. Irwin [*Kashmir*], p. 2. « The term "brocading" is misleading, because rather than discontinuous wefts which are wound around the last warp in which they are used to make the pattern as in the twill-weave tapestry, brocaders use a shuttle and run the weft across the whole width of the fabric but "float" the wefts along the back of the fabric where they do not wish the particular color to be employed in the design. This technique is used, for example, in the production of many tribal *gelim*s (flat-woven carpets) in Iran. Brocading produces a "good side" and a "bad side" to the fabric (where the floated wefts are exposed), but has the advantage being a relatively less time-consuming technique than shawl weaving. Also, it requires less fine yarn, and the weaving is less tight ».

1837. Goldsmid, I, p. 102.

1838. DCR, 1376 (1894), p. 30.

been suggested that shawls were used as covers (*sofrehs*) as well. This may be right, although in contemporary travelogues the authors invariably state that calico (*chit*) and other cotton fabrics were used for this purpose. Shawls were used as napkins to cover fruit trays and the like[1840]. Sometimes these varied end-uses have resulted in special combination words such as *shal-e kamar* (waist band shawl) or *shal-e kolah* and *shal-e sar* (head-dress shawl) just as in English similar combination words have come into being (e.g. shawl collar; shawl-room; shawl-dance)[1841]. The same type of shawl, generally 2.75 meters long with one plain color and borders with floral and *boteh* patterns, has also been called the *shal-e kamarbandi*[1842]. The *shal-e chaharqadi*, or head-scarf shawl, is another example of a combination word. This type of shawl was square and about 1.5 m x 1.5 m. Two types were distinguished: *lachak-toranj* which had a medallion design with four curls and bands around the edges; and *goldar*, which only had floral designs[1843]. This type of shawl was also referred to as *shalkesh* or as *shal dawr sari*[1844]. The shawl « most commonly made in Karman is in pieces of five or six yards long and three-quarters wide, which are cut up into outer coats for both sexes. It is also used by the rich for door hangings and tent linings, for caps, tray covers, and many other purposes. Long pieces of a single colour, embroidered with needlework at the ends, are used for turbans and waistcloths, and come nearer to the European idea of a shawl than anything else »[1845]. A shawl was sold by the piece, usually of a size sufficient to

---

1839. Greenfield, p. 311; Tahvildar, p. 100; Layard, p. 157; Fraser [*Travels*], II, p. 305, « my head was wrapped in various bindings of shawl and puttoo » against the cold.

1840. For a picture of a shawl presumbaly used as a *sofreh* see Scarce [Persian Shawl], p. 36 (Fig. 21); on its use as a napkin see Morier [*A Second Journey*], p. 220. For the use of calico as *sofreh* see, for example, Bélanger, II, p. 180, 380.

1841. See, for example, Morier [*A Journey*], p. 244; Mostawfi, I, p. 98; Dehkhoda, q.v. *shal*. Shawls which were wrapped twice around the waist, and of which both ends passed in front of the belly and back, were known as *shal-e lam alef lam*, because the wrapping required a motion akin to the writing of those letters (*ibid.*, I, p. 304, n. 1).

1842. Anavian and Anavian, p. 23. According to Thévenot (III, p. 37), in India « At all times when they go abroad, they wear a Chal which is a kind of toilet of very fine Wool made at Cachmir. These Chals are about two Ells long and an Ell broad ».

1843. Anavian and Anavian, p. 22.

1844. [*Farhang-e loghat*], p. 283.

1845. Goldsmid, I, p. 102. « Shawls in Persia are chiefly made use of for lining or covering the long loose robes, as barounies, oemas, Cc. as sashes to tie round the waist, or as turbans round the head. [...] But the material and texture of these shawls is of great

make an upper cloak. Shawls could also be sold, or given away, by the bundle (*boqcheh*). *Boqcheh* seems to refer to a package of 36 pieces of shawl, although elsewhere two *boqchehs* are said to have contained 66 pieces of shawl[1846].

There are many references to shawls in the travelogues of royalty, nobles and their servants[1847]. However, shawls were seldom used to wear around the shoulders as in India, and thus few so-called long shawls were used in Persia[1848]. Shawls were also used as presents during official ceremonies such as on the occasion of the signing of the Treaty of Paris in 1857, when 10 *taqeh-ye shal-e termeh* were listed as royal presents[1849]. A peculiar use of the shawl was the making of robes of honor (*khel'at*) which the shah presented to deserving persons. « The courtiers wear them when in full dress »[1850]. The deserving person could also be one who had been

---

importance [...] these imitations [shawls] would go far to supply the place of the Cashmere shawls. For this purpose, I cannot help thinking, that the wool of Kerman, particularly of that sort called khoolk, would answer remarkably well » (Fraser [*Caspian Sea*], p. 369). See also Waring, p. 58, 61.

1846. Zell al-Soltan, p. 155, 215. It may be that the number 33 was misread as 36.

1847. Fraser [*A Winter's Journey*], II, p. 19 « The Sepahsalar was most gorgeously clad in a yellow silk kabba, or dress, with a white spotted shawl around his waist, in which he had stuck a splendid jewelled dagger. His cloak was of fine shawl, lined with very handsome fur »; « a prince wearing a rich shawl dress » (p. 87); « nassakchees and yessawuls in their red barounies and shawl wrapped caps » (p. 88); « a prince with an exquisite shawl girdle » (p. 91); also p. 183 and 484. Brydges-Jones, p. 100 « on his head [the prince] wore a Persian cap, with a very beautiful shawl twisted around it; the Shah wore a cap around which was twisted a dark blue and white cashmire shawl (p. 243). Fraser [*Travels*], I, p. 52 and II, p. 265 where he notes the absence of a shawl in case of the chief minister as something out of the ordinary. Morier [*Journey*], p. 243-244; Keppel, p. 251 « the court dress is simple, but rich; the common sheep-skin is covered with a superb Cachemire shawl ». Tancoigne, p. 203; Porter, I, p. 324, 355, 466; Stuart, p. 185, 299; Bélanger, II, p. 212, 357; Ouseley, III, p. 134.

1848. Fraser [*Caspian Sea*], p. 369. This indeed gives India some claim to be regarded as the true home of the shawl, in the sense in which it became known in Europe, as Irwin [*Kashmir*], p. 2 has suggested.

1849. Farrokh Khan, II, p. 326.

1850. Sykes [*Persia*], p. 319. Polak [*Persien*], I, p. 153, mentions the ceremony of the reception of the *khel'at*, which either were cast off from the shah (*az tan-e mobarak*) or came from the royal wardrobe. He also remarks that Persians had no prejudice in accepting, buying and wearing used clothes (*ibid.*, I, p. 155). Arnold, p. 215, mentions the governor of Qom with a robe of honor « made from a Cashmere shawl, of which the

wrongly given the bastinado and thus received a shawl or some other costly present as compensation[1851]. Shawls also « cover the bier of a rich man on his way the grave »[1852]. Lambton mentions that among certain artisans, more particularly the butchers in Tehran, a special ceremony prevailed whereby a Kashmir shawl was placed on the shoulders of the nearest relative of the deceased[1853]. In the *ta'ziyeh* procession the so-called *qabr-e peighambar* (prophet's bier) was covered with Kashmir shawls[1854]. Mrs. Bishop mentions that the tomb of Fatima, sister of Imam Reza, in Qom was covered by a large brown shawl. Around the tomb, « Kerman, Kashmir and Indian shawls are laid down as carpets »[1855]. Shawls were also used to decorate places used and frequented by royalty. Fath 'Ali Shah's tents were lined throughout with Kashmir shawls. Some of these tents, therefore, cost up to £40,000[1856]. The stage of the *ta'ziyeh* that Naser al-Din Shah had built in the Golestan Palace grounds also was adorned with shawls. The latter were also used to dress up the actors and animals participating in the passion play[1857]. Naser al-Din Shah rewarded the overseers (*mobashers*) of the passion play theater with shawl robes of honor. « Three hours prior to the beginning of the passion play a table was set up on the stage on which more than 200 pieces of shawl were put. The overseers came one by one in

---

ground was white »; on p. 224, he mentions the governor of Kashan « dressed in a long robe of dark Cashmere »; Mostaufi, I, p. 98-99 gives a description of Qajar official dress and notes the changes therein over time. He notes that among the military the use of the shawl around the hat fell into disuse.

1851. Nezam al-Saltaneh, I, p. 254.

1852. Sykes [*Persia*], p. 319; see also Adams, p. 347 « the bier was covered with rich shawls ».

1853. Lambton, p. 26.

1854. Morier [*Second Journey*], p. 181. Special Kashmir shawls, known as *qabr-push* or tomb-cover, were imported into Persia, Irwin [*Kashmir*], appendix I.

1855. Bird, I, p. 169. Other costly fabrics were also used to cover tombs such as gold brocade or *zarduzi*, Khʷondamir, IV, p. 494; Bafqi, III, p. 53 (*zarbaft*) ; Le Bruyn, I, p. 167, 170 (brocade).

1856. Brydges-Jones, p. 238; S.W.G. Benjamin, p. 195, the tents « of the Shah and his courtiers are lined with embroidered cashmere ».

1857. Smith, p. 39 quoted by Scarce [Persian Shawl], p. 35. Shawls also played a role in the ta'ziyeh procession; the led horses were covered with shawls (Morier [*Second Journey*], p. 182, with drawing on next page), while the *ta'ziyeh* procession was opened « by a crowd of men of the lower orders, carrying standards [...] and banners of Cachemir shawls » (Tancoigne, p. 199); Sheil, p. 130; Ouseley, III, p. 170.

front of the Shah's booth, and after they had put on the costly piece, they made their obeisance »[1858].

Shawls also played a role during *'id-e qorban*, though it is not known whether this was a prank or occurred regularly. Three days prior to the sacrifice of the camel, Naser al-Din Shah sent a very big ram adorned with a rich shawl accompanied by two fat ewes to his two daughters who had gone to their husbands[1859].

Persian shawls had to compete with Kashmir shawls which traditionally were imported along with other fabrics from India[1860]. There were Persian merchants who specialized in the trade of Kashmir shawls, and were among the most important merchants of their city. For example, Hajji Mohammad Javad of Shiraz resided in Kashmir where he traded in Kashmir shawls, and Hajji Mohammad Hosein, his brother, did the same in Baghdad. Hajji 'Ali Reza Tajer Dehdashti was known as Kashmiri, because for many years he lived in Kashmir and traded in Kashmir shawls[1861]. It is, therefore, no surprise to learn that Kashmiri shawls were specially made for the Persian market. « At this city [wrote Moorcroft from the capital, Srinagar, in 1822] I find merchants from Gela and from other cities of Chinese Turkestan, from Uzbek, Tartary, from Kabul, from Persia, from Turkey, and from the provinces of British India engaged in purchasing and in waiting for the getting up of shawl goods differing as to quality and pattern in conformity to the taste of the markets for which they are intended in a degree probably not suspected in Europe »[1862]. In addition to lengths of cloth, furnishings for special dedicated end-uses were imported, such as:

khukhabutha : large compound flowers, consisting of groups of smaller ones
islimi : for saddle cloth, curtains, women's use
lahri-dar : waved like water
lungi : girdles
jarrab : short stockings, both flowered and striped
darparda : curtains
balapos or *palangposh* : quilts, covers
langota : waist belts

1858. Mo'ayyer al-Mamalek, p. 67.

1859. *Ibid.*, p. 61.

1860. Waring, p. 77 writes that Persian merchants « often undertake long journeys, frequently to Cashmere, where they supply themselves with shawls ».

1861. Fasa'i, II, p. 78; see also Issawi, p. 26.

1862. Irwin [*Kashmir*], p. 13 (emphasis added).

paipech : leggings
qabr-posh : shrouds
taqposh : covers or hangings to recesses, cupboards[1863].

Thus, the *shal* fabric was put to various uses, and came in different sizes, prices, patterns and designs. « The shawls are plain and [...] figures of a great variety of qualities and descriptions, which would not be intelligible without a reference to the articles themselves: they are also of many different breadths and lengths; and of prices from 1s/- to £14 each »[1864]. Shawls also were cut into long borders (*hashiyehs*), that were used to line and adorn clothes[1865]. Richly flowered shawls, or spotted ones with pines of great or smaller size on a rich background of black, green, yellow, crimson, or scarlet were greatly appreciated in the early Qajar period[1866].

As a consequence of the great variety in shawl sizes, designs and colors, these fabrics were known under various names. Shawls may be classified according to four criteria:

1. production center; 2. size; 3. color; 4. pattern.

The first classification was a simple one in view of the limited centers of production. Thus we find reference to the *shal-e Kashmir, shal-e Kerman, shal-e Mashhad* or *Khorasan, shal-e Yazd* and *shal-e Esfahan*[1867].

The second classification also was simple. Shawls were either square (*charqad*) or oblong (*kuseh*). Probably because of this, Polak mentioned a thin Kermani shawl that was close in quality to the European type of Kashmir shawl (i.e. oblong), which was known as *shal-e kuseh* and obtained 5-6 ducats[1868]. The *charqad* or kerchief versions were usually 2.5 arshins both in length and in width. The oblong ones were either 2.5 arshins long and 1.25 arshin wide, or 3 arshins by 1.5 arshin. Imitation Kashmir shawls were somewhat longer, and used to be twice as wide as the Persian ones. Moreover, there were Kerman woolen fabrics, considered to be

1863. Irwin [*Kashmir*], Appendix 1, p. 27-36. In this appendix a total of 40 types of shawl, manufactured inter alia for the Persian market are listed.

1864. Amanat, p. 83.

1865. Polak [*Persien*], II, p. 168.

1866. Fraser [*Caspian Sea*], p. 369.

1867. Blau, p. 107; Qazvini, p. 13, 44, 45.

1868. Polak [*Persien*], II p. 167-168; Hoseini, p. 371 (q.v. *shal*) states that a *shal-e kuseh* is « of natural color and a kind of plain shawl »; Afshar [*Kolliyat*].

inferior shawls, that were either entirely white or colored without patterns, measuring 5 arshins in length and 1 arshin in width. This size included the embroidered hems. These were sold at 3-5 tomans per piece, and were used to make kaftans, women's camisoles and other garments. However, they were inferior products that did not last long[1869].

The third classification is a varied one due to the many colors (*alvan* as against *sadeh* [plain]) in which shawls were produced. There was a great variety, such as *shal-e haft-rang* (seven- or multi-colored), *laki* (red), *lajevardi* (turquoise), *ahrami* (probably multi-colored and floral patterns), *khaki*, *zard*, (yellow), *zengari* (verdigris), and *zomorrod* (emerald)[1870].

With regard to the fourth classification, one finds reference to patterns such as *afshan* (floral), *boteh'i* or *zola va botehdar* (flame and *boteh* patterned), or *boteh va jiqeh* (aigrette), *gushehdar* (palm-leaf pattern), *shakh gavazn* (hartshorn), and *shal-e rahrah* or *shal-e moharamat* (striped shawls). There were two types of striped shawls: the *rah-e barik*, a narrow-striped shawl, and the *rah-e pahn*, or wide-striped shawl. Shawls with a flower design in a honeycombed pattern were referred to as *shal-e bandi*. Finally, there was the *shal-e abrah*[1871]. The most prized shawl was known as *shal-e reza'i*, which had a plain ground with a pattern in the center and borders all around. This type of shawl was usually square of form (also referred to as *charqad*) and was produced both in Kashmir and Kerman[1872]. According to

---

1869. Blau, p. 108. The length of a shawl is about 10 feet 6 inches by 3 feet 6 inches in width according to DCR 1376 (1892-3), p. 30.

1870. Blau, p. 107; Afshar [*Kolliyat*]; Fraser [*Caspian Sea*], p. 362, 366, 369; Polak [*Persien*], II, p. 168; Gleadow-Newcomen, p. 94; Anavian and Anavian, p. 22. *Termeh-ye laki* (red *termeh*) was an inferior kind of shawl, and ranked below that of *termeh-ye portuqali* or orange-colored *termeh* (Mostaufi, III, p. 423). A *shal-e laki* only cost 18 tomans (Farrokh Khan, V, p. 27). The *Bahar-e 'Ajam* mentions a *shal-e tus*, which most likely meant a khaki colored shawl rather than one made in Tus, see Dehkhoda, q.v. *shal*, and Hoseini. *Haft-rang* shawls were in particular made in Mashhad. According to Gluck and Gluck, p. 214, this term referred to multicolored shawls woven in narrow bands. There is no evidence whatsoever for Gluck's statement (*ibid.*) that at first overall designs such as paisley, boteh, birds and flowers were woven, while later busier designs were introduced.

1871. Blau, p. 107; Afshar [*Kolliyat*]; Polak [*Persien*], II, p. 168; Hoseini, p. 284; Anavian and Anavian, p. 22. According to Gluck and Gluck, p. 214, the *shal-e mohamarat* was a multi-colored shawl woven in wide bands. *Shal-e rah-e pahn va zomorrudi*; *shal-e abrah*; *shal-e goli*, Farrokh Khan, V, p. 240. See also note 1787 for *shal-e ebra*.

1872. Blau, p. 107.

the Anavians the *shal-e reza'i* was the finest and most well-known type of Kashmir brocade. They were brocaded with very large patterns (sometimes only one) extending over one meter. Their explanation that *reza'i* refers to a dealer who exported these shawls and greatly contributed to their development is not supported by textual evidence, and therefore must be considered as conjecture[1873]. Another statement by them is not borne out by the evidence: « The fineness of these brocades and the necessity of changing the color of the warps abruptly obliged the weaver to make the shawl in small bits and then assemble them. For this reason they are also referred to as assembled shawls »[1874]. Another well-known and sought after shawl was the *shal-e 'azim khani*; it is reported that one piece cost as much as 300 tomans at the turn of the 19th century[1875].

The Anavians, writing about assembled shawls, are clearly referring to the so-called *'amli* shawls. Irwin writes that « The traditional practice was for the patterned section of a shawl to be produced on a single loom. In the early 19th century, a new practice was introduced of dividing the work of a single shawl among two or more looms. Then the parts were handed over to the *rafugar* (needleworker) who joined them together. In 1821 Moorcroft describes this as a recent introduction »[1876]. The reason thus was economics, not technology. These shawls, therefore, were also referred to as patchwork shawls. It is, however, wrong to state, as Gluck does, that only Kashmir shawls were produced in this fashion, for Persian shawl weavers also produced patchwork shawls.

We have already seen that the embroidered, needleworked shawls were known as [*shal-e*] *termeh* [*-ye kermani* or *kashmiri*][1877]. This type of shawl was also known as *shal-e amiri* in commemoration of the endeavors of Amir Kabir to stimulate the Kerman shawl industry[1878]. It is more than likely that

1873. Anavian and Anavian, p. 22-23.

1874. *Ibid.*, p. 23.

1875. Bastani Parizi [*Farmanfarma*], p. 224.

1876. Irwin [*Kashmir*], p. 3.

1877. Zarrabi p. 255. Gmelin, III, p. 424 described the "Schall-tirmeh" as a white woollen fabric. According to Brugsch, II, p. 89, the *shal-e termeh* or *kashmiri* is the Kashmir shawl proper. Brugsch refers in this case to the needleworked or *'amli* shawl. See, however, Zarrabi, p. 250, who mentions *termeh-ye kermani* and *kashmiri* as two distinct fabrics. In Kermani parlance a *shal-e anguri* referred to an imitation *termeh* shawl (Dehkhoda, q.v. *shal*).

1878. See Mostaufi, I, p. 75 for the *shal-e Amiri*; also Qazvini, p. 14, 55. Anavian and Anavian, p. 22, are wrong to ascribe this term to the fact that this kind of shawl was

the *termeh* shawl was a Persian tradition copied by Kashmiri weavers. Moorcroft explicitly mentions that « the improved method [of *'amli* shawls] being learned subsequently from embroiderers of Kirman province in Persia »[1879]. Among the *termeh* shawls one distinguished several kinds such as *termeh-ye dula'i* (double-ply) and *termeh-ye selseleh* or embroidered *termeh*[1880].

• *Shawl Material*

D'Allemagne mentions that Persian shawls can always be recognized by their completely white fond, that they are made with goat hair, part of which is exported as raw material to Amritsar for the production of « d'habiles contrefaçon ». The key word here is "goat hair", for real shawls were not made of cotton, silk, sheep wool, or camel wool, but of goat wool. Moreover, not just any goat wool or *taftik*, but of the down or *kork* of the goats. A plain woolen shawl was referred to as *shal-e pashmeh'i*. The shawl was also imitated as printed cotton using shawl designs. This imitation shawl was also known as *shal-e pashmeh'i* just as the real thing, according to the Kermanshah customs register[1881].

Shawls were also made from silk and referred to as *shal-e abrishami*, or simply *abrishami*, meaning silken shawl[1882]. Already in 1818, Ouseley reports that in Kashan manufactures was made « a sort of [silken] shawls

---

highly valued by the aristocracy and rulers (*amir*). This is also clear from the existence of the term *shal-e Atabegi*, which refers to the *Atabeg-e A'zam*, or the leading politician in Persia between 1880-1907.

1879. Irwin [*Kashmir*], p. 4. See for pictures of these shawls, *ibid.*, p. 17, and plate 36.

1880. The *termeh-ye dula'i* was used to make *kolejeh* (cloak) and *sardari* (frock plaited about the waist), while *termeh-ye selseleh* was used to adorn a shawl used as girdle, both were used in winter time. The latter also was used for turbans worn by merchants (Zarrabi, p. 248-249). The *termeh-ye selseleh* is also described as a shawl « made of simple colors, and, subsequently covered with rich needleworked embroideries » (D'Allemagne, II, p. 152); see also Khaza'eli, p. 113. *Shal-e selselehduzi* was still being produced in Kerman by the end of the 19th century (Vaziri, p. 37). On *selselehduzi* see Gluck and Gluck, p. 222.

1881. Rabino [Kermanshah], p. 67.

1882. Polak [*Persien*], II, p. 172, states that the *shal-e abrisham* was typical for Yazd, which like the Indian fabric was woven with palm and arabesk patterns; it was also embroidered.

worn and esteemed in the most remote provinces of the empire »[1883]. This is confirmed by Porter who writes that « a particularly rich shawl, of silk fabric, is also made here [Kashan], and in as great request »[1884]. Such silken shawls were also manufactured in Gilan, Yazd, Tabriz and Isfahan. In the latter city some 110 silk shawl weavers were active around the 1870s[1885]. Another kind of silken shawl, known as *termeh-nama* or imitation *termeh*, was exported to India and Turkey around 1850[1886]. The most famous silken shawl was the so-called *Hosein Qoli Khani* type woven in Kashan, although its actual production probably started in Yazd[1887]. For according to Sykes it was a product of Yazd. When discussing the silken shawls of Yazd he writes « That known as Husein Kuli Khan, after its originator, who was a native of Kerman, consists of a fir-cone pattern on a plum-coloured ground, and is far from cheap, costing about 7s.6d. per yard »[1888]. For all its reputation only a few weavers made this shawl. Sykes, as British consul, observes that « an extremely pretty stuff of the pattern, called "Hussein Kuli Khan", is made all in silk; but for this class of material there are only three looms »[1889]. The Hosein Qoli Khan shawls

1883. Ouseley, III, p. 92.

1884. Porter, I, p. 388-389.

1885. Hoeltzer, p. 22, 45; see also the introductory section of this study regarding the coarse woollen-silken shawls woven in Mazandaran. In 1800, Malcolm writes « One made of Karmania wool and silk, which is denominated the Yezd shawl » (Issawi, p. 262).

1886. Amanat, p. 109, 114; Blau, p. 109; Brugsch, II, p. 90 says about the *termeh-nama* that it was a silken fabric with a figured weave of shawl-like patterns which was not durable, although it was well liked by the public. It may already have been manufactured in the 1830s, Stuart (p. 226) mentions that Kerman shawls and "Tirmalaman" (error for *termeh-nama* or simply for *termeh*?) are really to be admired. The term may also be related to a silken fabric referred to as "talamana" which was produced at Shamakhi in the 16th century (*Barbaro and Contarini*, I, p. 144).

1887. Keihan, III, p. 284; see also Naraqi, p. 260: « a seven-colored silken shawl, which was known by the name of its designer (Hosein Qoli Khan), was one of the masterworks of Kashan's *sha'rbaf-khaneh* (silk manufacturies) towards the end of the 19th century », and Jamalzadeh, p. 79.

1888. Sykes [*Ten Thousand*], p. 423. Sykes may be right, see Wills, p. 395 and next note. In the Persian translation of Sykes' book the shawl is referred to as Hajj Khalil Khani, as quoted by Khaza'eli, p. 112; see also Bastani Parizi [*Farmanfarma*], p. 182, 237 as well as Asef, p. 101.

1889. DCR 1662 (1894-5), p. 27.

were woven on harness looms, while the unused sections of the wefts on the underside were left floating[1890].

In Kerman and Yazd, cotton shawls were also woven, or shawls with a cotton warp or woof[1891]. Europeans also marketed cottons with shawl patterns; both fabrics were known as *shal-e panbeh'i*[1892]. This was especially done to to improve sales of printed cottons in the Iranian market.

« They have sometimes sent home a Cashmeer shawl the pattern of which suited the Persian taste, or had the design painted by Persian painters to send home. The prints made are chiefly 5 Col[or] Prints costing about fifteen to sixteen shillings at Manchester and we will say the old patterns sold for about S25/ here. The new designs are printed in the same calicoe have the same colours in them and the same work as the old ones and cost very little more but being new they have sold as high as S40/. I have seen some of these prints made to imitate cashmeer so exactly that until within a few feet you could not tell the difference, and the shawl which they resembled could not cost less than 5 or 6 pounds a yard, the print S 1/6. here »[1893].

The Market for Shawl

Persian shawls were mainly produced for the national market. According to Stolze and Andreas they generally were made only to order[1894]. Waring reports that « at Kirman they make shawls, which are worn by the poor people, and are sent all over Persia; but, speaking generally, they rely almost entirely on foreigners for furnishing them with articles of dress and luxury »[1895]. If Waring is right then these Kerman shawls must have been of the coarse variety, because the price of Kashmir quality shawls, as reported later in the century, clearly put them beyond the purchasing power of the poor. Also, information provided by other authors contradict Waring, and, in fact, mention that shawls were exclusively worn

1890. Irwin [*Kashmir*], p. 17. For pictures of a Hosein Qoli Khan shawl, which also usually copied Kashmir patterns, see Bier, p. 272-273. This type of shawl was sold at 7 shahis 6 d. per yard, *Historical Gazetteer*, I, p. 694.

1891. Khaza'eli, p. 113; Olmer, p. 34-35, states that in Yazd both the warp and woof of shawls were of cotton, while in Kerman both were of wool.

1892. Qazvini, p. 14.

1893. Schwartz, p. 84-85.

1894. Stolze and Andreas, p. 25.

1895. Waring, p. 76

by the rich[1896]. The only author who mentions that common people used pieces of shawl to adorn themselves is Fraser, although he in fact also confirms the exclusivity of shawls. He mentions that in Gorgan the women wore a dress of which « the sleeves are long and wide, and some gird it around the loins and lower part of the stomach with a strip of white cloth or coarse shawl. To have a good shawl for this purpose is a point of great ambition with the Toorkoman women »[1897]. From a letter from Charles Burgess in 1831 it is clear that Waring must have meant coarse shawls. « The best shals manufactured here [Kerman] are of coarser quality, but approaching the inferior Cashmeers. An immense export exportation of the commoner kinds takes place to all parts of Turkey and to India; some are as low as in price as 2s. 6d., containing nearly two square yards, and are worn by all the lower classes throughout Asia »[1898].

The British ambassador, Sir Hartford Brydges-Jones, had well understood the social importance of shawls. Thus, when he entered Shiraz, he « wore a shawl cloak, which, of course impressed the multitude with a very high opinion of his rank »[1899]. Tancoigne claims that « the king and the chah zades alone enjoy the privilege of wearing Cachemire shawls as girdles: those of the nobility are of gold cloth »[1900]. This is not borne out by information given by other contemporary travellers. According to Morier, « over the caba [*qaba*] comes the shal kemer, which is the bandage around the waist. This is made either of Cashmer shawl, or the common shawl of Kerman, or of English chintz, or of lowered muslin. The proper size is about eight yards long and one broad. To this is fastened (by a string neatly tied around it) a kunjur, or dagger, ornamented according to the wealth of the possessor, from an enamelled pummel set in precious stones, to a common handle of bone or wood »[1901]. Drouville confirms that « the Persians wear a shawl waist band, and more often than not, one can form

1896. See Drouville, I, p. 29; Morier [*A Journey*], p. 245, states that a shawl wrapped around a cap is a « distinction confined to the king, to the princes his sons, and to some of the nobility and great officers of state ».

1897. Fraser [*A Winter's Journey*], II, p. 370.

1898. Abrahamian, p. 288.

1899. Brydges-Jones, p. 102; see also Ouseley, I, p. 222.

1900. Tancoigne, p. 204.

1901. Morier [*A Journey*], p. 244.

an idea of the rank or wealth of an individual by judging [the value of] that shawl, and of the dagger that has been stuck in it »[1902].

Shawl clothing was expensive and consequently its use was restricted to the upper class. Fraser writes that « The Khan himself [Hosein Qoli Khan, *beglerbegi* of Ormiya] had on a shawl-cloak — it must have been worth more than one hundred pounds sterling »[1903]. This amount seems to be a bit on the high side, if Stuart is right when he writes that Mohammad Shah wore a shawl surcoat, which « seldom costs less than 25 pounds, often much more »[1904]. Men of the upper classes wear « a skirted coat buttoned in front, made of woollen cloth obtained from Europe, or of "kurk" or "barak", a waistcoat of the same materials. In winter many wear cloaks and jackets of cloth, Kashmir or Kirman shawl lined with otter or squirrel fur [...] The merchant and tradesman class wear turbans of Yezd shawl. [...] In the cold seasons a second gown (the kaba) is worn, also made of cloth or "barak". When out walking or visiting the loose "aba", or cloack of cloth, camel-hair cloth, "abar" [*sic*] or Kashmir, is thrown over the shoulders »[1905]. Consul Jones reports in 1870 that only the upper classes wore Kerman shawl, while the middle class wore imported European broadcloth[1906].

Shawls were also given on various occasions by visiting governors to local staff, to local dignitaries as well as by local magnates to the governor[1907]. These gifts were not bribes in the strict sense of the word, but tokens of reinforcement of the existing relationship between the parties concerned. As such the value and nature of the gifts given were of importance, since these either confirmed that relationship or not. Sir Percy Sykes, for example, refused to accept a quantity of snow and a lamb that was send to him by Sa'd al-Molk, the governor of Lorestan. He informed the governor that « he was neither a child that played with a lamb nor a Persian who drinks his lemon water chilled with snow. He added that Farmanfarma, the governor of Kerman, had send him a shawl and a horse,

1902. Drouville, I, p. 28-29.

1903. Fraser [*Travels*], I, p. 52; Perkins (opposite p. 184), who visited the Khan three days later, produces a drawing of the Khan showing him in his official dress with a striped shawl.

1904. Stuart, p. 185.

1905. DCR 976 (1890-91), p. 14. See also Wills, p. 318.

1906. AP 29, LXV (1871), p. 238.

1907. Nezam al-Saltaneh, I, p. 49, 166, 119, 145, 283.

which I accepted because of our personal friendship »[1908]. Shawls also were given to reward someone for a noteworthy activity such as a poet who received a Gujarati shawl from Mohammad 'Ali Khan, the Qashqa'i Ilkhan around 1860[1909].

In view of the role that shawls played in the social and economic life of the Persian elite it is also clear that Waring must have been mistaken or referred to the coarse home woven shawl. « Of all the fabrics that serve to make clothes, the Persian estimates the shawl products above all; in business transactions they are even used as if they were cash money. Because the fabrics do hardly loose any of their value over time, part of any well-to-do family's wealth has been invested in shawls. It is only with great reluctance that one divests oneself of this property, so that in time of need one rather hocks them to be redeemed at a later date. In this way shawls are inherited by several generations. Europeans look upon these rich clothes, embellished with intricate Palms and arabesques, maybe only as very expensive sleeping garments. Persians, however, view them with totally different eyes. However old and used a shawl may be, the bearer is proud of its ownership and looks down on somebody wearing a brand new shawl garment. It is a sign of good education, that one knows how to estimate the value of a horse, a carpet and a shawl reasonably correctly. Even when a shawl has been cut into small pieces it does not loose much of its value. In that case it is sold by weight in miskals [methqal = 4.6 grams] and used for borders and hems; one also makes purses, house caps, etc. from them, or one stitches the pieces together so cleverly that the stitches can hardly be seen. This is something that is done by stitchers [*rafugar*]. Almost all bribes are effected through the gift of shawls; the more expensive a shawl the less frequently Persian virtue, male or female, can withstand its [allure]. Old shawls are washed and retouched, and thus acquire a new freshness, so that the uninitiated believe them to be new »[1910].

Similar observations are made by Brugsch who states « their value has remained unchanged in Persia, such that pieces of real shawls are weighed with gold and are considered to be as small pieces of money. One pays for one methqal of shawl 10 shahis (about 2 silver Groschen) up to 2.5 qrans. In particular Jews are engaged in the trade of selling shawls, which is

1908. Nezam al-Saltaneh, I, p. 187.

1909. Bastani Parizi [*Farmanfarma*], p. 224.

1910. Polak [*Persien*], I, p. 153-154. For some instances where shawls were offered as bribes see Nezam al-Saltaneh, I, p. 96, 108, 177 and Qazvini, p. 85.

considerably profitable, because the Persians are accustomed to adorn the borders of their robes with these small pieces of shawl. The price of an entire shawl varies according to its quality from 20 to 300-400 ducats. A special difference between the real and imitation [shawls] is that the former do not consist of one piece, but of a piece that has been stitched together from many smaller pieces, but done in such a fashion that the pattern and design are not disturbed. Most shawls that are offered for sale are old, therefore often faded and with small holes »[1911]. Burgess informs us that money was lent on pledges of jewels and shawls[1912].

Ferrières-Sauvebœuf reports that shawls get more beautiful and soft with time. A used shawl, therefore, could be resold in Persia or India for the original purchase price, after having been in use for two years[1913]. Blau observes that shawls were sold by weight, i.e. per methqal. He was astonished that Persian shawl traders immediately knew its size as well whether it was a real or imitation one by weighing a shawl in their hands. He further remarks that real shawls were not made out of one piece; the distinction of a real shawl was that it had been assembled from various pieces that had been stitched together in such a fashion that this could hardly be seen. Unfortunately, imitation shawls also often were assembled, which also facilitated the manner in which shawls were traded, that is, in small pieces rather than as an entire fabric[1914].

Royalty and the rich especially had large and rich collections of shawls. Fraser reports that « this morning a room in the palace took fire, and before

---

1911. Brugsch, II, p. 90; Mostaufi, I, p. 160 mentions that these Jews were known as [*shal*] *moshtari*. « The edges of damaged shawls were removed and the [brocaded] bands were joined together » (Anavian and Anavian, p. 23). Thus, Gluck and Gluck (p. 214), are mistaken when they state that « In Kashmir it was woven in small pieces and joined together by invisible mending by special craftsmen, the rufugar. In Iran, however, larger pieces were woven ». These shawl brokers ran a risky business. Mirza Reza, Naser al-Din Shah's assassin, was such a shawl broker. Ten year's prior to the assassination he had to wait for two years for a payment from Na'eb al-Saltaneh, one of the Shah's sons, for a shawl that he had sold to him. Such purchases on credit by the rich were not exceptional. See Bastani Parizi [*Farmanfarma*], p. 277, 283, 220.

1912. Schwartz, p. 88.

1913. Ferrières-Sauvebœuf, II, p. 11.

1914. Blau, p. 107; this calls into question the view advanced by the Anavian and Anavian (p. 22) that only the *shal-e reza'i* was qualified as an assembled shawl. Because Blau's observations are confirmed by other contemporary observers it would seem that the Anavians are wrong.

it could be extinguished about three thousand tomauns, or £1500 worth of shawls, &c. were consumed »[1915]. This room may have been part of the *sanduq-khaneh* or the *rakhtehdar-khaneh* where the fabrics (including shawls) were stored for the making of robes of honor as well as the shah's clothes[1916]. The wife of Mirza Taqi Khan Amir Kabir and sister of Naser al-Din Shah received Lady Sheil, around 1851, in a room where the floor « was covered with fine Cashmeer shawls »[1917]. Private households also took care to store their valuable shawls. « Because of their preciousness and sentimental value, these fabrics were carefully preserved in specially constructed wooden boxes called sandoughcheh »[1918]. Shawls also were given to important religious establishments such as the shrine of Karbala. When the Wahabis attacked and looted Karbala in 1800, the administrator of the shrine noted the theft of 4,000 pieces of Kashmir shawl[1919].

Shawls figured prominently during the Nawruz ceremonies when princes and nobles presented their new year gifts to the shah as well as among presents brought by or given to ambassadors[1920]. In 1808, Fath 'Ali Shah was allegedly presented with « fifty-five mules, each covered with a fine Cashmire shawl, and carrying a load of 1,000 tomauns »[1921]. Other recorded events show that the usual number of shawls presented were much smaller[1922]. During the Nawruz ceremonies « great trays of confectionery, covered with gold cloth and shawls, were paraded on men's heads » through the bazaar[1923]. The shawl also played a role in the popular customs on the occasion of Nawruz. It takes place on the last Wednesday of the year (*chaharshanbeh suri*). Rural houses usually have a chimney-like hole in the center of the living room where the entire family congregates at night. On the eve of *chaharshanbeh suri*, people (especially young children) disguise

1915. Fraser [*A Winter's Journey*], II, p. 51-52.

1916. Mostaufi, I, p. 408.

1917. Sheil, p. 285.

1918. Anavian and Anavian, p. 10.

1919. Bastani Parizi [*Farmanfarma*], p. 215.

1920. Drouville, I, p. 126; Sepehr, I, p. 191; Among the presents Malcolm, the East India Company Envoy in 1800, presented to Fath 'Ali Shah were shawls (Hollingberry, p. 86). Tancoigne, p. 224; Ouseley, II, p. 212; Stuart, p. 239; Ouseley, II, p. 212, III, p. 259.

1921. Brydges-Jones, p. 412; for similar observations see Ouseley, III, p. 338; Porter, I, p. 329; and Fraser [*A Winter's Journey*], II, p. 93.

1922. Farrokh Khan, V, p. 240.

1923. Fraser [*Winter's Journey*], II, p. 12.

themselves and go over the rooftops of the houses of their relatives and friends. Then they throw their shawl through the chimney hole and ask for a new year's present. This custom is known as *shal atmakh* (Persian: *shal andakhtan*), the throwing of the shawl, also referred to as *shal avizan*. People inside the house usually guess or are somehow informed of the identity of each *shal atan* (shawl thrower). Therefore, they tie appropriate presents to each shawl. Usually, presents include woollen socks, silk handkerchiefs, colored eggs, nuts, sweets and so on. The occasion is also used to provide clothing and other forms of assistance to the poor in the form of gifts[1924].

Mohammad Hosein Shahryar, the most prominent Azari poet in the 20th c., has vividly reflected the tradition of *shal atmakh* in his native village of Qish Qorshaq in Khoshknab (between Qarah Chaman and Ardabil). In his 36 pieces of poetry in Azari, entitled *Heidar Babayah salam* (greetings to Heidar Baba), two specifically deal with the tradition of *shal atmakh*[1925]:

> It was Nawruz, and the night bird was singing
> The engaged girl was knitting her fiancé's socks
> Everybody was pushing his shawl into a hole
> Oh, what a beautiful tradition was shawl-throwing!
> How pretty it was to tie your fiancé's present to his shawl!

In the second verse Shahryar recollects:

> I cried and asked for a shawl.
> I got a shawl and quickly tied it to my belly.
> I ran to Gholam's house and threw my shawl.
> My aunt Fatemeh tied a pair of socks to my shawl.
> She remembered my grandmother and wept.

Shawls also figured prominently among presents exchanged between persons[1926]. Especially on the occasion of marriages, shawls played an important role, where these could be given as a present as well as serve a function in pre-nuptial ceremonies. This shawl was sometimes referred to as *shal va angoshtar* or the shawl and the ring, because when the groom came to ask for his bride he offered both a ring and a shawl. The shawl in use

1924. This information was kindly provided to me by Dr. Mohammad Faghfoory, a native of Azerbaijan, presently of Alexandria, Virginia (USA); see also Mohammadi, p. 338, who describes the same tradition and refers to it as *shal avizan*.

1925. Translation by Dr. Mohammad Faghfoory. Shahryar's poems were published in 1346/1967 in Tabriz, and the two verses are found on p. 37.

1926. For example, Naser al-Din Mirza, when he visited the Russian emperor as crown prince in 1253/1837-8, in Erevan, presented him with, inter alia, 50 pieces (*bafteh*) of *shal-e reza'i* (Sepehr, II, p. 51). See also Tancoigne, p. 100.

may have been the *shal-e qebaleh* or the (half) piece of shal in which the groom sent the marriage contract to the bride's house on the evening of the marriage[1927]. Among the Afshars in Azarbaijan it was a marriage custom to give the groom a shawl, which custom was locally known as *shallama*. The groom's shawl was distinguishable by secret signs agreed upon between the couple. The bride did not want her family to learn directly which her shawl was, but made this known through signs and hints given to her sisters or sisters-in-law[1928]. Shawls also were part of the brides' trousseau[1929].

8. Princely Persian dress (16th c.)

1927. Dehkhoda, q.v. *shal*.

1928. Mohammadi, p. 338; Afshar Sistani, p. 863; Fraser [*Winter's Journey*], II, p. 92; Anavian and Anavian, p. 10; coarse shawls were still woven among tribal groups for a woman's dowry, until recently (Martin, p. 125, 132).

1929. Begdili, p. 668 (*shal-e termeh*), p. 672 (*boqcheh-ye termeh*).

Table 7: Export of shawls from Persia to Russia and Turkey (1846-54)

(in assignate rubles)

Year	Russia	Turkey	Type of shawl*
1848	150.198	573.500	Kerman
		177.100	Kashmir
1849	98.026	451.000	Kerman
		1.150	Kashmir
1850	469.830	630.134	Kerman
	8.314	409.924	Kashmir
1854	110.356	77.551	Kerman
	1.214	26.600	Kashmir
1855	101.682	817.088	Kerman
	28.876		Kashmir

*The Kerman category includes other Kerman woolens.
Source: Kukanova, ed., p. 140-141, 146, 168, 183, 216, 220.

Kerman shawls were exported to India, Iraq, Egypt, Central Asia, and Turkey; in the latter case they were known as *shal bab-e Rum*[1930]. There was also export of Persian and Kashmir shawls to France[1931], to Russia via Tabriz[1932], and to Gilan[1933]. In fact, in 1855 the export of shawls from Persia via Trabzon amounted to 32,806,000 piasters, 60 percent of which were Kashmir and 40 percent Persian shawls, although in the preceding years it seems that more Kerman shawls than Kashmir shawls were exported (see Table 8)[1934]. A lower quality shawl, made from lamb's wool, was exported in large quantities to Turkey[1935]. Irwin's statement that in the second quarter of the 19th century Kashmir shawls were facing competition from Kerman shawls was probably owing to his belief that Kerman shawls started being made only then. But Persian shawls were also produced and

1930. Fraser [*Travels*], p. 363; Kinneir, p. 199; Waring, p. 76; Morier [*A Journey*], p. 238; Vaziri, p. 33; Polak [*Persien*], II, p. 168; Hoseini, p. 284.

1931. Blau, p. 107.

1932. Kukanova, ed, p. 140-141, 149, 168, 173, 182-183, 215-216, 219-220. These data refer to the period between 1846 and 1854.

1933. AP 34 (LXXXII) 1877, Gilan, p. 750; AP 29 (LXX) 1878-79, Gilan, p. 467; AP 35 (LXXXVI), 1874-75, Gilan, p. 1492.

1934. Blau, p. 108.

1935. Stolze and Andreas, p. 25, who probably referred to second quality shawls, which were « woven from the wool of a small sheep », according to Curzon, II, p. 245. For an overview of shawl exports from Persia based on British sources see Schneider, table 84, p. 341-343.

sold prior to that date and thus already competed with Kashmir shawls; in fact, they were even protected by a royal ban on the use of Kashmir shawls, as we will see[1936].

In the mid-19th century there was less appreciation for Persian shawls in Europe than now. In 1849 Burgess wrote « I am right glad that you have not sold the shawl, it is worth twenty or perhaps much more here, if I recollect right I was offered sixty tomauns for it at Tabreez, this would be about £27. But it appears your friends the Americans don't know the value of such things »[1937]. It was not only the Americans who failed to appreciate Persian shawls. Wills, writing some thirty years later, describes the totally indifferent appreciation of Persian shawls in Great Britain: « One of the means of making presents used by the great in Persia is the giving of Cashmere shawls; the gift of a shawl is supposed to be an honour as well as a money payment to the recipient. On taking it [a shawl] to England I was astonished to find that it was unappreciated, and still more surprised to learn that, as it was made in several strips, as are all the real Cashmere shawls that go to Persia, and fringeless, it was nearly absolutely valueless. I took it back to Persia and sold it for twenty pounds, my servant probably making a five pound commission on the transaction »[1938].

Although the European market had lost total interest in both the Kashmir and Persian shawls, demand for Persian shawls persisted in its traditional markets (Turkey, Caucasus, Central Asia) after 1880. « Shawls are made varying in price from 30 krans to 1,000 krans; the latter are almost entirely taken up by the Government and rich natives, whilst the cheaper ones go to the various towns in Persia; the largest demand comes from Constantinople, for which place special shapes and designs are worked. A small quantity also find their way into Russia and the Khanates »[1939].

According to Russian consular sources the price of Persian shawls exported to Russia varied between 50 kopeks to 60 assignate rubles per piece at the end of the 1840s[1940].

1936. Irwin [*Kashmir*], p. 17.
1937. Schwartz, p. 105.
1938. Wills, p. 274.
1939. DCR 1376 (1894), p. 30.
1940. Kukanova, p. 149.

Goedel reports that around 1849 the market price for shawls was as follows[1941]:

Kashmir shawls	25-600 ducats
Kerman shawls	6-40 ducats
Mashhad shawls	5-20 ducats

Prices in 1857, in the Tabriz market, were[1942]:

Mashhad shawls	2.5 x 1.25 arshins	66-80 qrans
Kerman shawls	2.5 x 1.25 arshins	15-60 qrans
White Kerman shawls	5 x 1 arshins	40-50 qrans
Half wool	5 x 1 arshins	30-40 qrans

According to de Rochechouart the price of Kerman shawls varied from 2 to 80 tomans, although the most commonly produced were sold for 6 to 15 tomans in 1862. Plain shawls cost 5 to 12 tomans. He adds that it took 18 months to embroider a very beautiful shawl, but only 8 days for an inferior type of shawl. Those in the price range of 10-15 tomans required a production time of two to two and a half months. All these shawls had one standard size of 3 m. x 1.50 m[1943].

According to Smith, « a shawl of the best description, three yards in length, takes about a year to make, and should cost from forty to sixty tomans (£16 or £24) »[1944]. However, shawls are of different qualities. « The finest, of three or three and half ells in length, require twelve of fifteen months for their completion, and are sold at forty or fifty tumans apiece; others, destined for the Constantinople market, and of much coarser texture, can be finished in a month or six weeks, and are sold for ten or fifteen krans »[1945]. In Tabriz, shawl weavers « accomplished only half an inch daily, and six months, they said, were necessary to complete a shawl

1941. Blau, p. 120; Blau himself [p. 108] reports that average prices for the Kerman shawls amounted to 30-35 tomans and for Mashhad shawls to 20-25 tomans.

1942. Blau, p. 121.

1943. MAE, Rochechouart to Gobineau, Kirman 5/11/1862, unfoliated. Samples of these shawls are attached to this letter. I thank Dr. Homa Nateq for bringing this source to my attention.

1944. Goldsmid, p. 187; see also F. J. Goldsmid. « II. Modern Persia », in *Encyclopaedia Britannica*, 9th ed., XIV, p. 100.

1945. Browne [*A Year*], p. 483.

of one and a half yards in length »[1946]. Stolze and Andreas report that the usual size of a shawl is 0.7 m x 3 m. The finest quality took one year to make and would cost 300-500 marks[1947]. The best Kerman shawls, according to Curzon, cost from £16 to £24[1948]. Olmer reports that shawls generally were 2.35 m long and 1.35 m wide, which took one month of weaving. They obtained prices varying between 60 and 110 francs[1949].

Generally, Mashhad shawls were of inferior quality compared with the Kerman product, according to Polak. This was also expressed in the difference in price, the Kerman shawls costing three times as much as Mashhad shawls, both in the regular 3 m x 1.25 m size. The latter cost 8-10 ducats, while the Kerman variety obtained 20-30 ducats[1950].

The news from Mashhad, however, brings a different message. « Shawls of a Kashmir pattern, called in Persian Meshedees [...] are held in greater esteem than those of Kerman » reports Ferrier in 1846[1951]. MacLean mentions that a merchant in Mashhad claimed that the Khorasan shawls were better than those made in Kerman. The latter were « imported into Meshed, where bales are made up for the Constantinople market usually containing 10 Kerman and 20 Meshed shawls. The trade is all to Turkey, Caucasia, and Transcaspia. A few are sent to India »[1952]. The *Historical Gazetteer of Iran*, however, states that « neither carpets, nor shawls can compare with the exquisite fabrics produced in Kirman »[1953].

The Shawl production

Our information on the system of shawl production is mainly from British travellers from the latter half of the 19th century. These travellers tell us about the shawl manufacturies, the working conditions, how shawls were woven, how young weavers were taught, and how much shawl weavers earned. Shawl weaving took place either at people's homes or in

1946. Southgate, II, p. 7.
1947. Stolze and Andreas, p. 25.
1948. Curzon, II, p. 245.
1949. Olmer, p. 35.
1950. Polak [*Persien*], II, p. 167. Others echo this sentiment. Blau, p. 108; Stolze and Andreas, p. 25; Bassett, p. 262; MAE, Rochechouart to Gobineau, 5/9/1862.
1951. Ferrier [*Caravan*], p. 125.
1952. MacLean, p. 47.
1953. *Historical Gazetteer*, II, p. 489.

special manufacturies[1954]. The authors, who did not visit people's homes, all agree that a shawl manufactory was uninviting and unwholesome to say the least. « The first thing that strikes one is that the actual workshops where the shawls are made are without doors or windows. The entrance is effected through a small square hole in the wall, about three foot from the ground, and light is sparingly admitted through small holes in the roof. When you have once scrambled inside (a process involving loss of dignity) and when your eyes have become accustomed to the darkness, and your nose to the smell of a number of filthy little saucers of stinking oil with burning wicks in them, three or four of which hang about each loom, then you see before you the sort of Black Hole in which Kasmir shawl are made »[1955].

The reason for the lack of ventilation was explained in the following manner:

« I asked why there were no windows to the place, and the skeleton [meaning the foreman] replied that it would be too cold. With these lamps the place was warm enough without clothing. It was just this: glazed windows and clothing were dearer than lamps without either »[1956].

According to Abbott, « the poor Shawl weavers are generally confined to a close and foul atmosphere, their apartments being shut up in Winter and Summer either to secure a proper degree of heat, or to exclude dust »[1957].

It would seem that those manufacturies visited by Europeans usually consisted of about three rooms; in each room between 10 to 30 people would be working. « A room will contain some four to ten looms, according to its capacity. I saw one of 28 feet by 14 feet, in which were eight looms all in work », reports Preece in 1894[1958]. According Smith, writing some 20 years earlier, « about sixty or seventy men and boys were seated in three rooms, working at looms placed horizontally before them »[1959]. The number of people working per loom was a function of the quality of the shawl. « The looms in which the finest shawls are produced,

---

1954. Amanat, p. 83-84.

1955. Goldsmid, I, p. 187; for similar remarks see Amanat, p. 84; Floyer, p. 324; DCR 1376, p. 30; Olmer, p. 35.

1956. Floyer, p. 324.

1957. Amanat, p. 84.

1958. DCR 1376 (1894), p. 30.

1959. Goldsmid, I, p. 187.

employ each three pair of hands; those for plain shawls requiring only one man to each »[1960].

Shawl workers in Persia, as in Kashmir, were exclusively male: young boys, who did the work requiring nimble fingers, while older men did the easier work and provided the supervision. De Rochechouart observes that three persons operated each shawl loom; he did not see anyone over 20 years of age, but many who were not even 10 years old[1961]. According to Olmer, especially young Jewish children were used for shawl weaving[1962], while Preece mentions that « some of the [Zoroastrian] men are employed in making a cloth called "shal" »[1963]. In the latter case the shawl may not necessarily have been a beautiful *kork* shawl, but rather an inferior product. The common shawl weavers were referred to in Kermani dialect as *kholush* (pl. *akhalish*), while the experienced shawl weavers were known as *khalifeh*[1964].

As in the case of carpets, the shawl patterns were committed to memory. « At each one [loom] stooped two or three miserable, sallow, half-naked children, their preternaturally thin hard finger going nervously, and their noses almost touching their work even while I engaged them in conversation [...] there were only about six distinct patterns, there being many variations of the same pattern. [...] Some of the children were working by memory, others were nearly perfect, but had to have small grimy pattern tacked up on the loom in front of them, which to my eye were difficult to understand. [...] Children were hired to learn [the patterns]. Some can only recollect one pattern at a time (and quite enough I thought), and when that pattern is no longer in demand, were out of employment and off pay until they learnt another. Some clever boys could remember two at a time »[1965].

According to Abbott the sickly appearance of the shawl weavers was partly attributable to the lack of ventilation and partly to their long working

1960. Amanat, p. 83
1961. MAE, Rochechouart to Gobineau, 5/11/1862.
1962. Olmer, p. 11.
1963. DCR 1376 (1894), p. 15.
1964. Bastani Parizi [*Farmanfarma*], p. 264-265.
1965. Floyer, p. 324-325.

hours[1966]. Perhaps for this reason poor people were referred to as *shalbaf* in the Kermani dialect[1967].

At the looms there was an appropriate mix of old and young weavers. « Each loom, worked by one man and two small boys, contained the fabric of one shawl. The man, always an experienced hand, sits in the middle, and the two boys on either side. They sit so close together that their arms actually interlace, but, nevertheless, their nimble fingers work away with great rapidity. Some of the children we saw working could not have been more than seven or eight years old, and children were by far the majority of workers. The boys and the men sit in holes with their feet under the web, which position brings their arms on a level with the shawl »[1968].

As in the case of carpet weaving, wrote Abbott in 1849, « the [shawl] weavers are taught from a Book, which they get by heart, and in which is described the proper succession of threads necessary to form each pattern; one of them repeats to the rest the lesson he has thus acquired, working himself at the same time, boys of 6, 7, and 8 years of age are thus employed; indeed the weavers of figured shawls are mostly children, whose small fingers are best adapted to the work, whilst grown up people attend principally to the plain weaving. In the former manufacture the reverse of the pattern appears uttermost in the loom »[1969].

Smith, in 1873, is more explicit about the learning by rote of the shawl patterns: « They make the shawls with the right side downwards, so that their eyes can be of very little use in guiding them, and they learn the patterns by heart. Extraordinary as it seems, these intricate patterns are learnt by heart and rote, not from painted pictures with long written explanations, but entirely from manuscript. We were informed that it would take a clever lad six months or more to learn a pattern, but that once learnt it was never forgotten. In one of the rooms the shawls in course of manufacture were of a very simple design, and adapted to beginners; a man was walking up and down reading out the patterns from a dirty and soiled manuscript. But the better shawls have all, as it were, to be learnt by heart »[1970].

1966. Amanat, p. 84.
1967. Hoseini, p. 284.
1968. Goldsmid, I, p. 186; see also Browne, p. 482.
1969. Amanat, p. 83.
1970. Goldsmid, I, p. 187; see also Olmer, p. 35.

In fact, to make things easier, it would seem that many weavers would weave only one color and one design all their lives or for as long as they were employed as shawl weavers[1971].

Preece provides some particulars about the weaving technique employed in Kerman: « The loom is perpendicular, and the pattern side is away from the work people, of whom three are employed on each shawl, the one in the centre directing the others what colours to work in from memory. The procedure generally in making shawls and carpets is very similar, except that in the shawl the ends of the wool are not cut off but are turned in, and remain to be carried on »[1972]. Smith adds to that, writing, « the threads of kurk, or goat's-hair, dyed, are cut in short lengths, and these are woven in by the fingers into the web of the shawl stretched horizontally before the maker »[1973]. Olmer offers additional details: « the warp was divided into four sections [lames] which could be moved by four pedals. The weave employed was either Batavia or Casimir. After each weave, the workers pass by hand the woolen yarn, which pass under the thread of the warp, by taking from 2 to 15, such that the end of the warp that sticks out is left idle till the next passage. The fabric is worked from the reverse side, for one passes a second thread, beats it, and start all over again »[1974]. We further learn that the shawls, when finished, were given a number of finishing touches. Preece writes: « I was given a full account of the number of stretchings, moistenings, rollings, etc. that a shawl has to go through after leaving the loom before being fit for sale, but they were only what all woollen manufactures require »[1975]. The person who washed the shawls after the weaving was completed was known as *shalshur*[1976]. The washing was necessary to remove excess indigo, or some other dye. As a side effect of the washing the shawls also became about 0.25 m longer[1977].

The wool used to make shawls was dyed rather than the shawls themselves. The wool was first washed in warm water to take the grease out, after which the washed wool was boiled in a decoction of *zaj-e sefid* (aluminum sulphate). To dye the wool blue, indigo was used, mixed with a

1971. *Farhang-e Iran Zamin*, XIX, p. 204.
1972. DCR 1376 (1894), p. 30.
1973. Goldsmid, p. 186-187.
1974. Olmer, p. 34-35.
1975. Floyer, p. 324-325.
1976. Hoseini, p. 284.
1977. Olmer, p. 35.

little sulphur, although care was taken to boil the dye before it was used. To get a green color, one only had to soak wool that had been dyed blue in a dye made of esperak or the extract of the yellow larkspur flower (weld, *Reseda luteola*). To dye wool red, cochineal *meshki* or *zaj-e sefid* was used. To get violet, indigo and cochineal was used, and for yellow boiled esparak; to get a dark yellow dye one added a little *runas* (madder). Pomegranate rinds mixed with *zaj-e siyah* (black vitriol) and gal-nuts were used to get a black dye. Henna and *gol-e behna* were used for gray; pomegranate rinds were used for brown and dried almond shells to get a a dusty gray[1978].

Silken shawls had designs similar to woollen Kerman shawls, but were made with the "tireur de lacs" method, i.e. with a draw loom. The warp was silken, dyed black, dark blue or dark violet. Five, six or even seven spools with different colors were used, which were filled with silk yarns. Sometimes some were equipped with yarns or with very fine wool. The vertical shafts, which corresponded with each passage of the spool, were made into one cord. All these cords were placed in a certain order, so that when one lifted them in that order the pattern or weave was produced. This ordering or selection of the cords was the job of the person who mounted the loom, the so-called draw-boy. It was a very delicate job, which required several days of work. A child climbed on top of the loom and after each passage of the spool he lifted one of the cords in the order in which they had been attached. The weaver then passed the various spools several times, whilst moving the pedals[1979].

Shawls were top-quality fabrics which obtained high prices in the market. This investment in quality was a function of the time spent on weaving a shawl. Consequently, « some of the best cloths, not more than ten feet in length, take as long as a month per foot in their manufacture, and they realise very high prices, even as much as nine or ten pounds sterling a yard »[1980]. This observation is confirmed by Smith, according to whom, « a shawl of the best description, three yards in length, takes about a year to make, and should cost from forty to sixty tomans (£16 or £24) »[1981].

1978. MAE, Rochechouart to Gobineau, 5/9/1862; on the use and identification of dyes see J. Dhamija, "Carpets. II", *EIr*, IV, p. 840-842.

1979. Olmer, p. 39-40.

1980. Savage-Landor, I, p. 437. The weaving referred to in Bambis is to be found in *ibid.*, p. 366.

1981. Goldsmid, I, p. 187.

These very costly and top-quality shawls were known as *shal-e sanginbaf* as was the weaver (*sanginbaf*) who made them[1982].

Not only were working conditions unhealthy, but the working hours were difficult. « That the work is unhealthy in the extreme, the pale sallow faces of the men and boys sufficiently testified; but it has also a serious effect in damaging the eyes; few of those whom we saw but had bleared and weak eyes, and many more wore spectacles. The emaciated bodies of the children were especially noticeable and very pitiable, and their arms seemed to be almost withered away. We were informed by the proprietor that the hours allotted to sheer work averaged fourteen a day! »[1983]

These long working hours are confirmed by Abbott and by Browne, who adds: « They have a half-holiday on Friday (from mid-day onwards), thirteen days' holiday at the Nawruz, and one or two days more on the great annual festivals, while for food they get nothing as a rule but dry bread »[1984]. It is worthwhile to remember that the long days were not different from the working hours in other industries in Persia[1985].

Despite the long working hours the weavers were neither well paid nor well treated. « Yes, they were beaten often, for mistakes in the pattern and, they die soon », according to the foreman of the shawl manufactory visited by Floyer[1986]. Around 1837, shawl weavers in Tabriz said that « their compensation was enough not to die upon »[1987]. In 1849, according to Abbott, « their miserable gains amount to 1 and 2 Kerans (11 d. to 1s.10d.) per week for common workers, and up to 5 Kerans (3s.2d. to 4s.6d.) for the most skilful »[1988]. De Rochechouart reports that « each loom is paid two and half krans per day » in 1862[1989]. In the 1870s, their nominal wages had increased. Nevertheless, Smith opined, « the men are badly paid, the best workers averaging about 1 s. a day, and the children about

1982. Hoseini, p. 284; Bastani Parizi [*Farmanfarma*], p. 271, such a *sanginbaf* or *shalbaf* could become very rich men, see *ibid.*, p. 246, 271.

1983. Goldsmid, I, p. 187.

1984. Browne (*A Year*), p. 482-483; « commencing in Winter at Sunrise, or even earlier, and lasting with a short interval for meals, until dark, that is from 9 to 10 hours. In Summer the work is carried out from daybreak until Sun is down; a long spell, especially as the weavers are principally children » (Amanat, p. 84).

1985. Floor [*Labour*], p. 100.

1986. Floyer, p. 324-325.

1987. Southgate, II, p. 7.

1988. Amanat, p. 84.

1989. MAE, Rochechouart to Gobineau, 5/11/1862.

2d. to 4d. »[1990]. In 1879 an employee of the Telegraph Office reports that the annual wages of the young workers ranged from three to ten tomans. An adult would make 10 to 25 tomans per year[1991]. According to Browne, reporting on the situation some 10 years later, « their wages, as I learned, begin at ten tumans (about £3) a year, and increase gradually to twenty-four or twenty-five tumans (about £7 10s.) », which means that things had not changed[1992]. At the turn of the 20th century the wages for a 10-hour working day were 0.45 francs[1993]. Wages for the weaving of silken shawls in Yazd were no better than for woollen ones in Kerman. For a 10-hour working day a weaver would receive 0.50 to 1 franc. During that day a weaver would produce half a meter of shawl, for which the two weavers would be paid 2.50 francs together. Each spool filled with silk cost 7 to 8 centimes, while a silken shawl would be sold for 7 to 10 francs per meter[1994].

In 1890 Curzon reiterated the judgment about the bad working conditions of the shawl weavers[1995]. Ten years later, however, around 1900, Sykes observed that « the boys do not appear to be overworked or unhealthy. There has certainly been a change for the better since Sir Frederic Goldsmid's Mission »[1996]. However, this opinion is not shared by Olmer, who writing five years later, reiterates what earlier authors have said about the unhealthy working conditions. He adds that the time between completing one shawl and beginning work on another took only five minutes, which he timed with his watch[1997].

• *Centers of production*

The center of shawl manufacturing was Kerman. The Kerman shawl industry had suffered from the Qajar-Zand wars at the end of the 18th century and many of its ancillary workers, in particular embroiderers and stitchers, had emigrated to India, where they contributed to the further

1990. Goldsmid, I, p. 187.
1991. *Farhang-e Iran Zamin*, XIX, p. 204.
1992. Browne [*A Year*], p. 483.
1993. Olmer, p. 35.
1994. *Ibid.*, p. 40.
1995. Curzon, II, p. 245.
1996. Sykes [*Ten Thousand*], p. 200.
1997. Olmer, p. 35.

development and production of the famous Kashmir shawls[1998]. Despite this handicap, by 1816, an important wool-manufacturing industry had come into being once again in Kerman. Malcolm, Morier, Drouville and Kinneir mentioned "Kirmaun" shawls among Persia's manufactories, while the former also reports that *kork* was exported to India[1999]. To stimulate the shawl industry, in about 1808 Fath 'Ali Shah (r. 1799-1834) « prohibited the use of Cashmere shawls, or rather confined it to the Princes of the blood, and some few individuals of very high rank. It is said that this edict has been issued principally with a view to improve and benefit the manufactures of Korman, where a shawl is now made of so delicate a texture as almost to rival that of Cashmere »[2000]. This policy apparently was successful for, according to Pottinger, « upwards of one-third of the inhabitants [i.e. 10,000 people] are said to be employed in its shawl manufacturies. The governor of Kerman also imposed a heavy tax on shawls, which had to bear a government stamp as a sign of having paid the tax »[2001]. Dubeux noted in 1834 that there was a large number of shawl looms in Kerman imitating those of Kashmir[2002]. Fraser observes that, although Kerman was the chief city, « most of the surrounding villages manufacture shawls, numuds and other woollens »[2003]. Nearby Mahan was also an important shawl manufacturing center and its output was

1998. Irwin, p. 3-4.

1999. Kinneir, p. 199; Morier [*A Journey*], p. 238; Issawi, p. 262-264; Malcolm [*History*], II, p. 529 « imitation of Cashmere shawls, which are made of the wool of Kerman ». Drouville (II, p. 209), adds that the Kerman shawls are very much esteemed all over Asia; Heude (p. 43) also mentions the export of « fine wool from Kirman » from Bushire.

2000. Brydges-Jones, p. 102, also for an entertaining story purporting to be the real reason for the prohibition of the use of Cashmere shawls. Morier [*A Journey*], p. 245, writes that « Cashmire shawls have been discouraged of late, in order to promote the domestic manufacture of brocade shawls ». Fath 'Ali Shah continued wearing Kashmir and other foreign shawls: see Fraser [*A Winter's Journey*], II, p. 103, who mentions that the Shah was « plainly dressed in a koordee of French grey shawl over a vest of brocade »; Porter, I, p. 355: the Shah's « under garments were composed of red Kashmere shawls of the richest work ».

2001. Pottinger, p. 225, 227 and note. The government stamp probably was referred to as *tamgha-ye qumash* as it was in the 17th century, see Golchin Ma'ani, p. 114, from Lesani-ye Shirazi's *Majma' al-Asnaf*.

2002. Dubeux, p. 17.

2003. Fraser [*Caspian Sea*], p. 354.

probably considered to be part and parcel of Kerman's shawl production[2004].

• *Shawl manufacturing outside Kerman*

Kork production was concentrated in, but shawl manufacturing was not restricted to, Kerman. The other main center for shawl weaving was Mashhad, which produced even more shawls than Kerman, albeit of an inferior quality, according to de Rochechouart[2005]. According to Vaziri, the master weavers in Mashhad were all from Kerman, as were the shawls' warp and woof[2006]. There also appears to have been some production of coarse shawls among the Turkomans of Astarabad and Semnan, part of which was traded[2007]. Some of the Kerman *kork* was sent to Mashhad and Yazd and other towns in Persia, as were its shawls[2008]. Malcolm mentions that shawls of Kerman wool were produced in Yazd. « Some new manufactures have been lately tried [in Yazd] that appear likely to meet with much success. One made of Karmania wool and silk, which is denominated the Yezd shawl, is the principal »[2009]. There was also some shawl manufacturing, albeit of the silken variety, in Isfahan[2010] and Tabriz[2011].

2004. *Historical Gazetteer*, IV, p. 278.

2005. MAE, Rochechouart to Gobineau, 5/11/1862; Stolze and Andreas, p. 25; Polak [*Persien*], II, p. 167.

2006. Vaziri, p. 33.

2007. *Historical Gazetteer*, II, p. 46; Rafi', p. 432. The information from the *Gazetteer* with regard to the Turkomans may be wrong. No other source reports that in the Astarabad area shawls were manufactured. However, *shali*, which is a kind of rice, was produced and traded there. This may have been the cause for the mentioning of shawl production among the Turkomans. See for example Dhabihi (p. 27) for a list of articles produced by the Astarabad area.

2008. Amanat, p. 84-85. For shawl imports by Gilan see AP 29 (LXXVIII) 1867-68, p. 297 and (LXV) 1871, p. 234; AP 23 (LVIII) 1872, p. 1187; AP 35 (LXXVI) 1874-75, p. 1474, 1491, and AP 34 (LXXXII) 1877, p. 751.

2009. Issawi, p. 262; this was a continuation of shawl weaving that had already begun in the 18th century, see supra; see also D'Allemagne (II, p. 152) who states that Yazd shawls were coarse, while their patterns are like those of Kerman. The warp and woof are of cotton. Silken shawls were also woven at Yazd.

2010. Polak [*Persien*], II, p. 167; Tahvildar, p. 101-102; Hoeltzer (p. 20): 110 *shalbaf*; in the early 1920s, there were still 30 shawl weavers active in Isfahan (Janab, p. 78).

Shawl weaving in Tabriz had been initiated by 'Abbas Mirza. The weavers had been brought from Kerman, against their will, probably to weave shawls for the military. Their looms were located in the citadel (*arg*)[2012]. Silken shawls were also woven in Yazd and Kashan, the most famous being the Hosein Qoli Khan variety[2013].

In 1825 Fraser reported thus on *kork* and shawl production in Birjand and Qa'en: « This district is celebrated for its felt manufactures, which supply a great part of Persia with the most beautiful numuds. Many articles are also made of Khoolk, such as coarse shawls, pieces for linings of winter garments, wrappers of various sorts, caps, stockings, gloves, &c., &c.; and it is alleged that in Kayn, and the villages around, there are eight thousand families of these weavers alone »[2014]. We do not know how important this activity remained, and whether it had similar ups-and-downs as the Kerman wool industry, but the Birjand wool industry was still active by the end of the 19th century[2015]. There was also some production of shawls in Kandahar, where 11 shawl weavers were active in 1880[2016].

2011. Perkins, p. 148: « Shawls are manufactured by the natives of Tabrees, though not so extensively nor of so superior a quality as in some Persian cities » (Shafi' Javadi, p. 227).

2012. Southgate (II, p. 6-7) speaks of « a company of workmen » without mentioning their number. Although woollen shawls were initially woven, later in the century only silken shawls were manufactured.

2013. Tancoigne, p. 214; Morier [*Second Journey*], p. 162, mentions a very beautiful fabric « known by the name of shawl kashai [*shal-e kashi*] » or Kashan shawl, which followed the Kashmir patterns. See also D'Allemagne (II, p. 152) who states that Kashan and Yazd imitated the Kerman patterns. The warp was of silk, generally black, dark blue, or dark violet. For the woof, one sometimes used as many as 7 to 8 spools of different colors (Issawi, p. 262).

2014. Fraser [*Narrative*], appendix p. 20.

2015. Lorini, p. 192; see also Savage-Landor, II, p. 99. According to the *Historical Gazetteer* (IV, p. 75), the woollen fabrics were *kork* and *barak*, which was probably the case. Forster, for example, reports in 1784, that in the Khorasan-Herat area « coarse woollens of a string texture are manufactured [...] a great part of which, made into garments, are exported into various parts of Northern Persia », extract from Forster's Travels, in *Pinkerton's Travels*, VII, p. 286.

2016. *Gazetteer of Afghanistan*, V, p. 245.

Historical development of the Shawl Industry

• *Safavid-Zand Period*

Despite the good beginning, the shawl industry suffered from imports of Indian and European textiles. In 1836, Mohammad Shah (r. 1834-1848) felt obliged to support the shawl industry by insisting that courtiers only wear the *nezami* dress, which is easier to wear and put on and is cheaper. One could have two *nezami* dresses made for the price of the old one. The latter lasted 5 months, while the new one lasts one year. About 2 korurs (one million tomans) went to Kashmir and India for the purchase of shawls (each year). For the *sanduq-khaneh* (royal wardrobe) alone 3,000 pieces of shawls were bought. People also spent preposterous amounts of money on their *jabbeh* (long over-coat), their waist bands, their *arkhaleq* (overcoat) and *kolejeh*. This money left Persia, but now with the use of the *nezami* dress not so much will be taken from the people, because one does not need the shawl. Arrogant people, who are hooked on shawls and *khazz* (silken stuff), preferred the long dress and sought to outdo their peers. This obliged normal people, who were not afflicted by these worldly extravangancies, to get similar clothes. These then had to spend 200 tomans to get a *termeh jabbeh*, or a Bokhara hat to show off. The *nezami* dress will be made of *qadak* (cotton fabric), *dara'i* (cotton-silk fabric) and plain Kerman shawl, while pelts from Shiraz will be used to make hats and *kolejeh*s, so that money does not have to leave for India and Kashmir needlessly[2017].

However, this ban was not respected, either by the business community and the courtiers, or by the shah himself. Lt. Col. Stuart, a member of a visiting British embassy at that time, reports that the shah sent some of his people to buy the same goods « of which he had himself so lately forbidden the purchase »[2018]. There seems to have been, nevertheless, an upturn in Kerman's shawl industry, although more likely due to economic reasons than the expected severity of Mohammad Shah's punishment. For in 1847, « Kerman's Woollen manufactures are on a limited scale, but appear to be thriving, particularly, since increased attention has been bestowed on the production of the finer kind of shawls. The weavers are skilful, and the quality of the Goats Wool obtained in the Province admits of a very fine

---

2017. Sepehr, II, p. 90. The British envoy confirms this when he writes that « the courtiers should gradually substitute Persian woollens and Kerman shawls for the broadcloth now used in their dresses », Issawi, p. 79.

2018. Stuart, p. 226; Charles Burgess was an English businessman, see Schwartz.

fabric. The wool employed for all but the coarsest kind of shawls is that of Goats. The manufacture is carried on in the homes of the weavers, I estimate that there are about 2,200 looms for shawl weaving. Together with 220 looms that produced other woolens such as cloaks, and coarse fabrics such as patu and barak these wool industry had an annual turnover of about 100,000 *tumans* or £40,000 to £45,000. An additional £7,000 was realized by 325 looms in nine surrounding villages »[2019].

In another report, written about the same time, Abbott states that the making of shawls and other woollen fabrics, « still form a thriving branch of Industry. [...] The manufacture has improved of late years, and with encouragement might, in the course of time, become of considerably more importance, both as regards quality and quantity »[2020].

Although, shawl manufacturing may not have been as booming as in 1816, « the manufacture of Shawls, etc. appears to consume nearly all the Goats Wool in the Country. The White is worth about 3.5 Kerans per Men and the Yellow and the Brown 2 Kerans in Spring, the season for the product »[2021]. « About 2,000 Mens of Goats Wool spun into thread are send yearly to Meshed for the Shawl manufacturing of that city » at the end of the 1840s[2022]. Goedel reports in 1849 that, Mashhad shawls as well as Kerman shawls were exported[2023].

• *Decline in Kerman's shawl industry*

Amir Kabir, chancellor between 1848-51, tried to stimulate the wool industry in Kerman. He included shawls in an industrial exhibition of Persian manufactured goods that he organized in Britain. He also stimulated the Kerman industry to produce products of equal quality with those of Kashmir. Amir Kabir succeeded in doing so, or Persian experts were unable to tell a Kerman shawl apart from a Kashmir one, and, in fact bought a Kerman shawl for 80 tomans believing it to be a Kashmiri one[2024]. As a

2019. Amanat, p. 83. Abbott estimated that 4,500 people were employed at the looms, although the inhabitants told him 9,000 people were employed at 5,000 looms; on working conditions see *ibid.*, p. 84; the highest value given for best shawls did not exceed 30 tomans or about £14 (*ibid*, p. 83).

2020. *Ibid.*, p. 151.

2021. *Ibid.*, p. 110. The duty at city gate was 6 shahis per man.

2022. *Ibid.*

2023. Goedel, p. 26.

2024. Qazvini, p. 54-55; Adamiyyat, p. 220.

result the Kerman shawls were also referred to as *shal-e amiri*, which obtained prices as high as 50-60 ducats, a price seldom fetched by the Kashmir shawls. It is far-fetched, however, when Adamiyat contends that this development also resulted in a fall of imports of Kashmir shawls into Persia, for which he adduces no evidence[2025]. For a time, Amir Kabir's policy bore the fruits of success, even after his death. The ban on trade of Kashmir shawls in Kerman, issued in 1854 by Mohammad Hasan Khan Sardar, governor of Kerman, sustained the shawl industry's viability for some time. The ban even stimulated the development of new shawl designs[2026]. Mirza Aqa Khan Nuri, the new prime minister, also took steps to ensure that henceforth all robes of honor were to be made of Kerman shawl[2027]. But this measure could not stem the downturn of the shawl industry. The demand for Kashmir shawls in France increased during the early 1850s; these were exported via Persia and Istanbul. At the same time, the imports and stock of Kashmir shawls into Persia had been reduced due to the ban on its trade, while the production of Kerman shawls had also declined. As a result, the price of shawls rose so high in Persia that Naser al-Din Shah (r. 1848-96) had to ban the export of shawls in the fall of 1857[2028].

When Khanikoff visited Kerman at the end of the 1850s there were only about 200 shawl manufactories still operating. He noticed that there was indeed a slump in the industry, for the number of manufactories had dropped from 2,200, as reported by Abbott[2029]. This may also explain why Blau reports that there was a vigorous trade in *taftik*, or goat hair, in the 1850s. Part of the production was exported to Germany and France. In Persia itself, *taftik* was mixed with wool for the production of carpets and other woven stuffs. Blau does not mention *kork*, but quotes a price for *taftik* in the Tabriz market at 4 qrans and 10 shahis per 1,000 methqals in 1858[2030]. This is confirmed by Polak who mentions that after Amir Kabir's

2025. Mostaufi, I, p. 69, 75; E'temad al-Saltaneh [*Ma'ather*], p. 101, mentions the promotion of the shawl weaving industry; Adamiyyat, p. 220; Issawi, p. 294-295.

2026. *Ruznameh-ye Vaqaye'-ye Ettefaqiyeh* (Tehran), No. 182, (1 Dhu'l-Qa'da 1270/26) July 1854.

2027. Sasani, I, p. 162.

2028. Blau, p. 107-108; E'temad al-Saltaneh [*Ma'ather*], p. 101; E'temad al-Saltaneh [*Montazam*], III, p. 208, 322; Adamiyat, p. 220. For a general discussion of the situation of the textile industry in Iran in the 19th century see chapter one.

2029. Khanikoff, p. 196.

2030. Blau, p. 71.

death the shawl industry suffered a decline and that the bulk of the *kork* clip was exported to India, because of the high prices obtaining there[2031].

Around 1860, Kerman was selling much of its *kork* to Kashmir rather than manufacturing shawls itself. Vakil al-Molk, then governor of Kerman, held the monopoly of the wool trade to India, which was very extensive. There was still some export of shawls to Turkey and Egypt[2032]. De Rochechouart gives a rather optimistic view of shawl production in Kerman in 1862. He notes that there were 1,000 looms in the city, that each produced three to four shawls per year. He further mentions that there were also 100 looms in Kerman, that produced each one shawl every two days, which were used as sashes and as *'abas* or coats. He was unable to procure an entire shawl of this kind and could only obtain a sample of the fabric. He also states that each year Kerman exported 4,000 shawls with a value of 800,000 francs or about 66,000 tomans. This seemingly thriving industry was located in a city and community that according to de Rochechouart was very poor[2033]. However, Polak mentions that *kork* was used mainly for the manufacturing of felts and woven stuffs. Shawls were made with it in particular, but part of the *kork* production was exported, through Yazd, to India[2034]. Persian sources also draw a depressed picture of the Kerman shawl industry in the 1860s. In April 1869, for example, Naser al-Din Shah had given instructions to the governor of Kerman, Vakil al-Molk II, to try to stimulate the Kerman industries such as shawl and carpet weaving[2035].

Around 1870, there were only about 120 shawl manufactories left, and 6 carpet manufactories, according to Smith[2036]. Vakil al-Molk had a private shawl factory, where « alone the finer qualities [are] produced »[2037]. « We learnt that the Karman shawls of the finer sort, made of kurk, were not in great demand for exportation, they being principally made to order. Great quantities of the inferior kinds, however, made of lambswool, were

2031. Polak [*Persien*], II, p. 168. Irwin, [*Kashmir*] p. 9 writes that the Kashmir shawl weavers « often compelled to adulterate goat-fleece with Kirman's sheep's wool » which seems to contradict the information from Persia which reports the export of goat-wool or *kork*. However, Kerman exported both wool (*pashm*) and goat hair (*kork*).

2032. Polak, II, p. 168.

2033. MAE, Rochechouart to Gobineau, 5/11/1862 (see sample 7). Blau (p. 108) also mentions this cheap and inferior type of shawl; see *supra* classification of shawls.

2034. Polak [Beitrag], p. 112.

2035. Bastani Parizi [*Farmanfarma*], p. 248-249.

2036. Goldsmid, I, p. 191.

2037. *Ibid.*, I, p. 101.

sent to the Turkish market. The local duty on the superior shawls was five per cent »[2038]. Smith also reports that there still was export of *kork* to India[2039]. This is also confirmed by a local source. « Wool and kurk from here [Jebalbarez, Eqta'] is mostly carried to Bandar 'Abbas, whence it is taken to India »[2040]. This may have been bad for the shawl weavers, but not for the owners of sheep and goats, who became rich men, because of the high price of *kork* and wool[2041].

Around 1865, the shawl weavers in Mashhad imported some 6,000 mans of *kork* from Kerman[2042]. In the early 1870s, Baker reported that « a cloth called kourk or barek, woven from camel down » was traded in Mashhad. He stated further that *barak* was a cloth made of goat hair[2043]. Around 1879, there were about 100 shawl and five carpet manufacturies in Kerman. Together with Mashhad, which boasted of 320 shawl looms, it was the center of shawl production in Persia[2044]. However, according to Vaziri there were about 12,000 shawl looms (*kar-khaneh*) in Kerman in 1292/1875, each loom employing two persons, or a total of 24,000 shawl weavers. A similarly high figure is given by a European official of the Telegraph department: 12,000 shawl weavers in 1879. Both these figures are much too high to be correct. According to Houtum-Schindler there were only some 20,000 males in Kerman in 1878, and only men wove shawls[2045]. Even if Vaziri meant to refer to Kerman and its peri-urban area, rather than to the city proper, his number is still too high. Referring to the same census as Houtum-Schindler, he states that there were 29,500 males in Kerman and its neighbouring villages. Vaziri may, therefore, have meant to write 1,200 shawl looms, which seems a more likely number, given the fact that (according to him) one-third of the population was engaged in

2038. Goldsmid, I, p. 190.

2039. *Ibid.*, p. 186-187.

2040. Vaziri, p. 120, 138.

2041. *Ibid.*, p. 158.

2042. AP 72 (1866), p. 210.

2043. Baker, p. 183 and note 11.

2044. Houtum-Schindler ([*Reisen*], p. 321) adds that in the past, which he does not specify, there were 300 shawl manufacturies. This last figure must refer to the period prior to 1870. He also observed that the Parsis only made very coarse ordinary shawls; Stolze and Andreas, p. 25; Curzon, I, p. 167.

2045. Vaziri, p. 33; *Farhang-e Iran Zamin*, XIX, p. 205; Houtum-Schindler [*Reisen*], p. 328, the statistical data had been collected by Vakil ol-Molk II, who had kept a detailed register of the city's population.

weaving[2046]. Furthermore, the shawl weaving industry was in a slump and many weavers had little or no work, and were very poor and hungry. Colonel Taqi Khan of the Kerman regiment, therefore, had a few uniforms made of shawl and sent these to Tehran with the suggestion that this be made a regular order for the Kerman shawl industry. For one uniform would not cost more than one tuman to make, and one order from one or more regiments would bring a lot of money into the community[2047]. The economic downturn of weaving activities coincided with a drought, lack of food, and an oppressive governor, which led to a revolt of the poor in general and the shawl weavers in particular, led by 'Ali Mohammad Shalbaf[2048]. Bastani Parizi states that this uprising was the first worker's revolt in Persia (he suggestively adds that it happened five years before Marx's death) and stops short of suggesting that due to the shawl workers' activities the Constitutional Revolution of 1906 could take place. However, the shawl weavers' uprising was not an exceptional event in the urban history of Persia, where many similar events occurred[2049].

In the early 1880s, *kork* was used for the production of shawls as well as exported to Kashmir through Bombay. Although no price is quoted for *kork*, the average price for *taftik* was 80 German marks per 100 kg in Tabriz[2050]. In 1882, Naser al-Din Shah again tried to stimulate the Kerman shawl industry, this time with more success. He issued a decree that all robes of honor that were given by him were to be made of Kerman shawl[2051]. The shawl industry in Mashhad, making shawls in the Kashmir style, was also supported[2052]. Ironically, the success of the Kerman shawl industry coincided with the almost total collapse of the Kashmir shawl

2046. Vaziri, p. 41, 35.

2047. *Farhang-e Iran Zamin*, XIX, p. 205; Bastani Parizi [*Farmanfarma*], p. 251.

2048. *Ibid.*, p. 254-259; see also *Farhang-e Iran Zamin*, XIX, p. 208-210.

2049. Bastani Parizi [*Farmanfarma*], p. 249-260, and in particular p. 254, 289; see also p. 277-285.

2050. Stolze and Andreas, p. 22.

2051. E'temad al-Saltaneh [*Montazam*], III, p. 208, 332; E'temad al-Saltaneh [*Ma'ather*] p. 101. He also promoted the production of better quality products such as the *hashiyeh-ye termeh* (*termeh* borders) which could not easily be distinguished from the so-called *'azim-khani* borders, E'temad al-Saltaneh [*Ma'ather*], p. 106.

2052. E'temad al-Saltaneh [*Ma'ather*], p. 101.

industry after 1870, due to lack of demand in Europe[2053]. Browne noted in 1888 that « of late, however, the shawl trade had been on the decline; and the proprietor of this establishment told me he was thinking of closing his workshops for a year »[2054].

When Preece visited Kerman in 1892-94, he observed that the weaving of shawls and the making of *namads* (felt carpets) were the city's two main industries[2055]. Four years later the wool industry in Kerman was « in a thoroughly prosperous condition. The coarse shawls are exported to Turkey, where they are used for ladies' dresses, but the finest qualities which cost up to £8 per square yard now find an increasing sale in Persia, where they quite hold their own with the Kashmir articles. The white shawls are manufactured with wet wool, but, I am assured that it is a mistake to suppose, as previous travellers have related, that a moist atmosphere is necessary during the process of weaving, no water whatever being used in connection with the embroidered article »[2056]. About the same time, there were 500 shawl weavers in Mahan, undoubtedly an integrated part of Kerman's productive and commercial effort[2057].

Despite the growth of the wool industry there was still some export of raw wool, in three qualities, but it was an unimportant aspect of the industry. A good deal was formerly sent to Kashmir and Amritsar, but by the mid-1890s this trade had fallen off. In 1894-95 not more than 4,000 mans of *kork* were exported to India with a value of 3,600 qrans or £720[2058]. This was due to a number of coinciding factors. Foremost among these was the introduction of the Jacquard mechanical loom and the Paisley looms, in the 1860s, which turned out shawls comparable to those of Kasmir at a much lower price. In addition, the closure of the French market to Kashmir shawls as a result of the Franco-Prussian war dealt a severe blow to the Kashmir shawl industry. While the market for shawls in Europe

2053. Irwin [*Kashmir*], p. 18. Persian shawls were not produced for the European and American market, however.

2054. Browne [*A Year*], p. 483.

2055. DCR 1376 (1894), p. 30.

2056. DCR 1671 (1896), p. 12; « Shawls are made varying in price from 30 krans to 1,000 krans; the latter are almost entirely taken up by the Government and rich natives, whilst the cheaper ones go to the various towns in Persia; the largest demand comes from Constantinople, for which place special shapes and designs are worked. A small quantity also find their way into Russia and the Khanates » (DCR, 1376 (1894), p. 30).

2057. *Historical Gazetteer*, IV, p. 278.

2058. DCR 1671 (1896), p. 11, 12, 14.

expanded, because the lower classes could afford the cheap Paisley shawls, the use of shawls by the upper class went out of fashion. The combination of these factors led to the impoverishment of the Kashmiri shawl makers[2059].

The situation was different in Kerman, which remained relatively unscathed by the events in Europe. This was due to the fact that the European market had never been important for Kerman shawls. Its traditional markets (the domestic market, Turkey, the Central Asian khanates, the Caucasus) were not yet affected by changes in weaving technology and fashion in Europe. A British consul in Kerman observed: « The shawl and carpet industries have doubled their output during the last few years, although during 1895 there has been a temporary check, owing to troubles in Turkey, where most of the shawls and a large percentage of the carpets are bought. Kerman shawls are made in qualities rivalling the products of Kashmir, and also as coarse as merino. They find no market in Europe, where even the Kashmir shawl is now but rarely seen »[2060].

One of the indications of the importance of the wool industry to Kerman was its income from customs revenues. « The income of the customs is mainly derived from charging an octroi of about 10 s. per 650 lbs. of wool, worth some £15 and £2 for a similar amount of "kurk" or fine goat wool, worth £18, £32, or £48, no distinction being made for quality. Similar dues, averaging 5 per cent, were levied on the export of shawls, and other manufactured goods »[2061].

A British commercial mission reports in 1904: « Little or no Kirmani wool finds its way to the sea, being nearly all utilised in the manufacture of carpets and shawls. There used at one time to be a fairly heavy export of wool from Kirman, and much more Khorasan wool was brought down to the coast than is now the case »[2062]. The shawl industry gave employment to a large number of people in Kerman. « The output of Kerman shawls, in

2059. Irwin [*Kashmir*], p. 18, 25.

2060. DCR 1671 (1896), p. 5; however, export of shawls to Constantinople (of a coarse quality), Tabriz, Shiraz (a few), Mashhad (a few) Baghdad (*ibid.*, p. 11). Shawls and *barak* continued to be exported from Mashhad to Russian territories and Afghanistan, DCR 976 (1890-91), Mashhad, p. 20-21.

2061. DCR 1671 (1896), p. 8.

2062. Gleadowe-Newcomen, p. 91; the wool produced in Bam district « is nearly all used in the manufacture of carpets; and none is exported to India » (*Historical Gazetteer*, IV, p. 41).

the production of which some 3,000 looms are employed, may be reckoned at £60,000. The greater quantity of Kerman shawls are made to order for Teheran where they are used for presentation as Khilats or robes of honour at No-roz »[2063]. The demand for wool, especially that from Kerman, in Persia itself did not diminish. There was a growing national and international demand for Kerman carpets, which had an annual turnover of about £50,000, somewhat less than that of shawls[2064].

The signs of the diminishing importance of the shawl industry were already clear by 1900. Sykes wrote: « Kerman was, until quite recently, more especially famous for its shawls, but to-day, its carpets claim precedence »[2065]. This turnabout started in 1294/1897-98, due to the enormous demand for carpets. Anyone with ten tomans to his name invested in one or more looms to start producing carpets, as a result of which many shawl looms were turned into carpet looms. This upsurge of carpet production lasted till 1320/1902-03 when the market was hit by a sudden drop in demand, which caused much damage to the Kerman economy[2066].

By 1910, shawls were still produced in Kerman and elsewhere. D'Allemagne gives a description of their production, as well as of the characteristics of the Kerman shawls[2067]. Kuss also mentions that shawls were still produced at Kerman. The cheapest, i.e. without embroidery, could be had already for 8-30 German marks. More elaborate and pricey shawls cost 60-200 marks, while the highest quality shawls cost as much as 500-800 marks[2068]. However beautiful the Kerman shawls were, the market was not interested in them anymore. The shawl manufactures in Kerman gradually became insignificant compared with the city's carpet weavers and even with those of Yazd. But shawls left their mark on the nascent Kerman carpet industry. Many of the shawl weavers and designers became weavers and designers of carpets. According to Edwards, who named this period between the late 1890s and the outbreak of World War I

2063. Gleadowe-Newcomen, p. 94; see also Sykes [*Ten Thousand*], p. 200. *Historical Gazetteer*, IV, p. 257; see however Abdullaev (p. 87 and 89), quoting Rittikh who visited Kerman in 1900, according to whom there were only 1,000 shawl looms in Kerman at that time, with an annual export of 300,000 tomans.

2064. « In Persia the carpets of Kerman have even a higher name than the shawls » (DCR 1376 (1894), p 30); Gleadowe-Newcomen, p. 94.

2065. Sykes [*Ten Thousand*], p. 199. See also *Historical Gazetteer*, IV, p. 257.

2066. Vaziri, p. 33-34.

2067. D'Allemagne, I, p. 151.

2068. Kuss, p. 148.

the "shawl period", « the designers of those early Kerman carpets borrowed freely from the Kerman shawls »[2069].

Mashhad, likewise, suffered a decline in shawl production. In 1905, there were still only about 70 shawl looms operating in Mashhad, whereas in 1890 their number had been about 320[2070]. In Kashan, apart from the Hosein Qoli Khani shawl, various other varieties were still woven which offered small patterns and were made in six or seven different colors (*shesh-rang* and *haft-rang*). They were beautiful to look at and cost 15 to 20 qrans per dhar' (roughly equivalent to one meter)[2071].

Since the late 1880s, the shawl industry had played a significant role, but by 1910 its importance had been reduced considerably. The reasons for this were: the growing use of European dress by the Iranian elite; the import of cheap imitations; and, finally, the impoverishment of the populace. « Formerly, all Persians, whether rich or poor, wore a waist band made of shawl, often with rich embroideries. Nowadays, if one carries a shawl at all, one has a woolen waist band, often of simple designs. The shawl production is estimated to amount to DM 400,000/yr now »[2072], while in the period 1912-14 Persia still exported some 1.3 to 1.6 million tomans in shawl[2073]. In 1924, there were only 5 shawl sellers in Tehran[2074]. However, in 1920, there were still 30 shawl manufactories in Tabriz, employing 180 workers[2075].

With the change in dress and customs — a trend accelerated by the Constitutional Revolution of 1906 — the use of robes of honor and other types of traditional clothing declined, and the demand for Kerman shawls

2069. Edwards, p. 207-208 and plates p. 203-208. The likelihood that shawl weavers became carpet weavers is reinforced by the fact that « the procedure generally in making shawls and carpets is very similar, except that in the shawls the ends of the wool are not cut off but are turned in, and remains to be carried on » (DCR, 1376 (1894), p. 30).

2070. AP 127 (1906), p. 9. *Historical Gazetteer*, II, p. 489.

2071. Jamalzadeh, p. 79.

2072. [*Die Wirtschaftlichen*], p. 268-269.

2073. Abdullaev, p. 89 quoting the Statistique, p. 173.

2074. Keihan, III, p. 331; at that time, there were still 30 shawl weavers in Isfahan. Also, in the same year, Isfahan imported Kerman shawls to a value of only 600 *tumans* and a quantity of 200 sangs of *kork*, costing 560 tomans (Janab, p. 78, 119).

2075. Sultanzadeh, p. 102; for the situation in Isfahan, see Janab, p. 78. It is not clear whether woollen, silk, or other types of shawls were woven, but they were most likely of the silken variety.

also diminished[2076]. The reduced demand, in part fueled by competition from the cheaper European imitation shawls[2077], expressed itself in a reorientation of the production capacity of the weaving industry towards the production of carpets and away from shawls. The final blow to the shawl industry came when the government abolished the use of robes of honor and traditional garb in general on 29 December 1928[2078]. Subsequently, the demand for shawls dropped almost to zero, although some production continued in Kerman[2079]. The use of goat wool, especially *kork*, was redirected to the Kerman carpet industry. In 1928, Amory observed: « Some of the grey-beards here refer to the time of Nasr-ed-Din Shah, only two generations ago, as days of comparative prosperity. Then Kirman turned out its famous carpets and its woven shals of goat's down or wool that compared not unworthily with the shawls of Kashmir. Now, the Kirmanis seem to be occupied only with rugs and opium »[2080]. A few years later another American visitor remarked: « Today, apart from its shawls, Kerman is noted chiefly for its carpets »[2081]. In modern times, some shawl production, especially of *termeh*, still continues in Kerman. English concluded that the shawl makers « are among the strongest guilds in Kerman in the 1960s, although there is no objective evidence for such a claim »[2082]. A contemporary report by the Handicraft Organization of Iran

2076. See Mostaufi, III, p. 422-424, for an interesting discussion on the change in official dress and the attitudes of various officials on this matter. Also, that the highest fiscal officials wore a white *termeh* coat (*jebbeh*), the next highest an emerald or *zomorrod termeh* coat, the next ranking officials a *portoqali* (orange) *termeh* coat and the lowest category of officials a *laki* (red) *termeh* coat.

2077. Bastani Parizi [*Farmanfarma*], p. 287, attaches too much importance to European competition to explain the disappearance of the Persian shawl industry in my view. Contemporary Iranian observers also held that view, see *ibid.* p. 288, quoting an interesting article from the newspaper *Habl al-Matin* of May 1906; see for a translation Issawi, p. 68.

2078. Hedayat [*Khatarat*], p. 382; Gabriel, p. 225, mentions that the manufacture of shawls had been prohibited in Kerman, because it required the use of child labour. Gabriel, however, confuses this prohibition with that of the general regulation covering the weaving arts, a ban which remained a dead letter. See Floor [*Labour*], p. 82-93.

2079. Keihan, III, p. 298.

2080. Amory, p. 171.

2081. Filmer, p. 135.

2082. English, p. 76. However, the 1966 census does not even have a separate professional category for shawl manufacturing and thus it is not possible to gauge the importance of the craft in the economy of Kerman. The fact that it did not warrant a

mentions that only in the village of Hutak, some 40 km outside Kerman were shawls woven. There were still some eight looms working, operated by weavers above 40 years of age[2083]. The *termeh* fabrics woven during the last decades are produced in somber colors, « as the recent generation has associated them with use in mourning. This is being overcome again with its use in ladies' suiting, bringing back even the metal-enriched brocades »[2084].

What is a Persian Shawl?

The Kerman shawls, though inferior to the best Kashmir shawls, are of surprising beauty, fineness and richness, all contemporary reporters agree[2085]. In what way were Kerman shawls considered to be inferior? The evidence is conflicting. Although all authors agree that the Kashmir shawls were superior to the Kerman shawls, most point out that it is very difficult to distinguish between the two. Only very few authors dare to suggest that they are able to do so. We will, therefore, review the arguments to determine whether indeed it is possible to identify characteristics of Persian shawls that mark them from the Kashmir ones.

Polak mentions that Kerman shawls, while comparable in design and color to those of Kashmir, were inferior in fineness and suppleness. He submits, however, that it was only after years of experience in the trade that one was able to judge the difference in quality between shawls and assess their market value. Polak adds that for a Persian, he undoubtedly means a well-to-do one, it was part of his education to judge a good shawl, carpet or horse. Polak did not trust a European's opinion on this point and continues that it takes a good eye to spot the difference between a Kerman and

---

special category in the census indicates that shawl weaving was insignificant. Based on my own, granted superficial, observations in Kerman in that same year the artisanal manufacturing of *shal-e termeh* was indeed a marginal economic activity.

2083. Khaza'eli, p. 113.

2084. Gluck and Gluck, p. 214.

2085. Polak [*Persien*], I, p. 153; Blau, p. 107; « the most esteemed are those coming from Kashmir » (Gleadowe-Newcomen, p. 94); « the texture of the finest shawls of the Persian Looms is considered equal to that of the best productions of India. They are of a very excellent and durable quality, and of the figured ones the colors and designs are admirable. The wool employed for all but the coarsest kind of shawls is that of Goats ». (Amanat, p. 83).

Kashmir shawl[2086]. This last point is confirmed by Murdoch Smith who opines: « The shawls of Kerman are not much inferior to those of Cashmere »[2087], and Blau, who states that « even experts find it difficult to distinguish » a Kerman shawl from a Kashmir one[2088]. This point is also made by the official Persian newspaper *Vaqe'e-ye ettefaqiyeh* in 1850, when it relates a story that experts were shown a Kerman shawl and were unable to tell whether it were Kerman or Kashmir shawl[2089]. Other contemporary observers, such as Major Smith, report that *kork* shawls, « unlike Kashmir, shrinking slightly on being wet ». He adds, « The shawls of Karman appear to differ slightly from those of Kashmir in being of worsted instead of the under-down of wool »[2090]. Based on her study of the weaving technique of shawls, Phyllis Ackerman echoes Polak when she states that Kerman shawls « are difficult to distinguish with any confidence from the Kashmiri productions »[2091].

Other observers, however, think that they had the ability to spot a Persian shawl. Benjamin, the American consul-general in Persia states: « in general scope the needlework of the province of Kerman is allied to that of Cashmere. It differs from that in being of coarser texture, although often wrought on very fine stuffs similar to those made of cashmere wool. The design is also ordinarily in wool, but sometimes it is of silk thread on fine cashmere, or on the fine wool-stuffs of Kerman which resemble cashmere. The shawls of Cashmere are intended for a different purpose, and are generally made by another process. The work of Kerman is very beautiful, although the design commonly consists of variations of what we call the palm-leaf pattern, which orientals affirm is properly intended as a conventional rendering of the cypress, the tree of immortality. It is worked with an exquisite union of rich, soft colors, associated with effective borders. The ground is generally scarlet or pure white »[2092].

According to d'Allemagne, writing some thirty years later, Persian shawls were easy to distinguish from the Kashmir ones, « because they often have an entirely white fond: in that case, the pattern shows large palm-

---

2086. Polak [*Persien*], II, p. 169.
2087. Smith, p. 48, quoted by Scarce [Persian Shawl], p. 28.
2088. Blau, p. 107.
2089. Adamiyyat, p. 220; for a translation see Issawi, p. 294.
2090. Goldsmid, I, p. 102.
2091. Pope and Ackerman, III, p. 2154.
2092. Benjamin, p. 334.

leaves [*boteh*] which sprout forth vigorously and constitute the shawl's borders. They [also] do not present that very soft harmony of the real Indian Kashmir shawls, whose colors harmoniously mix together, and constitute the characteristic of that kind of work »[2093].

Powell, writing in 1923, reports: « The Persian shawl should not be confused with the Kashmir shawls of which our grandmothers were proud possessors, and which were copied in great numbers by the Paisley looms. The Persian shawl, instead of being square, like the Kashmir, with triangles of embroidery in the corners and in the center an embroidered medallion, is a strip of solid needlework, about a yard wide and four yards long. The name of its maker, sometimes surmounted by the emblem of the Lion and the Sun done in silver thread, is frequently to be found in one corner of the finer specimens. The most chic design is the so-called "pineapple" pattern on a white ground. Such a shawl costs in Tehran from a hundred dollars upward. These shawls are not intended to be worn as a wrap, but to be cut into one of the long, tight-fitting coats, reaching almost to the heels, which are the garments worn by all Persian officials at court and on other state occasions »[2094].

Modern experts claim they can identify a Persian shawl. Irwin submits that both the Persian and Kashmir shawl are woven in the same twill-tapestry technique. However, Persian shawls show a bolder floral treatment and a more architectural emphasis in design. Also, their « predominant color is a rather deep red not at all characteristic of Kashmir »[2095]. The Anavians, as usual, without providing any explanation or proof, allege to have identified not only Persian shawls from the 18th century, but even to have been able to distinguish between those woven in Kerman and Yazd[2096]. Even Phyllis Ackerman could not withstand the urge to identify Persian shawls. She believed that she had been able to identify a Mashhad shawl, because of its floral character, imitating a Mashhad carpet pattern, and so unlike a Kashmir shawl[2097].

Jennifer Scarce is the last author who has claimed to be able to distinguish between a Kashmir and a Persian shawl. She maintains: « One

---

2093. D'Allemagne, I, p. 151.

2094. Powell, p. 255-256. Powell is wrong when he states that there were no square Persian shawls. The pineapple pattern he refers to is that of the floral *boteh* pattern.

2095. Irwin [*Kashmir*], p. 17.

2096. Anavian and Anavian, see various plates.

2097. Pope and Ackerman, III, p. 2154 and plate p. 1093.

contemporary piece acquired by Robert Murdoch Smith in 1888 for the Edinburgh collections shows that the Persian product is clearly distinguishable from that of Kashmir »[2098]. However, from her descriptive article we do not learn in what way the two, Persian and Kashmir shawls, can be distinguished from each other either. The only information that Scarce offers is that « certain motifs such as the floral *boteh* are shared with Kashmiri textiles but on examination are clearly distinguished because they are employed in Persian examples to create repeating patterns suitable for lengths of furnishing and clothing fabrics »[2099]. Unfortunately, Scarce does not offer a list of distinguishing marks that are peculiar for the Persian shawl only. She further submits that Persian shawls were made of goat fleece and wool fiber mixed to give a dense, firm weave (but so were Kashmir shawls as well) and that clear background colors were preferred (white, rich red and yellow). The foundation of the warps and wefts is woven in a 2 x 2 twill weave. « Orange, crimson, green, blue, and black pattern wefts are woven in a different twill weave passing over two and under one warp. Separate wefts are used for each unit of color and are only carried across as floats at the back of the weaving where intervals are short »[2100].

Despite the claims that it is easy to identify a Persian shawl, I submit that it is very difficult to do so. What is the evidence ? Authors who state that the two (Kashmir and Persian) shawls differ in quality, at the same time point that even contemporary experts found it difficult to distinguish between the two. Those that claim that they can tell them apart offer very little convincing evidence for such a claim, in fact none that can withstand critical scrutiny. Benjamin's remarks are of too general a nature to be relevant. He is also wrong when he states that Kashmir shawls are intended for a different purpose and are generally made by another process. D'Allemagne only states that Persian shawls have a white ground and that the colors of Kashmir shawls mix harmoniously together, which is a subjective argument, not necessarily a fact. Powell is clearly wrong when he states that there were no Persian square shawls. Irwin only offers a subjective appreciation not founded in fact, while Scarce's observations can be easily countered by what we know about Persian and Kashmir shawls.

2098. Scarce [Persian Shawl], p. 29.
2099. *Ibid.*, p. 23.
2100. Scarce [Persian Shawl], p. 29.

Information about the relatively better known Kashmir shawls as well as observations by contemporaries show that Scarce's contribution is not very helpful, for her description is equally applicable to them. Irwin writes that « the cone or pine [*boteh*] motif is standard for Kashmir shawls »[2101]. As we have seen above, Persian shawls were not only of the *boteh* type as is clear from the many different colors and other patterns used in them. Sykes reports that the finest shawls were of a « fir-cone [*boteh*] pattern of rich colours, generally used for the khalat or robe of honour, which constitutes the Governor's reinvesture at No Ruz. A white or grey quality closely resembles merino, and the striped varieties are exported to Constantinople and used for wearing round the waist, or for ladies's dress »[2102]. Furthermore, Moorcroft (the major source on Kashmir shawls) reports that the Persians preferred shawls in which the pattern « almost completely covers and conceals the colours of the ground »[2103]. The fact that Kashmir produced shawls specifically for the Persian market, taking into account their end-use and current fashion, makes it likely that Kashmiri shawl weavers wove repeating patterns suitable for lengths of furnishing and clothing fabrics in accordance with Persian taste and fashion[2104]. The need to market imitation shawls that were woven using Persian designs and patterns was not lost on Fraser when he writes that « in making shawls therefore for the Persian market, they should be fabricated both in shape and ornament, with reference to their use. Those which they chiefly admire are richly flowered all over, or spotted with pines of great or less size on a rich ground, as black, blue, green, yellow, crimson, or scarlet. A few of the striped patterns are liked, but the former are the best »[2105]. Even chemical analysis of the fibers may not yield convincing evidence to determine the origin of a particular shawl. For Persian wool was

2101. Irwin [*Kashmir*], p. 11.

2102. Sykes [*Ten Thousand*], p. 200.

2103. Irwin [*Kashmir*], p. 15.

2104. *Ibid.*, p. 13.

2105. Fraser [*Caspian Sea*], p. 369. He adds that « square shawl-handkerchiefs for the ladies should have a handsome center ornament, surrounded with happy devices, and rich corner ornaments, with a border to match ». British observers of the Kashmir shawl manufacturing industry confirm that great attention was given to the quality and pattern of its products as a function of which market these were targeted for, (Irwin [*Kashmir*], p. 13).

extensively used in the weaving of Kashmir shawls, and "Indian" wool likewise was used in the weaving of Persian Kashmir-like socks[2106].

Persian shawls probably were not of the *do-shaleh* type, i.e. their underside was visible, because two shawls were not stitched back-to-back[2107]. This conclusion seems tenable due to the fact that Fraser writes that European imitation shawls show « the rough and ragged appearance of their wrong sides; if this could be made more to resemble the real shawls, it would tend greatly to increase their sale »[2108].

Distinguishing between Kashmir and Persian shawls is also made difficult by the fact that contemporary authors disagree on the characteristics of the two types of shawls. Most authors agree that Persian shawls have either a white or scarlet ground[2109], and that they usually have a large palm leave pattern[2110], and are worsted[2111]. Others maintain that Kashmir shawls were usually in larger patterns, while Kerman shawls had smaller more numerous repeats[2112]. Given this difference in opinion, it seems impossible to identify a number of items that may permit identification of a certain type, most likely the most common and inferior types of Persian shawls. I leave this pleasant task to art historians and textile experts, who, perhaps, will be helped in this task by the information offered in this study. Examination of Persian shawls whose origin is known and uncontested, and their comparison with similar Kashmir shawls, may yield information that will help to settle the issue of what is a Persian shawl and what is not.

2106. On the export of Persian wool to Kashmir see chapter VI as well as Irwin [*Kashmir*], p. 7; on the use of Indian wool for Persian shawls see Blau, p. 108.

2107. Irwin [*Kashmir*], p. 10, describes the invention of this type of shawl for Kashmir.

2108. Fraser [*Caspian Sea*], p. 369.

2109. Benjamin; d'Allemagne, Powell; Irwin [*Kashmir*]; Scarce [Persian Shawl].

2110. D'Allemagne; Powell.

2111. Goldsmid, I, p. 102; Savage-Landor who visited Kerman in 1901 writes: « Kerman is celebrated for its cloth manufacture and felts. The cloth is of fine worsted, and is generally in pieces six yards long by three quarters of a yard wide. It is much used by the natives, both for hangings and for making clothes for men and women, being very soft and durable. Embroidered turbans and kamarbands are made from these cloths, especially on white cloth, generally of a fine quality ».

2112. Gluck and Gluck, p. 214.

9. 19th century Persian dress

(ndoor female dress - male dress - outdoor female dress)

VI. The Kerman Goat Hair or Kork

The reason why the discussion of the trade in goat hair or *kork* from the Kerman area warrants attention is that this trade acquired some international importance after 1658, when the two Companies, VOC and EIC, started to buy this commodity. The use and the trade of this wool certainly predates European interest. However, apart from being documented, European trade also made *kork* a more important commodity than it had been prior to 1658 or after 1769, when the EIC stopped trading in this commodity. In fact, apart from bullion, *kork* became the VOC and EIC's most important export commodity. Nevertheless, the wool trade was marginal to the total annual turnover of the VOC and EIC in Persia. In addition, the *kork* trade and its related manufacturing activities was of vital economic importance to the population of Kerman province.

In this study I will focus on the trade in *kork* after 1730, although I will also refer to data from the earlier period. The reason for this particular starting date is that the the wool trade between 1658-1730 has been discussed by Matthee[2113]. In what follows, therefore, I will discuss the nature and development of European commercial interest in *kork,* and the local importance of the *kork* trade.

What is kork?

Wool is produced in large quantities in Persia. It was, and still is, an important source of income for the pastoral and peasant population. In addition to sheep's wool and camel's wool, there was considerable production of, and trade in, goat hair or *taftik*[2114]. During the period between 1658-1769 there was considerable European interest in a very special type of goats' hair, viz., the down or *kork* of the goats. The standard Persian terms for wool, in the 19th and 20th centuries, are « coork and pasham; pasham is the outer and coarser wool and is dirtier than coork, i.e. the down like wool underlying it »[2115]. Thus, *kork,* was not a trade name for Kerman goats' hair, as is usually believed, but for all down-like wool. It

2113. Matthee [East India].

2114. Stolze and Andreas, p. 22; Blau, p. 71.

2115. Gleadowe-Newcomen, p. 91.

may have been used more to refer to the down grown at the roots of the hair of goats, but it seems to have been a generic term rather than a specialized one. This generic nature of the term has led various travellers, who reported on Kerman goat hair, into reporting that the wool, referred to as *kork*, came from sheep or camels[2116]. In this study, however, the term *kork* refers to Kerman goat wool.

Fine, soft goat hair, referred to in Persian as *kork*, *kurk*, *kulk* or *khulk*[2117], is the down undercoat underneath the rough outer hair of the goats. This fleece of the finest hairs on the under-belly serves to protect the goats against the cold winters and is shed during spring[2118]. It is produced by the Rayin goat, a variety of the *Capra ibex*, a Central Asian species, whose fleece is used to make Kashmir shawls. « They are small animals, weighing anywhere from 40 to 80 lbs., with black, brown, reddish, grey, or white coats. Their thick undercoat of down is their most valuable product »[2119]. The Persians distinguished four different types of *kork*, according to an 18th century Dutch report:

« [fol. 1083] there is pure white wool, which is used to weave and spin, and is called koerk tshengoe doessie [*kork-e chenguduzi*]; the second or red kind (the Company's choice) is used to make hats and nimets [*namad*] by the nemets makers [felt makers] and is called koerk kirmans [*kork-e kermani* or Kerman down]; the third kind, the grey-white wool, is mostly used like the first one, but it is not as good, it is called koerk safiet [*kork-e sefid* or white down]; the fourth kind is yellowish-red wool which is used like the second kind, but is not as good. It is called koerk nabattie [*kork-e nabati* or Nabati down], for from there hails the best clip. For one clip differs from the other as day from night. That from Boloek Aghta [*boluk-e Eqta'*] and Orsomoet [Orzuya?] and the village of Rahien [Rayin] is the best, and [fol. 1084] that from Sierjoen [Sirjan] is second best, but not as good as the first quality. From Serrint [Zarand] comes the third quality which is almost as good as the second quality. That from the province of Yazd is almost as [good as] the third [quality], but it contains much dirt and

2116. See for example Matthee [East India], mentioning Tavernier, Chardin, Bell, Hanway who identified *kork* with sheep's wool or camel's wool.

2117. See Fraser [*Caspian Sea*], p. 359: « this down, which the natives call khoolk »; Wulff, p. 209, 222; see also Dehkhoda, q.v. *kork*.

2118. Lumsden, p. 218; Irwin [*Kashmir*], p. 4-5; « If left too late it casts its wool and it becomes coarse and valueless » (DCR 1671, London, 1894, p. 31).

2119. English, p. 131.

hair, just as the wool that is obtained around this town. In fixing prices you need to take the place of origin into account. [fol. 1085] Therefore, try to get wool from the three first-mentioned places. It is more expensive, but better »[2120].

As is clear from the report quoted, the different kinds of *kork* also had different types of uses and colours. Moreover, *kork* was produced not only in Kerman, but also in Yazd province; moreover, there were quality differences between the various production locations. Of the various colours, the VOC only wanted the red. The EIC, likewise, preferred the red type, but also bought the other types of *kork*. For example, in June 1736, Auwannees, the VOC's Armenian wool buyer, reports that Savage, the EIC wool buyer, wanted all four colours, viz. red, yellow, pearly and purple[2121].

Historical development of the kork trade

Safavid, Zand and Afsharid periods

• *Production and use*

The production area of *kork* seems to have been concentrated in the area stretching from Ravar, 70 miles northwest of Kerman, to Sirjan, a town at equal distance towards the southwest of the city; to Rayin in the northeast and Orzuya in the southeast. In addition, *kork* was supplied by Yazd. However, the British reported that *kork* also was imported from as far as Herat in the 17th century[2122]. This may have been true, even if it happened only a few times, because goat hair and down was also collected in other parts of Persia and Afghanistan. Ferrier, in the 1850s, reports, for example, that the Hazaras manufactured « a cloth called *kourk* or *barek*, woven of an exceedingly fine and silky wool which grows on the belly of the camel; [...] a down similar to that which grows on the camel, but infinitely superior in quality, grows under the hair of goat, and cloth of incomparible beauty and

2120. VOC 2416, "Memorandum by Clement to van Loon", Kerman, 11/6/1736, fol. 1083-1086. « The white Kerman goat hair was used to make shawls, reason why mostly white goats were raised rather than colored ones. The red variery was in particular used for the production of namad and caps », VOC 2511, Auwannees to Koenad, 1/7/1740, fol. 592.

2121. VOC 2510, Auwannees to Koenad, 15/6/39, fol. 1326-1327.

2122. See Matthee [East India], notes 34-36, and 39.

quality is made of it »[2123]. In 1826, Fraser reports that *kork* is found, « not only in Kerman, but in more or less degree over all Khorasan, and the countries to the eastward; the mountains of which are favourable to the animals which produce it; but I do not believe it is to be had in any great quantities together »[2124].

Apart from the availability of goat hair from elsewhere, there was also the problem that the resource base of Kerman alone probably may not have been sufficient to produce the quantities of *kork* consumed locally and that exported by the British and the Dutch. According to English, the Kerman goats produced an average fleece weight of 0.5-0.75 kg in the 1960s[2125]. Dillon, who rightly points out that *kork* is combed out of the coarser hair, submits that English's figures refer to the combined weight of hair and down. Basing himself on a shepherd's estimate, Dillon suggests that goats produce between 25-400 grams of *kork* annually. Using this figure as the basis of calculation it means that to deliver 63,000 kg (the largest quantity ever exported by the EIC) you need at a minimum 157,500 goats or 2.5 million at a maximum. Using English's estimates, assuming that half the fleece was *kork* and that there were two clips per year, one would still need between 84,000 and 126,000 goats to produce the same amount of *kork*[2126]. In 1966, there were some 213,000 sheep and goats in the entire province of Kerman, of which probably two-thirds, or 144,000 animals, were goats[2127]. Assuming that goat husbandry practices have not changed much, it means that the Dutch report is right about the area on which was drawn for *kork*. This area included most of Kerman province and parts of

2123. Ferrier [*Caravan*], p. 192; he also remarks (p. 193) that the Hazaras « have lived for some years [in tranquillity which has been the result of] the development of their industry in the manufacture of kourks, with which they supply all this part of Asia ». Baker quoting Ferrier says that « a cloth called kourk or barek, woven from camel down » was traded in Mashhad. In the text itself (p. 183, n.), he states that *barak* is a cloth made of goats' hair.

2124. Fraser [*Caspian Sea*], p. 359.

2125. English, p. 133; his statement that goats had two clips per year is also borne out by Major Euan Smith who states « the goats are shorn twice a year, in the spring and autumn » (Goldsmid, I, p. 188); see, however, DCR 1671 (1894), p. 31, which states that « the underwool of the young animal is shorn early in spring », which appears to contradict English. A Dutch report, dated 1695, also mentions two clips, the second of which was less important (VOC 1549, fol. 590).

2126. Dillon, p. 235.

2127. *Ibid.*, p. 237.

Yazd province. In view of the EIC report, there may even have been *kork* supplied from Khorasan and Herat, on occasion. If we take the small geographical production base into account, it is likely that *kork* from other areas may occasionally have been passed off as being Kerman goat hair. However, under normal circumstances the province of Kerman would seem to have been able to meet market demand.

As far as the use of *kork* is concerned it was mainly used to make shawls and serge, or worsted cloth of which hats, caps, felt carpets or *namads* were made as well as various pieces of clothing such as shirts, trousers, and overcoats to adorn the bodies and the homes of the rich. A very specialized application was the robe of honour or *khel'at*[2128].

• *Export of goats*

Whatever the sources of supply, everybody agrees that the best wool was from Kerman. Because of the lack of control over the *kork* trade, which led to fluctuating prices and quantities, the Europeans wanted to get hold of the *kork* resource base, viz. *kork* shedding goats. The first export of goats by the EIC dates from 1668, which was followed by other attempts both by the EIC and VOC. The goats were sent to places as varied as Ceylon, India, and Cape of Good Hope to multiply and shed *kork*[2129]. However, outside their habitat the goats died. In spite of the disappointing experiences the VOC did not give up and regularly asked its factory at Bandar 'Abbas to send new groups of goats. In 1732, the VOC exported 47 Kerman goats[2130], while additional groups were sent in 1734, 1735, 1736, and 1754[2131].

• *Trade of kork*

It was important for the European companies to have good relations with the local governor and other government officials. For although both companies were authorized to trade in *kork* in Kerman by royal decree, a governor or other official could make a wool factor's life very difficult. The

2128. Tavernier, I, p. 95-96; Du Mans, p. 248-249; VOC 1798, fol. 6; see also Scarce [Vesture], p. 33-56.

2129. Matthee [East India], note 132.

2130. VOC 2254, de Cleen to governor-general, 19/7/1732, fol. 644.

2131. VOC 2323, Auwannees to de Cleen, 12/4/1734, fol. 831; VOC 2416, Clement to Koenad, 30/4/1735, fol. 1870; VOC 2416, Koenad to governor-general, 10/12/1736, fol. 449; VOC 2863, Schoonderwoerd to governor-general, 20/12/1754, fol. 42.

governor expected presents, or a loan when he was short of cash. When relations were good he would promise to pay back. In fact, sometimes he did, or part of the sum, and forgot about the rest. Or the governor gave an IOU ("I ow you", promissory note), which in practice meant that you would not get your money[2132].

The good offices of a governor required a *quid pro quo*. On arrival of the wool factor in Kerman he usually gave the governor some presents as well as a letter from the director in Bandar 'Abbas, asking for his assistance. The governor, in his turn, would write the director assuring him that he would assist the wool factor in the collection of *kork* and/or outstanding debts. Similar letters were usually sent by the governor's *vakil* or agent, the vizier and *kalantar* (mayor) of Kerman[2133].

Sometimes the good relations even paid off. Clement, for example, reports that when Mirza Reza, the new *saheb-ekhtiyar* or governor of Kerman arrived in that city on 25 June 1735, he received the VOC representatives more pleasantly than those of the EIC. When shortly thereafter Mirza Reza announced that all merchants had to sign an undertaking (*eltezam*) in which they promised not to send any copper money out of Kerman the EIC factor was also told to sign. Clement, however, did not have to do the same. For the governor said that this would be unfair to the VOC. The Dutch had made advances of 3,000 tomans copper money, and could not be expected to export merchandise only[2134]. Mirza Reza continued to shower favours on the Dutch. During a public meeting he offered Clement pack-animals when he needed them, and said that the Dutch were sincere and reliable. At the same time he criticized the British. Mirza Reza went so far as to visit Clement in his house on 5 October 1735. The governor was accompanied by the *Sheikh al-Eslam*, Towakkel Beg his favourite, the *kalantar* Mirza Yusef, the vizier Mirza Hassim, and various

2132. VOC 2323, Auwannees to de Cleen, 15/6/1734, fol. 834; VOC 2417, Clement to Koenad, 31/12/1735, fol. 3141; VOC 2416, Resolutie Gamron, 3/9/1736, fol. 3789 (presents to Nader Shah given by Auwannees); VOC 2417, Martijn to Koenad, 10/12/1736, fol. 3978; VOC 2511, Auwannes to Koenad, 20/2/1740, fol. 1350-1351.

2133. VOC 2323, Auwannees to de Cleen, 12/4/1734, fol. 833; VOC 2357, Mhamed Coelie Beecq, *vakil* of the governor of Kerman to Koenad, 29/5/1735, fol. 894; see also *ibid.* fol. 923, 4/8/1735, with letter from the governor; VOC 2510, Mhamed Sarieff Chan, governor of Kerman to Koenad, 30/5/1739 received, fol. 1225-1228 and fol. 1227-1228 similar letter from his vizier Miersa Hosein; VOC 2510, Moezaffer Chan, governor of Kerman to Koenad, 29/10/1739, fol. 1265.

2134. VOC 2416, Clement to Koenad, 22/7/1735, fol. 2109-2110.

other officials. The official party then had lunch at Clement's house. As a result of this visit the Dutch were the talk of the town, for they had been honored as no European had ever been before. The *Sheikh al-Eslam* had never before visited the house of a Christian, let alone eaten there[2135].

Such relations were useful when there were conflicts, for they provided easier access to the decision makers[2136]. On the other hand, if friendly governors made a request it also meant that the company had to respond in kind and find ways to satisfy the governor's request. Such was the case, for example, in 1739 when Muzaffar Khan requested broad cloth and shawls, which were unobtainable in Kerman[2137].

- Nature of the kork trade

At the beginning of each year (January) the company factors in Kerman advanced money to local wool merchants, often Banians. The latter, in their turn, advanced money to the owners of the goats in the wool producing villages. This system of *pish-furush* (or advanced sale) obliged the owners of the goats to sell their wool to the merchant who had advanced them the money. After their buying trip through the wool producing areas the wool merchants returned to Kerman. Here they remained till March, when they once again asked for an advance from the company brokers. Then they left once again to the villages to collect and pay the full amount of the contracted price of the wool. Thus, the wool trade was not based on a current account, for « if the vendor has more goods than the value of the money he has received, he will never agree to hand this surplus to the purchaser for just a cash payment without enjoying yet another fair advance supply for the following year, which means that the purchasers are and must always be indebted ».The same system bound the wool merchants to the companies. The former were supposed to settle their outstanding debts with the companies' factors, but if they were unable to, the merchants were credited for next year's clip. Apart from this mercantile operation, there were herd owners who brought *kork* to the market themselves, « which is auctioned by its owners, who are not dependent on anyone at the market and is bought

2135. VOC 2417, Clement to Koenad, 15/10/1735, fol. 3103-3107.

2136. *Ibid.*, Clement to Koenad, 25/11/1736, fol. 3281; *ibid.*, Clement to Koenad, 19/10/1736, fol. 3253.

2137. VOC 2511, Moezaffer Chan to Koenad, 8/2/1740 received, fol. 1286-1288; *ibid.*, Koenad to Auwannees, 10/2/1740, fol. 1267-1270.

more dearly than the rest »[2138]. Thus, most peasants and pastoralists only had indirect contact with the market, in most cases through a great number of middlemen. A similar situation prevailed in the silk trade in Persia at that time. In 1637, the VOC agent in Persia reported that « in order to buy 100 loads of raw silk, one would need at least 20 Dutchmen, not counting other servants, because the silk is purchased by the bundle from house to house, and from village to village »[2139]. This system has persisted till our time and prevailed in the Kerman hinterland in the 1970s. According to Dillon « the merchant and/or his representative comb the mountain valleys in the spring and then again in the late summer looking to buy the small amounts of fleece accumulated by the peasant families »[2140].

As was the case prior to 1730, the *kork* trade was affected by political interference, military operations, and natural disaster. These factors influenced the volume and conditions of trade, the price of *kork*, and the transportation rates. There were also continued attempts to raise the goats outside their natural habitat. However, there the added element of a collusion by the VOC and EIC to keep prices low, and thus stave off the threat of serious competition from Persian merchants. Another new factor was the general scarcity of cash and its depreciation.

- The European impact

After the defeat of the Afghan troops by Safavid forces at the end of 1729, it took some while before the situation in and around Kerman returned to normal. It was only on 13 September 1731 that the Dutch sent their experienced duo of wool factors back to Kerman. This team consisted of the brothers Auwannees (Hovhannes) and Gojatoer Giroen (Khac'atur Girun), who had been active in the wool trade for the VOC since 1708[2141]. They had orders to buy *kork* and goats, and were succesful in obtaining both.

2138. VOC 1999, Lispensier to Oets, fol. 347-350; for a summary of this report see Floor [*Conflict*], p. 39; in June 1735, Clement reports that due to extortion people are forced to sell small quantities of wool in lots of 4, 10, and 20 mans at 12.5 mahmudis, VOC 2416, Clement to Koenad, 8/6/1735, fol. 1896.

2139. Dunlop, p. 670.

2140. Dillon, p. 242.

2141. VOC 2254, Gamronsch Dagregister, fol. 965; Auwannees mentions in a letter dated 27/12/1737 to Koenad that he had already been engaged in the wool trade for 29 years, VOC 2417, fol. 4161.

The British had also sent a wool factor to Kerman, as a result of which the traditional competition between the two companies came into the open. To give the VOC wool factor a competitive edge, he was given an advance of 300 tomans to invest in pre-clip purchasing (*pish-kharid*) of kork. This was a departure from VOC procedure, which thus far had not allowed its factor to follow this practice. However, the High Government in Batavia had given its approval for an experiment along these lines in 1731. Auwannees was successful in purchasing wool and asked for more money. To ensure the purchase of larger quantities of wool the director in Bandar 'Abbas decided to give Auwannees more money. This had the desired result[2142].

This initial success soon met its first hurdle when Tahmasp Qoli Khan (the future Nader Shah) made unacceptable demands from the VOC. In response the Company stopped its operations in Kerman on 4 October 1732. Auwannees returned to Bandar 'Abbas, but before doing so he raised money privately himself and invested it in the purchase of *kork*. He also appointed a reliable agent to inform him about trade developments. What the Dutch heard they did not like. The EIC agent, Mr. Cadix, was very successful in establishing himself both with the local government and the traders. The EIC and Cadix himself had advanced 2,000 tomans (Dfl. 85,000) among the wool collectors. The VOC director therefore decided to send Auwannees to Kerman to capture at least some share of the *kork* market. He received 500 tomans as working capital, which was considered sufficient to get the required quantities of *kork* and to be able to compete with the EIC. Mr Cadix, meanwhile, died and was replaced by Widwell[2143].

The *kork* trade had become quite sophisticated. The main sellers were a number local merchants from the Kerman region. They, or rather their agents, collected the *kork* among the pastoralists and mountain peasants. The merchants from Righabad were the most important group of local sellers[2144]. An eventual deal between the latter and the VOC and/or EIC, generally served as a trendsetter for the market price[2145]. Clement, the VOC wool buyer, therefore, counseled his successor van Loon in 1736, « to act

2142. VOC 2254, Resolutie Gamron, 30/12/1731, fol. 752-754.

2143. VOC 2322, de Cleen to governor-general, 30/10/1733, fol. 71-77.

2144. VOC 2416, Clement to Koenad, 22/7/1735, fol. 2115; VOC 2416, Report Clement to van Loon, 11/6/1736, fol. 1087.

2145. *Ibid.*, Clement to Koenad, 22/7/1735, fol. 2116.

towards them, as if you need no wool, so as to urge them to take quick action. Also keep an eye on the British. It is better to conclude a market agreement with them. This helps to keep the price and the [local] merchants down »[2146]. He also advised van Loon to have an informant among the Righabad merchants, who would be able to keep the Dutch abreast of the daily discussions among the merchants themselves as well as with the British. In this way, the Dutch could keep surprises to a minimum[2147].

There were mainly four players in the Kerman *kork* market. Apart from the local wool merchants, there were the VOC and the EIC, and the local weavers, the last also being the least influential. Each of the four parties tried to set up the others against each other, on occasion, so as to gain by the other's loss. The governor of Kerman regularly interfered in this process, whether his involvement sollicited or not. This political interference did not serve any economic objective, such as supporting local industry, but rather to line the governor's pocket. This framework had been functioning more or less well since 1659 and provided a stable basis for the *kork* trade. After 1730, there were two major changes in this configuration. First, as of 1735, the VOC and EIC concluded an agreement, on an annual basis, to form a joint front *vis-à-vis* the local merchants to keep prices down. Second, in 1737, new players presented themselves in the market, who intended to upset the VOC-EIC apple-cart. The latter development was of a short duration. The VOC-EIC *kork* ring provided stability in the *kork* trade, during a period when Persia in general, and Kerman in particular, suffered from military turmoil.

In July 1735, the VOC and EIC agents in Kerman concluded an oral agreement to pay not more than 11 mahmudis per man of *kork* in the case of small quantities. This price would not be increased, unless both parties agreed to that increase. This bold step proved to be a very effective and profitable mechanism for both companies. Prior to that date they had been forced to pay high and fluctuating prices for bad quality wool as a result of their fierce competition for *kork*[2148]. This agreement was the result of the unwillingness of the Righabad merchants to sell *kork* at 12.5 mahmudis per Tabriz man. The merchants wanted the same price as in 1734, viz. 30-34 mahmudis. Both the Dutch and British were not interested to buy wool at

---

2146. VOC 2416, Report Clement to van Loon, 11/6/1736, fol. 1087-1088.

2147. *Ibid.*, fol. 1089-1090; undoubtedly the British did the same, while the Persian merchants used this role of informant also to their own advantage.

2148. Matthee [East India].

that price. As a result of their united front they were able to conclude the purchase of wool at prices ranging from 12-15.5 mahmudis per Tabriz man[2149].

Despite the success of the agreement Clement remained suspicious of the British. When Widwell arrived unexpectedly in Kerman on 24 April 1736, Clement wondered what he was up to. He became even more wary when he learnt that Cockill, the EIC agent, himself would come to Kerman. Nevertheless, Clement hoped that he would be able to reach a new price agreement with Widwell, for the *kork* harvest looked promising[2150]. Widwell had nothing up his sleeve, however. He entered into a price agreement with van Loon, who had replaced Clement. This time, the price was fixed at 12 mahmudis for large quantities and 10-10.5 mahmudis for small lots[2151].

Thus, the *kork* trading season began auspiciously for both companies. However, apart from problems of lack of pack-animals a more serious issue arose. Van Loon reports that two merchants had arrived in Kerman, who had been sent by Ebrahim Khan, Nader Shah's brother, to buy *kork*. They had 1,500 tumans in silver with them and wanted to buy only red wool, which they intended to sell in Gilan. In addition, there were also another four less well connected merchants in Kerman who had similar ideas. These four did not act, out of fear that both companies would prevent them from trading. However, they wanted to see whether Ebrahim Khan's merchants would buy. If the latter did, they also would buy wool and take it to Baghdad. Cockill was very disturbed about this development and visited van Loon in his house on 15 August 1736. Both companies agreed on a common policy. They announced to the Righabad and other principal merchants that if they would sell *kork* to these interloping merchants, that neither the VOC nor the EIC would buy their remaining *kork*. Because of this threat the Righabad merchants refused to sell their wool to the "foreign" merchants[2152]. However, these were able to buy some wool, after all. For later it is reported that they bought 3,000 lbs which they sent to Georgia,

2149. VOC 2416, "Report Clement to van Loon", 11/3/1736, fol. 1088; VOC 2357, Auwannes to Koenad, 22/7/1735, fol. 909; VOC 2416, Clement to Koenad, 22/7/1735, fol. 2099; *ibid.*, fol. 2116-2119; VOC 2417, Clement to Koenad, 26/8/1735, fol. 3071.

2150. VOC 2417, Clement to Koenad, 24/4/1736, fol. 3158-3162.

2151. *Ibid.*, van Loon to Koenad, 29/8/1736, fol. 3210.

2152. *Ibid.*, fol. 3213-3215.

Aleppo and Smyrna[2153]. The new competitors, however, were not able to upset the vested interests of the Dutch and the British. The latter kept their agreement with the Dutch, although in other areas of trade competed vigorously with the Dutch, for example in the purchase of asafœtida[2154].

- Transport and other problems

What upset both companies more at that time was the lack of pack-animals. Initially, the transport of wool posed no problem. Pack-animals were to be had, if one took care to engage the service of a caravan driver beforehand. The standard contractual arrangements did not change either. Half of the freight cost had to be paid up front, half on delivery. The maximum number of days in which the wool had to be delivered in Bandar 'Abbas were stated in the contract. The rates changes varied, depending on the availability of the animals as is shown in Table 3.

The freight could be paid in either silver (= heavy) or copper (= black) mahmudis. In addition, some of the contracts stipulate the payment of some kind of tip, referred to as "good will" or as "tobacco coin" (tabax penning), at a rate of one copper mahmudi per carga or 60 lb[2155].

Thus, there was no major change with the previous period in contractual arrangements. What had changed was the reliability, and even the availability of transport. This was due to the military operations carried out by Nader Shah, who had an insatiable need for money and pack animals. Even the Europeans suffered from Nader Shah's requirements for cash and animals. Company caravans en route to Bandar 'Abbas were unloaded and the animals were taken to Seistan to assist in the war effort. The goods were stored in Dastiyab, where the *kalantar*, Pir Mohammad Agha, had friendly relations with both companies. An order (*ta'liqeh*) from the governor of Kerman did not stop the *mohassel* (tax collector) who requisitioned the animals; the Shah's orders prevailed over any other he stated[2156]. Clement obtained a new order which gave the transportation of VOC goods even priority over royal grain transports[2157]. However,

2153. VOC 2416, Koenad to governor-general, 10/12/1736, fol. 195.
2154. VOC 2417, van Loon to Koenad, 29/8/1736, fol. 2319.
2155. *Ibid.*, fol. 3197, 3221.
2156. *Ibid.*, Clement to Koenad, 23/9/1736, fol. 3231-3234.
2157. *Ibid.*, Clement to Koenad, 19/10/1736, fol. 3253-3254.

Clement had to lodge a formal protest with the governor to get transportation, which the latter promised, but did not deliver[2158].

Because Nader Shah was expected to pass through Kerman on his way to Qandahar, apart from pack-animals and grain also cash was demanded from the population in the Kerman region. Everybody was forced to pay, and those unwilling, severely beaten. The local merchants and Banians had to pay 1,500 tomans, for example[2159]. The European companies did not escape either, and were told to pay each 100 tomans. After some discussion the EIC had to pay 50 tomans, while the VOC went scot-free, because the "factor", Martijn (who had replaced van Loon), was ill and was about to leave the city[2160].

Nader Shah spent the last week of December of 1736 in Kerman as a result of which the extortions and requisitions continued. During his visit, Mirza Taqi (one of the most influential courtiers), informed Auwannees (who had taken over from Martijn) that the Shah was interested in the wool trade. He had samples of the various types of wool collected to determine which ones were the most profitable ones. If the wool trade looked profitable the shah intended to send some merchants to buy wool and sell it in Gilan and Turkey. Auwannees tried to convince Mirza Taqi that this would be a bad idea. For the merchants and thousands of people depended for their livelihood on the Dutch company. Every year, merchants came to Kerman to buy merchandise from the Europeans. If the European companies would leave, the merchants would not come anymore either. This would be a blow to the economy of Kerman, he prophesized. The shah could of course do what he liked, but it would ruin the city. Mirza Taqi seemed sufficiently impressed by this argument to try to induce Nader Shah to give up the idea of dealing in *kork*[2161].

However, things had already been set into motion. The wool collectors left shortly after *Nawruz* (New Year) to the mountain villages[2162]. On 2 April 1737, Hajie Derwieds (Hajji Darvish) arrived from Isfahan with 2,000 tomans to buy wool and shawls and to export these to Turkey. An Armenian merchant, Hadje Hasan (Hajji Hasan), also had come with the same

2158. VOC 2417, Clement to Koenad, from Kiskoen village, 25/11/1736, fol. 3280-3281.

2159. *Ibid.*, Martijn to Koenad, 17/11/1736, fol. 3277.

2160. *Ibid.*, Martijn to Koenad, 10/12/1736, fol. 3978.

2161. *Ibid.*, Auwannees to Koenad, 13/2/1737, fol. 4146-4148.

2162. *Ibid.*, Auwannees to Koenad, 19/3/1737, fol. 4170.

intentions. In addition, there were some agents of Isfahani merchants with orders to buy *kork* as well. All of them had orders to buy as much *kork*, of the red variety, as possible[2163].

Despite the early alarm signals the interference by "outsiders" in the *kork* market remained insignificant. The VOC and EIC again concluded a price agreement and forced a price of 12 mahmudis per Tabriz man[2164]. The intruders did not return in 1739. This may be was due to the fact that the pest had broken out among the mountain goats[2165]. However, this time the local weavers presented themselves en force in the market due to orders from the vice-roy to supply the army with 3,000 caps. The *namad* or felt makers therefore bought all kinds of *kork* at 7-8 mahmudis of heavy city coinage per Tabriz man[2166]. Auwannees, therefore, was concerned that he would not be able to obtain the required 6,000 lb. He asked whether, if need be, he might make up the difference with yellow wool[2167].

On 3 June 1739, Auwannees reached an agreement with Savage. They agreed on a price of 6 mahmudis of heavy silver or 10.5 copper mahmudis for red wool per Tabriz man. The red wool would be split equally between the VOC and EIC. Savage would take all the other types of wool, provided Auwannees paid 0.20 heavy silver mahmudis or 7 copper paisas more than the cost price of the other types of wool. This resulted in a price of 10.8 copper mahmudis per Tabriz man of uncleant wool for the VOC[2168].

Because of the high mortality rate among the goats, which Auwannees reported to be 90%[2169], and the demands by Nader Shah for all kinds of woolen clothes, the European companies were unable to obtain much wool[2170]. Auwannees was ordered to get as little as possible, however, and also not to get any yellow wool, because the VOC had received orders to discontinue the Kerman wool trade. The VOC directors did not want *kork* any more, because its quality was bad, its price high, while it yielded a loss

2163. VOC 2368, Auwannees to Koenad, 7/4/1737, fol. 3806.
2164. *Ibid.*, Auwannees to Koenad, 3/5/1737, fol. 3806v.
2165. VOC 2477, Auwannees to Koenad, 19/2/1739, fol. 789 and fol. 792.
2166. VOC 2510, Auwannees to Koenad, 21/5/1739, fol. 1318-1319.
2167. *Ibid.*, fol. 1317-1324.
2168. *Ibid.*, Auwannees to Koenad, 10/8/1739, fol. 1336-1342; *ibid.*, 18/8/1739, fol. 1337-1339.
2169. *Ibid.*, Auwannes to Koenad, 8/7/1739, fol. 1330-1331.
2170. VOC 2511, Auwannees to Koenad, 22/1/1740, fol. 1337; *ibid*, 14/12/1739, fol. 1332; VOC 2510, Auwannees to Koenad, 19/11/1739, fol. 1354-1357.

of 28% in the Netherlands[2171]. Auwannees was ordered to return to Bandar 'Abbas and have his books audited[2172].

At the time that the Dutch decided to abandon the *kork* trade the French East India Company obtained permission to start trading in Kerman, where it was allowed to build a house, and send an agent; it would enjoy the same privileges as the VOC and EIC. However, the French Company did not avail itself of this privilege. In 1743 it closed down its factory in Bandar 'Abbas and discontinued its trading activities in Persia[2173].

Although the Dutch had abandoned the *kork* trade the British continued their trading activities in Kerman. Savage had been able to obtain only 1,300 Tabriz mans of *kork* in 1739, due to Nader Shah's orders for woolen coats and caps[2174]. Trade in Kerman suffered because of the continuing extortion by Nader Shah. Towards the end of 1741, a royal courier arrived with orders for the payment of 2,000 tomans. Savage and Auwannees had to pay each 100 tomans, although the governor promised to pay it back. Auwannees, however, received only 20 tomans in cash and an IOU for the remainder[2175]. In 1742 the Dutch report that Kerman was almost empty of people, who had to pay 20,000 tomans to Nader Shah[2176]. Although, the British continued their activities, due to Nader Shah's depradations, this branch of trade was almost completely stopped[2177]. In 1747 people in Kerman were so oppressed that they were « obliged to sell their goats in the market to raise money for their tax, & the villages circumjacent had been plundered and their goats destroyed »[2178].

2171. VOC 2511, Resolutie Garmon, 26/2/1740, fol. 287; VOC 2477, Koenad to Auwannees, 24/3/1739, fol. 822-225.

2172. VOC 2511, Resolutie Gamron, 26/2/1740, fol. 287. Auwannees stayed, however, in Kerman, because of outstanding debts (VOC 2511, Auwannees to Koenad, 24/6/1740, fol. 1357-1358); he was still in Kerman towards the end of 1741 (VOC 2584, Auwannees to Koenad, 10/11/1741, fol. 2270).

2173. VOC 2510, Auwannees to Koenad, 19/11/1739, fol. 1356-1357; Lockhart, p. 286.

2174. VOC 2511, Auwannes to Koenad, 22/1/1740, fol. 1337; Lorimer, p. 117.

2175. VOC 2584, Auwannees to Koenad, 10/11/1741, fol. 2270-2271.

2176. VOC 2593, Clement to governor-general, 31/10/1742, fol. 1778.

2177. Amin, p. 126.

2178. Lorimer, p. 118.

The post Nader Shah period

With the death of Nader Shah in 1747, it was hoped that stability would return to the region and trade would be restored. The EIC, whose agent had fled from Kerman in 1744 or thereabouts, reopened its factory there, and bought 1,200 lb of *kork*. The Dutch hesitated, because of the cost of maintaining a wool buyer in Kerman. To trade in Kerman one needed a trustworthy person, who also had to be given working capital to pre-purchase *kork*. To send a European to Kerman would add Dfl. 6,000 per year to the operating cost, however. After deliberation, the VOC director in Bandar 'Abbas decided to send someone to Kerman, as soon as he had found a trustworthy person and the roads were safe again[2179].

The next year the Dutch had an Armenian wool factor, The Parsan, representing them in Kerman[2180]. The British ordered 50,000 lb of *kork*, preferably red, « without any limitations as to the price », but obtained 400 lbs only[2181]. This was due to a very high demand for woolens which drove the price of Kerman wool upwards, to 80 stuivers per lb. This not only caused many troubles, but also the VOC and EIC factors to return empty-handed to Bandar 'Abbas. The directors of both companies discussed the situation and decided to send the wool factors back, but not to the city of Kerman. The wool factors were ordered to go into the mountain ranges outside Kerman and buy the *kork* directly from the herders. The maximum price the wool factors were allowed to pay was 25 stuivers per lb. Both companies would equally split the quantities obtained. The wool factors left Bandar 'Abbas on 30 April 1750 with an amount of Dfl. 3,000 in cash and some merchandise[2182]. This forage was not very successful. One of the VOC wool factors was not able to buy any wool, because the merchants in Kerman paid 60 mahmudis (Dfl. 18) per Tabriz man for uncleaned *kork*[2183]. The other one, The Parsan, arrived one month later with 86 lb of cleaned wool at a price of Dfl. 4:1:5 per lb. Trade in Kerman was at a total standstill[2184].

2179. VOC 2784, Schoonderwoerd to governor-general, 10/10/1748, fol. 102-104, 232.

2180. VOC 2766, Schoonderwoerd to governor-general, 25/12/1749, fol. 43.

2181. Amin, p. 126; Lorimer, p. 118.

2182. VOC 2766, Schoonderwoerd to governor-general, 10/5/1750, fol. 219. One stuiver is 5 cents, thus 20 stuivers equals one guilder.

2183. VOC 2787, Schoonderwoerd to governor-general, 17/2/1751, fol. 26-27.

2184. *Ibid.*, Schoonderwoerd to governor-general, 8/3/1751, fol. 81.

• *Traditional VOC-EIC rivalry revived*

The Dutch factory in Bandar 'Abbas was temporarily closed in 1752, but reopened in 1753. The "entente" with the British was over, however, and there was a restoration of the traditional rivalry. This was probably due to the fact that the directors of both companies had made urgent requests for large quantities of wool[2185]. The Dutch factor accused his EIC colleague of inciting the local shawl weavers to complain to the governor that the VOC was buying the entire wool clip, so that they could not earn their living anymore. The weavers said nothing about the EIC purchases. After having heard the case the governor declined to interfere. Shortly thereafter, the weavers complained again and this time the governor confiscated all VOC wool that was in stock. However, after payment of Dfl. 500 the governor released the wool. This action may either have been caused by a higher profile of the VOC or because the British were really behind it. The EIC agent was very much upset by Dutch endeavours to capture the wool trade. For Bandar 'Abbas had allowed the wool factor to bid 2 stuivers per lb. higher than the EIC. As a result the EIC only obtained 3,000 lbs[2186].

The wool trade suffered from internal troubles. The VOC wool factor and many merchants who had gone to Kerman had to wait for months, for nothing could be done. When the strife was over there was no trade. Nevertheless, similar quantities of *kork* could be shipped as in 1753, when the availabilty of wool also had been limited due to depradations upon livestock by robbers and government officials[2187]. A fierce competition between the VOC and EIC started. Both tried to outdo the other in getting its hands on as much *kork* as possible. There were still problems in Kerman. There was a lack of laborers, which had consequences for the cleaning of the wool. An additional problem was that the villagers and merchants only were willing to accept "saheb coroenis" (sahebqran), or silver coins. Both companies suffered from these constraints and had to send silver from Bandar 'Abbas. This, of course, made *kork* more expensive[2188]. The British won this competition, because they accepted all four types of *kork*. Of course, the EIC wool factor used the old stratagem of stating that his

---

2185. VOC 1007, 21/7/1753, fol. 309; Amin, p. 126.

2186. VOC 2843, Schoonderwoerd to governor-general, 1/10/1753, fol. 31; Lorimer, p. 119.

2187. VOC 2863, Schoonderwoerd to governor-general, 20/12/1754, fol. 42; Lorimer, p. 119.

2188. VOC 2864, Schoonderwoerd to governor-general, 24/7/1755, fol. 71.

VOC colleague was doing this and therefore he could not do otherwise. « He mentioned his apprehensions that a refusal to take the black sort of wool wou'd be attended with bad consequences, as the Dutch made no exceptions to any colour and used every means in their power to engross the whole investment »[2189]. These alleged causes for these apprehensions are not borne out by VOC sources.

Because of the continued shortage of labor in Kerman, *kork* remained in a poor state. It also remained expensive, for it could not be bought at less than 50 stuivers per lb. Despite these conditions the two companies continued their buying spree. In 1758, the VOC bought the largest quantity since 1750, but their wool factor had overextended himself and went bankrupt. The governor was asked to assist Auwannees in collecting his outstanding debts. The latter was also ordered to return to Bandar 'Abbas to give an accounting of himself. He owed the VOC Dfl. 17,262 and therefore excused himself by referring to the governor, who would not allow him to leave[2190]. At the end of 1758 the VOC closed its factory in Bandar 'Abbas. The VOC continued to buy some *kork* via its factory on Khark island, but as of 1761 it stopped trading in this commodity altogether[2191].

The British also had their problems. Although larger quantities of *kork* had been obtained, its quality had deteriorated. Therefore, the EIC suffered a loss on the sale of *kork*. The EIC directors therefore instructed their staff that « no more of the black sort should be sent them and that an attempt should be made to buy red without either black or white »[2192]. In the following years, the EIC was able to buy less wool than before, while the conditions under which it had to operate also became much more difficult. In 1761, the oppression in Kerman was such that the EIC director informed the wool factor that if he believed that he could not remain there « in any degree of security » he might return to Bandar 'Abbas. The wool factor obtained the governor's permission to leave and departed immediately. In 1763, the EIC abandoned its Bandar 'Abbas factory and moved to Bushire. From this new location the EIC obtained several thousands of Tabriz mans of *kork* in 1766. However, with the abandoning of the Bushire factory in 1769, due to a conflict with Karim Khan, the EIC also discontinued the

2189. Lorimer, p. 120.

2190. VOC 2885, 8/9/1756, fol. 2; VOC 2937, 24/9/1757, fol. 7; VOC 2968, 1/5/1759, fol. 10, 20.

2191. Floor [The Dutch], p. 441-460.

2192. Lorimer, p. 120.

wool trade[2193]. The continued internal troubles in Persia also precluded any revival of the trade in *kork*. A report written in the 1780s by EIC staff mentions as one of the possible exports of Persia « wool of the Kerman sheep [sic] »[2194]. A similar report, written by the EIC Residents in Basra in 1790, does not consider Kerman wool as an interesting export commodity. Not more than 3,000 Tabriz mans per year could be exported of it « on account of its increased use for shawl-making and prohibitions against its export by Ja'far Khan » the Zand ruler[2195]. The result of these developments was that with the revived interest of trade with Persia at the beginning of the 19th century, Europeans had forgotten about the existence of *kork*.

The Qajar period

Despite the destruction of Kerman in 1794 at the end of the Qajar-Zand conflict it did not take many years for the *kork* trade and wool manufacturing to become prominent again. This time, however, the *kork* trade remained an entirely Iranian affair. By 1816, it was thriving enough, mainly producing shawls, to be noticed. After an initial growth of the industry, in harmony with the positive development of the economy at large, the *kork* industry suffered a slump at the end of the 1840s. An attempt by Amir Kabir (1850) to stimulate the industry failed. Gradually, less shawls were woven, and more *kork* was exported to Kashmir. An attempt by Naser al-Din Shah (1882) to stimulate the shawl industry had more success, and led to a revival in the 1880s that lasted till the beginning of the 20th century. Finally, with the change in dress and competition from cheap shawl imitations, and better returns on capital investment in the carpet industry, shawl production was reduced to almost nothing.

• *Production and trade*

European interest in *kork* was not revived after stability had returned to Iran with the establishment of the Qajar dynasty. However, as a raw material for the production of all kinds of textiles such as caps, hats, coats, other types of clothing, and carpets *kork* continued to play a role in the economy of Kerman.

2193. Amin, p. 127.
2194. Issawi, p. 88.
2195. Lorimer, p. 167.

Because Europeans either did not know about *kork*, and/or were not interested anymore in *kork* as an export commodity, information about it is less frequent. The first European to draw attention to the availability of *kork* or "khoolk" as a possible export article in the beginning of the 19th century was Fraser. « I think there is little doubt, that if a sufficient quantity of this down, which the natives call khoolk, could be brought to England, it would very greatly improve the texture of our imitation shawls, and render them saleable in the east to a far greater extent than they now are »[2196].

In the 1880s, *taftik* or coarse goat wool, was produced mainly in the provinces of 'Eraq, Golpaigan, Khorasan, Kermanshah, Nehavand, Lurestan, and in particular in Kurdistan and Kerman. In the latter area the production of *kork* was in particular singled out as a high quality product[2197]. For the production of *kork* remained concentrated in Kerman, although there were also production in Yazd, Baluchistan, Seistan, Khorasan and Afghanistan. In 1826, Fraser reports that *kork* is found, « not only in Kerman, but in more or less degree over all Khorasan, and the countries to the eastward; the mountains of which are favourable to the animals which produce it; but I do not believe it is to be had in any great quantities together »[2198]. Ferrier, in the 1850s, reports, for example, that the Hazaras manufactured « a cloth called kourk or barek »[2199]. In Yazd, however, there was only a small number of pastoralists and therefore little wool production. What locally was manufactured was mostly imported from Kerman and Khorasan. « Of Goats wool about 1000 Mens (13,000 lbs) might under present circumstances be procured at Yazd; worth, for the red, brown and white qualities in December 1849, 6 Kerans per Men, (5s/6d for 13 lbs); it ranges in price from 5 to 8 Kerans according to circumstances »[2200]. In Fars, there was a good deal of goat wool

2196. « The price [of *kork*] in Khorasan was between two and three reals per maun Tabreez (about 5d. a pound), but it was full of goat's coarse hair and very foul; I understood it was to be had much finer, clearer, and even cheaper, in Kerman (Fraser [*Caspian Sea*], p. 359).

2197. Stolze and Andreas, p. 22; Malcolm singled kork out as a possible major export commodity. « Karmania Wool. This valuable article which is found only in Persia, is in constant demand in Europe. It might be increased to any quantity. Noting is required but attention to the goats of that province and taking every means to propagate the breed », Issawi, p. 266.

2198. Fraser [*Caspian Sea*], p. 359.

2199. Ferrier [*Caravan*], p. 192.

2200. Amanat, p. 106.

production, but « it is not a fine quality and is for the most part black, brown, and red »[2201]. For the 1890s, Lorini reports that, a type of goat's fleece with a reputation such as that of Smyrna is to be found at Birjand, that is used for the production of shawls. These shawls were exported via Bombay to Great Britain[2202]. Shawl wool was also exported from Herat and Kandahar to India. The production of shawl-like clothes was peculiar for Herat province, Badakhshan and the Hazaras[2203].

Apart from the availability of goat hair from elsewhere, there was also the problem that the resource base of Kerman alone probably may not have been sufficient to produce the quantities of *kork* consumed locally and that exported to India. Consequently, either local use or export to India suffered a shortfall depending on the relative price that *kork* obtained. Towards the end of the 19th century the Bam Narmashir district in Kerman province produced about 10,000 Tabriz mans of wool, half of which was *kork*. It was purchased by merchants, « who buy in small quantities from the herdsmen and farmers; some lots of the best are, however, sent in by Khans from their estates. This wool is all exported to Kirman, Yazd, Kum, and Isfahan »[2204]. According to English, in the 1960s the Kerman goats produced an average fleece weight of 0.5-0.75 kg[2205]. Dillon, who rightly points out that *kork* is combed out of the coarser hair, submits that English's figures refer to the combined weight of hair and down. Basing himself on a shepherd's estimate, Dillon suggests that goats produce between 25-400 grams of *kork* annually[2206]. Dillon's figures seem to be realistic when compared with data from Baluchistan-Seistan where, in 1961, some

2201. Amanat, p. 115.

2202. Lorini, p. 192; he probably referred to « barak, a kind of woolen cloth », mentioned by Savage-Landor, II, p. 99; see also chapter III.

2203. *Imperial Gazetteer*, p. 32, 35; In Badakhshan, the Wakhan « women clean and spin the wool, while the men weave it into cloth. The valuable wool of Tibet, from which the costly shawls of Kashmir are fabricated, is yielded by the goat of Wakhan » (Wood, p. 246). It therefore would seem that the production area of *kork* had not changed much as compared with the 18th century.

2204. *Historical Gazetteer*, IV, p. 41.

2205. English, p. 133; his statement that goats had two clips per year is also borne out by Smith who states « the goats are shorn twice a year, in the spring and autumn », Goldsmid, I, p. 188.

2206. Dillon, p. 235.

350,000 goats only produced some 14,000 kg of *kork*, or 0.4 kg per goat[2207].

• *The use of kork*

Kork was mainly used locally in the manufacturing of all kinds of traditional textile products. The main items were *barak* and *patu* as well as all kinds of other felt items[2208]. « Nothing can be softer or warmer than these *bareks*, but unluckily they are badly woven- if they were better made, they would be preferable to every other kind of cloth »[2209]. Drouville confirms this when he reports that « during winter time, the Persians wrap themselves in large coats. These coats, which they call Kurks, are excessively warm »[2210]. The product that stood out among the textile products woven from *kork*, however, was the shawl. The term shawl, as we use it, is quite incorrect, shawl meaning the stuff, not a particular article of dress[2211].

Apart from shawl and felt products, *kork* was also used in carpets. « The woof is made from the wool or kurk of the Kerman sheep or goat, and dyed by the weavers themselves. This kurk is a speciality of Kerman. It is the underwool of the young animal which is shorn in early spring. The hair of the goat and wool of the sheep are used seperately, never if possible are they used together in making the same carpet »[2212].

2207. Italconsult, table 14. This figure may be too high, due to underestimation of the number of goats, however, see *ibid.*, I, p. 105. The same goats also produced 210,100 kg of *mu* or hair, or 0.6 kg per goat, which, when adding to the two figures, tallies with the estimate made by English.

2208. Amanat, p. 84 ; Polak [*Persien*], II, p. 169-170 ; for details on the production of felt articles see Wulff, p. 214 ff.

2209. Ferrier [*Caravan*], p. 192; *Historical Gazetteer* (IV, p. 75) mentions among the products of Berjand « kurk (a species of cloth) ».

2210. Drouville, I, p. 29.

2211. See chapter V.

2212. DCR 1376 (1894), p. 31; Blau, p. 104 contradicts this, however, and so does Gleadowe-Newcomen, p. 93, who states that « the woof of Kerman carpets is nearly always cotton, and is made from Manchester and Bombay yarn and twist; the warp and pile are wool ».

• *The export of goats*

During the 18th century, because of its quality the European companies tried to raise their own herds of Kerman goats outside their natural habitat to increase the *kork* resource base. Fath 'Ali Shah (1798-1834) also tried to relocate Kerman goats to other parts of Iran to increase the quantity of *kork*. « They have been removed to different parts of the kingdom, by orders of Futtuh Allee Shah the King, where, although the animals appear to thrive, the wool loses its qualities: and, what is still more unaccountable, it cannot be wrought to any perfection elsewhere than at Kirman. It is very curious that a similar occurrence occurs with regard to the Province of Kashmeer »[2213]. Also attempts to raise the Kerman goats in Great-Britain and France were unsuccessful. The goats either died en route, developed diseases, or yielded extreemly low fleeces[2214]. At the end of the 19th century a British consular report summarizes the situation as follows: « The splendid quality of Kerman wool is confined to the province, all attempts at introducing the same sheep [sic] in other districts having failed to produce wool of the superlative excellence possessed by the homegrown article »[2215].

This may also explain why Blau reports that there was a vigorous trade in *taftik*, or goat hair, in the 1850s. Goat hair was sold in Tabriz in 1849 at 25-30 Turkish piasters per 4 'oqqeh. It was inter alia exported to France and Austria. In 1855, some 184 loads were exported, and some 106 loads in 1856. The price obtained directly from the seller amounted to 4 qrans 10 shahis per 1000 methqals[2216]. Around 1900, prices for *kork* produced in the Bam district obtained 8 to 14 qrans per Tabriz man, while coarse wool only realized 4 to 8 qrans[2217].

Although, shawl manufacturing may not have been as booming as in 1816, « the manufacture of Shawls, etc. appears to consume nearly all the Goats Wool in the Country. The White is worth about 3,5 kerans per Men and the Yellow and the Brown 2 Kerans in Spring, the season for the product » in the 1840s[2218].

2213. Pottinger, p. 225.
2214. Irwin [*Kashmir*], p. 26-28.
2215. DCR, 1671 (1896), p. 5-6.
2216. Blau, p. 71.
2217. *Historical Gazetteer*, IV, p. 41.
2218. Amanat, p. 110. The duty at city gate was 6 shahis per man.

By the 1850s part of the *kork* production was exported to Germany and France. In Persia itself, *taftik* was mixed with (sheep's) wool for the production of carpets and other woven stuffs[2219]. This is confirmed by Polak who mentions that after Amir Kabir's death (in 1852) the shawl industry suffered a decline and that the bulk of the *kork* clip was exported to India, because of the high prices obtaining there[2220].

Around 1860, Kerman was selling much of its *kork* to Kashmir rather than manufacturing shawls itself. During the period 1880-96 most of the *kork* was used in the Persian shawl industry. The reduced demand for shawls thereafter led to a reorientation of the production capacity of the Kerman weaving industry towards the production of carpets and away from shawls. Demand for shawls came to almost nothing. However, goat hair, especially its down or *kork*, continued to be used and much appreciated by the Kerman carpet industry.

At present, *kork* is still an important product for many pastoralists in Iran. For example, *kork* produced in Baluchistan-Seistan had « a good commercial value, and is almost totally exported for the production of high quality hosiery » in the 1950s-60s[2221]. *Kork*, of course, is also still being collected in Kerman province by e.g. the Komanchi and Afshar tribes around Kerman. To that end they keep almost exclusively red goats to sell *kork* at high prices in Kerman[2222]. Prices in 1961, for *kork* produced in Baluchistan-Seistan amounted to an average of 18,500 *riyal*s per 100 kg[2223]. *Kork* is still used in the production of carpets and shawls and is exported as well[2224]. The latter also holds for Afghanistan where some

---

2219. Blau, p. 71.

2220. Polak [*Persien*], II, p. 168. Irwin [*Kashmir*], p. 9 writes that the Kashmir shawl weavers « often compelled to adulterate goat-fleece with Kirman's sheep's wool » which seems to contradict the information from Persia which reports the export of goat's wool or *kork*. However, Kerman exported both wool and goat hair.

2221. Italconsult, I, p. 105.

2222. To-day, *kork* is still collected by e.g. the Komanchi and Afshar tribes around Kerman. To that end they keep almost exclusively red goats to sell kork at high prices in Kerman, Stoeber, p. 84. See also English, Dillon, and Wulff referred to above.

2223. Italconsult, table 14.

2224. See Government of Iran - Foreign Trade Statistics, commodity item 495 (*mu va kork*).

336,718 kg of Kashmir wool, with a commercial value of US$ 942,811 was exported to the USA in 1978-79[2225].

Conclusion

There seems to be no evidence for Dillon's thesis that new capitalist economic institutions, in particular urban herding contracts, had come into being in the Kerman area. True, there was a group of wool merchants operating in Kerman, but there is every reason to believe that this group was also active prior to the advent of the Europeans. Also, their *modus operandi* was that of *pish-furush*, a commercial system that predates European involvement in the wool trade. In fact, a similar system operated in the silk trade, another Persian commodity Europeans actively traded in. In both cases, it was the Europeans who adapted themselves to local commercial conventions rather than bringing about changes. Furthermore, the European factors also bought small quantities of wool from the herders themselves.

The fact the Europeans were never able to satisfy their demand for wool also mitigates against Dillon's thesis. Attempts to enlarge the supply base of *kork* failed. *Kork* from outside its "natural habitat" was of an inferior quality and was unwanted, whilst the export of goats to establish a production base outside Persia also failed. Prices were not stable either, as Dillon has it. Prices in the pre-1730 period fluctuated considerably due to fierce Dutch-British competition, and only between 1700-15 was there price stability. Between 1735-40, the VOC and EIC wool buyers were once again able to bring price stability to the market through a price agreement between the two Companies. This agreement was very effective as is shown in Table 10. The price dropped immediately with 50% as soon as the VOC-EIC agreement became effective. This was a remarkable achievement, given the fact that the wool trade still suffered from political interference, requisitions of pack-animals for military operations, natural disaster, and reduced supply. The appearance of Persian merchants in the Kerman wool market in 1736 was unable to change the situation. The Europeans continued to dominate the market, but not its supply.

2225. Democratic Republic of Afghanistan, State Planning Committee, Central Statistics Office: Statistics of Exports of Goods during 1978-1979, p. 71; similar exports also took place in preceding years, see the same publication for the earlier years. There are no data available for export of Kashmir wool after that date.

In fact, the European companies themselves brought more competition to the market, because they were unable to agree upon a new price agreement in 1753. After a brief, but hard fought competition for slinking *kork* supplies, the Dutch abandoned the trade in Kerman wool in 1758, due to its negative returns. The British continued, but for another decade only. Supply continued to decrease as did its quality.

What the Europeans could not control was the political and economic context of the Kerman wool trade. As is clear from Table 9, the annual turnover in this trade after having peaked in 1736 went fast down-hill, never to recover. This low turnover occurred despite a very high demand for *kork* from the European companies. The reduced supply was partly due to competing demand by Nader Shah to supply his army with warm clothing, partly due to very high mortality among the goat herd in 1739. The ensuing war and strife, with its demands for money and supplies, did not provide an incentive for the development of goat production or wool trade. European attempts to transplant the *kork* resource base, the Rayen goats, failed, for the goats either died outside their natural habitat or produced very little down. With the return of stability in Iran as of 1800, the Kerman wool industry slowly revived. European interest in *kork*, however, did not. Kerman began producing shawls again as well as a number of other felt and woolen products for the market. This industry was an exclusive urban industry producing for the urban market, for its products were expensive, some of its products requiring one year's work before being completed.

After initial success, the shawl industry was hit again and fell into a sudden decline, suffering from competition from Indian and European fabrics. Kerman started to export *kork* again, this time to India. Unfortunately, we do not know anything about the trading arrangements. No doubt, the well established *pish-forush* system was operative in the Kerman area to induce the pastoralists and peasants to sell their wool to the ambulatory middlemen. In the 1880s, with help from Naser al-Din Shah, the shawl industry made a come-back and became Kerman's most important economic activity for about 20 years. However, due to a change in taste, competition from cheaper imitations, and higher returns in the carpet industry, shawl manufacturing went virtually out of business by 1910. Only a limited capacity survived for the production of special items on command. *Kork*, of course, is still being collected and is used in the production of carpets.

Table 8 : Volume of kork shipped from Bandar 'Abbas (in lb)

Year	VOC	EIC
1732	13,452	
1733	65,348	115,759
1734	44,063	121,500
1735	19,620	
1736	86,637	141,750
1737		
1738	20,540	
1739	10,000	
1740	none	
1745	none	19,375
1746	none	37,500
1747	none	19,887
1748	none	16,281
1749	1,098	16,281
1750	n.a.	2,375
1751	none	-.-
1752	none	2,500
1753	5,767	16,906
1754	9,111	22,525
1755	17,844	37,437
1756	1,595	56,250
1757	21,828	86,250
1758	13,621	75,375
1759	-.-	-.-
1760	-.-	30,000
1761	some	11,250
1762	4,300	1,250
1763	none	28,125

Sources: VOC : 2254, fol. 644; 2322, fol. 137v; 2357, fol. 442; 2323, fol. 248; 2448, fol. 249; 2476, fol. 138; 2766, fol. 87; 2843, fol. 45; 2863, fol. 50; 3027, fol. 3; 3092, fol. 29. Ricks, appendix H, p. 418; Dillon, p. 224 (table 7-1) for the years 1733-36. The EIC data have been converted from Tabriz man (=6.25 lb) into pounds.

Table 9: Prices paid for kork by the VOC (1732-1755)

Year	Price (mahmudis)
1732	
1733	
1734	30-34
1735	17
1736	14
1737	12
1738	10.8
1739	10.5
1749	16

Table 10 : Cost for the transport of wool from Kerman to Bandar 'Abbas

Date	Rate per 100 mans or 630 lb		number of days
	silver mahmudis	copper mahmudis	
February 1734	120	32	
May 1734	125	25	
September 1735	90	25	
October 1735	85	-	
October 1735	90	-	
January 1736	113.7	25	
March 1736	100	30	
April 1736	120	27	
August 1736	88	120	27

Sources: VOC : 2323, fol. 825 and 834; 2417, fol. 3086, 3088, 3090, 3126, 3128, 3190, 3197, 3221, 3974-3975.

BIBLIOGRAPHY AND ABBREVIATIONS

Abbreviations

EIC : East India Company.
EIr : *Encyclopædia Iranica*, Ehsan Yarshater ed., London and Costa Mesa, 1982 f.
EI : *Encyclopædia of Islam*, 2nd ed., Leiden, 1960 f.
VOC : Dutch East Indies Company.

Archives

AP : Great-Britain, House of Commons, Parliamentary Papers, Accounts and Papers.

ARA : Algemeen Rijks Archief (General State Archives, the Hague)

- Incoming letters KA, which as of 1980 were relabeled as VOC. In the ARA a list is available providing the link between the KA and VOC archive numbers.
- Collectie Geleynsen de Jonge no. 25, Anonymous, *Description of Persia.*
- *Hooge Regering Batavia*, no. 896.

DCR : Great-Britain, Diplomatic and Consular Reports.

MAE : Archives du Ministère des Affaires Etrangères, (Quai d'Orsay, Paris). Perse, Mémoires et Documents, II.

Published Materials

Abdullaev : Z. Z. Abdullaev, Promyshlennost i zarozhdenie rabochego klassa Irana v kontse XIX-nachala XX vv., Baku, 1963.

Abrahamian : E. Abrahamian, "Early Trade of the Northern Provinces of Persia: A Document", in *Iranian Studies*, 16 (1983), p. 279-293.

Adamiyat : F. Adamiyat, *Amir Kabir va Iran*, Tehran, 1334/1955.

Adams : I. Adams, *Persia by a Persian*, n.p., 1900.

Afshar [*Kolliyat*] : Iraj Afshar, Kolliyat-e Athar-e Adib Qasemi-ye Kermani, Tehran, 1372/1995, index "Shal".

Afshar [*Yadgarha*] : Iraj Afshar, *Yadgarha-ye Yazd*, 2 vols, Tehran, 1355/1976.

Afshar [Zilu] : Iraj Afshar, "Zilu", in Annette Ittig ed., *The Carpets and Textiles of Iran, Iranian Studies*, 25 (1992), p. 31-36.

Afshar Sistani : Iraj Afshar Sistani, *Negahi be Azerbeijan-e Gharbi*, Tehran, 1369/1990.

Agashirunova : S. S. Agashirunova, *Material'naya kul'tura Lezgii, XIX- nachala XX vv*, Moscow, 1970.

'Ala'i : 'Ali Akbar 'Ala'i, "'Alaqehbandi", in *Honar va Mardom*, 124-5 (1351/1972).

[*'Alamara-ye Safavi*] : *'Alamara-ye Safavi*, ed. Y. Shokri, Tehran, 1350/1971.

[*'Alamara-ye Shah Esma'il*] : *'Alamara-ye Shah Esma'il*, ed. Asghar Montazer Saheb, Tehran, 1349/1970.

[*'Alamara-ye Shah Tahmasp*] : *'Alamara-ye Shah Tahmasp*, anonymous, ed. Iraj Afshar, Tehran, 1370/1991.

'Ali-ye Kateb : Ahmad b. Hosein b. 'Ali-ye Kateb, *Tarikh-e Jadid-e Yazd*, ed. Iraj Afshar, Tehran 1345/1966.

'Allami : Abu'l-Fazl 'Allami, *A'in-i Akbari*, 3 vols, I. tr. H. Blochmann; II, III. tr. H.S. Jarrett, Calcutta, 1868-94.

Amanat : Abbas Amanat ed., *Cities & Trade: Consul Abbott on the Economy and Society of Iran 1847-1866*, London, 1983.

Ames [Fashion] : F. Ames, "The Fashion of the Kashmir Shawl in France", in *Hali*, 5/1 (1982), p. 59-100.

Ames [*Kashmir*] : F. Ames, *The Kashmir Shawl*, The Antique Collectors, Woodbridge, 1986.

Amin : A. A. Amin, *British Interests in the Persian Gulf 1747-1780*, Leiden, 1976.

Amory : C. Amory Jr., *Persian Days*, Boston-New York, 1929.

Anavian and Anavian : G. Anavian and R. Anavian, *Royal Persian and Kashmir Brocade*, Tokyo, 1975.

Anet : Cl. Anet, *Through Persia in a motor car*, London, 1907.

Arnold : A. Arnold, *Through Persia by Caravan*, New York, 1877.

Asef : Mohammad Hashem Asef [Rostam al-Hokumeh], *Rostam al-Tavarikh*, ed. Mohammad Moshiri, Tehran, 1348/1969.

Ashraf : Ahmad Ashraf, *Mavane'-ye tarikh-e roshd-e sarmayehdari dar Iran: doureh-ye Qajariyyeh*, Tehran 1359/1970.

[*Asnad-e Siyasi*] : *Asnad va Mokatebat-e Siyasi-ye Iran*, ed. 'Abdol-Hosein Nava'i, Tehran, 1363/1984.

Astarabadi : Seyyed b. Morteza Hoseini Astarabadi, *Az Sheikh Safi ta Shah Safi*, ed. Ehsan Eshraqi, Tehran, 1364/1985.

[*Astarabadnameh*] : *Astarabadnameh*, ed. Masih Dhabihi, Tehran, 1348/1969.

Bafqi : Mohammad Mofid Mostaufi Bafqi, *Jame'-ye Mofidi*, 3 vols, ed. Iraj Afshar, Tehran, 1340-1/1961-2.

Baker : Valentine Baker, *Clouds in the East*, London, 1876.

Bakhash : Shaul Bakhash, *Iran: Monarchy, Bureaucracy & Reform under the Qajars 1858-1896*, London, 1978.

Barbaro and Contarini : *Travels to Tana and Persia by J. Barbaro and A. Contarini*, ed. Lord Stanley, Hakluyt No. 49, 2 vols in one, London, 1873.

Bardsiri : Mir Mohammad Sa'id Moshizi Bardsiri, *Tazkereh-ye Safavi-e Kerman*, ed. Bastani Parizi, Tehran, 1369/1990.

Barsavush : S. M. Hoseini Barsavush, *Farhang va joghrafiya-ye 'Aliabad Kotul*, Tehran, 1370/1991.

Barthold : W. Barthold, *An Historical Geography of Iran*, Princeton, 1984.

Bassett : J. Bassett, *Persia, the Land of the Imams*, New York, 1886.

Bastani Parizi [*Farmanframa*] : Mohammad Ebrahim Bastani Parizi, *Farmanframa-ye 'Alam*, Tehran, 1364/1985.

Bastani Parizi [*Ganj*] : Mohammad Ebrahim Bastani Parizi, *Ganj 'Ali Khan*, 3rd ed., Tehran, 1368/1989.

Bazin : Marcel Bazin, *Le Talech, une region ethnique au nord de l'Iran*, 2 vols, Paris, 1980.

Bazin et al : Marcel Bazin *et al*, *Gilan et Azarbayjan oriental*, Paris, 1982.

Bastiaensen : *Souvenir de la Perse safavide et autres lieux de l'Orient (1674-1678)*, ed. Michel Bastiaensen, Brussel, 1985.

Beattie : M. H. Beattie, *Carpets of Central Persia*, Sheffield, 1976.

Begdili : Gholam Hosein Begdili, *Tarikh-e Begdili - Madarek va Asnad*, Tehran, 1367/1988.

Bélanger : C. Bélanger, *Voyage aux Indes-Orientales pendant les années 1825 à 1829*, 2 vols in one, Paris, n.d.

Bell : John Bell, *Travels from St. Petersburg in Russia to Various parts of Asia in 1716, 1719, 1722, &c.*, in John Pinkerton ed., *A General Collection of Voyages and Travels*, London, 1811.

Benjamin : S.G.W. Benjamin, *Persia and the Persians*, London, 1887.

Berchet : Guglielmo Berchet, *La Republicca di Venezia e la Persia*, Torino, 1865, reprint 1976.

Bier : Carol Bier ed., *Woven from the Heart, Spun from the Soul*, Washington D.C., 1987.

Binning : R.M.B. Binning, *Journal of Two Years' Travels*, 2 vols, London, 1852.

Bird : Isabella Bird (Mrs. Bishop), *Journeys in Persia and Kurdistan*, 2 vols, London, 1891, reprint 1988.

Birge : J. K. Birge, *The Bektashi order of dervishes*, London, 1937.

Blau : Otto Blau, *Die commerzielle Zustaende Persiens*, Wien, 1858.

Boré : Eugène Boré, *Correspondance et Mémoires d'un Voyageur en Orient*, 2 vols, Paris, 1840.

Brett : Katherine B. Brett, *Origins of Chintz*, London, 1970.

Brosset : M.F. Brosset, *Histoire de la Georgie depuis l'antiquité jusqu'au XIXe siècle*, 4 vols in two, St. Petersburg, 1849-58.

Browne [History] : Edward G. Browne, *A Literary History of Persia*, 4 vols, London, 1924.

Browne [A Year] : Edward G. Browne, *A Year Amongst The Persians*, London, 1893, reprint 1970.

Brugsch : H. Brugsch, *Die Reise der K.K. Gesandtschaft nach Persien 1861-1862*, 2 vols, Berlin, 1863.

Brydges-Jones : H. Brydges-Jones, *An Account of the Transactions of H. M.'s Mission to the Court of Persia*, London, 1824, reprint 1976.

[Burgess] : *Letters from Persia written by Charles and Edward Burgess, 1822-1855*, ed. Benjamin Schwartz, New York, 1942.

Bushev [Besposhlinnaya torgovliya] : P. P. Bushev, "Besposhlinnaya torgovliya Russkikh kuptsov v Irane v 1732-1747 gg." in N.A. Kuznetosova ed., *Iran - istoria i kultura v srednie veka i novoe vremia*, Moscow, 1980.

Bushev [Iranskii kuptsina] : P. P. Bushev, "Iranskii kuptsina Kazem beg v Rossii, 1706-1709 gg", in A. Z. Arabadzhiana and N. A. Kuznetsova eds., *Iran - sbornik statei*, Moscow, 1973.

[Carmelites] : *A chronicle of the Carmelites in Persia and the Papal mission of the seventeenth and eighteenth centuries*, anonymous, 2 vols, London, 1939.

Cassin : J. Cassin, "Chand-Dar - The Moon-Shawls of Kashmir", in *Hali* 3/4 (1981), p. 290-293.

Chardin : Jean Chardin, *Les Voyages*, 10 vols, ed. L. Langlès, Paris, 1811.

Chenciner and Mogomdkhanov : Robert Chenciner and Magomedkhan Mogomdkhanov, "Persian Exports to Russia from the Sixteenth to the Nineteenth Century", in *Iran*, 30 (1992), p. 123-130.

Cook : John Cook, *Voyages and Travels through the Russian Empire, Tartary, and Part of Persia*, 2 vols, Edinburgh, 1770.

Coolhaas : W. Ph. Coolhaas, *Generale Missieven van Gouverneurs-Generaal en Raden aan Heren XVII der Verenigde Oostindische Compagnie*, 8 vols, The Hague, 1960 f.

Curzon : R. G. Curzon, *Persia and the Persian Question*, 2 vols, London, 1890.

Dal Farra : Marta Dal Farra, "A 'Safavid Cadabi' in the Royal Ontario Museum Reconsidered", in *Iranian Studies*, 22 (1992), p. 81-90.

D'Allemagne : H. d'Allemagne, *Du Khorasan au Pays des Backhtiyaris*, 2 vols, Paris, 1911.

De Cerceau : M. de Cerceau, *The Compleat History of Thamas Kouli Khan, Late Sovereign of Persia*, in 2 parts, London, 1748.

Dehkhoda : Ali Akbar Dehkhoda, *Loghatnameh-ye Dehkhoda*, Tehran, 1946-1979.

De la Harpe : M. de la Harpe, *Abregé de l'histoire générale des voyages*, Paris, 1780.

Della Valle [Voyages] : Pietro Della Valle, *Voyages*, 2 vols, Paris, 1663.

Della Valle [Extract] : "Extract of the Travels of Della Valle", in John Pinkerton ed., *A General Collection of Voyages and Travels*, IX, London, 1811.

De Windt : Harry de Windt, *A Ride to India*, London, 1891.

Dhabiyan : *Safarnameh-ye Baron Fiyudur Kurof 1834-1835*, tr. Eskander Dhabiyan, Tehran, 1372/1993.

[Die wirtschaftlichen] : "Die wirtschaftlichen Verhaeltnissen Persiens", in *Berichte und Handel*, XIV, Heft 7, Berlin, 1910.

Diba : Leyla S. Diba, "Clothes - Safavids", *EIr* , q.v.

Dickinson and Welch : Dickinson and Welch, *The Houghton Shahnama*. 2 vols, Cambridge, 1981.

Digard : Jean-Pierre Digard, *Techniques des nomades baxtyari d'Iran*, London and Paris, 1981.

Dillon : R. J. Dillon, *Carpet Capitalism and Craft Involution in Kirman, Iran: A Study in Economic Anthropology*, (unpublished thesis Columbia University, 1976).

Dhabihi : Masih Dhabihi, *Astarabadnameh*, Tehran, 1348/1969.

Dhoka' : Yahya Dhoka', *Lebas-e zanan*, Tehran, 1336/1957.

Doerfer : G. Doerfer, *Türkische und Mongolische Elemente im Neupersischen*, 4 vols, Wiesbaden, 1963-1975.

Donboli : 'Abd al-Rahman Razzaq Donboli, *Ma'ather-e Soltaniyya*, ed. Gholam Hosein Sadri Afshar, Tehran, 1351/1972.

Don Juan : *Don Juan of Persia, a Shi'ah Catholic 1560-1604*, tr. G. le Strange, New York-London, 1926.

Dozy : R. P. Dozy, *Dictionnaire détaillé des noms des vêtemens chez les Arabes*, Leiden, 1843; tr. H. 'A. Harawi, *Farhang-e lebas-e mosalmanan*, Tehran, 1345/ 1966.

Drouville : G. Drouville, *Voyage en Persie pendant les années 1812 et 1813*, 2 vols, Paris, 1819, reprint 1976.

Dubeux : Louis Dubeux, *La Perse*, Paris, 1841.

Du Mans [*L'estat*]: Raphaël Du Mans, *L'estat de la Perse en 1660*, ed. Ch. Schefer, Paris, 1890.

Du Mans : *Raphael Du Mans*, ed. Francis Richard, 2 vols. Vol. I, Biographie. Correspondance; vol. II, Estats et Mémoire, in *Moyen Orient & Océan Indien, XVIe-XIXe s.*, IX, Paris, 1995.

Dunlop : H. Dunlop, *Bronnen tot de geschiedenis der Oostindische Compagnie in Perzie*, The Hague, 1930.

Edwards : Cecil Edwards, *The Persian Carpet*, London, 1953, 4th ed. 1975.

Ehsani : 'Abdol-Hosein Ehsani, *Majmu'eh-ye qalamkar-e Iran*, Tehran, 1350/1971.

English : P. W. English, *City and Village in Iran. Settlement and Economy in the Kerman Basin*, Madison, 1966.

Erdmann : K. Erdmann, *Oriental Carpets and Their History*, London, 1976.

Esfahani [*Nesf-e jahan*] : Mohammad Mehdi b. Mohammad Reza al-Esfahani, *Nesf-e jahan fi ta'rif-e Esfahan*, ed. Manuchehr Sotudeh, Tehran, 1340/1961.

Esfahani [*Ketab*] : Mir Seyyed 'Ali Reza Janab al-Esfahani, *Ketab al-Esfahan*, Isfahan, 1303/1924.

Esfahani [*Kholasat*] : Mohammad Ma'sum b. Kh^{w}ajegi Esfahani, *Kholasat al-Siyar*, ed. Iraj Afshar, Tehran, n.d.

E'temad al-Saltaneh [*Ma'ather*] : E'temad al-Saltaneh, Mohammad Hasan Khan [Sani' al-Douleh], *Al-ma'ather wa'l-athar*, Tehran, 1307/1889 (litho).

E'temad al-Saltaneh [*Montazam*] : E'temad al-Saltaneh, Mohammad Hasan Khan [Sani' al-Douleh], *Montazam-e Naseri*, 3 vols, Tehran, 1300/1883.

E'tezad al-Saltaneh : 'Aliquli Mirza E'tezad al-Saltaneh, *Iksir al-Tavarikh*, ed. Jamshid Kayanfar, Tehran, 1370/1991.

Falsafi : Nasrollah Falsafi, *Zendegani-ye Shah 'Abbas*, 5 vols, 3rd. ed., Tehran, 1344.

[*Farhang-e loghat*] : *Farhang-e loghat va estelahat-e mardom-e Kerman*, ed. A.-Q. Hoseini, Tehran, 1370/1991.

Farrokh Khan : *Majmu'a-ye Asnad va Madarek-e Farrokh Khan Amin al-Douleh*, ed. K. Isfahaniyan and Q. Rushani (Zafaranlu), 5 vols, Tehran, 1346-57/1967-78.

Fasa'i : Hajj Mirza Hasan Hoseini Fasa'i, *Tarikh-e Farsnameh-ye Naseri*, 2 vols, Tehran, 1314q/1892 (litho).

Feilberg : C. G. Feilberg, *Les Papis*, Copenhagen, 1952.

Ferrier [*Caravan*]: J. P. Ferrier, *Caravan Journeys and Wanderings in Persia, Afghanistan etc.*, London, 1857.

Ferrier [An English View] : R. W. Ferrier, "An English View of Persian Trade in 1618. Reports from the merchants Edward Pettus and Thomas Barker", in *Journal of the Economic and Social History of the Orient*, 19 (1976), p. 182-214.

Ferrier [*British-Persian Relations*] : R. W. Ferrier, *British-Persian Relations in the 17th century* (unpublished dissertation Cambridge University, 1970).

Ferrier [*The Arts*] : R. W. Ferrier, *The Arts of Persia*, London, 1991.

Ferrières-Sauveboeuf : Comte L. F. de Ferrières-Sauveboeuf, *Mémoires historiques, politiques et geographiques des voyages du comte de Ferrières-Sauveboeuf faits en Turquie, en Perse et en Arabie depuis 1782 jusqu'en 1789*, 2 vols, Paris, 1790.

Feuvrier : Dr Feuvrier, *Trois ans à la cour de Perse*, Paris, n.d.

Figueroa : *G. Silva y Figueroa, L'ambassade de Silva Figueroa en Perse*, tr. de Wicquefort, Paris, 1667.

Filmer : H. Filmer, *The Pageant of Persia*, New York, 1936.

Flandin and Coste : E. Flandin and P. Coste, *Voyage en Perse de M.M. Eugène Flandin, peintre, et Pascal Coste, architecte, 1840-41*. 2 vols, Paris, 1851.

Floor [A Description] : Willem Floor, "A Description of Masqat and Oman anno 1673/1084 Q", in *Moyen Orient & Ocean Indien XVI-XIXe s.*, 2 (1985),p. 1-69.

Floor [*Conflict*] : Willem Floor, *Commercial Conflict between Persia and the Netherlands 1712-1718*, in University of Durham Occasional Paper Series, No. 37, 1988.

Floor [*Fiscal History*] : Willem Floor, *A Fiscal History of Iran in the Safavid and Qajar Periods*, New York, 1999.

Floor [Guilds and futuvvat] : Willem Floor, "Guilds and futuvvat in Iran", in *Zeitschrift der Deutschen Morgenländischen Gesellschaft*, 134 (1984), p. 106-114.

Floor [*Hokumat*] : Willem Floor, *Hokumat-e Nader Shah*, tr. Abu'l-Qasem Serri, Tehran, 1367/1988.

Floor [*Industrialization*] : Willem Floor, *Industrialization in Iran 1900-1941*, in University of Durham Occasional Paper Series, 23, Durham, 1984.

Floor [*Labour*] : Willem Floor, *Labour Unions, Law, and Conditions in Iran 1900-1941*, in University of Durham Occasional Paper Series, No. 26, 1985.

Floor [Persian Silk] : Willem Floor, "The Persian Silk Trade in the Seventeenth Century", in Ch. Melville ed., *Safavid Persia. The History and Politics of an Islamic Society*, London, 1996, p. 323-368.

Floor [The Decline] : Willem Floor, "The Decline of the Dutch East Indies Company in Bandar 'Abbas (1747-1759)", in *Moyen Orient & Ocean Indien, XVI-XIXe s.*, VI, Paris, 1989, p. 45-80.

Floor [The Dutch] : Willem Floor, "The Dutch on Khark Island - A Commercial Mishap", in *International Journal of Middle Eastern Studies*, 24 (1992), p. 441-460.

Floor [The merchants] : Willem Floor, "The merchants in Qajar Iran", in *Zeitschrift der Deutschen Morgenländischen Gesellschaft*, 126 (1976), p. 101-135.

Floor [Traditional] : Willem Floor, "Traditional Crafts and Modern Industry in Qajar Iran", in *Zeitschrift der Deutschen Morgenländischen Gesellschaft*, 141 (1991), p. 317-352.

Floyer : E. A. Floyer, *The Unexplored Baluchistan*, London, 1882.

Forster : "Extract from Forster's Travels in N. Persia (1784)", in John Pinkerton ed., A General Collection of Voyages and Travels, London, 1811.

Francklin : William Francklin, Observations made on a tour from Bengal to Persia in the years 1786-1787, London, 1790, reprint 1976.

Fraser [Caspian Sea] : James B. Fraser, Travels and Adventures in the Persian Provinces and the Southern Banks of the Caspian Sea, London, 1826.

Fraser [Narrative] : James B. Fraser, Narrative of a Journey into Khorasan in the Years 1821 & 1822, London, 1825, reed. Delhi, 1984.

Fraser [Travels] : James B. Fraser, Travels in Koordistan, Mesopotamia, 2 vol., London, 1840.

Fraser [Winter's Journey] : James B. Fraser, A Winter's Journey from Constantinople to Teheran, 2 vol. in one, London, 1838, reprint 1973.

Freygang : Madame de Freygang, *Letters from the Caucasus and Georgia*, London, 1823.

Fryer : John Fryer, *A New Account of East India and Persia Being Nine Years' Travels, 1672-1681*, 3 vols, Hakluyt Second Series, London, 1909-15.

Fumeni : 'Abdol-Fattah Fumeni, *Tarikh-e Gilan*, ed. Manuchehr Sotudeh., Tehran, 1349/1970.

Fursat : Fursat Husayni Shirazi, *Athar-i `Ajam*, litho, Tehran 1314/1896-7.

Gabriel : A. Gabriel, *Im Weltfernen Orient*, Muenchen-Berlin, 1929.

Gaube and Wirth : H. Gaube and E. Wirth, *Der Bazar von Isfahan*, Wiesbaden, 1978.

Gazetteer of Afghanistan : *Historical and Political Gazetteer of Afghanistan*, Kandahar-Graz, 1980.

Gervers : Veronika Gervers, "Oriental Carpets from Eastern Europe", in Jennifer Scarce ed., *Islam in the Balkans - Persian Art and Culture of the 18th and 19th Centuries*, Edinburgh, 1979.

Gleadow-Newcomen : A. H. Gleadow-Newcomen, *Report of a commercial mission to Persia*, Calcutta, 1904.

Glukhohed : V. S. Glukhohed, *Problemi ekonomicheskogo razvitia Irana*, Moscow, 1968.

Gluck and Gluck : J. Gluck and S. Gluck, *A Survey of Persian Handicraft*, Tehran-Tokyo, 1977.

Gmelin : S. G. Gmelin, *Reise durch Russland*, 3 vols, St. Petersburg, 1774.

Gobineau : comte Arthur de Gobineau, *Trois Ans en Asie*, 2 vols, Paris, 1922.

Goedel : R. Goedel, *Ueber den pontischen Handelsweg und die Verhaeltnisse des europaeisch-persischen Verkehres*, Wien, 1849.

Goetz : Hermann Goetz, "The History of Persian Costume", in Alexander Pope and Phyllis Ackerman, *A Survey of Persian Art, from Prehistoric Times to the Present*, London-New York, 1938-39, III, p. 2227-2256.

Golchin Ma'ani : Ahmad Golchin Ma'ani, *Shahr-ashub dar she'r-e farsi*, Tehran, 1346/1967.

Goldsmid : Sir Frederic J. Goldsmid, *Eastern Persia, An Account of the Journeys of the Persian Boundary Commission 1870-71-72*, 2 vols, London, 1876.

Golestaneh : Abu'l-Ghasan b. Mohammad Amin Golestaneh, *Majmal al-Tavarikh*, ed. Modarres Razavi, Tehran, 2536/1977.

Golriz : Mohammad Ali Golriz, *Minudar ya Bab al-jenna-ye Qazvin*, Tehran, 1337/1958.

Golzari : Mas'ud Golzari, *Safarnameh-ye Astarabad va Mazandaran va Gilan*, Tehran, 2535/1976.

Gopal : Surendra Gopal, *Indians in Russia in the 17th and 18th Centuries*, New Delhi, 1988.

Gramlich : Richard Gramlich, *Die Schiitischen Derwischorden Persiens, Dritter teil: Brauchtum und Riten*, 3 vols, Wiesbaden, 1981.

Greenfield : J. Greenfield, *Die Verfassung des persischen Staates*, Berlin, 1904.

Hackluyt : Richard Hackluyt, *The Principal Navigations, Voyages, Trafiques and Discoveries of the English Nation*, 8 vols, New York, 1927.

Hadow [1923] : R. H. Hadow, *Report on the Trade and Industry of Persia to June, 1923*, London, 1923.

Hadow [1925] : R. H. Hadow, *Report on the Trade and Industry of Persia dated April, 1925*, London, 1925.

Hale : F. Hale, *From Persian Uplands*, New York, n.d.

Hanway : Jonas Hanway, *An Historical Account of the british Trade over the Caspian Sea*, 4 vols in three, London, 1753.

Hardin and Duffied : Ian R. Hardin and Frances Duffied, "Characterization of Metallic Yarns in Historic Persian Textiles by Microanalysis", in Howard L. Neddles and S. Haig Zeronian eds, *Historic Textile and Paper Materials*, American Chemical Society, Washington DC, 1986, p. 231-252.

Hedayat [Khatarat] : Mehdi Qoli Hedayat, *Khatarat va Khaterat*, Tehran, 2nd ed., 1344/1967.

Hedayat [*Rauzat*] : Reza Qoli Khan Hedayat, *Tarikh-e Rauzat al-Safa-ye Naseri*, 10 vols, Qom, 1339/1960.

Helfgott : Leonard M. Helfgott, "Production and Trade - The Persian Carpet Industry", in Carol Bier ed., *Woven from the Heart, Spun from the Soul* , Washington DC, 1987.

Herbert : Thomas Herbert, *Travels in Persia*, 1627-1629, ed. W. Foster, New York, 1929.

Herzig : Edmund Herzig, "The Volume of Iranian Raw Silk Exports in the Safavid Period", in *Iranian Studies*, 25 (1992), p. 41-80.

Heude : W. Heude, *A Voyage up the Persian Gulf in 1817*, London, 1819.

Historical Gazetteer : *Historical Gazetteer of Iran*, L. Adamec ed., 4 vols, Graz, 1981.

Hobson-Jobson : H. Yule and A.C. Burnell, *Hobson-Jobson, A glossary of Anglo-Indian colloquial words and phrases...*, London, 1969.

Hoeltzer : E. Hoeltzer, *Persien vor 113 Jahren*, trad. Mohammad Assemi, Tehran, 1975.

al-Hokama : M. H. Asef Rostam al-Hokama, *Rostam al-tavarikh*, ed. M. Moshiri, Tehran, 1348/1969).

Hollingberry : W. Hollingberry, *A Journal of Observations made during the British Embassy to the Court of Persia in the years 1799, 1800 and 1801*, Calcutta, 1814, reprint Tehran, 1976.

Holmes : William Richard Holmes, *Sketches on the Shores of the Caspian*, London, 1845.

Hotz : A. Hotz, *Reis van de gezant der O.I. Compagnie Joan Cunaeus naar Perzie in 1651-1652*, Amsterdam, 1908.

Housego : J. Housego, "18th Century Persian Carpets: Continuity and Change", in *Oriental Carpet & Textile Studies* , III/1, London, 1987.

Houtum-Schindler [Reisen] : A. Houtum-Schindler, "Reisen im suedlichen Persien (1879)", in *Zeitschrift der Gesellschaft fuer Erdkunde zu Berlin*, 16 (1881), p. 318-331.

Houtum-Schindler [Shah Isma'il] : A. Houtum-Schindler, "Shah Isma'il", in *Journal of the Royal Asiatic Society*, 1897, p.

Imperial Gazetteer : *Imperial Gazetteer of India: Afghanistan and Nepal*, reprint Lahore, n.d.

Irwin [Indian Textile] : John Irwin, "Indian Textile Trade in the Seventeenth Century", in *Journal of Indian Textile History*, 1 (1955), p. 59-65

Irwin [*Kashmir*] : John Irwin, *The Kashmir Shawl*, H. M. Stationery Office, London, 1973.

Irwin and Hall : John Irwin and Margaret Hall, *India Painted and Printed Fabrics*, 2 vols, Ahmadabad, 1971.

Issawi : Charles Issawi, *The Economic History of Iran 1800-1914*, Chicago, 1971.

Italconsult : *Italconsult* (for the Plan Organisation), Socio-economic Development Plan for the South-East Region, 5 vols, Rome, 1970, IV (Agriculture).

Ittig : Annette Ittig ed., "The Carpets and Textiles of Iran", = *Iranian Studies*, 25 (1992).

Ja'fari : Ja'far b. Moh. b. Hasan Ja'fari, *Tarikh-e Yazd*, ed. Iraj Afshar, Tehran 1338/1959.

Jamalzadeh : Seyyed Mohammad 'Ali Jamalzadeh, *Ganj-e Shayegan*, Berlin, 1335/1916.

Janab : Mir Seyyed 'Ali Reza Janab, *Ketab al-Esfahan*, Isfahan, 1303/1924.

Javadi : Hasan Javadi et al., *Du Resaleh* [Two Qajar Essays on Men and Women], Washington, 1992.

Kaempfer [Am Hofe] : Engelbert Kaempfer, *Am Hofe des Persischen Grosskoenigs*, tr. Walter Hinz, Leipzig, 1940.

Kaempfer [Reisetagebuecher] : Engelbert Kaempfer, *Die Reisetagebuecher*, ed. K. Meier-Lemgo, Wiesbaden, 1968.

Kakasch : Kakasch von Zalonkemeny, *Iter Persicum*, Altenburg, 1609.

Kashefi : Maulana Hosein Va'ez Kashefi Sabzevari, *Fotovvatnameh-ye Soltani*, ed. Mohammad Ja'far Mahjub, Tehran, 1350/1971.

Kateb : Ahmad b. Hosein b. 'Ali Kateb, *Tarikh-e Jadid-e Yazd*, ed. Iraj Afshar, Tehran, 1345/1966.

Keppel : G. Keppel, *Personal Narrative of a Journey from India to England in 1824*, London, 1827.

Kermani [*Tarikh*] : Ahmad Majd al-Eslam Kermani, *Tarikh-e enqelab-e mashrutiyat-e Iran*, 3 vols, ed. Mahmud Khalilpur, Isfahan, 1347/1968.

Kermani [*Manaqeb*] : Awhad al-Din Kermani, *Manaqeb-e Awhad al-Din Kermani*, ed. B. Foruzanfar, Tehran, 1347/1968.

[*Ketabshenasi*] : *Ketabshenasi-ye teknolozhi-ye sonnati-ye Iran*, 3 vols, Government of Iran, Ministry of Culture and Education, Tehran, 1367/1988.

Keyvani : Mehdi Keyvani, *Artisans and Guild Life in the later Safavid Period*, Berlin, 1982.

Khaki Khorasani : *The Diwan of Khaki Khorasani*, ed. W. Ivanov, Bombay, 1923.

Khanikoff : N. de Khanikoff, *Mémoire sur la partie méridionale de l'Asie centrale*, Paris, 1862.

Khaza'eli : Madhri Khaza'eli, "Tarikhcheh-ye sanaye'-ye nassaji-ye Kerman", in Mohammad Rasul Daryagasht ed., *Kerman dar qalamru-ye tahqiqat-e Irani - majmu'eh-ye maqallat*, Tehran, 1370/1991.

Khavafi : Abu'l-Qasem Shehab al-Din Ahmad Khavafi, *Monsha al-Ensha*, ed. Rokn al-Din Homayunfarrokh, 2 vols, Tehran, 1357/1978.

Kh^{w}ondamir : Kh^{w}ondamir, Habib al-Siyar, 4 vols, ed. Mohammad Dabir-Siyaqi, 3rd. ed., Tehran, 1362/1983.

Kinneir : J. M. Kinneir, *A Geographical Memoir of the Persian Empire*, London, 1813.

Klein and Ackerman : Vladimir Klein and Phyllis Ackerman, "A Russian Document on Persian Textiles", in Alexander Pope and Phyllis Ackerman, *A Survey of Persian Art, from Prehistoric Times to the Present*, London-New York, 1938-39, III, p. 2163-2174.

Kochwasser : Friedrich H. Kochwasser, "Persien im Spiegel der Reisebeschreibung von Heinrich von Poser (1620/25)", in Wilhelm Eilers ed., *Festgabe deutscher Iranisten zur 2500 Jahrfeier Irans*, Stuttgart, 1971, p. 80-93.

Kotov : *Khozhenie Kuptsa Fedota Kotova v Persiyu*, ed. N. Kuznetsova, Moscow, 1958.

Kukanova : N. G. Kukanova, "K voprosu o torgovle rossii s Iranom v 50-80 godi XVIII v", in N. A. Kuznetsova ed., *Iran - sbornik statei*, Moscow, 1971, p. 72-83.

Kukanova, ed. : N. G. Kukanova, ed., *Russko-iranskaya torgovla 30-50-e godi XIX veka, Sbornik dokumentov*, Moscow, 1984.

Kuss : W. Kuss, *Handelsratgeber fuer Persien*, Berlin-Tehran, 1911.

Kuznetsova [*O genezise*] : N. A. Kuznetsova, *O genezise kapitalizma v stranakh vostoka*, XV-XIX vv., Moscow, 1962.

Kuznetsova [Urban Industry] : N. A. Kuznetsova, "Urban Industry in Persia during the 18th and 19th centuries", in *Central Asian Review*, XI (1963), p. .

Lambton : A. K. S. Lambton, *Islamic Society in Persia*, London, 1954.

Laufer : B. Laufer, *Sino-Iranica*, Chicago, 1991.

Layard : A. H. Layard, *Early Adventures in Persia, Susiania and Babylonia*, London, 1894, reprint 1971.

Le Bruyn : Cornelius Le Bruyn, *Travels into Moscovy, Persia and part of the East-Indies*, 2 vols, London, 1737.

Lesani-ye Shirazi : Lesani-ye Shirazi, *Majma' al-Asnaf*, n.p., 1961.

Levi-Strauss : M. Levi-Strauss, *Le Châle cachmire en France au XIXe siecle*, Musée Historique des Tissus, Lyon, 1983.

Lingeman : E. R. Lingeman, *Report on the Finance and Commerce of Persia 1925-1927*, London, 1928.

Lockhart : Laurence Lockhart, *Nadir Shah*, Cambridge, 1938.

Lockyer : Charles Lockyer, *An Account of British Trade in India*, London, 1711.

Lorimer : J. G. Lorimer, *Gazetteer of the Persian Gulf*, Calcutta, 1915, reprint 1970.

Lorini : E. Lorini, *La Persia contemporanea e sua questione monetaria*, Rome, 1900, reprint 1976.

Lumsden : H. M. Lumsden, *The mission to Kandahar*, Calcutta, 1860.

MacAllan : Richard MacAllan, "The English East India Company and Its Role in the Carpet Trade of 17th Century India and Persia", in *Oriental Carpet & Textile Studies*, III/2, London 1989, p. 105-115.

MacLean : H. W. MacLean, *Report on the Conditions and Prospects of British Trade in Persia*, London, 1904.

Malcolm [*History*] : John Malcolm, *The History of Persian*, 2 vols, London, 1815, reprint Tehran, 1976.

Malcolm [*Five Years*] : Napier Malcolm, *Five Years in a Persian Town*, London, 1905.

Malekzadeh : Mehdi Malekzadeh, *Tarikh-e enqelab-e mashrutiyat-e Iran*, 7 vols, Tehran, 1328/1949.

Mankowski : T. Mankowski, "The art of carpet making B. Some documents from Polish sources relating to carpet making in the time of Shah 'Abbas I", in Alexander Pope and Phyllis Ackerman, *A Survey of Persian Art, from Prehistoric Times to the Present*, London-New York, 1938-39, III, p. 2431-2432.

[*Maqalat*] : *Maqalat-e Shams-e Tabrizi (daftar-e avval)*, ed. M. 'A. Movahhed, Tehran, 1368/1989.

Mar'ashi : Mir Teymur Mar'ashi, *Tarikh-e Khandan-e Mar'ashi-ye Mazandaran*, ed, Manuchehr Sotudeh, Tehran, 2536/1977.

Mar'ashi Safavi : Mirza Mohammad Khalil Mar'ashi Safavi, *Majma' al-Tavarikh*, ed. 'Abbas Eqbal, Tehran, 1328q/1915.

Marsh [*The Tennesseean*] : D.W. Marsh, *The Tennesseean in Persia and Koordistan*, Philadelphia, 1869.

Marsh [*A Ride*] : H.C. Marsh, *A Ride Through Islam*, London, 1877.

Martin : M. Martin, "City and Country: Rural Textile Production in Northeastern Iran", in Carol Bier ed., *Woven from the Heart, Spun from the Soul*, Washington DC, 1987, p. 121-133.

Matthee [East India] : Rudi Matthee, "The East India Company Trade in Kerman Wool, 1658-1730", in Jean Calmard ed., *Etudes Safavides*, Paris-Tehran, 1993, p. 343-383.

Matthee [*Politics*] : Rudi Matthee, *Politics and Trade in Late Safavid Iran* (unpublished thesis UCLA, Berkeley, 1991).

Matthee [The Career] : Rudi Matthee, "The Career of Mohammad Beg, Grand Vizier of Shah 'Abbas II", in *Iranian Studies*, 24 (1991), p. 17-36.

McKenzie : C. F. McKenzie, *Safarnameh-ye shomal*, tr. Mansoureh Ettehadiyeh (Nezam Mafi), Tehran, 1359/1980.

Membré : Michele Membré, *Relazione*, ed. G. Scarcia, Rome, 1969. English translation, see Morton.

Mervi : Mohammad Kazem Mervi, *Tarikh-e 'Alamara-ye Naderi*, 3 vols, ed. Mohammad Amin Riyahi, 2nd ed., Tehran, 1369/1990.

Mikosch : E. Mikosch, "Catalogue of Kashmir Shawls in the Textile Museum", in *The Textile Museum Journal* (1985), p. 23-54.

Millspaugh : A. C. Millspaugh, *The American Task in Persia*, New York, 1925, reprint 1973.

Minadoi : John-Thomas Minadoi, *The History of the Warres between the Turkes and the Persians*, London, 1595, reprint 1976.

Mirza Rafi'a : Mirza Rafi'a, *Dastur al-Moluk*, ed. Mohammad-Taqi Danesh-Pazhuh, Tehran, 1356/1977.

Mo'ayyer al-Mamalek : Dust 'Ali Mo'ayyer al-Mamalek, *Yaddashtha'i az Zendegani-ye khosusi-ye Naser al-Din Shah*, Tehran, 1351/1972.

Mokamalli : Mohammad Kazem Mokamalli, "Charuq-duzi dar Zanjan", in *Honar va Mardom*, 167 (2537), p. 54-60.

Mohammadi : 'Ali Mohammadi, *Ketab-e Afshar*, n.p., n.d.

Monajjem : Molla Jalal Monajjem, *Tarikh-e 'Abbasi ya ruznameh-ye Molla Jalal*, ed. S. Vahidniya, Tehran, 1366/1987.

Monshi : Eskander Beg Monshi, *Tarikh-e 'Alamara-ye 'Abbasi*, 2 vols, ed. Iraj Afshar, Tehran, 1350/1971.

Moqimi : M. E. Moqimi, *Joghrafiya-ye tarikhi-ye Shirvan*, Tehran, 1370/1991.

Morier [*A Journey*] : James Morier, *A Journey through Persia, Armenia and Asia Minor in the Years 1808 and 1809*, Philadelphia, 1816.

Morier [*A Second Journey*] : James Morier, *A Second Journey through Persia ... between the Years 1810 and 1816*, London, 1818.

Morton : A. H. Morton, *Mission to the Lord Sophy of Persia (1539-1542)*, London, 1993.

Mostaufi : 'Abdollah Mostaufi, *Sharh-e zendagani-ye man*, 3 vols, Tehran, n.d.

Mueller : Gerhard Friedriech Mueller, *Sammlung Russischer Geschichte*, 9 vols, St. Petersburg, 1732-1764.

Mukminova [*Differentsiatsiia*] : R. G. Mukminova, *Sotsialn'aia Differentsiatsiia Naseleniia Gorodov Uzbekistana XV-XVI*, Tashkent, 1985.

Mukminova [*Ocherki*] : P. G. Mukminova, *Ocherki po istorii remesla v Samarkande i Buxare v XVI veke*, Tashkent, 1976.

Nami Esfahani : Mirza Mohammad Sadeq Musavi Nami Esfahani, *Tarikh-e Giti-Gosha*, ed. S. Nafisi, Tehran, 1317/1938, 2nd ed., 1363/1984.

Napier : G. C. Napier, "Extract from a Diary of a Tour in Khorassan", in *Journal of the Royal Geographical Society*, 46 (1876), p. 62-171.

Naraqi : Ehsan Naraqi, *Tarikh-e ejtema'i-ye Kashan*, Tehran, 1340/1961.

Nasiri : Mohammad Reza Nasiri, *Asnad va Mokatebat-e Tarikhi-ye Iran, doureh-ye Afshariyeh*, Tehran, 1364.

Nasrabadi : Mirza Mohammad Taher Nasrabadi, *Tadhkereh-ye Nasrabadi*, ed. Vahid Dastgerdi, Tehran, 3rd ed., 1361/1982.

Natanzi : Mahmud b. Hedayatollah Afushti Natanzi, *Naqavat al-athar fi dhekr al-akhyar*, ed. Ehsan Eshraqi, Tehran, 1350/1971.

Nava'i [*Shah Tahmasp*] : 'Abdol Hosein Nava'i, *Asnad va Mokatebat-e Shah Tahmasp-e Safavi*, Tehran, 1349/1970.

Ness : Mrs. Patrick Ness, *Ten Thousand Miles in Two Continents*, London, 1929.

Neves Aguas : *Viagens por terra da India a Portugal*, ed. Neves Aguas, Lisbon, 1991.

Nezam al-Saltaneh : Nezam al-Saltaneh, *Khaterat va Asnad-e Hosein Qoli Khan Nezam al-Saltaneh Mafi*, 2 vols, ed. Mansoureh Nezam-Mafi *et al.*, Tehran, 1361/1982.

Nicolas : M. Nicolas, *La mode du châle cachmire en France*, Musée de la Mode et du Costume, 1982.

Niebuhr : Carsten Niebuhr, *Reisebeschreibung nach Arabien*, Kopenhagen, 1774, reprint 3 parts in one, Tuebingen, 1975.

Niño Jesus : Florencio del Niño Jesus, "A Persia (1604-9), Peripecias de una embajada pontificia que fue a Persia a principios des siglo XVII", in *Biblioteca Carmelitana-Teresiana de Misiones*, II, Pamplona, 1929.

Norden : Hermann Norden, *Under Persian Skies*, Philadelphia, n.d.

Nouveaux Mémoires : *Nouveaux Mémoires des Missions de la Compagnie de Jésus dans le Levant*, IX, Paris, 1755.

O'Donovan : E. O'Donovan, *The Merv Oasis*, 2 vols, London, 1882.

Olearius : Adam Olearius, Vermehrte und Newe Beschreibung der Muscowitischen und Persianischen Reyse, ed. D. Lohmeier, Schleswig, 1656, reprint Tuebingen, 1971.

Olivier : G.-A. Olivier, *Voyage dans l'empire Ottomane, l'Egypte, et la Perse*, 6 vols, Paris, 1807.

Olmer : L.-J. Olmer, "Rapport sur une mission scientifique en Perse", in *Nouvelles Archives des Missions Scientifiques et Littéraires*, XVI, Paris, 1908.

Otter : Jean Otter, *Voyage en Turquie et en Perse*, 2 vols, Paris, 1748.

Ouseley : W. Ouseley, *Travels in various countries of the East: more particularly Persia*, 3 vols, London, 1819-23.

Pacifique de Provins : Père Pacifique de Provins, *Le voyage de Perse*, ed. Godefroy de Paris and Hilaire de Wingene, Assisi, 1939.

Parodi : S. Parodi, *Cose e Parole nei "Viaggi" di Pietro della Valle*, Firenze, 1987.

Perkins : J. Perkins, *A Residence of Eight Years in Persia*, Andover, 1843.

Pinkerton : John Pinkerton ed., *A General Collection of Voyages and Travels*, London, 1811.

Polak [Beitrag]: J. E. Polak, "Beitrag zu den agrarischen verhaeltnissen in Persien", in *Mitteilungen der K-K. Geographischen Gesellschaft zur Wien*, 1862, p. .

Polak [*Persien*] : J. E. Polak, *Persien, das Land und seine Bewohner*, 2 vols, Leipzig, 1865.

Pope and Ackerman : Alexander Pope and Phyllis Ackerman, *A Survey of Persian Art, from Prehistoric Times to the Present*, 6 vols, London-New York, 1938-39.

Porter : R. K. Porter, *Travels in Georgia, Persia, Armenia, etc. during 1817-1820*, 2 vols, London, 1821.

Pottinger : H. Pottinger, *Travels in Baluchistan and Sind*, London, 1816.

Powell : E. A. Powell, *By Camel and Car to the Peacock Throne*, New York, 1923.

Purchas : Samuel Purchas, *Hakluytus Posthumus or Purchas, His Pilgrimes*, 8 vols, Glasgow, 1905.

Qajar : Jalal Mirza Qajar, *Nameh-ye Khosrowan*, Bombay, 1324/1906-7.

Qandahari and Lotfi : F. Taheri Qandahari and M. Taheri Lotfi, *Ketabshenasi va rahnama'i-ye sanaye'-e dasti-ye Iran*, Tehran, 1369/1990.

Qari : Maulana Mahmud Nezam Qari, *Divan-e albeseh*, ed. Mohammad Moshiri, Tehran, 1359/1980.

Qazvini: Mohammad Shafi' Qazvini, *Qanun-e Qazvini enteqad-e ouza'-ye ejtema'i-ye Iran doureh-ye Naseri*, ed. Iraj Afshar, Tehran, 1370/1991.

Qomi : Qazi Ahmad ibn Sharaf al-Din al-Hosein al-Hoseini al-Qomi, *Kholasat al-Tavarikh*, 2 vols, ed. Ehsan Eshraqi, Tehran, 1363/1984.

Rabino [Barfrush] : H. L. Rabino, "Report on the Trade and General Condition of the City of Barfrush and the Province of Mazanderan for the Year 1910-11", DCR No. 4812, London, 1911, p. 1-27.

Rabino [Kermanshah] : H. L. Rabino, "Report on the Trade and General Conditions of the City and Province of Kermanshah", DCR, Miscellaneous Series, No. 590, London 1903.

Rabino and Lafont : H. L. Rabino and F. Lafont, "Notes agricoles et industrielles. Le commerce et l'agriculture dans la Perse du Nord", dans *Revue du Monde Musulman*, 23 (1913), p. 166-197.

Rafi' : 'Abd al-Rafi' Haqiqat Rafi', *Tarikh-e Semnan*, Semnan, 1352/1973.

Rawlinson : Sir Henry Rawlinson, "Notes on a Journey from Tabriz to Takhti-Soleiman [Oct. 1838]", in *Journal of the Royal Geographical Society*, 10 (1841), p. 1-64.

Rennicke : E. Rennicke, *The Art of Paisley*, New York, 1980.

Riazul Islam [*Calender*] : Riazul Islam, *A Calender of Documents on Indo-Persian Relations*, 2 vols, Karachi, 1979.

Riazul Islam [*Relations*] : Riazul Islam, *Indo-Persian Relations*, Tehran, 1970.

Rice : Clara C. Rice, *Persian Women & Their Ways*, London, 1923.

Ricks : Thomas Ricks, *Politics and Trade in Southern Iran and the Gulf, 1745-1765*, (unpubl. thesis, Indiana University, 1974).

Rittikh : P. A. Rittikh, *Otchet o poedzke v Persiyu ... v 1900 g.*, 2 vols, St. Petersburg.

Roe : Sir Thomas Roe, *The Embassy to the Moghul*, ed. William Foster, London, 1926.

Roemer : H. R. Roemer, *Persien auf dem Weg in die Neuzeit*, Beirut, 1989.

Rowe : A. P. Rowe, "The Woven Structures of European Shawls in The Textile Museum Collection", in *The Textile Museum Journal* (1985), p. 55-59.

Rumlu : Hasan Rumlu, *Ahsan al-Tavarikh*, ed. N. Seddon, Baroda, 1931.

[*Ruznameh*] : *Ruznameh-ye Mirza Mohammad Kalantar-e Fars*, ed. 'Abbas Eqbal, Tehran, 1325/1946.

Saba : Mohsen Saba, "A Note on Lebas ol-Taqva", in *Tahqiqat-e eqtesadi*, VIII/21 (1971), p. 103-106.

[*Safarnameh*] : *Safarnameh-ye Astarabad va Mazandaran*, ed. Mas'ud Golzari, Tehran, 2535/1976.

Safavi : Rahimzadeh Safavi, *Shahr-e jangha va tarikh-e zendegani-ye Shah Esma'il Safavi*, Tehran, 1341/1962.

Sanson : Sanson, *The Present State of Persia*, London, 1695.

Sasani : Khan Malek Sasani, *Siyasatgaran-e doureh-ye Qajar*, 2 vols, Tehran, 1352/1971.

Savage-Landor : H. Savage-Landor, *Across Coveted Lands*, 2 vols, New York, 1903.

Savory : *'Alamara-ye 'Abbasi*, tr. R. M. Savory: *History of Shah 'Abbas the Great*, 2 vols, Boulder, Colorado, 1978.

Scarce [Persian Shawl] : Jennifer M. Scarce, "The Persian Shawl Industry," in *The Textile Museum Journal* (1988-89), p. 22-39.

Scarce [Vesture] : Jennifer M. Scarce, "Vesture and Dress, Fashion, Function and Impact", in Carol Bier ed., *Woven from the Heart, Spun from the Soul*, Washington D.C., 1987, p. 33-56.

Schefer : Charles Schefer, *Le voyage de M. d'Aranon*, Paris, 1887.

Schillinger : Franz Casper Schillinger, *Persianische und Ost-Indianische Reis*, Nuernberg, 1707.

Schlimmer : J. L. Schlimmer, Terminologie Medico-Pharmaceutique: Française - Persane, Tehran, 1874, reprint 1970.

Schmitz : Barbara Schmitz, "On a special hat introduced during the reign of Shah 'Abbas the Great", in *Iran*, 22 (1984), p. 103-112.

Schneider : Manfred Schneider, *Beitraege zur Wirtschaftsstruktur und Wirtschaftsentwicklung Persiens 1850-1900*, Stuttgart, 1990.

Schwartz : Benjamin Schwartz, *Letters from Persia written by Charles and Edward Burgess 1828-1855*, New York, 1942.

Sepehr : Sepehr, Mirza Mohammad Taqi, *Lesan al-Molk. Nasekh al-Tavarikh*, 3 vols in one, ed. J. Qa'emmaqami, Tehran, 1337/1958.

Seyf [Technical Changes] : Ahmad Seyf, "Technical Changes in Iranian Agriculture, 1800-1906", in *Middle Eastern Studies*, 20 (1984), p. 147-149.

Seyf [Silk Production] : Ahmad Seyf, "Silk Production and Trade in Iran in the Nineteenth Century", in *Iranian Studies*, 26 (1983), p. 51-72.

Shafi' Javadi : Shafi' Javadi, *Tabriz va Peiramun*, Tabriz, 1350/1971.

Shahanshahi [*Tarikhcheh*] : Soheila Shahanshahi, *Tarikhcheh-ye pushesh-e sar dar Iran*, Tehran, 1374/1995.

Shahri : Ja'far Shahri, *Tarikh-e ejtema'i - Tehran dar qarn-e sizdahom*, 6 vols, Tehran, 1368/1989.

Shalchi : A. Shalchi, *Farhang-e govayshi-ye Khorasan-e bozorg*, Tehran 1370/1991.

Shamlu : Vali Qoli b. Da'ud Qoli Shamlu, *Qesas al-Khaqani*, ed. Hasan Sadat Naseri, Tehran, 1371/1992.

Shari'at-Niya [*Orupa'iha*] : Sayyed Hesam al-din Shari'at-Niya, *Orupa'iha va Lebas-e Iraniyan*, Tehran, 1372/1993.

Sharifzadeh [Golabtun] : Seyyed 'Abdol-Hamid Sharifzadeh, "Golabtun", in *Mirath-e Farhangi*, 2 (1369/1990), p. 34-35.

Sharifzadeh [Sha'rbafi] : Seyyed 'Abdol-Hamid Sharifzadeh, "Sha'rbafi", in Mirath-e Farhangi, 8-9 (1372/1993), p. 52-64.

Sheil : Lady Sheil, *Glimpses of Life and Manners in Persia*, London, 1856, reprint 1973.

Shirazi : 'Abdi Beg Shirazi, *Takmelat al-Akhbar*, ed. 'Abdol-Hosein Nava'i, Tehran, 1369/1990.

Shushtari : Mir 'Abd ol-Latif Khan Shushtari, Tohfat al-'Alam, ed. Samad Muhed, Tehran, 1363/1984.

Silva y Figueroa : Don Garcia de Silva y Figueroa, *Commentarios de D. García de Silva y Figueroa que de parrte del rey de España don Felipe III hizo el rey Xa Abas de Persia*, Madrid, 1903.

Sistani : Malek Shah Hosein Sistani, *Ehya al-Moluk*, ed. Manuchehr Sotudeh, Tehran, 1345/1966.

Smith : Robert Murdoch Smith, *Persian Art*, South Kensington Museum Art Handbooks, London, 1876.

Smith : Ronald Bishop Smith, *The First Age of the Portuguese Embassies, Navigations and Peregrinations in Persia (1507-1524)*, Bethesda, 1970.

Soltan-Ahmad Mirza : 'Azud al-Douleh Soltan-Ahmad Mirza, *Tarikh-e 'Azudi*, ed. 'Abdol-Hosein Nava'i, Tehran, 1355/1976.

Soltani : M. 'A. Soltani, *Joghrafiya-ye tarikhi va tarikh-e mofassal-e Kermanshahan "Bakhtaran"*, Tehran, 1370/1991.

Southgate : H. Southgate, *A Tour Through Armenia and Mesopotamia*, 2 vols, New York, 1840.

Stewart : David Stewart, "The Humor of the Scholars: The Autobiography of Ni'mat Allah al-Jazairi (d. 1112/1701)", in *Iranian Studies*, 22 (1991), p. 47-81.

Stirling : Edward Stirling, *The Journals of Edward Stirling in Persia and Afghanistan 1828-1829*, ed. Jonathan L. Lee, Naples, 1991.

Stoeber : G. Stoeber, *Die Afshar. Nomadismus im Raum Kerman*, Marburg, 1978.

Stolze and Andreas : F. Stolze and F. C. Andreas, *Die Handelsverhaeltnisse Persiens*, Gotha, 1885.

Stranszens : Jan Struys, *The most perrilous and most unhappy voyage of John Struys*, London, 1683.

Stuart : Lt. Col. C. Stuart, *Journal of a Residence in Northern Persia*, London, 1854.

Sultanzadeh : A. Sultanzadeh, *Sovremennaya Persiya*, Moscow, 1922, translated as "Iran-e Mo'aser", in *Avetis Makailian [Sultanzade], selected writings, Historical Documents: The Workers', Social-Democratic and Communist Movement in Iran (1903-1963)*, IV, Florence, n.d., p. 65-104.

Sykes [Persia] : Ella Sykes, *Persia and its People*, London, 1910.

Sykes [Ten Thousand] : Sir Percy M. Sykes, *Ten Thousand Miles*, London, 1902.

[*Tadhkirat al-Muluk*] : *Tadhkirat al-Muluk*, ed. and tr. Vladimir Minorsky, London, 1943.

[*Tadhkereh*] : *Tadhkereh-ye Shah Tahmasp*, ed. 'Abdol-Shokri, Berlin, 1343q/1924.

Tahvildar : Mirza Hosein Khan Tahvildar, *Joghrafiya-ye Isfahan*, ed. Manuchehr Sotudeh, Tehran, 1342/1963.

Talibof : 'Abd al-Rahim Talibof, *Ketab-e Ahmad*,

Tancoigne : J. M. Tancoigne, *A Narrative of a Journey into Persia*, London, 1820.

Tavakkol : M. R. Tavakkol, *Joghrafiya va tarikh-e Baneh-ye Kordestan*, 2nd ed., Tehran, 1363/1984.

Tavernier : Jean-Baptiste Tavernier, *Les Six Voyages de Turquie et de Perse*, 2 vols, Paris, 1676, reed., 1711.

Temple : B. Temple, *Report on the Trade and Transport Conditions in Persia to January, 1922*, in Great Britain, Department of Overseas Trade, London, 1922.

Texeira : *The travels of Pedro Texeira*, ed. and tr. W.F. Sinclair, London, 1902.

[*The Indian Heritage*] : *The Indian Heritage: Court Life and Arts under Mughal Rule*, Victoria and Albert Museum, London, 1982.

[*The Kashmir Shawl*] : *The Kashmir Shawl*, Yale University Art Gallery, New Haven, 1975.

Thévenot : J. de Thévenot, *The Travels of M. de Thévenot into the Levant*, London, 1686, reprint 1971.

Tusi : Asadi Tusi, *Loghat al-Fors*, ed. M. Dabir Siyaqi, Tehran, 1336/1957.

Valentyn : Francois Valentyn, *Oud en Nieuw Oost-Indien*, 5 vols, Dordrecht, 1726.

Van Linschoten : J. H. van Linschoten, *The voyage of Jan Huygen van Linschoten to the East Indies*, ed. and tr. A. C. Burnell and P. A. Tiele, 2 vols, London, 1885.

Van Santen : H. W. van Santen, *Verenigde Oost-Indische Compagnie in Gujarat en Hindustan, 1620-1660*, Meppel, 1982 (thesis Leiden).

Vaziri [*Joghrafiya*] : Ahmad 'Ali Khan Vaziri, *Joghrafiya-ye Kerman*, ed. Bastani Parizi, Tehran, 1354/1977.

Vaziri [*Tarikh*] : Ahmad 'Ali Khan Vaziri, *Tarikh-e Kerman*, ed. Mohammad Ebrahim Bastani Parizi, 2nd ed., Tehran, 1352/1973.

Von Hammer : J. von Hammer, *Geschichte des osmanischen Reiches*, 10 vols, Budapest, 1827-35.

Waring : E. S. Waring, *A Tour to Sheeraz*, London, 1807.

Wills : C. J. Wills, *In the Land of the Lion and the Sun*, 2nd ed., London, 1893.

Wilson : S. G. Wilson, *Persian Life and Customs*, New York, 1895.

Wirth : E. Wirth, *Der Orientteppich und Europa*, Erlangen, 1976.

Wood : John Wood, *A Journey to the Source of the River Oxus*, London, 1872, reprint Karachi, 1976.

Wulff : Hans E. Wulff, *Traditional Crafts of Persia*, Cambridge, 1966.

Ydema : Onno Ydema, *Carpets & Their Datings in Netherlandish Paintings, 1500-1700*, Leiden-Zutphen, 1991.

Zarinebaf-Shahr : Fariba Zarinebaf-Shahr, *Tabriz under Ottoman Rule*, diss. Univ. of Chicago, 1991.

Zarrabi : 'Abd ol-Rahman Zarrabi, *Tarikh-e Kashan*, ed. Iraj Afshar, Tehran, 1342/1963.

Zell al-Soltan : Mas'ud Mirza Zell al-Soltan, *Tarikh-e Sargozasht-e Mas'udi*, Tehran, 1325/1907-08.

Moyen Orient & Océan Indien, XVIe-XIXe siècles

Derniers volumes parus :

8 - *Européens en Orient au XVIIIe siècle* (202 pages)

Gérald DUVERDIER, Propagande protestante en langues orientales aux XVIIe et XVIIIe s.

M. GHARAVI, Un médecin des Lumières, Simon de Vierville et son voyage en Perse.

Willem FLOOR, The Dutch on Khark island : the end of an era. The Baron Von Kniphausen's adventures.

9 - *Raphaël du Mans, missionnaire en Perse au XVIIe s.*

Francis RICHARD

vol. 1 : Biographie et Correspondance (318 pages)
vol. 2 : Estats et Mémoires (403 pages)

10 - *Sources européennes sur le Gujarat* (210 pages)

sous la direction d'Ernestine CARREIRA

Aniruddha RAY : Malet collection on Cambay (Gujarat) at the end of the 18th Century.

Michelguglielmo TORRI : Surat, its hinterland and its trade, c. 1740-1800 : The British documents.

Luis Frederico DIAS ANTUNES : Diu, the Commercial activity of a small harbour in Gujarat (1680-1800) :The Portuguese documents.

Ernestine CARREIRA : La correspondance de Francisco Gomes Loureiro, un négociant portugais au Gujarat.

Celsa PINTO : Late Eighteenth-Early Nineteenth Century Daman. Source Material in the Goa Archives.

Lakshmi SUBRAMANIAM : Towards a Commercial history of India's Western littoral: some reflections on the holdings of the Maharashtra state archives.

Om PRAKASH : Archival source material in the Netherlands on the history of Gujarat in the early modern period.

Jeremy FRANKS : The Observant Braad: a Swedish enquirer in Gujerat in the 1750s.

Florence D'SOUZA : Voyageurs européens au Gujarat au XVIIe siècle.

www.ingramcontent.com/pod-product-compliance
Lightning Source LLC
Chambersburg PA
CBHW071413230926
51846CB00001B/74